African American Architects

AFRICAN AMERICAN ARCHITECTS

A Biographical Dictionary 1865–1945

EDITED BY
DRECK SPURLOCK WILSON

ROUTLEDGE
AN IMPRINT OF TAYLOR & FRANCIS INC.

NEW YORK LONDON

Published in 2004 by

Routledge
29 West 35th Street
New York, NY 10001
www.routledge-ny.com

Published in Great Britain by
Routledge
11 New Fetter Lane
London EC4P 4EE
www.routledge.uk.co

Routledge is an imprint of Taylor & Francis Books, Inc.

Copyright © 2004 by Taylor & Francis, Inc.

Printed in the United States of America on acid-free paper.

10 9 8 7 6 5 4 3 2

All rights reserved. No part of this book may be reprinted or utilized in any form or by any electronic, mechanical, or other means, now known or hereafter invented, including any photocopying and recording, or any information storage or retrieval system, without permission in writing from the publishers.

Library of Congress Cataloging-in-Publication Data

African-American architects : a biographical dictionary, 1865–1945 / edited by Dreck Spurlock Wilson.
     p. cm.
Includes bibliographical references and index.
   ISBN 0-415-92959-8 (hardback : alk. paper)
 1. African American architects—Biography—Dictionaries.
I. Wilson, Dreck Spurlock.
NA736.A47 2003
720'.92'396073—dc21

Cover art by Aaron Douglas, "Building More Stately Mansions" (1944). Fisk University Galleries. Oil on canvas.

Contents

Preface	vii
Introduction	ix
Acknowledgments	xiii
Contributors	xv
Alphabetical List of Entries	xvii
Entries A to Z	1
General Bibliography	469
Appendix—Buildings Sorted by State and Country	471
Index	517

Preface

African American architects have contributed significantly, albeit often anonymously, to the architectural heritage of America. The veil of anonymity, made denser by racism, has resulted in a dearth of documentation about their role as architects. There are only a few archival repositories with holdings on African American architects. In the District of Columbia, the Moorland-Spingarn Research Center's "Archive of African American Architects" is the largest, composed principally of the papers of ALBERT IRVIN CASSELL, HOWARD HAMILTON MACKEY SR., and HILYARD ROBERT ROBINSON and the ephemera of 140 other architects. The Athenaeum in Philadelphia is the repository for the firm ledgers of the Office of Horace Trumbauer, which *de facto* becomes a repository for Trumbauer's African American senior designer, **Julian Francis Abele**. At the time that this dictionary was being compiled, the Filson Society in Louisville tendered the winning bid during an on-line auction and rescued the papers of **Samuel M. Plato** from an unknown fate. There are only a few other repositories where serious scholars can go to research the contributions of late nineteenth century and early twentieth century African American architects. *African American Architects: A Biographical Dictionary 1865–1945* is intended to rectify the dearth of that documentation if only incompletely in order to "correct or reform the exclusionist tradition of our histories."[1] Some almost comical situations arose due to the dearth of information. Three different contributors claimed their person was "the first" Black architect in the state of Virginia. Often contributors made assumptions about their architect, thinking that a date in the 1920s or 1930s was "early" because they were unaware of architects who were practicing in the 1890s and 1900s. In essence, this dictionary will correct the historic record.

Note
1. Valencia Hollins Coar, *A Century of Black Photographers: 1840–1960* (Providence: Rhode Island School of Design), 1983 p. 15.

Introduction

African American Architects: A Biographical Dictionary 1865–1945 is a single-volume reference work for architectural historians, historic preservationists, architects, historians, curators, students, and the general public seeking to provide reliable information on late nineteenth century and early twentieth century African American architects. The *Dictionary* is composed of 168 entries that were provided by more than 100 contributing authors. The entries, which range in length from 250 to 4,000 words, are arranged alphabetically, internally cross-referenced, and supplemented by photographs of architects and the buildings that they designed. The *Dictionary* includes a building list and, whenever possible, a selected bibliography for each architect. To assist scholars with authoritative references, a general bibliography is included at the end of the dictionary.

The format for this biographical dictionary is modeled after the *Concise Dictionary of American Biography* (DAB), which was first published in 1927 by Scribner & Sons and due to its popularity is in its fifth edition, having been reprinted in 1997.[1] The convention used by DAB's editors was to recruit subject-matter experts or contributors to provide short biographies. This convention was adopted by the editors of this dictionary. Acknowledged for its scholarship and accuracy, the *DAB*, revised through 1997, however it failed to include an African American. Charles Birnbaum and Robin Karson's *Pioneers of American Landscape Design,* the format of which parallels the DAB and the subject matter (i.e., landscape architects) of this dictionary, includes only one African American—surveyor, Benjamin Banneker (1731–1806). Banneker's connection to landscape architecture is tenuous at best and attribution for having re-drawn "the plans from memory" of Pierre Charles L'Enfant's District of Columbia street grid lacks evidentiary proof.[2] Of course, without the inclusion of Benjamin Banneker and having over-looked George Washington Carver horticulturist/agronomist/agriculturist, (1864–1943) they would not have had any African Americans in their book. Since they were apparently not aware of African American landscape architects such as DAVID AUGUSTUS WILLISTON, JOSEPH MANUAL BARTHOLOMEW SR., JASMINIUS WILSONNI RUDOLPHUS GRANDY III, and LOUIS HARVEY BANKS. It is because of these kinds of omissions that this biographical dictionary was compiled.

For this biographical dictionary, the editors used the descriptive term "African American" to describe a racial group. The adjective "Black" is used interchangeably with African American to characterize ancestry, not skin color. Owing to the 100 or so contributors who submitted entries and their individual writing styles, the terms "Negro" and "colored" are used occassionally in historic context, not to be disparaging, but in an attempt to be historically synonymous. The editors approved of their usage in this context. Sometimes an architect's racial identity was decided by examining vintage photographs, cross-referencing them in African American biographical dictionaries, or—when all else failed—asking relatives and colleagues.

The question of racial identity was a tricky one, individually addressed for each entry. Most of the male architects and all of the female architects felt that "race" was crucial to their identity and relied on their ethnicity to obtain clients. For some race was seen as a negative factor in their professional advancement and therefore it was expedient to play down their ethnicity; for others, it was a philosophic stance—they felt an emphasis on race was divisive to national unity. Inclusion in the dictionary should not be not be construed as representing that person's beliefs about race.

The definition of "architect" used by the editors was that the person had to conceive a design and visually present it by means of a sketch, floor plan, drawing, scale model, or mock-up with sufficient detail so that others could build it. Certainly licensure confers the title, but the starting threshold year of 1865 precedes licensing laws for all states and the District of Columbia. Most jurisdictions required an examination for licensing, but some jurisdictions grandfathered-in applicants who could prove that they had been in practice a certain number of years prior to enactment of the licensing law, which was the case with ROBERT L. ROBINSON and brothers CALVIN LUNSFORD and MOSES MCKISSACK III among many others. Some jurisdictions required a college degree in order to qualify to take the examination. The intent of the examination was that a person's qualifications could

INTRODUCTION

be measured and in theory this would be an objective measure of the architect's knowledge. However, simply by showing up, the test-taker's racial identity could be deduced by the White proctor and the specter of racial bias could be introduced. Therefore, possessing a license was not a qualifier for inclusion in this dictionary.

To be inclusive rather than exclusive, the editors included designers who were professionally tangential to architects if they were formally educated in the fine arts or civil engineering or demonstrated a design *ouvre*. This more elastic definition made it possible to include a historic preservationist, a lithographer, two pattern makers, four landscape architects, five bridge designers, and a score of architectural engineers.

The dictionary focuses on African American architects who practiced in the United States between 1865 and 1945. The starting year was chosen because it corresponds to the end of the Civil War, when the majority of African Americans were freed from slavery. In theory they had more control over their lives and increased choices with regard to the type of work in which they wanted to engage. There were exceedingly more opportunities to obtain an education, and nascent vocational schools, industrial institutes, colleges, and universities sprang into existence creating in their wake a clientele for African American architects. Although there were certainly *antebellum* African Americans, such as Youngstown, Ohio architect PLYMPTON ROSS BERRY and Chicago's RICHARD MASON HANCOCK, a pattern maker, it is the editors' view that they were "exceptions" to the national stereotype of African Americans being naive designers or artless copiers. The presumption that was formative in setting the book ending year was that the number of African American architects dramatically increased after World War II due in large part to the GI Bill, which made a college education financially attainable. The notoriously unreliable Compendium of the United States Occupational Census for 1940, enumerated sixty-eight Black male architects and 15,347 White ones.[3] The Occupational Census for 1950 enumerated 180 Black architects and 22,400 White ones.[4] Nineteen forty-five was a porous year to choose as the ending year because architects who began their apprenticeship or architectural education prior to 1945, and continued their career beyond 1945, were included. However, establishing the book ending year as 1945 created the fortunate circumstance of being able to interview living subjects. Architects CLARENCE CROSS, CHARLES IRVIN CASSELL, and ROBERT PRINCE MADISON contributed their own autobiographies. At the time this dictionary went to press, other living subjects included preservationist ALMA FAIRFAX MURRAY CARLISE, landscape architect EDWARD LYONS PRYCE; and architects ALBERTA CASSELL BUTLER, LEWIS WENTWORTH GILES JR. ROY ANTHONY SEALEY and GOLDEN JOSEPH ZENON JR. Their authentic voices provide a nuanced reality about being a minority within a majority profession.

Initially, the names of architects considered for the dictionary came from the editors' familiarity with topical journals, African American history books, biographical dictionaries, and archived oral histories. To add to those names, State Historic Preservation Offices were surveyed. Over 250 architects (244 males and 7 females) were identified and screened for eligibility. However, it was only possible to identify contributors for 168 architects. Regrettably, 83 architects, who were otherwise eligible, were not included. The editors hope that this dictionary will motivate others to undertake further research.

Contributors to the dictionary were solicited from among the national and, in one instance, international community of architectural historians, historic preservationists, architects, historians, librarians, curators, genealogists, researchers, professors, graduate students, and relatives of architects. For the better-known ones—such as "architect to the stars" PAUL REVERE WILLIAMS, the "dean of African American architects" JOHN ANDERSON LANKFORD, and Booker T. Washington's son-in-law WILLIAM SIDNEY PITTMAN—it was relatively easy to find a contributor. Five architects have been the subject of university theses: WALTER THOMAS BAILEY, JAMES HOMER GARRETT, VERTNER WOODSON TANDY, PAUL REVERE WILLIAMS, and SAMUEL M. PLATO.[5] The authors of these theses were logical choices to recruit as contributors. The author of *Clarence "Cap" Wesley Wigington, An Architectural Legacy in Ice and Stone* was the logical person to ask to contribute to the dictionary.[6] Sometimes architectural historians or historic preservationists who were known to the editors were asked to submit an entry on an architect in their geographic locale. In addition, if an architect's children or collateral relatives were found, they sometimes were asked to submit an entry on their family member.

To provide historic context on Black architectural schools and departments that trained the majority of the race's architects, nine architectural programs are profiled: CLAFIN UNIVERSITY, FLORIDA AGRICULTURAL & MECHANICAL UNIVERSITY, HAMPTON INSTITUTE, HOWARD UNIVERSITY, NORTH CAROLINA AGRICULTURAL & TECHNICAL STATE UNIVERSITY, PRAIRIE VIEW AGRICULTURAL & MECHANICAL COLLEGE, SOUTHERN UNIVERSITY SCHOOL OF ARCHITECTURE, and TUSKEGEE

INTRODUCTION

NORMAL & INDUSTRIAL INSTITUTE. Narrative histories for the schools are offered, recalling architectural faculty who were instrumental in founding and advancing the program at their respective school, architectural pedagogy, curriculum development, and outstanding graduates.

Eight so-called "Negro Buildings" that were designed by African American architects (with two exceptions) for African Americans at seven southern regional fairs and one world's fair are included. They were a building type that existed for no other reason than segregation, but much racial pride must have been contained within their walls. One must consider the all-Negro Board of Managers who organized the building into existence, the architect who designed it, the craftsmen who built it, and the fairgoers who experienced it. The fairs with "Negro Buildings" were (in chronological order) COTTON STATES AND INTERNATIONAL EXPOSITION in Atlanta, Georgia (1895); TENNESSEE CENTENNIAL AND INTERNATIONAL EXPOSITION in Nashville (1897); SOUTH CAROLINA INTERSTATE AND WEST INDIAN EXPOSITION in Charleston (1901); ALABAMA STATE FAIR in Montgomery (1906); JAMESTOWN TER-CENTENNIAL EXPOSITION in Virginia (1907); APPALACHIAN EXPOSITION in Knoxville, Tennessee (1910); CENTURY OF PROGRESS EXPOSITION in Chicago, Illinois (1933); and TEXAS CENTENNIAL EXPOSITION in Dallas (1936). Negro Buildings, like their brethren exposition buildings, were not meant to be permanent so their demolition is more palatable than the demolition of culturally and architecturally significant buildings designed by Black architects.

Simmona Simmons-Hodo, associate editor and University of Maryland at College Park and Baltimore County bibliographer, compiled a comprehensive survey of literature on African American architects as an aid for architectural historians and other scholars who are interested in undertaking further research. The general bibliography provides a starting point for serious scholars of domestic architecture. An abridged bibliography for each architect is provided to assist readers who wish to research the specific architect in more depth.

A determined search was undertaken to find a photographic portrait of each architect, and was by and large a success. For many of these architects this is the first time their likeness has been published. The formal portraits should intrigue because of their historic implications and because many of them were photographed by early African American photographers such as Addison N. Scurlock (1883–1964) in Washington, D.C., James Van Der Zee (1886–1983) in Harlem, New York, and Prentice Herman Polk (1898–1984) in Tuskegee, Alabama. These photographers were members in good standing of the same extended fine arts family as were the early Black architects. It was more than coincidence that the areas in which clusters of Black architects were found—such as Washington, D.C.; Harlem; Cincinnati; and Tuskegee—were also where Black photographers were found. They, too, competed artistically and commercially in a highly contested branch of art and were not welcomed by the majority culture.

This dictionary includes a building list for each architect that identifies the client or building name, address at the time the building was constructed (when known), city, state, and year built. The purpose of the list is twofold; it provides information so that the reader can go on a site visit to these historic structures, and it represents an index of sites and structures that deserve consideration for historic landmark designation. It is disappointing to review the building list for some architects and realize that almost their entire known body of work has been demolished. Deliberate demolition of these buildings was generally government driven and demolition by neglect generally can be blamed on the indifference of the community. It is a damning statement of the avarice and ignorance of history that unravels the cultural and social fabric of Black neighborhoods.

During compilation of the dictionary, questions arose about these architects as a group. Did they know each other? Why did some migrate to the same, non-Black universities such as Cornell University, Ohio State University, and the University of Illinois? Were there professional networks available to them? Who were their patrons? Were societal pressures on female architects any different than those on their male peers? How did female architects fare within this male-dominated profession? An attempt was made to provide answers to these questions in the context of each architect's biography. Invariably, the question arises as to whether Black architects produced anything resembling an African American architectural style. The dictionary is a biographical compilation and was not intended to be a *treatise* on architectural styles. However, the building photographs provide a visual reference to begin to answer that aesthetic question.

> In sketching the life of a particular personality, the student of history finds himself face to face with some of the most serious and dangerous problems in connection with the reconstruction of the past. There is the danger that the writer may oversimplify the period in which his subject lived and thus mislead his readers into thinking that they can understand all the forces that

INTRODUCTION

shaped the history of the period by becoming acquainted with one person.... One must keep in mind the fact that sweeping generalizations based on the life of one person are neither good history nor good biography.[6]

Notes

1. *Concise Dictionary of American Biography.* N.Y.: Scribner, 1997.

2. E. Lynn Miller, "Banneker, Benjamin," in *Pioneers of Landscape Design*, eds. Charles Birnbaum and Robin Karson (NY: McGraw-Hill, 2000), p. 10.

3. Compendium of the United States Occupational Census for the Year 1940 Subject "Architect," (D.C.: Government Printing Office, 1940). Also see the compendium for the year 1950.

4. 1950 population census, special reports occupational characteristics, vol. IV, part 1, chapter B, p. 29.

5. Carson A. Anderson, "The Architectural Practice of Vertner W. Tandy: An Evaluation of the Professional and Social Position of a Black Architect" (master's thesis, University of Virginia, 1982); Wesley H. Henderson, "Two Case Studies of African-American Architects' Careers in Los Angles, 1890–1945: Paul Williams, FAIA and James Garrott, AIA" (Ph.D. dissertation, University of California, 1992); and Jon Smith, The Architecture of Samuel M. Plato, 1902 to 1921, (Master's thesis, Ball State University, 1998).

6. David Taylor, *Clarence "Cap" Wesley Wigington, An Architectural Legacy in Ice and Stone.* (St. Paul: St. Paul Foundation, 2000).

7. John Hope Franklin, "James Boon, Free Negro Artisan," *Journal of Negro History,* (April, 1945): 150.

DR. WESLEY HOWARD HENDERSON,
ASSOCIATE EDITOR

SIMMONA SIMMONS-HODO,
ASSOCIATE EDITOR

DRECK SPURLOCK WILSON,
EDITOR

Acknowledgments

The dearth of reliable information about late nineteenth century and early twentieth century African American architects created the need for *African American Architects: A Biographical Dictionary 1865–1945*.

Research support for the *Dictionary* was provided by the Graham Foundation for the Advanced Studies in the Fine Arts.

The 168 entries in this dictionary could not have been produced without the 115 contributing authors who embraced the project as if it was their own, which, in essence, it was. They "voluntarily" spent hours searching for documentation about the life and career of their subject architect and looking for photographic portraits of their architect or vintage photographs of the various schools of architecture and "Negro Buildings." Even more hours were spent condensing the disparate information they collected into an insightful, annotated biography or history. To each contributing author, most of whom I have never met, on behalf of the editors and the architects profiled herein whose careers you brought into sharper focus, we thank you. Gracious appreciation is likewise extended to the contributing authors who captured the forgotten institutional histories of the Reconstruction Era schools of architecture and the seldom told histories about the "Negro Buildings at Expositions."

Dr. Wesley Howard Henderson was an assistant professor at the University of Texas at Austin, School of Architecture when he agreed to become associate editor of the *Dictionary* and take on the enormously time-consuming responsibility of editing the 168 entries submitted by contributors, many of whom had never been published before. His time was additionally encroached upon when he volunteered to contribute six biographical entries of his own. In actuality, the dictionary could not have been compiled without him.

My discovery of bibliographer Simmona E. Simmons-Hodo, head of Reference Services at the University of Maryland at Baltimore County and adjunct faculty at the University of Maryland at College Park, and her agreeing to become an associate editor added a significant talent to the editorial team. Her near-encyclopedic familiarity with architectural publications and African Americans helped to expand the comprehensiveness of the general bibliography and elevated the quality of individual bibliographic references associated with each entry.

The obscure information that needed to be mined and the mostly forgotten photographs that needed to be dusted off and brought into the public domain made reliance on reference librarians, archivists, government historic preservationists, architectural historians, curators, and collection and historic photograph specialists an absolute necessity. To a person they were knowledgeable generous with their time and on numerous occasions led us to ancillary information.

The associate editors, Dr. Wesley Howard Henderson and Simmona E. Simmons-Hodo, and I are grateful to Mark O'Malley, associate project editor for reference publications at Routledge, whose experience in editing dictionaries adroitly and patiently guided us as we labored to edit the *Dictionary*. Routledge Reference Publishing Director Sylvia Miller is the person most responsible for fashioning my embryonic proposal into a publication. My gratitude to her is limitless.

Chrome Photographic Services Digital Imaging in Washington, D.C. processed film and converted slides into photographic prints for almost all of the images in the dictionary. Graphic Artist Byron Wade in Newberry Park, California digitally restored many images, destined for the dictionary. His painstaking attention to detail dramatically improved many of the images.

Unto myself, I take responsibility for the selection of entries contained herein.

DRECK SPURLOCK WILSON
WASHINGTON, D.C.

Contributors

Kira M. Alston
Carson A. Anderson
Carolyn Ashkar
Jane Bettistea
Ancella R. Bickley
Bonita Billingsley-Harris
Lisa M. Boone
Stanford Britt
Marshall V. Brown Jr.
Annette K. Carter
Lilian B. Cartwright
Charles I. Cassell
Anthony Chibbaro
Andrew Chin
Donna K. Christian
Curtis Clay
Yves Coleman
Robert T. Coles
Clarence Cross
Diane Davis
Kerry Davis
Elizabeth M. Dowling
William M. Drennen Jr.
Edward D. Dunson Jr.
DeWitt S. Dykes Jr.
Wendel Eckford
Hazel R. Edwards
Joellen ElBashir
Patsy M. Fletcher
Thomas L. French
James Gabbert
Bryan C. Green
Judith E. Greene
Margaret M. Grubiak
Phylis Hammonds
Ronald N. Helms
Wesley H. Henderson
Mark Hewitt
Donald Hibbard

Caroline M. Hickman
William C. Hine
Samuel J. Hodges III
Susan Horner
Ginger Howell
Granville Hurley Jr.
Ruth E. Hurwitz
Louise D. Hutchinson
E. Renee Ingram
Lauren Jacobi
Doris F. Johnson
Alice E. Jones
Audrey Jones
Katherine M. Jourdan
Eric Key
Walter E. Langsam
William Lebovich
Lizzetta LeFalle-Collins
Glen B. Leiner
Sarah Lenahan
Jack Lufkin
John S. Lupold
Robert P. Madison
Joel W. McEachin
Ronnie McGhee
Joyce Mendelsohn
William Milligan Sr.
Kaye L. Minchew
Melvin L. Mitchell
Mary Ann Neeley
Angel D. Nieves
John C. Norman, Jr.
Anthony Opalka
Susan G. Pearl
T. Thomas Potterfield Jr.
Peggy S. Ratliff
Roosevelt Ratliff
David Riehle
Carol Roark

Harry G. Robinson III
Maisah B. Robinson
Elizabeth Rosin
Robert W. Rydell
Mary H. Sadler
Tim Samuelson
Constance E. Sarto
Nancy Schwartz
Perre deClue Scott
Vincent A. Shivers
Richard Singletary
Calvin H. Sinnette
John H. Spencer
Wesley Springer
Richard M. Standifer
Albert M. Tannler
David V. Taylor
Beverly Tetterton
Philip Thomason
John H. Thompson
Christine Trebellas
Micki Waldrop
Monica L. Walker
Joyce D. Washington
Roberta Washington
L. Roger Watson III
Danette Welch
Sophonia Welch
Craig L. Wilkins
Barbara C. Williams
Douglas A. Williams
Paul K. Williams
Lisa Willis
Dreck S. Wilson
Elizabeth Wilson
Thomas O. Wisemiller
Thomas M. Wolf
Sarah H. Zurier

Alphabetical List of Entries

Abele, Julian Francis
Alabama State Fair Negro Building, Montgomery
Alexander, Archibald Alphonse
Appalachian Exposition Negro Building, Knoxville, Tennessee
Archer, Romulus Cornelius Jr.
Bailey, Walter Thomas
Bankhead, Lester Oliver
Banks, Louis Harvey
Barnett, Carl Eugene
Bartholomew, Joseph Manual Sr.
Bates, Robert Charles
Bellinger, Louis Arnett Stewart
Berry, Plympton Ross
Birch, Edward Eginton
Birch, Ernest Octavius
Blanche, John Henry Jr.
Blodgett, Joseph Haygood
Boles, Henry Clifford
Bow, Cyril Garner
Bowman, Charles Sumner
Boyde, Thomas Wilson Jr.
Brent, Calvin Thomas Stowe
Brent, John Edmonson
Brookins, Sanford Augustus
Brooks, Elizabeth Carter
Brown, Albert Grant
Brown, Georgia Louise Harris
Brown, Grafton Tyler
Brown, Leroy John Henry
Brown, Richard Lewis
Buffins, Robert Lester
Butler, Alberta Jeannette Cassell
Carlisle, Alma Fairfax Murray
Cassell, Albert Irvin
Cassell, Charles Irvin
Century of Progress Exposition De Saible Cabin, Chicago, Illinois
Claflin University, Manual Training Department
Coleman, William Emmett Jr.
Cook, Julian Abele
Cook, Ralph Victor
Cooke, William Wilson
Cotton States and International Exposition Negro Building, Atlanta, Georgia
Cross, Clarence
Decatur, William Jefferson
Delany, Henry Beard
Dickinson, Charles Edgar
Drayton, Clyde Martin
Duke, Charles Sumner
Dykes, DeWitt Sanford Sr.
Edwards, Gaston Alonzo
Elliott, Curtis Graham
Farrar, Daniel J. Sr.
Ferguson, Arthur Wilfred
Ferguson, George Alonzo
Fields, Robert Lionel
Fisher, Orpheus Hodge
Florida Agricultural & Mechanical University, School of Architecture
Ford, Wade Alston
Foster, George Washington Jr.
Fry, Louis Edwin Sr.
Furman, Ethel Madison Bailey
Garrott, James Homer
Giles, Lewis Wentworth Jr.
Giles, Lewis Wentworth Sr.
Grandy, Jasminius Wilsonni Rudolphus III
Greene, Beverly Loraine
Griffin, Francis Eugene
Hamilton, Calvin Pazavia
Hampton Institute, Department of Architecture
Hancock, Richard Mason
Harris, Clinton Stevens
Hatton, Isaiah Truman
Hazel, William Augustus
Henderson, Cornelius Langston Sr.
Hill, Joseph E.
Hilliard, Leroy
Hoban, Stewart Daniel Sr.
Holloway, John Bunyon Jr.
Howard University, Department of Architecture
Hurley, Granville Warner Sr.
Hutchins, James Edward
Ifill, Percy Costa
Jackson, Leon Quincy
Jamestown Ter-centennial Exposition Negro Building, Virginia
Jenkins, Willie Edward
Johnson, Conrad Adolphus Jr.
Johnson, Harvey Nathaniel
Jones, George Maceo
Jones, William Thomas
King, Horace
King, John Thomas
Lankford, Arthur Edward
Lankford, John Anderson
Lightner, Calvin Esua
Livas, Henry Lewis
Mackey, Howard Hamilton Sr.
Madison, Robert Prince
McKissack, Calvin Lunsford
McKissack, Moses III
Melby, John Alexander
Meredith, Amaza Lee
Merrick, John
Michael, John Henry
Mickels, Elon Howard
Miller, Edward Charles
Moore, John Aycocks
Moses, William Henry Jr.
National Technical Association
Norman, John Clavon Sr.
North Carolina Agricultural & Technical State University, School of Mechanic Arts
O'Neal, Kenneth Roderick
Parker, Helen Eugenia
Parker, Joseph Lincoln
Pelham, Frederick Blackburn
Persley, Louis Hudson
Pittman, William Sidney
Plater, James Alonzo
Plato, Samuel M.
Prairie View Agricultural & Mechanical College, School of Architecture
Price, Henry James
Pryce, Edward Lyons
Ransom, Leon Andrew Jr.

ALPHABETICAL LIST OF ENTRIES

Rayfield, Wallace Augustus
Reese, Lawrence
Roberson, Francis Jefferson
Roberson, Francis Rassieur
Roberts, Walter Lenox Jr.
Robinson, Hilyard Robert
Robinson, Robert L.
Robinson, William J.
Rosemond, John Henry
Rousseve, Ferdinand Lucien
Russell, Charles Thaddeus
Sealey, Roy Anthony
Smith, William W.
South Carolina Interstate and West Indian Exposition Negro Building, Charleston
Southern University, School of Architecture
Spears, Prince W.
Streat, William Alfred Jr.
Sulton, John Dennis
Tandy, Vertner Woodson
Taylor, Robert Robinson
Taylor, Robert Rochon
Tennessee Centennial and International Exposition Negro Building, Nashville
Texas Centennial Exposition Hall of Negro Life, Dallas
Thompson, Martha Ann Cassell
Thornton, William Ferguson
Tuskegee Normal & Industrial Institute, Mechanical Industries Department
Vaughn, Ralph Augustine
Vaughn, Roscoe Ingersoll
Walker, Josiah Joshua
Washington, Booker Taliaferro III
Washington, Robert Edward Lee
Welch, John Austin
Wheat, Clarence Buchanan Sr.
White, Columbus Bob
White, Donald Frank
White, Richard Cassius
Whittaker, Miller Fulton
Wigington, Clarence Wesley
Williams, Paul Revere
Williston, David Augustus
Wilson, John Louis Jr.
Woodson, Howard Dilworth
Young, Edward Walter Owen
Zenon, Golden Joseph Jr.

Julian Francis Abele
(1881–1950)

Josephine Faulkner Webster

Julian Francis Abele was one of the most prolific American architects of the Gilded Age and ensuing Country Estate Era between 1890 and 1920s, having designed over 200 buildings as senior designer for the Office of Horace Trumbauer in Philadelphia. He considered himself an *artiste* beyond racial classification—neither Black nor White. Abele was the living embodiment of Dr. W. E. B. DuBois' characterization of "double consciousness": outwardly Black, living in White America "an American, a Negro; two souls, two thoughts, two unreconciled stirrings, two warring ideals in one dark body."[1]

Julian Abele was wellborn on April 21, 1881, to an Olde Philadelphia family that traced their presence back to William Penn's grand religious experiment more than 200 hundred years ago. Julian's father, Charles Abele, was born a freedman in Chester, Pennsylvania, in 1841. He fought for Emancipation, was wounded, and settled in nearby Philadelphia, where he worked as a laborer at the U.S. Treasury Customs House, a coveted patronage position. Julian's mother, Mary Jones Abele, was a milliner and collateral descendent of Absalom Jones, the first rector of the African Church of Philadelphia.

Julian Abele was the eighth of eleven siblings. In 1893 he enrolled at Philadelphia's Institute for Colored Youth (ICY), founded by the Society of Friends or Quakers in 1852. In June 1897 Abele graduated from the ICY and won a $15 prize for the senior who attained the highest mathematics score. His aunt, Julia Jones, who taught drawing at the ICY, steered Julian toward a career in architecture.

In the fall of 1897, at age sixteen, Julian Abele was admitted to the Pennsylvania Museum and School of Industrial Arts. The world-famous museum, which also operated an industrial arts school, offered a prestigious education in the fine arts and technical industries. Abele graduated June 9, 1898, with a Certificate in Architectural Design, the first of his race to do so.[2] He further distinguished himself by winning the $25 Frederick Graff Jr. Prize awarded to the highest-ranked evening student. In the fall of 1898 Abele was accepted into the University of Pennsylvania, School of Architecture. The practicing architects who comprised the faculty taught architecture not as a science, but as a fine art in *l'espirit des l'Ecole des Beaux-Arts* in Paris. Abele's matriculation was filled with first placements in juried competitions and honors such as being elected president of the University of Pennsylvania Architectural Society. On June 18, 1902, Abele became the first Black graduate from the School of Architecture and only the second African American to earn a baccalaureate degree in architecture, following ROBERT ROBINSON TAYLOR.[3] In the fall of 1902, Abele passed the entrance examinations to the Pennsylvania Academy of the Fine Arts. His decision to pursue yet another Certificate in Architectural Design was probably influenced by his desire to further his training in oil and watercolor painting rather than advanced architectural training. On May 30, 1903, Julian Abele received a Certificate of Completion in Architectural Design from the Academy, once again becoming the first of his race to do so.[4]

In the summer of 1906, aided by Warren Poivers Laird, the director of the School of Architecture at the University of Pennsylvania, Julian Abele was hired as a junior architect by Horace Trumbauer (1868–1938). Trumbauer, whose architectural training was gained via apprenticeship, wanted a talented *Beaux Arts–*trained designer who could transform the extravagant demands of his mainline Philadelphia, 5th Avenue Manhattan, and Newport clients into huge mansions, glamorous hotels, and awe-inspiring public libraries. By 1908 Abele was senior designer for the office, and was responsible for the "look" of all major buildings. As a testament to his allegiance to Trumbauer, the rare opportunity to design significant buildings, and his high salary, Abele spent his entire forty-four-year career with the Office of Horace Trumbauer.

The scenario was repeated so often it became redundant. Marriages collapsed, inter-marriages among the wealthy were celebrated, Trumbauer gained another commission, and Abele gained another opportunity to demonstrate his architectural prowess.

In 1915 Louise Cromwell Brooks, the daughter of Eva Cromwell Stotesbury, hired Trumbauer, who assigned Abele to design "Eccleston." Inspired by Richard Castle's "Powerscourt" (1731) in Ireland, the eighteenth-century English Georgian country house had forty-five rooms, making it the largest private residence in Baltimore County, Maryland.

In 1916 Louise's mother, Eva Cromwell Stotesbury, and stepfather, Edward Stotesbury, who was senior vice president of J. Pierpoint Morgan's Philadelphia investment and banking office, commissioned Trumbauer, who then assigned Abele to design "Whitemarsh Hall." The limestone behemoth was a *grande trianon* with a total of 147 rooms.

Edward Stotesbury, also a member of Philadelphia's Fairmont Park Commission, hired the Office of Horace Trumbauer in 1927 to design the Philadelphia Free Library at 19th and Franklin Parkway. The rusticated limestone Corinthian colonnade portico and sculptural pediment were patterned by Abele from the *Ministiere de la Marine* (1731) in Paris by Jacques-Ange Gabriel.

Julian Abele married late in life to Paris émigré Marguerite Bulle on June 6, 1925. The bride was a graduate of the Conservatorie de Music in Paris with an emphasis on piano and organ. By their ninth wedding anniversary the marriage had disintegrated. Marguerite abandoned her husband, adolescent son, and infant daughter. Julian Abele never remarried.

In 1920 James Cromwell, Eva's only son, wed Delphine Dodge, the only daughter of Anna Dodge,

The Free Library of Philadelphia, *Print and Picture Collection, The Free Library of Philadelphia*

heiress to the Dodge Brothers Motor Company. Anna Dodge retained Trumbauer, who assigned Abele to design a Washington, D.C., mansion for Delphine called "Marly" (1930). At the same time that "Marly" was on the drawing boards, Abele was designing "Rose Terrace" (1931) for Anna Dodge on the shores of Lake Saint Claire in Grosse Pointe, Michigan. James Cromwell, after divorcing Delphine Dodge in 1928, married Doris Duke, who was the daughter of James Duke, president of both the American Tobacco Company and Southern Power Company. James Duke, whose trust indenture built Duke University, was one of Trumbauer's top patrons. Abele had previously designed James Duke's eighteenth-century, French academic style, 5th Avenue, New York City townhouse (1909). Julian Abele, without ever stepping foot on Duke University's campus to avoid the dehumanizing Jim Crow laws in North Carolina, designed eleven Georgian-style and thirty-eight Collegiate Gothic–style buildings for the new university from 1925 to 1940.

Julian Abele died alone in his Philadelphia row house after suffering a heart attack on April 18, 1950. He had been among a cadre of Gilded Age architects who favored not originality, but the interpretation of historic precedence. He was buried in Eden Cemetery in Collindale, Pennsylvania. There would be no massive mausoleums like the ones he designed for cigar manufacturer Charles Eisenlohr (1912), traction magnate Peter A. B. Widener (1915), and manufacturer Thomas Develon Jr. (1932). Abele's gravestone, as was the man, is unobtrusive.

Notes
1. William E. B. DuBois, *The Souls of Black Folk* (Chicago: McClurg & Co., 1931), p. 3.
2. Pennsylvania Museum and School of Industrial Art, "Commencement Program 1898," Philadelphia Museum of Art Archives.
3. University of Pennsylvania, The record, "Julian Francis Abele," *Class of 1902* (Philadelphia: University of Pennsylvania, 1902), p. 9.
4. Pennsylvania Academy of the Fine Arts, Student Records, "Julian F. Abele Registration Card," Archives of American Art, roll 4316, Washington, D.C.

Bibliography
American Institute of Architects Philadelphia Chapter. *21st Annual Architectural Exhibition of the T-Square Club.* Philadelphia: Philadelphia AIA, 1915.
Maher, James T. *The Twilight of Splendor.* Boston: Little Brown & Co., 1975.
Mao, Jackson B. "The Architecture of Horace Trumbauer Firm." Master's thesis, Drexel University, 1975.

DRECK SPURLOCK WILSON

BUILDING LIST

Name	Address	City	State	Year	Comments
Baker, Raymond T. "Marly"	2300 Foxhall Rd., NW	Washington	DC	1931	Now Belgium ambassador's residence
Beneficial Savings Bank	826 East Allegheny Ave.	Philadelphia	PA	1923	Kensington branch
Berwind, Herminie "Knollhunt"	Spruce Tree & Berwind Rds.	Radnor	PA	1908	
Brokaw, Howard C.	Northern Blvd.	Brookville	NY	1916	Now Muttontown Golf Club
Brooke, George A. "Almonbury"	Mill & Conestoga Rds.	Villanova	PA	c1925	
Brooks, Walter, Jr.	10729 Park Heights Ave.	Owings Mill	MD	1915	
Bucknell University	Rte. 15 in front of stadium	Lewisburg	PA	1923	Mathewson Gateway
Carhart, Amory S.	3 East 95th St.	New York	NY	1913	Now *Lycee Francais*
Chateau Crillon	222 S. 19th St.	Philadelphia	PA	1928	
Clanerda Presbyterian Church	34th & Girard Sts.	Philadelphia	PA	1912	
Clews, James B. "La Lanterne"	Wolver Hollow & Piping Rock	Brookville	NY	1929	
Colver Presbyterian Church	7th & Reese Ave.	Colver	PA	1913	
Continental Hotel	820 Chestnut St.	Philadelphia	PA	1922	Now Continental Hotel
Cramp, Theodore W. "Portlege"	464 S. Roberts Rd.	Bryn Mawr	PA	1910	
Darlington, H. S.	Mill & Conestoga Rds.	Villanova	PA	1911	Now American Missionary Fellowship
Dixon, Fitz E. "Ronaele Manor"	Church Rd. & Washington Ln.	Elkins Park	PA	1923	demolished
Dodge, Anna	12 Lakeshore Rd.	Grosse Pointe	MI	1931	"Rose Terrace," demolished
Dows, David "Charlton Hall"	Brookfield SE of Hempsted	Brookville	NY	1916	
Drexel, John R. "Fairholme"	237 Ruggles Ave.	Newport	RI	1910	
Duke, James B.	1 E. 78th St.	New York	NY	1909	Now NYU Institute of Fine Arts
Duke's Chapel	807 Old Oxford Rd.	Bragtown	NC	1926	
Duke University Botany Bldg.	Campus	Durham	NC	1929	
Duke University Chapel	Campus	Durham	NC	1929	
Duke University Dormitories 1–5	Campus	Durham	NC	1925	
Duke University Engineers' Dormitory	Campus	Durham	NC	1925	
Duke University Faculty Houses 1–11	Campus	Durham	NC	1930	

JULIAN FRANCIS ABELE

BUILDING LIST (continued)

Name	Address	City/County	State	Year	Comments
Duke University Gymnasium	Campus	Durham	NC	1940	
Duke University Hospital	Campus	Durham	NC	1938	
Duke University Indoor Stadium	Campus	Durham	NC	1939	
Duke University Perkins Library	Campus	Durham	NC	1926	
Duke University Physics Bldg.	Campus	Durham	NC	1947	
Duke University Private Patient's Bldg.	Campus	Durham	NC	1938	
Eisenlohr, Otto	3812 Walnut St.	Philadelphia	PA	1911	Now Univ. of Pa. President's Residence
Elmendorf Farm	3931 Park Pike	Fayette County	KY	1911	
Episcopal Hospital	Front & Lehigh Sts.	Philadelphia	PA	1933	
Fifth Baptist Church	18th & Spring Garden Sts.	Philadelphia	PA	1924	
First Church of Christ, Science	138 Lakeview Ave.	West Palm Beach	FL	1927	
Free Library	1901 Vine St.	Philadelphia	PA	1917	
Grace, Joseph P. "Tullaroan"	North Service Rd.	Manhasset	NY	1920	Now Deepdale Golf Clubhouse
Grace Presbyterian Church	444 Old York Rd.	Jenkintown	PA	1909	
Hahneman Medical College Out-Patient's Bldg.	15th north of Race St.	Philadelphia	PA	1947	
Harvard University Institute of Geographical Exploration	2 Divinity Square	Cambridge	MA	1930	
Harvard University Widener Library	Harvard Yard near Mass. Ave.	Cambridge	MA	1913	
Huff, George	1600 New Hampshire Ave. NW	Washington	DC	1906	Now Argentine Embassy
Jefferson Medical College Curtis Clinic	1015 Walnut St.	Philadelphia	PA	1929	
Jenkintown Bank & Trust Co.	400 Old York Rd.	Jenkintown	PA	1924	Now First Union Bank
Keswick Theatre	291 Keswick Ave.	Glenside	PA	1928	
Knight, Edward C. Jr. "Stonybrook"	Stonybrook Rd.	Middletown	NJ	1927	
Lafayette College *Chi Phi* House	W. Campus Dr. & Sullivan Ln.	Easton	PA	1909	
Martin, John C.	Greenwood & Church Rds.	Wyncote	PA	1922	Now Rabbinical College
McFadden, George H.	200 South Ithan Ave.	Rosemont	PA	1923	
Mitchell, Frank P.	1815 Q St., NW	Washington	DC	1912	Now Argentine ambassador's residence
Montgomery, Robert "Ardrosson"	Newtown Rd. at Abraham's Ln.	Villanova	PA	1911	
New York Evening Post	75 West St.	New York	NY	1925	
North Broad Street Station	2601 N. Broad St.	Philadelphia	PA	1928	
Northern Home for Children	Ridge Ave. & Laurison St.	Philadelphia	PA	1927	
Ogontz School for Girls	1600 Woodland Rd.	Rydal	PA	1916	Now PSU Southerland Hall
Parson, Hubert T.	Cedar & Norwood Ave.	West Long Branch	NH	1927	Now Monmouth College Wilson Hall
Pere Marquette Hotel	501 Main St.	Peoria	IL	1923	
Philadelphia Stock Exchange	1409 Walnut St.	Philadelphia	PA	1912	
Philadelphia YMCA	1007 Lehigh Ave.	Philadelphia	PA	1912	North Branch
Phipps, Henry C.	345 Lakeville Rd.	Great Neck	NY	1916	Now Great Neck School Admin. Bldg.
Phipps, John S. "Westbury House"	71 Old Westbury Rd.	Westbury	NY	1911	
Pulitzer Bldg.	Park Row & Franfort St.	New York	NY	1907	
Rice, Eleanor *Miramar*	Bellevue & Yzanga Ct.	Newport	RI	1930	
Ritz-Carlton Hotel	Broad St. below Chestnut	Philadelphia	PA	1911	
St. Paul's Episcopal Church	Ashbourne & Old York Rds.	Elkins Park	PA	1912	
Stotesbury, Edward T. "Whitemarsh Hall"	Paper Mill & Willow Grove	Chestnut Hill	PA	1916	
University of Pennsylvania Irvine Auditorium	34th & Spruce Sts.	Philadelphia	PA	1928	
Watson, James E. "High Gate"	801 Fairmont Ave.	Fairmont	WVA	1909	Now Ross Funeral Home
Widener Memorial Home	2800 Atlantic Ave.	Longport	NJ	1911	Now Gospel Hall Home
Widener, Peter A. B.	3822 Ridge Ave.	Philadelphia	PA	1915	Mausoleum
Wildenstein Gallery	19 East 64th St.	New York	NY	1931	
Windber Hospital	600 Somerset Ave.	Windber	PA	1930	
Zimmerman, Daniel	800 Georgian Pl.	Somerset County	PA	1915	Now Inn at Georgian Place
Zoological Society	34th & Girard Ave.	Philadelphia	PA	1912	

Alabama State Fair Negro Building
Montgomery (1906)

Alabama's capital city was the site of the state fair in 1906, as it had been on other such occasions. Located on the Alabama River and with excellent railroad connections, Montgomery was the center of wholesale trade for central Alabama. It was home to an African American population that was in the majority in Montgomery County and sometimes outnumbered Whites in the city. Since the adoption of the new state constitution in 1901, most Blacks and a large number of Whites had been disfranchised. "Separate but equal" had entered the vocabulary, and segregation was a factor in almost every area of Montgomery and state life. There was a strong connection, however, between the races.

Alabama state fairs went back to antebellum days and continued as popular entertainment for people bolstered by prestigious awards for the accomplishments of those engaged in agriculture. By the turn of the twentieth century, the fair was being held at the fairgrounds, north of the city, and was eagerly anticipated by most of the citizenry. Birmingham also had fairs, as did other cities in Alabama, but the Montgomery fair was very popular.

Sponsored by the Alabama Agricultural Association, the fair encouraged African American entries, and the White directors invited the "Negroes of the state to participate."[1] According to the *Montgomery Advertiser*, the largest local newspaper that was distributed statewide, there was enthusiasm in the acceptance of the invitation. In the tone and attitude of the day, a reporter wrote,

> The Negroes have, without cost to the management, erected a building on the fair grounds which reflects credit upon the Negroes who built it and made the architectural plans for same and upon the whole State Fair Management as well.
>
> Under the direction of Booker T. Washington of Tuskegee Institute, they have worked up interest throughout the State and have put together a collection of exhibits which shows the progress of the Negroes of Alabama. The exhibits focused on the "educational, moral and industrial life of the Negroes."[2]

The Negro Building, designed by WALTER THOMAS BAILEY of TUSKEGEE INSTITUTE, was "L" shaped with exterior dimensions of 72 × 90 feet. Inside were an exhibit room, 50 × 75 feet; a dining room, 22 × 30 feet; a kitchen and pantry; general waiting room; and rooms for men and women. Three entrances led into the exhibit room from narrow halls. Two rows of columns in the exhibit room, spaced 13 feet on center,

Alabama State Fair Negro Building, *Montgomery Advertiser*[3]

supported the roof. The ceilings were 24 feet high with eleven large windows that were 7 feet wide and 13 feet tall. The reporter added that these windows, with their oval tops, were one of the most attractive exterior features.

The reporter continued with the description:

> Extending around the exterior of the building is a base four feet high. On this base pilasters are placed extending to the corners. The whole exterior is weatherboarded and painted. The interior walls are not covered in any way, but are left with studs exposed. Situated on the corner of two streets, it occupies a very prominent position and thus its pleasing architectural lines are shown to great advantage. This location on two streets gives a splendid opportunity to give easy entrance to all parts of the building, especially the dining room and main exhibit room.[4]

Saturday, October 27, 1906, was set aside for "Negro Day" with an extensive program planned including parades by secret societies, a speech by BOOKER TALIFERRO WASHINGTON, and talks by other leaders of the race. Governor William D. Jelks offered remarks as well. Trotting horses raced in the afternoon, and nighttime fireworks concluded the day.

In urging Negroes to attend, Booker Taliferro Washington stated that the officers of the fair had given great encouragement to them, and he hoped that all would show their appreciation by turning out in great numbers. He added that "thousands of white people in Alabama have visited the Negro Building and have expressed their great satisfaction at the evidences that the race is making."

The Alabama State Fair Negro Building was demolished after the fair closed.

Notes
1. "Negroes of Alabama Have A Fine Display at Fair," *Montgomery Advertiser 25,* October 1906, p. 10.
2. "Today Is Negro Day at Alabama Agricultural Fair," *Montgomery Advertiser 27,* October 1906, p. 1.
3. "Negroes at Fair Urge Law and Order League," *Montgomery Advertiser 28,* October 1906, p. 1.
4. Ibid., p. 1.

Bibliography
"Robert Robinson Taylor." In *Cyclopedia of the Colored Race.* Montgomery, Ala.: National Publishing Co., 1919.

MARY ANN NEELY,
MONTGOMERY, ALABAMA

Archibald Alphonse Alexander
(1888–1958)

Harmon Foundation

"Engineering is a tough field at best and it may be twice as tough for a Negro," a professor told Archie Alexander, a student at the State University of Iowa in Iowa City, in 1909. Moreover, the professor had "never heard of a Negro engineer."[1] Forty years later Carter G. Woodson, founder of the Association for the Study of Negro Life and History, wrote that Alexander overcame these words of discouragement, and admired Alexander as "The most successful Negro businessman in America."[2] *Ebony Magazine* echoed these sentiments in two 1949 articles profiling accomplished and wealthy African American businessmen, including Alexander. His commercial success as an architectural engineer is noteworthy for a very unusual business structure: an inter-racial partnership.

Alexander was born in 1888 in Ottumwa, Iowa, where there were approximately 500 Blacks out of a total population of 14,000 people. His parents were Price and Mary Alexander. Price earned a living as a coachman and janitor. One of young Archie's play activities was building dams with his eight brothers and sisters in a creek behind his home. In 1899 the family moved to a small farm outside Des Moines when his father became head custodian at the Des Moines National Bank, a prestigious job for a Black man. In Iowa's capital city, Alexander attended Oak Park Grammar School, Oak Park High School, and the now-defunct Highland Park College for one year.

Alexander's engineering education began in earnest at the State University of Iowa (now University of Iowa). Alexander also played for the school football team, earning the nickname "Alexander the Great," and joined the *Kappa Alpha Psi* fraternity. During the summer he worked as draftsman for Marsh Engineers, a Des Moines bridge-designing firm. In 1912 Alexander received his bachelor of science degree; he was the university's first Black football player and engineer. He continued his education at the University of London for some coursework in bridge design in 1921, and obtained his civil engineering degree in 1925 at the State University of Iowa. Alexander received an honorary doctorate in engineering from HOWARD UNIVERSITY in 1947.

Alexander's first years in the business world seemed to bear out his professor's prediction. Every engineering firm in Des Moines turned down his employment application. Initially discouraged, he became a laborer in a steel shop at Marsh Engineering, earning $10 per week. Within two years he was earning $70 per week in charge of bridge construction in Iowa and Minnesota.

In 1914 Alexander started his own engineering company, A. A. Alexander, Inc. To extend his construction projects beyond minority clients, in 1917 he became partners with white contractor George F. Higbee, a Marsh acquaintance. Alexander & Higbee, Inc. specialized in bridge construction, sewer systems, and road construction. Alexander lost his partner in 1925 when Higbee died from an injury suffered in a construction accident.

Shortly after Higbee's death, Alexander received his largest contract to date—the construction in 1927 of a $1.2 million central heating and generating station for the University of Iowa. Perched along the Iowa River, it is still in use. The following year, he finished two other projects for his *alma mater*: a power plant and tunnel under the Iowa River that were designed to pipe steam, hot water, and electricity from the power plant to the campus on the other side of the river.

A year after completing these projects, Alexander teamed with his second White partner, Maurice A. Repass, a football teammate who was also an engineering graduate. He joined forces with Alexander in 1929 when they bid for a Michigan contract. The City of Grand Rapids awarded the new partnership the contract to build a $1 million sewage treatment plant in 1930. Columbus, Nebraska, also hired Alexander & Repass to build the Loup River Power Plant in 1933. As the Great Depression worsened, the firm struggled to stay in business despite its good reputation. The partners laid off all of their workers and grabbed any sort of work, such as repairing sidewalks, patching streets, and other miscellaneous building and repair jobs—doing the work themselves.

Alexander & Repass fortunes improved considerably after they affiliated with Des Moines' Glen C. Herrick, a prominent White contractor and road builder. Herrick, who was under contract to develop a canal system in Nebraska, had accompanying bridge work and hired Alexander & Repass for the task. Herrick also provided financing for a number of projects by Alexander & Repass. The firm's next large project also occurred in the Cornhusker state, where, in 1935, they designed and began construction of the Union Pacific Railroad Bridge crossing the North Platte River. At about the same time, the firm was awarded bridge-building projects in Des Moines.

A salutory reputation, proven ability, solid financial resources, and capitalization positioned the firm to bid on projects in other parts of the country. The expanding area of federal contracts brought on by the war effort enabled Alexander & Repass to successfully bid on the construction of the airfield at the U.S. Army air base in Chewhaw, Alabama, the 99th Pursuit Squadron Air Base and Pilot Training School, where the Tuskegee Airmen trained.

During World War II, Alexander & Repass opened a second office in Washington, D.C. This became a profitable necessity because the federal government accepted their bids for a number of lucrative and publicly visible construction projects around the nation's capital. Alexander designed the granite and limestone Tidal Basin Bridge and Seawall, which employed 160 workers and cost $1 million to build. Other Washington, D.C., projects included the K Street elevated highway and underpass from Key Bridge to 27th Street, NW; the $3.5 million Whitehurst Freeway alongside the Potomac River, which carried traffic around Georgetown; and the overpass that took Riggs Road under the tracks of the Baltimore & Ohio Railroad. Alexander also designed and his company built the Frederick Douglass Memorial Estate Apartments in Washington, D.C.'s Anacostia neighborhood in 1955.

Archie Alexander's role as designer in his other construction projects is not documented. His role in the partnership was to pursue contracts. "Some of them act as though they want to bar me but I walk in, throw my

Steam Plant, University of Iowa,
University of Iowa Archives

cards down and I'm in. My money talks," Alexander once asserted, "just as loudly as theirs."[3] Known for a "commanding personality and imposing appearance," Alexander, with his football-player bulk, was a capable taskmaster and known for his directness, honesty, and bluntness.[4] Repass served as the inside man, reviewing contracts and handling mechanical details.

Alexander's stature in the Black community in both Des Moines and the nation's capital garnered him a leadership role in a number of civic-improvement and race-relations efforts. His many civic involvements around the country included being a trustee at both TUSKEGEE INSTITUTE and HOWARD UNIVERSITY, a member of a 1934 team that investigated the economic development potential of Haiti (at the request of the Haitian president), and national polemarch of the *Kappa Alpha Psi* Fraternity. Other achievements included receiving the Harmon Award in 1926 for outstanding achievement in Negro business and winning the National Association for the Advancement of Colored People's Spingarn Medal in 1934 as the second most successful Negro in American business. In Iowa Alexander served as state chairman of the Iowa Republican Party and was a board member of the Colored Young Mens Christian Association. He headed the Des Moines branch, National Association for the Advancement of Colored People; served on the Des Moines Inter-racial Commission; chaired the Polk County, Iowa, draft board; and presided over the Negro Community Center.

Alexander's prominence did not allow him to escape the tentacles of racism. One of the worst examples occurred in 1944 when he purchased a large house in a fashionable White Des Moines neighborhood and had to fight a restrictive racial covenant. The first morning after he moved into his home, he and his wife Audra woke up to a burning cross in their front lawn.

The culmination of his public service was his selection by President Dwight David Eisenhower in 1954 to serve as governor of the Virgin Islands, which turned out to be an unhappy experience. His blunt, outspoken style and aggressive agenda to develop the islands did little to endear him with the population. Moreover, because he had already begun to develop business interests in South America and the Caribbean he was being accused of cronyism and as a result was being attacked by a growing number of members of the island's legislature. Alexander lasted in this position for eighteen months, resigning partially because of declining health.

Following his unsatisfying foray into politics, Alexander retired and moved back to Des Moines. He died of a heart attack three years later in 1958.

Notes
1. Charles E. Wynes, "Alexander the Great, Bridge Builder," *Palimpsest* (1985): 80.
2. Mary McGaffin, "Alexander and White Partner Amaze Capital," *Des Moines Sunday Register*, 18 December 1949, p. 116.
3. "Alexander Won't Let Color Handicap Him in Getting Jobs," *Ebony Magazine* (December 1949): 60.
4. Ibid.

Bibliography
Bergman, Leola N. *Studies in Iowa History: The Negro in Iowa*. Iowa City: State Historical Society of Iowa, 1969.

"Personal Papers of Archie Alexander." Special Collections Department, University of Iowa Libraries, Iowa City, Iowa.

Peters, J. Jerome. *The Story of Kappa Alpha Psi*. Philadelphia: Kappa Alpha Psi Fraternity, 1967.

JACK LUFKIN,
CURATOR, STATE OF IOWA MUSEUM

STRUCTURE LIST

Name	Address	City	State	Year	Comments
4th Avenue Viaduct	Over Des Moines River	Des Moines	IA		
Alexander, Archie	2901 5th Ave.	Des Moines	IA	1913	
Chicago, Rock Island & Pacific Bridge	Over Missouri River	Kansas City	MO		Kansas City short-line
College Street Viaduct	Loup Rock Island tracks	Iowa City	IA		
River Power Plant	Platte River Basin	Columbus	NE	1933	
Des Moines River Highway Bridge	Over Des Moines River	Mt. Pleasant	IA		
Des Moines Sewage Disposal Plant	300 Vandalia Dr.	Des Moines	IA		
East 14th Street Viaduct	Over Des Moines River	Des Moines	IA	1937	
Fluer Drive Bridge	Over Racoon River	Des Moines	IA	1937	
Francis Scott Key Bridge	Over Potomac River	Washington	DC		Widening
Frederick Douglass Public Dwellings	1200 Alabama Ave., SE	Washington	DC	1941	Hilyard Robinson, assoc. Architect
Grand Rapids Sewage Plant	NR. Grand River	Grand Rapids	NE	1930	
Independence Avenue Bridge	Over Tidal Basin	Washington	DC		
James River Bridge	Over James River	Mitchell	SD		
Union Pacific Bridge	Above North Platte River	North Platte	NE	1935	
University of Iowa Steam Plant	Campus	Iowa City	IA	1927	
University of Iowa Power Plant	Campus	Iowa City	IA	1928	

Appalachian Exposition Negro Building, Knoxville, Tennesssee (1910)

The Negro Building was heralded as one of the most beautiful buildings constructed for the Knoxville, Tennessee, Appalachian Exposition of 1910.

> What colored man could visit the magnificent structure at the head of the lower lake and know that it is a product of colored mind and muscle from its very conception in the architect's brain to the last nail driven by black hands without experiencing a thrill of inspiration?[1]

asked Dr. Henry M. Green, president of the Colored Department, in his speech for the fair's opening ceremonies in Chilhowee Park. The media agreed. "It is doubtful, very doubtful, if ever a more perfect presentation of progress and achievements of the Negro race has ever been made in the South."[2]

JOHN HENRY MICHAEL, head of the Mechanical Department at Knoxville College, designed the building while his business partner William Stacy supervised its construction by Knoxville College carpentry students and the Stacy & Michael Contracting Company. The Appalachian Exposition's architectural commission had asked for plans for a 6,600-square-foot structure to be built in a combination of Oriental and Modern styles and the building resulting from the plans Michael submitted to fit those criteria came to be called the greatest exhibit of the Colored Department.

Fifty feet wide, sixty feet long, and thirty feet tall, the 2-story stucco building occupied a hill at the north end of the park's lower lake. Its silhouette was outlined by hundreds of tiny electric lights that illuminated its white facade for fairgoers across the entire park to see after dark. Inside it featured a monumental double stairway leading to a mezzanine that overlooked a 25 × 50 foot open court of exhibition space on the floor below. Additionally, a fully equipped hos-

Appalachian Exposition Negro Building, *McClung Historical Collection, Knox County Public Library*

pital emergency area was installed in two rooms at the far end of the second floor and staffed by doctors and nurses from Knoxville College ready to treat "colored" fairgoers in need of medical assistance.

Knoxville's Appalachian Exposition was the first such large-scale fair held in the city. Inspired by the recent Atlanta COTTON STATES AND INTERNATIONAL EXPOSITION of 1895, the Appalachian Exposition was intended to present a regional—if not national—forum for Knoxville, not only to celebrate the city's coming of age as an industrial center of the South, but also to showcase its beauty, its resources, and its position as a ripe spot for further economic and commercial growth. The Appalachian Exposition was a success for Knoxville's civic boosters and was so popular that it was repeated in 1911 and again in 1913 as the National Conservation Exposition.

All the other original buildings built for the fair were renovated or completely reconstructed in preparation for the subsequent expositions. However, the Negro Building and the Main Building from the first Appalachian Exposition were deemed exemplary structures by the architectural commission and allowed to stand as they were. Later, Chilhowee Park passed into private ownership and eventually fell into disrepair, during which time the Negro Building was demolished. Today, Chilhowee is once again a public park, but all that remains of the Negro Building is a memory.

Notes
1. Henry M. Green, "Negroes' Day at Exposition," *Daily Journal and Tribune (Knoxville)*, 25 September 1910, p. 2.
2. "Buildings of the Appalachian Exposition," *Daily Journal and Tribune, (Knoxville)*, 1 September 1910, p. 3.

Bibliography
Ash, Stephen V. *Meet Me at the Fair! A Pictorial History of the Tennessee Valley Agricultural & Industrial Fair.* Knoxville: The Fair Company, 1985.
Booker, Robert J. *And There Was Light!* Virginia Beach: Donning Company, 1994.
Goodman, William, ed. *The First Exposition of Conservation and Its Builders.* Knoxville: Lithographing Company, 1914.

DANETTE WELCH,
KNOX COUNTY PUBLIC LIBRARY,
CALVIN M. MCCLUNG HISTORICAL COLLECTION

Romulus Cornelius Archer Jr.
(1890–1968)

Washington Evening Times

Romulus C. Archer Jr. was born in Norfolk, Virginia, on March 11, 1890. His father, Romulus Cornelius Archer Sr., was a plastering contractor in Norfolk and probably the motivator behind his son's decision to become an architect. His mother, Mary Poindexter Archer, was a homemaker. Romulus Jr. graduated from Norfolk Public High School after five years of study in 1908. He was the oldest of five siblings, and had two brothers, William A. and Andrew E., and two sisters, Mary E. and Carey V. Romulus Jr. went on to enroll at Norfolk Mission College, where he remained until 1910. For the next several years, Archer studied architecture through the International Correspondence School in Scranton, Pennsylvania, a path of study also chosen by SAMUEL M. PLATO, JOHN ANDERSON LANKFORD, and many others. Archer's final year of formal architecture education was received at Columbia University, where he studied for one year in 1913.

Archer enlisted in the U.S. Army on March 11, 1918. Late entering World War II, he did not see combat after being assigned to the regimental band, where he was promoted to the rank of corporal. He was honorably discharged approximately a year and a month later on April 8, 1919. Archer would return to active duty during World War II as a mechanical drafting instructor.

From June 1 until November 15, 1921, Archer was employed briefly as one of the few Black architects in the U.S. Treasury Department, Office of Supervising Architect in Washington, D.C. Probably the only other Black professional in the office was supervising architect WILLIAM WILSON COOKE. Also in 1921 Archer joined Florida Avenue Baptist Church, located in northwest D.C., and he remained a member for nearly fifty years.

In December 1921 Archer opened a solo practice from his home. Two years later, with his business fortunes improving, he relocated to an office building at 1449 Florida Avenue, NW, near U Street, NW, D.C.'s bustling Black business corridor. In January 1926 the D.C. Board of Examiners and Registrars of Architects issued license No. 117 to Archer, making him the second Black architect in D.C. to be licensed, following John Anderson Lankford.[1] The three architects Archer selected "to certify to his character, competency and qualifications" were D.C.-based architects Lankford, ROSCOE INGERSOLL VAUGHN, and Lee L. Wise, an African American architect based in Portsmouth, Virginia, who Archer probably knew from his earlier years in nearby Norfolk. Archer's office was known as a training ground for inexperienced Black architects, and the Young Mens Christian Association in 1964 named him "Citizen of the Year" for apprenticing so many young architects.

Romulus Jr. married Louise Williams in the 1920s. She was a public school teacher formerly from Durham, North Carolina. No children were born to their union, and she died in 1948. Romulus Jr. married a second time, to Nettie Archer, who passed away in 1965. They had no children.

Archer fashioned a career as an architect of structures located predominantly in the northeast Brook-

First Baptist Church, *Pamela Scott*

land neighborhood of D.C. He designed apartment buildings, churches, and medium-sized commercial buildings. During the 1920s and 1930s he designed eleven houses in Brookland, all of which were red brick Georgian style—the style preferred by his Howard University and federal employee clients. Archer's building list also included five churches in Washington, D.C., and churches in Norfolk, Lynchburg, and Danville, Virginia. Archer's full-time office staff probably never exceeded five employees. Three who were with him the longest were architectural draftsmen Frederick W. Thomas, Clayton Kelly, and Gustavus N. Bull.

Archer was a long-time treasurer of the D.C. chapter of the NATIONAL TECHNICAL ASSOCIATION and a member of the American Art Society.

Romulus Archer Jr. died November 29, 1968, in the Beverly Nursing Home located in Washington, D.C.[2] His funeral was held at Florida Avenue Baptist Church, where he had been baptized forty-seven years earlier. Corporal Archer chose burial in Arlington National Cemetery.

Notes
1. D.C. Board of Examiners and Registrars of Architects "Romulus Cornelius Archer Jr.," Certificate No. 117, issued 15 January 1926.
2. "Romulus C. Archer Jr., 77, Architect Here for 40 Years," *Washington Post*, 1 December 1969, p. B6.

DRECK SPURLOCK WILSON

BUILDING LIST

Name	Address	City	State	Year	Comments
____ Baptist Church	209 K St., NE	Washington	DC	1954	
____ Apartments	910 Shepherd St., NW	Washington	DC	1947	
____ Apartments	337 Oakdale Pl., NW	Washington	DC	1939	
____ Baptist Church	935 Florida Ave., NW	Washington	DC	1926	
____ duplex	501–03 Oakwood St., SE	Washington	DC	1941	
____ duplex	512–16 Oakwood St., SE	Washington	DC	1940	
____ duplex	525–27 Oakwood St., SE	Washington	DC	1941	
____ duplex	528–30 Oakwood St., SE	Washington	DC	1940	
____ duplex	532–34 Oakwood St., SE	Washington	DC	1940	
____ duplex	536–38 Oakwood St., SE	Washington	DC	1940	
____ duplex	519–21 Oakwood St., SE	Washington	DC	1940	
____ duplex	520–24 Oakwood St., SE	Washington	DC	1940	
____ house	634 O St., NW	Washington	DC	1939	

ROMULUS CORNELIUS ARCHER JR

BUILDING LIST (continued)

Name	Address	City	State	Year	Comments
Allen Realty Co. House	452 Lebaum St., SE	Washington	DC	1938	
Allen Realty Co. House	456 Lebaum St., SE	Washington	DC	1938	
Allen Realty Co. House	460 Lebaum St., SE	Washington	DC	1938	
Anchor Apartments	1901–16th St., NW	Washington	DC	1934	
Archer, Romulus	215 Florida Ave., NW	Washington	DC		
Asbury Methodist Church	1110 K St., NW	Washington	DC	1950	Alterations
Brooks, J. R.		Washington	DC	1957	
Capitol View Baptist Church	5201 Ames St., NE	Washington	DC	1947	Demolished
Chandler, George M.	1416 Hamlin St., NE	Washington	DC	1955	
Chandler, George M.	2960–13th St., NE	Washington	DC	1956	
Church of God	1512 K St., SE	Washington	DC	1948	
Curtis, J. S.	1413 Hamlin St., NE	Washington	DC	1935	
D'April Brothers Housing		Wheaton	MD		Tract houses
David, George	3790 Nichols Ave., SE	Washington	DC		Demolished
Dillard Apartments	2nd & A Sts., NE	Washington	DC	c1925	
Ephesus 7th Day Adventist Church	3985 Massachusetts Ave., SE	Washington	DC	1956	
Executive Motel	1635 New York Ave., NE	Washington	DC	1957	
First Baptist Church	50th & B Sts., SE	Washington	DC	1924	
First Baptist Church	623 Florida Ave., NW	Washington	DC		
Franklin, Homer	1518 Jackson St., NE	Washington	DC	1938	
Froe, U. M.	1509 Girard St., NE	Washington	DC	1937	
Galilee Baptist Church	523–55th St., NE	Washington	DC	1938	Demolished
Garrett Congregational Methodist Episcopal Church		Norfolk	VA	1920	Demolished
Grant Street Holiness Church		Norfolk	VA	1920	Demolished
Hamline Methodist Episcopal Church	1500–9th St., NW	Washington	DC	1946	Alterations
Holy Trinity Apostolic Church	1618–11th St., NW	Washington	DC	1955	Alterations
Jackson, F.	1352 Newton St., NE	Washington	DC	1950	
Johnson, Morris	1515 Jackson St., NE	Washington	DC	1950	
Jones Memorial Methodist Church Education Bldg.	5600 G St., NW	Washington	DC	1952	
Kapnick Apartments	4428 Benning Rd., NE	Washington	DC	1945	Demolished
Kramer, J. W.	623 Mellon St., SE	Washington	DC	1937	
Kramer, J. W.	625 Mellon St., SE	Washington	DC	1937	
Kramer, Leon A.	532 Lebaum St., SE	Washington	DC	1937	
Kramer, Leon A.	460–62 Mellon St., SE	Washington	DC	1939	
Kramer V. W.	515 Lebaum St., SE	Washington	DC	1937	
Loyal Street Baptist Church	468 Halbrook St.	Danville	VA	1924	
Macedonia Baptist Church	2625 Stanton Rd., SE	Washington	DC	1946	
Mentrotone Baptist Church	5126 B St., SE	Washington	DC	1955	
New Hope Free Church Parsonage	1104 W St., NW	Washington	DC	1938	
Okert, D. M.	1415 Oak St., NW	Washington	DC	1935	
Robinson, H. J.	1300 Hamlin St., NE	Washington	DC	1941	
Saterwhite Store	1212 U St., NW	Washington	DC	1922	
Shaw United Methodist Church	2525–12th Pl., SE	Washington	DC	1954	
Shop-Rite Liquor Store	6333 New Hampshire Ave.	Takoma Park	MD		
Southern Baptist Church	134 L St., NW	Washington	DC	1938	
St. Paul Congregational Methodist Church	401 I St., SE	Washington	DC	1924	
Tabernacle Baptist Church	719 Division Ave., NE	Washington	DC	1936	Demolished
Virginia Baptist Convention School	Campus	Lynchburg	VA	1924	
Virginia Theological Seminary Administration Bldg.	Campus	Lynchburg	VA	1920	
Yenching Palace Restaurant	3524 Connecticut Ave., NW	Washington	DC	1945	

Walter Thomas Bailey
(1882–1941)

Courtesy of the University of Illinois Archives

Walter Thomas Bailey was born in Kewanee, Illinois, on January 11, 1882. He was the son of Emanuel and Lucy Reynolds Bailey. A graduate of Kewanee High School, he entered the University of Illinois in Champaign in September 1900. He undertook studies in the architectural program and was a member of the student "Architects' Club." He married Josephine L. McCurdy on October 15, 1904, and they had two daughters—Edyth Hazel born in 1905 and Alberta Josephine born in 1913.

After graduating from the University of Illinois in June 1904 with a bachelor of arts in architecture, Bailey returned to Kewanee, where he worked as a draftsman in the office of architect Henry Eckland. By February 1905 he had returned to Champaign, where he briefly worked in the architectural office of Spencer & Temple. A turning point in Bailey's career came in September 1905 when he went to work for Booker T. Washington's TUSKEGEE INSTITUTE, where he headed the school's Mechanical Industries Department and also supervised the architectural and planning aspects of the campus.

Bailey left Tuskegee Institute in 1916 to open his own office in Memphis, Tennessee, where he maintained a successful practice specializing in churches. While in Memphis Bailey obtained beneficial business contacts through the lodges of the Knights of Pythias, an African American fraternal organization. These contacts resulted in many commissions. Most notably, this connection netted Bailey the largest project of his career and one of the major African American building projects of the early twentieth century—the 8-story National Pythian Temple in Chicago. Conceptualized in 1922, the building was planned to be the headquarters of the Knights of Pythias and to house the lodge's combined national offices, numerous meeting halls, and rent-producing stores and offices. The site was in the heart of Chicago's thriving Bronzeville "city-within-a-city" Black business community on the South Side, which already had several major commercial buildings that were developed and built with Black capital during the 1910s and 1920s. Estimated to cost over $1 million dollars, it was bragged about as "the largest building financed, designed and built by African Americans" and towered above its more modestly scaled neighbors.[1]

When construction began in 1924, Bailey moved his architectural practice to Chicago, where he was the first licensed Black architect in the city. He rented an office in the Overton-Hygenic Building, a Black-owned office building near the construction site. Financial difficulties caused construction to proceed slowly. By 1928 the massive, yellow brick exterior enlivened by terra-cotta ornaments with Egyptian motifs had been completed, but the interiors remained unfinished. Bailey relocated his architectural office to a space in the mostly vacant building. The lodge eventually lost ownership of the property, and it was finally built out as multi-family housing as part of a Works Progress Administration project. Abandoned in the 1970s, the building was demolished in 1980.

Despite the fact that Chicago's Black business community was noted for its sponsorship of new buildings during the 1920s, Walter Bailey had few substantial commissions—aside from the ill-fated Knights of Pythias Temple—during this period. His subsequent architectural practice was largely devoted to smaller commercial, church, and remodeling projects. With the onset of the Great Depression, his practice shrank significantly, paralleling the widespread financial collapse of Chicago's African American business community as a whole.

Bailey's final major project was the design for the First Church of Deliverance (1939) in Chicago, a streamlined *Art Moderne* church that radically broke with established traditions of ecclesiastical architecture. The unconventional design was undoubtedly guided by the forward-thinking ideas of its pastor, Reverend Clarence Cobbs, who was among the pioneering Black ministers to broadcast his sermons on the radio. The project was an extensive rebuilding and extension of a factory building that Reverend Cobbs had previously remodeled for the church. Instead of the soaring verticality of typical churches, Bailey's design hugged the ground with horizontal ribbons of glazed terra cotta, alternating with expanses of glass block. Inside, a wide expansive sanctuary had a low acoustically treated ceiling that allowed the space to double as a broadcast studio, complete with all the modern radio technologies. Clearly, Cobbs and Bailey collaborated to redefine the form and needs of the modern African American church. The building still stands, but was modified in December 1945 following a fire. The alterations involved the addition of a canopy and double towers on the facade as well as modifications to the interior. The building was given protective "Chicago Landmark" status on October 5, 1994.

On February 21, 1941, Walter Thomas Bailey died in Chicago at the age of fifty-nine.[2] The cause of death was pneumonia caused by complications from

Knights of Pythias Building, *Chicago Historical Society*

heart disease. According to his obituary, Bailey was working on two projects at the time of his death.[3] The first was the interior remodeling of the Olivet Baptist Church, one of the most prominent of Chicago's African American churches. Bailey also reportedly was working on the Ida B. Wells Homes, a large public housing project for African Americans on Chicago's West Side; it was dedicated the year of his death. However, Bailey is not listed as one of the official architects of the project and therefore most likely worked on the Ida B. Wells homes in a secondary capacity.

Notes

1. Lee Bey, "Black Designer All But Forgotten," *Chicago Sun Times*, 9 February 1998, p. 13.
2. "Architect Aids on Col. Wolfe School Dies," *Urbana Courier*, 3 February 1941, p. 4.
3. Commission on Chicago Landmarks, *First Church of Deliverance*, (Chicago: Commission on Chicago Landmarks, Department of Planning and Development, 1994), p. 4.

Bibliography

Graves, John. The mosiac templars and African American enterprise, leadership, and culture in Arkansas; Little Rock's Ninth Street as a lens to interpret black achievement. www.mosiactemplarspreservation.org/history.

Kriz, Mikel. "Walter T. Bailey and the African-American patron." Master's thesis, University of Illinois, 2002.

Taitt, John. *The Souvenir of Negro Progress*. Chicago: The De Saible Association Inc., 1925.

TIM SAMUELSON, CITY OF CHICAGO HISTORIAN

BUILDING LIST

Name	Address	City	State	Year	Comments
Alabama Agricultural Fair Negro Bldg.	Fairgrounds	Montgomery	AL	1906	
Colonel Wolfe School	4th & Healey Sts.	Champaign	IL	1905	
First Church of Deliverance	4315 S. Wabash Ave.	Chicago	IL	1939	Alterations
Fraternal Savings & Trust Bank	Beale St. at Church Park	Memphis	TN	1924	Demolished
Ida B. Wells Homes	38th St. & Rhodes Ave.	Chicago	IL	1940	
Knights of Pythias Bath House & Sanitarium	358 Beale Ave.	Hot Springs	AR	1923	
Knights of Pythias Bldg.	3737 S. State St.	Chicago	IL	1924	Demolished
Knights of Pythias Bldg.		Nashville	TN	1924	
Momence Country Club	Along Kankakee River	Momence	IL	1928	Plans only
Mosaic State Temple Bldg.	9th & Broadway	Little Rock	AR	1922	
Mt. Moriah Lodge No. 28 Free & Accepted Masons	1223 Emerson St.	Evanston	IL	1929	
Olivet Baptist Church	3101 S. King Jr. Dr.	Chicago	IL	1941	Alterations
Woodmen of Union Bath House	Malvern Ave. at Gulpha	Hot Springs	AR	1924	Now National Baptist Hotel

Lester Oliver Bankhead
(1912–1997)

Elvenia Bankhead

Lester Bankhead, the eldest of six children, was born on April 20, 1912, in Union, South Carolina. His parents were John Hayes Bankhead and Pearl Eugenia Eskew.[1]

Lester's early education was provided by his mother in a one-room Rosenwald School in Cherokee County, South Carolina. Information about his secondary information is vague. Finally oral history says that he was taught at home and he possibly attended Simms High School.[2] His father was a minister and farmer, and his mother was trained as a teacher at TUSKEGEE INSTITUTE. Although he grew up on a farm in Cherokee County, unlike most African Americans during the time, his family owned their own land and were not sharecroppers. Lester credited his mother with recognizing his skills in math and drawing and providing him with inspiration to look toward architecture as a future life endeavor. His mother told him on numerous occasions that he would "grow up to be an architect."[3]

Although his mother died of influenza when he was twelve, Lester Bankhead never lost sight of her desire that he receive a technical education. Bankhead had hoped to attend Tuskegee Institute, but lack of financial support forced him to seek training elsewhere. He wrote to Voorhees College in Denmark, South Carolina, and inquired if there were any jobs on campus for a barber. When a college official acknowledged that they needed a barber, Bankhead enrolled at Voorhees College in 1937 and graduated with a degree in agriculture and a certificate in carpentry in 1941.[4] While at Voorhees College, Bankhead was singled-out for his drafting ability and was given the opportunity to assist drafting instructors with work on campus buildings and tutoring other students.

After graduating from college, Bankhead was drafted into the U.S. Army in 1942. After completing basic training and ordnance training at Fort McClellan, Alabama, his unit was ordered to Casablanca, Morocco, to liberate North Africa during World War II. Bankhead rose to the rank of sergeant in the Ordnance Corps.[5]

Bankhead moved to Los Angeles after discharge from the U.S. Army in 1945. He married Mary Wright in 1946 and they had two children, Patricia and Elvenia. He settled just a few blocks from Central Avenue, then the hub of Black life in Los Angeles. While in Los Angeles, Bankhead continued to improve his skills and education. He attended the University of California at Los Angeles extension school, Otis Art Institute, Los Angeles City College, and Los Angeles Trade Technical College. Bankhead attempted to find work with Los Angeles architect PAUL REVERE WILLIAMS. According to Bankhead, Williams would not hire him because his skills were beyond entry level. Bankhead found various opportunities to develop his skills as an architect. For a time he worked for Roab Construction Company and eventually began practicing on his own in the 1950s. One of his first buildings was an apartment building on Washington Boulevard.

By 1962 Bankhead had received a contractor's license from the state of California and founded Bankhead's Building Design Services, which later became the Lester O. Bankhead Design Group. He also continued working as a barber while he sought contracts and commissions. He opened Bankhead's Barbershop shortly after arriving in Los Angeles.

Bankhead was among a handful of pioneering Black architects in Los Angeles. Although he faced the racial prejudice of his times, he—like Paul Revere Williams—was able to obtain work from some of Hollywood's celebrities. He designed palatial houses for actor Loren Green of *Bonanza* fame; Kelly Lang, a well-known Los Angeles news anchor; and H. B. Barnum, noted music producer and arranger for Frank Sinatra, and Smokey Robinson and the Miracles.[6]

Bankhead's main emphasis was church design, and he is credited with designing ten churches. Bankhead's notable church designs include Chapel of Faith Baptist Church, Greater Life Missionary Church, New Jerusalem Missionary Baptist Church, Miracle Baptist Church, Trinity Baptist Church, and the United Revelation Church of God in Christ. Although Bankhead's work marks a reasonable contribution, his work did not achieve the notoriety of other Black architects during his era such as Paul Revere Williams or JAMES HOMER GARROTT. Many of Bankhead's designs were in the Modernist style. Like many architects of his era who had to do more with less, Bankhead utilized contemporary architectural devices to give modestly funded buildings a sense of form. The New Jerusalem Missionary Baptist Church of Los Angeles is a fine example of Bankhead's architectural style.

Bankhead's contribution to architecture in Los Angeles was his willingness to mentor promising young African American architects. Bankhead is credited with apprenticing over forty young Black architects. He believed in service to his community and encouraged women to pursue careers in architecture. He took his two children, Patricia and Elvenia, to job sites and taught them basic drafting. Always looking to encourage young people in the discipline of life, Bankhead remarked, "there is no such thing as time, only life circumstances."[7]

Voorhees College honored Bankhead as one of "100 Distinguished Alumni" at the Association for Equal Opportunity in Higher Education in 1988. Lester Oliver Bankhead died in Los Angeles in 1997; he was eighty-five.[8]

Notes
1. Interview with Lester Bankhead, by Wesley Henderson, Los Angeles, California, 1992, University of California at Los Angeles Oral History Program, p. 6.
2. Ibid., p. 81.
3. Interview with Elvenia Bankhead (daughter of Lester Bankhead), Los Angeles, California, 18 August 2002.
4. Lester O. Bankhead, certificate in carpentry, Voorhees College, 1937.
5. Henderson, p. 72.
6. Interview with Patricia Bankhead (daughter of Lester Bankhead), Los Angeles, California, 18 August 2002.
7. Patricia Bankhead, interview.
8. Inglewood Grace Chapel Funeral Program, "In Loving Memory of Lester O. Bankhead," 15 February 1997, frontispiece.

WENDEL ECKFORD, POMONA, CALIFORNIA

New Jerusalem Missionary Baptist Church, *Elvenia Bankhead*

LESTER OLIVER BANKHEAD

BUILDING LIST

Name	Address	City	State	Year	Comments
Apts	4400 Washington Blvd.	Los Angeles	CA		
Barnum, H. B.			CA		
Chapel of Faith Baptist Church	7931 S. San Pedro St.	Los Angeles	CA		
Miracle Baptist Church	8318 S. Central Ave.	Los Angeles	CA		
New Jerusalem Missionary Baptist Church	430 Santa Fe Ave.	Compton	CA		
Trinity Baptist Church	2040 W. Jefferson Blvd.	Los Angeles	CA		
United Revelation Church of God in Christ	655 E. 43rd St.	Los Angeles	CA		

Louis Harvey Banks
(1868–1935)

Louis Harvey Banks was born in Caroline County, Virginia, on January 26, 1868, to Esau and Alice Banks—both natives of Virginia.[1] Louis appears in the 1870 U.S. Census with his parents. Esau was a farmer in Bowling Green Township, Caroline County, Virginia. Louis was the oldest of ten children. Where and when he may have attended school is not known.

Louis Banks was a glassworker and living in Ford City, Pennsylvania, when he married Margaret "Maggie" Enty at Templeton, Armstrong County, Pennsylvania, on October 2, 1894. They had one son, Thornton Kenneth Banks, who was born September 2, 1895, in Ford City, Armstrong County, Pennsylvania.

Louis Banks moved his family to Toledo, Ohio, circa 1900. He first appears in the *Toledo City Directory* in 1901 as a grinder for the Edward Ford Plate Glass Company, which opened in Rossford, Ohio, two years earlier.

Because of his love of flowers, Louis Banks went into business for himself as a landscape architect/gardener around 1913. It is possible that he may have learned horticulture from one of his brothers, Chastine Banks, who was also a landscape gardener and joined his brother in Toledo around 1918. Louis Banks designed residential gardens in the Old West End and Ottawa Hills. There are no records of the families for whom he worked. The Old West End is a neighborhood of Victorian mansions just west of downtown Toledo. Construction of the palatial homes in the Old West End began in the 1870s. During the late nineteenth and early twentieth centuries, the wealthiest and most prominent families of Toledo lived in this area. Ottawa Hills began in the early 1900s as an upper-class community planned by E. H. Close, a local realtor who platted several neighborhoods in Toledo. The village was planned with spacious estates, and 35 of the original 100 acres were set aside for parkland. Ottawa Hills celebrated its grand opening on August 1, 1915. Louis Banks employed a crew of two or three laborers. His own garden at 628

Louis Banks House, *Toledo-Lucas County Public Library*

LOUIS HARVEY BANKS

Pinewood Avenue in Toledo was one that people came from all over the city to see.[2]

Louis Banks was widowed when Maggie died on November 28, 1928, in Templeton, Pennsylvania. She had moved back home with her sister when she developed tuberculosis. Louis Banks died March 19, 1935, of cancer of the stomach and was buried in historic Woodlawn Cemetery in Toledo on March 22, 1935.[3]

Notes

1. Louis Banks's death certificate lists his birth date as January 26, 1875. However, U.S. Census entries for 1870 and 1880 in Caroline County, Virginia, and for 1910, 1920, and 1930 in Lucas County, Ohio, all give an age consistent with a birth year of 1868.

2. Interview with Calvin K. Banks Sr. (grandson of Louis Banks), Toledo, Ohio, 26 August 2002. Tape held by Local History Department, Toledo–Lucas County Public Library, Toledo, Ohio.

3. Ohio Department of Health, Columbus, Ohio, "Louis Banks Death Certificate," No. 854, issued March 1935; Historic Woodlawn Cemetery, Toledo, Ohio, "Louis H. Bank [sic], Burial Record"; Center for Archival Collections, Bowling Green State University, micro-publication, roll 1.

Bibliography

Kapp, Marion, and Jared Cardinal. "History of Ottawa Hills." *Toledo History Scrapbook*. Toledo, Ohio: Local History and Geneology Department, Toledo–Lucas County Public Library, 1981.

DONNA KAY CHRISTIAN,
GENEALOGY DEPARTMENT,
TOLEDO-LUCAS COUNTY PUBLIC LIBRARY

LANDSCAPE PROJECT LIST

Name	Address	City	State	Year	Comments
Banks, Louis H.	628 Pinewood Ave.	Toledo	OH	1915	

Carl Eugene Barnett
(1895–1978)

Ancella Bickley

Carl Eugene Barnett was born in Keyser, West Virginia, on January 7, 1895. His parents were Carter Harrison Barnett and Caroline "Callie" Jackson Barnett. He had one sibling, Nelson LeRoy Barnett. In 1897 Carl Barnett and his family moved from Keyser to Huntington, West Virginia, where he remained until he became of school age. At that point he and his brother were sent to their maternal grandmother in Granville, Ohio, because his parents felt that the Granville public schools were better. When Carl Barnett's father took a job in Columbus, Ohio, the family was reunited there. Carl Barnett graduated from North High School in Columbus in 1912. He enrolled at Ohio State University in the fall of 1914 and graduated in 1918 with a bachelor of science degree in architectural engineering.

Unable to find work in the architectural profession, Carl Barnett accepted employment as a teacher of manual training and science at the all-Black Kelly Miller School in Clarksburg, West Virginia. While in Clarksburg he met Carrie Thomas, who became his wife in 1921. The couple had no children. Long widowed, Barnett later married a Huntington woman, Viney Dotson, who also preceded him in death.

In 1920 Barnett took a position as a teacher of carpentry and mechanical drawing at Central State University in Wilberforce, Ohio. He returned to West Virginia in 1922 and began teaching at Henry Highland Garnet High School in Charleston.

Barnett sat for and passed the state of West Virginia licensing examination and on July 23, 1924, received certificate No. 133, the third architectural license issued to a Black architect in West Virginia.[1] In spite of being licensed, however, opportunities to practice his profession in West Virginia eluded Barnett. He returned to Columbus, Ohio, and took a job as an architectural engineer with the Black-owned C.W. Bryant Construction Company from August 1925 to November 1927. From 1927 to 1929 Barnett maintained a solo practice with an office at 1005 East Long Street in Columbus.

Barnett designed the Long-Garfield Filling Station and developed the plans and specifications and supervised the construction of the Adelphi Savings and Loan Building. According to his nephew, Nelson L. Barnett Jr., Carl Barnett found this Columbus period to be professionally rewarding but financially disastrous, and in 1930 he returned to Huntington, West Virginia, to teach art, European history, and mechanical drawing at Douglass High School.[2] Barnett supplemented his teaching income by opening Notan Studio, a photography business, and by preparing permit drawings for houses. He retired from teaching in 1960.

In his practice, Carl Barnett designed larger structures, including the Mount Zion Baptist Church in Fairmont, West Virginia, and renovations on his home church, the First Baptist Church of Huntington. How-

CARL EUGENE BARNETT

First Baptist Church, *Notan Studio*

ever, he considered the design of small houses his architectural specialty. Barnett designed and built houses for professors while he was at Central State University and he designed and built his own home while he was teaching in Huntington.

In 1965, when he was seventy, Barnett engaged in what was probably the biggest architectural undertaking of his career—he was commissioned to design and supervise the building of the replacement for Huntington's First Baptist Church, which had been destroyed by fire.

On December 18, 1978, Carl Eugene Barnett died in Huntington.[3] He was buried in Huntington's Springhill Cemetery.

Notes

1. West Virginia Architectural Records Office, Huntington, W. Va., "Carl Eugene Barnett," License no. 133, issued 23 July 1924.
2. Nelson L. Barnet Jr., "A Short History of Seven Generations of Barnetts," unpublished, Columbus, Ohio, 1987.
3. "Carl Eugene Barnett," *Herald Dispatch*, 21 December 1978.

Bibliography

Barnett, Nelson LeRoy Jr. *Aesculapius Ebony,* unpublished, 1987.

ANCELLA R. BICKLEY,
RESEARCHER, THE VILLAGES, FLORIDA

BUILDING LIST

Name	Address	City	State	Year	Comments
Adelphia Savings & Loan Bldg.		Columbus	OH	1928	
Barnett, Carl E.		Huntington	WV		
First Baptist Church	801 6th Ave.	Huntington	WV	1965	
Frances, D. S.	1825 Dalton Ave.	Huntington	WV	1942	
Long-Garfield Filling Station		Columbus	OH	1926	
Mt. Zion Baptist Church		Fairmont	WV		
Ohio State University Testing Laboratory	Campus	Columbus	OH	1928	

Joseph Manual Bartholomew Sr.
(1881–1971)

Ruth Creech

Joseph M. Bartholomew Sr. was born in a modest house on the corner of Cherokee and Ester Streets in New Orleans, Louisiana, on August 1, 1881. He was one of four children. His father was an African American cook and his mother was of Cajun descent.

Joseph Batholomew attended public school in New Orleans, but did not advance beyond the eighth grade. In his preteens he began caddying at the nearby Audubon Park Golf Course, where he taught himself to play. He soon became so proficient at the game that he began teaching others. When Freddie MacLeod, the 1908 U.S. Open champion, became the club professional at Audubon Park, he recognized Bartholomew's golfing abilities and persuaded Bartholomew to caddie for him.

In 1922 a group of wealthy White golfers in the New Orleans area decided to build a golf course in Metairie, a suburb of New Orleans. Many of them had hired Bartholomew initially as a caddie and then later for private instructions. Moreover, they were impressed with his groundskeeping skills and felt that he could be relied on to build a first-rate course. To further refine his golf course design skills, they sent him to New York to study with Seth Raynor, a renowned golf course architect. After a year under Raynor's tutelage, Bartholomew returned to New Orleans to start construction on his first golf course. Prior to his return, however, the aspiring golf course architect had the foresight to make plasticine models of some of the famous bunkers, greens, and fairways that Raynor had used for instructional purposes. The scale models proved invaluable to Bartholomew in later years.

The site chosen for the new course was in an obscure section of Metairie. Fearful that jealous competitors might attempt to sabotage his progress, Bartholomew worked at night. After the Metairie course was completed—to the praise and satisfaction of club members—Bartholomew endured the bitter sting of racial prejudice. Because segregation was the order of the day, he was not permitted to play on the course that he had designed and built. Nevertheless, when word of his accomplishment at Metairie spread through the White golfing community, Bartholomew was deluged with offers to design and construct other golf courses.

In the following few years, he built the Number One and Number Three courses at City Park, the all-Black nine-hole course at Pontchartrain Park, and a course in the suburb of Algiers; all in New Orleans. Throughout Louisiana, he designed and built courses in Hammond, Abita Springs, Covington, and Baton Rouge. At each one, except for the segregated Pontchartrain Park facility, Bartholomew was denied access to play on the courses he had created.

As the years passed, the successful golf course architect acquired a number of pieces of heavy earth-moving equipment. Initially he rented equipment to local (predominately White) contractors. When he realized that the heavy construction equipment provided significant financial return, Bartholomew decided

Pontchartrain Park Municipal Golf Course, *Courtesy of New Orleans Planning Commission*

to venture into excavation, foundation construction, and large-scale landscaping projects. Soon he established one of the largest, Black-owned construction firms in New Orleans.

With profits from his construction firm, Bartholomew invested in an insurance company. He then began to acquire real estate and shortly thereafter became a partner in a land-development company. Finally, with the purchase of an ice cream manufacturing plant, Bartholomew's new worth had grown to the extent that he was described in a national business magazine as someone who was "an instinctive money-maker and worth half a million [dollars]."[1]

A quiet, modest man who shunned the limelight, Joseph Bartholomew was a devout Catholic, as well as a devoted husband and father. He married Shreveport-born Ruth Seque in 1918 and the couple had twin daughters and a son. Joseph Bartholmew had a generous spirit and in addition to providing substantial financial support to historically Black Xavier University and Dillard University he helped a number of local Black businessmen. On his property in Harahan outside of New Orleans, Bartholomew built a private seven-hole golf course, where he frequently taught local youngsters and invited members of the African American community to play free of charge.

Joseph Bartholomew died in his home on October 12, 1971. Four months later he was inducted into the Greater New Orleans Hall of Fame, the first African American so honored. On July 2, 1979, the newly renovated Pontchartrain Park Municipal Golf Course, now expanded to eighteen holes, was officially renamed the Joseph M. Bartholomew Sr. Municipal Golf Course in honor of the facility's initial landscape architect.

Notes

1. "Negro Businessman of New Orleans," *Fortune Magazine*, November 1949, p. 112.

Bibliography

McDaniel, Pete. *Uneven Lies: The Heroic Story of African-Americans in Golf*. Greenwich: American Golfer, 2000.

Sinnette, Calvin H. *Forbidden Fairways: African Americans and the Game of Golf*. Chelsea, Mich.: Sleeping Bear Press, 1998.

CALVIN H. SINNETTE,
RETIRED PHYSICIAN AND AFRICAN AMERICAN
GOLF HISTORIAN, ARLINGTON, VIRGINIA

LANDSCAPE PROJECT LIST

Name	Address	City	State	Year	Comments
Abita Springs Golf Course	7343 Oliver St.	Abita Springs	LA		
Bartholomew, Joseph	Colonial Club Dr.	Harahan	LA	1940	7 Hole Course (Demolished)
City Park No. 1 Golf Course	1040 Filmore	New Orleans	LA	1923	
City Park No. 3 Golf Course	1040 Filmore	New Orleans	LA	1923	
Covington Country Club Golf Course	200 Country Club Dr.	Covington	LA	1954	
Hammond Country Club Golf Course		Hammond	LA	1921	Now Oak Knoll Country Club
Metairie Golf Course	580 Wood Vine Ave.	Metairie	LA	1922	
Pine Wood Country Club Golf Course	405 Country Club Blvd.	Slidell	LA	c1963	
Pontchartrain Park Municipal Golf Course	6514 Congress Dr.	New Orleans	LA	1924	Renamed Bartholomew Golf Course
Web Park Golf Course	1352 Country Club Dr.	Baton Rouge	LA	1926	

Robert Charles Bates
(c1872–unknown)

Robert C. Bates was born circa 1872. His father was a farmer and his mother was a housewife in Columbia, South Carolina.

It is likely that Bates gained his training in mechanical drawing from correspondence courses like the ones offered by the Scranton Correspondence School in Pennsylvania. Although only two years removed from graduation from CLAFLIN UNIVERSITY's Normal School for teachers, he was appointed by the Freedmen's Aid and Southern Education Society as general superintendent of manual training at his *alma mater*. By the fall of 1890, Bates was teaching "the properties of bodies, the rudiments of natural philosophy, drawing and design."[1] Each of the 820 students who was enrolled at Claflin University during the year of his appointment were required to take at least one hour per day of a shop trade. Those enrolled in the architectural drawing course were exposed to much more than the basics of mechanical drawing. Bates introduced students to the history of architecture, historic styles of architecture, ornamentation, principles of architectural design, construction details, proper ventilation, strength of various timber, and sound construction supervision practices. He considered that his students were in the loftier training of "architecture" and not "vocational" training. Bates' course in architectural drawing was the first architecture course taught at a historically Black university, pre-dating ROBERT ROBINSON TAYLOR's course at TUSKEGEE INSTITUTE by several years.

In 1893 Robert Charles Bates compiled a series of his class lectures into a book, *The Elementary Principles of Architecture and Building*. In the introduction he wrote that his purpose was "to make a concise statement of the rudimentary principles of architecture as an art, and impart instruction in regard to what constitutes good building."[2] This 147-page book was possibly the first book on architecture authored by an African American. The quality of the book was uneven, which, in an unflattering way, exposed Bates' lack of formal training because his knowledge about architecture was gleaned from pattern books and periodicals, and correspondence courses.

It is believed that Robert Bates was the architect for the Claflin University Chapel (1890), the Claflin Library (1899), and the John F. Slater Manual Training Building. It is known, however, that he designed additions to Boston architect C. H. McClare's Main Building (1894). Bates added well-proportioned, 4-story

Claflin University Main Building, *The Christian Educator*

towers to the north and south ends of the building in 1899 and a classroom annex in 1900. It took students from the Industrial Department—who were supervised by Bates—five years to construct the towers and annex. Fire destroyed the Main Building in 1913. The trustees of the Slater Fund and its president, Rutherford B. Hays—who were generous donors to the Freedmen's Aid and Southern Education Society—expressed high praise of Bates.

In 1897 the state of South Carolina withdrew its financial support to Claflin University and transferred its Morrill Act land grant funds "across the fence" to the State Colored Normal, Industrial, Agricultural, & Mechanical College. Coinciding with the state's action, Bates decided to leave Claflin University. He moved to upstate New York to teach mechanical drawing at the New York State Reformatory at Elmira. The $1,800 annual salary lured him, as did the opportunity to teach in the well-equipped vocational shops in America's first adult reformatory, which offered indefinite sentences based on conduct, individual psychological counseling, and liberal parole polices. He remained in Elmira until 1900.

Dedicated to teaching juvenile delinquents and orphans, an article in *The Christian Educator* announced that Bates had accepted an offer to teach at the Jacob Tome Institute, presumably refering to the one in Port Deposit, in northeast Maryland. The institution was founded by White philanthropists who moralized that they were faced with "a large colored population among us . . . in a desperate state of ignorance . . . children found guilty of incorrigibility, vagrancy and stealing . . . some children had lost one or both of their parents . . . others removed from their homes . . . because both of their parents were 'intemperate.'"[3] From 1900 to 1940 Robert C. Bates taught vocational trades. It is presumed that Bates would have designed and led his students to construct needed buildings over the course of his four-decade employment; however, documentation to support this supposition has not been found.

The circumstances and place of Robert Charles Bates' death are not known.

Notes

1. Zack Rice, "Claflin University: Educating African-Americans for Architecture and Building" (paper presented at the 47th annual meeting in Philadelphia, Pennsylvania of the Society of Architectural Historians, April 1994), p. 4.
2. Robert Bates, *The Elementary Principles of Architecture and Building* (Boston: Geo. H. Ellis, 1892), p. 8.
3. Ibid.
4. Laura Rice, *More Than Meets the Eye: History of Maryland through Prints, 1750–1900* (Baltimore: Maryland Historical Society, 2002), p. 1.

DRECK SPURLOCK WILSON

BUILDING LIST

Name	Address	City	State	Year	Comments
Claflin University Chapel	Campus	Orangeburg	SC	1890	
Claflin University Main Bldg.	Campus	Orangeburg	SC	1899	North & south towers
Claflin University Main Bldg.	Campus	Orangeburg	SC	1900	Classroom annex
Claflin University Manual Training Bldg.	Campus	Orangeburg	SC		

Louis Arnett Stewart Bellinger
(1891–1946)

Carnegie Library of Pittsburgh

Louis Arnett Stewart Bellinger was born on September 29, 1891, in Sumter, South Carolina.[1] His parents were native South Carolinians; they had five sons, George, Louis, Henry, Walter, and Eugene, and daughters, Esther and Cassandra.

Louis Bellinger attended elementary and secondary schools in Charleston, graduating from Shaw School in 1906 and from Avery Normal Institute in 1910. In September 1910 he entered the College of Arts and Sciences at HOWARD UNIVERSITY. At Howard University Bellinger focused on mathematics, physical sciences, and architectural engineering; he also studied Greek, Latin, and German. He withdrew from the university in June 1913 for an unspecified reason, but returned and graduated with a bachelor of science degree in architecture on June 3, 1914.

Bellinger accepted a teaching position in Florida at Tessenden Academy. Around this time he married Ethel Connel, who was born in New Jersey, was two years younger than her husband, and became a music teacher at Robert Vann Elementary School in Pittsburgh, Pennsylvania. The Bellingers had no children.

In 1916 Louis Bellinger joined the faculty of Allen University in Columbia, South Carolina, as a teacher of mathematics. He spent part of 1917 in the military, returning to the university in 1918. The following year the Bellingers arrived in Pittsburgh, where Louis Bellinger began a twenty-six-year career in architecture.

"Bellinger, Louis A. S., Arch[itect]" appeared in the 1919 *Pittsburgh City Directory*.[2] In 1922 Bellinger opened an office at 525 Fifth Avenue, across from the Allegheny County Courthouse in downtown Pittsburgh, took out a listing in the classified directory, and designed a house for an unidentified client in Pittsburgh's Greenfield neighborhood. The house and a 1923 apartment building on Junilla Street in the Hill District are Bellinger's first documented Pittsburgh commissions.

In 1923 Bellinger became an assistant architect in the office of the city architect, John P. Brennan. During his three-year term of employment, he designed a police station and remodeled park buildings. He also took a course in advanced construction at Carnegie Institute of Technology.

Bellinger's return to full-time private practice in 1926 was marked by a major commission not in Pittsburgh, but in Philadelphia—the Publication Building for the African Methodist Episcopal Book Concern at 19th and Pemberton Streets.

Early in 1927 Bellinger designed a building in Pittsburgh that became his best known. The Pythian Temple, dramatically sited in the 2000 block of Centre Avenue, was built for the Knights of Pythias fraternal lodge and provided meeting rooms and a drill area as well as commercial space and an auditorium open to the public. Construction began in the summer of 1927—Bellinger served as general contractor—and the formal opening was celebrated on March 25, 1928.[3] The brick building occupies the entire hillside block between Wylie and Centre Avenues. The 3-story Wylie Avenue side is simply patterned brick;

Knights of Pythias Temple, *Archives Service Center, University of Pittsburgh*

over the doorway is inscribed "Pythian Temple A.D. 1927." The 4-story Centre Avenue side is ornamented with terra-cotta crenellations, crests, and finials in the Tudor style, befitting a fraternal knighthood. (The doorway's grand Tudor arch has been covered or removed.) The auditorium held 1,500 and was "decorated in classical style, with myriad lights, finished walls, box seats, hardwood floor and a new innovation in seating arrangement"[4] to transform the main floor into a basketball court. Popular Black entertainers were soon appearing on the Pythian Temple stage. Eight years later the building was sold and remodeled by architect Alfred M. Marks as the New Granada Theatre.

In January 1928, as the Pythian Temple was nearing completion, Bellinger participated in the pioneering exhibition of African American art sponsored by the Harmon Foundation of New York City. He submitted a "Proposed Plan for Church and Apartments."[5] Later that year Bellinger designed his own house; he and Ethel lived on the second floor of the duplex at 530 Francis Street. Documented projects during the remainder of the decade are relatively modest: two small apartment buildings, two houses, and various remodeling jobs.

With the onset of the Great Depression, Bellinger gave up his downtown office and sold his home. Around 1933 he and Ethel moved to 3171 Centre Avenue, which became his office as well as home address. His largest recorded project during the 1930s was an apartment building designed for Albert S. Knott in 1932. Bellinger was again invited to display his work at the Harmon Foundation exhibition held in 1933; his entry, possibly a design of a Masonic Temple, was damaged in transit and never displayed.

Bellinger's solution to economic adversity was to take a position in late 1936 or early 1937 as an inspector for the City of Pittsburgh Bureau of Building Inspection. He held the position for approximately three years (through 1939), and then, after an unsuccessful attempt to reestablish his private practice in 1940, he worked as an inspector again in 1941 and 1942.

Bellinger's only documented work from 1943 to 1944 was a church basement renovation. In 1945, near the end of World War II, business improved. On July 10, 1945, he was elected to membership in the American Institute of Architects.[6] By late December Bellinger was juggling three commissions. On February 3, 1946, he died[7] at the age of fifty-four.

Louis Bellinger was buried in historic Allegheny Cemetery. He was eulogized on the front pages of the *Pittsburgh Courier* and the *Builders' Bulletin* (Pittsburgh's premier building industry journal). His education, professional affiliations such as the Pittsburgh chapter of the American Institute of Architects and the NATIONAL TECHNICAL ASSOCIATION, and work for both public and private sectors of the community were respectfully noted.

LOUIS ARNETT STEWART BELLINGER

Much of Bellinger's work remains undocumented; virtually all of his documented buildings have been altered or demolished. The Pythian Temple—nominated to the National Register of Historic Places—survives, but is endangered. Louis Bellinger persevered in a time of limited opportunity and economic hardship to become, and remain, an architect. That may be his greatest achievement.

Notes

1. Although Bellinger's Howard University Certificate of Applicant for Admission (prepared by his Avery Institute teacher, Mattie May Marsh) gives his birthplace as Charleston, Sumter is the location identified in the Allegheny County Census of 1920.
2. *Pittsburgh City Directory,* "Bellinger, Louis A. S., Arch.," (Pittsburgh: Polk & Co., 1919), p. 515.
3. "Many Witness Corner-Stone Laying of Phythian Temple," *Pittsburgh Courier,* 31 March 1928, p. 11.
4. The description of the interior appears in a reporter's recounting of an interview with Bellinger when the project was announced. *Pittsburgh Courier,* 12 March 1927, p. 1.
5. Harmon Foundation, *Negro Artists: An Illustrated Review of Their Achievements* (New York: Harmon Foundation, 1935), p. 43.
6. American Institute of Architects, Pittsburgh Collection, Membership Records, "Louis Bellinger," Carnegie Mellon University Architecture Archives.
7. "Louis A. Bellinger, Architect, Buried," *Pittsburgh Courier,* 9 February 1946, p. 1.

Bibliography

Builders Bulletin. Pittsburgh Builders' Exchange, vol. 3, 1919, through vol. 30, 1946.
Cederholm, Theresa Dickason. *Afro-American Artists: A Biobibliographical Directory.* Boston: Boston Public Library, 1973, p. 22.
Kidney, Walter C. *Pittsburgh's Landmark Architecture: The Buildings of Pittsburgh and Allegheny County.* Pittsburgh: Pittsburgh History and Landmarks Foundation, 1997.
Smoot, Pamela A. "The First One-Hundred Years of Ebenezer Baptist Church of Pittsburgh, Pennsylvania, 1875–1975." Master's thesis, Tennessee State University, 1979.

ALBERT M. TANNLER,
HISTORICAL COLLECTIONS DIRECTOR,
PITTSBURGH HISTORY AND LANDMARKS FOUNDATION

BUILDING LIST

Name	Address	City	State	Year	Comments
House	Greenfield nr. Hazelwood Ave.	Pittsburgh	PA	1922	
African Methodist Episcopal Book Concern	19th & Pemberton Sts.	Philadelphia	PA	1926	
American Legion Post No. 7	207 Jefferson St.	Fairmont	WVA	1945	
Bellinger, Ethel C.	530 Francis St.	Pittsburgh	PA	1928	
Burchett Apts.	Junilla St.	Pittsburgh	PA	1923	
Ciaramella, John	5100 2nd Ave.	Pittsburgh	PA	1929	
Crunkleton, J. H.	Camp & Finland Sts.	Pittsburgh	PA	1945	Addition
Cutts, W. G., Dr.	1921 Perrysville Ave.	Pittsburgh	PA	1927	
Greenlee Store	1401 Wylie St.	Pittsburgh	PA	1933	Alterations
Iron City Lodge Post No. 17	1847 Centre Ave.	Pittsburgh	PA	1945	Alterations
Johnson, Luther H.	2105 Centre Ave.	Pittsburgh	PA	1945	Demolished
Knights of Pythias Temple	2009 Centre Ave.	Pittsburgh	PA	1927	Demolished
Knott Apartments	2803 Centre Ave.	Pittsburgh	PA	1932	Alterations
Mutual Real Estate Co.	2801 Wylie Ave.	Pittsburgh	PA	1928	Alterations
Pittsburgh Police Station		Pittsburgh	PA	1923	Demolished
Prince Hall Temple Association Lodge and Apartments	2611 Centre Ave.	Pittsburgh	PA	1928	Alterations
Rodman Street Baptist Church	6011 Rodman St.	Pittsburgh	PA	1929	Alterations
Sixth Mt. Zion Baptist Church	Joseph St. nr. Larimer Ave.	Pittsburgh	PA	1930	Demolished
Smith, Robert T.	85 Sylvania Ave.	Pittsburgh	PA	1928	Demolished
St. John's Evangelical Baptist Church	4535 Chatsworth Ave.	Pittsburgh	PA	1943	Plans only
St. Mark African Methodist Episcopal Church	1409 Montier St.	Wilkinsburg	PA	1927	Plans only

Plympton Ross Berry
(1834–1917)

Mahoning Valley Historical Society

Plympton Ross Berry was born a free man of color in Mount Pleasant, Pennsylvania, in 1834. When Plympton Berry was six, his father, Thomas D. Berry, relocated the family to Lawrence County, Pennsylvania, where the Berry family became the first African Americans to live in the New Castle area.[1] Thomas Berry operated a successful barbershop. Plympton, known to all as "Ross," was trained at an early age to be a bricklayer.

At the age of sixteen, P. Ross Berry worked on his first major building, the construction of the Lawrence County Courthouse and jail.[2] This project was a monumental task for such a young man; nonetheless, Berry rose to the occasion. It is not known where Berry obtained the "look" of the courthouse—perhaps from a periodical. As stated in an 1852 edition of *The New Castle Gazette*, "It [the courthouse] will stand for the ages as a monument of youth vigor and taste. For a century to come our citizens will be content with their public building, nor desire to tear them down to erect more splendid ones."[3] Construction commenced in 1850 and was completed in 1852. The cost of the building was $32,000.[4] Over the years there have been three additions not executed by Berry, and the original clock tower has been removed. The courthouse is listed on the National Register of Historic Places.[5]

Berry married Mary Long in 1857. Nine children were born to their union. All of Plympton and Mary's children were educated, including their daughters, which was another unique accomplishment for the era. The girls were taught music, and the boys, bricklaying.

In 1861 Berry moved his family west across the Pennsylvania state line into Ohio. The family settled in Youngstown. Although Youngstown was just a hamlet in 1860, the town was on the verge of a construction boom. Berry's contracting company was involved in many of the town's major building projects between 1860 and 1880. For years he was the only building contractor listed in the *Youngstown City Directory* and one of the few builders with architecture experience. Buildings designed and built by Berry included banks, schools, hotels, factories, churches, and a courthouse. There are sixty-five documented structures attributed to Berry as either brick mason, architect, or builder. Among the residences designed and constructed by Berry was Youngstown's first mansion. Youngstown was the home of Governor David Tod, who commissioned Berry to build a mansion in 1867. Some months after the mansion was completed it caught fire; the governor insisted that no one other than Berry rebuild the mansion. The Tod mansion was an elaborate 35 × 60 foot building that cost $50,000 to build. The front-to-rear wings were 93 × 73 feet. The first floor consisted of nine rooms and the second floor had eleven rooms. The roof was dark slate bordered with green slate. The mansion was demolished in 1929.

After the Civil War, Berry's reputation as a master builder with architecture experience grew. He was kept busy with contracts to construct buildings in

Rayen School, *Vince Shivers*

other towns. Berry owned his own brickyard, where he burned a unique, reddish orange brick for some of his jobs. Work took Berry to Mercer, Oil City, and New Castle, Pennsylvania; and Struters, Poland, and Warren, Ohio. In addition to Civil War veterans that he hired, Berry taught bricklaying to his oldest son, Thomas. In 1881 Berry and thirty-five mostly White bricklayers met to charter Local 8 Bricklayers Union in Youngstown, which remains active today.

P. Ross Berry was a well-respected businessman in the community. In 1878, when the City of Youngstown called on its philanthropists to contribute money to build the city's first courthouse, Berry donated $1,000—a significant contribution by the standards of the day. Later Berry was awarded the contract to provide bricks for the Mahoning County Courthouse.

Berry was also well known within the African American community. During crises he was known to call individuals together to seek resolutions to conflicts. In 1867 Berry was one of the organizers of the "Emancipation Ball and Dinner." African Americans came from all over northeastern Ohio and western Pennsylvania to attend. When local members of the U.S. Colored Troops returned after the Civil War, Berry offered them training and jobs with his construction company. Although the majority of the laborers who worked for Berry were African American, he also employed several White workers. The sight of a Black man supervising White laborers was rare.

P. Ross Berry started to lighten his work schedule around 1901, after almost fifty years of bricklaying, designing, and building. He continued supervising construction projects until 1916. He died in 1917 and was laid to rest in the historic Oak Hill Cemetery in Youngstown. An obelisk similar to ones found in Egypt marks his grave.

Notes

1. Population Schedules of the Eighth Census of the United States, Pennsylvania, Lawrence County, 1850, National Archives.
2. "Plympton Ross Berry," files of Lawrence County Historical Society, New Castle, Penn.
3. "Courthouse," *New Castle Gazette*, 1 June 1852, p. 2.
4. L. H. Everts & Company, *History of Lawrence County, 1770–1877* (Philadelphia: L. H. Everts & Company, 1877), p. 31.
5. U.S. Department of Interior, National Park Service, "Lawrence County Courthouse," 21 June 1978, National Register of Historic Places.

Bibliography

Brenner, William A. *Downtown and the University*. Youngstown: Brenner Company, 1976.

VINCENT AJAMU SHIVERS,
RESEARCHER, YOUNGSTOWN, OHIO

BUILDING LIST

Name	Address	City	State	Year	Comments
Covington Street School	706 Covington St.	Youngstown	OH	1890	Demolished
Dollar Bank	Central Square	Youngstown	OH	1901	Now National City Bank
First Baptist Church	Market & Boardman Sts.	Youngstown	OH	1863	Demolished
First Presbyterian Church	201 Wick Ave.	Youngstown	OH	1866	Demolished
Front Street School	Front & Hazel Sts.	Youngstown	OH	1871	Demolished
Grand Opera House	Public Square	Youngstown	OH	1872	Demolished
Hitchcock, William	Wick Ave.	Youngstown	OH	1863	Demolished
Homer Hamiltion & Co.	Boatman & Canal Sts.	Youngstown	OH	1861	Demolished
Howell's Business Block	2 W. Federal St.	Youngstown	OH	1865	Demolished
Lawrence County Courthouse	430 Court St.	New Castle	PA	1852	
Mahoning County Courthouse	E. Market & Wick Sts.	Youngstown	OH	1875	Demolished
McMillian Free Library	Market & Front Sts.	Youngstown	OH	c1899	Demolished
New Discipline Church	23 W. Washington St.	New Castle	PA	1868	
Ohio Govenor's Mansion	429 Holmes St.	Youngstown	OH	1868	Demolished
Rayen School	20 W. Wood St.	Youngstwon	OH	1861	Now Youngstown Board of Education Bldg.
St. Columbia Cathedral	W. Wood & Hazel Sts.	Youngstown	OH	1863	Demolished
St. Joseph's Cathedral	Rayen St. & Wick Ave.	Youngstown	OH	1881	Demolished
Tod House Hotel	Public Square	Youngstown	OH	1869	Demolished
West Side Schoolhouse	755 Mahoning Ave.	Youngstown	OH	1877	
Youngstown City Jail	Boardman & Hazel Sts.	Youngstown	OH	1866	Demolished

Edward Eginton Birch
(1888–1974)

William Gordon

Little is known about African American architects in the Cincinnati area between the subject years of 1865 and 1945. Because Cincinnati and most of northern Kentucky city directories have been "color blind" since at least the Civil War, a common way of identifying the race of an architect is of no use here. The most valuable and virtually only firsthand source of Cincinnati's African American community, including its history back to the beginning of European settlement, is *Cincinnati's Colored Citizens, Historical, Sociological, and Biographical*, written by the editor of the Black weekly the *Union*, Wendell Phillips Dabney (1865–1952).[1] He references a number of Black builders in Cincinnati during the late nineteenth and early twentieth centuries, but refers to only four architects: WALLACE AUGUSTUS RAYFIELD, the Birmingham, Alabama-based architect of Antioch Baptist Church in Cincinnati (1926); CURTIS GRAHAM ELLIOTT, an architect at Howard University's Building and Grounds Department who is a descendant of the Elliott Brothers who operated a successful construction company in Wyoming, a close-in suburb of Cincinnati; a one-sentence mention of "A. Townsend," about whom we know nothing; and Edward Birch.

Edward E. Birch, the youngest of three brothers, was born on October 31, 1888, to Samuel and Jane Busch Birch of Winchester, Kentucky. Edward's oldest brother was ERNEST BIRCH. The family resided at 125 3rd Street in a modest house. Edward completed high school in the Winchester public schools and attended HAMPTON UNIVERSITY from 1907 to 1908, pursuing studies in architectural engineering. He worked in Hampton Institute's laundry to pay his tuition. Birch apparently withdrew before earning his diploma.

From about 1908 until 1934, Edward and his brother, ERNEST OCTAVIUS BIRCH, a graduate of Kentucky Normal and Industrial Institute for Colored Persons, practiced together. Attribution for buildings designed by the brothers could not be differentiated. Edward Birch's business card stated that he was an architect and consulting engineer doing business out of his home at 1123 Yale Avenue in the Walnut Hills neighborhood of Cincinnati. Up until 1945, he listed himself in the *Cincinnati City Directory* as an "architect" even though he was not licensed by the state of Ohio.[2]

Edward Birch designed Brown Chapel African Methodist Episcopal Church; the cornerstone was installed in 1929, but the church was not completed until 1951. Brown Chapel was built on land donated by Lane Presbyterian Theological Seminary, where the Reverend Lyman Beecher and his daughter, Harriet Beecher Stowe, were associated. In the early years worship services were held in the basement, which was nothing more than a shell. Some years later the church was put under roof. The original roof was flat but over the years was replaced with a more utilitarian gable and hipped roof.

Brown Chapel African Methodist Episcopal Church, *Walter E. Langsam*

Edward Birch married Eva Downey Birch in 1908, but they were separated by 1916. They had one son, Augustine Edward Birch, who was eight years old when his parents divorced. Augustine, after serving with the heroic 99th Pursuit Squadron (the "Tuskegee Airmen"), returned to Cincinnati and worked for the Cincinnati Recreation Department and retired from the Cincinnati Bureau of Employment Services. Edward Birch re-married to Susie Whittaker Birch of Cincinnati.

In 1923 Edward Birch designed an 8-room, $80,000 hospital addition at the rear of the home of Dr. A. F. Lyons in the predominately White community of Fort Thomas near Covington, Kentucky, across the Ohio River from Cincinnati. During World War II, Edward Birch received U.S. Civil Service status as an assistant engineering draftsman in the Engineering Division at Wright Patterson Airfield in Dayton, Ohio.

Edward E. Birch died on July 31, 1974. As a long-time member of the First Church of Christ, Scientist in Walnut Hills, his passing was mourned quietly.

Notes
1. Wendell Dabney, *Cincinnati's Colored Citizens, Historical, Sociological, and Biographical* (Cincinnati: Dabney Publishing Co., 1926).
2. Roger Clark, *Architects' Directory from the Cincinnati City Directories* (Cincinnati: Cincinnati Historical Society, 1989), N. P.

WALTER E. LANGSAM,
ARCHITECTURAL HISTORIAN AND HISTORIC
PRESERVATION CONSULTANT, CINCINNATI, OHIO

BUILDING LIST

Name	Address	City	State	Year	Comments
Brown Chapel African Methodist Episcopal Church	2804 Alms Pl.	Walnut Hills	OH	1929	
Lyons Hospital	727 N. St. Thomas Ave.	Covington	KY	c1940	Additon

Ernest Octavius Birch
(1885–1951)

The Birch family was from Winchester, Kentucky, where Ernest, the older of three boys, was born on September 16, 1885. He attended public schools in Winchester.

Ernest and his brother, EDWARD EGINTON BIRCH, were associates for twenty-five years (1908 to 1933), a partnership that likely began after Edward left HAMPTON UNIVERSITY and joined his older brother in Cincinnati. They were among the first two Black architects in the city. Ernest Birch attended Kentucky Normal and Industrial Institute for Colored Persons in Frankfort from 1900 to 1903. He started in the normal school hoping to become a teacher and switched to carpentry. The carpentry shop would later be housed in the beautiful stone Trades Building (1909), which was designed by WILLIAM SIDNEY PITTMAN and constructed by legendary local stonemason James C. Brown. Toward the end of his life Edward Birch took extension courses at the University of Cincinnati Evening College in 1945 and returned in 1948.

Neither brother was licensed, but that did not stop them from advertising themselves in the *Cincinnati City Directory* as "architects." They worked together as Birch Bros., first at 835 West 7th Street in the West End near downtown Cincinnati, then the center of professional and fashionable African American life. In the 1920s their office was at 3146 Gaff Avenue in Walnut Hills, where Ernest Birch continued to live until his death. Beginning in 1934, Ernest Birch was employed as a facilities maintenance engineer for Rubel Baking Company.

He married Emma Birch and they lived together in their Walnut Hills home located in a historically Black Cincinnati neighborhood. The couple had no children.

During his leisure time, Ernest Birch was a member of the Cincinnati Colored Young Mens Christian Association of Cincinnati.

Ernest O. Birch died of a heart attack on March 3, 1951.[1] His funeral was held at Bethel Baptist Church, where it is more than likely he was a member. He was buried in Union Baptist Cemetery, the oldest cemetery in Cincinnati for Blacks, dating to 1831 and located in the Price Hill neighborhood of Western Hills, Ohio.

Note

1. "Ernest O. Birch," *Cincinnati Enquirer*, 4 March 1951, p. 6.

WALTER E. LANGSAM,
ARCHITECTURAL HISTORIAN AND HISTORIC PRESERVATIONIST, CINCINNATI, OHIO

Ernest Birch (right) inside the Kentucky Normal & Industrial School Trades Building, *Kentucky State University Archives and Special Collections*

John Henry Blanche Jr.
(1908–1960)

Eva Blanche

John Henry Blanche Jr. was born November 11, 1908, in Charleston, South Carolina, the youngest of three sons born to John H. Blanche Sr. His mother died before he reached four years old. When his father died a short time later, he was taken in and reared by his mother's first cousin, Hattie Bynum.

John Blanche received his early education in the public schools of Charleston, South Carolina. When he was in the eighth grade he met MILLER FULTAN WHITTAKER, a student recruiter from South Carolina State Colored Agricultural & Mechanical Institute. At that time the college had a high school component. While in Charleston recruiting students to attend high school, Whittaker invited John Henry Blanche to Orangeburg to enroll. Blanche accepted his invitation and began matriculating at the institute in the ninth grade. Whittaker saw great potential in John Henry Blanche and became his mentor and surrogate father. Moreover Whittaker, as the first Black registered architect in South Carolina, was committed to teaching the young, astute, and talented Blanche all that he knew so that he might one day become successful. On completion of high school at South Carolina State Colored Normal Institute, Blanche remained and began his undergraduate education majoring in building and woodworking. During his matriculation at the college, Blanche supported himself in the practical use of his major and was often in great demand because of his talent in building and woodworks. Blanche served an architectural apprenticeship with Whittaker. For his senior final project, Blanche designed Dukes Gymnasium. He graduated in 1930. Later Blanche received his master of arts degree from the University of Pennsylvania in 1939.

After graduating from college, John Henry Blanche began a teaching career in Greenville, Newberry, and Rock Hill, South Carolina. In 1936, when Sterling High School in the Greenville School District was out for summer vacation, Blanche returned to his *alma mater* to work for the summer. There he met Eva Mae Gibbs, a Home Economics major from Pamplico, South Carolina. Their relationship grew and in 1937, while she was a senior, he proposed to her and asked her father for her hand in marriage. Although her father sanctioned the marriage, Eva told John that he would have to wait five years because she wanted to work and show her parents her appreciation for their support during the pursuit of her college education.[1] On June 6, 1942, the couple married. No children were born to their union.

In the fall of 1936, at the invitation of Whittaker, who was now president of the South Carolina State College, Blanche resigned from public school teaching and returned to South Carolina State as a tenure-track instructor and eventually became an associate professor of architectural engineering.

While at South Carolina State College, Blanche also served as band director for two years in the absence of Reginald Thomasson. At South Carolina State he taught Drawing 301, a course that was a requirement of all students. Blanche also served as a role model for many students. During one summer he met Barbara Thompson, who was then a junior in high school. Barbara Thompson's aunt, Mamie Thompson, introduced her to Blanche because Barbara had an interest in drawing. Blanche worked with her and assisted her in developing her drawing skills. Later, when she entered South Carolina State College, she decided to major in architectural engineering because there was no organized art program. Thus Barbara Thompson, under Blanche's tutelage, became the first female to major in and complete an architectural engineering degree at South Carolina State College.

When Blanche came to South Carolina State College he was not a registered architect. However, he designed many buildings under Whittaker's license, such as the Mechanical and Engineering Building at South Carolina State College. It was Whittaker who encouraged him to take the examination to receive his architect's license. Blanche was hesitant because of the blatant practice of discrimination against African Americans during the time. However, in 1948 he went to the University of South Carolina to take the Architectural Board of Examinations. He was the only Black out of thirteen people who were taking the examination. Blanche was not allowed to take the exam in the same room with the Whites, where there were canted drafting tables and overhead fluorescent lighting. Whereas the other test takers were comfortable and provided with the drafting tools they needed to take the exam, Blanche was placed in a small storage room. The room contained a 40-watt lightbulb, a stool, and a flat board, which was elevated with bricks. He could not even go into the cafeteria for lunch, but had to bring lunch with him. Despite the hardships, Blanche was informed by Dean Rowe of the School of Architecture that he had passed the State Board of Examinations to become a registered architect. Blanche was licensed to practice not only in South Carolina but also in North Carolina.

Blanche's architecture career began when he designed Dukes Gymnasium as his senior final project in 1929. He also designed the Science Building at CLAFLIN UNIVERSITY in Orangeburg, South Carolina; the Gymnasium and Home Economics Buildings at Morris College in Sumter, South Carolina; and the plans for Layman Hall and Reid's Hall at Allen University; and supervised the renovation of the Girls Dormitory. Additionally, he created plans for many hotels, including the Holiday Inn Motel in Orangeburg, which later became the South Campus of South Carolina State University; and the Slumberland Motel located in Orangeburg. At the time of his death in 1960, he was completing two buildings for Benedict College in Columbia, South Carolina.

One of the few Black architects in South Carolina, Blanche's services were always in demand. He was called to design many churches, including Antioch Baptist Church in Bowman, St. Mark Baptist Church in St. George, Mt. Zion African Methodist Episcopal Church in Florence, Lovely Hill Baptist Church in Holly Hill, and Orangeburg Lutheran Church in Orangeburg. He also designed the parsonage for his home church, Williams Chapel African Methodist

Dukes Gymnasium, South Carolina State University, *Eva Gibbs Blanche*

Episcopal Church in Orangeburg, South Carolina, contributing his free time and service to the planning and supervision of the church parsonage; and aided and supervised the renovation of the church itself, Williams Chapel African Methodist Episcopal Church. Blanche created the plans for several prominent citizens' homes in Orangeburg, including those of the president of South Carolina State College, Dr. Maceo; James L. Wells Sr.; and the late Mr. Rhude Cherry, a prominent businessman who was the owner of Cherry Feed & Seeds. Blanche also designed his own home.

Blanche was a gifted architect, a musician, and a quiet man who did not participate in arguments. John Blanche died on January 14, 1960, at Orangeburg Regional Hospital.[2]

Notes
1. Interview with Eva Gibbs Blanche (wife of John Blanche), Orangeburg, South Carolina, 17 October 2002.
2. "Final Rites: Mr. John Henry Blanche," *Times and Democrat*, 17 January 1960, p. 1.

PEGGY STEVENSON RATLIFF,
CHAIR, DIVISION OF HUMANITIES
AND SOCIAL SCIENCES AND PH.D,
ROOSEVELT RATLIFF JR., PHD,
ASSISTANT VICE-PRESIDENT
FOR LEADERSHIP DEVELOPMENT,
CLAFLIN UNIVERSITY

Bibliography
"John Blanche," personal folder, South Carolina State University Historical Collection Whittaker Library, Orangeburg, South Carolina.

BUILDING LIST

Name	Address	City	State	Year	Comments
Aiken Low-Income Housing		Atlanta	GA		700 Dwelling units (du)
Allen University Girls Dormitory	Campus	Columbia	SC	1950	Alteration
Allen University Ministers' Hall	Campus	Columbia	SC		Now Faith Hall
Antioch Baptist Church	7640 Charleston Hywy.	Bowman	SC		
Benedict College	Campus	Columbia	SC		
Blanche, John H., "Home on the Hill"	2689 Magnolia NE	Orangeburg	SC	1945	
Claflin University Science Bldg.	Campus	Orangeburg	SC		
Holiday Inn Motel	415 Calhoun Dr.	Orangeburg	SC		Now South campus
Lovely Hill Baptist Church	631 Hesseman Ave.	Holly Hill	SC		
Morris College Home Economics Bldg.	Campus	Sumter	SC		
Mt. Zion African Methodist Episcopal Church	1305 E. Cheves St.	Florence	SC		
Orangeburg Lutheran Church	610 Ellis Ave.	Orangeburg	SC		
Slumberland Motel	1440 Five Chop Rd.	Orangeburg	SC		
South Carolina State University Dukes Gymnasium	Campus	Orangeburg	SC	1931	
St. Mark's Baptist Church	Ridge St.	Saint George	SC		
Williams Chapel African Methodist Episcopal Church Parsonage	1198 Glover St.	Orangeburg	SC	c1950s	
Williams Chapel African Methodist Episcopal Church	Glover St.	Orangeburg	SC		

Joseph Haygood Blodgett
(1858–1934)

Courtesy of Thomas G. Carpenter Library, Eartha M. M. White Collection, University of North Florida

Although he had very little formal education, Joseph Haygood Blodgett became one of the most respected and successful African American business and community leaders in Jacksonville, Florida, during the first quarter of the twentieth century. Born in Augusta, Georgia, on February 8, 1858, Blodgett left the farm as a teenager and moved to Summerville, South Carolina, where he hauled phosphate and later cut cross ties for the South Carolina Railroad Company. Blodgett relocated to bustling Jacksonville, Florida, in the 1890s, reportedly with only one dollar and ten cents in his pocket.[1]

From this humble start in Jacksonville, Blodgett, who initially worked for the railroad, went on to open his own drayage business that was later expanded to include a wood yard, restaurant, and farm. By 1898 he had entered the construction and real estate business and had constructed numerous houses and offices, many located on parcels he owned. Blodgett lost most of his buildings in the Great Fire of May 3, 1901, which destroyed almost all of downtown Jacksonville, including parts of the outlying, adjacent neighborhood of LaVilla. He borrowed five thousand dollars from the State Bank of Florida and revived his construction and real estate businesses and by 1919 had designed and constructed 258 houses—100 of which he kept and rented out.[2] In 1910 Blodgett was one of only five African American architect-builders in the Jacksonville area.

By 1919 Blodgett had designed and built his own elegant residence, "Blodgett Villa" on West 8th Street in the middle-class African American neighborhood known as Sugar Hill. While residing at "Blodgett Villa," he and his wife, Sallie Barnes Barnett of Barnwell, South Carolina, entertained many notable visitors, including the principal of TUSKEGEE INSTITUTE, BOOKER TALIAFERRO WASHINGTON. Blodgett went on to design and build many houses in Sugar Hill and the Durkeeville area that were characterized by his trademark 2-story residences with a small upper porch over a larger lower porch. Blodgett reportedly designed and built similar houses in Durham, North Carolina; Savannah, Georgia; Springfield, Massachusetts; and Oklahoma City, Oklahoma. One of the more noted buildings designed and constructed by Blodgett in 1915 was the Lawton-Pratt Funeral Home at 525 West Beaver Street in the LaVilla section of downtown Jacksonville.

In his obituary, the *Florida Times Union* proclaimed Joseph H. Blodgett a leader among the African American community as well as one of the wealthiest Blacks in Duval County.[3] This declaration was based not only on his business success, but also on his demonstrated community leadership and civic involvement. For example, immediately after the 1901 fire, Blodgett was tapped by Black community leaders to direct a Colored Relief Association to coordinate relief efforts among the African American community. A strong and active supporter of both his church, Ebenezer United Methodist Church, and Edward Waters College, Blodgett also supported the local chapter of the Negro Business League.

Lawton-Pratt Funeral Home, Evelyn Hillman Kennebrew

Because of declining health due to high blood pressure, Blodgett retired from his businesses by the early 1920s and relocated to one of his houses on Hart Street in Durkeeville, where he died on June 5, 1934.[4]

Notes
1. Monroe Nathan Work, ed., *Negro Year Book: An Annual Encyclopedia of the Negro, 1918–1919* (Tuskegee: Negro Year Book Publishing Company, 1919) p. 435.
2. Camilla P. Thompson, "Joseph H. Blodgett: Pioneer Achiever," Mrs. Perry's Free Press, 15 May 1997, p. 13.
3. "Joseph H. Blodgett, One of City's Best Known Negroes, Dies," *Florida Times Union*, 6 June 1934, p. 22.
4. Ibid.

Bibliography
Crooks, James B. "Changing Face of Jacksonville, Florida, 1900–1910." *Florida Historical Quarterly* (April 1984), p. 462.
———. *Jacksonville after the Fire, 1901–1919: A New South City*. Jacksonville: University of North Florida Press, 1991.

JOEL W. MCEACHIN,
SENIOR HISTORIC PRESERVATION PLANNER,
JACKSONVILLE PLANNING AND
DEVELOPMENT DEPARTMENT

BUILDING LIST

Name	Address	City	State	Year	Comments
Blodgett, Joseph H., "Blodgett Villa"	W. 8th St.	Jacksonville	FL	1919	
Blodgett, Joseph H.	Hart St.	Jacksonville	FL	c1920	
Lawton-Pratt Funeral Home	525 W. Beaver St.	Jacksonville	FL	1915	
Sugar Hill single-family housing	Various addresses	Jacksonville	FL	1920s	Approx. 258 houses

Henry Clifford Boles
(1910–1979)

Henry "Hank" Boles was born on February 22, 1910, in Oxford, Mississippi. His father was William Robert Boles, a cobbler, and his mother was Willa Wright Boles. He attended LeMoyne Junior College in Memphis, Tennessee, where he graduated in 1927. On August 28, 1938, he married Myrtle C. Spralley of Kansas City, Missouri, with whom he had three children, Henry Jr., Robert and Gail. After a brief stint at Crane Business College in Chicago, Illinois, at the age of twenty-nine Boles entered the Illinois Institute of Technology (IIT), also in Chicago, where he studied under Mies van der Rohe (1886–1969). Boles received his bachelor of science degree in architecture in 1943. From 1929 until the end of his undergraduate education, Boles supported himself and his family by working as a clerk for the United States Postal Service.

Following his graduation from Illinois Institute of Technology, Boles spent the remaining two years of World War II, from January 1943 to April 1945, as an assistant plant engineer at Aero Parts Manufacturing Company in Wichita, Kansas. His early architectural career was a succession of short job stays and much moving. For six months in 1945 he worked in the Washington, D.C., office of HILYARD ROBERT ROBINSON, an architect who had a strong interest in housing for the working class and poor. After teaching architectural design at PRAIRIE VIEW AGRICULTURAL & MECHANICAL COLLEGE from October 1945 to April 1946, Boles traveled back to the nation's capital, where he was employed in the office headed by HOWARD HAMILTON MACKEY SR. for three months as an architectural draftsman. Boles then worked for the National Capital Housing Authority from August 1946 to May 1947, focusing on public housing. He then was an architectural draftsman in Washington, D.C. for Howe & Foster and Berla & Able for the remainder of 1947.

At the end of 1947, Boles moved to Boston, Massachusetts, to work in the office of Walter F. Bogner, a colleague of Walter Gropius at the Harvard University School of Architecture. For the following two years, Boles was the chief draftsman in the firm of Samuel Glaser & Associates while he also studied for his master of architecture degree at Harvard University. Boles received his degree in 1949, after one year of study under Gropius.

Boles spent the next four years in government service. From February 1950 to November 1951, he worked for the Public Housing Administration and U.S. Army Corps of Engineers in Boston. From the end of 1951 to 1954, Boles was in Monrovia, Liberia, as chief architect for the Point Four Program created under the Truman administration to provide technical and economic assistance to underdeveloped countries. It was in this position that Boles completed his first known designs, housing for United States technicians (1952–54) and the Monrovia Elementary School (1954).

Upon returning to the United States in 1954, at the age of forty-four, Boles moved back to Massachusetts, where he remained for the rest of his career. He ran his own practice in Boston for three years although his commissions from this period remain unidentified. In 1957 Boles and partner Paul Parks, an African American civil engineer educated at Purdue University and the Massachusetts Institute of Technology, formed Associated Architect & Engineer and were later joined by William Spilman, an engineer. The firm established itself with commissions for the Methuen Junior High School and Saint Stephen's Episcopal Church Parish Hall. Boles apparently received the bulk of his commissions after dissolving the firm in 1969. He designed the Westfield State College Student Union–Library and several housing complexes for the elderly in Methuen, Athol, and Dennis, Massachusetts. He also designed fire stations in Tewksbury and Boston.

Boles's life was marked by a distinguished record of public service. A long-time resident of South Dennis, Massachusetts, Boles served as the town's only African American Selectman from 1973 to 1977. He also served on the South Dennis Board of Health, Planning Board, and Design Review Panel, where he was particularly concerned with the quality of low-cost housing, and he was a member of the Old King's Highway Interim Regional Planning Committee and Historic District Committee. He was a trustee and member of the board of investment of the Bass River Savings Bank, president of the Dennis Taxpayers Association from 1966 to 1969, and a member of the Greater Boston Chamber of Commerce. Professionally, Boles was a member of the American Institute of Architects and the Boston Society of Architects Ethics Committee, and he served as a critic for the Boston Architectural Center. He was also a warden of the Christ Church Episcopal in Harwichport, Massachusetts, and was active in the National Association for the Advancement of Colored People.

Henry Boles, who was described as "serious, courtly, and somewhat elegant" as well as self-controlled and principled, died from cancer on January 29, 1979, at the age of sixty-eight in Hyannis, Massachusetts.[1] His funeral was held at Saint David's Episcopal Church in South Yarmouth, Massachusetts, a church he had designed in 1970. He was buried at the Blue Hills Cemetery in Braintree, Massachusetts. Boles's architectural education under Mies van der Rohe at Illinois Institute of Technology and Walter Gropius at Harvard University placed him firmly within the Modernist movement as a designer. His Modernist identity is reflected in his designs, which show strong rectangular forms with little ornamentation, and in his urban renewal projects such as Marksdale Gardens (1965) in Roxbury and Brunswick Gardens (c1977) in Dorchester, Massachusetts. His architectural career encompassed both the rise and decline of Modern architecture. His design philosophy can be summed up by an observation he made during an interview: "I think right now we're getting into the period with our modern architecture that has come to many other periods . . . that period where the urge to do something extreme sort of gets in the way of the sensible."[2]

Saint David's Episcopal Church, *Courtesy of Saint David's Episcopal Church*

HENRY CLIFFORD BOLES

Notes
1. "Henry C. Boles, 68, Dies: Dennis Official, Architect," *Boston Evening Globe*, 31 January 1979, p. 13.
2. John B. Value, "Partnership for Logic, Beauty," *Boston Evening Globe*, 23 April 1964, p. 22.

Bibliography
American Institute of Architects (AIA). "Henry C. Boles" Folder, Box 53, RG 803. American Institute of Architects Archives, Washington, D.C.

"Henry C. Boles." Paul V. Galvin Library, Illinois Institute of Technology, University Archives. Deceased Donors Series, Accession no. 1991.06.

MARGARET M. GRUBIAK
GRADUATE STUDENT,
UNIVERSITY OF VIRGINIA
SCHOOL OF ARCHITECTURE

BUILDING LIST

Name	Address	City	State/Country	Year	Comments
Agricultural Experiment Station	Suakoko	Monrovia	Liberia	1953	
Athol Elderly Housing	Lakeville Rd.	Athol	MA	1972	
Blue Hill Avenue Fire Station	976 Blue Hill Ave.	Boston	MA	1974	
Boles, Henry C.	97 Great Western Rd.	South Yarmouth	MA	c1960	
Brewster Baptist Church	1648 Main St.	Brewster	MA	1976	Addition
Brunswick Gardens	Brunswick St.	Dorchester	MA	c1977	
Captain Farris House	308 S. Main St.	South Yarmouth	MA		
Dennis Elderly Housing	Center St.	South Dennis	MA	1974	
Knights of Columbus Home of Council	462 Broadway	Methuen	MA	1961	
Marksdale Gardens	95 Humboldt Ave.	Roxbury	MA	1965	
Massachusetts Bureau of Bldg. Constr. Office & Garage		Plymouth	MA	1977	
Methuen Elderly Housing		Methuen	MA	1974	
Methuen Fire Station	24 Lowell St.	Methuen	MA	1967	West End
Methuen Junior High School	1 Ranger Rd.	Methuen	MA		
Mines & Geology Bldg.		Monrovia	Liberia	1955	
Monrovia Elementary School		Monrovia	Liberia	1954	
North Street Fire Station	830 North St.	Tewksbury	MA	1976	
Phalanx Housing					
St. David's Episcopal Church	205 Old Main St.	South Yarmouth	MA	1970	
St. Stephen's Episcopal Church Parish Hall	419 Shawmutt Ave.	Boston	MA	1961	
U.S. Post Office	321 Main St.	Wakefield	MA	1975	Addition
Washington Park Shopping Center		Roxbury	MA		
Westfield State College Student Union–Ely Library	Campus	Westfield	MA	1973	

Cyril Garner Bow
(1899–1963)

Charcoal by James Porter, 1928. *Courtesy of Howard University Gallery of Art Permanent Collection.*

As an architect, Cyril Bow was educationally and professionally associated with ALBERT IRVIN CASSELL. Choosing to enroll at Cornell University and the most productive years of his professional career were linked to Cassell.

Cyril was born on June 15, 1899, in Buffalo, New York. He attended Lafayette High School, which was located in an affluent, all-White neighborhood of West Buffalo. He entered high school at age sixteen in 1915 and graduated four years later. A member of the alumni association believes that Cyril Bow was the first African American to graduate from Lafayette.

In the fall of 1919, Bow entered the School of Architecture at Cornell University in Ithaca, New York. His admission to the School of Architecture broke their tradition because another Black, Albert Cassell, was admitted in the same first-year class: during the second decade of the twentieth century it was unusual to find two or more Blacks in the same School of Architecture at the same time at a non-Black university. It was rare but not unprecedented for Cornell's School of Architecture to admit Blacks because they had admitted and subsequently graduated RALPH VICTOR COOK more than two decades earlier in 1898 and VERTNER WOODSON TANDY a decade after that in 1908.

Racial prejudice prevented White fraternities from rushing Negro pledges and the university prohibited Negroes from residing in dormitories in 1906. So Tandy and six other non-architecture students had founded the first Black fraternity in America, *Alpha Phi Alpha*, so they would have a communal house to stay in and be able to academically support each other. When Bow and Cassell arrived on campus in September 1915, they were enthusiastic and relieved to be rushed by the *Alphas*. Bow earned 101 credits during the six years he was enrolled (1919–25), but finally left without earning a diploma. Six years was two years longer than it took to complete the course in architecture, according to the catalog of Cornell University, which suggests that Bow was not a full-time student. He was likely working his way through school or could not come up with the lump sum full-time tuition.

Bow left Ithaca near the end of 1925 and settled in Washington, D.C., in a rental row house on S Street, NW, at the bottom of the hilltop campus of HOWARD UNIVERSITY. His fraternity brother, Albert Irvin Cassell, had preceded him to Washington, D.C., where he was already university architect at Howard. Initially Bow worked for Cassell when the latter directed Howard University's Department of Building and Grounds and afterward for the office of Albert I. Cassell. From 1926 until 1951, Bow served Albert I. Cassell as his most trusted employee and chief draftsman in charge of drawing production, the drafting room, and draftsmen-architects therein, such as CLYDE MARTIN DRAYTON and CLARENCE BUCHANAN WHEAT.[1]

CYRIL GARNER BOW

Clarence Short House, Dreck Spurlock Wilson

The only known buildings attributable to Bow that should not be attributed to Cassell are an apartment building (1939) at 4208 Benning Road, NE, in Washington, D.C., and four houses in the Deanwood neighborhood of the District of Columbia, which Bow probably took on as moonlighting jobs.

Cyril Bow married Marguerite Smith after her 1924 graduation from Howard University's School of Music. She taught vocal music in the D.C. public schools for thirty-three years.

Artist and art historian James Porter (1905–71), who was at the center of the "New Negro Movement" during the 1920s and professor of art at Howard University for forty years, counted Cyril Bow as one of his close friends, which suggests that Bow mingled in the art intelligentsia circles of Black Washington. In 1925 Porter sketched a charcoal portrait of a contemplative Bow, which is held in the permanent collection of the Howard University Art Gallery.

Bow was an active member of the NATIONAL TECHNICAL ASSOCIATION.

Cyril Bow died on February 9, 1963. He was buried in Harmony Cemetery in Suitland, Maryland, alongside his wife.

Notes
1. Cyril G. Bow to Thomas M. Locraft, Secretary-Treasurer, D.C. Board of Examiners and Registrars of Architects, 12 December 1951, "Reference for Clyde Drayton," D.C. Archives.

Bibliography
Howard University Gallery of Art. *James A. Porter, the Memory of the Legacy*. D.C.: Howard University Gallery of Art, 1992.

SOPHONIA WELCH,
CORNELL UNIVERSITY, SCHOOL OF ARCHITECTURE

BUILDING LIST

Name	Address	City	State	Year	Comments
Apartment Bldg.	4208 Benning Rd., NE	Washington	DC	1939	
Guilford Baptist Church	320 V St., NW	Washington	DC	1945	Demolished
Landis, Sylvia	1011 Irving St., NE	Washington	DC	1940	
Lee, Robert	2917 14th St., NE	Washington	DC	1939	
McDuffie, Clyde	1427 Hamlin St., NE	Washington	DC	1941	
Short, Clarence	1424 Girard St., NE	Washington	DC	1939	

Charles Sumner Bowman
(c1873–unknown)

Charles Sumner Bowman was born in Mississippi circa 1873.[1] His mother, Mattie [*sic* Marta] Bowman, worked as a maid and laundress in Vicksburg while raising Charles and his three siblings, Lilly, Paul, and Victoria. Mattie was widowed by the age of twenty-eight and the identity of Charles' father is not known.

Bowman entered the junior class of the Normal Department at TUSKEGEE INSTITUTE as an evening student in 1895.[2] The Tuskegee Institute evening school program enabled those students who were unable to afford the expenses of day school to earn money working on campus during the day to pay for their tuition. The period during which Bowman attended Tuskegee Institute was one of rapid expansion, and, along with his classmates, he participated in the construction of any number of campus buildings, learning all aspects of mechanical drawing and carpentry trades. Bowman completed his senior year in the Mechanical Industries Department in May 1899. Following in her older brother's footsteps, Charles' younger sister Victoria appears in the 1899 to 1900 *Tuskegee Institute Catalog* as a member of the "A" Preparatory Class.

After graduation, Bowman found employment with Western University in Quindaro, Kansas, as the first director of its newly formed Industrial Department. Western University was the only institution of higher learning for African Americans in Kansas. The African Methodist Episcopal denomination organized Western University in 1896 from the remnants of the defunct Freedman's University, which had been established around 1865. Inspired by BOOKER T. WASHINGTON's success at TUSKEGEE INSTITUTE, the Western University trustees lobbied the state legislature for funds to establish a State Industrial Department that would train young men and women in critically needed labor skills.

A leading advocate for the new industrial program was Kansas Governor William Stanley, who made a moving statement in support of the industrial school at the opening of the 1898 to 1899 legislative session. Citing the national fame and success of Booker T. Washington's industrial education program, Stanley noted that public appropriations had augmented private donations Washington received. He concluded by throwing his support behind the program, urging "that the Quindaro movement be given aid and encouragement by the state."[3] Following Stanley's speech the legislature passed the *Bailey Bill*, creating the State Industrial Department.

The first group of Industrial Department instructors, including Bowman, were graduates of Tuskegee Institute, Fisk University, Lincoln University at Jefferson City, and other historically Black colleges and universities. Hired as director of industries in 1899, the following year Bowman conducted the Military Department drill and held the position of assistant superintendent of the Industrial Department. Bowman instructed courses in carpentry, woodworking machinery, cabinetmaking, and architectural and mechanical drawing. In the introduction to the carpentry course in the 1899 university catalog, Bowman describes the importance of building construction "along scientific lines." The skills taught at Western University enabled young men to "[build] for themselves" and to "find . . . a most lucrative employment as a means of livelihood."[4] The 1900 to 1901 university catalog lists nine first-year and seven second-year students in the architectural drawing and carpentry course. The majority are from the two Kansas Cities with a few from other Kansas towns, including Leavenworth, Topeka, and Ellsworth, and one from the Indian Territory near Lawrence, Kansas.

The legislation establishing the State Industrial Department at Western University included an appropriation for the construction of an Industrial Department building. The cornerstone of Stanley Industrial Hall, named for Governor Stanley, was laid in 1900. As director of industries, Bowman probably designed and supervised construction of this 3-story Romanesque-style building. The pride of Western University, it had a high limestone water table that contrasted with the dark red brick upper stories. The first two floors contained large, bright, and airy classrooms, whereas the upper floor housed fully outfitted dormitory rooms for fifty men.

Stanley Industrial Hall, Western University, *Annual Catalogue of Western University, 1902–1903,* Kansas State Historical Society

Bowman left Western University in 1902 to establish his own architectural practice in Kansas City, Kansas. With an office located at 524 Minnesota Avenue, he advertised his services in Hoye's *Kansas City, Kansas Directory* (1903). During the next two decades, Bowman rented office space at 500 Minnesota Avenue (1907–12), 1016 North 5th Street (1920–22), and 428 Minnesota Avenue (1924–25).

Charles Bowman married Etta B. Buford on August 2, 1904, in Kansas City, Kansas. She was a former student of music and typing at Western University. Their years together appear to have been short. After 1905, records show Charles Bowman listed as "single."

Bowman disappears from records for Kansas City, Kansas, between 1913 and 1919. His whereabouts during this period are unknown. A listing for his architectural practice reappears in 1920 and last appears in the 1924–25 *Kansas City, Kansas Directory*, which is the last record of his presence in Wyandotte County.

The only private commission attributable to Bowman is a brick apartment building constructed circa 1904 in Kansas City, Kansas, for Dr. Isham H. Anthony, an African American physician and vice president of the Wyandotte Drug Company.[5] Having worked as an architect for over twenty years, undoubtedly Charles Sumner Bowman contributed to the built environment of Kansas City, Kansas. Unfortunately no records survive to identify his mark.

The date of Charles Sumner Bowman's death and the location of his grave site are not known.

Notes
1. U.S. Census Bureau, *Federal Population Schedules and Indexes* (D.C.: U.S. Census Bureau, Population Division, 1870–1930). Records place Bowman's birth date between March 1873 and June 1876.
2. Tuskegee Institute, *Catalog of the Tuskegee Normal and Industrial Institute* (Tuskegee: Tuskegee Institute, 1895–1900), p. 212.
3. Western University, *Annual Catalogue of Western University, 1898–1899* (Quindaro: Western University Industrial Student Printers, 1899), p. 5.
4. Ibid., p. 35.
5. Richard K. Dozier, "Tuskegee: Booker T. Washington's Contributions to the Education of Black Architects" (Arch.D. dissertation, University of Michigan 1990), p. 74. Dozier describes the building as a project for Dr. J. H. Anderson [*sic*]. City directories carry a listing for a Dr. Isham H. Anthony who it is believed was the client.
6. *Hoyes' Kansas City and (Kansas City, Kans., Rosedale, Kans. and Argentine, Kans.) Directory*, Kansas City: Hoye's Directory Company 1903, p. 23.

Bibliography

Tuskegee Normal and Industrial Institute. *Catalogue of the Tuskegee Normal and Industrial Institute.* Tuskegee: Tuskegee Normal School Steam Press, 1895–1900.

Western University. *Annual Catalogue of Western University.* Quindaro: Western University Industrial Student Printers, 1899–1903.

CHARLES SUMNER BOWMAN

KERRY DAVIS AND ELIZABETH ROSIN,
HISTORIC PRESERVATION SERVICES, LLC,
KANSAS CITY, MISSOURI

BUILDING LIST

Name	Address	City	State	Year	Comments
Anthony, Dr. Isham H.	Apartment Bldg., 1512 N. 5th St.	Kansas City	KS	c1904	Demolished
Western University Stanley Industrial Hall	Garfield Ave. & 27th St.	Quindaro	KS	1900	Demolished

Thomas Wilson Boyde Jr.
(1905–1981)

Rochester Museum and Science Center

Thomas Wilson Boyde Jr. was born on Christmas Day 1905 in Washington, D.C., the third of four children of Thomas Wilson Boyde Sr., a chauffeur, and Sadie Underwood Boyde.[1] The family lived in the LeDroit Park neighborhood near Howard University.

Boyde graduated from Dunbar High School in 1923. His yearbook describes him as "military, mathematical, and courteous"; an officer in a prize-winning cadet battalion; and president of the Dunbar Officers' Club.[2] Although not accepted to the U.S. Military Academy at West Point—his first choice—Boyde was admitted to Brown University to study engineering but stayed only one year. As a sophomore, Boyde attended the University of Minnesota; as a junior, the University of Michigan; and after a senior year at Syracuse University, he graduated with a bachelor of architecture degree in 1928. While in college, Boyde pledged *Omega Psi Phi* fraternity.

In the late 1920s, architecture students at Syracuse University were instructed in the *Beaux Arts* tradition. Boyde studied with Professors Revels, Hallenbeck, Sargent, and Lear, the last an exacting teacher who had trained in Paris. While at Syracuse, Boyde won notice in several student competitions.

After graduation, Boyde worked in New York City and Albany, New York, but little is known about his early professional life. Surviving records indicate that he worked for Schultz & Weaver; VERTNER WOODSON TANDY; Voorhees, Gmelin, & Walker; and the New York State Architect's Office.

In 1930 Boyde responded to an employment advertisement for an architectural designer. The job was in Rochester, New York, with the firm of Sigmund Firestone, a Romanian-born architect. Unaware that Boyde was African American when he invited him to interview, Firestone polled his staff to see if they would object to working with a man of color before offering Boyde a position working on the $4 million Monroe County Home and Infirmary.

For the Monroe County Home and Infirmary, Boyde executed Lombard Romanesque–style features that included "elaborate stone carvings (gargoyles, grotesques, and other symbolic motifs) and patterned, polychromatic masonry (alternating bands of red brick, light colored stone, and glazed terra cotta tiles)."[3]

Funded just as the Great Depression began, the Monroe County Home and Infirmary was attacked as a "palace" for the poor because of its "lavish" expenditures. Boyde responded by portraying the project's detractors unflatteringly in stone and using symbolic motifs such as Saint George slaying the dragon to depict the political struggle.[4] Several grand juries investigated the project's finances but the architects and contractors were cleared each time. After the final investigation, newspaper columnist Paul Benton attacked the "atrocious" architecture and the secrecy of the grand jury process, saying "the longer [the] facts . . . are kept a dark and fearsome secret, the longer the Sovereign Voter is going to simmer in uncertainty.

And ... the deeper will grow his conviction that the Senegambian he thinks is in the woodpile is very, very black indeed."⁵ Just three days earlier Ku Klux Klan members had burned a cross nearby, and the night Benton's column appeared, a suspicious fire almost destroyed the new buildings.

For the remainder of the Great Depression, Boyde worked for Sigmond Firestone, the Works Progress Administration, Frank Quinlan, and others in Rochester. In 1937 he returned briefly to Washington, D.C., at the request of ALBERT IRVIN CASSELL to work as an inspector on HOWARD UNIVERSITY's Founders Library and prepare drawings for other projects such as Mayfair Gardens. In 1940 Boyde obtained his New York State architect's license.

During World War II, Boyde worked as an engineer in military aircraft and ordnance plants in the Buffalo area. In 1947 he started his own firm in Rochester. One of his first projects was the Frederick Douglass Homes for the Negro Housing and Planning Council. Drawing on his knowledge of the trendsetting public housing in Washington, D.C., Boyde tried to meet the housing needs of Rochester's African American population, which had increased from 3,000 in 1930 to 8,000 after the war. The project—which included stores, a social hall, and twenty-three apartments—was never realized.

Boyde's successes came from the postwar expansion of Rochester's suburbs. His projects were a mix of houses and tracts, apartment buildings, motels, office buildings, restaurants and franchises, supermarkets, industrial buildings, shopping plazas, and bowling alleys. In 1949 Boyde was invited to join the Rochester Society of Architects. He joined, but was never an active member.

Boyde was proudest of his house designs and continued to do all of the firm's residential work, even after hiring Martin Rose and William Leitch to help with commercial and industrial projects between 1962 and 1970. An admirer of architect Frank Lloyd Wright, Boyde was an accomplished Modernist known for his solid construction. His buildings had simple, clean lines and often featured overhanging roofs, curved walls that he dubbed "Mae Wests," and corner windows. Boyde also did numerous projects for nonprofit organizations including several Black churches; the Black women's Masonic organization the Eastern Star; and a day-care center.

Although not active in politics, Boyde, along with a small group of Black professionals who were close friends, made several mostly unsuccessful attempts in the 1960s and early 1970s to address the growing need for diverse housing in Rochester. Hired by the

Detail from Monroe County Home and Infirmary, *Rochester Museum & Science Center*

Rochester Housing Authority to design the city's first federally funded housing projects, Boyde was replaced midway through the project because officials wanted a denser occupancy, which meant more apartments. In 1968 Boyde's design for a *Kindergarten*–3 school with low- and moderate-income housing, sponsored by the Urban League, was abandoned when negotiations to purchase the property fell through. The group then incorporated as Applied Urban Research Associates and applied for federal Model Cities funds, but contracts were awarded instead to F.I.G.H.T., an activist organization that worked with the urban poor and whose leaders were Black ministers.

Boyde married Jennie Jones on July 19, 1930, and they had three children. Boyde's family and friends describe him as highly intelligent, a storyteller with a playful sense of humor, absorbed in his work, a trusting person who made deals with handshakes instead of contracts, and more fond of the art of architecture than the business of it. A friend and contemporary

THOMAS WILSON BOYDE JR.

noted with admiration that although Boyde faced prejudice in his career, he worked continuously in his chosen field from graduation on, practicing the profession that he loved.[5] It is all the more remarkable that he did so in Rochester, a city that at mid-century had a small Black population and no appreciable Black middle-class.

Boyde suffered from multiple sclerosis during the last years of his life and his practice dropped off in the mid-1970s. He died on September 12, 1981.

Notes

1. U.S. Department of Commerce, Bureau of the Census, "Twelfth Census of the United States, 1900, Schedule No. 1—Population," District of Columbia, S.D. 1, E.D. 127, Sheet 7.
2. Dunbar High School, Liber Anni: *Historical Sketch and Review of the Class of 1923* (D.C.: Dunbar High School, 1923), n.p.
3. Bero Associates, "Monroe Community Hospital Masonry Survey" unpublished, Rochester, New York n.d.
5. Louis Regner, "Grand Jury Says Hospital Costs May Need Probe," *Rochester Democrat and Chronicle*, 11 April 1933, p. 13; Paul Benton, "Frankly Speaking," *Rochester Times Union*, 6 June 1933, p. 6; "$4,000,000 County Home Threatened When Blaze Breaks Out in Basement," *Rochester Democrat and Chronicle*, 7 June 1933, p. 15.
6. Interview with Dr. William Knox, Newton, Massachusetts, 5 July 1994.

Bibliography

"Thomas Wilson Boyde Jr. Papers," Schuyler Towson Research Library. Rochester Museum and Science Center, Rochester, New York

Schmidt, Carl Frederick. *Architecture and Architects of Rochester.* Rochester: Rochester Society of Architects, 1959.

JUDITH E. GREENE,
PROJECT ARCHIVIST,
WIDENER LIBRARY, HARVARD UNIVERSITY

BUILDING LIST

Name	Address	City	State	Year	Comments
Aero Industries	1140 Brooks Ave.	Gates	—	1953	Demolished
Aprilano, Frank	286 Ashbourne Rd.	Brighton	NY	1955	
Arieno, Charles J.	281 Pardee Rd.	Irondequoit	NY	1951	
Aronson, Victor	3409 W. Lake Rd.	Canandaigua	NY	1953	
Axelrod, Milton P.	56 Varinna Dr.	Brighton	NY	1952	
Baird Sanitarium	301 Lake Ave.		NY		
Balonek, Frank	857 Main St.	Mumford	NY	1952	
Bay View Hotel		Irondequoit	NY	c1951	
Betsy & Betty Beauty Salon	42 East Ave.	Rochester	NY	1948	Interior design only
Blue Label Foods Plant	460 Buffalo Rd.	Rochester	NY	1936	Sigmund Firestone Assoc. architect
Brodsky, Maurice	411 Rawlinson Rd.	Irondequoit	NY	1950	
Camellaci, Raymond	242 Oakridge Dr.	Irondequoit	NY	c1955	
Carver House	192 Ormond St.	Rochester	NY	1943	
Cellura, Alfred	75 Deerfield Dr.	Irondequoit	NY	1952	
Collins, Lawrence	4425 Douglas St., NE	Washington	DC	1939	
Connors, Joseph S.	569 Hurstbourne Rd.	Irondequoit	NY	1949	
Daltin Restaurant	72 Franklin St.	Rochester	NY	1950	
Dattilo, Atty. Philip B., Sr.	1920 Culver Rd.	Irondequoit	NY	1948	
Davis, Harry I.	2627 English Rd.	Greece	NY	1951	
DeRyke Dairy	1985 Ridge Rd. East	Irondequoit	NY	1947	
Dinner Bell Restaurant	476 Monroe Ave.	Rochester	NY	1947	
Dorschel, John	3833 East Ave.	Pittsford	NY	1952	
Dorschel Motors	67 Ridge Rd. West at Lake Ave.	Greece	NY	1948	
Duffy's Hotel	102 Clinton Ave. North	Rochester	NY	1954	Demolished
Eastman Hotel Rainbow Lounge & Coffee Shop	215 Chestnut St.	Rochester	NY	1947	
Eisenstat, William P.	150 Thackery Rd.	Brighton	NY	1952	
Empire Parkway Restaurant	2235 Empire Blvd.	Webster	NY	1950	
Ernie's Place Restaurant	4653 Lake Ave.	Rochester	NY	1954	
Famous Brand Shoes	405 Main St. East	Rochester	NY	1953	
Fasino, Joseph	597 Van Voorhis Ave.	Irondequoit	NY	1955	
Ferris, Newell A.	772 Penfield Rd.	Brighton	NY	1948	

BUILDING LIST (continued)

Name	Address	City	State	Year	Comments
Fountainbleau Restaurant & Bar	75 Clinton Ave. North	Rochester	NY	1952	Storefront & interior
Franklin House Restaurant	72 Franklin St.	Rochester	NY	c1960	
Frati, Mario J.	304 Greeley St.	Rochester	NY	1953	
Friederich, Adam G.	442 Edgemere Dr.	Greece	NY	1955	
Friedman, Jules	321 Council Rock Ave.	Brighton	NY	1953	
Frijhy, Frank S.	2086 Norton St.	Rochester	NY	1950	
Gargano, Frank A.	158 Orland Rd.	Irondequoit	NY	1949	
Genesee Steel Co.	1460 Lyell Ave. (rear)	Rochester	NY	1949	
Genesse Valley Trust Bldg.	45 Exchange St.	Rochester	NY	1929	Voorhees, Gmelin & Walker Assoc. architects
Gianforti, Bert C.	2153 Baird Rd.	Penfield	NY	1954	
Gibbin, Dr. Clifford L.	4048 East Ave.	Pittsford	NY	1946	
Ginghamtown Restaurant & Motel	409 Lake Shore Dr.	Canandaigua	NY	1953	
Giordano, Joseph J.	3883 St. Paul Blvd.	Irondequoit	NY	1947	Address changed when street was extended
Goldstein, David G.	6 San Rafael Dr.	Pittsford	NY	1954	
Green, Harry, Jr.	307 Greeley St.	Rochester	NY	1948	
Grossman, Milton	401 Pelham Rd.	Brighton	NY	1954	
Guzetta, Matthew	80 Woodman Park	Rochester	NY	1946	
H & E Sandwich Shop	280 Alexander St.	Rochester	NY	1950	Berkley Hotel
Hedges Grill	955 Joseph Ave.	Rochester	NY	1951	Birch Room addition
Heicklen, Morris	70 Varinna Dr.	Brighton	NY	1950	
Hicks, George T.	99 Norman Rd.	Brighton	NY	1951	
Hoffman, Harry L.	222 Pelham Rd.	Brighton	NY	1950	
Huntington, Harry B.	3280 East Ave.	Brighton	NY	1947	
Interlichia, Philip C.	172 Hillcrest St.	Rochester	NY	1953	
Jon-Jose Beauty Salon	839 Clinton Ave. South	Rochester	NY	c1952	
Kapp, Sam	225 Lake Front	Irondequoit	NY	1955	
Kasdins, Jacob	259 Ashbourne Rd.	Brighton	NY	1953	
Kroll's Great Expectations Shop	645 Clinton Ave. North	Rochester	NY	1949	
Lanzatella, Philip J.	160 Wisner Rd.	Irondequoit	NY	1951	
Leonardo, Henry F.	245 Edgemere Dr.	Greece	NY	1949	
Leonardo, Richard A.	2500 St. Paul Blvd.	Irondequoit	NY	1950	
Levy, Bennett	256 Rhinecliff Dr.	Brighton	NY	1948	
Lipson Furniture Co.	681 Fillmore Ave.	Buffalo	NY	1952	
Lipson, Avrome Y.	34 Louvaine Dr.	Tonawanda	NY	1950	
Litwin, Emil	20 Varinna Dr.	Brighton	NY	1952	
LoCurcio, Ralph D.	226 Thomas Ave.	Irondequoit	NY	1948	
Lopatin, Harold H.	345 Pelham Rd.	Brighton	NY	1954	
Low-income housing	8 Prince St.	Rochester	NY	c1968	Plans only
Mammano, Joseph T.	125 Tottenham Rd.	Irondequoit	NY	1954	
Mangurian, Harry T.	666 Corwin Rd.	Brighton	NY	1955	
Masonic Temple	68 Perine	Dansville	NY	1953	Addition
Matteson, Harlan J.	50 Lattimore Rd.	Rochester	NY	1947	
Mercurio, Frank	304 Simpson Rd.	Irondequoit	NY	1948	
Miracle Diner	755 Hudson Ave.	Rochester	NY	1954	
Monroe County Home and Infirmary	435 East Henrietta Rd.	Rochester	NY	1933	Now Monroe Hospital; Sigmund Firestone assoc. architect
Morris, Atty. Ira H.	55 Esplanade Dr.	Brighton	NY	1955	
Murray Shoe Store	643 Clinton Ave. North	Rochester		c1950	
Nazareth College of Rochester Admn. Bldg.	Campus	Rochester	NY	1941	Frank Quinlan Assoc. architect
Nazareth College of Rochester Auditorium	Campus	Rochester	NY	1941	Frank Quinlan Assoc. architect
Nazareth College of Rochester Classroom Bldg.	Campus	Rochester	NY	1941	Frank Quinlan Assoc. architect

THOMAS WILSON BOYDE JR.

BUILDING LIST *(continued)*

Name	Address	City	State	Year	Comments
Nazareth College of Rochester Dormitory	Campus	Rochester	NY	1941	Frank Quinlan Assoc. architect
Noah's Ark Auto Accessories	836 Goodman St. North	Rochester	NY	c1958	
Noah's Ark Auto Accessories		Syracuse	NY	1955	Westvale Shopping Plaza
Palermo, Biagio	92 Oaklawn Dr.	Irondequoit	NY	1946	
Papa, Frank C.	100 Shaftsbury Rd.	Brighton	NY	1951	
Papa, Samuel R.	261 Orchard Park Blvd.	Irondequoit	NY	1948	
Parks, Joseph F.	175 Winona Blvd.	Irondequoit	NY	1948	
Passero, Anthony P.	22 Grantham	Irondequoit	NY	1953	
Passero, Joseph D.	2190 Culver Rd.	Rochester	NY	1952	
Pierleoni, Ennius	1293 Jay St.	Rochester	NY	1951	
Piscitello, Frances	125 Woodman Park	Rochester	NY	1954	
Pluto, Andrew	97 Simpson Rd.	Irondequoit	NY	1953	
Prager, Sol L.	333 Council Rock Ave.	Brighton	NY	1952	
Prato, Samuel	41 Woodman Pk.	Rochester	NY	1946	
Queen's Colony Subdivision	Various addresses	Brighton	NY	1954	48 houses
Raffelson, Jacob	80 Wilshire Rd.	Brighton	NY	1948	
Rause, Arthur A.	271 Council Rock Ave.	Brighton	NY	1951	
Reagan, Edward B.	20 Coleridge Rd.	Rochester	NY	1951	
Ring, Dr. Ellis	45 Torrington Dr.	Brighton	NY	c1943	
Ritts, Donald B.	440 Claybourne Rd.	Brighton	NY	1950	
Rochester Bakery	1252 Goodman St. North	Rochester	NY	1948	
Rogacs, Joseph	179 Haviland Park	Greece	NY	1950	
Romack, Paul	2330 W. Henrietta Rd.	Brighton	NY	1951	
Romeo, Frank J.	588 Rocket St.	Rochester	NY	1949	
Romeo, Philip	134 Laurelton Rd.	Irondequoit	NY	1950	
Rowe, Vincent	2200 Culver Rd.	Rochester	NY	1951	
Russi, Arthur M.	28 Tottenham Rd.	Irondequoit	NY	1947	
Rutner Iron Company	11 Nester St.	Rochester	NY	1951	
Santa, Sam R.	41 Esplanade Dr.	Brighton	NY	1955	
Scardino, Samuel P.	295 Orchard Park Blvd.	Irondequoit	NY	1951	
Schifano, Benedict F.	163 Wyndham Rd.	Irondequoit	NY	1954	
Segal, Morris	306 Pelham Rd.	Brighton	NY	1953	
Shannon, Harry D.	116 Westview Terr.	Rochester	NY	1948	
Sherman, Barney R.	55 Rhinecliffe Dr.	Brighton	NY	1948	
Sleephy Hollow Motel	2631 Monroe Ave.	Brighton	NY	1954	
Storrer, Herman L.		Henderson Harbor	NY	1954	Summer cottage
Sutphen, George T.	76 Baycrest Dr.	Irondequoit	NY	1953	
Thurston, Lewis M.	505 Penfield Rd.	Brighton	NY	1949	
Times Square Hotel & Club	45 Exchange St.	Rochester	NY	1950	Alterations
Walters, Adelaide	90 Cloverdale St.	Rochester	NY	1953	
Ward, Clarence A.	212 Baycrest Dr.	Irondequoit	NY	1952	
Ward, John C.	1703 Creek St.	Penfield	NY	1941	
Weis, Linus R.	60 Penfield Rd.	Brighton	NY	1950	Demolished
Wilinsky, Dr. Isadore J.	198 San Gabriel Dr.	Rochester	NY	1947	
Wolk, Paul	69 Torrington Dr.	Brighton	NY	c1943	
Your Flower Shop	165 Clinton Ave. North	Rochester	NY		

Calvin Thomas Stowe Brent
(1854–1899)

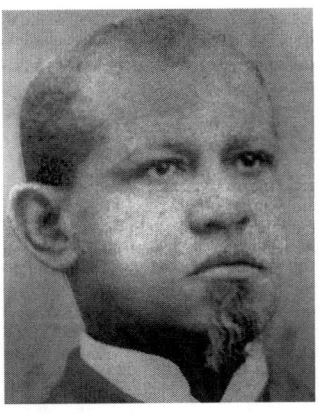

Janice Rollins

According to contemporary sources Calvin Brent was the first African American architect in the District of Columbia and the only one practicing in the last quarter of the nineteenth century. Although little is known about the man, his architectural training, or his practice, city building permits reveal that Brent worked in all quadrants of the city, designing at least eighty-two houses, two stores, and six churches during his twenty-five-year career.[1]

Calvin Brent was born in 1854, the seventh of eight children to John and Elizabeth Edmonson Brent. Calvin's father was an industrious man who had been able to purchase his own freedom and that of his fiancée.[2] He was also a founder and the first pastor of the John Wesley African Methodist Episcopal Zion Church, one of the early independent Black congregations in the city. Born into a free, financially secure family that was able to provide its children with some formal education, Calvin Brent was in the position to take advantage of the opportunities that opened for African Americans in the brief period after the Civil War and before the Reconstruction Era.

In a family reminiscence, his son recalled that Calvin Brent "learned his profession as an apprentice to Plowman and Weightman, a firm of architects on E Street, NW east of 7th Street," in about 1873.[3] This would have been a common way to acquire professional training at that time. No architect named Weightman has been found, but the other firm member was probably Thomas M. Plowman, who was originally from Philadelphia but was working in Washington, D.C., by 1864. During a four-year partnership with Nathan G. Starkweather, Plowman was responsible for the design of several major projects in the city, including the Freedmen's Savings and Loan Building. By the time Brent would have been in his office, Plowman was practicing alone and serving as the Inspector of Buildings for the District of Columbia.

The earliest building with which Brent's name is associated is Saint Luke's Episcopal Church, founded by African American minister Alexander Crummell. This landmark Gothic-style chapel was begun in 1876, and twenty-two-year-old Brent apparently drafted the plans.[4] Most of Brent's commissions date from the mid-1880s through 1893, when an economic depression slowed Washington, D.C.'s real estate boom. Many of his buildings stood in areas of the city that have been redeveloped, and only two churches and twenty-nine houses remain. Brent's projects fall solidly within the brick building tradition that characterized Washington, D.C., architecture in the late nineteenth century. His name sometimes appears as both architect and builder on city permits, and he was probably closer to the skilled builders of the city than to its high-style architects. Brent's expansiveness was probably also constrained by the budgets of his clients. Although he had a few White clients, most of Brent's patrons were from the African American middle class and were tied to him through family, neighborhood, or church connections.

Brent married Albertine Jones in 1874 and through marriage was related to some of the most socially prominent families in Washington, D.C. The Wormley family, Dr. John Francis, Douglass Syphax, and others commissioned Brent to design speculative housing for them; however, except for designs for his brother-in-law, Garrett Wormley, he does not seem to have designed the homes of the wealthiest African Americans. Despite pleas from the Union League and chiding by the editor of the *Washington Bee*, these commissions and those of the elite churches went to White architects.

Four churches occupied Brent's time in the early to mid-1880s. The first and largest of these was the now-demolished Fourth (Metropolitan) Baptist Church at 13th and R Streets, NW. Begun in 1882 when Brent was twenty-eight, this was one of the largest African American churches in the city—a major accomplishment for both the architect and the young congregation that had been founded by ex-slaves only twenty years before. The brick building had Gothic details and symmetrically placed towers—a facade arrangement common to four of Brent's church designs.

Most of Brent's residential projects were the common brick row houses of 2 or 3 stories with full-height bays built in Washington, D.C., in the late nineteenth century. These were usually built singly or in groups of two or three. Brent is known to have designed three coordinated groups of speculative housing. One provided rental income for John Wesley African Methodist Episcopal Zion Church. Another was a handsome ensemble of nine buildings with oriel windows and stone trim that he built for the African American developer William A. Stewart (still standing at 4th and E Streets, NE, on Capitol Hill). The third consisted of ten houses at the intersection of Grant Street and Florida Avenue, NW, and included a towered corner home for his brother-in-law, Garrett Wormley. Calvin Chase, editor of the *Washington Bee*, praised this development as an example of African American enterprise.[5]

Calvin Brent's first wife and the mother of his seven children was Albertine Jones, a seamstress and the daughter of a successful feed merchant who donated the land for the first modern school for African American children in the city. After her death, Brent married Laurelia Brown, a widow of independent means who owned a large house on Striver's Row (1700 V Street, NW) and a produce stall in the Centre Market. Throughout most of his life, Brent resided at the corner of 18th and L Streets, NW, first in the house his father had built in 1842 and then in the brick house he designed to replace the original frame building. The property remained in the family until it was demolished in 1947.

Fourth Metropolitan Baptist Church, *Courtesy of Fourth Metropolitan Baptist Church*

Brent died suddenly at the age of forty-five in 1899 at what should have been the height of his career.[6] He was held up as an example to the group of young college-educated architects that appeared in Washington, D.C., a few years after his death. His significance lies in his role as a pioneer who chose to enter a profession previously closed to members of his race and who persevered in that profession despite economic recessions and the growing restrictions of the Reconstruction era. Brent was born into a capital city where slavery was protected and African Americans were restricted by law to a few occupations. When these restrictions were lifted at the close of the Civil War, Brent was positioned through social standing, education, and talent to take advantage of the professional opportunities that were available for the first time.

Notes
1. District of Columbia Building Permits, National Archives, Record Group 351, Microfilm Group M-1116. Dr. Harrison Mosley Ethridge, one of the first scholars to extensively re-

search African American architects in Washington, D.C., looked through permits issued by the District of Columbia and found more than fifty on which Brent's name appears. Because building permits were issued sporadically in the 1870s and the architect's name was not always filled-in, this may not represent the total of Brent's commissions.

2. John H. Paynter, *Fugitives of the Pearl* (Washington, D.C.: Associated Publishers, Inc., 1930), p.   . This book chronicles the story of Elizabeth Brent's siblings who were among the group of Washington, D.C., slaves who attempted a daring escape aboard the schooner *Pearl*. Publicity about the harsh treatment they received after being recaptured helped fuel the abolitionist movement. The book contains a romantic account of John and Elizabeth Brent's courtship.

3. Alfred P. Brent, "Business, Education, Religious Background of Ancestors, Predecessors," Harrison Ethridge Collection, Washington, D.C.

4. Harrison Ethridge, "St. Luke's Episcopal Church," Historic American Buildings Survey No. DC-359, Prints and Photographs Division, Library of Congress.

5. Calvin Chase, *Washington Bee*, 12 July 1890, n.p.

6. Calvin Chase, *Evening Star*, 16 November 1899, n.p.

Bibliography

Paynter, John N. "A Tribute to Mr. Brent—Obituary." *Colored American*, 2 December 1899, n.p.

Pinkett, Harold T. *National Church of Zion Methodism: A History of John Wesley A. M. E. Zion Church*. Baltimore: Gateway Press, 1989.

NANCY SCHWARTZ,
ARCHITECTURAL HISTORIAN,
GARRETT PARK, MARYLAND

BUILDING LIST

Name	Address	City	State	Year	Comments
Augusta, Dr. A. T.	1136 3rd St., NW	Washington	DC	1886	Houses & store demolished
Beason, J. T.	1219 Jackson St., NW	Washington	DC	1897	Alterations
Becket, L. M.	520 C. St., SE	Washington	DC	1893	
Beckley, M. D.	2125 12th St., NW	Washington	DC	1892	Demolished
Booker, Nelson	1119 19th St., NW	Washington	DC	1890	Demolished
Branson, Stephen	1219 25th St., NW	Washington	DC	1893	Demolished
Branson, Stephen	1245 25th St., NW	Washington	DC	1893	Demolished
Brent, Calvin T. S.	118 5th St., SE	Washington	DC	1893	
Brent, Calvin T. S.	916 20th St., NW	Washington	DC	1892	Demolished
Brent, Calvin T. S.	1016 18th St., NW (rear)	Washington	DC	1891	Demolished
Brent, John E.	1000 blk. 18th St., NW	Washington	DC		Demolished
Brent, John E.	1800 L St., NW	Washington	DC	1892	Demolished
Brent, John E.	1838 18th St., NW	Washington	DC	1889	Demolished
Brown, Laurelia	1704 V St., NW	Washington	DC	1891	
Clark, Michael	1453 Alley, NW	Washington	DC	1890	Demolished
Clark, Michael	1131 15th St., NW	Washington	DC	1890	Demolished
Clarke, Thomas H.	1106 G St., NE	Washington	DC	1892	
Clarke, Thomas H.	2234 11th St., NW	Washington	DC	1891	
Colbert, Robert R.	1629 O St., NW	Washington	DC	1881	Demolished
Davis, Elizabeth	1143 19th St., NW	Washington	DC	1891	Demolished
Ebenezer Methodist Episcopal Church Parsonage	332 4th St., SE	Washington	DC	1891	Demolished
Fourth (Metropolitan) Baptist Church	1225 R St., NW	Washington	DC	1882	Demolished
Francis, John R.	1619 Corcoran St., NW	Washington	DC	1889	Demolished
Francis, John R.	E. side 21st St., NW btwn. E & F Sts.	Washington	DC	1885	Demolished
Freeman, William L.	1905 K St., NW	Washington	DC	1890	House/barbershop demolished
French, Alfred	2212 F St., NW	Washington	DC	1887	
Grady, Washington	2123 N St., NW	Washington	DC	1892	
Hoffman, Jarrett F.	660 Morton Pl., NE	Washington	DC	1890	House & store
Howard, J. H.	1724 8th St., NW	Washington	DC	1886	Demolished
Jones, Cleo	2118 K St., NW (rear)	Washington	DC	1891	Demolished
Keith, John	1900 L St., NW	Washington	DC	1890	Demolished
Liberty Colored Baptist Church	1700 Blk. E St., NW	Washington	DC	c1879	
Lucas, William E.	461 E. St., SW	Washington	DC	1889	Demolished
Madison, James G.	1127 23rd St., NW	Washington	DC	1893	Demolished
Miles Memorial Colored Methodist Episcopal Church	1110 3rd St., NW	Washington	DC	1890	Demolished

CALVIN THOMAS STOWE BRENT

BUILDING LIST (continued)

Name	Address	City	State	Year	Comments
Minton, Theophilus J.	1327 T St., NW	Washington	DC	1886	
Mt. Jezreel Baptist Church	511 E. St., SE	Washington	DC	1883	
Mt. Jezreel Baptist Church Parsonage	511 E. St., SE	Washington	DC	1891	
Mt. Zion Baptist Church Parsonage	2902 O St., NW	Washington	DC	1896	
Murray, Daniel	S. side N St., NW btwn. 19th & 20th Sts.	Washington	DC	1878	Demolished
Naylor, William T.	1133 20th St., NW (rear)	Washington	DC	1890	Demolished
Pierre, William	510 21st St., NW	Washington	DC	1886	Demolished
Rogers, J. L.	1737 S. St., NW	Washington	DC	1892	
St. Luke's Baptist Church	Shephard St. nr. Bright Wood	Washington	DC	1890	Demolished
St. Luke's Episcopal Church	1514 15th St., NW	Washington	DC	1876	
Stewart, Edward	1407 1st St., NW	Washington	DC	1892	Demolished
Stewart, William A.	401–413 E St., NE	Washington	DC	1889	Rowhouses
Stewart, William A.	443–445 4th St., NE	Washington	DC	1889	Rowhouses
Syphax, Douglass P.	1833 8th St., NW	Washington	DC	1891	Demolished
Third Baptist Church	1546 5th St., NW	Washington	DC	1892	Alterations
Union Wesley American Methodist Episcopal Zion Church	E. side of 23rd St., NW nr. L St.	Washington	DC	1884	Demolished
Wales, S. S.	814–818 G St., NW	Washington	DC	1890	Rowhouses demolished
Wells, Samuel	1808 18th St., NW	Washington	DC	1888	Demolished
Wesley African Methodist Episcopal Zion Church	1120 Connecticut Ave., NW	Washington	DC	1884	Demolished
Wesley African Methodist Episcopal Zion Church Parsonage	1120 Connecticut Ave., NW	Washington	DC	1889	Demolished
Wesley African Methodist Episcopal Zion Church	1112 DeSales Ct., NW	Washington	DC	1889	Demolished
Wesley Zion Church	211 O St. SW	Washington	DC	1893	Demolished
Wormley, Garrett	SE corner Barry Pl. & Florida Ave., NW	Washington	DC	1890	10 houses; 7 demolished
Zion Baptist Church	337 F St., SW	Washington	DC	1891	Demolished

John Edmonson Brent
(1889–1962)

University Archives, State University of New York at Buffalo

Buffalo, New York, at the turn of the nineteenth century, was the eighth largest city in the United States, with a population of 350,000. It had more millionaires than any other city in the nation. Buffalo had hosted the Pan American Centennial Exposition in 1901 to showcase the extraordinary achievements made possible by the development of electrical power from nearby Niagara Falls.

Buffalonians had the taste, talent, and money to import great architects such as Henry Hobson Richardson, Louis Sullivan, Stanford White, Daniel Burnham, and Frank Lloyd Wright. Perhaps that is why Buffalo's first African American architect, John Edmonson Brent, came to Buffalo in 1912. It may be that he thought this industrial city could employ his talents to create great architecture regardless of his skin color.

John Edmonson Brent, named after his paternal grandfather, was born in 1889 and raised in one of the most sophisticated cities of Black culture—Washington, D.C. In addition, his father CALVIN THOMAS STOWE BRENT, was the first African American architect in the District of Columbia and had his own architectural practice as early as 1876. To be both African American and the son of an architect at that early date was extremely rare.

John Brent was educated in the public schools of Washington, D.C. He had little opportunity to watch his father—who died in 1899 when John was ten—practice his profession. It was probably his father's occupation as an architect that influenced John Brent's decision to go to TUSKEGEE INSTITUTE sometime in the early 1900s to study architecture. Tuskegee Institute was by then the preeminent Black architectural school in the nation.

Brent studied carpentry for two years at Tuskegee Institute and then architecture for one year, graduating in 1907. He returned to Washington, D.C., for one year, working briefly at HOWARD UNIVERSITY's Building and Grounds Department, followed by one year of working with VERTNER WOODSON TANDY in New York City before enrolling at the School of Architecture at Drexel Institute in Philadelphia. Drexel Institute must have been a finishing school for a number of African Americans in architecture because WILLIAM SIDNEY PITTMAN among others graduated from there. While at Drexel, Brent was awarded a scholarship and graduated from the full course in architecture in 1912.

In 1912 Buffalo's African American population was probably less than 1,500 persons, and most males were working in steel mills or for the Pullman Company rail car shops. Perhaps it was the aura of Louis Sullivan and Frank Lloyd Wright that lured John E. Brent from sophisticated Washington, D.C., to industrial Buffalo. He came in 1912, and apparently in a few days found work in the office of Max G. Beierl. He later moved to the office of H. Osgood Holland, where he worked on plans for the new Hutchinson High School. Later he worked in the office of Waterbury & Mann on the Wanakah Country Club. Brent was also employed in the office of Julius E. Schulty and for two years worked in the office of North, Shelgren, & Swift.

JOHN EDMONSON BRENT

In addition to being actively involved in architecture, John and his wife, Neeton, lived in the Cold Springs neighborhood and were involved in the African American community. With the expansion of industry, cheap labor was in demand and plants such as Lackawanna Steel and others sent trains to the South to bring African Americans to Buffalo. Many came seeking employment, but found that living conditions were horrible. There was a lack of decent housing, medical care, and decent schools. John E. Brent, an architect trained to see things as they can be, was instrumental in organizing the first local chapter of the National Association for the Advancement of Colored People. He was active in Saint Phillip Episcopal Church, where he received the Bishop's Medal for meritorious service, and was also a founding member of the Michigan Avenue Colored Young Mens Christian Association. He and his wife raised June Lewis and Robert Milliner, who still reside in Buffalo, as their own children.

Brent was working for the office of Oakley & Schallmore when he was selected by the Board of Directors of the Young Mens Christian Association (YMCA) as architect for their new building in 1922. He left Oakley & Schallmore to open his own office. John Brent was the second African American architect in the United States to design a YMCA—the first was William Pittman, who designed the 12th Street YMCA (1900) in Washington, D.C. The Buffalo "Y" located on Michigan Avenue and Cypress Street was a 4-story, red brick building of Georgian style. It contained a gymnasium, swimming pool, game rooms, meeting rooms, and approximately fifty dormitory rooms. Originally budgeted at $175,000, the final construction cost was $285,000. A cafeteria addition was added by others in 1960.

After the completion of the Young Mens Christian Association, Brent worked on several smaller commissions, including an office for dentist Dr. Myron McGuire; a summer cottage for social worker Clara Payne in rural Eden; and a contemporary house for Mitchell Miles—brother of heavyweight boxing champion Joe Louis's manager, Marshall Miles—on Genesee Street in Cheektowaga, next to the airport. Brent worked for many years as a municipal architect for the City of Buffalo Parks Department, which was headed by landscape architect Roeder Kinkel, who designed many of the buildings at the Buffalo Zoo. Brent's initials appear on many of the drawings for the zoo, including two entrance gates, bear pits, and other zoo structures.

John Brent died on October 20, 1962.[1] Other than the Michigan Avenue YMCA and the handful of buildings shown in his Building List, John E. Brent

Michigan Avenue YMCA, *University Archives, State University of New York at Buffalo*

did not have the opportunity to follow in the footsteps of Frank Lloyd Wright and Louis Sullivan in Buffalo. However, he was a mentor to Negro youth.

Note
1. John E. Brent, *Buffalo Evening News*, 23 October 1962, p. 30.

Bibliography
"John E. Brent, Second (sic) Negro Architect in the U.S. to Have Charge of Building Y for Colored Men." *Buffalo American*, 4 May 1926, n.p.
Schwartz, Nancy. "Calvin Brent, Washington's First African American Architect." Unpublished manuscript, Garrett Park, Md., 1990.

ROBERT T. COLES, FAIA, PRESIDENT,
ROBERT TRAYNHAM COLES, ARCHITECTS, P.C.,
BUFFALO, NEW YORK

BUILDING LIST

Name	Address	City	State	Year	Comments
McGuire Medical Office	482 Jefferson Ave.	Buffalo	NY		
Michigan Avenue YMCA	585 Michigan Ave.	Buffalo	NY	1926	
Miles, Mitchell	4000 Genesse St.	Cheektowaga	NY	c1935	
Payne, Clara		Eden	NY		Summer cottage

Sanford Augustus Brookins
(1877–1968)

Marsha Dean Phelts

Sanford Brookins was one of two African American architect-builders active in Jacksonville, Florida, during the first half of the twentieth century. He was born on May 9, 1877, in Macon, Georgia, to George and Charlotte Brookins. George Brookins was a farmhand. Sanford received training at the Dorchester Academy—probably the one in Liberty County, Georgia—before relocating to Jacksonville in 1904. After serving as a construction foreman for twelve years, Brookins established his own contracting business and was particularly active in house construction. By 1925 Brookins was credited with the design and construction of over 150 houses, with an additional nine houses designed and built for which he maintained ownership as investment property. With the continued growth of his business, Sanford Brookins and his wife, Leola Calloway Brookins, and daughter Daisy moved to a new home at 601 West 8th Street in the popular Sugar Hill neighborhood of Jacksonville in 1924.[1]

Many of the houses designed and constructed by Brookins were in Sugar Hill and in the newer subdivision known as Durkee Gardens, which was located between West 8th Street and West 13th Street northwest of downtown Jacksonville. Marketed to Jacksonville's growing Black middle-class, this subdivision of predominately 1-story brick houses opened between 1934 and 1940. Contracted by real estate developer George P. Mason in 1925, Brookins was also responsible for the construction of several residences in the prominent White neighborhood of Riverside. Brookins is also credited with the construction of at least two summer cottages at American Beach, including his own summer home at 5485 Waldon Street that was completed in 1936, one year after the beach resort opened. In response to state-sanctioned segregation, American Beach was one of the earliest oceanfront resorts developed for African Americans. Located on Amelia Island in Nassau County, Florida, American Beach was carved from three large beachfront parcels purchased and platted between 1935 and 1946 by the Pension Bureau of the Afro-American Life Insurance Company of Jacksonville, Florida.[2]

Brookins was a member of the Trustee Board of Bethel Baptist Institutional Church. He had retired from his business by 1965.

Sanford A. Brookins was living with his daughter when he died on June 22, 1968, in Compton, California, and was buried in the family plot at Memorial Cemetery in Jacksonville.

Notes
1. Florida Blue Book Publishing Company, *The National Negro Blue Book, North Florida Edition* (Jacksonville: Florida Blue Book Publishing Co., 1926), p. 21.
2. Joel McEachin, *Historic Building Survey of American Beach Nassau County, Florida* (Nassau County: American Beach Property Owner's Association, 1998), p. 31.

Sanford Brookins House, *Marsha Dean Phelts*

Bibliography

Historic Property Associates. *Historic Building Survey of Urban Core Southwest of the City of Jacksonville.* Jacksonville, Fla.: Jacksonville Planning and Development Department, 1997.

JOEL W. MCEACHIN,
SENIOR HISTORIC PRESERVATION PLANNER,
JACKSONVILLE PLANNING
AND DEVELOPMENT DEPARTMENT

BUILDING LIST

Name	Address	City	State	Year	Comments
Brookins, Sanford A.	601 W. 8th St.	Jacksonville	FL	1924	
Brookins, Sanford A.	5458 Waldon St.	Amelia Island	FL	1936	Summer cottage
Durkee Gardens single-family houses	Various addresses	Jacksonville	FL	1920s	150 houses

Elizabeth Carter Brooks
(1867–1951)

David Angel Nieves

Elizabeth Carter Brooks was an educator, club woman, architect, philanthropist, and real estate developer who was born in the whaling town of New Bedford, Massachusetts. The child of a former slave, she demonstrated her commitment to racial equality by providing African Americans with the tools for race betterment through advances and opportunities in social welfare. Brooks's mother, Martha Webb, was a manumitted slave from the plantation owned by President William Harrison Tyler in Norfolk, Virginia. Tyler had sent Martha Webb north to Bedford Village (originally New Bedford) before the Civil War to receive an education. New Bedford was well known at the time among Blacks for providing refuge to freed slaves and free seamen from West Africa, the Cape Verde Islands, and the Caribbean. New Bedford was a strategic stop on the Underground Railroad, and, according to oral history, Martha Webb helped numerous runaway slaves escape to the North.[1]

Black citizens of New Bedford had unique opportunities—access to capital, racially integrated public schools, established neighborhoods, and places to work. Beginning in 1716, the town's Quakers began a public campaign against chattel slavery, and by 1785 the town had ridded itself of human bondage within its limits. Several camouflaged tunnels and underground hideaways located throughout the city attest to the aid provided to slaves by some of the town's wealthy and influential Quaker families. The town's African American community comprised the highest percentage of Black citizens of any New England town between 1850 and 1880, with some 30 percent of them claiming southern birth.[2]

Elizabeth Carter attended New Bedford High School, the Harrington Normal Training School, and Swain Free School. Founded in 1881, the Swain Free School provided to its students a thorough course of instruction in the fundamental principles of design and their practical application. By the turn of the nineteenth century, the school was engaged in a familiar classic curriculum preparing its students to continue the work of the various architecturally significant "historic styles" in addition to sculpture and painting through the study of books, photographs, sketches, and drawings. Despite Victorian conventions, Brooks was able to attend the school without regard to her gender or race, due in large part to the overall acceptance accorded New Bedford's African Americans. Despite the virtual exclusion of women from architecture, Brooks became one of the few Black women of the era who could be considered both architect and patron.

Carter began her teaching career in around the 1890s at Howard's Orphan Home in Brooklyn, New York. She became an active member of the Woman's Loyal Union, an organization of prominent Brooklyn-based African American women committed to teaching and "race uplift" efforts. In 1895, as an outgrowth of the First National Conference of the Colored Women of America, the National Federation of Afro-

American Women was formed. Carter was one of twelve organizers and became the Federation's first recording secretary. Carter then helped form and served as president of the Northeastern Federation of Colored Women's Clubs. From 1908 until 1912, she served as the fourth president of the National Association of Colored Women.

Presumably Elizabeth Carter returned to New Bedford as the William H. Taylor School's first Black female teacher circa 1900, where she taught for over twenty-nine years. Her childhood dream of providing a home for New Bedford's elderly citizens had come true back in 1897 with the opening of the New Bedford Home for the Aged. In 1908, after several temporary locations, Carter designed a permanent home at 396 Middle Street, which was built by Henry W. and Benjamin Tripp, contractors. The Colonial-style Home for the Aged still exists. It stands 2½ stories tall, topped with a hip roof. There are six dormers: two in the front, two in the rear, and one on either side. The front facade features a flat-roofed portico and balustrade supported by four Doric columns. The home is clad with clapboard and rests on a sturdily built granite block foundation.

In 1918, during World War I, Carter was asked by the War Council of the National Board of Young Women's Christian Association to supervise the construction of the Phyllis Wheatley Young Women's Christian Association in Washington, D.C., designed by Shroeder & Parish Architects.[3] The building for Black women and girls at 901 Rhode Island Avenue, NW, was completed in 1920. She remained president of the New Bedford Home for the Aged until 1929, when she married Bishop W. Sampson Brooks of the African Methodist Episcopal denomination and Bethel Church. After retiring from teaching she moved along with her husband to San Antonio, Texas, where she remained until her husband's death in 1934. Elizabeth Carter Brooks returned to New Bedford and served as president of the New England Conference Branch Woman's Mite Missionary Society.

Brooks is a rare figure among African Americans, not only because she designed institutions for race betterment, but because she was also involved in some of the earliest attempts to preserve historic Black sites. Soon after returning from Texas, Brooks purchased the Sergeant William H. Carney house on behalf of the Martha Briggs Educational Club. Carney was an enlistee in the all-Black 54th Massachusetts Regiment during the Civil War and fought in the disastrous battle at Fort Wagner, delivering the Union flag to his regiment and shouting the now-famous words, "the Old Flag never touched the ground."[4] Over the years, the Sergeant Carney Memorial House has became a shrine honoring the Black Union troops who fought in the Civil War. Like many women reformers of her day, Brooks understood that these monuments to "race history" were an important part

New Bedford Home for the Aged, *Deborah Hynes Photography*

of the African American cultural landscape and deserved to be preserved.

Brooks continued to serve as an active member of several organizations through the 1930s, even serving as the local secretary of New Bedford's National Association for the Advancement of Colored People.

Elizabeth Carter Brooks died on July 13, 1951.

Notes

1. Barbara Clayton and Kathleen Whitley, *Guide to New Bedford* (Guilford, Conn.: Globe Pequot Press, 1979), p. 37.
2. Earl Francis Mulderink III, "We Can: African American and Irish-American Community Life in New Bedford, Massachusetts, during the Civil War Era" (Ph.D. diss., University of Wisconsin at Madison, 1995), p. 2.
3. Martha McAdoo, "Phylis Wheatley YWCA Passes a Milestone," *The Women's Press*, May 1925, p. 358.
4. Carl Cruz, "My Uncle, Sergeant Carney," Petersburg, N.H., January 1999, p. 1

Bibliography

Davis, Elizabeth Lindsay. " Lifting as They Climb." D.C.: National Association of Colored Women, 1933.

Swain Free School. Archives and Special Collections. *New Bedford Massachusetts, Eighteenth Year, 1899–1900*. New Bedford: E. Anthony & Sons Printers, 1899. University of Massachusetts at Dartmouth Library.

Waters, Jane C. *A Guide to New Bedford's Black Heritage Trail*. New Bedford: privately published, 1976.

ANGEL DAVID NIEVES,
ASSISTANT PROFESSOR,
SCHOOL OF ARCHITECTURE,
PLANNING, AND PRESERVATION
UNIVERSITY OF MARYLAND AT COLLEGE PARK

BUILDING LIST

Name	Address	City	State	Year	Comments
Carney, Sgt. William H.	128 Mill St.	New Bedford	MA	c1930	Restoration
New Bedford Home for the Aged	396 Middle St.	New Bedford	MA	1908	

Albert Grant Brown
(1881–1924)

Courtesy of the Cultural Center

Albert Grant Brown was born on a farm in Campbell's Creek, West Virginia. His father was Benjamin Brown, who farmed in Campbell's Creek, kept boarders, and served as a deacon in the African Methodist Zion Church in Malden. His mother was Margaret Ferguson Brown, who served the community as a midwife. Maggie Brown was a master's child from Hale's Ford, Virginia, who was born at about the same time and in the same vicinity as BOOKER TALIFERRO WASHINGTON. Washington helped organize the Sunday school at the African Methodist Zion Church and later became principal of TUSKEGEE INSTITUTE.

Albert had three older brothers: Daniel, born in 1871; William Clayton, born in 1873; and Benjamin, born in 1877. He also had three sisters: Gertrude, Sarah, and Bessie. The family was raised on the farm and in a 2-story house in Dana, West Virginia, just a few miles from the farm.

Although coal had been mined for the salt industry in the area as early as 1820, and Booker T. Washington was a coal miner there in the 1860s, with the completion of the railroad through the Kanawha Valley in 1873 the demand for mines and miners increased rapidly. Albert's two oldest brothers went to work in the mines. They decided among themselves that they did not want their younger brothers to be forced into such a life. With their help, both Albert and Benjamin, on passing elementary education classes at Black Hawk Hollow Negro School, attended West Virginia Colored Institute in Farm, West Virginia.

Albert Brown was a diligent student. He played halfback on the football team; was granted a commission as a 1st Lieutenant Ordnance Officer in the West Virginia Colored Institute Corps of Cadets in 1902; and in June of 1903, after completing the Normal Course of Study, was awarded a diploma. It must have been at this time that he traveled to Tuskegee Institute in Alabama for additional instruction in mechanical arts. Family oral history says that Albert was welcomed to Tuskegee Institute by Booker T. Washington himself and was not permitted to pay for his education "because he was family."[1]

On completion of his studies at Tuskegee Institute, Brown returned to West Virginia and began teaching mechanical and freehand drawing at his *alma mater*. The African American population of Charleston was developing a more stable economic base and several entrepreneurs were developing real estate in the triangle district of downtown Charleston. The Knights of Pythias Hall was built in 1905 at Dickinson and Washington Streets, at that time across from the State Capitol, with Albert G. Brown as the architect. An article in *The Advocate* praised, "A.G. Brown, now a teacher in drawing in this his alma mater, is recognized in Charleston, where his work comes in competition with the best white architects, as one of the best in his profession."[2]

As a faculty member at West Virginia Collegiate Institute (the name was changed in 1908), Brown participated in the lively life of the school. He coached

Knights of Pythias building, *West Virginia State Archives, James Randall Collection*

football and track and eventually became director of athletics during an era in which the school was an acknowledged leader in Negro collegiate sports. He also became interested in photography. It appears he was the school (and family) photographer for all teams and all occasions. His photographs show a consistent balance of composition and form that are indicative of an architectural aesthetic. He often appears in pictures he is taking.

The only significant Albert Brown building still standing of which there could be found explicit records is Saint Paul Baptist Church in Saint Albans, West Virginia. Church historian Eugene H. Washington wrote, "The church commissioned in 1920 an architect, A. G. Brown, Manual Arts Instructor at West Virginia Collegiate Institute, to work with Freddie Graves . . . to design and resolve those necessary details that would serve as plans for the construction of a new church home."[3] Brown's church with some modifications stands today as it did when completed on Christmas Day 1925.

Both the Knights of Pythias building and Saint Paul Church show a sensitive awareness of the styles of the day. The Knights of Pythias has an Italianate-style cornice; detailed brickwork in the fenestration; and a balanced, symmetrical facade. Capping the front elevation is an ornate marquee. Saint Paul Church, on the other hand, is an imposing brick structure. There is a massive bell tower at the street corner and large Gothic-style arch windows in both the tower and the two elevations facing the street. The interior is most remarkable, with its quiet wood-paneled sanctuary and choir loft, which imparts a peacefulness of contemplation in the sanctuary of the church. Saint Paul Baptist Church is a refined memorial to the young architect, who was thirty-nine years old when the church was begun and who died before construction was completed.

Albert G. Brown was a beloved and respected member of the Institute community. Although he owned several houses, he continued living in the dormitories throughout his career. He was an immaculate dresser and nifty dancer, and was sought after for a variety of social activities. Brown was an innovator who understood the necessity of good organization. His dedication to a solid foundation and especially athletic opportunity for West Virginia's Blacks set the stage for West Virginia Collegiate Institute to become a national leader in vocational education for the race.

Albert Brown's life was cut short on August 28, 1924. He had been admitted to the hospital for a hernia operation, contracted pneumonia, and died soon thereafter. His funeral was held at First Baptist Church in Charleston, where Reverend Mordecai

Wyatt Johnson, future president of Howard University, officiated. Brown is buried at Spring Hill Cemetery.

Notes
1. Interview with Anna Gilmer (niece of Albert Brown), April 2001, Shepherdstown, W. Va.
2. "W. Va. Colored Institute," *The Advocate*, 21 April 1910, p. 1.
3. Eugene H. Washington, *Miracle on B Street Continues* (St. Albans, W. Va.: The Church, 1998), p. 5.

Bibliography
"The Eye." *El Ojo: Alpha Zeta Chapter of Alpha Phi Alpha Fraternity,* 1923.
Harlan, John. C. *History of West Virginia State College, 1891–1965.* Institute Dubuque, Iowa: Brown Book Company, 1968.

WILLIAM M. DRENNEN, JR.,
FORMER HISTORY INSTRUCTOR,
WEST VIRGINIA STATE COLLEGE,
AND FORMER COMMISSIONER
OF WEST VIRGINIA CULTURE AND HISTORY

BUILDING LIST

Name	Address	City	State	Year	Comments
Knights of Pythias	Washington & Dickinson Sts.	Charleston	WV	1905	Demolished
St. Paul Baptist Church	821 B St.	St. Albans	WV	1920	

Georgia Louise Harris Brown
(1918–1999)

Sarah Brown

Georgia Louise Harris is believed to be the second African American woman licensed as an architect in the United States. She was born in Topeka, Kansas, on June 12, 1918, to Carl Collins and Georgia Watkins Harris. Preferring to be called Louise, she was the middle of five children born to a father who was a shipping clerk and a stay-at-home mother who for a period of time taught school and studied classical music. From an early age, Louise exhibited an interest in drawing and painting, as well as working on cars and farm equipment with her brother Bryant, who was several years older. After graduating from Seaman High School in North Topeka, Louise Harris attended Washburn University from 1936 to 1937 (her mother's alma mater).

In 1938 Louise Harris followed her brother to Chicago. A year later she took her first architectural course—a night class at the Armour Institute of Technology (now Illinois Institute of Technology). The course was taught by Mies van der Rohe (1886–1969), who had recently arrived from Germany and went on to become a world-renowned architect. Louise Harris would describe contacts with Mies van der Rohe as some of the most interesting times of her life.

The year 1940 found Louise Harris back in Kansas, this time at the University of Kansas in Lawrence. Enrolled in the School of Engineering and Architecture, she graduated in June 1944 with a bachelor of science degree in architecture. Her stay at the university was not without reminders of racism and sexism. She recalled being asked several times by one professor if she didn't think she should be in domestic science instead of architecture.[1]

In 1941 Louise married James A. Brown, who had been her brother's roommate in Chicago. Back in Chicago, Louise Brown found a job working for KENNETH RODERICK O'NEAL in 1945 and worked there until 1949.

Louise Brown passed the registration examination on her first try and was licensed as an architect in Illinois on July 19, 1949.[2] She had a special interest in structural design. From 1949 until 1953, she worked at Frank J. Kornacker & Associates, a civil engineering firm that specialized in the effect of wind stress on high-rise buildings. Louise Brown was the only professional female in the eight-person firm. While there, she produced the structural calculations for various reinforced steel and concrete buildings, including the Promontory and Lake Shore apartment buildings designed by her former instructor, Mies van der Rohe.

These were very active years for Brown. Unable to reconcile her career and marriage, she divorced in 1952 and sent her two children to live with her parents in Topeka. While working full-time for Kornacker & Associates, she studied civil engineering at night at the Illinois Institute of Technology and moonlighted with an associate in their own engineering and architectural firm designing houses, churches, and office buildings. Brown was active in the Chicago chapter of *Alpha Alpha Gamma*, a professional association of female architects; she was probably their first Black member. This period of her life was also a time of reflection about her future. Although she was careful not to limit herself, Louise Brown was acutely aware that opportunities for advancement were limited by her race.

Brown had read about Brazil, particularly Brasilia, the newly designed capital. She was excited about what was happening there architecturally and considered it an opportunity to practice architecture free of racial boundaries. In addition to her already heavy schedule, she began studying Portuguese with a Brazilian friend. In 1953 she went to São Paulo, Brazil, and by 1954 had moved there permanently.

In 1954, while working for the architectural firm of transplanted American Charles Bosworth, Brown opened Escandia Ltda., an interior design firm. In Bosworth's office, she worked on plans to renovate the City Bank of New York office building in São Paulo. In her own firm, she designed several installations for the Ibirapuera City Park for the Fourth City Centennial in addition to designing interiors and wood furniture for offices and residences.

In the firm of Headeager Bosworth do Brazil, Brown worked as designer and project manager on a foundry/office/restaurant complex in Osasco, Brazil, and a large Pfizer Corporation complex in Guarulhos. From 1963 to 1965, she worked for RACZ Construction, where she designed and supervised the construction of a 100,000-square-foot factory and administration building; and from 1965 to 1966, Brown prepared research studies, designs, and cost estimates for prefabricated buildings for Headeager do Brazil.

From 1967 to 1968, Brown was responsible for the renovation of several farm buildings on a ranch in Angatuba, including an airport with a 5,500-foot runway, for the Krupp family. For the next two years, she was project manager and site supervisor with RACZ Construction and was responsible for the construction of the 376,740-square-foot Kodak Brasileire Comerico film factory in São Jose dos Campos. In 1970 Brown traveled to Japan, Iran, and India, sketching and recording her thoughts about the architecture and the people.

From the time of her arrival in São Paulo, Brown attracted the attention of several wealthy Brazilians

Matarazzo House, *Sarah Brown*

who admired her creativity and flair. From 1971 to 1985, she designed dozens of homes and associated furniture for these families. Brown also designed small commercial projects. When designing private homes, she paid great attention to details such as how the personality of each member of a household was expressed in the house's design. In her private practice she also had the reputation as a restoration architect.

In 1993 Louise Harris Brown retired from her practice and returned to the United States. Following surgery for cancer and suffering from Alzheimer's disease, she unexpectedly went into a coma. Two weeks later on September 21, 1999, at the age of eighty-one, Louise Harris Brown died.

Notes
1. Georgia Louise Harris, "Brief Autobiography" (longhand), February 1984. In the possession of cousin Howard K. Harris, Washington, D.C.
2. State of Illinois, Department of Registration and Education, "Louise Harris Brown," Certificate No. 3417, issued 19 July 1949.

Bibliography
"A Blueprint for Success." *Ebony Magazine*, June 1984, 56.

ROBERTA WASHINGTON, RA,
PRINCIPAL, ROBERTA WASHINGTON ARCHITECTS, PC,
NEW YORK, NEW YORK

BUILDING LIST

Name	Address	City	State/Country	Year	Comments
Aranha, Paulo	Morumbi	São Paulo	Brazil	1986	
Beer, Robert	Araquava Farm, Santo Amaro	São Paulo	Brazil	1979	
Behmer, ___	Rua Conde D'Eu, Santo Amaro	São Paulo	Brazil	1968	
Bohlen und Halbach *Ranchero*	Angatuba	São Paulo	Brazil	1967	
Bottene, Brown	Dircinha Garden	São Paulo	Brazil	1975	
Carrera, Bermudez	Ave. B (606)/Rua 6	São Paulo	Brazil	1976	
CIT Co.	Maripora	São Paulo	Brazil	1978	Planning study
dos Reis, Jair Sorbelini	Aracaraguama	São Paulo	Brazil	1977	
Elene, Nilson	Rua Ibaragui, Vila Mariana	São Paulo	Brazil	1980	
Ericsson of Brazil	São Jose dos Campos	São Paulo	Brazil	1972	Racz Construction Co.
Fagundes, Jose O.	Vila Madalena	São Paulo	Brazil	1979	
Ford Motor Co. of Brazil		Osasco	Brazil	1957	Office of Hedeager Bosworth
Fourth City Centennial	Ibirapuera City Park	São Paulo	Brazil	1955	
Guglielmi, Julio	Ibirapuera	São Paulo	Brazil	1974	
Hoverter, ___	Rua Porto Feliz, Carapicuiba	São Paulo	Brazil	1980	
Hughes, Peter A.	Santo Amaro	São Paulo	Brazil	1974	
Kodak of Brazil, Industrial & Commercial Division	São Jose dos Campos	São Paulo	Brazil	1970	Racz Construction Co.
Lake Shore Drive Apts.	2970 N. Lake Shore Dr.	Chicago	IL	1950	Reinforced concrete design
Lunt Lake Apts.		Chicago	IL	1950	Reinforced concrete design
Marchesini, Hugo B.	Rua Pio IV/Rua Oagikaule	São Paulo	Brazil	1987	
Marchesini, Hugo B.	Juliete Farm	São Paulo	Brazil	1976	
Matarazzo, ___	Rua Miranda Guerra, 500	São Paulo	Brazil	1967	
Michineves, Eduardo	Maripora	São Paulo	Brazil	1978	
National City Bank of New York	Ave. S. Joao & Ave. Ipiranga	São Paulo	Brazil	1954	Office of Charles Bosworth
Pfizer Corp. of Brazil		Guarulhos	Brazil	1960	Office of Hedeager Bosworth
Prairie Court Apts.		Chicago	IL	1950	Reinforced concrete design
Pravaz-Recordati Laboratories		São Paulo	Brazil	c1963	Office of Hedeager Bosworth
Promontory Apts.	5530 S. Shore Dr.	Chicago	IL	1950	Reinforced concrete design
Reydon, Frederick	Santo Amaro	São Paulo	Brazil	1979	
Ruthofer, Eva M.	Interlagos	São Paulo	Brazil	1977	
Sampaio, Marcio	Rua Liveiro Saraiva, 65	São Paulo	Brazil	1986	
Terron, ___	Interlagos	São Paulo	Brazil	1975	
Von Erlea, ___	Rua Managua Esq. R. Ilimani	São Paulo	Brazil	1968	

Grafton Tyler Brown
(1841–1918)

The 1850 U.S. Census places Grafton Brown's parents in Harrisburg, Pennsylvania, one year before his birth, February 22, 1841.[1] The census also lists his father, Thomas, as a laborer, and his mother, Wilhemina, as a homemaker. As a free man, Thomas Brown worked with the abolitionist movement in Harrisburg to help free others.

At the age of fourteen, Grafton Brown began to work in a print shop in Philadelphia as a clean-up boy, but soon learned lithography by watching the lithographers. The print shop produced maps, city views, bank notes, stationary, death certificates, and dry goods labels. Most of the lithographers in Harrisburg and Philadelphia were German immigrants who came from a long lineage of lithographers, following the invention of the first lithographic press in Germany in 1798.

C. C. Kuchel—a German lithographer from whom Brown had learned the trade—left Philadelphia for San Francisco, California, to seek his fortune. Soon thereafter, Brown followed Kuchel to San Francisco. Brown first appears in the *San Francisco Directory* in 1861 as a boarder at the What Cheer House. Opened in 1852, it housed one of San Francisco's earliest public libraries and was known for its lithographic views and paintings of California scenes hung in its lobby. Brown's early maps of claims and city boundaries in the Nevada Territories and subsequent city views of towns and ranches in the Bay Area literally documented settlements and the selling of the American West. Following his apprenticeship with C. C. Kuchel, during which he drew scenes such as "Comstock Lode Map" and "Virginia City," Brown eventually assumed Kuchel's business upon the latter's death and established G. T. Brown & Co. in 1867. In that same year, Brown is also listed in connection with lithographic printers Frederick Brandt, Gilman Davis, and Patrick Murray in the *San Francisco Directory*. Gilman B. Davis is still listed as an employee of Brown's in the 1875 *San Francisco Directory*, along with Alfred Gilbert. Brown's company printed sheet music, bill mastheads, city views, and maps.

Brown's largest and most celebrated lithography commission was the "Illustrated History of San Mateo County" (1878). This work consisted of seventy-two views of ranches and towns in San Mateo County. The views were finely drawn for exactness and recognition. Brown continued to produce lithographs in other areas of the Pacific Northwest, working from photographs, as well as rendering images freehand.

In 1882 Brown is listed in the *San Francisco Directory* as a lithographic artist working at 540 Clay Street and residing in Oakland. This listing represents a significant shift in Brown's interests and self-identification. Increasingly Brown began to define himself as a painter. His earliest known painting is "Mt. Hood, Oregon," painted during the same period that his company printed "Bird's Eye View of the City of Portland, Oregon" and "Proposed Terminus of the Northern [*sic*] Pacific RR." By 1882 Brown had left the United States to join the Amos Bowman Geologi-

Residence, Ranch & Dairy of V. Guerrero, *California African-American Foundation*

cal Survey party as a draftsman as they worked east of the Cascade Mountains along the Fraser River in the Caribou country of Victoria, British Columbia. When Brown completed his employment with the survey company, he settled in British Columbia, with its fancy hotels and shops. Brown opened a painting studio in Victoria, advertising himself as a landscape artist. This was the first time that he referred to himself as an "artist." He painted over twenty-two views of Victoria locales and had one-person art exhibits at the Occidental Hotel. His work was well received by visitors to the hotel as well as *Victoria Colonist* newspaper art critics.

By 1885 Brown had left Canada to return to the United States, journeying through Washington, where he painted several scenes of Mount Tacoma, and into Oregon, where he painted most of his landscapes of the Pacific Northwest. From 1886 to 1890, he is listed in the *Portland Oregon Directory* as an artist. Brown joined the Portland Art Club in 1889 before leaving the area to paint well-known sites such as Yosemite Valley in California and Yellowstone National Park in Wyoming. His landscape paintings conveyed the vastness of the unspoiled wilderness of the West. Brown relocated once more, to Saint Paul, Minnesota, where he worked as a draftsman for the U.S. Army Corps of Engineers, Saint Paul District. He was employed by the corps from November 1, 1892, to November 30, 1897.

From 1897 to 1903, he was listed as George T. Brown, draftsman, and again as George, artist. During this time he worked for the Great Northwest Railway (1899), Saint Paul City Engineer's Office (1900–1), and as a draftsman with the Saint Paul Commissioner of Public Works (1902–9). The last listing for Grafton Brown, in 1910, lists him as a civil engineer. It is likely that Grafton T., George T., and Grafton J. were all the same person. In 1911, 1914, and 1915, he is again listed as a draftsman in the City Engineer's Office. In 1916 he is listed as a draftsman with the Commissioner of Public Works. There is no listing in 1917 and the next notice is of his death on March 2, 1918:

> G. T. Brown, 77 years old, 646 Hague Avenue, for years a draughtsman in the city civil engineering department, died late yesterday. He had been ill for five years. Born in Harrisburg, Penn., February 22, 1841, Mr. Brown came to St. Paul 25 years ago. He is survived by his widow. Funeral arrangements have not been made.[2]

The purpose of Brown's drawn city views and maps were to sell the West, but in later painted landscapes he seemed to revere the land for its natural beauty rather than for its commercial potential. His paintings had a double significance of visually sharing his experiences in the wilderness with his viewers and preserving the scenes for future generations just as landscape painter John Moran, who was first led to Yosemite Valley by John Muir, had done.

In San Francisco, Brown was referred to as a "mulatto" or "quadroon."[3] Grafton Tyler Brown survived the racial obstacles experienced by most free Blacks because his complexion was light enough to "pass," which is suggested by the varying racial characterizations documented in official records. Assuming an alternative racial role possibly allowed Grafton Brown to fluidly redefine himself and his career throughout his life.

Notes
1. U.S. Census Report, "Free Inhabitants in West Ward," Harrisburg Borough, County of Dauphin, State of Penna, 31 August 1850, p. 63.
2. "G. T. Brown, Aged City Employee, Dies at 77," *St. Paul Sunday Pioneer Press*. 3 March 1916, p. 1.
3. R. G. Dunn & Company Collection, Baker Library, Graduate School of Business, Harvard University, Cambridge, Massachusetts. His father, mother, one sister, three brothers, and grandmother are all listed as mulatto.

Bibliography

Ireland, Willard E. "G. T. Brown, Artist." *Okanagan Historical Society*, 1948, p. 166.

LeFalle-Collins, Lizzetta. "Grafton Tyler Brown: Selling the Promise of the West." In *The International Review of African American Art*. Juliette Harris, ed 1995, p. 26.

Parker, Elizabeth, and James Abajian. *A Walking Tour of the Black Presence in San Francisco during the Nineteenth Century.* San Francisco: San Francisco African American Historical and Cultural Society, 1974.

Peters, Harry T. *California on Stone.* Garden City, N.J.: Doubleday, Doran & Company, 1935.

LIZZETTA LEFALLE-COLLINS,
ART HISTORIAN
OAKLAND, CALIFORNIA

LITHOGRAPH LIST

Title	City	State	Year	Comments
Astoria, Clatsop County	Clatsop County	OR	1870	
Bird's Eye View of the City of Portland, Oregon	Portland	OR	1870	
Cerro Gordo	Inyo County	CA	1874	
City of Portland	Portland	OR	c1861	
Clinton Mound Tract	Alameda County	CA		
Comstock Lode Map	Placerville	CA	1860	
Firk's View	San Francisco	CA	1868	
Forman Shaft	Silver City	ID	1881	
Illustrated History of San Mateo County	San Mateo	CA	1878	
Important Auction of 100 Lots in Oakland	Oakland	CA	1875	
Iron Clad Mine	Oakland	CA	c1875	
Lake Ranch of R. T. Ray	San Mateo	CA	1878	
Lake Tahoe	Lake Tahoe	CA		
Late Collison between the Trains	Simpson's Station	CA	1869	
Map of *Buena Vista* Homestead	Buena Vista	CA	1868	
Map of Highland Park	Oakland	CA	1878	
Map of Horton's Addition	San Diego	CA	c1868	
Map of Jones Tract	Alameda County	CA		
Map of Oakland	Oakland	CA	c1875	
Map of the Bodie Mining District	Bodie	CA	1877	
Map of the Central Land Company	Oakland	CA		
Map of the Comstock Lode	Storey County	NV	1875	
Map of the Leonard Tract	Berkely	CA	1875	
Map of the Sausalito Land & Ferry Co.	Sausalito	CA		
Map of the Town of Redwood City	Redwood City	CA		
Map of Yolo County	Yolo County	CA	1870	
Ocean View Ranch	San Mateo	CA	1878	
Plan of the Town of St. Helen's	St. Helen's	WA	c1875	
Ranch & Dairy of V. Guerrero	San Mateo	CA	1878	
San Felix Station	San Mateo	CA	1878	
San Francico View	San Francisco	CA	1869	
San Francisco Looking South from North Point	San Francisco	CA	1877	
Silver City, Idaho Territory	Silver City	ID	1866	
Stockton Fire Department	Stockton	CA		
Sunny Vale Homestead	San Francisco	CA		
View of Fort Churchill	Weeks	NV	c1869	
View of San Diego	San Diego	CA	c1857	
View of Santa Rosa	Santa Rosa	CA	1855	
Virginia City	Virginia City	NV	1861	
Virginia City Territory	Virginia City	NV	1864	
Walla Wall, Washington Territory	Walla Walla	WA	1866	

Leroy John Henry Brown
(1912–1993)

Moorland-Spingarn Research Center

Leroy J. H. Brown was born in Charleston, South Carolina. Little is known about his early life. Brown entered South Carolina Agricultural & Mechanical College in Orangeburg, South Carolina—then known as the Colored Normal Industrial Agricultural & Mechanical College—sometime around 1932, with the goal of becoming an architect. He received a bachelor of science degree in mechanical arts in 1936.[1]

Within a year after graduating, Brown went to Washington, D.C., and worked for a time at the War Production Board as an architectural engineering draftsman. He returned to his *alma mater* and taught there during World War II. While there, he taught alongside HENRY LEWIS LIVAS, who would go on to teach at HAMPTON INSTITUTE while also heading up a successful architectural practice.[2]

Brown returned to Washington, D.C., in 1941 to enroll in the architecture program at the School of Engineering and Architecture at HOWARD UNIVERSITY. Brown received a bachelor of science degree in architecture in 1944. A year later, he joined the faculty of the Department of Architecture in the School of Engineering and Architecture at Howard University. For a brief period, during the sabbatical absence of department chairman HOWARD HAMILTON MACKEY SR., Brown served as acting chairman. Brown's teaching assignments included design, descriptive geometry, shades and shadows, perspective drawing, building construction, and structural analysis. Generations of successful architects all over the United States and in Africa, India, and Asia acknowledge a debt of gratitude to Brown's rigorous freshman and sophomore courses.

Brown's extensive exposure to industrial vocational education had an influence on the curriculum at Howard University. He quietly championed for the idea of ensuring that by the end of the first two years of the program, a student had acquired the skills to be productive in a professional office. Brown was also instrumental in ensuring that graduates were well prepared for the architectural registration exam, and stressed that graduates should be able to handle all engineering design and construction drawings requirements of small- to modest-sized buildings.

In 1949 Brown married Angella M. Smith, a teacher in the D.C. public school system. They would remain married until his death forty-four years later. They had no children.

Brown opened an office in Washington, D.C., in the early 1950s at 215 Florida Avenue, NW. By 1955 Brown had received his master of architecture degree from The Catholic University of America School of Engineering and Architecture. He was one of the earliest African Americans to receive an architecture degree from Catholic University. Brown became a member of the American Institute of Architects in 1956. He maintained registration in Maryland and Virginia, as well as in the District of Columbia, where he also served on the D.C. Board of Examiners and Registrars of Architects from 1962 to 1967.[3]

Brown's commissions included numerous designs for African American business owners and professionals in need of income-producing offices and apartment buildings that could also house their practices. During the early years of his practice from 1952 to 1965, Brown also designed D.C. public school additions and churches.

Until his retirement from Howard University in 1977, Brown combined full-time teaching duties with his leadership of a small but significant professional practice. He was a staunch admirer of former department chairman HILYARD ROBERT ROBINSON's articulate advocacy of affordable and sturdily built public housing for African Americans. In 1962 Brown moved his office to 1832 North Capitol Street, NW. His first significant commissions came from the National Capital Housing Authority to design additions to several public housing projects. The two most notable projects were apartment buildings at Parkside Dwellings and a thirty-four-townhouse addition to Robinson's nationally acclaimed Langston Terrace. From the beginning, Brown's practice was a source of apprenticeship work for Howard University architecture students.

In the early 1960s, Brown joined the NATIONAL TECHNICAL ASSOCIATION. Brown took over the duties of editor in chief of the *NTA Journal*, which published scholarly articles written by and about African Americans in the technical fields. Brown wrote an editorial for each issue and occasional feature-length articles to promote his passionate advocacy of Black economic advancement and the need for Black institutions to seek to control federal housing and urban renewal programs targeted for Black communities. Years in advance of the 1960s urban rebellions, Brown was advocating for the need for intensive collaboration between the Federal Housing Administration and historically Black colleges and universities in the revitalization of urban Black communities. By 1967 Brown had moved into a small office building that he owned and designed at 3310 Georgia Avenue, NW, ten blocks north of Howard University.

Brown's social and professional activism propelled him into a leadership role in the Capital City Collaborative, a coalition of local African American architectural firms established in the late 1960s. The coalition wrested the ten acre Shaw Urban Renewal Area survey of existing conditions contract from the D.C. Redevelopment Land Agency after the 1968 riots. The coalition also forged a joint venture with Skidmore Owings & Merrill Architects and Engineers to produce a master plan for the west downtown Mount Vernon Square campus of the University of the District of Columbia. However, the project was never built.

While continuing his full-time teaching duties at Howard University into the late 1970s, Brown executed several modest but socially significant commissions. The most notable was a K–6 elementary school, later renamed Malcom X. In 1973 he designed an addition to the Hilyard Robinson–Paul Williams–designed School of Engineering and Architecture building for the Chemistry Department. Although many of the buildings on Howard University's campus had been designed by African American architects, this was the first commission awarded to an *alumnus*. Brown was also the architect for the Capitol Heights Metro Station in Prince George's County, Maryland.

Brown retired from Howard University in 1977, but continued his private practice for another five years. Brown resided at 22 Bryant Street, NE. He remained active in the Bloomingdale Civic Association until nearly the end of his life. Mayor Marion S. Barry

Chemistry Building, Howard University, *Moorland-Spingarn Research Center*

LEROY JOHN HENRY BROWN

Jr. declared February 26, 1988, as "Leroy J. H. Brown Day" in the District of Columbia in recognition of Brown's civic and professional contributions. Brown died peacefully of natural causes at the age of eighty on July 10, 1993, at the Washington Hospital Center.

Notes

1. "Papers of Leroy Brown," Moorland-Spingarn Research Center, Archive of African American Architects, Washington, D.C.
2. Ibid. Brown papers.
3. District of Columbia Board of Examiners and Registrars. "Leroy J. H. Brown," License No. 693, issued 15 June 1950.

MELVIN MITCHELL, FAIA,
RETIRED DIRECTOR OF THE INSTITUTE OF
ARCHITECTURE, LANDSCAPE ARCHITECTURE AND
PLANNING, MORGAN STATE UNIVERSITY

BUILDING LIST

Name	Address	City	State	Year	Comments
Asbury United Methodist Church	11th & K Sts., NW	Washington	DC	1978	Addition
Capitol Heights Metro Transit Station	E. Capitol & Southern Ave.	Capitol Heights	MD	1979	
Chamberlain Vocational High School	1345 Potomac Ave., SE	Washington	DC	1966	
Fire Engine Company No. 2	2225 5th NE	Washington	DC	1977	
Howard University Chemistry Bldg.	Campus	Washington	DC	1973	Addition
Langston Terrace Public Housing	2100 Benning Rd., NE	Washington	DC	1964	34 du addition
Malcolm X Elementary School	1351 Alabama Ave., SE	Washington	DC	1970	
Nazreth Baptist Church	3935 7th St., NW	Washington	DC	1956	Addition
Parkside Dwellings	4500 Quarles St., NE	Washington	DC	1964	
Pilgrim Baptist Church	700 I St. NE	Washington	DC	1968	
Seventh District Police Station	2455 Alabama Ave., SE	Washington	DC	1972	

Richard Lewis Brown
(1854–1948)

Joel McEachin

Born into slavery in Abbeville, South Carolina, Richard Lewis Brown came to align himself between two traditions in the history of the architecture profession: master builder and gentleman-architect. Having risen through the building trades as a carpenter, he came to be relied on to advise and manage the construction of numerous institutional buildings in early-twentieth-century Jacksonville, Florida, and was commissioned to design some of them as well. Merging the usually divergent roles of designer and constructor, Brown took complete control of several projects.[1] He was the consummate master builder and like so many gentleman-architects who preceded him lived the life of a Renaissance man, adroitly maneuvering through diverse interests and vocations. "Jacksonville's first known black architect" was also a farmer, printer, carpenter, minister, and politician.[2]

Little is known about Brown's early life. At the close of the Civil War, he and his family migrated to Lake City, Florida, before settling in Jacksonville. It is speculated that he attended Stanton Normal School, where he would have learned to read and decipher. In 1875 he married Louisa Certain and immersed himself into a full religious, civic, and family life. As a staunch member of the African Methodist Episcopal church, Brown served as an elder and for a number of years pastored a church as well. By 1881 he was elected to the first of two consecutive terms in the Florida House of Representatives. Postreconstruction-era Jacksonville—Florida's largest city well into the 1920s—saw the African Methodist Episcopal denomination powerfully galvanize civic engagement among its members. In spite of constant upheaval and conflict on so many fronts, Blacks were elected and appointed to numerous positions at all levels of state and city government.[3] Brown purchased several acres of land in East Jacksonville, part of which was eventually deeded to the Duval County public schools for an elementary school named in his honor. By the 1890s he was a father; Louisa gave birth to three children: Daisy, Elexina, and Richard Lewis Jr.

The growth of his new family paralleled the growth of Brown's business. These skills would prepare him for the imminent growth in building construction that occurred in Jacksonville after the great fire destroyed so much of the city in May 1901. In those opening decades of the twentieth century, the Duval County School Board hired Brown to build and repair its schools. This experience with school architecture reached its fullest expression in Brown's work on the Edward Waters College campus in West Jacksonville.

Founded by the African Methodist Episcopal denomination in 1870 as Brown Theological Institute, Edward Waters College evolved from a high school in the 1880s to a full-fledged college in 1891. It took its current name from an early African Methodist Episcopal bishop. For several years after the 1901 fire, the school maintained temporary accommodations before a substantive building campaign was initiated in 1912.

81

Mount Olive African Methodist Episcopal Church, *Davis & Vedas in Jacksonville's Architectural Heritage*

The centerpiece of the campus was Centennial Hall, so named to commemorate the 100th anniversary of the African Methodist Episcopal denomination. Designed by the Seattle-based architectural firm Howells & Stokes and built by Richard Lewis Brown, the 1916 structure is the oldest building on the campus and cost $30,000 to build. By 1919 Brown had become superintendent of industries at Edward Waters, where he oversaw the completion of the school's campus. All the while he prepared to make his own most notable and lasting statement in ecclesiastic architecture.

Brown must have appreciated the classic details that Howells & Stokes freely quoted, including the 2-story pavilion marking the entrance with paired, engaged columns and the roof's cupola—since removed in a 1979 renovation. Brown added his own exuberant design for Mount Olive African Methodist Episcopal Church to Howells and Stokes's restrained incorporation of such elements.

In desperate need of a larger sanctuary, the church's building committee chose congregation member Richard Lewis Brown to design and construct the new building in 1920. Brown took complete control over the aesthetic elements as well as the structural matters. Like so many of his local and national contemporaries in architecture, his was an eclectic interpretation of predominant academic styles. In the case of Mount Olive African Methodist Episcopal Church, Brown refers mostly, but not exclusively, to the Louis eighteenth-century historical tradition. Grand balustrade staircases ascend to a powerful and solid trinity of columns in the portico, and a profusion of round and arched windows further embellish an already dynamic facade of rich brown mortar and buff, rough-hewn concrete block. The whole voluminous composition, resting on a base of smoother-surfaced concrete block, reinvents aesthetic principles that were set forth as early as the Renaissance era and were refined at the Ecole des Beaux-Arts in Paris. Without the benefit of an academic understanding of these historical eras and design centers, gentleman-architect Brown was, nevertheless, attentive to the aesthetic forces dominating early-twentieth-century American architecture. For centuries the designs of gentleman-architects had been marked by varying degrees of eclecticism over and above purely academic style. Moreover they, like Brown, understood how aesthetics could express the role and significance a building had in society. His project at Mount Olive African Methodist Episcopal Church spoke to the church's function in the Black community as a source of spiritual nourishment, as well as a catalyst for educational advancement and economic improvement.

The Industrial Revolution—with its great advancements in construction technology—had increasingly served to divide the laborers of architecture. A kind of professional ghettoization occurred, leaving clear distinctions between architects and builders and engineers. Brown was among the last of a diminishing generation of gentleman-architects: those who took on the roles of both designer and constructor.

Richard Lewis Brown's achievement, then, reaches beyond the distinction of being Jacksonville's first known Black architect. He not only built buildings but through the works of his life also built human bridges. The gentleman-architect sought to improve the spiritual, civic, and educational life of his people, and as a master builder he bridged the ever-widening professional divide between those who designed architecture and those who built it in late-nineteenth- and early-twentieth-century America. So aligned, Richard Lewis Brown, was emblematic of the most time-honored traditions in the field of architecture.

Richard Lewis Brown died in Jacksonville at the age of ninety-four on August 24, 1948.

Notes
1. Sharon Weightman, "Builder, Politician, Architect R. L. Brown Left His Mark on City," *Florida Times-Union*, 19 February 1995, p. A1.
2. Canter Brown, *Florida's Black Public Officials, 1867–1924*, (Tuscaloosa: University of Alabama Press, 1998), p. 77.

Bibliography
Wood, Wayne W. *Jacksonville's Architectural Heritage: Landmarks for the Future*. Rev. ed. Gainesville: University Press of Florida, 1996.

RICHARD M. STANDIFER,
VISUAL ARTIST, MIAMI, FLORIDA

BUILDING LIST

Name	Address	City	State	Year	Comments
Apartment Bldg.	1208 Florida Ave.	Jacksonville	FL		
Edward Waters College Centennial Hall	Campus	Jacksonville	FL	1916	
Mt. Olive African Methodist Episcopal Church	841 Franklin St.	Jacksonville	FL	1921	

Robert Lester Buffins
(1892–1981)

Harmon Foundation

A footnote in the history of African American architecture, Robert Lester Buffins was one of thirteen practicing architects and four recent graduates of the Department of Architecture represented in HOWARD UNIVERSITY's pioneering "Exhibition of the Work of Negro-Architects" mounted in 1931.[1] Although Buffins would go on to lead a full, positive, and productive career in architecture, his career was one of unfulfilled aspirations.

Born in Memphis, Tennessee, on November 24, 1892, to Robert and Effie Buffins, he grew up, married Rebecca Velma Jackson, and worked at various jobs, including Pullman railroad porter and U.S. Postal Service clerk in the city of his birth. Around 1916 Buffins, his wife, and six children moved to Chicago, Illinois, where he initially worked for the U.S. Postal Service. Tragedy struck the young family during the mid-1920s, when Rebecca as well as four of their children died, victims of the influenza epidemic.

Trying to fulfill his dream of becoming an architect, Buffins attended trade school and junior college in Chicago and took correspondence courses in drafting. He eventually was hired as a draftsman in the "Loop" office of CHARLES SUMNER DUKE. While with Duke, Buffins designed three apartment buildings and two bungalows in Chicago, Brookfield, and Lyons, Illinois. Buffins's years in Chicago also saw the development of a lifelong friendship with GEORGE MACEO JONES.

It appears that Buffins's employment with Charles Sumner Duke was the extent of his professional training, but was sufficient to land him a position as an architectural draftsman at the Pearl Harbor Naval Base in the Territory of Hawaii. Arriving in 1929, he was greeted by his supervisor, a Southerner, who told him, "I asked for a draftsman, not a colored man."[2] His unpleasant welcome notwithstanding, Buffins remained with the U.S. Navy for twenty-six years, advancing to the position of naval architect by the time of his retirement in 1955.

Buffins's professional work was primarily limited to assignments at the naval base, although around 1930 he took the license examination several times but did not pass it. He did, however, occasionally design houses in Hawaii, including a dwelling in Lihue, Kauai, for Doctor and Mrs. San Yee Chang, which he entered in the seminal 1931 Howard University Exhibition. He also designed his own home in Honolulu, which was completed in 1945.

The decision to design his own residence was in part prompted by a shift in the architect's personal life. In the midst of World War II, on January 13, 1943, Lester Buffins married Yurie Tanaka, a Japanese American from Hawaii. They had one daughter, Nola. His marriage to someone ancestrally linked with the recent enemy coupled with Buffins's earlier membership with the leftist-leaning Americans for Democratic Action further complicated his wartime career and led to him being investigated by the Shipyard Loyalty Board at Pearl Harbor and by the House Committee on Un-American Activities. On both occasions he was eventually exonerated.

Unknown client, Brookfield, Illinois, *Yuri Tanaka Buffins*

Following the war, Buffins attended night school at the University of Hawaii and in 1958 received a bachelor of arts degree in Spanish. After his retirement from the U.S. Navy, he taught drafting and blueprint reading at Farrington High School in Honolulu until 1962. Next he worked three years for the University of Hawaii Facilities Maintenance Department. He continued working as a draftsman for several years on a contract basis for Kentron Company, a construction firm.

Robert Lester Buffins died in Honolulu on July 18, 1981, leaving behind his wife, three daughters, eleven grandchildren, and nine great-grandchildren.[3]

Notes

1. Department of Architecture, Howard University, "Exhibition of the Work of Negro-Architects," Howard University Gallery of Art, 12–28 May 1931.
2. Nola Buffins (daughter of Lester Buffins), interview, Honolulu, Hawaii, 8 December 2002.
3. "Robert Lester Buffins," *Honolulu Advertiser*, 21 July 1981, p. D8.

DONALD HIBBARD,
ARCHITECTURAL HISTORIAN, KANEOHE, HAWAII

BUILDING LIST

Name	Address	City	State	Year	Comments
Apartment Bldg.		Chicago	IL		36 dwelling units (du)
Apartment Bldg.		Chicago	IL		44 du
Bungalow		Lyons	IL		
Bungalow		Brookfield	IL		
House		Brookfield	IL		
House		Lihue Kauai	HW	1931	
Triplex		Chicago	IL		3 du
Buffins, Robert L.	327 Dalene Way	Honolulu	HW		
Chang, San Yee		Kauai	HW		
Duchess Apts.		Chicago	IL		
Parker House Sausage Co.		Chicago	IL		

Alberta Jeannette Cassell Butler
(1926–)

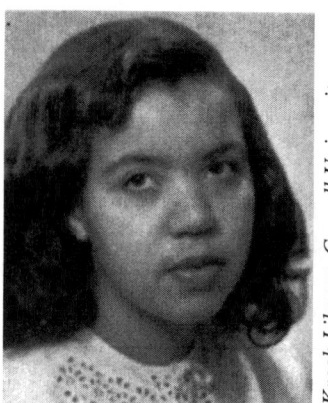

Alberta Jeannette Charlotte Cassell was born on November 22, 1926. She was the third child of ALBERT IRVIN CASSELL and Martha Ann Mason Cassell. She has an older brother, CHARLES IRVIN, and an older sister, MARTHA ANN, both of whom are architects.

Her mother, who was originally from Baltimore, Maryland, became a Baltimore Public School teacher after finishing Coppin Normal School. Her father graduated from Cornell University's School of Architecture in 1919.

Alberta attended James Monroe Elementary School, and Garnet Patterson and Banneker Junior High Schools, and graduated from Dunbar High School in 1944, all in Washington, D.C.

Alberta's brother, Charles Irvin Cassell, entered the School of Architecture at Cornell in 1942, served in the U.S. Army Air Corps for two years, and received his bachelor of architecture degree at Rensselaer Polytechnic Institute in Troy, New York, in 1951. Alberta's uncle, Oliver Burnett Cassell, received his bachelor of civil engineering degree at Cornell University. Alberta entered Cornell University in 1944. During her sophomore year she was a member of the four-student team that won a national contest for the design of a shopping center in Ithaca, New York. She also received an award during her sophomore year for having the highest grade in the School of Architecture. Alberta Cassell graduated from the School of Architecture in 1948. Her sister, Martha Ann Cassell Thompson, who was also enrolled at Cornell University, graduated the following year. The Cassell sisters were the first two African American women to receive the bachelor of architecture degree from Cornell University.

Alberta Cassell worked in her father's architectural office for two years after graduation, and when he began to direct his attention toward real estate development, she took a position in May 1951 as an architectural engineer at the Naval Research Laboratory in Washington, D.C.

In May 1961 she accepted a position as an engineering draftsman with the Military Sea Lift Command. She then became a naval architect with the U.S. Naval Sea Systems Command, where she worked from February 1971 until February 1982. Unfortunately, in 1982 she was forced to retire on disability.

In 1950 Alberta married Francis Butler, a mechanical engineering graduate of HOWARD UNIVERSITY. They had two children: Carl Butler, born in 1951; and Mira Butler, born in 1953. Carl Butler received his degree in arts and aircraft design at the University of Massachusetts in 1969 and worked for an aircraft firm in Los Angeles. Mira Butler completed her studies in computer science in 1977 at the University of the District of Columbia and accepted a position as computer analyst at the National Center for Disease Control.

Alberta Cassell is a member of the *Alpha Kappa Alpha* Sorority, the *Alpha Alpha Gamma* Society for Women Architects, the Association of Scientists and

Engineers (U.S. Navy), and the Association of University Women.

Since retiring on disability, Alberta Cassell's passion has been writing children's fairy tales and photographing flowers and butterflies. She is currently writing a book titled *The Little White Butterflies*.

CHARLES IRVIN CASSELL, FAIA,
WASHINGTON, DC

Alma Fairfax Murray Carlisle
(1927–   )

Lilian Burwell Cartwright

Alma Fairfax Murray was born in Alexandria, Virginia, on July 9, 1927. She was the younger of two children born to Clarence Murray and Alma Pinn Murray; her sister, Madeline, was ten years older. Alma Murray's father worked for the U.S. Postal Service, and her mother was an elementary school teacher in Alexandria and at one time operated her own nursery school in Alexandria.

Alma Murray attended Parker Gray Elementary School and Lyles Crouch Elementary School in Alexandria, Virginia. She went on to attend Shaw Junior High School and Dunbar Senior High School in Washington, D.C., and graduated from Dunbar in 1944. It was during her high school years that she felt "drawn to study architecture and architectural history."[1] A high school aptitude test confirmed her interests and potential ability in this profession, which were further nurtured by relatives who owned real estate and built their own homes. Her father owned numerous rental properties in the District of Columbia. Alma Murray helped out by wall stenciling some of the dwellings. Her maternal grandfather, Samuel Madden, was a carpentry instructor in one of the D.C. public schools and built his own home in Washington, D.C. Alma Murray grew up in a home in Alexandria on Northwest Street that was built by her paternal great-uncle, Benjamin Berry.

Alma Murray graduated *cum laude* from HOWARD UNIVERSITY in 1950 with a bachelor of architecture degree.[2] During her time at Howard University, she worked for various professors and also worked for a commercial arts studio, where she designed brochures.

Murray met David Kay Carlisle at a party in Washington, D.C., and after a short courtship they married on July 28, 1953, in Alexandria, Virginia. They had three children: David Jr., Carolyn, and Judith. David Kay Carlisle Sr. was a graduate of the U.S. Military Academy at West Point, where he majored in electrical engineering. He served as a commissioned officer in the U.S. Army. The family moved with him to different posts around the country. Alma Carlisle stayed at home raising their three children during the 1950s and 1960s.

Alma Carlisle returned to the working world for a short time in the 1960s when she was employed by the Office of Facilities at the D.C. Public Schools. She was a project manager whose duties were to coordinate the work of architects hired to design new schools, and she planned and coordinated the renovations of some of the district's schools, including her *alma mater*, Dunbar High School. She specialized in historic preservation, which has always been and continues to be her primary interest. However, she once designed a house located in North Carolina for a close friend.[3]

Alma and David Carlisle moved to Los Angeles, his hometown, in 1975. She began a career with the City of Los Angeles that lasted in various capacities from 1975 to 1996. From 1975 to 1981, she was in the Department of Public Works as an architectural assistant in the Architectural Division. She prepared contract documents, drawings, and specifications for improvements to buildings owned by the City of Los Angeles, and monitored federally funded construction projects for compliance with construction schedules and disbursements.

From 1981 to 1994, Alma Carlisle was an architectural associate in the Environmental Management Division for the city of Los Angeles. She surveyed twenty-seven neighborhoods, which resulted in the designation of four Historic Preservation Overlay Zones. Although the surveys were not authored by one person alone, Carlisle was very involved in ones for Melrose Hill (1984) and Whitley Heights (1990). She also surveyed more than fifty City of Los Angeles historic and cultural monuments. Additionally, she wrote and reviewed California Environmental Quality Act documents.

In 1994, Alma Carlisle returned to the Department of Public Works as an architectural associate in the Architectural Division, remaining there until 1996. Her duties included preparing architectural design specifications and contract documents for the adaptive reuse of municipally owned historic buildings such as the former Eagle Rock Branch Library.

Alma Carlisle's husband, David, died on January 15, 2000.

In 2001 Alma Carlisle joined the firm of Myra L. Frank & Associates in Los Angeles as a senior architectural historian and is presently still with them. She is a credentialed and certified architectural historian who researches and documents the architectural and cultural history of buildings and gathers biographical information on owners and architects. Her work also includes environmental review and research.

Alma Carlisle continues to live in Los Angeles while working and pursuing her interests in gardening, travel, and American history. She is a member and past president of the Los Angeles City Historical Society, a member of the West Adams Heritage Association, and a member of *Tau Beta Pi* national engineering honor society.

Her daughter, Carolyn Carlisle Raines, gave this assessment of her mother:

> My mother is an original. She was a very inspirational person in many ways. Even as a child, I knew my mother was different from other people of her generation because she worked, had a career, and had a life outside of the house that meant something to her. I always admired her very much. From the youngest age I can remember, I just assumed that women were equal to men and so I felt that I could do and be anything I wanted to. That was the message my mother gave me, my sister, and my brother. My mother is very unique in her taste as it relates to clothing, furniture, and more. She is a person who is not afraid to think outside of the box. She has always been a path breaker. She has always taught people to be whatever you want to be. To me, my mother is an original who has never been held to any stereotype. I never thought women were limited in any way.[4]

Notes

1. Interview with Alma Fairfax Murray Carlisle, interview by author, Los Angeles, Calif., 12 May 2002.
2. Howard University, Student Records, "Alma Murray," Office of the Registrar.
3. Documentation for this house could not be located.
4. Interview with Carolyn Carlisle Raines (daughter of Alma Carlisle), College Station, Texas, 29 September 2002.

LILIAN BURWELL CARTWRIGHT,
PRESIDENT, CREATIONS BY LILIAN,
HOUSTON, TEXAS

Albert Irvin Cassell
(1895–1969)

Charles Irvin Cassell

Albert Cassell was a prominent mid-twentieth-century Washington, D.C., architect. At his death, he left behind a widow, Flora B. McClarty Cassell, and several children from two marriages. Three of his children—Charles, Martha, and Alberta—followed in their father's footsteps, attending Cornell University and becoming architects. Cassell was best known for his long association with HOWARD UNIVERSITY. In his capacity as its campus planner and architect in the 1920s and 1930s, Cassell brought order to a chaotic siting of buildings and landscape and created a unified visual character that gave Howard University its architectural and intellectual symbol, Founders Library. Cassell was also well known for his Mayfair Garden (also known as Mayfair Mansion), an early and rare housing project for middle-class African Americans that he conceived during the Great Depression and built during World War II. This was his earliest effort to address the critical shortage of safe, decent, and affordable housing for Blacks. Throughout his long career, he applied his considerable architectural and business acumen to providing better housing for African Americans.

Albert Irving Cassell was born on June 25, 1895, to Albert Truman Cassell and Charlotte Cassell in Towson, Maryland. Within a year the family moved to nearby Baltimore, where Cassell attended segregated public schools. In 1909 at the age of fourteen, Cassell exhibited ambitious goals by starting to learn drafting from RALPH VICTOR COOK, who taught at Douglas High School. In 1914 Cassell graduated from a four-year carpentry program at Douglas High School. In the fall of 1915 he entered the architecture program at Cornell University. Cook was an 1898 graduate of Cornell University and made sure that Cassell received additional academic preparation before entering Cornell's architecture program.

After completing two years of college, Cassell enlisted in the U.S. Army to fight in World War I. After serving in France, but not in combat, he was honorably discharged in 1919 as a second lieutenant in the 351st Heavy Field Artillery Regiment. That same year, Cornell University awarded him a degree, although he never returned to complete his remaining two years.[1] Cornell awarded "war degrees" to Cassell and other students who interrupted or ended their academics to fight in the war.

After employment at TUSKEGEE INSTITUTE, where he and WILLIAM AUGUSTUS HAZEL designed five buildings, and in Bethlehem, Pennsylvania, where Cassell was the chief draftsman for architect Howard J. Wiegner, Cassell went to work in late 1920 for Hazel at Howard University. Hired as associate architect and construction supervisor for the Home Economics Building and as an instructor, Cassell became university architect and head of the Architecture Department when Hazel left in 1922. Cassell's complex relationship with Howard University ended in 1938 when the university's president, Dr. Mordecai Wyatt Johnson, fired him. Cassell sued the university, which countersued. The long simmering feud between the two men—with each accusing the other of various improprieties—was finally resolved in 1941, when a D.C. Superior Court judge ruled in Cassell's favor and he negotiated a small settlement from Howard University.

In his eighteen years at Howard University, Cassell performed admirably as surveyor, land manager (acquiring adjacent parcels for the university), and architect. He created Howard's "Twenty Year Plan" and designed the gymnasium, field house, armory, College of Medicine, Home Economics Building, Chemistry Building, heating plant, three women's dormitories, and underground utility tunnels.[2] In the single most important building at Howard University, Founders Library, Cassell evoked the Georgian Revival style and massing of Independence Hall in Philadelphia. This gave Howard University a symbolic expression that was similar to the Georgian-style buildings at Harvard University, and perhaps made concrete the aphorism that Howard was the Harvard of historically Black colleges and universities. This building symbolized to the administration and students that Howard University was a major—and perhaps the premier—educator of Black college students.

Cassell used the Georgian Revival style in all the buildings on campus to create a visual order where there previously had been none. He furthered this sense of architectural unity by his careful planning of the campus and siting of buildings. His layout overcame the hilly terrain that literally divided the university into two campuses. In one building, Founders Library, he created an architectural and educational symbol for the university, and in the larger scheme of his work at Howard University he created a unified whole of which Founders Library was the most visible element.

Despite his substantial efforts at Howard University, Cassell found time for other institutional clients—such as Masonic temples; Provident Hospital in Baltimore, Maryland; and Virginia Union University in Richmond—as well as commercial and residential clients. Building on his career at Howard University, he went on to design several dormitories and administration buildings at Morgan State College in Baltimore during the next twenty years. In his later years, he associated with other Black architects to form the architectural firm of Cassell, Gray, & Sulton, continuing his institutional architectural practice. Later clients for Cassell, either working independently or with the firm, included the Washington Diocese of the Roman Catholic Church, several Protestant churches, municipal projects with the District of Columbia government, and the Pentagon.

In addition to Mayfair Gardens, Cassell designed several World War II public housing projects for Blacks. In Arlington, Virginia, Cassell designed and

Howard University Founders Library, *William Lebovich*

supervised construction of the George Washington Carver Public Housing. Built in 1942, several of the 2-story apartment buildings still stand. Devoid of any historic period details, the buildings are sited to create generous front yards and backyards that are larger than typical service areas. Like the Carver project, Soller's Point in Dundalk, Maryland (adjacent to Baltimore), was built in 1942 to house Black war workers and their families. Of Cassell's three federally funded public housing projects completed during the war, the James Creek dwellings in southwest Washington, D.C., were the most expensive at $2 million dollars. Sharing with Carver the stripped-down European Modern style, the James Creek project was presented in a major national architectural magazine as an example of well-designed public housing. Cassell was the only architect not named in the magazine article, presumably because he was a Negro.

Unlike these three federal housing projects, which were erected without major problems, the housing projects that Cassell conceived, designed, and owned (at least in part) did not go as well. "Calverton" was never built because he could not secure needed subsidizes from the U.S. Department of the Interior. Mayfair Garden was built and is still used as housing, having been renovated within the last few years, but Cassell was swindled out of majority ownership by his partner and later was subpoenaed to testify before Congress concerning bribes paid to a Federal Housing Administration official to secure a federal loan guarantee. Despite this major setback in his career (his membership in the American Institute of Architects was suspended), Cassell persisted in trying to develop Chesapeake Heights on the Bay, a 520-acre summer-resort community for Blacks with 305 free-standing houses, a motel, shopping center, parking lots, pier, marina, beach, and clubhouse fronting on the Chesapeake Bay. He described it as a "dream of large and pleasant homes for men of all nations" in the sales brochure.[3] He started purchasing the land in the 1930s and built roads and several houses, but upon his death in 1969 the project ended.

To conceive of providing bayside housing for Blacks during the Great Depression, when there was not even adequate numbers of basic housing for Blacks, suggests the optimism, ambition, and self-assurance of Cassell. That he failed at Chesapeake Heights on the Bay and Calverton, and was swindled out of Mayfair Garden, is not surprising given the overwhelming obstacles he faced. Given the restrictive period in which he worked, his accomplishments are considerable.

Notes

1. "Albert Cassell," Deceased Alumni Files and Information for War Records, Cornell University Archives, Ithaca, N.Y.
2. "Howard University-Bldgs," National Archives, Record Group 66, Box 75, Project Files 1910–54.
3. Joellen ElBashir and Helen Rutt, "Chesapeake Heights on the Bay" brochure, Archive of African American Architects, Moorland-Spingarn Research Center, Washington, D.C., March 1995.

Bibliography

"Albert Cassell," Roper Library, Morgan State University Archives, manuscript collection miscellaneous records.
"Cassell Family Papers." In the possession of granddaughter, Gabrielle Lange, Silver Spring, Md.
"Centennial Exhibit of Albert I. Cassell, 1895–1995," Howard University, Founders Library, 17 November 1995.
Ethridge, Harrison M. "Founders Library." Historic American Buildings Survey, HABS No. DC-364-5, n.d.

WILLIAM LEBOVICH, ARCHITECTURAL HISTORIAN
AND ARCHITECTURAL PHOTOGRAPHER,
SILVER SPRING, MARYLAND

BUILDING LIST

Name	Address	City/County	State	Year	Comments
Birney Elementary School	Nichols Ave. & Shulman Rd., SE	Washington	DC	1969	Addition
Booker T. Washington Memorial		Malden	WV	1926	Plans only
Campbell Ave Church	2567 Nichols Ave., SE	Washington	DC	1917	
Carver War Public Housing	S. Rolfe & 13th Sts.	Arlington	VA	1942	
Catholic Diocese	Morris Rd., SE	Washington	DC		
Cheaspeake Heights on the Bay	Various Addresses	Calverton	MD	1932	Plans only
Corinthian Baptist Church	500 I St., NW	Washington	DC		
Crockett, Edward	1827 1st St., NW	Washington	DC		
Crownsville Hospital Housing & Recreation Center	1520 Crownsville Rd.	Crownsville	MD	c1950	
Friendship Baptist Church					
Glenarden City Hall	8600 Glenarden Pkwy	Glenarden	MD		
Howard University Armory	Campus	Washington	DC	1925	Demolished

ALBERT IRVIN CASSELL

BUILDING LIST *(continued)*

Name	Address	City	State	Year	Comments
Howard University Baldwin Hall	Campus	Washington	DC	1951	Howard
University Chemistry Bldg.	Campus	Washington	DC	1936	
Howard University College of Medicine	Campus	Washington	DC	1927	
Howard University Crandall Womens Dormitory	Campus	Washington	DC	1931	
Howard University Dining Hall & Home Economics Bldg.	Campus	Washington	DC	1922	Demolished
Howard University Douglas Mens Dormitory	Campus	Washington	DC	1936	
Howard University Founders Library	Campus	Washington	DC	1937	
Howard University Frazier Womens Dormitory	Campus	Washington	DC	1931	
Howard University Greene Stadium and Football Field	Campus	Washington	DC	1926	
Howard University Gym	Campus	Washington	DC	1925	Demolished
Howard University Power Plant	Campus	Washington	DC	1934	
Howard University President's Home	Campus	Washington	DC		Alterations
Howard University Truth Womens Dormitory	Campus	Washington	DC	1931	
Howard University Wheatley Hall	Campus	Washington	DC	1951	
Howard University Womens Gym	Campus	Washington	DC	1922	
James Creek Public Housing	1st & M Sts., SW	Washington	DC	1942	
Kimball Elementary School	Minnesota Ave. & Ely Pl., SE	Washington	DC	1964	Addition
Maryland School for Colored Girls	Campus	Glenn Burnie	MD	1936	
Masonic Temple	1000 U St., NW	Washington	DC	1932	Alterations
Mayfair Garden	Hays St. & Kenilworth Ave., NE	Washington	DC	1946	
Morgan State College Harper Womens Dormitory	Campus	Baltimore	MD	1951	
Morgan State College O'Connel Mens Dormitory	Campus	Baltimore	MD	1964	
Morgan State College Soldiers Armory	Campus	Baltimore	MD	1957	
Morgan State College Student Christian Center	Campus	Baltimore	MD	1941	
Morgan State College Talmadge Field House	Campus	Baltimore	MD	1969	John Gray, assoc. architect
Morgan State College Tubman Women's Dormitory	Campus	Baltimore	MD	1941	
Murphy, Carl T.	2406 Overland Ave.	Baltimore	MD		
Odd Fellows Temple	9th & T Sts., NW	Washington	DC	1932	
Odd Fellows Temple	Saratoga & Cathedral Sts.	Baltimore	MD	1925	
Omega Psi Phi Fraternity		Washington	DC		
Pemberton, Stafford	53rd Pl., SE	Washington	DC		
Pilgrim African Methodist Episcopal Church	612 17th St., NE	Washington	DC		Alterations
Plummer, Robert	3030 12th St., NE	Washington	DC		
Provident Hospital and Free Dispensary	Mosher St.	Baltimore	MD	1928	Alterations
Public housing	Paca & St. Mary's Sts.	Baltimore	MD		
Seaton Elementary School	10th St. & Rhode Island Ave.	Washington	DC	1965	
Soller's Point War Housing		Dundalk	MD	1942	
St. Luke Episcopal Church Parish	15th & Church Sts., NW	Washington	DC	1960	Alterations
St. Paul's Baptist Church	Alameda & Springfield Sts.	Baltimore	MD	1967	
Thomas, Edward	Anacostia Dr., SE	Washington	DC		
Tuskegee Institute Trade Bldgs.	Campus	Tuskegee	AL	1919	5 trade bldgs.
Virginia Union University Hartshorn Womens Dormitory	Campus	Richmond	VA	1928	
Washington Vocational School	38 O St., NW	Washington	DC	1938	Alterations
Wheately YWCA	901 Rhode Island Ave., NW	Washington	DC		Alterations

Charles Irvin Cassell
(1924–)

Charles Irvin Cassell was born on August 5, 1924, in Washington, D.C. He was the first child of ALBERT IRVIN CASSELL and Martha Ann Mason Cassell. Subsequently, he was joined by Martha Ann (b. 1925), Alberta Jeanette (b. 1926), and Albert Thomas (1929).

Charles's mother, originally from Baltimore, Maryland, attended schools in that city and became a teacher after finishing Coppin Normal School. His father was director of the Building and Grounds Department at HOWARD UNIVERSITY. As a child, Charles carried the lunch made by his mother to his father, who was too busy to stop to go out for lunch.[1]

Charles attended James Monroe Elementary School, Garnet Patterson Junior High School, and Dunbar Academic High School, all in Washington, D.C. Having "skipped" the second semester of the fourth grade, he graduated from high school in mid-term of February 1942.

From February 1942 to September 1942, Charles attended (part time) Cardozo Business High School, where he took typing and shorthand, and Armstrong Technical High School, where he enrolled in the architectural drafting class.

Albert Cassell sent three of his four children to Cornell University, two of whom graduated from the School of Architecture. Martha finished in the class of 1948 and Alberta followed in the class of 1949. Albert's brother, Oliver Burnett Cassell, also graduated from Cornell University and became a successful building contractor in Washington, D.C. Charles was at Cornell University for two years when he entered the U.S. Army in 1944. Drafted into the U.S. Army Air Corps, he trained to become a fighter pilot at the 99th Pursuit Squadron Airfield, designed by HILYARD ROBERT ROBINSON and close to TUSKEGEE INSTITUTE, where his father had designed several trade buildings. After being honorably discharged, he enrolled in the School of Architecture at Rensselaer Polytechnic Institute in Troy, New York, and graduated in the class of 1951.

Charles worked with his father after graduating from Rensselaer Polytechnic Institute. When his father turned his focus toward the development of a new town in Calvert County, Maryland, adjacent to the Chesapeake Bay, Charles accepted a position with the U.S. Navy's Bureau of Yards and Docks, where he designed quarters, theaters, and hospitals. His next position was with the Veterans Administration, where he designed hospitals for the agency to be located throughout the country. His last position with the federal government was with the General Services Administration. In that position, he traveled throughout New England and advised the agency with regard to the demolition, rehabilitation, and construction of federal facilities.

During his government service, he continued working with his father on schools and firehouses. While working with his father, Charles also gained experience in new town development as his father proceeded to plan for Chesapeake Heights on the Bay, an independent town for African Americans where they could live and thrive free of the discrimination and segregation that permeated the Washington, D.C., region. Although racial and political obstacles prevented the completion of that project, Charles Cassell learned much about land acquisition, site planning, and marketing real estate.

In April 1960 Charles Cassell received his architecture registration in the District of Columbia.[2]

From the late 1960s to the mid-1980s, Charles Cassell became involved in the civil rights movement in Washington, D.C. Among his various activities were advocacy of the right of District of Columbia citizens to vote for the President of the United States; advocacy in Congress for an elected Board of Education for D.C., 1968; and serving as vice chairman of the Emergency Committee on the Transportation Crisis, 1978 to 1980; president of the D.C. Statehood Party, a movement that advocated statehood for the nation's capital, 1981 to 1982; and chairman of the D.C. Statehood Constitutional Convention, an elected body that wrote a constitution for the emergence of the capitol city into statehood, 1982 to 1985.

In 1968 he was appointed a professor of urban planning at the Federal City College, and in 1975 he accepted a position as assistant to the vice president for planning at Federal City College. In 1976 he became director of facilities development for the new University of the District of Columbia. In this position, he supervised the design and construction of nine buildings on the northwest campus, including tennis courts, an amphitheater, and an Olympic-sized swimming pool. From 1988 until retirement, he was vice president of administrative services.

In 1981 Charles Cassell began a career as an advisor to the National Trust for Historic Preservation, 1996 to 2001; trustee of the Committee of 100 on the Federal City, 1998 to the present; chairman of the D.C. Historic Preservation Review Board, 1993 to 1996; and vice president of the D.C. Historic Preservation League, 1990 to 1994.

Charles Cassell married Elaine Bridgette in 1947, during his first year at Rensselaer Polytechnic University. Before they divorced, they had two daughters, who graduated from the Law School at Harvard University. His second and present wife of nineteen years, Linda Wernick Cassell, is director of development for the American Society of Association Executives in Washington, D.C.

Since 1988 Charles Cassell has been a private consultant in urban planning, historic preservation, and architecture.

Notes

1. Interview with Charles Cassell, by Dreck Spurlock Wilson, Washington, D.C., 22 November 1981.
2. D.C. Board of Examiners and Registrars of Architects, "Charles I. Cassell," Certificate No. 1077, issued April 1960.

CHARLES IRVIN CASSELL, FAIA,
WASHINGTON, D.C.

BUILDING LIST

Name	Address	City	State	Year	Comments
University of the District of Columbia Administration Bldg.	Campus	Washington	DC	1976	Supervising architect
University of the District of Columbia Auditorium	Campus	Washington	DC	1976	Supervising architect
University of the District of Columbia Library	Campus	Washington	DC	1976	Supervising architect
University of the District of Columbia Life Sciences Bldg.	Campus	Washington	DC	1976	Supervising architect
University of the District of Columbia Music & Dance Bldg.	Campus	Washington	DC	1976	Supervising architect
University of the District of Columbia Physical Activities Ctr.	Campus	Washington	DC	1976	Supervising architect
University of the District of Columbia Physical Science Bldg.	Campus	Washington	DC	1976	Supervising architect
University of the District of Columbia Power Plant	Campus	Washington	DC	1976	Supervising architect
University of the District of Columbia Technology Bldg.	Campus	Washington	DC	1976	Supervising architect

Century of Progress Exposition De Saible Cabin, Chicago, Illinois
(1933)

For those who saw it, the 1933 to 1934 Chicago Century of Progress Exposition was one of the greatest spectacles of the twentieth century. Held in the midst of the Great Depression and just fourteen years after Chicago's 1919 race riots, the fair reminded visitors of America's national progress over the preceding century and held out hope for a brighter future. For African Americans, this fair, like its predecessors, proved enormously frustrating, especially as it became clear that few Blacks would find work at the fair and that few African American exhibits would be included among the displays. As the racist policies of the fair came into focus, it became clear that if African Americans were to have any focal point for calling attention to their contributions to Chicago's history, their hopes would have to rest on a replica of Jean Pointe Baptiste De Saible's log cabin originally built by a fur trapper of African and French descent who was generally assumed to have been the founder of Eschecagau, a native American name which was Anglicized to Chicago.

The De Saible cabin replica was tiny in comparison with Negro buildings erected at southern expositions and was totally inadequate to represent the contributions of African Americans to Chicago's and America's "century of progress." The fact that the cabin was placed on the exposition's Midway, which included concessions that went out of their way to ridicule African Americans, compromised the exhibit's educational value in the eyes of some commentators.[1] Nevertheless, the De Saible cabin was a source of pride for those who fought hard to have it included in the fair and it became a destination point for African American visitors to the fair.[2]

The De Saible cabin was the brain child of Annie Oliver, one of the leaders of a Black women's organization, the De Saible Memorial Society. She worked in tandem with representatives of the Chicago Urban League to win the support of Black alderman Robert R. Jackson, who succeeded in getting a small appropriation from the City of Chicago to support the project. With these funds in tow, project backers hired CHARLES SUMNER DUKE to prepare plans for a replica. When it was finally erected, the cabin was initially built near the northeast corner of a replica of Fort Dearborn at 26th Street and Lake Michigan and listed as part of the social science exhibits.[3] Before the close of the fair's 1934 season, the cabin was moved to the northwest corner of the fort and finally relocated farther west, probably occupying a portion of the site that, in 1933, had been occupied by the Irish Village concession. It is worth noting that it took the better part of five years for Exposition authorities to agree to include the De Saible cabin as part of the fair and that the African Americans who promoted the cabin felt obliged to minimize De Saible's African American ancestry in order to get the project accepted by Exposition organizers.[4]

Despite, or maybe because of, these compromises, African Americans were determined to utilize the De Saible cabin to set the record straight. No exact records exist about the number of African American visitors to the Century of Progress Exposition, but it is clear that those who could afford the admission charge to the fairgrounds made certain to visit the cabin, where, in addition to finding a momentary respite from the discriminatory practices that awaited them elsewhere on the fairgrounds, they had the opportunity to recall the contributions of African Americans to Chicago's origins.[5]

Exactly what drove Exposition managers to relocate the cabin and shift its site ever more squarely in the area of the fair reserved for Midway concessions is unclear. Since the Midway featured several manifestly degrading shows—including an Old Plantation minstrel show and an African Dips concession that allowed fairgoers to throw balls at a target that would drop an African American performer into a bucket of water—one could argue that by putting the De Saible cabin on the Midway, Exposition managers sought to erase the African-French origins of Chicago. At the same time, it should be noted that the Exposition corporation paid for fireproofing the cabin, thus making it possible to reopen for a second year. To say that

De Saible Log Cabin (replica), Century of Progress World's Fair, 1933, *Chicago Historical Society*

Exposition authorities were, at best, ambivalent about the cabin is an accurate, if not altogether complete, characterization of management attitudes during both exposition seasons.

In small form, the controversies over the De Saible cabin replicated the larger struggles between African Americans and Century of Progress Exposition managers over the matter of equal treatment for African Americans at the fair and in American society more generally. By 1934, African Americans and their White supporters had had enough. Through some brilliant political maneuvering in the downstate Illinois legislature, they managed to delay a re-allocation of funds to the exposition organizers until world's fair authorities agreed to end discriminatory practices on the fairgrounds.[6] In an era of national racial apartheid, this was no small accomplishment and one that is impossible to understand fully, apart from knowing the contested history of the De Saible cabin at the Chicago Century of Progress Exposition.

Notes

1. Dewey R. Jones, "A Day at the Fair," *Chicago Defender*, 16 June 1934, p. 10.
2. Christopher Robert Reed, "In the Shadow of Fort Dearborn: Honoring De Saible at the Chicago World's Fair of 1933–34," *Journal of Black Studies*, June 1991, p. 398.
3. "Break Ground on Fair Site for De Saible Log Cabin," *Chicago Defender*, 29 April 1933, p. 10.
4. Dewey R. Jones, "Crowd at Dedication of De Sabile Cabin in World's Fair," *Chicago Defender*, 17 June 1933, p. 1.
5. Inez Duke, "World's Fair Helped to Make Known De Saible's Place in Our History," *Chicago Defender*, 17 November 1934, p. 11. Inez Duke was the wife of Charles Sumner Duke.
6. August Meier and Elliott Rudwick, "Negro Protest at the Chicago World's Fair, 1933–34," *Journal of the Illinois State Historical Society* (Summer 1966): 161.

Bibliography

Rydell, Robert W., *Worlds of Fairs: The Century of Progress Exposition*. Chicago: University of Chicago Press, 1993.

ROBERT W. RYDELL, PROFESSOR OF HISTORY,
MONTANA STATE UNIVERSITY

Claflin University, Manual Training Department
(1872)

Claflin University was the first college or university for Blacks to offer a course in architectural drawing, beginning in 1890. ROBERT CHARLES BATES, general superintendent of the Manual Training Department, created and taught the course. Mechanical drafting was offered by most industrial arts departments, but it was not meant to be artistic or approach the professional level as did the drawing course taught by Bates.

Claflin College of Agriculture & Mechanics' Institute for Colored Students was located in Orangeburg, South Carolina, on the former site of the Orangeburg Female Seminary alongside the South Carolina Railroad tracks. The college was founded in 1869 during the Reconstruction era, by the White, northern branch and Black South Carolina Conference of the Methodist Episcopal church, financially supported by the Freedmen's Aid and Southern Education Society. A modest annual appropriation was provided by the State of South Carolina through the federal Morrill Act. The Freedmen's Society operated segregated normal schools and colleges and even medical and dental schools for both races throughout the South.[1] The school was named after Lee Claflin, a wealthy abolitionist, and his son, William Claflin, then governor of Massachusetts. The college was incorporated on March 12, 1872, and was governed by a six-member corporation, a fourteen-member integrated board of trustees dominated by ministers, and a three-member providential committee who made sure the college operated in a "thoroughly Christian" manner.

The introduction of architectural drawing was consistent with the school's emphasis on fine arts, which included freehand drawing and painting from figures and casts. The colloquially named "university" was organized into a grammar school (Kindergarten to sixth grade), normal school for preparing teachers, preparatory school, and college program. Students seeking a profession in the preparatory school and college program could choose among the natural sciences, literature, French, art, Latin, Greek, German, mathematics,

Claflin University architectural drawing class (William Cooke standing on the right), *The Christian Educator*

history, political science, vocal music, and, of course, Christianity. At the zenith of its enrollment in 1890, there were over eight hundred students in the grammar, normal school, and preparatory school and thirteen students in the college program—the same number of students taking architectural drawing. A modest $8.50 a month covered tuition, room and board, laundry privileges, and bathing.

During the presidency of Reverend L. L. Dunton, who served for over twenty-five years, Claflin University boasted one of the largest infrastructures of any of the almost twenty student-built buildings of the Freedmen's schools. The major buildings included four trade buildings, a School of Manual Training, Webster Memorial Chapel, a memorial hall, a main administrative building, a library, boys' and girls' dormitories, a classroom building, and a 2-story demonstration barn.

The Industrial Trades and Manual Training Department was housed in a row of four trade buildings. There were twenty-four shops. Carpentry was the first shop, organized in 1880, followed by shops offering blacksmithing, carpentry, cabinetmaking, house painting, tailoring, laundering, bricklaying, wagonmaking, and agriculture, which farmed 150 acres adjacent to the school. For females there was cooking, housekeeping, nursing, sewing, and dressmaking. As the Manual Training Department matured, the addition of architectural drawing was understandable.

Civil engineer and professor of pure and applied mathematics William J. DeTreville, from a prominent White South Carolina family, was the first to teach mechanical drawing at Claflin, beginning in 1884. After his dismissal in 1890, the former superintendent of carpentry, ROBERT CHARLES BATES, a Claflin graduate, was appointed drawing instructor.

> The Architectural and Mechanical Drawing courses were regarded at Claflin as "of first importance" in the Manual Training Department. For all of Claflin's Manual Training classes the students produced drawings of their projects prior to constructing them.[2]

In 1891 there were thirteen students enrolled in architectural drawing. Despite offering architectural drawing, the only known student who went on to become an architect was WILLIAM WILSON COOKE. After graduating from Claflin University, Cooke returned to his *alma mater* in 1894, as first assistant to Bates. When Bates resigned to accept a position at the New York State Reformatory in Elmira, Cooke was elected general superintendent of the department and drawing instructor. He upgraded the architectural drawing course to include the architectonic orders and rendering techniques in pencil and ink.

In 1896 the State of South Carolina switched their Morrill Act appropriation from Claflin University to South Carolina State Normal, Industrial, Agricultural, & Mechanical College, which was next door. The course concentrations at Claflin in the fine arts were deemphasized and the architectural drawing class was dropped from the curriculum.

Notes

1. The Freedmen's Aid and Southern Education Society operated the following schools for Blacks: Bennett College in Greensboro, North Carolina; Clark College in Atlanta, Georgia; Cookman Institute in Jacksonville, Florida; Dillard University in New Orleans, Louisiana; Gammon Theological Seminary in Atlanta, Georgia; Huston-Tillotson College in Austin, Texas; Meharry Medical College in Nashville, Tennessee; Morgan College in Baltimore, Maryland; Morristown Junior College in Morristown, Tennessee; Philander Smith College in Little Rock, Arkansas; Rust College in Holly Spring, Mississippi; and Wiley College in Marshall, Texas. These schools all had campuses varying from two to ten buildings that, in the philosophy of self-help (with several exceptions), were designed by faculty, making the Freedmen's Aid and Southern Education Society the most prolific patron of Black architects in the decades during and following The Reconstruction Era.

2. Zack Rice, "Claflin University: Educating African Americans for Architecture and Building" (paper presented at 47th annual meeting of the Society of Architectural Historians, Philadelphia, Pennsylvania, 26 April 1994).

DRECK SPURLOCK WILSON

William Emmett Coleman Jr.
(1922–1987)

Yves Francis Coleman

William Coleman Jr. was born on April 14, 1922, in Baltimore, Maryland. His father, William Sr., was the Baltimore manager of North Carolina Mutual Insurance Company, founded by JOHN MERRICK and six others. His mother, Mabel West, formerly from Richmond, Virginia, was employed by another pioneer Black business entrepreneur, banker Maggie Walker, and later worked at all-Black Provident Hospital as records manager. William Jr., his brother Walter, and sisters Helen and Nancy all attended the segregated Frederick Douglass High in Baltimore. William learned mechanical drawing from longtime mechanical arts and manual training teacher, RALPH VICTOR COOK. "William was something of a child prodigy who was a math wiz."[1] He graduated near the top of his class of almost three hundred at the age of sixteen in 1938.

Maryland's Jim Crow laws prevented him from attending the only state university with a program in architecture, the University of Maryland at College Park. The State of Maryland paid his tuition to attend an out-of-state university. He chose the University of Illinois at Urbana-Champaign, which he entered in 1939. To pay for room and board, Coleman earned money writing term papers for upperclassmen. He was good at it and considered himself a writer as well as an architect. He stayed at the University of Illinois for two years and then transferred to Yale University in May 1942. Nine months later he was drafted into the U.S. Army. An outspoken conscientious objector, Coleman was stationed successively at various posts, the first of which was Jefferson Barracks, an Army Air Corps Training Center in Missouri, where he was under the illusion that he was being sent to a limited-assignment medical corps unit, when in fact he worked as a classification specialist. He was then a clerk typist and aircraft dispatcher for the flight training school at Chehaw, Alabama, where the "Tuskegee Airmen" trained. Next he was assigned to the regional veterans hospital at Greensboro, North Carolina, as an assistant recording case histories and administering psychotherapy under the supervision of psychiatrist Morris H. Adler. His experiences embittered him about the military and he spent much of his off-duty time writing a lengthy manifesto on conscientious objectors.

Coleman was discharged from the U.S. Army in 1946 and resumed his studies at Yale University. He graduated in June 1947 with a master of architecture degree, and won the prestigious Prix de Beaux Arts, which provided him with a stipend to study French academic architecture at the Sorbonne University in Paris. From June 1947 until April 1948, however, he lived in New York City, where he was a close friend of Maya Deren, a vanguard filmmaker. Sometime in 1947, Coleman designed a country house, "Treetops," for sultry torch singer Libby Holman, whose trademark song was a cover of "Body and Soul." The Holman commission would be William Coleman's last domestic commission because he left America and settled in Paris, France, in April 1948.

Coleman sporadically attended classes in literature at the Sorbonne from 1948 to 1950, with the intention of writing a terminal paper titled "The Theme of Morality in French Modern Literature." He probably took classes at the Sorbonne in order to receive money from his Prix de Beaux Arts. In France Coleman lived a Bohemian life and in the coffee houses of Paris he met several writers and journalists such as Frederic de Towarniki (translator of the German philosopher Heidegger), Albert Camus, and Jean Paul Sartre. Coleman had already envisioned himself as a writer and now he also wanted to become a translator. He began translating, from French to English, Simone de Beauvoir's book about the United States but after doing a large amount of work discovered that the rights were already sold to someone else.

In March 1950 William Coleman married Violante do Canto (1923–), the daughter of famed Portugese sculptor Ernesto Canto da Maya (1890–1981). During their two years of marriage Violante do Canto Coleman worked as a translator. To their union, one son, Yves Francis Coleman, was born, on October 6, 1950. After two years of marriage, William and Violante divorced. William Coleman worked as a translator for L'Architecture d'Aujourd'hui journal. From 1954 to 1957 Coleman went to work in London, England, as an architect for a large architectural firm. However, his strong opinions and prickly personality often provoked conflicts with his colleagues and supervisors.

Coleman quit architecture when he returned to France in 1957. His divorce from architecture was so complete that when Albert Camus proposed to introduce Coleman to Le Corbusier (1887–1965) he declined the invitation. Coleman bought a plot of land in the south of France with the intention of designing and constructing a home while he lived off his savings. During this time he met Chester Himes, a Black American novelist. In 1960, totally broke, Coleman returned to Paris and from then on worked as a technical translator. He was employed for several years by a translator's agency called Polytra, which gave him more and more responsibilities. At some point Polytra closed, and Coleman became a sort of middleman between the agency's former clients and unemployed translators.

In Paris Coleman had very few contacts with the American Black community. He always considered the value and interest of a person and not the color of their skin or nationality. Coleman was a close friend of dynamic jazz bassist Charlie Mingus, jazz musician Albert Nicholas, and author Richard Wright.

Coleman never returned to America although he maintained his American citizenship. Basically what

Libby Holman Reynolds "Treetops," *Robert Yelin, Hay Photographers*

he appreciated in France was that although France obviously sheltered racist individuals, there was not an overt color line.

In 1986 Coleman learned that he had lung cancer, despite the fact that he had stopped smoking years ago. Coleman died in *Creteil* at *Henri Mondo* Hospital, which specialized in cancer treatment, on December 2, 1987, at the age of sixty-four.[2] His ashes were strewn over a *petite* garden in the cemetery of Fontaine-Sainte-Martin in Valenton, close to Paris.

Notes

1. Nancy Coleman (sister of William Coleman), interview, Lasarre, Quebec, 30 December 2002.
2. "William Coleman Dies in Paris at Age 63 [*sic*], Was Architect, Expatriate," *Baltimore Afro-American,* 13 January 1987, p. 1.

YVES FRANCIS COLEMAN,
SON OF WILLIAM COLEMAN JR.,
PARIS, FRANCE

BUILDING LIST

Name	Address	City	State	Year	Comments
Reynolds, Libby H.	Merriebrooke Ln.	Stamford	CT	1947	"Treetops"

Julian Abele Cook
(1904–1986)

Courtesy of Columbian Harmony Society

Julian A. Cook was born on April 10, 1904, to John Francis Cook III (1867–1932) and Elizabeth Rebecca Abele Cook (1865–1943) in Bonners Ferry, Idaho. His birthplace was in the Kotenai Valley along the Wild Horse Trail that led to the gold fields of British Columbia about forty miles north. His father had received a coveted appointment from President Benjamin Harrison to be U.S. postmaster for Bonners Ferry. Educated as a pharmacist at HOWARD UNIVERSITY (1888), John Cook operated the town's only apothecary in the old Bonner Hotel while being the only Negro among the Bonners Ferry population of five hundred. Elizabeth Cook was a calligrapher. When she joined her new husband in Bonners Ferry after their wedding in 1894, she earned money preparing mining deeds, stock certificates, and bills of sale. Bonners Ferry was rugged country for a sophisticated easterner. On top of that, John Cook suffered a succession of calamitous financial setbacks and took out his frustration on his wife. In 1906 Elizabeth Cook took Julian, his two sisters, and his brother and left her husband behind in Bonners Ferry to return to Philadelphia, her hometown. Her unmarried brother, architect JULIAN FRANCIS ABELE, took them in. Living under the roof of his uncle and namesake, Julian Cook's ambition to become an architect was understandable.

Julian Cook attended Central High School in Philadelphia, which enjoyed a well-deserved reputation for training students in the fine arts. At Central High School, Julian was friends with HOWARD HAMILTON MACKEY SR., WILLIAM HENRY MOSES JR., and GRANVILLE WARNER HURLEY SR. After graduating in 1922, Cook was admitted to Pennsylvania State University in State College, where William Moses Jr. had also enrolled. Cook withdrew after one year and transferred with sixteen credits in September 1923 to the University of Pennsylvania School of Fine Arts, where his uncle had distinguished himself by becoming the first African American to graduate from the School of Architecture.[1] Cook withdrew from the university with an "honorable dismissal" in 1926, without enough credits to earn his degree. Cook found employment with the City of Philadelphia Transit Department tracing construction details onto drawings. In 1930 he was hired by ALBERT IRVIN CASSELL as a draftsman and assigned to work on three women's dormitories for Howard University that Cassell was designing. During Cook's architectural career, he was never recognized as a designer, but rather as a technically proficient architect who excelled at project management, construction supervision, and contract administration. In March 1932 Cassell moved Cook off of his office payroll and onto the payroll of the Howard University's Buildings and Grounds Department, where in various capacities he remained for forty-two years. Cook prepared the construction drawings for retrofitting the old Carnegie Library into the School of Religion. In 1933 he prepared the installation drawings for a new organ in Rankin Chapel. He also led the design effort to renovate Clark Hall. From 1944 until 1946 he was superintendent of buildings and grounds and was responsible for the design, construction, and field supervision of all university buildings.

Julian Cook married Ruth McNeil of Fayetteville, North Carolina, in 1929. Their only child, Julian Abele Cook Jr., became a U.S. District Court judge for the Eastern District of Michigan.

For less than a year, at the onset of World War II, Cook taught architectural drafting for the Engineering Defense Training Unit in Washington, D.C. In 1943 Julian Cook received his D.C. architect registration.[2] Cook was an active member of *Omega Psi Phi* fraternity and the NATIONAL TECHNICAL ASSOCIATION.

Julian Cook died on July 8, 1986.[3] He is buried in Harmony Memorial Cemetery in Suitland, Maryland.

Notes

1. University of Pennsylvania, Official Transcript, "Julian Able [sic] Cook," 17 May 1935.
2. D.C. Board of Examiners and Registrars of Architects, "Julian Abele Cook," Certificate No. 438, issued 17 February 1943.
3. Rankin Memorial Chapel Funeral Program, "Funeral Services for Julian Abele Cook 1904–1986," Howard University, 12 July 1986.

Bibliography

Gatewood, Willard, *Aristocrats of Color: The Black Elite*. Fayetteville: University of Arkansas, 2000.
Wormley, Stanton L., ed. *Genealogy of the Cook Family of Washington, D.C.* D.C.: Columbian Harmony Society, 1984.

DRECK SPURLOCK WILSON

BUILDING LIST

Name	Address	City	State	Year	Comments
Howard University Carnegie Library	Campus	Washington	DC	1932	Renovations
Howard University Clark Hall	Campus	Washington	DC	1933	Demolished

Ralph Victor Cook
(1875–1949)

Columbian Harmony Society

Ralph Victor Cook taught to hundreds of Negro secondary students the art of architectural and mechanical drafting, a significant number of whom went on to become architects. At Douglass High School in Baltimore, Maryland, he was one of the first African American public school teachers and administrators in Maryland when he was hired in 1901. He taught there for forty-five years before retiring in 1946.

Ralph Cook was born in Washington, D.C., to John Francis Cook II and Helen Appo Cook, a housewife. John Cook was a public school teacher and in 1867 was appointed a clerk in the office of the collector of taxes for the District of Columbia by President Ulysses Simpson Grant. Ralph was the fifth and youngest child of John and Helen Cook. His siblings were: Elizabeth (b. 1864), John (b. 1866), George (b. 1869), and Charles (b. 1871). Ralph attended public schools in Washington, D.C., and was living with his family on 6th Street, NW, near HOWARD UNIVERSITY, when he matriculated at Cornell University in 1892. There he studied architectural and mechanical engineering, graduating in 1898 with a bachelor of science degree in mechanical engineering. His thesis was titled "Stress and Strain Relations of Rubber on the Friction of Aluminum-Zinc Alloys."[1]

When Cook began teaching at Douglass High School, he taught fourteen periods of mechanical drawing and fifteen periods of shop per week. One hundred and sixty-one students were enrolled in the Department of Manual Training and Mechanical Drawing that year; half were freshmen in the newly consolidated normal and secondary school. His faculty colleagues included other well-known African American educators, such as Dwight O. W. Holmes, who later became the first Black president of Morgan State University in Baltimore.

Cook's friendship with Holmes continued and produced several joint construction projects in Baltimore. They both attended summer school at Columbia University in New York City and influenced other faculty to do the same. They also were among the organizers of the American Tennis Association, which was incorporated in 1916 to promote the sport of tennis and is today the oldest African American sports organization in the United States.

Among Cook's civic interests was the Baltimore Urban League. The Urban League's "Lung Block Survey" attained national prominence by focusing attention on a densely populated area of West Baltimore, which was the rumored to harbor tuberculosis. During the 1920s and 1930s, dilapidated row houses in the neighborhood were demolished, making way for a public elementary school. Ralph Cook's first wife, Corona, died in 1911. There were no children from his first marriage. A child from his second marriage died in infancy.

Cook's interests were shared by his second wife, whom he married in 1918 at the age of forty-three. Vivian Johnson Cook was a prominent educator as well. She started her teaching career at TUSKEGEE INSTITUTE and moved to Baltimore after her marriage. She was the first African American female appointed to an administrative post in the Baltimore City public schools when she became vice principal of the Booker T. Washington Junior High School. She also was the first female to serve as principal of a coeducational high school when she was appointed principal of Dunbar Junior-Senior High School, with an enrollment of 3,800 students.

Ralph and Vivian Cooke traveled extensively in Africa, Europe, and the Near East. Ralph Cook died at age seventy-four on September 1, 1949.

Notes
1. Ralph Cook, "Stress and Strain Relations of Rubber on the Friction of Aluminum-Zinc Alloys" (B.S. thesis, Cornell University, 1898).

Bibliography
Wormley, Stanton L. *Genealogy of the Cook Family of Washington, D.C.* Washington, D.C.: Columbian Harmony Society, n.d.

GINGER HOWELL,
GRADUATE STUDENT,
INSTITUTE OF ARCHITECTURE,
LANDSCAPE ARCHITECTURE, AND PLANNING,
MORGAN STATE UNIVERSITY

William Wilson Cooke
(1871–1949)

Vera E. Cooke

William Wilson Cooke was born on December 27, 1871, in Greenville, South Carolina. His father, Wilson Cooke (1819–1897), was the slave son of Vardry McBee, the putative founder of Greenville, South Carolina. Wilson Cooke and his free Black wife, Margaret Magdelena Walker Cooke, lived on West Coffee Street in a house provided by McBee. Wilson Cooke variously was a tanner, owned a barber shop, and owned a grocery. A prominent colored citizen of Greenville during the Reconstruction era, he was a Republican delegate to the 1868 South Carolina Constitutional Convention. William completed normal and parochial schools before he was fourteen. A sickly child, he was pulled out of school and went to work as a clerk in his father's grocery. Later when his health improved he was an apprentice carpenter starting in 1885. William's older three sisters and brother all attended CLAFLIN UNIVERSITY, where their father had a building named after him. Claflin University would also figure prominantly in William's destiny. He enrolled there in the fall of 1888, in the Literary and Industrial Department.

Claflin University was administered by the Freedman's Aid and Southern Education Society with supplemental funding provided by the State of South Carolina. The Freedman's Aid and Southern Education Society managed more than twenty schools all over the South: segregated ones for Blacks such as Wiley College, Morgan State College, Cookman Institute, and Rust University in Holly Springs, Mississippi, which offered a course in architectural drawing; and separate schools for Whites.

All students, whether they were enrolled in the liberal arts or manual training departments, were required to take a shop course. Cooke enrolled in the architectural drawing course taught by ROBERT CHARLES BATES, the department's general superintendent and architectural and mechanical drawing instructor. Cooke graduated in the spring of 1893 with a college preparatory diploma in liberal arts. The following fall, Cooke returned to Claflin University as first assistant to Professor Bates. Despite his youth and lack of practical experience, he taught architectural drawing.

In October 1894 Cooke was elected by the trustees of Georgia State Industrial College for Colored Youth in Savannah as superintendent of the Industrial Department, where he introduced carpentry and masonry into the Manual Training Department. The first building ever designed by Cooke was Meldrim Hall (1896), which was built by faculty and students in the manual trades, however the building burned down in 1917. Cooke resigned in 1897 and returned to his *alma mater* to replace Robert Bates as general superintendent of manual training and industrial arts. After returning, Cooke designed Lee Library (1898) a 60-foot-long, T-shaped, pressed-brick building that cost $5,000 to build using student labor. Cooke designed a "Souvenir Two Hundred Dollar Cottage"—a prototypical, stick-built cottage whose plans and specifications could be mail-ordered from Claflin University—which was modeled at the Fourth Educational and Industrial Conference, held in the spring of 1898. Cooke expanded the architectural drawing course to include the study of architectonic orders and introduced drawing requirements such as delineating shades and shadows and rendering in ink and watercolors, and he changed the name of the course to preparatory course in architecture. Cooke also designed the John F. Slater School of Manual Training Building (1900), the building that housed his classes. While serving as general superintendent, Cooke attended a course on architecture at Boston School of Technology in the summer of 1900 and the following summer attended a course on history and interpretation of art at Columbia University in New York City. Back at Claflin University he took additional liberal arts classes and was awarded a bachelor of science in technology degree in 1902.

Cooke found steady employment in his profession with the Freedmen's Aid and Southern Education Society starting in 1902 and lasting for five years. The Freedmen's Aid and Southern Education Society of the Methodist Episcopal denomination financially supported Claflin University; thus they were probably delighted to hire one of their prized graduates. While employed by the society, Cooke designed the Dining Hall and Girls' Home (1901) and Main Building (1905) at Cookman Institute in Jacksonville, Florida. An integral element of the Methodist Episcopalian's Reconstruction-era activities in Jacksonville, the school on the south side of West 8th Street opened as an academy in 1872. It was one of the first schools of higher learning for African Americans in Florida. At his *alma mater*, Cooke was the architect for the Louise Stokes Girls' Dormitory (1904); Louise Soules Home for Girls (1905); the $52,000 administrative building, Adella M. Tingley Memorial Hall (1908); and the brick 3-story Mary E. Dunton Boys' Dormitory (1907). Cooke was also the architect for the Booker T. Washington Hospital (1905) at Voorhees Industrial School, which must have been a *coup* because Voorhees Industrial School was programmatically aligned with the "Tuskegee Machine" and its stable of architects— namely ROBERT ROBINSON TAYLOR and WILLIAM SIDNEY PITTMAN. William Wilson Cooke designed the wood-shingle, white house (1903) on the prominent corner of Boulevard and Oak in Orangeburg, South Carolina, John Hammond Fordham, the only Black lawyer in Orangeburg and a popular member of the state Republican Party who even served as coroner for the town. The house cost $1,327 and was sized to accommodate Fordham's wife and nine children.[1] A three-window bay projects from the right side of the house as one walks toward the long and narrow porch, and the porch roof is supported by paired columns. These architectural details were familiar to the architect, having been emphasized in the preparatory course in architectural drawing that he had taught.

In March 1907, Cooke sat for and passed the three-day federal civil service examination given at a site in Boston.

He was not allowed to take the examination in the District of Columbia because of his race. He was told to report to work for the U.S. Treasury Department

U.S. Post Office, Marietta, Ohio, *Vera E. Cooke*

Supervising Architect's Office. Unaware of his race, his arrival at the Treasury Department building in downtown Washington, D.C., caused quite a stir.[2] His probationary appointment was as an architectural draftsman at an annual salary of $1,400, making him the first African American to serve in a professional capacity in the Supervising Architect's Office. He successfully served his six-month probationary term and on September 21 was permanently appointed an architectural draftsman. However, his annual salary was $200 less. In 1909 Cooke was transferred to Field Operations, where he supervised the construction of federal courthouses and post offices in Pennsylvania, Ohio, Illinois, and West Virginia. Cooke remained with the Supervising Architect's Office until 1918, a relatively long time, eleven years.

Cooke's only known private commissions in Washington, D.C., were a single-family house (1908) on Kearney Street, NE, in the historic Deanwood community and alterations to Asbury Methodist Church for family friend and presiding elder Matthew Wesley Claire.

Cooke was promoted and transferred to the War Department in October 1918 as director of vocational guidance and training, responsible for training all-Negro labor battalions at Wilberforce University in Ohio for overseas duty. Cooke discontinued his civil service appointment after three years with the War Department.

William Cooke was married to Anne Miller Cooke, the daughter of Thomas E. Miller, who was the first president of South Carolina State Normal, Industrial, Agricultural, & Mechanical College. The Cookes' two children, Anne and Lloyd, chose professions dissimilar from their father's. After attending Spellman College and Atlanta University, Anne Cooke Reid earned her doctoral degree from Yale University. She founded and was the first director of the Drama Department at Howard University. Lloyd Miller Cooke was the first African American to run cross-country track for the University of Wisconsin, where he earned a chemistry degree in 1937. He continued his academic career by earning a doctoral degree in cellulose chemistry from McGill University in Montreal, Canada, in 1941. A renowned chemist, Lloyd Cooke published a popular textbook on chemistry, won the William Proctor Prize for Scientific Achievement in 1970, was director of community affairs for Union Carbide in New York City, and was appointed to the National Science Foundation Board.

From 1921 to 1929 William Wilson Cooke was in private practice at 1828 Broadway in Gary, Indiana. His largest commission was the Gothic-style Trinity Methodist Episcopal Church and the co-located John Stewart Memorial Settlement House (1925), on whose board of directors he served. Other private commissions in Gary were Saint John's Hospital for hero physician Dr. McMitchell and the first African Methodist Episcopal Church. In the 1920s and 1930s, the Ku Klux Klan was active all over Indiana. Cooke led an anti-Klan group in Gary that opposed the "Bow-Tie Amalgamation," a group of negroes that formed a secret alliance with the Klan and conspired against their own race. He was a director of the Gary Building and Loan Association, whose borrowers represented potential clients. He obtained his state architect license on October 14, 1929, becoming the first of his race to be licensed to practice architecture in the state of Indiana.[3] For two years he served as assistant property assessor for the Lake County, Indiana, government. The Wall Street stock market crash on "Black Monday" in 1929 put him out of business. He was saddled with a lot of debt, but was proud of the fact that although it took him a long time, he repaid all of his creditors.

In 1931 Cooke returned to the Supervising Architect's Office as a construction engineer. He designed and supervised the construction of small-town post offices in Ohio, Illinois, Missouri, Michigan, Wisconsin, and Minnesota.[4] He retired from federal service in 1942.

William Wilson Cooke died at home, 2319 Adams Street in Gary, Indiana, on August 25, 1949, at the age of seventy-seven.[5] He was interred at Fern Oak Cemetery in Griffith, Indiana.

Notes
1. Eugene Robinson, "Looking Homeward at Four Generations," *Washington Post*, 13 December 1981, p. C1.
2. U.S. Treasury, Supervising Architect's Office, "Personnel Card for William W. Cooke," College Park, Maryland, National Archives II, Record Group 56.
3. State of Indiana Board of Registration for Architects, "William Wilson Cooke," Certificate No. 165, issued 14 October 1929.
4. "William Wilson Cooke," *The Journal of Negro Education*, (February 1942): n.p.
5. "W. W. Cooke, Outstanding Negro, Is Dead," *Gary Post-Tribune*, 26 August 1949, p. 19.

Bibliography
Hall, Clyde W. *One Hundred Years of Educating at Savannah State College, 1890–1990*. East Peoria, Ill.: Versa Press, 1991.
"William Wilson Cooke." *The Christian Educator*, (August 1902): p. 11.

DR. BARBARA COOK WILLIAMS,
ASSISTANT PROFESSOR, UNIVERSITY OF IDAHO

BUILDING LIST

Name	Address	City	State	Year	Comments
Commercial Bldg.	2137 Broadway St.	Gary	IN		Now furniture store
House	1019 Kearney St., NE	Washington	DC	1908	
Asbury United Methodist Church	11th & K Sts., NW	Washington	DC		Alterations
Campbell Friendship House	21st & Washington Aves.	Gary	IN		
Claflin University Administrative Bldg.	Campus	Orangeburg	FL		
Claflin University Dunton Boys Dormitory	Campus	Orangeburg	SC	1907	
Claflin University Lee Library	Campus	Orangeburg	SC	1898	
Claflin University President's Residence "Dunwalton"	Campus	Orangeburg	SC		
Claflin University Slater Training Bldg.	Campus	Orangeburg	SC	1900	
Claflin University Soules Home for Girls	Campus	Orangeburg	SC	1905	
Claflin University Souvenir Cottage	Campus			1898	Plans only
Claflin University Stokes Girls Dormitory	Campus	Orangeburg	SC	1904	
Claflin University Tingley Memorial Hall	Campus	Orangeburg	SC	1908	
Cookman Institute Dining Hall and Girls Home	Campus	Jacksonville	FL	1901	
Cookman Institute Main Bldg.	Campus	Jacksonville	FL	1905	
First African Methodist Episcopal Church	2001 Massachusetts St.	Gary	IN	1923	
Fordham, John, atty.	415 Boulevard St.	Orangeburg	SC	1903	
Georgia State Industrial College for Colored Youth, Meldrim Hall	Campus	Savannah	GA	1896	Destroyed by fire
St. John's Hospital	28 E. 22nd St.	Gary	IN	c1920	
Stewart Settlement House	15th Ave. & Massachusetts St.	Gary	IN	1925	
Trinity Methodist Episcopal Church	15th Ave. & Massachusetts St.	Gary	IN	1925	
U.S. Post Office	48 Chestnut St.	Lancaster	PA	1931	
U.S. Post Office	420 W. 2nd St.	Defiance	OH	1914	
U.S. Post Office	110 Cottage St.	Ashland	OH	1917	
U.S. Post Office	35 W. Union St.	Athens	OH	1911	
U.S. Post Office	Front St.	Marietta	OH		
U.S. Post Office	305 N. Main St.	Bowling Green	OH	1914	
U.S. Post Office	214 N. 4th St.	Ironton	OH		
U.S. Post Office	244 N. Seltzer St.	Crestline	OH	1941	
U.S. Post Office	101 E. Main St.	Coldwater	OH	1940	
U.S. Post Office	410 W. Franklin St.	Appleton	WI		Demolished
U.S. Post Office		Millville	WI	1938	
U.S. Post Office	211 S. Dickason Blvd.	Columbus	WI	1938	
U.S. Post Office	522 N. 9th St.	Sheboygan	WI	1932	
U.S. Post Office	1902 3rd St.	Hibbing	MN		
U.S. Post Office	400 4th St.	International Falls	MN	1935	
U.S. Post Office	132 S. Main St.	Bluffton	OH	1940	
U.S. Post Office	425 W. Genesse St.	Iron River	MI		
Voorhees Industrial School Washington Hospital	Campus	Denmark	SC	1905	
Wesley Methodist Church	101 E. Court St.	Greenville	SC		

Cotton States and International Exposition Negro Building, Atlanta, Georgia
(1895)

The Negro Building at Atlanta's Cotton States and International Exposition, 1895, set a meaningful and inspiring precedent in the United States. Considered a sociological experiment, the building and exhibit proved a success for the Cotton States Exposition and the African American race.

The idea of an exhibit portraying the progress of African Americans since Emancipation was initially proposed to Atlanta businessman Samuel Inman by Bishop Wesley John Gaines of the African Methodist Episcopal Denomination and the Honorable Henry A. Rucker. Inman then brought the suggestion before the directors of the exposition company in 1894. The officials approved the exhibit and accordingly created the Negro Department to manage the logistics of the exhibit.

The possibility of a building to house African American exhibits became a reality when African Methodist Episcopal Bishop Wesley John Gaines of Georgia, Abraham Grant of Texas, and BOOKER TALIAFERRO WASHINGTON, principal of TUSKEGEE INSTITUTE, accompanied a delegation of exposition supporters to Washington, D.C., to lobby Congress for sponsorship and contributions. With little time to prepare their speeches, the three men helped secure Congressional appropriations in the amount of $200,000.

Irvine Garland Penn, of Lynchburg, Virginia, was elected chief of the Negro Department in January 1895. Penn took on the project and was in charge of fulfilling the Negro Department's resolve to display the "best product of their race in various industries and pursuits that have been opened to them."[1] With the assistance of ten state commissioners, Penn secured money for building and operating expenses and exhibit materials from fourteen states and the District of Columbia. Clarke Howell, editor of the *Atlanta Constitution*, noted the excitement of the exhibit: "In every state of the South the negroes are organizing for the collection of their exhibit, and they already have met with such success as to give assurance that their unique exhibit, valuable as it will be, as a historic contribution of social development, will be one of the most attractive centers of the exposition."[2]

Located in the southeastern corner of the exposition grounds, near the Jackson Street entrance, the Negro Building was described as "unpretentious, but pleasing in appearance and in good taste," and lauded as an impressive and unique addition to the Cotton States and International Exposition.[3] Two African American contractors from Georgia—JOHN THOMAS KING of La Grange and J. W. Smith of Atlanta—built the building. A reporter for the *New York Observer Exposition Supplement* wrote, "every timber in the Negro building was laid by Negro mechanics . . . no white labor has been employed in the construction of the building, and the whole edifice from foundation to the roof is the product of the industry of the colored worker."[4]

The Negro Building, along with nine other structures at the Cotton States and International Exposition, was designed by Bradford Lee Gilbert (1859–1934), a nationally recognized New York architect who utilized "liberal dimensions and taste of architecture" in his plans.[5] The Negro Building was

> classed in a simplified Romanesque mode . . . characterized by simple rectilinear massing, arch-headed windows, and square pyramidally roofed towers. Featuring facades composed of rectilinear glazing and accented at each end by square towers . . . the tower motif was repeated pedimented [sic] central entrance pavilion.[6]

The building, made of wood and concrete, occupied 25,000 square feet. Two *bas-relief* sculptures placed on either side of the entrance pediments illustrated the progression of African Americans. The diametrically opposed medallions depicted the period of slavery with

> the slave mammie with the 1-room log cabin, the log church, the rake and basket in 1865" and the period

COTTON STATES AND INTERNATIONAL EXPOSITION NEGRO BUILDING, ATLANTA, GEORGIA

Cotton States and International Exposition Negro Building, *Atlanta History Center*

since Emancipation with "the face of Frederick Douglass . . . near him is the comfortable residence, the stone church and symbols of the race's progress in science, art and literature, all representative of the new negro in 1895.[7]

Exposition patrons of every race were welcomed to experience the Negro exhibition, and entrance fees were not charged for admittance into the Negro Building. The interior of the structure provided space for up to 269 exhibits and a restaurant for exposition patrons. Exhibits featuring agriculture products and farming techniques shared space with displays devoted to the education of African Americans and the manufacture of products and machines. In the official history of the Cotton States and International Exposition Walter Cooper stated, "The exhibit in the building is very extensively educational from a literary point of view."[8] One of the most notable displays, and one of the first viewed upon entering the building, hailed from D.C.'s Amateur Art Club. A statue "The Negro with Chains Broken But Not Off," by W. C. Hill allegorically summed up the condition of African Americans since Emancipation.

The sociological experiment, which was started in Atlanta in 1894, proved a rousing success for the African American race and the Cotton States and International Exposition. In addition to the Negro Building and the exhibits housed within, the presence of African Americans at the exposition has been well remembered. The speech of Booker T. Washington at the opening ceremony, later known as the "Atlanta Compromise," began the one-hundred-day exposition in which the African Americans were well represented. The buildings were demolished several years after the Cotton States and International Exposition closed. All that remains now is its historical legacy and Piedmont Park in northwest Atlanta in which it stood.

Notes

1. *Preliminary Prospectus of the Cotton States and International Exposition Company* (Atlanta: Franklin Printing and Publishing Company, 1894), p. 12.
2. Clark Howell, "The Worlds Event for 1895: The Cotton States and International Exposition," *The Review of Reviews* 61 (1895): 163.
3. *Report of the Board of Commissioners Representing the State of New York at the Cotton States and International Exposition Held at Atlanta, Georgia, 1895* (Albany, N.Y.: Wynkopp Hallenbeck Crawford Company, 1896), p. 197.
4. "Cotton States International Exposition," *New York Observer*, Suppl. (27 June 1895): 863.
5. Howell, p. 163.
6. F. H. Coons, "The Cotton States and International Exposition in the New South Architecture and Implications," master's thesis, University of Virginia, 1988, p. 30.

7. Walter G. Cooper, *The Cotton States and International Exposition and South Illustrated, Including the Official History of the Exposition* (Atlanta: Illustrator Company, 1895), p. 60.

8. Ibid., p. 60.

Bibliography

The Official Catalogue of the Cotton States and International Exposition Atlanta, Georgia, U.S.A., September 18 to December 31, 1895, Illustrated. Atlanta: Claflin & Mellichamp Publishers, 1895.

MICKI WALDROP, RESEARCH ASSOCIATE,
ATLANTA HISTORY CENTER

Clarence Cross
(1916–)

Clarence Cross

Clarence Cross was born on January 15, 1916, in a log cabin in Allensville, Kentucky. The grandson of slaves, his parents were Napoleon and Omelia Tinder Cross. His elementary education was in the public schools of Allensville and in Nashville, Tennessee. In 1927 his family moved to Kokomo, Indiana, where he completed his high school education.

Dating from his teens, Cross had an interest in drawing and building construction. Following graduation from high school, he participated in a Works Progress Administration arts education program. An oil painting that he made in this program was exhibited many years later at the 1939 New York World's Fair.

In 1940 Cross entered TUSKEGEE INSTITUTE with financial assistance from Mr. and Mrs. Robert J. Hamp, the family for whom his mother worked as a maid and he worked as a helper. He majored in carpentry until January 1942 when he was drafted into the U.S. Army. Cross served two years stateside with the 367th and 364th Infantries and twenty-one months overseas in the Asia-Pacific theater. During his military service, he took classes in architectural drawing, cost estimating, specification writing, and contract writing at the University of Washington in 1945. One of the honors he earned was being selected to serve in an honor guard for President Franklin Delano Roosevelt. He was honorably discharged in December 1945.

In 1946 Cross reentered Tuskegee Institute with financial assistance from the GI Bill. His major was architecture. One instructor, Milton Love, was particularly influential. Love was a graduate of Tuskegee Institute and had taught there for many years prior to Cross's arrival. Love taught Cross the history of architecture, applied mechanics, architectural design, specifications and contracts, and surveying. After graduating at the top of his class in 1949, Cross returned to Kokomo. There, as a member of American Legion Post No. 177, he designed and supervised construction of the new post home. He served as commander of the post in 1950.

In his continuing quest for education, Cross took architectural engineering courses from Wilson Engineering Corporation in Cambridge, Massachusetts, in 1953. He also took courses in Air Force management at the University of Dayton in 1967, and attended structural steel design conferences at Purdue University during 1971. Cross had a special interest in churches; therefore he attended national workshops on church design in New York, Chicago, Washington, D.C., and Minneapolis.

Cross moved to Dayton, Ohio, in 1951. He was employed by the Architectural Section, Base Civil Engineering for Wright-Patterson U.S. Air Force Base near Dayton, and became a registered architect in Ohio in 1958.[1] Two years later he became a registered architect in Indiana.[2] Along the way to obtaining registrations, Cross worked in Tuskegee, Alabama; Philadelphia, Pennsylvania; and Kokomo, Indiana. He retired from the federal government in 1971, with the title of chief architect, base unit leader, and head of the architectural

Tabernacle Baptist Church, Dayton, Ohio, *Clarence Cross*

unit of the civil engineering division. His duties included supervision of high school and college students on summer internships, and he was technical supervisor of civilian and military personnel in his unit. In addition, he was the facilities manager for Wright-Patterson Field and Engineer Manager and was responsible for multi-million-dollar construction projects.

Cross maintained a small private practice from 1958 to 1969, in addition to his federal job. In 1969 Cross became a founding partner in the architectural and engineering firm of Cross, Curry, de Weaver, Randall, & Associates. This inter-racial firm was largely responsible for the design and working drawings for the Charles Drew Health Center, Model Cities Neighborhood Facility, Southwest Shopping Center, Dayton Fire Station No. 13, and Parks Copeland Building for the Tabernacle Baptist Church, all in Dayton. The firm was one of three selected to design the multi-million-dollar Rapid Transit Authority office and garage. In 1997 the firm was dissolved.

Churches were Cross's favorite building type, and he is particularly proud of the Second Baptist Church (1958) in Ford City, Pennsylvania. He was the designer but not the architect of record for the church. Other churches that he designed include the Greater Nebo Baptist Church (1962) and the Tabernacle Baptist Church (1985), both in Dayton. He is a member of the latter.

Clarence Cross married Mary Elizabeth Thompson on April 11, 1953. They had no children. He and his wife (who is not a Tuskegee Institute graduate) were founding members of the Dayton, Ohio, Tuskegee Alumni Club. Cross donated the initial gift of books to establish the nucleus of the Tuskegee Institute architectural library. In 1964 Cross also established the Milton Love Prize, in memory of his favorite teacher, which is given each year to the graduating senior showing the most potential in architecture. On two occasions prior to 1981, he furnished the funds for two $400 competition prizes for students in architecture.

At the height of the civil rights movement in Dayton, Cross became a member of the West Side Citizens Council, Congress of Racial Equality, and the Dayton Alliance for Racial Equality. Cross's other memberships include the Dayton chapter of the American Institute of Architects, Ohio Society of Architects, National Trust for Historic Preservation, and Ohio Association of Railroad Passengers, and he is a life member of Tuskegee University Alumni Association.

Notes
1. State of Ohio Board of Examiners of Architects, "Clarence Cross," Certificate no. A5802839, issued 24 January 1958.
2. State of Indiana Board of Registration for Architects and Landscape Architects, "Clarence Cross," Certificate no. AR00031521, issued 29 December 1960.

Bibliography
"Clarence Cross." In *Who's Who in the Midwest*. Chicago: Marquis Who's Who, Inc, 1972–73, 1974–75, and 1976–77.

CLARENCE CROSS
DAYTON, OHIO

BUILDING LIST

Name	Address	City	State	Year	Comments
Charles Drew Health Center	1323 W. 3rd St	Dayton	OH		
Dayton Fire Station No. 13	1723 W. 3rd St.	Dayton	OH		
Dayton Rapid Transit Office & Garage		Dayton	OH	1971	
Greater Int. Nebo Baptist Church	172 Colgate Ave.	Dayton	OH	1962	
Model Cities Neighborhood Center	1520 Germantown Ave.	Dayton	OH	1971	
Second Baptist Church	4th Ave.	Ford City	PA	1958	
Southwest Shopping Center		Dayton	OH		
Tabernacle Baptist Church	380 S. Broadway St.	Dayton	OH	1958	
Tabernacle Baptist Church Parks Copeland Bldg.		Dayton	OH	1985	

William Jefferson Decatur
(1874–unknown)

Judith Jones

William Jefferson Decatur was born on October 16, 1874, in Atlanta, Georgia. His parents were Isaac and Olivia North Decatur. He received a bachelor of arts degree from Atlanta University in 1899 and took courses at the University of Chicago.

From 1899 to 1901, Decatur was assistant superintendent of industries at Tougaloo College in Mississippi. The school was administered under the auspices of the American Missionary Association. From 1901 to 1904, he was superintendent of industries at Talladega College in Alabama, which was the *alma mater* of his father-in-law, Jefferson Davenport Ish. From 1904 to 1905, Decatur was an architect and builder in Atlanta, Georgia. Decatur's best-known building is the Henry A. Rucker Building (1906) at the corner of Auburn and Piedmont Avenues within the Martin Luther King Jr. Historic District.[1] The building is named for the prominent Negro Republican who served as Georgia's federal tax collector at the turn of the twentieth century. The Rucker Building was the first Black-owned and Black-designed office building in Atlanta. Decatur and his partner William Long were contractors for the building.

From 1906 to 1912, William Decatur was an instructor in the School of Applied Sciences at HOWARD UNIVERSITY. On September 9, 1908, he married Harriett Mae Ish of Little Rock, Arkansas. No children were born to their union. In 1912 Decatur was director of vocations at Wilberforce University in Ohio. In 1912, he became principal of Manassas Industrial School in Virginia. The last information found on Decatur was that in 1927 he was president of the Colored Industrial School of Cincinnati, Ohio.

Note
1. "African American Architects and Builders/Contractors in Georgia," Office of Historic Preservation, George Department of Natural Resources, Atlanta.

Bibliography
Mather, Frank Lincoln. *Who's Who of the Colored Race*. vol. 1. Detroit: Gale Research Co., 1915.

MAISAH B. ROBINSON, PH.D.,
ATLANTA, GEORGIA

Rucker Building, *Georgia Department of Natural Resources, Historic Preservation Division, 1993. Jim Lockhart*

BUILDING LIST

Name	Address	City	State	Year	Comments
Rucker Bldg.	Auburn & Piedmont Aves.	Atlanta	GA	1906	Demolished

Henry Beard Delany
(1858–1928)

New York Public Library

Henry Beard Delany was born a slave on February 5, 1858 in Saint Mary's, Georgia, the son of Thomas Delany, a ship and house carpenter, and Sarah, a house slave on the rock plantation. During his childhood, the family moved to Fernandina, Florida, where he worked on his father's farm, learned bricklaying and plastering, and attended a school supported by the Freedmen's Bureau. Henry Delany and his brothers all learned a trade. Following in the shoes of one of his older brothers, he became a mason. Henry Delany enrolled at Saint Augustine's School in Raleigh, North Carolina, in 1881, where he studied theology and graduated from the academic course in 1885. He remained at Saint Augustine's as a faculty member until 1908, teaching music and religion; he was also chaplain, vice principal (1889–1908), and supervisor of building projects.

On October 6, 1886, Henry Delany married Nannie James Logan of Danville, Virginia, who taught home economics and domestic science at Saint Augustine's. Delany Residence Hall (c1929) was named in recognition of her fifty-year association with the school. Their ten children, all born on Saint Augustine's campus, became teachers, doctors, lawyers, and dentists. In 1993, two daughters, Sadie and Bessie, published their autobiography of the Delany family, *Having Our Say—The Delany Sisters' First 100 Years*, which became a popular Broadway play.[1]

On June 7, 1889, Henry Delany was ordained a deacon in Raleigh's Ambrose Episcopal Church, where he assisted in services and was ordained a priest in 1892. Representing the Diocese of North Carolina, he was a member of the Commission for Work among Colored People from 1889 to 1904, visiting congregations in North Carolina counties and assisting in organizing schools for Blacks. He also made monthly visits to prisoners in the county workhouse. In 1908 he was named archdeacon for Negro work in the diocese, necessitating his resignation from Saint Augustine's faculty; however, the family continued to live on the campus where Nannie Delany was a teacher and matron. Shaw University awarded Henry Delaney an honorary doctor of divinity degree in 1911.

On May 15, 1918, Delany was unanimously elected suffragan bishop in charge of Negro work in the Diocese of North Carolina. He was the first African American bishop elected in North Carolina and only the second in the nation.

Saint Augustine's Chapel was designed by Delany in 1895. During construction he served as a mason and quarry master. The chapel was built with student labor. The stone was quarried from a site on campus. The original design was a rectangular stone structure with a tower. It was modified with a north transept in 1904. The tower was replaced by a transept in 1917.

The interior of the chapel continues the strong medieval feel of the exterior and features an impressive stone altar separated from the pulpit by an arch stone balustrade. The marble mansa contains five circles—symbolic of the body wounds on Christ. Each circle contains stones brought from Mantime Prison in Rome and the Appian Way. The chapel also has a font

Taylor Hall, Saint Augustine's College,
Saint Augustine College

pool and baptismal pool. Diamond-paned and multi-colored leaded glass windows punctuate the walls and carry inscriptions commemorating Saint Augustine's most influential faculty and benefactors, including Henry Delany.

The chapel is the oldest of three nineteenth-century buildings on the campus that were designed by Delany. Taylor Hall was built in two parts. Delany and his students built the first section, Benson Library, in 1898 as an L-shaped stone structure. In 1902 the rectangular stone structure on the west end was added and named Taylor Hall. The name came to indicate the entire building after the construction of the second Benson Library.

Saint Agnes Hospital dates from 1909 and is a 3-story stone cruciform structure that served as a hospital until 1961. For many years it was the only hospital for Blacks in North Carolina. The hospital was designed by Paul A. Davis of Philadelphia, with Delaney serving as on-site architect and construction supervisor.

Henry Delany died in 1928, at his home on Saint Augustine's campus. His funeral was conducted in Saint Augustine's Chapel, which he had designed. He was buried in Mount Hope Cemetery in Raleigh, North Carolina.

Note
1. Sarah Delany and A. Elizabeth Delany, *Having Our Say—The Delany Sisters' First 100 Years* (New York: Kodansha America, 1993), p. 26.

Bibliography
Davis, Lenwood G. *A Travel Guide to Black Historical Sites and Landmarks in North Carolina.* Winston-Salem: Bandit Books, 1991.

Henry, Phillip N. *The Heritage of Blacks in North Carolina.* Charlotte: The African American Heritage Foundation, 1990.

Jones, Alice Eley. *African American Builders and Architects in North Carolina, 1526–1998.* Raleigh: Preservation North Carolina, 1998.

Simmons-Henry, Linda, and Linda H. Edminsten. *Culture Town-Life in Raleigh's African American Communities.* Raleigh: Historic Districts Commission, 1993.

ALICE ELEY JONES, AUTHOR AND OWNER
OF HISTORICALLY SPEAKING

BUILDING LIST

Name	Address	City	State	Year	Comments
St. Augustine's, Benson Library	Campus	Raleigh	NC	1898	
St. Augustine's, Chapel	Campus	Raleigh	NC	1895	
St. Augustine's, Taylor Hall	Campus	Raleigh	NC	1902	Addition

Charles Edgar Dickinson
(1908–1964)

Lincoln Collection, Page Library

Charles E. Dickinson was born in Columbus, Ohio, on August 12, 1908, to Charles and Jessie Dickinson. He had one brother, Jessie Dickinson Jr., who became an attorney in Milwaukee, Wisconsin. During his childhood, Charles worked alongside his father on landscaping jobs. He attended public schools in Columbus, Ohio.[1] He received a bachelor of landscape architecture degree in 1930, a master of science in landscape architecture in 1945, and a doctor of philosophy degree in 1950, all from Ohio State University.[2] Dickinson served as an instructor and campus landscape architect at Palmer Memorial Institute, a day and boarding school in Sedalia, North Carolina, and taught at TUSKEGEE INSTITUTE from 1931 to 1932 and at South Carolina State University in Orangeburg from 1934 to 1940.[3]

Dickinson was a professor of horticulture in the Agricultural Department and campus landscape architect at Lincoln University of Missouri from December 1940 to November 1964. He was a familiar figure on Lincoln's campus, planning much of the landscape around Richardson's Fine Arts Center, Jason Gymnasium, and the Student Center, and designing the greenhouse where flora horticulture was taught.[4] Dickinson planted Norfolk pines near the main entrance of Lincoln University, which remained for many years until they were dug up for security purposes in the 1980s. The silver maples that he planted can still be seen on the campus. Dickinson also designed most of the flower gardens on campus, and was the consultant landscape architect for Page Library, collaborating with LOUIS EDWIN FRY SR., who was the architect for the library. He also served as a consultant landscape architect on city-sponsored projects in the "Brothel"—a very impoverished area in southeast Missouri. In addition, Dickinson collaborated on the landscape design for the Young Mens Christian Association building in Jefferson City, Missouri.[5]

Dickinson was known throughout the university community for his expertise and creativity, as well as his versatility, efficiency, knowledge, productiveness, and cooperativeness. The Horticultural Building—Dickinson Research Center—was named in his honor. According to his students and colleagues, he was quiet, reserved, and professional. George Enlow, who was one of his first students at Lincoln University and became a teacher of horticulture at Grambling University, stated that Dickinson was an excellent instructor.[6] Dickinson's contemporary, Lucius Jones, told of how Dickinson helped him to plant trees in such a way that the boundaries of the house he bought were marked.[7] Dickinson brought the trees from his house and planted them in Jones's yard. He used chicken manure to fertilize the trees.

Dickinson was one of the founders of the Hawthorne Club of Jefferson City, which was very much involved with horticulture and floriculture. He assisted many local residents with landscaping their homes and never charged for any of the work or ad-

123

CHARLES EDGAR DICKINSON

Lincoln University campus, *Lincoln Collection, Page Library*

vice he gave to the community or its residents. He also planted and grew Poinsettias, which he gave away to university staff each Christmas. At university convocations and programs, his Poinsettias customarily adorned the auditorium stage.

Charles Dickinson married Edith Waterman of Orangeburg, South Carolina. She worked for the state of Missouri for many years. They did not have any children, but nieces and nephews were always visiting.

In 1964 Charles Dickinson was entering his twenty-fourth year on the faculty at Lincoln University when he suffered a fatal heart attack at the age of fifty-six.

Notes

1. Interview with Gracie Dawson (librarian of Page Library at Lincoln University), Jefferson City, Mo., 10 October 2002.
2. *The Makio, Ohio State University Yearbook*, "Charles E. Dickinson" (Columbus: Ohio State University, 1930), p. 372.
3. "Charles Dickinson," Tuskegee Institute Archives, Tuskegee, Ala.
4. Interivew with Lucius Jones (Lincoln University printer), Jefferson City, Mo., 11 September 2002.
5. Interview with George Enlow (professor of Horticulture), Lincoln University, Jefferson City, Mo., 26 September 2002.
6. Ibid.
7. Lucius Jones interview.

Bibliography

Testimonial Banquet, "In Memory of Charles E. Dickinson." Ethnic Studies Center, Lincoln University, Jefferson City, Mo., 19 November 1964.

ELIZABETH WILSON,
LIBRARIAN, PAGE LIBRARY, LINCOLN UNIVERSITY

LANDSCAPE PROJECT LIST

Name	Address	City	State	Year	Comments
Jones, Lucius	1006 Lafayette St.	Jefferson City	MO	1954	
Lincoln University Fine Arts Center	Campus	Jefferson City	MO	1958	
Lincoln University Greenhouse	Campus	Jefferson City	MO	1952	
Lincoln University Jason Gym	Campus	Jefferson City	MO	1959	
Lincoln University Scruggs Student Center	Campus	Jefferson City	MO	1964	

Clyde Martin Drayton
(1915–1983)

Quincy Drayton

Clyde Martin Drayton was born on March 1, 1915, in Southern Pines, North Carolina. Drayton graduated from Armstrong Technical High School in Washington, D.C., in 1932. From there he entered HOWARD UNIVERSITY School of Architecture and Engineering in 1935. After graduating from Howard University, Drayton found gainful employment as a draftsman for ALBERT IRVIN CASSELL in Washington, D.C. For twelve years Drayton "had a very important part in the designing and the supervising to completion of approximately ten million dollars ($10,000,000) worth of construction."[1] The projects ranged from vocational schools, housing developments, and shopping centers to children's clinics, religious buildings, and houses. After years of busy and detailed work as a draftsman and privately heading a small architecture practice, Drayton founded the Clyde Drayton Architectural Firm in 1942. He also worked for LOUIS EDWIN FRY SR. "Drayton designed numerous commercial establishments in Washington, D.C., including Blackie's House of Beef and Ed Murphy's Supper Club on Georgia Ave."[2] Two notable houses designed by Drayton were the L. M. Bevins residence on Irving Street, NW, and the Julius Bryan residence on Hamilton Street, NE. He was the recipient of the Capitol Hill Society's Restoration of the Year Award.

Drayton worshipped at Galbraith African Methodist Episcopal Church in the District of Columbia and was a member of the NATIONAL TECHNICAL ASSOCIATION and Shepard Park Civic Assocation.

Due to failing health, Drayton closed his office in 1966, but continued to work from his home until he died of cardiac arrest at Howard University Hospital on March 12, 1983. Survivors included his wife, Etta Katherine Izzard Drayton, a D.C. public school principal; two children, Joyce Ann Love and Clyde M. Drayton Jr.; two grandsons; and six great-grandchildren.

Notes
1. D.C. Board of Examiners and Registrars of Architects, "Clyde Martin Drayton," Certificate no. 1415, issued 6 December 1951.
2. "Clyde Martin Drayton," *Washington Afro-American*, 26 March 1983, p. 15.

L. ROGER WATSON III, ARCHITECT INTERN,
STOIBER & ASSOCIATES, WASHINGTON, D.C.

Julius O. Bryan House, *L. Roger Watson*

BUILDING LIST

Name	Address	City	State	Year	Comments
Bethelem Baptist Church	2458 King Jr. Dr., SE	Washington	DC	1954	
Bevins, L. M.	1427 Irving St., NW	Washington	DC	1954	
Brown, W. T.	4916 Blaine St., NE	Washington	DC	1950	
Bryan, Julius D.	1403 Hamilton St., NE	Washington	DC	1949	
Collins, Lawrence		Brentwood	MD	1948	Shopping center & apts.
Conway Hotel		Colton Pt.	MD	1945	
Fides Settlement House	219 I St., NW	Washington	DC		
Files, Herbert	123 50th St., NE	Washington	DC	1944	
Gibson, T. J.	4018 Lane St., NE	Washington	DC	1950	
Gregg, William H.	5200 E. Capitol St., SE	Washington	DC	1950	
Jones, D.		Ardmore	MD	1944	
Keister, J. B.		Camp Springs	MD	1950	Rental housing
Minter, Sylvester	1400 Jackson St., NW	Washington	DC	1960	
Newman Club	2417 1st St., NW	Washington	DC	1951	
Pendleton, William H.	5333 Blaine St., NE	Washington	DC	1949	
Woods, Lawrence	4319 Anacostia Ave., NE	Washington	DC	1948	

Charles Sumner Duke
(1879–1952)

Amy Duke Billingsley

Charles S. Duke was born on July 21, 1879, in Selma, Alabama. His father, Jesse Chisholm Duke, who had been born a slave, was owner, publisher, and editor of *The Herald* newspaper. Charles's mother, Willie Black Duke, was from a prominent family of entrepreneurs. His maternal grandfather, Harrison Black, a slave and a master carpenter, built plantation houses and churches throughout Demopolis, Alabama. The Dukes had more means than most African American families in that day and time, and could afford domestic help and private schools for Charles and his siblings. However, the family, including Charles and his siblings, David, Edward, Thomas, Ester, and Rosebud, were forced to flee for their lives from a lynch mob when Jesse Duke published a fiery editorial decrying lynching.[1] They safely reached Pine Bluff, Arkansas, and settled there.

Charles Duke fought racial discrimination by setting an example. He completed high school and earned a bachelor's degree from Branch Normal College, which is now Arkansas Agricultural & Mechanical College. He also took classes at HOWARD UNIVERSITY and Phillips Exeter, a prestigious private preparatory school in Exeter, New Hampshire. At Phillips Exeter, Duke became president of the debate team, a member of the Honor Society, and the first Black graduate, in 1901. Later, in 1904, he was the first African American to earn a bachelor of arts degree in mathematics from Harvard University and was also the first African American to earn a master of science degree in civil engineering from the University of Wisconsin in 1913.

The early 1900s offered few professional job opportunities for an African American architectural engineer. Therefore, in the fall of 1907, Duke became the principal of Public School No. 19 in Indianapolis, Indiana. It was one of the first Indiana public schools for the education of Black children. On June 11, 1908, Duke married the former Estelle Taylor of Saginaw, Michigan, and later that year found a job with the Chicago Northwestern Railroad as a foreman engineer to assist with the design of new freight lines. A year after that, he became the engineer in charge of the $1.5-million Southwest Land and Lake Tunnel in Lake Michigan for George Jackson Company of Chicago.

In August 1913 the City of Chicago Department of Public Works hired Duke as the first African American engineer draftsman. In December 1920 Duke completed the sixteen-hour written exam to become licensed in the state of Illinois with dual registration in architecture and engineering.[2] Duke enlisted in the all-Negro 8th Regiment of the Illinois National Guard in 1916. Brigadier General John "Black Jack" Pershing commanded the infantry division across the border and into Mexico in pursuit of bandit/revolutionary Pancho Villa.

In 1922 Duke established a private consulting firm specializing in architectural engineering. Duke engineered three Christian Science churches and a nursing home for the elderly in association with architect Charles Draper Faulkner (1890–1979).[3] As an architectural engineer, Duke designed hotels, churches, and houses in Chicago. He was the project engineer

Shiloh Seventh Day Adventist Church, *Estelle Taylor Duke*

for the 8-story Knights of Pythias building that was designed by WALTER THOMAS BAILEY. The $1-million structure was the first Black-owned and -financed high-rise in Chicago.

During his career, Duke made it his mission to help African Americans who were living in poverty by campaigning for better housing. In 1926 Chicago mayor Bill Thompson appointed Duke to the Chicago Zoning Commission—its only African American member. He was appointed to the President's Commission on Public Housing in 1928. In that role, Duke helped to secure funds to design and build the first public housing project in Chicago, the Ida B. Wells Homes, named for the African American journalist and civil rights pioneer.

On August 24, 1929, Duke convened a national meeting of Negro architects, engineers, and scientists to form the NATIONAL TECHNICAL ASSOCIATION "as a minority voice for excellence in mathematics, science, engineering and technology."[4] As its first president, Duke worked to encourage African Americans to enter technical fields, to support them in their careers, and to expand their professional opportunities. For Chicago's Century of Progress World's Fair in 1933, Charles Duke, assisted by his wife, designed a replica of the De Saible Cabin, a log cabin built by Black Frenchman Jean Pointe Baptist De Saible, the first permanent settler in the territory that became Chicago.

When the Great Depression forced Duke to close his practice, he went to work for the U.S. Resettlement Bureau, Homestead Subsistence Division in Washington, D.C. He supervised one of the largest staffs of Black architects and engineers in the United States. They prepared master plans and designed federally subsidized public housing throughout the South, including the Homestead Project in Hampton, Virginia, designed by HILYARD ROBERT ROBINSON and now known as Aberdeen Gardens.

In 1946 Duke became a supervising engineer with the Public Works Administration in the Virgin Islands. He oversaw a $10-million, five-year capital improvement project that included the construction of a potable water route, a sewer system, two health clinics, hospitals, a high school, and the first highway in Saint John. The "Duke Catchment" in Saint Thomas is a landmark of his legacy.

In March 1952, Duke revived his private practice in Chicago. Three months later, on June 11, he died from a blood clot following surgery for cancer at the Mayo Clinic in Rochester, Minnesota. In his honor, almost three decades later, Chicago mayor Jane Byrne proclaimed August 14, 1980, "Charles Duke Day."

Notes

1. Allen Jones, "The Black Press in the New South," *The Journal of Negro History* (Summer 1979): 215.
2. Illinois record of engineers examination and license applications, "Charles S. Duke," no. 991, issued 13 December 1920. State of Illinois Archives.
3. Charles Draper Faulkner was the architect and Duke was the architectural engineer for First Church of Christ Scientist, Montclair, New Jersey; Fourth Church of Christ Scientist, Milwaukee, Wisconsin; First Church of Christ Scientist, Muskegan, Michigan; and the Oakhaven Old People's Home, Chicago,

Illinois, included in Charles Draper Faulkner's *Christian Science Church Edifices* (Chicago: Charles Draper Faulkner, 1946).

4. Jesse C. Duke (son), p. 3 (typescript). In the possession of Amy Billingsley, Washington, D.C.

Bibliography

Carter, Elmer A. "Charles Sumner Duke, C.E." *Opportunity Magazine* (April 1942): 16.

"Charles S. Duke." *Journal of Negro Life* (April 1932): 117.

Hewes, Harry. "Noted Engineer Builds Memorial to His Genius in Isles." *Chicago Defender,* 4 June 1949, p. 13.

Fiftieth Anniversary Report. Harvard University. Class of 1905 report, "Charles Sumner Duke." Cambridge, Mass.: Harvard University, 1956, p. 149.

Downing, L.K. "Engineer-Elder Statesman-Student Advisor." *National Technical Association Journal* 3, no. 2 (Fall 1952): 8.

Duke, Charles S. "The Negro Technical Worker." *Opportunity Magazine* (April 1941): 100.

BONITA BILLINGSLEY HARRIS,
GREAT GRANDDAUGHTER, CHEASPEAKE, VIRGINIA

BUILDING LIST

Name	Address	City	State	Year	Comments
92nd Street Bridge	Over Chicago River	Chicago	IL	1914	
Becker Brothers Photographic Studio	2448 W. 63rd St.	Chicago	IL		Demolished
Chicago Avenue Bridge	Over Chicago River	Chicago	IL	1914	
Coastline Apts.	73rd & Lake Michigan Dr.	Chicago	IL		
De Saible Log Cabin	26th St. at Lake Michigan	Chicago	IL	1933	Chicago World's Fair
First Church of Christ, Scientist	8 Hillside Ave.	Montclair	NJ	1927	
First Church of Christ, Scientist	280 W. Muskegon Ave.	Muskegan	MI	1931	
Fourth Church of Christ, Scientist	Downer Ave. & Kenwood Blvd.	Milwaukee	WI	1931	
Grand Avenue Bridge	Over Chicago River	Chicago	IL	1913	
Hedges-Rayfield Motor Co.	9070 S. Chicago Ave.	Chicago	IL	1933	Demolished
Jackson Boulevard Bridge	Over Chicago River	Chicago	IL	1916	
Lake Street Bridge	Over Chicago River	Chicago	IL	1916	
Oakhaven Old People's Home	113th Pl. & Western Ave.	Chicago	IL	1922	
People's Church & Metropolitan Community Center	Pershing Rd. & Vernon Ave.	Chicago	IL		
Sheridan Beach Hotel	7301 N. Sheridan Rd.	Chicago	IL	1923	
Shiloh Seventh Day Adventist Church	4559 S. St. Lawrence Ave.	Chicago	IL	1925	Now Mt. Eagle M. B. Church
Southwest Land & Lake Tunnel	68th St. & Lake Michigan	Chicago	IL	1814	
Tudor Apts.	66th & Yale Ave.	Chicago	IL	1921	
Walters African Methodist Episcopal Zion Church	38th & Dearborn Sts.	Chicago	IL	1914	Demolished
Washington Boulevard Apts.	2547 W. Washington Blvd.	Chicago	IL		Demolished
Washington Street Bridge	Over Chicago River	Chicago	IL	1913	
Webster Avenue Bridge	Over Chicago River	Chicago	IL	1916	
Ida B. Wells Homes	454 E. Pershing Rd.	Chicago	IL	1941	

DeWitt Sanford Dykes Sr.
(1903–1991)

DeWitt Sanford Dykes Jr. Collection

DeWitt S. Dykes Sr., before becoming an architect at age fifty-one, served as an ordained minister and administrator in the Methodist church. He was born on August 16, 1903, in Gladsden, Alabama. His parents were Henry Sanford Roland Dykes and Mary Anna Wade Dykes. Henry Dykes earned his living as a brick mason and served as a lay minister in the Methodist church. Mary Anna Dykes kept house and cared for their six children. DeWitt was the fifth of six children and second oldest son. By the early 1910s, the Dykes family had relocated to Newport, Tennessee, where DeWitt received his early education.

Henry Dykes trained his sons in brick masonry. DeWitt was a quick learner and became an experienced brick mason by age fourteen. His interest in masonry construction led to his desire to become an architect. Henry Dykes was skeptical that his son could earn a living as an architect because of racial discrimination and the undependable support of Black individuals and institutions. As a result, DeWitt Dykes chose the Christian ministry as a profession.

DeWitt Dykes received most of his education at schools supported by the Methodist church. From 1919 to 1926, Dykes studied in the pre-college division of Morristown Normal & Industrial College in Morristown, Tennessee, which was managed by the Freedmen's Aid and Southern Education Society. He then entered another Freedmen's Aid school, Clark University in Atlanta, Georgia, receiving an *artrius* bachelor's degree in 1930. During his junior and senior years at Clark University, Dykes studied at Gammon Theological Seminary, another Freemen's Aid school in Atlanta, from which he received a bachelor of divinity degree in 1931. Recipient of a scholarship, Dykes entered the graduate program at Boston University School of Theology and earned a sacred theology master's degree in 1932. While he was studying to become a minister, Dykes earned money as a brick mason. During a summer stint in Detroit, Michigan, in 1925, he studied drafting at Cass Technical High School's evening school.

In November 1932 Dykes married Violet Thomasine Anderson in Bristol, Virginia. She was one of DeWitt's classmates at Morristown College's high school. DeWitt and Violet became the parents of Reida and DeWitt Jr., who became a librarian and history professor, respectively. In 1943 Violet Dykes died from inadequate health care. Seven years later, DeWitt married Viola Gertrude Logan, a principal in the Knoxville, Tennessee, public school system.

From 1932 to 1954, Reverend DeWitt Dykes was the pastor of churches in the East Tennessee Annual Conference of the Methodist church. Shortly after moving to Knoxville, Tennessee, in 1946, to supplement his income, he worked as a brick mason on several buildings designed by locally prominent White architect Francis F. Painter. In March 1951 Dykes was employed as an instructor in masonry in the vocational program of Austin High School in Knoxville. He taught Negro veterans in evening school until April 1953.

Mount Zion Baptist Church, *DeWitt Sanford Dykes Jr. Collection*

Starting in 1954, Dykes worked as an administrator for the United Methodist denomination. He became a staff member of the Division of Missions, Section of Church Extension, Department of Finance and Field Service from January 1956 until his retirement in 1968. Dykes was responsible for determining the financial feasibility of constructing Methodist churches, evaluating building sites, analyzing Building and Zoning Codes, performing design reviews, supervising construction, and administering payment draws. Because Dykes was not registered, Dykes submitted floor plans that he had prepared to the director of the Department of Architecture, Norman G. Byar, who was a licensed architect in the Philadelphia office of the Division of Missions. During his years with the Division of Missions, Dykes designed seventy-two Methodist churches and other religious buildings, as well as a community fire hall in Frakes, Kentucky.[1] Independent of the Methodist church, Dykes designed six churches under the license of Knoxville engineer Milo C. Fear. In 1960 Dykes took courses in architecture from the International Correspondence School of Scranton, Pennsylvania, and received a certificate of completion in 1965.

In 1968 Dykes took the oral part of the examination to become a registered architect. A year later, he took the written examination in building construction and professional administration. He became a registered architect in the state of Tennessee on March 5, 1970, and was also accepted into membership of the American Institute of Architects in 1970.[2] He gained his registration in the state of Virginia in 1973.

Dykes practiced from an office in his home on Dandridge Avenue in Knoxville from 1970 to 1976. He moved his practice to several office buildings from 1976 to 1986, occasionally apprenticing architectural students from the University of Tennessee. Dykes designed three churches in Knoxville for African American clients, a mortuary, and several public buildings. He also competed for pubic building commissions and was awarded several contracts. The last building he designed was a day-care center in 1988.

Dykes's health steadily declined in the late 1980s and he died peacefully at home in Knoxville on August 4, 1991.

Notes
1. Bill Dockery, "Born to Build: The Architectural Career of DeWitt Dykes, Sr.," *The Appalachian Magazine* (spring 1999): 9.
2. Tennessee Board of Architectural and Engineering Examiners, "DeWitt S. Dykes," Certificate no. 7209, issued 5 March 1970.

Bibliography
Smith, Jessie C. *Notable Black American Men*. Detroit: Gale Research, 1999.

DE WITT SANFORD DYKES JR.,
PROFESSOR OF HISTORY, OAKLAND UNIVERSITY

DEWITT SANFORD DYKES SR.

BUILDING LIST

Name	Address	City	State	Year	Comments
Alexander Chapel Methodist Church	1 Moon St.	Cartersville	GA	1962	
Asbury Methodist Church	4810 Narrow Paved Rd.	Lynchburg	SC	1961	
Bass Chapel Methodist Church Education Bldg.	5064 Bass Chapel Rd.	Greensboro	NC	1963	Demolished
Bentley Street Christian Church	417 Bentley	Knoxville	TN	1966	
Bethel Methodist Church	331 N. Mechanic St.	Pendleton	SC	1961	
Bethlehem Methodist Church		Bay Spring	MS	1957	
Brooks Temple Methodist Church		Midway	NC	1959	
Burns Methodist Church	5616 Farrow Rd.	Columbia	SC	1963	
Canaan Methodist Church	171 Hwy 61	Ridgeville	SC	1967	
Centenary Methodist Church	830 S. 6th St.	Hartsville	SC	1962	
Central Valley Methodist Church		Central Valley	CA	1959	
Cherry Hill Methodist Church	3225 Round Rd.	Baltimore	MD	1962	
Clinton Chapel African Methodist Episcopal Zion Church	546 College Ave.	Knoxville	TN	1977	
Community Methodist Church	136 Carver Rd.	Staunton	VA	1962	
County Line Methodist Church		County Line	GA	1962	
Dykes, DeWitt S.	2139 Dandridge Ave.	Knoxville	TN	1953	
Emmanuel Methodist Church	17th & York Sts.	Philadelphia	PA	1965	Alterations
Emmanuel Presbyterian Church	3023 Selma Ave.	Knoxville	TN	1964	
Fairlee Methodist Church Parsonage		Chestertown	MD	1964	
Flat Rock Methodist Church	4250 Flat Rock Rd.	Lithhonia	GA	1966	
Frakes, Kentucky Fire Station	Henderson Settlement	Frakes	KY	1967	
Friendship Methodist Church		Ehrhardt	SC	1962	
Golden Age Retirement Village	1109 Beaman Lake Rd.	Knoxville	TN	1982	Community Tectonics, assoc. architects
Grace Methodist Church	1711 Albany St.	Brunswick	GA	1963	
Grace Methodist Church	3145 Washington St., SW	Covington	GA	1966	
Green Pond Methodist Church	1045 E. Hwy 55	Clover	SC	1962	
Greenville Methodist Church	353 Maple Branch Rd.	Reevesville	SC	1963	
Harris Methodist Church	4601 Old Cusseta Rd.	Columbus	GA	1963	
Harris Temple Methodist Church	7915 Flower Ave.	Tampa	FL	1962	
Haven Chapel Methodist Church	220 Raccon Valley Rd.	Powell	TN	1966	
Hopewell Methodist Church	103 Mine St.	Jefferson	SC	1958	
Hopewell Methodist Church		Village Springs	AL	1963	
Howard Chapel Methodist Church	508 S. Washington St.	Dublin	GA	1967	
Jerusalem Methodist Church	Hwy 501 & Jerusalem Church Rd.	Laurinburg	NC	1966	
John Wesley Methodist Church		Easley	SC	1967	
John Wesley Methodist Church		Pinnopolis	SC	1967	
Johnson Recreation Center	507 Mulvaney St.	Knoxville	TN	1977	Addition
Laughlin Memorial Methodist Church	1417 Huffine Rd.	Greensboro	NC	1967	
Lenon-Seney United Methodist Church Sanctuary	2049 Dandridge Ave.	Knoxville	TN	1976	
Lentral Valley Methodist Church		Central Valley	CA	1959	
Logan Temple African Methodist Episcopal Zion Church	2744 Selma Ave.	Knoxville	TN	1963	
Lonsdale Day Care Center	1212 New York Ave.	Knoxville	TN	1988	
Martin Chapel Methodist Church	1746 Ohio Ave.	Knoxville	TN	1960	
McKendree Methodist Church	205 Paca St.	Cumberland	MD	1962	
McQueens Chapel Methodist Church	629 6th Ave. Dr. SW	Conover	NC	1958	Plans only
Mechanicsville Methodist Church	184 Lake Ashwood Rd.	Mechanicsville	SC	1961	
Mt. Calvary Baptist Church	1807 Dandridge Ave.	Knoxville	TN	1974	
Mt. Carmel Methodist Church Education Bldg.		Bamburg	SC	1962	
Mt. Olive Baptist Church	1601 Dandridge Ave.	Knoxville	TN	1969	
Mt. Nebo Baptist Church	1183 Bills Creek Rd.	Lake Lure	NC	1964	
Mt. Nebo Methodist Church	9975 NW 143rd St.	Alachua	FL	1967	
Mt. Pleasant Methodist Church	2010 Lincoln Ave.	Opa Locka	FL	1959	Plans only
Mt. Pleasant Methodist Church		Basin	MS	1960	
Mt. Pleasant Sayreton Methodist Church	4048 Church St. N.	Sayreton	AL	1964	
Mt. Tabor Methodist Church Education Bldg.	3100 Freeman Mill Rd.	Greensboro	NC	1964	

BUILDING LIST (continued)

Name	Address	City/Twp.	State	Year	Comments
Mt. Vernon Salem Methodist Church	3302 Church Hill Rd.	Church Hill	MD	1961	
Mt. Zion Methodist Church	1000 Cedar St.	Pocomoke City	MD	1961	
New Hope Methodist Church	301 SE 2nd Ave.	Hawthorne	FL	1964	
Philadelphia Methodist Church	157 Philadelphia Dr.	Rockingham	NC	1958	
Pleasant Hill Methodist Church	119 Dorsey Dr.	Villa Rica	GA	1963	
Riley Chapel Methodist Church		Handsboro	MS	1959	
Salem Methodist Church Education Bldg.	Claussen Rd.	Florence	SC	1962	
Seney Chapel Methodist Church		Knoxville	TN	1965	
Sertoma Sunshine Center	2335 Dandridge Ave.	Knoxville	TN	1976	Eugene Burr, assoc. architect
Shiloh Presbyterian Church	904 Biddle	Knoxville	TN	1967	
Simpson Memorial Methodist Church	1144 W 6th St.	Riveria Beach	FL	1960	
Smith Chapel Methodist Church	3225 Pacific Ave.	Austell	GA	1962	
St. James East Thomas Methodist Church	701 11th Gouroute W.	Birmingham	AL	1960	
St. James Methodist Church	920 Main St., N.	Warrior	AL	1967	
St. Mark's Methodist Church		DeKalb	MS	1956	Plans only
St. Matthew's Methodist Church	Somerton Rd. & Paris Ave	Trevose Twp.	PA	1959	
St. Paul Methodist Church	NE Cr. Hwys. 43 & 14	Eutaw	AL	1960	
St. Paul Methodist Church	310 Main St.	Stevenson	AL	1962	
St. Stephens Methodist Church	213 Yazoo St.	Yazoo City	MS	1959	
St. Stephens Methodist Church	600 Highway St.	Madison	NC	1960	
St. Stephens Methodist Church	303 W. Center St.	Hastings	FL	1967	
Tiller's Chapel Methodist Church	9240 County Rd. 22	Centre	AL	1959	Now St. Marks Methodist Episcopal Church
Trinity Methodist Church	2979 Lincoln Blvd.	Ft. Meyers	FL	1962	
Trinity Methodist Church	528 Maxwell Ave.	Greenwood	SC	1966	
Trinity Methodist Church	520 S. Sanford Ave.	Sanford	FL	1967	
Trinity Methodist Church Education Bldg.		Camden	SC	1962	
Union Wesley Methodist Church	RD 365	Clarksville	DE	1958	
Unionville Methodist Church	971 High Falls Park Rd.	Unionville	GA	1961	
Unity Mortuary	1425 McCalla Ave.	Knoxville	TN	1978	
Wesley Methodist Church		Carthage	MS	1957	
Wesley Methodist Church	1008 Hwy 315	Branceville	SC	1963	
World's Fair Merchanding and Snack Shops	913 Clinch Ave.	Knoxville	TN	1982	Relocated to Water Wonderland in Texas
Wrights Chapel Methodist Church	2133 32nd Ave. N.	Birmingham	AL	1962	

Gaston Alonzo Edwards
(1875–1943)

Hazel Ruth Edwards

Gaston Alonzo Edwards was born in Belvoir, Chatham County, North Carolina, on April 12, 1875. He was one of six children of Mary Edwards and William Gaston Snipes. She was Black and he was White. Like many African Americans born in rural nineteenth-century towns, he lived in humble conditions and began working at an early age to help support the family. He cut wheat by day and hair by night to earn money toward his college education. His travels often led him past the Chatham County Courthouse in Pittsboro. His passion for the building's classical design inspired him to become an architect. At age twenty-one, he entered the Agricultural and Mechanical College for the Colored Race at Greensboro (now NORTH CAROLINA A&T UNIVERSITY). He graduated from the architecture program in 1901. Between 1901 and 1903, he pursued graduate studies in architecture at Cornell University in Ithaca, New York.

After college, Edwards went to Raleigh, North Carolina, to establish the Mechanical Department of the Institution for Education of the Deaf, Dumb, and Blind (a segregated school for Blacks). He later accepted the position of teacher of natural science and superintendent of the Men's Industrial Department at Shaw University in Raleigh, and soon established himself as an educator and manager. Edwards started his academic career simultaneously with his architectural career and came to be known as Professor Edwards.

While at Shaw University, his reputation as an architect spread throughout the state and brought him notoriety. Edwards was responsible for Shaw University's Building Program during his fifteen-year tenure there. He also was the first Black to design and construct buildings for the American Baptist Home Mission Society.[1] He designed a Masonic Temple and other buildings in Raleigh. The Masonic Temple Building, located near the Shaw University campus, is a 3-story, brick and stone building with Italianate features. Constructed in 1907 to house the Widow's Son Lodge No. 4 and the Excelsior Lodge No. 21 of the Free and Accepted Masons, the building was added to the National Register of Historic Places in 1984.

One of the notable buildings Edwards designed while at Shaw University is the Leonard Medical

Leonard Medical School, Shaw University, *Shaw University Archives*

School (1912). The commission was originally given to a White architect. After careful analysis of the proposed design, Edwards discovered a major, life-threatening flaw. He decided not to interfere, but later had a dream in which several people died as a result of this flaw. He felt compelled to tell the appropriate officials, who promptly fired the architect and hired Edwards to complete the project. There were many similar instances when he was asked by White clients to consult on a project, but was not hired outright because he was Black.

A 1908 article in the *Afro-American Ledger* newspaper described Edwards as "a rising young Architect."[2] His reputation as an architect was growing due in part to his "limited concern for frills and fads of architecture and strict adherence to the three F's in designing—fit, firm, fair."[3]

On June 12, 1912, North Carolina governor William W. Kitchin appointed Edwards as a delegate to the third annual Negro National Educational Congress held in Saint Paul, Minnesota. Three years later, in 1915, the General Assembly of North Carolina passed an act requiring all architects to be examined, licensed, and registered. Edwards successfully passed the exam, becoming the first registered Black architect in North Carolina.[4] He advertised this fact by stating on his business card, "Never build without a plan, consult G. A. Edwards—the only Negro licensed to do business in North Carolina."[5]

Edwards continued working toward improving the physical environment of the Shaw University campus. He met and married a Shaw music student in 1909. He and Catherine Ruth Norris were wed on September 1, 1909. They had five children, four of whom were born in Raleigh.

The Edwards family lived in Raleigh until 1917, when Edwards was elected president of Kittrell College in Kittrell, North Carolina. This small African Methodist Episcopal institution was established in 1886 and until 1917, when Edwards become president, had neither a high school nor a college accreditation. It owned fifty-nine acres and four dilipidated buildings. When he resigned in 1929, Kittrell's holdings were 275 acres with nearly a half-mile frontage on U.S. Route 1—the major highway from Richmond, Virginia, to Raleigh, North Carolina. The appraised value of the property increased from $60,000 to $1 million and the institution had been raised from the standard of a high school to an industrial arts college.

After twelve years at Kittrell College, Edwards moved his family to Durham to practice architecture and design the North Carolina Mutual Life Insurance building. The economic boom of the late 1920s led to many commissions. Shortly after the family had moved to Durham in 1929, however, the stock market crashed—the Great Depression had begun. A proud but realistic man, Edwards accepted a position as principal of Lyon Park Elementary School and later Whitted School (now Hillside Park High School). He continued to practice architecture in Durham, where he designed and built houses for many of Durham's leading families.

Edwards was a prominent figure in Durham, serving on the board of directors of the Mechanics and Farmers Bank, Bankers Fire Insurance Company, and Southern Fidelity Insurance Company. He was an active member of the Durham Committee on Negro Affairs. At his funeral, C. C. Spaulding, president of the North Carolina Mutual Life Insurance Company and the Mechanics and Farmers Bank, described him "as being a most important asset due to his wise counsel, cooperative spirit, and even temperament."[6]

When Edwards died of a heart attack on October 5, 1943, he was reported to be the only Black architect licensed to practice in the state—a distinction he had held for nearly thirty years.

Notes

1. Clement Richardson, *The National Cyclopedia of the Colored Race* (Montgomery, Ala.: National Publishing Co., 1928), p. 332.
2. "Success in Many Fields: Rising Young Architect Who Designed Masonic Temple at Raleigh," *The Afro American Ledger*, 28 August 1909, p. 3.
3. Ibid.
4. State of North Carolina, Office of Sheriff, Wake County. "Gaston Alonzo Edwards," Certificate no. 5, issued 4 February 1916. The license certificate was dated September 8, 1916. The date on the certificate stub has been altered to suggest that the certificate was initially issued in 1915. Edwards is listed by the North Carolina Board of Architecture, Numerical Listing of Applicants on line 54, Certificate by Exempt, July 22, 1915. The significance of the difference between between two dates is not known.
5. Gaston Edwards buisness card. In the possession of the author.
6. "Gaston Alonzo Edwards," *Durham Journal and Guide*, 16 October 1943, p. 1.

Bibliography

Simmons-Henry, Linda, and Linda Edmisten. *Culture Town, Life in Raleigh's African American Communities*. Raleigh: Raleigh Historic Districts Commission, 1993.

HAZEL RUTH EDWARDS,
GRANDDAUGHTER OF GASTON EDWARDS
AND ASSISTANT PROFESSOR,
GRADUATE PROGRAM IN CITY
AND REGIONAL PLANNING,
INSTITUTE OF ARCHITECTURE,
LANDSCAPE ARCHITECTURE, AND
PLANNING, MORGAN STATE UNIVERSITY

BUILDING LIST

Name	Address	City	State	Year	Comments
Masonic Temple	427 S. Blount St.	Raleigh	NC	1907	
Shaw University Leonard Medical School	Campus	Raleigh	NC	1912	
Shaw University Tyler Hall	Campus	Raleigh	NC	1910	

Curtis Graham Elliott
(1906–1970)

Sue Elliott Carroll

Curtis Elliott was born on October 10, 1906, into a prominent Cincinnati family who were successful general contractors and respected civic leaders. Curtis's father, Wallace Claude Elliott, originally from Nicholasville, Kentucky, and three uncles operated Elliott Brothers, Contractors, a construction company based in the commuter railroad suburb of Wyoming, Ohio, where they lived. Elliott Brothers were known for their rock-faced "composition" concrete block houses and tight-bond new brick streets. Curtis Elliott's mother, Anna Graham Elliott, also originally from Nicholasville, kept busy caring for her eleven children.

Curtis entered the racially integrated Wyoming High School in 1921 after completing the all-Black Oak Avenue School. He received his high school diploma in 1925.

Curtis's father insisted he work for the construction company during the summers and long school breaks such as holidays. Working as a construction laborer understandably led to his decision to become an architect. He chose HOWARD UNIVERSITY'S SCHOOL OF ARCHITECTURE, where he enrolled in 1926. Elliott distinguished himself as a student and was selected as one of two student representatives sent to the first annual convention of the NATIONAL TECHNICAL ASSOCIATION held in Chicago in 1929.[1] Elliott graduated with a bachelor of science in architecture in 1931.

A month before receiving his diploma, with no practical experience, Elliott nevertheless was invited to be among the exhibitors in the first "Exhibition of the Work of Negro Architects" presented by the Department of Architecture at Howard University May 12 to May 28, 1931.[2] He submitted a class project—a modest-looking, single-family residence he had designed for a make-believe client.

Breaking from family tradition, Curtis Elliott did not return to Wyoming, Ohio, to join the family construction company. He instead joined Howard's Department of Buildings and Grounds, where he spent his entire professional career of three decades.

Curtis Elliott's first marriage was to Blanche Price of Washington, D.C. His second marriage was to Jennie Johnson. Curtis Elliott had no biological children. He was stepfather to Reginald B. Elliott, his second wife's son.

Curtis Elliott died from cancer at Freedman Hospital in Washington, D.C., on February 4, 1970. In recognition of his years of dedicated service to Howard University, his body lay in state in the university's Rankin Memorial Chapel. He was interred in Lincoln Memorial Cemetery in suburban Suitland, Maryland.

Notes

1. Jennie J. Elliott, "The N.T.A.: An Account of Its Activities, 1925–1957," (master's thesis, Howard University, 1958), p. 15. (She is Curtis Elliott's second wife.)
2. Howard University Department of Architecture, "Exhibition of the Work of Negro Architects," May 12–28, 1931, pamphlet, in the collection of the Moorland-Spingarn Research Center.

Bibliography

Guckenberger, George B. *Wyoming: A Retrospective.* Cincinnati: Mott Studio, 2000.

DRECK SPURLOCK WILSON

Daniel J. Farrar Sr.
(1862–1923)

Richmond Planet Newspaper

Born in 1862, in Charlottesville, Virginia, Daniel Farrar was educated in Richmond public schools. At age eighteen he dropped out of school to apprentice with his father, Joseph E. Farrar (1830–1892), a successful Richmond contractor and former member of the Board of Aldermen of Richmond. Rachel Willis Hill Farrar, his mother, was a homemaker. Daniel worked with his father for three years and then worked the following seven years as a journeyman carpenter.

In 1887 Joseph Farrar retired from his contracting business and was succeeded by his son Daniel, his son-in-law Henry J. Moore, and his brother John E. C. Farrar. The new business was known as Farrar, Moore & Co. but did not last long in this configuration. In October 1887, John Farrar withdrew from the firm. It was renamed Farrar & Moore and operated from an office at 3rd and Duval Streets. In addition to owning the building occupied by the firm, the men rented out several other buildings that they owned. The *Daily Planet* praised the partnership: "Some of the handsomest dwellings in the city have been built by them."[1]

By 1895 the firm had completed two contracts with the City of Richmond, employing two crews of workmen and apprentices. The partnership of Farrar & Moore dissolved sometime between 1897 and 1900, at which time both Daniel Farrar and Henry Moore independently advertised themselves as contractors. In 1902 Farrar advertised his new firm as "D. J. Farrar, Contractor and Builder, All Kinds of Carpentry. Special attention paid to taking Contracts for Building of any Style or Architecture."[2] He continued to advertise his services as a builder and contractor until his death in 1923.

On May 17, 1888, Daniel Farrar married Leah B. Holmes. The couple had two daughters, Alma and Leah, and two sons, Joseph and Daniel Jr. Daniel Jr. followed in the footsteps of his father and grandfather, becoming a third-generation carpenter and contractor.

Daniel Farrar Sr. designed and erected a variety of buildings throughout Virginia, including Smallwood Memorial Institute Administration Building in Claremount, Virginia; Mechanics Bank Building in Richmond, Virginia; Second Street Bank in Richmond, Virginia; and the 2-story frame Grand Fountain, United Order of True Reformers Hall in the all-Black Richmond neighborhood of Fulton.

DANIEL J. FARRAR SR.

True Reformers Meeting Hall, Virginia Historical Society

Daniel Farrar Sr. was a member of Ebenezer Baptist Church in Richmond. He was also a member of the Capital City Lodge of the Elks, 33rd Degree Scottish Rite Mason; Nobles of the Mystic Shrine; and the Richmond Lodge of the AF&AM. Farrar Sr. served as secretary and treasurer of the Evergreen Cemetery Association. He died on March 17, 1923, after suffering with an affliction for ten months. In his obituary, Daniel Farrar Sr. was characterized as "quiet, unassuming, but faithful in his obligations."[3]

Notes
1. "D. J. Farrar," *Daily Planet*, 9 February 1895, p. 1.
2. "Prominent Builder and Contractor Is Laid to Rest," *Daily Planet,* 17 March 1923, n.p.
3. "Noted Builder Death Victim in Richmond," *Chicago Offender*, 17 March 1923, n.p.

Bibliography
Burrell, G. W., and D. E. Johnson. *Twenty-Five Years [sic] History of the Grand Fountain of the United Order of True Reformers, 1881–1905.* Richmond: True Reformers, 1909.

Green, Bryan C., Loth Calder, and William M. Rasmussen. *Lost Virginia Architecture.* Charlottesville: Howell Press, 2002.

Wells, John E., and Robert E. Dalton. *The Virginia Architects, 1835–1955: A Biographical Dictionary.* Richmond: New South Architectural Press, 1997.

BRYAN CLARK GREEN,
ASSOCIATE CURATOR FOR PRINTS AND PHOTOGRAPHS,
THE VIRGINIA HISTORICAL SOCIETY

BUILDING LIST

Name	Address	City	State	Year	Comments
Dammals, Isaac	13 W. Leigh St.	Richmond	VA	c1890	
Dismond, Dr. Samuel H.	112 W. Leigh St.	Richmond	VA	c1890	
Henderson, William	2806 E. Leigh St.	Richmond	VA	c1890	
Hill, Robert T.	733 N. 3rd St.	Richmond	VA	c1890	
Jones, Dr. Robert E.	110 E. Leigh St.	Richmond	VA	c1890	
McCurdy, Hugh A.	1013 W. Grace St.	Richmond	VA	c1890	
Quarles, Alexander P.	1002 N. 3rd St.	Richmond	VA	c1890	

BUILDING LIST (continued)

Name	Address	City	State	Year	Comments
Second Street Bank		Richmond	VA		
Shepherd, John M.	36 W. Jackson St.	Richmond	VA	c1890	
Smallwood Institute Administration Bldg.	Campus	Claremont	VA		
Strother, Charles	1014 W. Leigh St.	Richmond	VA	c1890	
Trainum, Alexander	621 N. 29th St.	Richmond	VA	c1890	
Turner, Beverley F.	24 W. Leigh St.	Richmond	VA	c1890	
True Reformers Meeting Hall		Richmond	VA	1895	Demolished
Wyatt, William	414 N. 8th St.	Richmond	VA	c1890	

Arthur Wilfred Ferguson
(1898–1978)

Illinois State Historical Library

Arthur Ferguson was born on September 18, 1898, in the District of Columbia. He was the son of prominent dentist Dr. David Arthur Ferguson from Ohio and Antoinette Victoria Carter Ferguson from Washington, D.C. David Ferguson was the first Black applicant to successfully come before the Virginia State Board of Dental Examiners in 1900. Arthur had one sibling, Irma Vivian Ferguson Spencer, who later moved to Los Angeles, California.

Arthur Ferguson's educational experience began at Saint Paul's Normal & Industrial School in Lawrenceville, Virginia, which he attended from 1912 to 1916.[1] He spent two years at Oberlin High School in Ohio and graduated in 1918. He enrolled at HOWARD UNIVERSITY and received his bachelor of science degree in architecture on June 8, 1923.[2] While at Howard University, Ferguson was actively involved in the Reserve Officers Training Corps and played intramural tennis and football.

After graduating from Howard University, Ferguson taught architectural subjects, surveying, and mechanical drawing at his *alma mater*. He also worked for the U.S. Department of Interior as an architectural engineer engaged in steel and concrete design, construction supervision, surveying, and architectural design.

Arthur Ferguson had a distinguished military career.[3] He served in the U.S. Army Reserves at Camp Perry, Ohio, as a company officer. In May 1929, Ferguson was posted to TUSKEGEE INSTITUTE. He continued his rise through the ranks as a first lieutenant in the Infantry Reserves at Camp Devens, Massachusetts, in 1931, and ultimately was promoted to company commander at Fort Howard in Maryland in 1935.

By 1938 Ferguson was a civilian employed by the noted Washington, D.C., architect HILYARD ROBERT ROBINSON and his Los Angeles–based partner PAUL REVERE WILLIAMS at Robinson & Williams, located at 1927 11th Street, NW. When America entered into World War II, Ferguson was called to active duty.

During World War II, Ferguson served as company commander, 336th Infantry Regiment, starting in 1941. The all-Black 366th Infantry Regiment was activated at Fort Devens and led by Black officers, unprecedented in the history of the U.S. Army. Prior to this activation, White officers commanded all-Black units. The 366th Infantry Regiment was thrust into combat in North Africa and Italy.

At the end of the war, Ferguson was assigned to the Reserve Officer Training Corps unit at Winston-Salem State College in North Carolina and subsequently reassigned as ROTC instructor at NORTH CAROLINA AGRICULTURAL & TECHNICAL College in Greensboro.

In 1946 Ferguson married Margaret Wilkins of Springfield, Illinois, who was a social worker with the Children's Service Bureau of Sangamon County, Illinois.[4] They had no children.

In August 1948 Arthur Ferguson was promoted to captain and assigned to the recently reorganized 370th

Infantry Battalion in the European theater. He served as tactical officer and was responsible for officer training classes (which averaged forty officers per class), processing and de-processing, issuance of supplies and equipment, billeting, formations, and troop inspections. In early 1949 Ferguson was assigned to the Battalion Executive Office of the 373rd Infantry Battalion, First Constabulary Brigade at Wurzburg Military Post in West Germany. The 373rd was responsible for administration lodging and logistic support during garrison operations.

Captain Ferguson returned to the United States in April 1949 and was assigned as company commander of the 3rd Battalion, 15th Infantry Division, stationed at Fort Benning in Georgia.

From 1951 to 1953, Ferguson served as a professor of military science and tactics at South Carolina State Agricultural & Mechanical College in Orangeburg.

By 1954 Ferguson had risen to lieutenant colonel and was assigned to the Korea Civil Assistance Command Public Works Branch. He was sent to Seoul, Korea, in advance of the branch deployment to start a $2-million program for rehabilitation of government buildings. Ferguson advised the Republic of Korea government engineers, performed plan reviews, and prepared cost estimates for a new capitol annex. He also was the supervising architect for the design of a hospital for the Baptist Mission in Pusan, Korea and was the lead cost estimator for the rehabilitation of the Seoul Central Government Building, Korean Government Housing, Chamber of Commerce offices, Son Dai Moon Police Station, and the National Library, all in the Republic of Korea. Ferguson also prepared cost estimates for the rehabilitation of twenty-five buildings for the Suwon Agricultural College and another twenty-four buildings for the affiliated Suwon Agricultural Laboratory. From 1954 to 1955, Ferguson provided technical assistance on public works projects to the Republic of Korea prime minister and ministers of home affairs, justice, public health, and education and agriculture. Ferguson retired from the U.S. Army in 1965.

After mustering out of the military, Ferguson returned to Springfield, Illinois. He was active in many civic and social organizations including *Alpha Phi Alpha* Fraternity, St. Luke's Episcopal Church, Kamar Temple No. 56 of the Shriners, Knights Templar Prince Hall Commandry, Masonic Order (33rd degree Mason), NATIONAL TECHNICAL ASSOCIATION, and the Retired Officers Association.

Arthur Wilfred Ferguson died of cancer on February 3, 1978, at Saint John's Hospital in Springfield, Illinois.[5] He was buried at Oak Ridge Cemetery in Sangamon County, Illinois.

Notes
1. St. Paul's College, alumni notes section, "The Southern Missionary," (March 1920): 44.
2. "Record Number of Degrees Given at Howard," *Washington Post*, 9 June 1923, p. 8.
3. Chronological Record of Military Service and Efficiency Reports, "Arthur Ferguson," National Personnel Records Center, St. Louis, Missouri.
4. "Ferguson Family Papers, 1937–1977," Manuscript Collection, Illinois State Historical Library, Springfield, Illinois.
5. "Arthur Ferguson," *State Journal-Register (Springfield)*, 21 June 1967, n.p.

Bibliography
"Arthur Ferguson." In *Boyd's Directory of the District of Columbia, 1920–1923*. D.C.: R. L. Polk & Company, 1923.

"Headquarters 373rd Infantry Battalion (Sep.) Annual Historical Report." Army Post Office 169, U.S. Army, Review CSHIS-5, National Archives, Washington, D.C.

E. RENEE INGRAM,
PRESIDENT AND FOUNDER,
AFRICAN AMERICAN HERITAGE
PRESERVATION FOUNDATION

BUILDING LIST

Name	Address	City	Country	Year	Comments
Baptist Mission Hospital		Pusan	Korea	1954	
Chamber of Commerce	45 Namdae eunno	Seoul	Korea	1954	
Korean Housing Corp.		Seoul	Korea	1954	
National Library	Ahyen-Dong	Seoul	Korea	1954	
Seoul Central Bldg.	136 Serin-Dong	Seoul	Korea	1954	
Son Dai Moon Police Station		Seoul	Korea	1954	
Suwon Agricultural College	Campus	Seoul	Korea	1954	
Suwon Agricultural Laboratory	Campus	Seoul	Korea	1954	

George Alonzo Ferguson
(1895–1979)

Ferguson Family Collection

George Alonzo Ferguson practiced architecture in Washington, D.C., from the 1920s to the 1950s, designing churches, commercial buildings, and houses. He joined with HOWARD DILWORTH WOODSON and ROSCOE INGERSOLL VAUGHN in the architectural/engineering firm Woodson, Vaughn & Ferguson as the firm's principal architectural designer. He was also prominent among a group of Black architects who taught at Armstrong Technical High School in the District of Columbia.

Ferguson was born on October 2, 1895, in Washington, D.C., and graduated from Armstrong Technical High School in 1913. He entered the Urdana School of Architecture at the University of Illinois in 1913. His design for a Gothic-style office building for a student competition received a mention and was published in the School of Architecture's club magazine. He was the first Black and third graduate of the School of Architecture in June 1917.

Ferguson married Maude Mileam of Urbana, Illinois, in 1917. They had two sons, Roger and George Jr. and four daughters, Thelma, Angela, Mary, and Carole. After her untimely death he married Mary Leona Burden of Marion, Indiana, in 1920. He served briefly as a first lieutenant in the U.S. Army during World War I in France. He worked for architect SAMUEL M. PLATO in Marion, Indiana, from 1919 to 1921, and then returned to Washington, D.C., to practice architecture and to teach architectural drafting and drawing at Roosevelt High School and Armstrong Technical High School.

Ferguson was in partnership with Howard Dilworth Woodson and Roscoe Ingersoll Vaughn for several periods: Woodson, Vaughn & Ferguson, 1922 to 1924; Vaughn, Ferguson & Company, 1924 to 1931 (which closed during the Great Depression); Vaughn, Ferguson & Company, 1938 to 1941 (ending when Ferguson enlisted in World War II); and separately with both Woodson and Vaughn from 1946 into the 1950s. Ferguson's affidavit to the D.C. Board of Examiners of Architects lists him as the designer of a number of the firm's buildings.[1]

Ferguson's work ranged from residential to commercial—the latter category included a number of churches and offices. His designs in just one Washington, D.C. neighborhood—the commercial corridor of U Street, NW (Hamilton Printing Company and National Benefit Building)—are handsomely rendered in brick with stone detailing. Ferguson was adept at using elements of diverse historical styles for varying building types. The National Benefit Building and the Mattingly house both exhibit an elegant use of classical vocabulary, whereas the Hamilton Printing Company facade has an Art Deco appearance. The Federal Life Building has elements of the Roman order with pylons flanking the entrance.[2]

The *1924 D.C. Registration Law* for architects exempted professionals like Ferguson on the basis of experience prior to 1924. Ferguson practiced as an architect without being registered until 1952, when he was granted registration on the basis of experience.

National Benefit Building, *Caroline Hickman*

Like his partner in the firm, Roscoe Ingersoll Vaughn, Ferguson was a longtime drafting instructor at his *alma mater*, Armstrong Technical High School, teaching there from 1921 to 1965. He revised the curriculum to include more advanced work. The Armstrong program became a "feeder" to the SCHOOL OF ARCHITECTURE AT HOWARD UNIVERSITY during the 1920s and 1930s. Under his direction, students in the drafting classes designed a Young Men's Christian Association building in Arlington, Virginia, and a Boys Club in Fairmount Heights, Maryland.

Ferguson served in the Reserve Officers Training Corps and was a leader in the D.C. 428th Infantry Reserve. He distinguished himself during World War II as a battalion commander and regimental executive officer in the 366th Infantry and in 1944 assumed command of a regiment in Italy. Colonel West Hamilton, who was his reserve commander in France and later a client, characterized Ferguson as "a tower of strength" who had the "affectionate respect of confidence of all who knew or served with him."[3] Andrew L. Johnson served with Ferguson in the 366th Infantry as regimental chaplain and recommended him for architect registration in 1952. He wrote in glowing terms about Ferguson, "Of all the men that I know living today, there are none I would place ahead of George Alonzo Ferguson when character, personality, honesty, dependability, and ability are concerned."[4]

Ferguson was an active member of Mount Zion United Methodist Church in Washington, D.C., and maintained a summer home in Columbia Beach, Maryland, an all-Negro community on the Chesapeake Bay.

Ferguson died on March 10, 1979, in Washington, D.C., after suffering from a heart ailment.[5]

Notes
1. D.C. Board of Examiners and Registrars of Architects, "George Alonzo Ferguson," Case Files, Box 20, D.C. Archives.
2. "D.C. Building Permits no. 6571 and no. 3882," National Archives. Washington, D.C.
3. D.C. Board of Examiners and Registrars of Architects, Case Files.
4. Ibid.
5. "George A. Ferguson, 84, Taught at Armstrong, Roosevelt Highs," *Washington Post*, 10 March 1970, p. 64.

Bibliography
Lee, J. V. *Deanwood Historic Study: The Role of Black Architects in the Development of Deanwood*. Washington, D.C.: n.p., 1987. D.C. Historic Preservation Office.

CAROLINE MESROBIAN HICKMAN, ART AND ARCHITECTURAL HISTORIAN, WASHINGTON, D.C.

BUILDING LIST

Name	Address	City	State	Year	Comments
Bannister, C. C.	2950 Chain Bridge Rd.	Washington	DC	1924	Demolished
Federal Life Bldg.	715 Florida Ave., NW	Washington	DC	c1924	
Friendship Baptist Church	900 Delaware Ave., SW	Washington	DC	1965	

GEORGE ALONZO FERGUSON

BUILDING LIST (continued)

Name	Address	City	State	Year	Comments
Hamilton Printing Co.	1353 U St., NW	Washington	DC	1932	
Israel Baptist Church	682 11th St., NE	Washington	DC	1932	
Jones, Dr. W. W.	409 58th St., NE	Washington	DC	c1924	
Martin, George W.	New York Ave, NW	Washington	DC	c1924	Apartments
Mattingly, Robert	922 S St., NW	Washington	DC	1928	
Metropolitan Baptist Church Monument Hall	1225 R St., NW	Washington	DC	1950	Addition
Mt. Airy Baptist Church	1100 N. Capitol St., NW	Washington	DC	c1924	Alterations
Mt. Bethel Baptist Church	71 Rhode Island Ave., NW	Washington	DC	1958	
Mt. Moriah Baptist Church	3rd & L Sts., NW	Washington	DC	c1924	Demolished
National Benefit Bldg.	1209 U St., NW	Washington	DC	c1924	
National Training School for Women & Girls, Chapel	Campus	Washington	DC		
National Training School for Women & Girls, Dormitory	Campus	Washington	DC		
Penn, Garfield A.	4720 Sheriff Rd., NE	Washington	DC	1923	
Pilgrim Baptist Church	3rd & Van Sts., NE	Washington	DC	c1924	Demolished
Saunders Apartments	11th St., NW	Washington	DC	c1924	
Shephard, Dr. O'Donne	Upshur St., NW	Washington	DC		

Robert Lionel Fields
(1918–1985)

Robert Lionel Fields was born on May 18, 1918, in Charleston, South Carolina, the eldest son of Mamie Garvin Fields and Robert Lucas Fields. He was educated at Avery Institute in Charleston. Because at the time there were no secondary schools in Charleston for an African American aspiring to become an architect, at the age of fourteen his parents sent him to Armstrong Technical High School in Washington, D.C. Upon completing high school, Field entered HOWARD UNIVERSITY, where he earned a bachelor of science in architecture in 1945.

Fields began his career in architecture in the offices of prominent Washington, D.C., architect HOWARD HAMILTON MACKEY SR. Fields worked for

Delaware Avenue Baptist Church, *Dreck Spurlock Wilson*

ROBERT LIONEL FIELDS

Mackey from 1940 until 1945, when he opened his own office. Fields operated his own architectural practice until 1951, when he became an employee of the U.S. Navy, Bureau of Yards and Docks, Engineering and Technical Services Division. Fields left the Bureau of Yards and Docks in 1955 to join the office of Murphy & Locraft. He remained at Murphy & Locraft until 1972, when he once again opened his own practice, Robert Lionel Fields Architects & Planners.

During his second tenure in private practice, Fields worked on several major projects for Howard University. His projects included major renovations to the Lucy Diggs Slowe Hall, the Chemistry Building, and the bookstore.[1] He also designed the Howard University Museum, located within Joel Springarn Memorial Library.

Fields was a member of the American Institute of Architects, the American Society of Testing and Materials, the Construction Specifications Institute, Howard University 1000 Club, and *Omega Psi Phi* Fraternity.

Robert Fields died of congestive heart failure on January 26, 1985, at the age of sixty-six.

Note

1. "Robert Lionel Fields, Noted Architect," *Washington Afro-American*, 9 February 1985, p. 65.

ANNETTE K. CARTER,
ARCHITECTURAL DESIGN GROUP,
ALEXANDRIA, VIRGINIA

BUILDING LIST

Name	Address	City	State	Year	Comments
Delaware Avenue Baptist Church	1105 Delaware Ave., SW	Washington	DC	1950	
Georgetown University Theatre	Campus	Washington	DC		
Georgetown Visitation Prepatory School for Girls	1524 35th St., NW	Washington	DC	1978	
Howard University Chemistry Bldg.	Campus	Washington	DC		Alterations
Howard University Museum	Campus	Washington	DC		Alterations
Howard University Lucy Diggs Slowe Hall	Campus	Washington	DC		Alterations
Howard University Student Bookstore	Campus	Washington	DC		Alterations
Mt. Carmel Baptist Church	3800 Ely Pl., SE	Washington	DC		
Our Lady Queen of Peace Church	3730 Ely Pl., SE	Washington	DC	1951	
Randall Universal United Methodist Church	1002 46th St., NE	Washington	DC	1948	
Sacred Heart Home	5805 Queens Chapel Rd.	Hyattsville	MD	c1960	Addition

Orpheus Hodge Fisher
(1900–1986)

Courtesy of the Marian Anderson Collection of Photographs, Rare Book & Manuscript Library, University of Pennsylvania

Orpheus Hodge Fisher was born on July 11, 1900, in Oxford, Pennsylvania, the eighth child of Pauline Conklin Fisher of the Dominican Republic and George Albert Fisher of Baltimore, Maryland. Pauline Fisher died soon after Orpheus's birth and the family moved to Wilmington, Delaware. Fisher's father was an instructor at Lincoln University in Pennsylvania. Fisher attended the Central Friends Seminary in Philadelphia until ninth grade, when he transferred to Wilmington Central High School in Delaware.

Throughout the 1920s, Fisher worked at a number of jobs in Philadelphia, where he was part of a community of African American architects that included the renowned JULIAN FRANCIS ABELE. In a 1946 publicity release written by Marian Anderson's agent, Fisher named his employers during this period, including Zantzinger, Medary & Borie of Philadelphia.[1] He allegedly also worked for the Stanley Company of America, designing theaters in Philadelphia.

By February 1928, Fisher was working for Heacock & Hokanson Architects in Philadelphia. That same year, Fisher and a co-worker started their own company. They bought a golf course in a Philadelphia mainline suburb intending to reduce it from thirty-six holes to eighteen holes and build houses on the remaining land. The Great Depression put an end to this venture, and Fisher went to New York City in search of employment. This entrepreneurial spirit and professional flexibility was the one constant in Fisher's career and remained with him throughout his life.

As with many things, Orpheus Fisher's route to New York, where he spent his thirties, was not direct. From 1929 to 1930, Fisher was in Nova Scotia, Canada, helping to design the Glace Bay Power Plant. In 1930 he was working for the RCA Victor Company in Camden, New Jersey. It was probably during this stint that he worked on Rockefeller Center, because RCA was the Center's biggest tenant.[2] Perhaps it was during this period when Fisher also worked for United Engineers & Construction Company.[3] Fisher said that it was designing a home for the president of the company, DeWitt P. Robinson, that sparked his interest in residential design. This interest strongly influenced his later career choices.

In 1932 Fisher lived in Brooklyn and worked for the New York City Board of Education, Bureau of Construction and Maintenance. Later that year he worked for the American Cottonpickers Corporation in Manhattan performing unspecified tasks.

Although he met his second wife and great love, Marian Anderson, in 1915 when both were still in high school, they drifted apart. Fisher had such light skin that he passed for White, and in 1924 he married Ida Gould, a White woman. The marriage was not successful and the couple separated. Ida Gould's family raised their son James, born in 1925, with minimal contact with Fisher. It was not until the summer of 1935 that Orpheus Fisher and Marian Anderson rekindled their feelings for one another. This period coincides with professional stability for Fisher. From 1934 to 1939,

Fisher worked for the 1939 New York World's Fair Corporation.

In 1935 Fisher attended a concert by Marian Anderson at Carnegie Hall. They had not seen each other for more than two years. He knew, just as he had when they were teenagers, that he wanted to marry Marian. She, now in her late thirties, felt established enough in her professional singing career to consider marriage. However, Marian Anderson's constant international touring made it difficult for a romance to progress. Another obstacle was the fact that Fisher was still married to Ida Gould. Their divorce was not finalized until late 1940. This period of chaste courtship fostered continuous correspondence between Marian and Orpheus. Their letters document the extensive renovations Fisher carried out between 1938 and 1940 on Marian Anderson's Philadelphia residence. Fisher joined two rowhouses and applied a Georgian-style facade. He intended for these changes to signify the importance of the occupant.

Marian Anderson considered her long-distance architectural project as part of a grand scheme to return to America, retire, and settle down with Fisher. His responsibility, in addition to renovating her home in Philadelphia, was to find a suitable home for the two of them. In Danbury, Connecticut, Fisher located fifty acres of rolling farmland with a Victorian farmhouse and barn. Because Marian Anderson was African American and Fisher looked White, they suffered racial discrimination in their attempts to buy a home in Danbury. They ended up purchasing twice the amount of land than they had originally intended, probably a capitulation to race issues. However, by 1942 they owned their future home. Marian and Orpheus married on July 17, 1943, in Danbury and moved into the farmhouse. They were residents of Danbury for the remainder of their lives.

The 1940s saw Fisher shift professionally. Although the couple maintained a residence in New York City, in March 1943 Fisher resigned from his job there and began working for the Barden Corporation of Danbury, which manufactured indispensable ball bearings needed for the war effort. The job switch allowed him to end the lengthy commute between Danbury and New York City and to begin work on his proudest architectural achievement, "Marianna Farm."

Marian and Orpheus devoted themselves to developing "Marianna Farm" into a working farm. In addition to farming, Fisher operated a commercial kennel from 1946 to 1952. Fisher designed his wife's studio and the farmhouse. Both buildings were cleanly designed and 1-story with minimal ornamentation.

From the 1940s through the 1970s, Fisher received numerous solicitations from people interested in com-

Mariana Farm, *Courtesy of the Marian Anderson Collection of Photographs, Rare Book & Manuscript Library, University of Pennsylvania*

missioning projects or interviewing him. No evidence was found that Fisher either encouraged or accepted any of the offers.[4] He continued his work in Danbury, which included running a real estate company in which both Orpheus and Marian acted as landlords. Fisher also traveled extensively with his wife, supporting her singing career and civil rights appearances.

Orpheus Fisher died at Danbury Hospital in 1986 after an extended illness. His memorial service was held at the New Hope Baptist Church in Danbury.

Notes

1. Fisher said he worked on buildings at Yale and Princeton Universities. In the early 1920s, Zantzinger, Medary & Borie designed two dormitories on Princeton University's campus. The Howard Henry and Walter L. Foulke Memorial Dormitories were built between 1921 and 1923. In 1932 Zantzinger, Medary & Borie designed Sheffield Hall, Sterling Tower, and Strathcona Hall on Yale University's campus. Fisher could have been referring to these buildings.

2. Richard C. Wald. "How to Live with a Famous Wife," *Ebony Magazine* (August 1958): 52. Fisher claimed to have worked on Rockefeller Center, the Empire State Building, the Chrysler Building, and the Metropolitan Life Insurance Company Building.

3. United Engineers & Construction Company was the fourth largest builder in New York City at the time the Empire State Building was under construction. The company may be the link between Fisher and the Empire State Building. While working for United Engineers & Construction Company, Fisher traveled twice to Pernambuco, Brazil. He wrote, "many years ago I designed an air hangar for the airport there." Orpheus Fisher to Marian Anderson, n.d., 1937, Marian Anderson Papers, University of Pennsylvania Library.

4. Solicitations to Fisher came from the president of Hampton Institute, who expressed an interest in commissioning Fisher to design a home 8 January 1949; Lee-Lincoln Foundation referencing the design of a racially integrated community 3 March 1965; and Norma Skurka, *New York Times* design editor requesting an interview, 24 May 1974.

Bibliography

Anderson, Marian. Collection of Photographs, 1898–1992. Ahnenberg Rare Book and Manuscript Library, University of Pennsylvania, Philadelphia, Penn.

Keiler, Allen. *Marian Anderson: A Singer's Journey.* New York: Scribner, 2000.

RUTH E. HURWITZ,
ARCHITECTURAL HISTORIAN,
NEW YORK, NEW YORK

BUILDING LIST

Name	Address	City	State	Year	Comments
Anderson, Marian	762–764 Martin St.	Philadelphia	PA	c1940	Alteration
Anderson, Marian	Joe's Hill Road	Danbury	CT	1953	"Marianna Farm"
Marian Anderson Studio	Joe's Hill Road	Danbury	CT	c1942	"Marianna Farm"
New Hope Baptist Church	10 Cherry St.	Danbury	CT	1977	

Florida Agricultural & Mechanical University, School of Architecture
(1910)

Florida Agricultural & Mechanical (A&M) University was founded on October 3, 1887, as the State Normal College for Colored Students. In 1891 the college received $7,500 under the second Morrill Act for agricultural and mechanical arts education; thus, it became Florida's land grant institution for African Americans. The college was moved from Copeland Street in the western area of central Tallahassee to its present location just south of downtown, and its name was changed to the State Normal and Industrial College for Colored Students. The name was changed again in 1909 to Florida Agricultural & Mechanical College for Negroes. In 1953 the college's name was changed by legislative action to Florida Agricultural & Mechanical University.

The education of students in building trades at Florida Agricultural & Mechanical University officially began almost one hundred years ago, when the institution began offering a bachelor of science degree in mechanical arts in 1910. A review of the university's 1920s and 1930s catalogs indicates that mechanical arts students learned various construction trades, including carpentry, plumbing, and brickmaking. The course schedule also listed architectural drafting and construction supervision classes. In addition students were required to work construction projects three days a week. The requirement came from faculty, some of whom "had degrees in architecture, even if they weren't called that."[1]

The students' architectural skills became honed as they assisted professors in the design and construction of buildings on and around campus. For example, mechanical arts professor John Swilley designed and built, adjacent to the campus, the house for Dr. Leonard Foote, who was the founder of the Schools of Pharmacy and Nursing. In 1906 professors and students began building a library on campus that was underwritten by philanthropist Andrew Carnegie. Completed in 1908 and subsequently named Carnegie Library, the structure is one of hundreds of libraries throughout the nation underwritten by Carnegie. A well-proportioned, four-columned front porch distinguishes this Classical Revival–style building, which now houses the Florida Agricultural & Mechanical University Black Archives Research Center and Museum. The library was listed on the National Register of Historic Places in 1978. Similarly, "Sunshine Manor," a 2-story Anglo-Colonial Revival–style house, was the official residence for three university presidents. Built by mechanical arts students in 1936, it is used today as the Florida Agricultural & Mechanical Student Counseling Center. The students also helped to build Rosenwald Schools, named after Sears, Roebuck, & Company philanthropist Julius Rosenwald. The rural schoolhouses were part of a program backed by philanthropists from Standard Oil and Sears, Roebuck, & Company. One was built in the 1930s on the corner of Gamble Street and Martin Luther King Jr. Boulevard adjacent to the campus.

In 1942 the college secured a promise from the federal government to construct a training facility; $70,000 of federal funds were provided conditional on a temporary structure being erected. Prior to the start of construction, U.S. Army officials commandeered all available lumber for use on the nearby Dale Mabry Airfield. The college staff person in charge of building the temporary structure, Maxwell Samuel Thomas, stated, "I knew we should begin on the building because [if] the federal government officials came here and we had not begun, they would withdraw their promise of funds."[2] Acting quickly, Thomas and other faculty surveyed the campus and the college farm for tall pine timber. A sawmill was erected on campus and the lumber was cut to build the temporary structure.

Maxwell Samuel Thomas was born on June 24, 1907, in Ocala, Florida. He received his high school education at Howard High School, and learned carpentry from his father, Robert J. Thomas, a successful contractor who included his son in the family-owned business. Thomas earned a bachelor of science degree in building construction at HAMPTON INSTITUTE in 1932, and a master's degree in industrial education at Colorado State University in 1947. Thomas began his professional career in 1932 as a high school vocational teacher of carpentry and cabinetmaking, and as a football coach in Little Rock, Arkansas. In 1935 he worked as a construction foreman for W. H. Aiken Construction Company, in Atlanta, Georgia. After leaving Atlanta in 1936, he taught industrial arts in Asheville, North Carolina, and served as an educational advisor with the federal Civilian Conservation Corps. Thomas came to Tallahassee in 1938, as the state itinerant teacher trainer of trades and industrial education for the Florida Department of Education. How he came to be associated with Florida Agricultural & Mechanical University was explained by his testimony, "I was working . . . as a teacher trainer in industrial education at Florida Agricultural & Mechanical University because in those days, Blacks who worked in state government in Tallahassee were headquartered at A&M."[3] His presence allowed him to serve both, sometimes simultaneously, and in several capacities. By 1942 Thomas was named director of vocational training at Florida Agricultural & Mechanical University and in 1947 he was named dean of the Division of Mechanical Arts, which later became the Division of Engineering and Mechanical Arts. It was during this period that he came to be popularly called just "Dean" as a sign of respect and admiration. He served as the Florida Agricultural & Mechanical University coordinator of planning and development until he retired in 1977. Thomas continued to contribute to the university and Tallahassee community until he died in 1983.

To honor his contributions to the university, the Florida Department of Transportation named the South Adams Street overpass for Thomas in 1987. This bridge serves as the primary vehicular connection between the State Capitol Complex in downtown Tallahassee and campus.

In 1987 the university also renovated a laundry facility built in the 1920s and renamed it the M. S. Thomas Industrial Arts Laboratory. The 6,254-square-foot structure houses part of the College of Environmental Science, Technology, and Agriculture, which offers a bachelor of science degree in construction engineering. The space includes an industrial arts laboratory, art shops, graphic art shops, photography laboratory and darkroom, classrooms, offices, and storage areas.

In 1975 the State of Florida legislature provided funding to establish a fully accredited School of Architecture. A 3-story building designed by Peter Runpel for the program was constructed in 1980, and was renovated and expanded in 2000. The architecture program offers a bachelor of architecture, master of architecture, and master of landscape architecture degrees. In 2003, there were 200 students and twenty-five faculty.

Notes

1. Gerald Ensley, "Building the Future," *Tallahassee Democrat*, 9 February 1997, p. 5.
2. Interview with Maxwell S. Thomas, Tallahassee, Fla., 7 May 2002.
3. Thomas interview.

Bibliography

Eaton, James, Murell Dawson, and Sharyn Thompson. *The Architectural Survey of Florida Agricultural and Mechanical University*. Tallahassee: Florida Bureau of Historic Preservation, 1995.

Neyland, Ledell. *The History of Florida A&M University*. Tallahassee: Florida A&M University Foundation, 1963.

ANDREW CHIN,
ASSOCIATE PROFESSOR,
SCHOOL OF ARCHITECTURE
FLORIDA AGRICULTURE & MECHANICAL UNIVERSITY

Wade Alston Ford
(1886–1949)

Doris Ford Johnson

Wade Alston Ford, an architect of superlative reputation and academic excellence, was born on April 9, 1886, in Lake View, South Carolina. He was reared by his parents, English and Katie Ford, on their 150-acre plantation.

Ford attended the Lake View Grade School and earned his high school diploma from Allen University Normal School in Columbia, South Carolina. He then enrolled at South Carolina State Agricultural & Mechanical College in Orangeburg where he graduated in 1921 with a normal degree in mechanical drawing at the age of thirty-five.[1] Being older and more mature helped Ford to become academically superior to his younger classmates. Because of this, he earned nine "vacations," which enabled him to return home from his classes and work on the family plantation. His outstanding academic achievements earned him top honors in his graduating class.

Mount Olive Baptist Church,
Doris Ford Johnson

After graduation he returned home to the plantation. He worked as an architect-carpenter in Lake View, bordering communities, and other rural South Carolina towns. In 1922 he was hired to design and supervise the construction of Mount Olive Baptist Church at 301 Church Street in Mullins, South Carolina.[2]

Around 1927 Ford designed Saint John African Methodist Episcopal Church at 702 Mill Street in Marion, South Carolina, and helped to build it.

On April 21, 1928, Wade Ford married Ruth Nance, daughter of Armstrong and Ella Nance of Lake View. She taught in public schools in Dillon County, South Carolina. Three daughters—Mammie, Blondell, and Doris—were born to this union.

Ford learned quickly that his architectural fees were not sufficient to support his growing family. He resorted to building and renovating farm buildings and other ancillary structures.

When his parents' 2-story home was ruined by fire, he renovated it into a 1-story structure at 923 Old Kemper Road. In 1937 he designed and built another house at 938 Old Kemper Road, approximately three-fourths of a mile away, also on family-owned property. He harvested the lumber needed for the house from the longleaf timber on his own land. The house remains in the family as the home of his daughter, Doris Ford Johnson.

In 1942 Ford was hired by the Lake View School District to teach Black and White disabled veterans in carpentry, bricklaying, and related trades. In 1944 Ford designed and supervised the construction of Salem African Methodist Episcopal Church at 8381 Salem Church Road in Bucksport, South Carolina.

Wade Ford suffered a cerebral hemorrhage and died at home on January 31, 1949.[3] He is buried in the Union Cemetery in Lake View, South Carolina.

Notes
1. State Agricultural and Medical College, "Wade Alston Ford," Orangeburg, n.p., 1921, p. 8.
2. Fannie Leonard Simmons, "Mt. Olive Baptist Church," National Register of Historic Places Registration Form, U.S. Department of Interior, National Park Service, 1 July 1999, p. 1.
3. "Wade Alston Ford," Department of Commerce, Division of Vital Statistics, State Board of Health, State of South Carolina, 31 January 1949.

Bibliography
South Carolina Department of Archives and History. *African American National Register Sites of Historical Markers in South Carolina*. Orangeburg: South Carolina Department of Archives and History, 2000.

DORIS FORD JOHNSON,
DAUGHTER OF WADEFORD AND MASTER TEACHER
AND MEDIA SPECIALIST (RETIRED),
LAKE VIEW HIGH SCHOOL,
LAKE VIEW, SOUTH CAROLINA

BUILDING LIST

Name	Address	City	State	Year	Comments
Ford, Wade A.	938 Old Kemper Rd.	Lake View	SC	1937	
Mt. Olive Baptist Church	301 Church St.	Mullins	SC	1922	
Salem African Methodist Episcopal Church	8381 Salem Rd.	Bucksport	SC	1944	
St. John African Methodist Episcopal Church	702 Mill St.	Marion	SC	1927	

George Washington Foster Jr.
(1866–1923)

Jeanne Foster Higginbotham

George Washington Foster Jr. was born on December 18, 1866, in Newark, New Jersey. His father, George Sr., was a carriage striper and his mother, Isabella Davis Foster (a descendant of Jefferson Davis), was a housewife. Around 1880 the family moved to New York City. It is believed that Foster attended Cooper Union for the Advancement of Science and Art in Manhattan, a selective, private, tuition-free school that offered degrees in engineering and architecture.[1]

About 1888 Foster was hired as a draftsman in the office of prominent New York architect Henry J. Hardenbergh (1847–1918), well known for his designs of apartment houses, office buildings, and hotels.[2] In that period, the firm was preparing plans for the original Waldorf Hotel (1890) on Fifth Avenue and 34th Street. Foster is also believed to have worked in New York for the Chicago-based architectural office of Daniel H. Burnham & Co. in the construction of the Fuller Building (renamed the Flatiron Building), which was completed in 1903. In 1897 Foster won a medal at the TENNESSEE CENTENNIAL AND INTERNATIONAL EXPOSITION for his paintings "Cloister of San Pablo at Barcelona" and "Chateau Crillion"; it was the same competition in which WILLIAM AUGUSTUS HAZEL competed.

In 1889, at age twenty-three, George W. Foster Jr. married Carrie Augusta Jackson and for several years they lived on Long Island. Then in 1902, they moved with their three children to Park Ridge, New Jersey, to a spacious house at 102 Colony Avenue, which ultimately accommodated their large family of ten children. The house, which Foster had designed and where he lived until his death in 1923, is listed in the New Jersey Black Historic Places Survey.[3]

On March 19, 1908, Foster became the second African American licensed to practice architecture in the state of New Jersey.[4] That same year, he entered into partnership with VERTNER WOODSON TANDY to establish the firm of Tandy & Foster—combining his excellent delineating talents with Tandy's architectural engineering skills. Their office was located at 1931 Broadway in an African American neighborhood known as San Juan Hill in the west 60s in Manhattan near present-day Lincoln Center. The firm's commissions included a number of churches and apartment houses in Harlem.

The most prominent commission that Tandy & Foster received was the Saint Philip's Protestant Episcopal Church and Parish House, built between 1910 and 1911 in Harlem. The new building was the fourth home of the church, which was originally established in lower Manhattan in 1818 as the city's first African American congregation of Protestant Episcopalians. Following the movement of parishioners uptown, Saint Philip's was the first church constructed in Harlem that was designed by a Black architect for a Black congregation. Foster designed Saint Philip's in the neo-Gothic style with an impressive facade of contrasting orange Roman brick and cast-stone aggregate trim rising from a granite base. Pointed-arch, stained-glass windows were ornamented with tracery in the English Perpendicular style. The adjoining Parish House in the Queen Anne style is believed to be primarily the work of Foster.[5]

Foster received his license to practice in the state of New York on December 1, 1916. That same year he is listed with a different partner as Tillack & Foster in Park Ridge, New Jersey. His last office was located in River Edge, New Jersey, in association with contractors Lawlor & Hayes. In addition to his own residence, Foster designed houses in northern New Jersey; Berea, Kentucky; and Mexico City, Mexico.

Foster's most significant commission was Mother African Methodist Episcopal Zion Church (known as Mother Zion), New York's first Black congregation, established in 1876 and the founding church of a

Mother African Methodist Episcopal Zion Church, *Joyce Mendelsohn*

nationwide conference of churches that were prominent in the abolitionist movement. Located in Harlem, the sixth home of the congregation was erected between 1923 and 1925 at a cost of $450,000. Foster designed a distinguished neo-Gothic-style façade of rough gray stone laid in random ashlar trimmed in white terra cotta. Dominating the 95-foot-wide facade is a central gable pierced by a large pointed-arch stained-glass window above three pointed-arch entrances set within the entrance portico.[6]

George W. Foster Jr. died of pneumonia on December 20, 1923, shortly after his fifty-seventh birthday. He did not live to see construction of Mother Zion completed. He is buried in Westwood Cemetery, Westwood, New Jersey.

Notes

1. Interview with Jeanne Higginbotham (George Foster Jr.'s granddaughter), by Carson Anderson, Philadelphia, Pa., 6 June 1978.
2. Schuyler Warmflash, "George Washington Foster Jr., An Early Black Architect," in *Bergen County Historic Sites Survey*, (Parmus: Bergen County Office of Cultural and Historic Affairs, September 1983), p. 32.
3. Bob Craig, "11 New Jersey Black Historic Places Survey," Trenton: New Jersey Historical Commission, 1985, p. 7.
4. New Jersey State Board of Architects, "George W. Foster Jr.," Certificate no. 280, issued, 19 March 1908.
5. Carson Anderson to Bob Craig, 25 April 1983, p. 2. Letter in the possession of the editor
6. Moore, Christopher, and Andrew Dolkart. *Mother African Methodist Episcopal Church Designation Report.* New York: New York Landmarks Preservation Commission, 1993.

Bibliography

Savage, Charles. *St. Philips Protestant Episcopal Church Designation Report.* New York: New York Landmarks Preservation Commission, 1993.

JOYCE MENDELSOHN,
AUTHOR AND TEACHER, NEW SCHOOL UNIVERSITY,
NEW YORK, NEW YORK

BUILDING LIST

Name	Address	City	State	Year	Comments
Foster, George W.	102 Colony Ave.	Park Ridge	NJ	1902	
Mother African Methodist Episcopal Zion Church	140 W. 137th St.	New York	NY	1923	
St. Philips Protestant Episcopal Church	204 W. 134th St.	New York	NY	1910	
St. Philips Protestant Episcopal Church Parish Hall	208 W. 134th St.	New York	NY	1910	Demolished
Woodcliff Lake School	134 Woodcliff Ave.	Woodcliff Lake	NJ	1910	Plans only

Louis Edwin Fry Sr.
(1903–2000)

Louis Edwin Fry Jr.

Louis Fry Sr. was born January 10, 1903, in Bastrop, Texas, the youngest of two sons to Pleasant Ann Fry and Henry Bowers Fry. He attended Emile High School and graduated from the twelfth grade in 1918 at age fifteen. Following graduation, Fry left Bastrop to attend PRAIRIE VIEW AGRICULTURAL AND MECHANICAL COLLEGE (A&M) where he earned a bachelor of science in mechanic arts in 1922. In 1923 Fry enrolled at Kansas State University in Manhattan, where he earned a bachelor of science in architectural engineering in 1927.

Fry's first job after completing Kansas State University was to return to Prairie View Agricultural and Mechanical College to teach math and engineering. Fry was asked by the campus architect to design a new dormitory for women, later named Evans Hall (1928). Fry also designed the fifty-bed hospital (1929) in Prairie View, which was demolished in the 1980s. He was the second African American to practice architecture in the state of Texas.

In 1927 Fry married Obelie Swearinger of Kansas City, Missouri. Prior to their marriage she was a cook. Their first born, Louis Jr., became an architect and their second born, Gladys, became a professor of folklore at the University of Maryland at College Park.

In 1929 Fry returned to Kansas State University and earned a master of science in architecture a year later. After completing his master's degree at Kansas State University, Fry was hired by ALBERT IRVIN CASSELL, who at the time was designing two buildings for HOWARD UNIVERSITY. Fry was hired as a senior designer, replacing HILYARD ROBERT ROBINSON, who was leaving to study public housing in Germany.[1] Fry contributed to the design of the women's dormitory complex (begun by Hilyard Robinson), Douglas Hall classroom building, the Chemistry Building, Founders Library, the power plant, the university entrance gates, and the master plan for the campus. Fry left Cassell's office in 1935 when he received an offer from TUSKEGEE INSTITUTE to teach.

Although architecture classes had been taught at Tuskegee Institute since 1893, Fry became the first head of the newly organized Department of Architecture. He laid the foundation for future accreditation of the Tuskegee Architecture Department and completed the master plan for the campus. While at Tuskegee Institute, Fry also designed nine buildings on the quadrangle at Alabama State University in Montgomery.

In 1940 Fry was appointed campus architect at Lincoln University in Jefferson City, Missouri. Again Fry left his mark on a college campus by designing the Journalism Building and Page Library. Completed in 1947, the library, although Georgian in style to match the existing buildings, featured many innovative ideas such as opening the stacks for easier access, a concept not yet widely used at the time.[2] In 1983 Page Library was placed on the National Register of Historic Places a contributing building to the the Hilltop Campus Historic District encompassing Lincoln University. In collaboration with CHARLES EDGAR DICKINSON, Fry completed the master plan for Lincoln University.

In 1944 Fry took a sabbatical from Lincoln University to enroll in Harvard University's Graduate School of Design seeking a master of architecture degree. Among the celebrated faculty of the School of Design was Walter Gropius (1883–1969) from whom Fry took classes. Fry graduated in 1945, the first African American to earn the master of architecture degree from Harvard University. After graduation, Fry worked briefly for Marcel Breuer (1902–1981) as a draftsman.[3] He then returned to Lincoln University and resumed teaching and serving as campus architect.

In 1947 Fry was asked by Dr. Lewis K. Downing, dean of the Howard University School of Engineering and Architecture, to join the School of Architecture faculty. Fry accepted on the condition that he could continue his private practice and finish the buildings he had started for Lincoln University and Alabama State University. Fry taught at Howard University from 1947 until 1972, and—along with HOWARD HAMILTON MACKEY SR., then head of the School of Architecture—was instrumental in gaining accreditation for the School of Architecture.

Despite the distance, Fry continued to design buildings for Tuskegee Institute, Alabama State University, and Lincoln University. Fry operated his practice as a sole proprietor until 1954, when he asked JOHN AUSTIN WELCH, a longtime friend, to become a partner. The firm of Fry & Welch designed sixteen major campus buildings in five states. Welch handled day-to-day administrative matters and drawing production, whereas Fry was the office's designer. Fry & Welch designed approximately one-third of the buildings on Tuskegee Institute's campus and were associate architects to Paul Rudolph on the new chapel. The partnership lasted until 1969, despite the fact that in 1957 Welch became dean of the School of Mechanical Industries at Tuskegee Institute.

In 1960 Louis Edwin Fry Jr., a graduate of Howard University, joined his father's firm. Father and son designed Mount Carmel Apartments—the first air-rights housing development in the District of Columbia, and Takoma Elementary, Fort Lincoln Elementary, and Marie Reed Elementary for the District of Columbia public school system.

Throughout his career, Louis Fry Sr. taught architecture at the collegiate level. He felt that it was important for African American students to have practicing architects as role models and that architecture instructors should maintain a strong private practice so that students could aspire to do the same.

In 1967 Louis Edwin Fry Sr. was named a fellow of the American Institute of Architects for his contribution to the education and practice of architecture.

Fry was registered in Alabama, Maryland, Missouri, Pennsylvania, and the District of Columbia. He served as a member of the D.C. Board of Examiners and Reg-

Page Library, Lincoln University, *courtesy of Lincoln University Archives*

istrars for Architects, completing the last two years of the term relinquished by Hilyard Robert Robinson and then serving an additional three-year term of his own.

Louis Edwin Fry Sr. died in his sleep on June 13, 2000, three days before a testimonial dinner in his honor was to be held at Harvard University.

Notes
1. Louis Edwin Fry Sr., "His Life and His Architecture" (typescript), 1980, p. 88. Copy held by the office of Fry & Welch, Washington, D.C.
2. Ibid., p. 100.
3. Ibid., p. 137.
4. "Architect Louis Fry Sr.; Led Program at Howard," *Washington Post*, 13 June 2000, p. B5.

Bibliography
Fry Jr., Louis, "Remarks at Howard University Dinner to Honor Mr. Louis E. Fry Sr." (Transcript in the possession of Harry Robinson, Washington, D.C.) 16 June 2000, p. 3.
Fry, Louis E. "Where Is the Sun?" In *Research Journal*. Vol. 1, no. 1, Jefferson City: Lincoln University Press, (Spring 1947): 7.
"Young Negro Architect Praised for Designing Tuskegee's New Infantile Paralysis Hospital." *Oklahoma Eagle*, 10 February 1940, p. 1.

ANNETTE K. CARTER,
ARCHITECTURAL DESIGN GROUP,
ALEXANDRIA, VIRGINIA

BUILDING LIST

Name	Address	City	State	Year	Comments
Alabama State College Library	Campus	Montgomery	AL	1962	Addition
Alabama State College Arena–Auditorium	Campus	Montgomery	AL	1954	
Alabama State College Classroom Bldg.	Campus	Mobile	AL		
Alabama State College Classroom Bldg.	Campus	Montgomery	AL	1954	
Alabama State College Dining Hall	Campus	Montgomery	AL		
Alabama State College Mens Dormitory	Campus	Montgomery	AL	1960	
Alabama State College Science Bldg.	Campus	Montgomery	AL	1962	
Alabama State College Swimming Pool Bldg.	Campus	Montgomery	AL	1962	
Alabama State College Womens Dormitory	Campus	Montgomery	AL		architects
Davis, Dr. Stephen		Washington	DC	1962	
Ft. Lincoln Elementary School	3100 Ft. Lincoln Dr., NE	Washington	DC	1967	Now Marshall Elementary School
Gray, Dr. James C.		Washington	DC	1962	
Lincoln University Journalism Bldg.	Campus	Jefferson City	MO		
Lincoln University Mens Dormitory	Campus	Jefferson City	MO		
Lincoln University Page Library	Campus	Jefferson City	MO	1954	
Lincoln University Womens Dormitory	Campus	Jefferson City	MO		
Marie Reed Elementary School	2200 Champlain St., NW	Washington	DC		
Montana Terrace Public Housing	1625 Montana Ave., NE	Washington	DC	1965	
Morgan State University Classroom Bldg.	Campus	Baltimore	MD		
Mt. Carmel Apts. Housing	200 K St. NW	Washington	DC	1960	HWA & TAMS, assoc.
Phelps High School Greenhouse	704 26th St. NE	Washington	DC	1965	
Prairie View A&M Womens Dormitory	Campus	Prairie View	TX	1928	Now Evans Hall
Prairie View A&M Gym	Campus		TX	1929	Demolished
Prairie View A&M Hospital	Campus	Prairie View	TX	1929	Demolished
Takoma Elementary School	7010 Piney Branch Rd., NW	Washington	DC		
Tuskegee Institute Andrews Hospital	Campus	Tuskegee	AL	1962	Alterations
Tuskegee Institute Chapel	Campus	Tuskegee	AL	1960	Assoc. architect
Tuskegee Institute Food Processing Plant	Campus	Tuskegee	AL	1954	
Tuskegee Institute Infantile Paralysis Hospital	Campus	Tuskegee	AL	1940	
Tuskegee Institute Mens Dormitory	Campus	Tuskegee	AL	1962	
Tuskegee Institute Moton Hall	Campus	Tuskegee	AL		
Tuskegee Institute School of Nursing	Campus	Tuskegee	AL	1962	William Metcalf, assoc. enginr.
Tuskegee Institute Vocational Bldg.	Campus	Tuskegee	AL		
Tuskegee Institute Womens Dormitory	Campus	Tuskegee	AL	1962	
United House of Prayer	1117 7th St., NW	Washington	DC	1964	

Ethel Madison Bailey Furman
(1893–1976)

J. Livingston Furman

Ethel Madison Bailey was born July 6, 1893, in Richmond, Virginia. She was the daughter of Margaret M. Jones Bailey and Madison J. Bailey. She became the earliest known African American female architect in Virginia.

Ethel Bailey's life was shaped by architecture. Her father, the second licensed Black contractor in the city of Richmond, built the family home at 3025 Q Street, in the Church Hill district of Richmond. The house also served as her father's office. Madison J. Bailey was both father and mentor. Throughout Ethel's childhood, while attending segregated public schools, she would accompany her father to construction sites, observing the construction techniques and materials and listening to jargon associated with the building trade. Over time Ethel Bailey began to undertake some of the drafting work required by her father's construction business.[1]

Ethel Bailey's formal education began in the Richmond public school system, where she attended Armstrong High School before her family relocated to Pennsylvania. In 1910 she graduated from Germantown High School in north Philadelphia.

Ethel Bailey married William H. Carter, a barber, on October 12, 1912, in New Jersey. They had two children: Thelma Carter Henderson, born in 1914, in Buffalo, New York; and Madison Carter, born in 1916, in Lakawana, New York. By 1918 Ethel Bailey had divorced Carter, married Joseph D. Furman, and resumed her training in architectural drafting. Details are vague, but family oral history informs that Madison J. Bailey arranged for his daughter to receive architectural training from a private tutor in New York circa 1915. Private tutoring was an educational path employed by women such as Theodate Pope Riddle (1867–1946) to overcome the gender discrimination they commonly faced. Furman would not complete her formal education until the late 1940s. Between 1944 and 1946, Furman received formal training in architecture at the Chicago Technology College.

Ethel Furman returned to Richmond while her second husband, who was a Pullman porter for the New York Central Railroad spent much of his time on the road between New York and Richmond. She raised their son, J. Livingston Furman, and her two children from her previous marriage. Ethel and Joseph Furman lived in the house built by her father on Q Street where like her father before her she also had her office.

Furman began her architectural career with her father's contracting business. Her association with her father strengthened her ties to the building community, evidenced by her inclusion in the annual "Negro Contractors' Conference" held in 1927 at HAMPTON INSTITUTE. A notable example of her early work is the Wilder house, at 933 North 28th Street, in the Church Hill district of Richmond. Furman designed and her father constructed the birthplace and childhood home of Lawrence Douglas Wilder, the first elected post-

Fourth Baptist Church,
Kimberly M. Chen

Reconstruction-era Black governor in the United States in 1989. The Wilder house typifies Furman's desire to provide her clients with functional buildings at reasonable costs.[2]

Furman often scaled her designs to meet the needs of her clients. Reducing architectural details to a minimum in an effort to reduce expenses, she never compromised on the quality of materials or structural details. Although best remembered for her functional dwellings, Furman also designed many churches, including two in Liberia, Africa. In Richmond, an early example of her church designs is Saint James Holiness Church (1939). The education wing of Fourth Baptist Church (1961), also in Richmond, represents both the diversity and longevity of Furman's career.

Ethel Furman received awards for her community leadership. In 1954 the East End Civic League awarded Furman the "Walter Manning Citizenship Award" and in 1959 she was named to the *Richmond Afro-American* "Community Honor Roll." More than nine years after her death in 1976, Furman's impact on the community was acknowledged when in 1985 the City of Richmond renamed a neighborhood park in her honor.

With some two hundred buildings credited to Furman, it is significant that she has not been included in the architectural discourse in Virginia. Furman's earliest works and published references to her as an architect predate any known female architects and more specifically any Black female architects in Virginia.[3]

AMAZA LEE MEREDITH designed her own home "Azurest South" in 1939, well after Ethel Furman had begun her architectural career. Mary Ramsay Channel Brown (1907–   ) is recognized as the first licensed female architect in Virginia. In 1935 Brown completed her studies at Cornell University and received her license as an architect. She began her career in the early 1940s working primarily in Portsmouth, Virginia.[4] Furman, however, established her architectural career well before Meredith and Channel, completing the Wilder house in 1923. Many of Furman's earliest buildings have been demolished. This may partially explain why she has been recognized as a civic leader while her contributions to the architectural history of Virginia have gone largely unnoticed.

Notes

1. Interviews with J. Livingston Furman and Josephine Furman (son and daughter of Ethel Furman), by Jessica Breeden, Richmond, Va., 11 November 1996.

2. L. Douglas Wilder (former governor of Virginia), interview by Sonia M. Burke, Richmond, Va., 1 October 1982, quoted in "Ethel Bailey Furman: Her Story" (typescript), 16 April 1992, University of Virginia Library. In an interview for the Church Hill Oral History Collection, Virginia Black History Archives, James Branch Cabell Library, Virginia Commonwealth University, L. Douglas Wilder stated that he was born on January 17, 1931, in the house at 933 North 28th Street, delivered by a midwife.

3. "Mrs. Ethel Furman, 3025 Q Street, Richmond, Va., of Whom the Boast Is Made That She Is the Only Architect of Her Sex and Race in the Old Dominion," *Pittsburgh Courier*, 23 January 1937, n.p.

ETHEL MADISON BAILEY FURMAN

4. John E. Wells and Robert E. Dalton, *The Virginia Architects, 1835–1955: A Biographical Dictionary* (Richmond: New South Architectural Press, 1997), p. 49.

Bibliography

Breeden, Jessica Lloyd. "Ethel Bailey Furman: Richmond Architect" (typescript), 1996. Cabell Library, Virginia Commonwealth University, Richmond.

Brownell, Charles E., Calder Loth, William Rasmussen, and Richard Guy Wilson. *The Making of Virginia Architecture.* Richmond: Virginia Museum of Fine Arts, 1992.

Susan Gergen Horner,
Architectural Historian,
Richmond, Virginia

BUILDING LIST

Name	Address	City/County	State	Year	Comments
Apostolic Faith Church	2206 Ford Ave.	Richmond	VA		Demolished
Cauthorne, Leland S.	Rte. 650	Goochland County	VA	1955	
Cedar Street Memorial Baptist Church	716 N. 24th St.	Richmond	VA		Baptistery
Dickerson, Isaac	Rte 621	Goochland County	VA	c1950	
Edwards, Thomas N.	Rte. 33, Davis Hgwy.	Chesterfield County	VA	c1950	
Fourth Baptist Church	2800 P St.	Richmond	VA	1961	
Mt. Carmel Church	Highway 684	Noel	VA	1955	
Mt. Nebo Baptist Church	Rte. 168, Barhamsville	Kent County	VA		
Mt. Olive Baptist Church	8775 Mt. Olive Ave.	Henrico County	VA	1974	
Mt. Pleasant Baptist Church	Old Bermuda Hundreds	Chesterfield County	VA		
Pleasant, Nathan	Rte. 711	Powhatan	VA	c1950	
Rising Mt. Zion Baptist Church	Williamsburg Rd., Box 259	Sanston	VA	1976	
Snead, James	Rte 2, Box 368	Richmond	VA	1968	
Snead, Junius	Springfield Rd., Rte. 2	Glen Allen	VA	1968	
Snead, Mack	Blair Rd., Rte. 649	Goochland County	VA	1968	
Snead, Samuel	Blair Rd., Rte. 649	Goochland County	VA	c1968	
Snead, Thomas M.	SR 615 Road	Goochland County	VA	1965	
Springfield Baptist Church	7226 Creighton Rd.	Hanover County	VA	1976	
St. James Baptist Church	Blair Rd., Rte. 649	Goochland County	VA	1972	
St. James Baptist Church	Gumtree Rd.	Beaverdam	VA		Addition
St. James Holiness Church	14 E. 30th St.	Richmond	VA	1939	Demolished
St. James Holiness Church	16 E. 29th St.	Richmond	VA	1956	
Union Baptist Church	Rte. 611	Quinton	VA		Addition
Union Hope Baptist Church	Rte. 168, Barhamsville	Kent County	VA		Addition
Wilder, Robert J.	933 N. 28th St.	Richmond	VA	c1923	Demolished

James Homer Garrott
(1897–1991)

Negro History Bulletin

James Homer Garrott was born on June 19, 1897, in Montgomery, Alabama. His parents were James Henry Garrott and Fanny Walker Garrott. His father was a builder and helped to erect buildings on the campus of TUSKEGEE INSTITUTE including the chapel designed by ROBERT ROBINSON TAYLOR. His mother was remembered as being artistic and musical.

The Garrott family moved to Los Angeles in 1903, when James Homer was six. He graduated from Los Angeles Polytechnic High School in 1917.

Garrott's first documented employment was with Pasadena architect George P. Telling from 1924 to 1926. Garrott's next employment was with Cavagliere Construction Company of Los Angeles from 1926 to 1928. Garrott opened his own office after passing the California architect licensing examination in 1929.[1]

Garrott's most important early commission was the headquarters of Golden State Mutual Life Insurance Company, a Black-owned firm based in Los Angeles. This Spanish Colonial–style building was on the main commercial arterial of the African American community, Central Avenue, and opened in December 1928. The Golden State Mutual Life Insurance Company also used an African American contractor, Louis Blodgett.[2]

Few of Garrott's early buildings have been documented. One that has is a speculative house in Pasadena that was completed in 1930 for Clarence A. Jones. Spanish Colonial in style, the house cost $5,000 to build. The contractor was another African American, Woodford Terry.[3]

Garrott designed a four-unit Spanish Colonial–style apartment building in 1927, at 1151 West 27th Street in Los Angeles near the campus of the University of Southern California. Garrott also renovated a *café* at 1551 North Vine in Hollywood in 1938 and a store at 602 Santa Monica Boulevard in Hollywood in 1938.[4]

Garrott's second wife was Helen Duncan, whom he wed on February 13, 1942, in Yuma, Arizona. They had no children.

Garrott closed his practice because of the slowdown of civilian construction due to World War II. He went to work at Douglas Aircraft in Santa Monica. At age forty-eight he enrolled in the architecture program at the University of Southern California, whose curriculum had recently changed from the Ecole des

Beaux-Arts model to a Modernism derivative from the Bauhaus. Judging from his school projects, Garrott favored Modernism. Although he did not graduate from University of Southern California, Garrott's career was reborn by his enrollment there.

He re-opened his office in 1946, after the construction restrictions of World War II ended. By 1951 Garrott had designed an uncompromisingly Modern-style 1-story office building for himself at 2311 Hyperion Avenue in the Silverlake area and his home at 653 Micheltorena Street, not far from his office. His career seemed to be on the upswing. Garrott published an article on motels in *Architect and Engineer*, was profiled in *Negro Who's Who in California,* and was the subject of a lengthy interview in the *Negro History Bulletin* in which he claimed to have designed 200 houses and twenty-five churches.[5]

During this period of career rebirth in 1946, Garrott applied for membership in the Southern California Chapter of the American Institute of Architects. His application was endorsed by PAUL REVERE WILLIAMS and by Gregory Ain (1908–1988), a respected architect who was politically active in local progressive causes.

Garrott was also politically active. Frank Wilkinson, a dedicated Los Angeles housing activist, offered that Garrott was a member of an informal group of people he called "progressives."[6] Wilkinson included in that group well-known local architects Robert Evans Alexander (1907–1992), Reginald Johnson (1882–1952), and architect Richard Neutra (1892–1970) and others from related fields such as photographer Julius Shulman, husband and wife architect-designers Charles and Ray Eames, and landscape architect Garrett Eckbo (1910–2000). Many in this loose confederation were tarred by McCarthyism and blacklisted. Although it is difficult to prove that Garrott was blacklisted, he had few commissions between 1950 and 1954 at the peak of McCarthyism.

Garrott benefitted professionally from being politically well connected. Frank Wilkinson said that Garrott made friends with another liberal activist, Kenneth Hahn, who went on to become an influential Los Angeles County supervisor from 1952 to 1993.[7] It can be inferred that this connection helped Garrott to receive nine commissions from the Los Angeles County government between 1954 and 1969.

Garrott's best-recognized work is the Westchester Municipal Building. Completed in 1960 for the City of Los Angeles, it still functions as a satellite city hall and branch public library. The building is located in the Westchester neighborhood of Los Angeles, on the corner of Manchester and Lincoln Boulevards.

Chester M. Moss House, *Julius Shulman*

In the twilight years of Garrott's career, he was a mentor to inexperienced African American architects in Los Angeles including LESTER OLIVER BANKHEAD, Clyde Grimes, Charles G. Lewis, and Harold Williams. A testament to the high regard in which Garrott was held was evidenced by the Minority Architects and Planners of Los Angeles, which honored him with its "Award for Lifetime Achievement" in 1975. The first recipient a year earlier had been Paul Revere Williams. Garrott was elevated to emeritus status in the American Institute of Architects in 1974.

James Garrott died in Los Angeles on June 9, 1991.

Notes

1. California State Board of Architectural Examiner's Reports "James Garrott," no. 1642, issued 1929.
2. Golden State Mutual Life Insurance Company donated their records to the University of California at Los Angeles, University Research Library, Department of Special Collections. Interview with Edgar Johnson, Golden State Mutual Life Insurance Company, Executive Officer, Los Angeles, California, 7 August 1992.
3. The newsletter of the Urban Conservation Office, *The Bungalow Reader*, no. 5 (May 1988): n.p.
4. *Southwest Builders and Contractors*, 21 January 1938, p. 54; and *Southwest Builders and Contractors*, 4 August 1938, p. 65.
5. James Garrott, "Calistoga Motel," *Architect and Engineer* (May 1947): 16; "James Garrott," *Negro Who's Who in California* (Los Angeles: California Eagle Publishing Company 1948) p. 84; Marguerite Cartwright, "James Garrott, California Architect," *Negro History Bulletin* (April 1955), 151.
6. Interview with Frank Wilkinson (Los Angeles housing activist), Los Angeles, 10 April 1992.
7. Wilkinson interview.

Bibliography

"James Garrott." American Institute of Architects Archives, Washington, D.C.

WESLEY HOWARD HENDERSON

BUILDING LIST

Name	Address	City	State	Year	Comments
Apartment Bldg.	1151 W. 27th St.	Los Angeles	CA	1927	
Bodger County Park Director's Bldg.	14700 Yokon Ave.	Hawthorne	CA	1960	
Calistoga Motel		Calistoga	CA	1947	
Carson County Public Library	151 E. Carson Blvd.	Carson	CA	1969	
City Terrace Park Pavilion and Pool	1126 Hazzard Ave.	East Los Angeles	CA	1962	
Del Aire County Park Director's Bldg.	12601 S. Isis Ave.	Hawthorne	CA	1960	
Florence-Firestone Health Clinic	8019 Compton Ave.	Los Angeles	CA	1952	
Florence-Firestone Sheriff's Station	8019 Compton Ave.	Los Angeles	CA	1952	
Garrott, James H.	653 Micheltorena St.	Los Angeles	CA	1951	
Garrott Office Bldg.	2311 Hyperion Ave.	Los Angeles	CA	1951	
Golden State Mutual Insurance Company	4261 S. Central Ave.	Los Angeles	CA	1928	
Hamilton Methodist Church	6330 S. Figueroa St.	Los Angeles	CA	1950	
Hauser, Dr. Eric		Santa Fe	NM	1952	
Jones, Clarence A.	70 W. Mountain Ave.	Pasadena	CA	1930	Spec. house
Laguna Park Senior Citizen Bldg.	3646 Whittier Blvd.	East Los Angeles	CA	1967	
Lawndale Administrative Center Health Clinic	14616 Grevillea Ave.	Los Angeles	CA	1957	
Lawndale Administrative Center Library	14616 Grevillea Ave.	Los Angeles	CA	1957	
Margolis, Ben		Hollywood	CA	1961	
Moss, Chester M.		Westwood Hills	CA	1955	
Store	602 Santa Monica Blvd.	Los Angeles	CA	1938	
Tufeld, Richard		Los Angeles	CA	1959	Garden bldg.
Victoria County Park Director's Bldg.	419 E. 192nd St.	Carson	CA	1960	
Vine Street *Cafè*	1551 N. Vine St.	Los Angeles	CA	1938	Alternations
Westchester Municipal Bldg.	Lincoln & Manchester Blvds.	Los Angeles	CA	1960	

Lewis Wentworth Giles Jr.
(1923–   )

Lewis Giles Jr., was the youngest son of LEWIS WENTWORTH GILES SR. He was born in Washington, D.C., on July 25, 1923. His mother, Gladys Wheatley Giles, was a housewife. Attending college and aspiring to a professional career were drilled into him by his father. Lewis's older brother, Julian, who was not artistically inclined like his father and brother, chose a career in medicine, rising to the prestigious position of director of the Veterans Hospital not far from TUSKEGEE INSTITUTE, which was the only Veterans Hospital staffed entirely by Black doctors and nurses.

Lewis Jr., attended Armstrong Technical High School in Washington, D.C., where he took mechanical drawing, which was taught all four years by GEORGE ALONZO FERGUSON, a friend of his father's who occasionally visited the Giles's home on Hunt Place, NE.[1] Lewis Jr. grew up in the Hunt Place home designed by his father. He loved the house so much that he was certain that when he grew up he wanted to become an architect—a fact that was reinforced by his father being an architect. Lewis Jr. graduated from Armstrong Technical High School in 1940. His father often regaled him about his collegiate days in Urbana-Champaign at the University of Illinois, and therefore Lewis Jr. barely considered nearby HOWARD UNIVERSITY'S SCHOOL OF ARCHITECTURE and instead chose the University of Illinois. After four years, Lewis Jr. was awarded his bachelor of science degree in architectural engineering in 1944, earning the enduring respect of his father, who withdrew from the university before earning his degree. Lewis Giles Jr. was drafted into the U.S. Navy after graduation. Even though he possessed a *bona fide* degree from a major university, the rigidly segregated U.S. Navy assigned him to be a training clerk at Great Lakes Naval Base north of Chicago and later to an electronics unit stationed in Chicago.

Lewis Giles met Patricia Parker from Chicago, Illinois, while both were students at the University of Illinois. They wed and had two children, Alan and Kay. The marriage lasted until 1962. Five years afterward Lewis met and married Minerva Dawson, from Washington, D.C. Together they had a daughter, Julie Giles Cooke.

Honorably discharged from the U.S. Navy, Giles Jr. joined his father's office in 1946 as an architectural draftsman. From 1947 to 1948, he took graduate courses in architectural design at The Catholic University of America. In 1949 he went to work for HILYARD ROBERT ROBINSON drafting the construction drawings for Bethune Women's Dormitory and the School of Engineering and Architecture at Howard University. In 1952 son and father formed Giles & Giles, Architects. Father-son office pairings were not that unusual because the fathers, who were from the old school, generally welcomed their sons, who were more contemporary architectural designers and better educated in terms of engineering principles. Examples of such pairings were ALBERT IRVIN CASSELL and his son CHARLES IRVIN CASSELL, LOUIS EDWIN FRY SR. and his son Louis Jr., MOSES MCKISSACK III and his son William Deberry, ROBERT ROBINSON TAYLOR

Beulah Baptist Church, *Dreck Spurlock Wilson*

and his son ROBERT ROCHON TAYLOR, and FRANCIS JEFFERSON ROBERSON and his son FRANCIS RASSIEUR.

From 1959 to 1968, Lewis Giles Jr. was an architect with the Naval Facilities Engineering and Architectural Specifications Branch of the Department of the Navy. He then transferred to another federal agency, where he was chief of the Specifications and Estimates Branch of the U.S. Postal Service, Facilities Department, from 1968 to 1971.

Giles was registered to practice architecture in the District of Columbia in 1952 and in Maryland the following year.[2] He also passed the grueling four-day, thirty-six-hour examination given by the National Council of Architectural Registration Boards. He joined the American Institute of Architects years later in 1964, and was also a certified construction specifier.

Giles returned to the Department of the Navy in 1971 and remained until 1985. He rose quickly through the ranks from specification writer to assistant director of the Specifications and Cost Division to head of the Architectural Division to director of the Architectural Division to chief architect of the Architectural Division, which was the top civilian authority in the Naval Facilities Engineering Command.

Giles Jr. moonlighted through the 1970s and 1980s designing churches for African American congregations—such as Beulah Baptist Church and Purity Baptist Church in Washington, D.C—which were the philosophic and programmatic opposite of the government-issue buildings he designed for the U.S. Navy.

Notes

1. Interview with Lewis Giles Jr., Columbia, Md., 20 October 2002.
2. D.C. Board of Examiners and Registrars of Architects, "Lewis Wentworth Giles, Jr.," Certificate no. 839, issued 24 June 1952.

DRECK SPURLOCK WILSON

BUILDING LIST

Name	Address	City	State	Year	Comments
House	2721 King Jr. Ave., SE	Washington	DC		
House	E. Capitol St. above Benning Rd., NE	Washington	DC	c1960	
Beulah Baptist Church	5820 Dix St., NE	Washington	DC	1967	
Brooks, E.	S. Dakota nr. Michigan Ave., NE	Washington	DC	c1960	
Collins, Dr. William K.	117 49th St., NE	Washington	DC		
Deanwood Professional Arts Bldg.	4645 Deane Ave., NE	Washington	DC	1955	
East Capitol Church of Christ	E. Capitol St. & Benning Rd., NE	Washington	DC	1968	
Purity Baptist Church	1325 Maryland Ave., NE	Washington	DC	c1970	Addition
Tabernacle Baptist Church	719 Division Ave., NE	Washington	DC	1953	Demolished

Lewis Wentworth Giles Sr.
(1894–1974)

Lewis Wentworth Giles Jr.

Lewis Giles was born on November 6, 1894, in Amelia County, Virginia, southwest of Richmond, to Lewis and Hattie Giles. The family moved to Washington, D.C., and Lewis Giles became one of the district's first Negro policemen. Hattie Giles was a homemaker. The younger Lewis enrolled at Armstrong Technical High School in the District of Columbia in 1908, where he graduated after five years.

After graduating from high school, Lewis Giles concluded that the University of Illinois at Urbana-Champaign, with a track record for enrolling Blacks to study architecture, was a good choice so he enrolled there in 1914. During his matriculation he was one of the founders of *Alpha Phi Alpha* Fraternity at the University of Illinois. Giles was drafted into the U.S. Army in 1917, which forced him to withdraw from the School of Architecture at the end of his junior year before he had earned enough credits to receive his diploma.

Giles trained at Camp Dix in Wrightstown, New Jersey, and joined the 349th Field Artillery's all-Black 92nd Buffalo Division commanded by John "Black Jack" Pershing. He taught field armaments at La Courtine Artillery Training School in France and drew cartographic panoramas relied on by forward spotters.

After his honorable discharge, Giles found employment back in Washington, D.C., as an architectural draftsman with ISAIAH TRUMAN HATTON, beginning in 1918 and lasting until Hatton's death in 1921. Giles was the chief draftsman for the Southern Aid Building (1918). Hatton died May 21 under mysterious circumstances, and Giles as his only employee came under suspicion. He was arrested and spent several nights in jail. No charges were filed and Giles was released three days after his arrest.

Lewis wed Gladys Wheatley from Decatur, Illinois, on August 23, 1920, in Champaign, Illinois. He met his future bride while attending the University of Illinois. They had two sons: Julian W. Giles, who became a physician and was a director of the all-Black Veterans Hospital in Tuskegee, Alabama and LEWIS WENTWORTH GILES JR.

After his dispiriting experience involving Hatton, Giles practiced solo. In 1921 he opened an office at 1200 U Street, NW, the same building where Hatton's office had been located, and continued at this location until 1929. He relocated the office to his home in 1929, where he maintained his practice until his death in 1974. He was registered in the District of Columbia to practice architecture in 1951, only after a change in the law required architects to be licensed.[1] Giles specialized in residential architecture, and frequently employed the Georgian style in his designs, including those for his own home at 4428 Hunt Place, NE, in the historic Deanwood neighborhood of far northeast Washington, D.C.

At the age of eighty, Lewis Giles Sr. was still on the job crawling on his hands and knees in the crawl space of a house he was inspecting when he bumped his head on a low-projecting pipe. He went to his doctor to have the bruise examined. The doctor sent him home, instructing him to rest. He died on May 28, 1974, from an undiagnosed hematoma. Lewis Giles Sr. is buried in Lincoln Memorial Cemetery in Suitland, Maryland.

Notes
1. D.C. Board of Examiners and Registrars of Architects, "Lewis Wentworth Giles," Certificate no. 1274, issued 20 March 1951.

Bibliography
Giles, Lewis W. *Master Specifications*. New York: Pageant Press, 1957.

DRECK SPURLOCK WILSON

Gladys Giles House, *Dreck Spurlock Wilson*

BUILDING LIST

Name	Address	City	State	Year	Comments
House	761 10th St., NW	Washington	DC	c1950	Demolished
House	621 G St., SE	Washington	DC	c1950	
House	1207 Girard St., NE	Washington	DC	c1924	
House	337 F St., SW	Washington	DC		Demolished
House	2617 Bowen Rd., SE	Washington	DC	c1924	Demolished
House	747 Alabama Ave., SE	Washington	DC	1936	
House	2034 12th St., NW	Washington	DC	1923	Alterations
House	2638 Stanton Pl., SE	Washington	DC	1945	
House	1218 Wisconsin Ave., NW	Washington	DC	1945	Addition
Alabama Courts Apts.	741 Alabama Ave., SE	Washington	DC	1936	
Bennett, Helen Z.	1409 Franklin St., NE	Washington	DC	1935	
Bernheimer, L.	1252 9th St., NW	Washington	DC	1942	Demolished
Brown, Grace A.	1218 Kearney St., NE	Washington	DC	1934	
Brown, Sterling	1222 Kearney St., NE	Washington	DC	1934	
Caton Apts.	2800 O St., NW	Washington	DC	1939	
Caton Apts.	2806 O St., NW	Washington	DC	1939	
Church of God Church	2030 Georgia Ave.	Washington	DC	1932	Demolished
Clandny Apts.	626 O St., NW	Washington	DC	1944	Demolished
Cohen, Samuel L.	809 44th St., SE	Washington	DC	1938	
Cohen, Samuel L.	916 44th St., SE	Washington	DC	1927	
Conter African Methodist Episcopal Zion Church	903 Division Ave., NE	Washington	DC	1963	
Church for David Smith	4919 E. Capitol St., SE	Washington	DC	1944	Demolished
Davis Apts.	3322 Sherman Ave., NW	Washington	DC	1933	

LEWIS WENTWORTH GILES SR.

BUILDING LIST *(continued)*

Name	Address	City	State	Year	Comments
Dixon, J. A.	44th St., SE	Washington	DC	1927	
Dodd, Randolph	906 48th St., NE	Washington	DC	1928	
Dodd, Randolph	1023 49th St., NE	Washington	DC	1928	
Duvall, Malcolm	1229 10th St., NW	Washington	DC	1927	
Edmondson, Gladys	2930 14th St., NE	Washington	DC	1939	
Eisinger, Jane	20 7th St., NE	Washington	DC		
Ellis, Lacy B.	5011 Nash St., NE	Washington	DC	1926	
Fairview Apts.	615 Alabama Ave., SE	Washington	DC	1936	
First Church of Christ Holiness	1219 Hamlin St., NE	Washington	DC	1958	
Freeman, Frank	1210 Irving St., NE	Washington	DC	1954	
Geiman Apts.	214 13th St., SE	Washington	DC	1928	
Giles, Gladys W.	4424 Hunt Pl., NE	Washington	DC	1929	
Gott, Howard S.	1017 49th St., NE	Washington	DC	1928	
Gott, Howard S.	1035 49th St., NE	Washington	DC	1928	
Gott, Howard S.	1031 49th St., NE	Washington	DC	1927	
Gott, Howard S.	1045 49th St., NE	Washington	DC	1926	
Gott, Howard S.	4720 Meade St., NE	Washington	DC	1926	
Gross, William E.	4423 Hunt Pl., NE	Washington	DC	1926	
Hall, Alvin C.	3322 Brothers Pl., SE	Washington	DC	1938	
Hirsch Apts.	1390 Nicholson St., NW	Washington	DC	1940	
Hite, Ronald T.	1322 Perry St., NE	Washington	DC	1957	
Holy Trinity Church	1215 49th Pl., NE	Washington	DC	1950	
Jason, Robert S.	2901 15th St., NE	Washington	DC	1937	
Johnson, Catherine W.	111 Raleigh St., SE	Washington	DC	1941	
Kaufman Store & Apts.	568 Lebaum St., SE	Washington	DC	1941	
Lewis Bldg.	2001 11th St., NW	Washington	DC	1922	
Lewis, R. A.	1348 Newton St., NE	Washington	DC	1927	
Lunduer Apts.	613 Portland St., SE	Washington	DC	1936	
Lutes, Bertie M.	1418 Girard St., NE	Washington	DC	1965	
Metrotone Baptist Church	5207 B St., SE	Washington	DC	1945	Demolished
New Hope Church Parsonage	1104 W St., NW	Washington	DC	1938	
New Mt. Olive Baptist Church	58th & Grant, NE	Washington	DC	1936	
Phylis Apts.	3740 12th St., NE	Washington	DC	1939	
Pilgrim African Methodist Episcopal Church	612 17th St., NW	Washington	DC	c1941	Addition
Pincus Apts.	401 Douglas Ave., SE	Washington	DC	1937	
Plummer, Roy U.	1345 Irving St., NE	Washington	DC	1941	
Prohaska Apts.	2810 O St., NW	Washington	DC	1939	
Rahn, Joseph	1318 Perry St., NE	Washington	DC	1959	
Randall, John	1315 Hamlin St., NE	Washington	DC	1936	
Rhines, John T.	1011 6th St., SW	Washington	DC	1938	Demolished
Rock Creek Baptist Church	4201 8th St., NW	Washington	DC	1955	
Rubbert, M. Frank	2331 Calvert St., NW	Washington	DC	1930	
Simon Apts.	542 Mellon St., SE	Washington	DC	1935	
St. John Baptist Church	53rd & Call Pl., SE	Washington	DC	1945	
Striner, Benjamin	617 Mellon St., SE	Washington	DC	1942	
Talbert, Ella M.	3212 Brothers Pl., SE	Washington	DC	1936	
Talbert, Ella M.	3331 King Jr. Ave., SE	Washington	DC	1941	Street name changed
Tater, William	1311 Girard St., NE	Washington	DC	1925	
Tepper, Joseph L.	326 45th St., NE	Washington	DC	1926	Demolished
Tepper, Joseph L.	926 45th Pl., NE	Washington	DC	1926	
Tepper, Joseph L.	4621 Hunt Pl., NE	Washington	DC	1926	
Tepper, Joseph L.	4623 Hunt Pl., NE	Washington	DC	1926	
Tepper, Joseph L.	4643 Hunt Pl., NE	Washington	DC	1926	
Tepper, Joseph L.	809 46th St., NE	Washington	DC	1923	
Thomas, George	1418 Jackson St., NE	Washington	DC	1939	
Wiggins, Elsie C.	2901 14th St., NE	Washington	DC	1939	
Williamson, Alphonso	1401 Franklin St., NE	Washington	DC	1934	
Williamson, Alphonso	2711 14th St., NE	Washington	DC	1956	
Wilma Gardens Apts.	3639 King Jr. Ave., SE	Washington	DC	1938	
Wilson Manor Apts.	511 Mellon St., SE	Washington	DC	1940	
Wineland, Lloyd G.	455 Newcomb St., SE	Washington	DC	1939	

Jasminius Wilsonni Rudolphus Grandy III
(1919–2001)

Grandy Family

J. W. R. Grandy III, horticulturist and landscape architect, was born in the town of Windsor in Bertie County, North Carolina, in the second decade of the 20th century. His father was Moses Grandy and his mother was Cornelia Speller Grandy. Because his name sounded unusual and looked like it had been lifted from 17th-century Swedish botanist Carolus Linnaeus's *Scientifice Plant Classification*, he preferred to be known by his initials, J. W. R. The family of seventeen children and parents raised cotton, corn, and soybeans; they also planted a garden grown from seeds purchased via the mail from Sears, Roebuck, & Company. Encouraged by his father and mother, J. W. R. would later expand on his agricultural upbringing to study the scientific applications of horticulture and aesthetic applications of landscape architecture.

After his father died, Grandy was determined to escape the backbreaking labor of farming to exercise his mind.[1] He graduated from the public schools of Bertie County and went on to attend NORTH CAROLINA AGRICULTURAL & TECHNICAL UNIVERSITY. He earned his bachelor of science degree in horticulture in 1940. "I was walking by the greenhouse one day and went in and helped a man with some plants. All the ones I worked with lived and I was given a job for $16 a month."[2] He and a few classmates opened the first Black-owned floral shop in Greensboro, North Carolina, around 1939. His love of ornamental horticultural would later become his inspiration for his trademark campus decorations from Christmas to Commencement.

Grandy pursued advanced studies in landscape architecture at Cornell University between 1940 and 1942. A conscientious student, he frequently built scale models of his landscape projects. He worked odd jobs to pay his tuition with some assistance from a few wealthy classmates who befriended him,[3] and ate well while working as a chef for several White-only fraternities on campus.

Before completing the requirements for a master of landscape architecture degree at Cornell University, Grandy returned home in order to save the family farm. With his father deceased and crop prices bottoming out, the family farm was threatened with foreclosure. They were successful, however, in raising the money to keep the farm in the family for another generation.

With an interest in teaching, Grandy obtained a faculty position at SOUTHERN UNIVERSITY SCHOOL OF ARCHITECTURE in Baton Rouge, Louisiana. For one year he taught horticulture. The following year, Grandy returned to his home state and joined the faculty at North Carolina Agricultural & Technical State University. Within the Department of Plant Science & Technology, Grandy was an instructor of horticulture and landscape architecture design until his retirement forty-two years later.

As a member of the faculty, he frequented the offices of colleagues in the department, particularly the chair of botany, Dr. Artis P. Grives. Dr. Grives' secretary was an advisor, along with Grandy, to the New Farmers of America and an attraction between them

JASMINIUS WILSONNI RUDOLPHUS GRANDY III

J. W. R. Grandy with scale model of North Carolina A&T University campus, *Grandy Family*

grew. J. W. R. Grandy married Ruth Dilliard of Eden, North Carolina, in the autumn of 1962. The couple made their house a home with the birth of a baby girl named Shirley and a son, J. W. R. IV.

By 1975 Grandy had become superintendent of grounds at North Carolina Agricultural & Technical University. In his private practice, he designed residential projects such as the one for famed civil rights attorney S. Kenneth Lee. Commercial projects were fewer, but he did design an industrial campus for Burlington Industries, commissioned by president Spencer Love. Grandy's commissions, however, were always second to his love of teaching. Grandy left a rich legacy of landscape architectural education and practice. He was an inspiring force among the faculty at the first historically Black college or university to earn accreditation for its undergraduate program in landscape architecture.

Grandy was a man of faith and was active in several churches. In 1940 he joined Institution Baptist Church in Greensboro, teaching Sunday school and singing tenor in a church quartet. He was also a supporter of Christian View Baptist Church in Spencer, Virginia. He was later confirmed at Grace Lutheran Church in Greensboro in 1998.

J. W. R. Grandy died on August 9, 2001.[4] His funeral was held at Grace Lutheran Church. He is buried in Lakeview Memorial Cemetery in Greensboro, North Carolina.

Notes
1. Interview with Ruth D. Grandy (wife of J. W. R. Grandy), Greensboro, North Carolina, 11 November 2002.
2. "J.W.R. Grandy, III," *Greensboro News Record*, 19 August 2002, p. B6.
3. Ruth Grandy interview.
4. *Greensboro News Record*, p. B6.

Bibliography
Dunn, Samuel J. "Professor Grandy Retires After 42 Years." *Environmental Observer*, vol. IV (June 1985): North Carolina A & T archives.

Spruill, Albert. "J. W. R. Grandy III: A Golly Good Professor." *Peacemaker*, 18 May 1985, p. 7.

DOUGLAS A. WILLIAMS,
INSTRUCTOR, INSTITUTE OF ARCHITECTURE,
PLANNING, AND LANDSCAPE ARCHITECTURE,
MORGAN STATE UNIVERSITY

LANDSCAPE PROJECT LIST

Name	Address	City	State	Year	Comments
Lee, Atty. S. Kenneth	1021 Broad Ave.	Greensboro	NC	1960	
North Carolina A&T University	Campus	Greensboro	NC	1975	

Beverly Loraine Greene
(1915–1957)

University of Illinois Archives

Beverly Greene is believed to have been the first African American female licensed as an architect in the United States. At age twenty-seven she gained registration in the state of Illinois on December 28, 1942.[1]

Beverly Greene was born in Chicago on October 4, 1915, the only child of James A. Greene, a lawyer, and Vera Greene, a housewife. They lived in a comfortable home on the south side of Chicago at 4637 South Wabash Avenue.

Beverly Greene received a bachelor of science degree in architectural engineering from the University of Illinois at Urbana-Champaign in 1936 and a master of science degree in city planning and housing from the same university one year later. A White classmate, Rudard Jones, remembered her: "Beverly got on just fine, from what I could tell; there wasn't any problem, but she was very retiring type of person. She wasn't at all forward or belligerent."[2]

Greene returned to her hometown and worked for the Chicago Housing Authority. According to KENNETH RODERICK O'NEAL, her being hired by the Chicago Housing Authority was a milestone given her race and gender.[3]

In 1945 she moved to New York City because she had read in the newspaper that Metropolitan Life Insurance Company was developing "Stuyvesant Town," a large private housing project in lower Manhattan. She read that they "did not intend to allow Negroes to live in the proposed project and I knew that certainly they wouldn't hire me. But there I was wrong. I was the very first person they did hire as an architect."[4] However, she quit after several days to accept a scholarship pressed on her by Columbia University to study city planning. A yearbook at Columbia University confirms her presence. She received her master's degree in architecture on June 5, 1945.

Between 1947 and 1955, Greene worked for the architectural firm headed by Isadore Rosefield, who specialized in health care and hospital design. Greene was one of two Black employees, the other being architect CONRAD ADOLPHUS JOHNSON JR., who along with his wife Clivetta were her friends. Greene made friends easily and counted PERCY COSTAS IFILL and his wife and Billy Strayhorn, Edward "Duke" Ellington's irreplaceable composer, and actress Lena Horne among her confidants.

Greene also worked with noted architect Edward Durell Stone (1927–1974) on a section of the arts complex at Sarah Lawrence College, in Bronxville, New York, in 1952 and for a theater at Stone's alma mater, the University of Arkansas, in 1951.

Greene was a member of the Council for the Advancement of the Negro in Architecture, which was formed in New York City to advance the careers of Black architects—similar in mission to the NATIONAL TECHNICAL ASSOCIATION.

Sometime after 1955, Greene worked for another noted architect, Marcel Breuer (1902–1981), who had an office in New York City. She is credited with working on some of his major projects. One of them was

BEVERLY LORAINE GREENE

Christian Reformer Church, *Roberta Washington*

the UNESCO United Nations headquarters in Paris, completed in 1958. She also worked on buildings for New York University, in University Heights, beginning in 1956 and completing them in 1961.

Greene died at age forty-one in New York City on August 22, 1957. A memorial service was held at Unity Funeral Home, 2352 Eighth Avenue in Manhattan, a building she designed, according to an obituary in the *New York Amsterdam News*. The newspaper went on to say, "Notables attending the invitational service included Lennie Heyton, Billy Strayhorn, and Dr. Arthur Logan. Marion Bruce sang." Greene had no immediate family in the city. Her remains were transported back home to Chicago, where her funeral was held. The newspaper obituary also listed an independent project, Christian Reformation Church, 121st Street at 7th Avenue in New York City.

Notes

1. Illinois Record of Architects Examination and License Applications, "Beverly L. Greene," Certificate No. 3002, issued 28 December 1942. State of Illinois Archives.
2. Interview with Rudard A. Jones, University of Illinois classmates of Beverly Greene, Urbana, Ill., 4 April 2001, University of Illinois Archives Alumni Oral History Project Files, Record Series 35/3/49.
3. "Woman Architect Blazes a New Trail for Others," *Amsterdam News* 23 June 1945, n.p.
4. "Miss Beverly L. Greene," *Chicago Daily Tribune*, 26 August 1957, p. 15.

Bibliography

"Beverly Greene." *Jet Magazine,* 5 September 1957, p. 45.

ROBERTA WASHINGTON, PRINCIPAL,
ROBERTA WASHINGTON ARCHITECTS,
NEW YORK, NEW YORK

BUILDING LIST

Name	Address	City	State	Year	Comments
Christian Reformation Church	121st & 7th Ave.	New York	NY	1956	Now Christian Parish for Spiritual Renewal
New York University	Campus	New York	NY	c1956	
Sara Lawrence College Theater	Campus	Bronxville	NY	1952	
United Nations Headquarters	6 place de Fontenoy	Paris	FR	1958	
Unity Funeral Chapel	2352 8th Ave.	New York	NY	1954	
University of Arkansas Theater	Campus	Fayetteville	AK	1951	

Francis Eugene Griffin
(1910–1973)

Courtesy of Detroit chapter, American Institute of Architects

Francis Eugene Griffin was born on September 10, 1910, in Battle Creek, Michigan, the second of four sons of William Edward Dunston Griffin and Genevieve Tucker Griffin. William Griffin worked as a chef at the Battle Creek Country Club before becoming a custodian at the Post Building in Battle Creek. The Griffin family belonged to Mount Zion African Methodist Episcopal Church in Battle Creek, where Genevieve Griffin was pianist and choir director for many years. Francis finished high school in Battle Creek, and received a diploma in February 1928. He enrolled in the University of Michigan from 1928 to 1931 and resumed study at the university from 1933 to 1935. Apparently Griffin had finished all requirements for a bachelor of science degree in architectural engineering by June 1935, but there is some uncertainty as to when the University of Michigan officially awarded him the degree. In 1939, when Griffin applied for registration as an architect in Washington, D.C., he wrote on the application that his baccalaureate degree was awarded in June 1935. However, University of Michigan records indicate that Griffin received the degree in 1944. There is no evidence that Griffin studied at University of Michigan or another school after June 1935.

Griffin worked as a maintenance assistant for North Carolina Agricultural & Technical College in Greensboro, North Carolina, for six months—September 1935 to February 1936. He then moved to Washington, D.C., and was employed as a draftsman, designer, and occasionally as a specification writer. He worked for JOHN ANDERSON LANKFORD from 1936 to 1938 and then for HOWARD HAMILTON MACKEY SR. from 1939 to 1941. In March 1939 Griffin applied for registration as an architect in the District of Columbia based on education and experience. His application was approved on January 16, 1940,[1] and he was employed as a draftsman and construction supervisor in the Building and Grounds Department at HOWARD UNIVERSITY. He was also employed by the War Department's Holabird Quartermaster Depot in Baltimore, Maryland, from 1940 to 1941. From 1941 to 1943 Griffin maintained a small private practice out of his home at 5325 Ames Street, NE, in Washington, D.C. He was then a cost estimator for ALBERT IRVIN CASSELL on Mayfair Mansion from 1943 to 1945.

By 1946 Griffin had moved to Detroit to become a principal in the new firm of White & Griffin, Architect-Engineer Associates. Griffin became a partner with DONALD FRANK WHITE, who had been a student at the University of Michigan's School of Architecture during Griffin's matriculation. The White & Griffin firm continued until 1958. The firm was known as a training ground for Black architects and engineers. Griffin was admitted to membership in the Detroit chapter of the American Institute of Architects on August 15, 1946.

In the mid-1950s Francis Griffin and Don White worked in the Republic of Liberia, West Africa. They were members of a team of technicians that included faculty from PRAIRIE VIEW AGRICULTURAL & MECHANICAL COLLEGE sent by the federal government to

Considine Recreation Building

help the Booker T. Washington Institute in Harbel, Liberia, transform itself into a technical school similar to land grant colleges in the United States. Francis Griffin and Donald White modernized the curriculum, improved the physical facilities of the institute, and developed a campus master plan to guide future expansion. In the 1960s Griffin was being considered for a position in Ghana, West Africa, which apparently never materialized.

On his return from Liberia in the late 1950s, Griffin became a principal in a new firm, Ward, Griffin & Agee, named for Harold Edward Ward, Francis Griffin, and Aubrey Caston Agee. In the 1970s the firm's name became Francis E. Griffin Associates, Architects & Planners. It was difficult maintaining enough commissions to support the office. From 1962 to 1969 Griffin was employed as a senior assistant architect engineer in the design section of the City of Detroit Housing Commission.

Griffin was a leader in the National Technical Association, holding several offices at both the local and national levels including the position of national membership chairman in the late 1940s. An organization for African American professionals, the National Technical Association assisted African Americans in overcoming barriers in occupational training and job opportunities. Griffin was also active with the Black Architects Group in Detroit.

Francis Griffin married Mallie Hill Griffin on August 6, 1936. Mallie Hill was a native of Fruitland Park, Florida, and an active member of the alumni association of Florida Agricultural & Mechanical University. She became an employee of the Detroit public schools. Two children were born to this union, Clifford and Evelyn.

Francis Griffin died of cancer in Detroit, Michigan, on February 14, 1973.[2] He was buried in Oak Hill Cemetery in Battle Creek, Michigan.

Notes
1. Board of Examiners and Registrars of Architects, "Francis Eugene Griffin," Certificate no. 367, issued 16 January 1940.
2. "Battle Creek Burial for Noted Architect," *Michigan Chronicle*, 24 February 1973, p. 1A.

Bibliography
Johnson, Nathan. "The Black Architect in Michigan." Michigan Challenge. 9 June 1969, p. 26.
"Membership Folder for Francis Griffin." American Institute of Architects, Detroit chapter.
"Working in Liberia." *Detroit Times,* 19 August 1955, p. 27.

DeWitt Sanford Dykes Jr.,
Professor of History, Oakland University

BUILDING LIST

Name	Address	City	State	Year	Comments
Aijalon Baptist Church	6419 Beechwood St.	Detroit	MI	1950	
Considine Auditorium	8904 Woodward Ave.	Detroit	MI	1973	
Considine Sculpture Court	8904 Woodward Ave.	Detroit	MI	1973	

Calvin Pazavia Hamilton
(1923–2001)

Calvin P., as he preferred to be called, was born in Wilmington, Delaware, on June 14, 1923. His parents were Harrison R. Hamilton and Mattie Jenkins Hamilton, originally from Chestertown, Maryland. His father was a railroad porter and his mother worked for Wilmington's Department of Public Works. Together they raised five children at 320 East 10th Street in Wilmington. Calvin was the second son and fourth child.

Calvin attended Wilmington Public Elementary School No. 29. A diligent student, he was an avid reader and excelled at math. However, it was at Howard High School, which was established in 1869 as the first public high school for African Americans in the state of Delaware, that Hamilton's interest in architecture was sparked. Until 1928 Howard High School was the only high school in the state for Black Delawareans. As a result, it attracted the state's brightest Black students. Known for its high academic standards, Howard High School flourished under the scholarly and dedicated faculty led by Edwina Kruse, its first Black principal. For her efforts, she became the first female awarded an honorary doctoral degree by Lincoln University in Pennsylvania. Also on the faculty was Alice Dunbar Nelson, former wife of poet Paul Laurence Dunbar and author of the first extensive study of Negroes in Delaware. In the 1920s, as a result of the philanthropy of Peter S. DuPont, the old Howard High School was replaced, on the same site, by a modern facility equipped with technological advances. It was into this environment that Calvin Hamilton arrived. He was exposed to architecture through drafting and shop courses, and graduated with honors in 1941.

Hamilton's intention to continue on to college was interrupted in 1942 when he was drafted into the U.S. Army to fight in World War II. After being honorably discharged in 1946, he enrolled at HOWARD UNIVERSITY, where he majored in architecture. He studied under the notable faculty that included Frank West, LEROY JOHN HENRY BROWN, and HOWARD HAMILTON MACKEY SR. Hamilton graduated in 1951 and returned to Wilmington although he continued his architectural studies for a while at the University of Pennsylvania. After leaving the University of Pennsylvania, Hamilton was employed by W. Ellis Preston

(1907–1980) as a draftsman. Hamilton worked for W. Ellis Preston for a relatively long time, from 1952 to 1968. Projects out of Preston's office included several buildings at Delaware State University, a historically Black university in Dover. Hamilton contributed to the working drawings for the Womens Dormitory, an addition to Conrad Hall, and the imposing Luna I. Mishoe Science Building (1962). A large firm, W. Ellis Preston also designed office buildings, churches, schools, and private residences and thus provided Hamilton with a solid and varied experience. In addition, Preston himself served for a many years on the Zoning Commission for the City of Wilmington and on the State Board of Examiners of Architects, thus providing a civic role model for Hamilton. Having completed the required three-year internship while employed at Preston, Hamilton took the grueling, four-day Delaware certification examination in 1962 and passed with high scores. *Center Line*, the newsletter of the Delaware chapter of the American Institute of Architects, noted in its October issue that "Calvin P. Hamilton has become registered in the state of Delaware."[1] Hamilton had the distinction of being the first Black registered architect in Delaware. He later became registered in Maryland, New Jersey, and Pennsylvania.

While pursuing his career in a profession and in a city in which he was the only member of his race to practice, Hamilton involved himself in many civic interests to offset the social isolation of his profession. He was a lifelong member and a trustee of Ezion United Methodist Church, and served the Walnut Young Mens Christian Association as chairman of the board. He was also a member of the Wilmington chapter of the National Association for the Advancement of Colored People and *Kappa Alpha Psi* Fraternity. Among his favorite activities were those offered by the Mes Amis Club. In fact, it was at one of its pinochle game nights that he met his future wife. Marguerite (Peggy) Daniels had moved to Wilmington from Smyrna, Delaware, and worked as an elevator operator in the Traffic Department of the DuPont Company. She was an avid pinochle player whose skilled playing and good looks captivated Hamilton. They married in 1959. Although they had no children, they were surrogate parents to many youngsters in their neighborhood.

Calvin Hamilton also worked for J. Phillip Fox (1926–1972) in Newark, Delaware. Fox formerly worked for DuPont Company, Wilmington's major employer at the time. In 1961 Fox retired and opened his own practice. Soon after, his firm was hired to design public housing for the Newark Housing Authority and Glasgow Lodge, a motel/apartment building in nearby Glasgow.

After thirteen years of working for others, Hamilton opened his own architectural firm—Calvin P. Hamilton, Associated Architects—in 1968 at 218A

Ezion-Mt. Carmel
United Methodist Church,
Patsy M. Fletcher

9th Street West in Wilmington. The office quickly became known for its integrated professional staff of men and women. Hamilton was known as an exacting professional both in personal bearing and in product. He was a man for whom no detail was too small. The degree of isolation he experienced as the only African American architect in the state led him to become quite protective of his projects. At the same time, being the "first and only" for a number of years—especially during a period of attempts at racial integration—resulted in a number of commissions. His renovations included churches such as Ebenezer Baptist and Bethlehem 8th Street Baptist. His renovation of the historic Ezion Methodist Episcopal Church (1886) can no longer be admired because of its controversial demolition in 1971, to make way for a new civic center. Hamilton, however, served as associate architect along with A. Hansel Fink & Associates of Philadelphia for the replacement, Ezion-Mt. Carmel United Methodist Church. Located on two acres at 8th and Walnut, the impressive ultramodern 2-story Ezion-Mt. Carmel United Methodist Church has been described as "contemporary and full of light."[2]

Hamilton's design signature can also be seen in the auditorium, gymnasium, and career center additions to his *alma mater*, Howard High School. He was also the architect for Longshoremen's Hall, Gray Funeral Home, and the William Anderson Community Center. Hamilton's projects included several houses and multifamily housing projects, the most prominent of which was Westtown Village. Comprised of two developments for a redeveloped area of Wilmington, West Center Village (fifty-five du) and Westtown Plaza (forty-four du) provided almost one hundred units of affordable and attractive homes for low-income residents. Another subsidized housing project was Brandywine Village I, designed by Hamilton in Millsboro, Delaware. Hamilton was also the architect for the Ulysses S. Washington Herbarium and its distinctive perimeter wall at Delaware State University. The Colonial style of the brick wall and colorful metal features are sensitive to the nearby Agricultural School and herbarium. His design for the Terry Building at Delaware Technical and Community College in Dover brought him considerable acclaim for the "open-concept" library, which at the time was quite innovative. Although its rear facade has been altered, a photograph of the nighttime view of its *jalousie* windows was featured prominently in the college's publicity materials.

In addition to designing public buildings, Hamilton used his professional expertise to serve the public. He was a *pro bono* consultant specializing in the *Wilmington Building Code*. He was appointed to the New Castle County Board of Assessment Reviews in 1967 and became its chairman three years later. He also served on the State Bureau of Housing and the Wilmington Board of Appeals and Standards. While compiling impressive accomplishments in the professional arena, Hamilton never forgot his roots. Over the years he made a practice of giving back to his community through various civic, social, and religious organizations to which he belonged. For his boundless contributions he received numerous accolades from the Veterans of Foreign Wars, City of Wilmington, and the Afro-American Society of Delaware, among others.

Calvin P. Hamilton died June 17, 2001, at age seventy-eight. He is interred in Delaware Veteran's Memorial Cemetery in Bear, Delaware.

Notes
1. "General Notes," *Center-Line* (Delaware Chapter, American Institute of Architects) October, 1962, p. 2.
2. Interview with Franklin W. Hamilton Sr., (brother of Calvin) by author, Wilmington, Del., 21 May 2003.
3. "Calvin P. Hamilton," *The News Journal*, 24 June 2001, p. B4.

Bibliography
"Ezion Will Build Bi-Level Church." *Evening Journal*, 30 September 1971, p. 3.
"Picturing Heroes of the Past, Present." *News Journal-Local Section*, 23 February 2002, p. 1.
Wilmington Housing Authority. "Annual Report and Statement of Progress through March 31, 1969." Wilmington, Del., 1969.

PATSY M. FLETCHER
CONSULTANT, ECONOMIC AND COMMUNITY
DEVELOPMENT, PUBLIC HOUSING MANAGEMENT,
RESIDENT INITIATIVES, AND DIVERSITY ISSUES
WASHINGTON, D.C.

CALVIN PAZAVIA HAMILTON

BUILDING LIST

Name	Address	City	State	Year	Comments
Asbury Gardens Apts.	2nd & Walnut Sts.	Wilmington	DE		
Bethlehem 8th Street Baptist Church	1725 W. 8th St.	Wilmington	DE		Office & chapel
Brandywine Village I	401 Monroe St.	Millsboro	DE		
Butler, Dr. Charles		Coatsville	PA		
Delaware State University Boundary Wall	Campus	Dover	DE	1995	
Delaware State University Washington Herbarium	Campus	Dover	DE	1999	
Delaware State University Women's Dormitory	Campus	Dover	DE	1961	
Delaware Tech. and Comm. College Terry Bldg.	1832 N. DuPont Pkwy.	Dover	DE	1975	
Ebenezer Baptist Church	731 Vandever Ave.	Wilmington	DE		Alterations
Ezion-Mt. Carmel United Methodist Church	800 N. Walnut St.	Wilmington	DE	1972	Assoc. architect
Ezion United Methodist Episcopal Church	9th & French Sts.	Wilmington	DE		Demolished
Gray Funeral Home	201 N. Gray Ave.	Wilmington	DE		Now Congo Funeral Home
Haven United Methodist Church	1709 W. 3rd St.	Wilmington	DE		Alteration
Howard High School	401 E. 12th St.	Wilmington	DE		Auditorium, gym, & career center
Lockett, Jesse	3100 W. 4th St.	Wilmington	DE		
Longshoremen's Hall	200 S. Claymont St.	Wilmington	DE	1967	
Mt. Joy United Methodist Church	453 Townsend St.	Wilmington	DE		Alterations
Nix, Theopholis	2807 W. 4th St.	Wilmington	DE		
People's Settlement	408 E. 8th St.	Wilmington	DE		Old and new wings
Porter, Luther		Belvedere	PA		Alterations
Redding, Dr. Lewis	Lockley Rd.	Glen Mills	PA		Alterations
Talbert, E.	307 W. 3rd St.	Wilmington	DE		
Westown Square	2nd & Madison Sts.	Wilmington	DE	1972	
Westown Village	2nd & Madison Sts.	Wilmington	DE	1970	100 dwelling units (du)
William Anderson Community Center	501 N. Madison St.	Wilmington	DE	1972	
Wilmington, City of		Wilmington	DE	1969	Housing survey

Hampton Institute, Department of Architecture
(1871)

Hampton Institute is a private, nonsectarian university whose past is rooted in the aftermath of the Civil War. At the end of the Civil War, a new generation of young northern White men, their experiences forged in the war, discovered a new specific role for themselves. They were to serve as guides for those who made up the vast lower class, just as they had commanded its members as officers during the Civil War.

> These postbellum northern men thought a good deal about how to restore the nation, how to make the South a place safe for Yankee investment, and what to do with the freed slaves. The future of America was in industry and the agrarian South somehow had to be brought into the process.[1]

As a member of this group, Samuel Chapman Armstrong shared this vision. Armstrong, who was ultimately to be the founder and first principal of Hampton Institute, "believed that the freed people should not be ciphers in the process that would reconstruct the New South; rather, they should be active participants and contributors."[2]

In 1866 the issue of what to teach and how to educate the masses was still being debated. "A solution was found that was tolerable to both northern benevolent groups and the freedmen. A small *cadre* of dedicated white teachers would remain in the South to train the most able of the Black freedmen, so that they could become the teachers and leaders of their race."[3]

Toward that end, freedmen's aid societies, missionary associations, and the Freedmen's Bureau joined together in the creation of Black normal schools and colleges in the South. The American Baptist Home Mission Society, the Freedmen's Aid Society of the Methodist Episcopal Church (North), and the Presbyterian Board of Missions all established schools that in the next half century developed into Black colleges. Foremost among these groups was the American Missionary Association, which in 1867 and 1868 founded eight teacher-training schools in Macon, Savannah, and Atlanta, Georgia; Charleston, South Carolina; Louisville, Kentucky; Nashville, Tennessee; Talladega, Alabama; and Hampton, Virginia.

On a bright spring day, April 6, 1868, in Elizabeth City County, Virginia, young Brevet Brigadier General Samuel Chapman Armstrong pronounced his Hampton Normal and Agricultural Institute open to students. "I stand now where I have long aimed to stand," Armstrong exulted, "I can say to any noble, aspiring, whole-souled colored youth of either sex in the South—'Here you can come ragged and poor as you are, and become the men and women you wish to become.' "[4]

Armstrong's design for Hampton Institute was a cogent, appropriate response to the needs of the freedmen in southeastern Virginia circa 1868. Armstrong created a school that would give members of the Black masses skills that would enable them to achieve gradual progress in the political, social, and economic circumstances. Moreover, it would prepare these graduates to go out and teach these same skills to larger numbers of the Black population.

By 1871, the curriculum was expanded to include studies in the "normal course," a "commerce course," and a "mechanical course." The mechanical course included lessons in freehand drawing and mechanical drawing. By 1879, the mechanical course had evolved into "the trade school course." In addition to attending classes, students worked as brickmakers, masons, and carpenters. Many campus buildings at that time were designed by faculty and built by students.

In 1880 the Huntington Industrial Works was established. Located on campus at that time was a kiln for the making of bricks, a sawmill, and a woodworking shop. The 1882 school catalog stated that students who wished to learn trades must serve apprenticeships of three to four years while attending night school during the entire time. The trade school program grew over the years. The Armstrong and Slater Memorial Trade School Building, designed specifically for the teaching of trades, opened in 1896. Coursework included carpentry, bricklaying, plastering, frame construction, and house painting. Students spent time in the Huntington Industrial Works planing, woodworking, and working in the lumberyard and brick kiln. Hampton Institute graduates worked as carpenters, masons, and contractors. Some used their skills to design and build houses, small commercial buildings, and churches (CHARLES THADDEUS RUSSELL graduated in 1899 with a certificate in carpentry).

General Armstrong's idea of training the head, the heart, and the hand and promoting self-help, self-discipline, and self-esteem grew and developed. In 1922 the Trade School opened a Department of Building Construction with a two-year builder's course.

Department of Building Construction

H. Whittemore Brown, Director
Aim—The aim of the two-year Builder's Course, offered by the Department of Building Construction, is to develop:
 Accurate Business Methods
 Skillful Field Management
 Thorough Knowledge of Building Materials and Trades
 Sound Structural Sense
 Discriminating Architectural Taste
 Broad Human Interests [5]

In 1923 a four-year builder's course was added.

Builder's Course

Aim—To train skilled builders by thorough instruction in business methods, field management, building materials, trade practice, structural design, and principles of architecture.

The four-year builder's course, leading to the degree of Bachelor of Science, combines the technical instruction in these subjects with a broad cultural training. In addition to being well-trained in building construction, graduates of this course have an excellent preparation for teaching scientific and technical subjects in secondary schools and colleges.[6]

The curriculum included coursework in architectural drawing, principles of architecture, reading floor plans, preparing working drawings, structural design, and building materials. Graduates of the four-year builder's course went on to become contractors, practice architecture, and pursue graduate degrees in engineering or architecture.

On January 1, 1930, Hampton Normal and Agricultural Institute shortened its name to Hampton Institute. On January 24, 1933, Hampton Institute was accredited by the Southern Association of College and Secondary Schools as a class A school. The trade school advanced to college level.

Nineteen thirty-four was a landmark year in the history of the program in architecture. It was in this year that WILLIAM HENRY MOSES JR. joined the faculty to teach architectural drafting. Moses, with a bachelor of science in architecture from Pennsylvania State University, was the first formally educated African American architect to join the faculty. Moses became the driving force behind the development of a professional curriculum in architecture. As a result of his hard work the 1941 to 1942 catalog stated:

Architecture

Under Hampton Institute's plan of reorganization, architectural design and architectural engineering are being added, and the curriculum in building construction is being integrated with the two new courses of study.

The complete curriculum for each of these courses will be announced later. The candidate in any one of these fields will, upon satisfactory completion of his course, be awarded the B.S. degree.

Architectural Design

The work in architectural design will include basic instruction in the art, science, theory, and history of architecture, study of form and color, free design, sculpture, and modeling. The work of the studio and the drafting room will be combined in such a way as to supplement each other efficiently. Courses will be offered in English, foreign language, science, mathematics, and the social studies. The aim of the course is to train creative architectural designers, who will have the necessary preparation in engineering, professional procedure, business fundamentals, and cultural background to meet the educational requirements of state examining boards for certification.

Architectural Engineering

In the curriculum in architectural engineering, construction is the major subject instead of design. The technical and mechanical requirements in architecture are stressed and advanced courses in structural design are required. Here also, cultural courses in the arts and sciences will be required. The training fits graduates to employ, organize, and direct intelligently the specialties required in modern building projects and prepares them to meet the educational requirements of state examining boards for structural engineers.

Building Construction

The advanced two-year curriculum in building construction is designed to supplement a three-year curriculum in any one of the building trades. In addition to structural design, surveying, and the principles of architecture, the student receives basic training in the practices and procedures of the building trades—estimating, field superintendence, plant maintenance, business methods, and engineering law. This program assumes that the cultural courses will have been covered, for the most part, in the three previous years. Graduates under

HAMPTON INSTITUTE, DEPARTMENT OF ARCHITECTURE

Hampton Institute Drafting Class, *Hampton University Archives and Museum*

this curriculum will be prepared to serve in various technical capacities in the field of construction, to teach vocational subjects, and to take examinations for civil service jobs related to construction.[7]

The 1942 to 1943 catalog listed a two-year curriculum in building construction, a four-year curriculum in architectural design, and a four-year curriculum in architecture engineering with William Moses Jr. as acting chairman and Benson L. Dutton as faculty.

In the years 1945 to 1946, the three programs separated from the trade school and were reorganized into a new Division of Trades and Industries. Under Moses's leadership and urging, the administration in 1946 approved the formation of a Department of Engineering and Architecture, which included a two-year program in building construction, a four-year program in architectural design, and a four-year program in architectural engineering. William Moses Jr. was the acting chairman with Benson Dutton, Duane Grant, and HENRY LEWIS LIVAS as faculty.

Over the next few years, Moses, with the support of faculty, made curriculum changes to improve and develop a five-year program in architecture that would meet national accreditation standards. The year 1951 saw the initiation of the Division of Technology with a Department of Architecture and Engineering, which included a five-year program in architecture and a five-year program in building construction and engineering. The program in architectural engineering was phased out. Anthony Johns, who was to become the chairman of the Department of Architecture at HOWARD UNIVERSITY and later the chairman of the Department of Architecture at Morgan State University, was the last graduate of the architecture/engineering program, in 1955. In 1956 the first students graduated from the five-year program. Although the program remained relatively strong over the next ten years, it never achieved accreditation.

In 1965, after thirty-one years on the faculty and twenty-three years as chairman, William Moses Jr. relinquished his chairmanship. In that year, Bertram Berenson was appointed chairman with a mandate to achieve accreditation. The following year the Department of Architecture was elevated to a division with Bert Berenson as director. This was the first listing as the Division of Architecture offering the professional bachelor of architecture degree. The Department of Building Construction Engineering remained in the Division of Technology with Henry Livas as chairman until it was phased out at the end of the 1968 to 1969 academic year. In 1969, years of hard work culminated in the achievement of William Moses's dream when the Division of Architecture received a two-year accreditation.

In the spring of 1970, Bertram Berenson resigned as division director. John H. Spencer, a member of Hampton Institute's first five-year class in architecture (1956), returned to his *alma mater* as the new division director. Spencer used his experience in teaching and in professional practice to mold the directions of the division. He continued the curriculum development program revisions and consolidation. The program was strengthened with the identification of program and course standards, goals and directions, and student evaluation statements. The Division of Architecture was revisited by the National Architectural Accrediting Board in 1972 and received a maximum five-year accreditation. In the years that followed, Spencer worked to increase program excellence and to gain national recognition.

In the fall of 1972, academic restructuring at the university level lowered the Division of Architecture to a department in the Division of Social and Environmental Studies. A second restructuring in 1979 moved the Department of Architecture to the School of Pure and Applied Sciences, and a third restructuring in 1993 placed the department in the newly created School of Engineering and Technology.

Over the years the department's reputation for producing well-educated graduates grew; it responded to Armstrong's goal of producing solid citizens to go out and serve; and reached an early 1970s goal of producing educated, competent, African American architects.

In 1995 John H. Spencer stated that it was time for revitalization and new directions and resigned as chairman after twenty-five years. Associate Professor Solil Banerjee served as acting chairman until January 1997, when Bradford C. Grant—a graduate of the University of California at Berkeley with teaching experience at Berkeley, at San Luis Obispo California Polytechnical, and the University of Cincinnati—was appointed department chairman. Bradford Grant and faculty are committed to carrying Samuel Chapman Armstrong's dream and legacy into the new millennium.

Notes

1. Robert Francis Engs, *Educating the Disfranchised and Disinherited* (Knoxville: University of Tennessee Press, 1999), p. xiii.
2. Ibid.
3. Ibid.
4. Ibid.
5. *Hampton Institute Catalog* (Hampton: Institute Press, 1922), n.p.
6. *Hampton Institute Catalog* (Hampton: Hampton Institute Press, 1923), n.p.
7. *Hampton Institute Catalog* (Hampton: Hampton Institute Press, 1941–1942), n.p.

Bibliography

Hampton Institute Catalog 1896–97. Hampton, Va.: Institute Press, 1897.
Johnston, Francis B. Johnston Photographic Collection. Prints and Photograph Division, Library of Congress.

JOHN H. SPENCER, FORMER CHAIRMAN
AND EMERITUS PROFESSOR OF ARCHITECTURE,
HAMPTON UNIVERSITY

Richard Mason Hancock

(1832–1899)

Richard Mason Hancock was born on November 22, 1832, in New Bern, North Carolina. Both of his parents were also born in North Carolina. Richard attended a private school for free Negro children and by the age of thirteen he began apprenticing as a carpenter with his father, William H. Hancock. Craven County Court records indicate William Hancock was legally "bound" to builder Uriah Sandy as an apprentice from age fourteen.[1] Under North Carolina's apprenticeship system, "usually a single free Negro child was bound out to an individual for the purpose of learning a specific trade."[2]

In 1817—the same year that William Hancock's apprenticeship began—builders Uriah Sandy and Daniel Merrill constructed First Presbyterian Church in New Bern. Interestingly, one of the church's founding members was a free Black woman.

Richard Hancock worked alongside his father for nine years mastering the carpentry trade and then headed for New Haven, Connecticut. As an employee of Atwater & Treat and Dolittle & Company he worked as a carpenter joiner. Arriving in Lockport, New York, he spent the next two years working as a ship carpenter and built canal boats. Hancock subsequently was hired by Holly Manufacturing, where he learned a new trade, patternmaking.

In *An Encyclopedia of the Iron & Steel Industry*, patternmaking is defined as a "highly skilled craft of modeling the desired casting in wood, metal or other material," and a pattern is described as "a model, in wood, metal or other suitable material, of the required casting or a full scale reproduction of a part used as a guide in cutting."[3] Reverend William J. Simmons was referring to Hancock when he stated that "patternmaking . . . requires first of all a complete mastery of carpentry, besides an acquaintance with higher mathematics, a knowledge of draughting and constant exercise of the very best judgment."[4]

In the early years, Holly Manufacturing assembled household appliances including flatirons and sewing machines. In 1862 Birdsill Holly, company owner and inventor, patented the direct pressure water supply system commonly known as the fire hydrant. Hancock did not stay long in New York State. He moved west to Chicago, where he would live and work for the next thirty years.

Hancock's profession as a patternmaker took on special significance in Chicago. Not only did he hire on with Eagle Works Manufacturing—the largest foundry east of the Mississippi River—but he became assistant foreman of Eagle's Pattern Shops around 1867 and foreman around 1872, which was a rare position of importance to be occupied by a Negro. Eagle Works' *Chicago City Directory* advertisement read, "Do you want Steam Engines or Boilers? Patent Fire Evaporators, Saw mills, Flouring mills, Patent Stamp mills for Pike's Peak or Lake Superior, Patent Sugar Cane mills, Patent Steam Coil Evaporators and Machinery of all descriptions."[5]

The tradesmen supervised by Hancock were White, and nearly the entire group went on strike to protest against their Negro foreman. Management replaced those workers, and Hancock remained foreman. By 1873 Eagle Works had shut down, and Liberty Iron Works/ Fraser, Chalmers & Co. became its successor. The new owners grew the company to incredible heights, employing over seven hundred laborers. The 1875 *Lakeside Annual Directory of the City of Chicago* declared the new company's ambitious mission:

> Having been for the past years Partners and Managers of Eagle Works Manufacturing Company (these works now being closed), and having purchased all their large stock of Machinery Patterns, embracing the most complete and extensive set of Engines, Gears, Pulleys and miscellaneous Patterns in the Northwest, we are prepared to continue its business in all branches with unequalled facilities, to fill orders for all descriptions of work and repairs without the usual delay and expense in getting up new patterns.[6]

Hancock took great pride in his patternmaking, family, and community. He was a ranking member of the Masons and a founding member and choir master of Saint Thomas Episcopal Church in Chicago. With his first wife, Jane, whom he married in Chicago on June 6, 1867, he had two children: Fanny and George. George followed in his father's footsteps as a patternmaker with Liberty Iron Works. Richard Hancock married a second time. They did not have any children of their own.

Richard Hancock died on June 4, 1899. The cause of his death and location of his grave are not known.

Notes

1. James H. Craig, *The Arts and Crafts in North Carolina, 1699–1840* (Winston-Salem: Museum of Early Southern Decorative Arts, Old Salem Inc., 1966), p. 341.
2. John Hope Franklin, *The Free Negro in North Carolina, 1790–1860* (New York: Russell & Russell, 1969), p. 124.
3. A. K. Osborne, *An Encyclopedia of the Iron and Steel Industry* (New York: Philosophical Library, 1956), p. 308.
4. William Simmons, *Men of Mark: Eminent, Progressive, and Rising* (Cleveland: Rewell & Company, 1887), p. 406.
5. "Eagle Works," in *Halpin & Bailey's Chicago City Directory* (Chicago: Halpin & Bailey, 1862), p. 116.
6. "Liberty Iron Works," in *Lakeside Annual Directory of the City of Chicago* (Chicago: Lakeside Company, 1875), front flyleaf C.

LISA M. BOONE,
RESEARCHER/WRITER, CORAL SPRINGS, FLORIDA

Clinton Stevens Harris
(1900–1992)

Perre deClue Scott

Clinton S. Harris was born on May 9, 1900, in the Winfield neighborhood in the borough of Queens, New York City.[1] He was the second of five children born to Purcell Warren Harris and Lucy Jeanette Stevens. According to his sister, Evelyn Harris Millford, Clinton showed an interest in architecture at a very young age and could be found at the public library looking at picture books with buildings.

Purcell Harris was a laborer for the Washington Irving family in Tarrytown, New York, and consequently was frequently not at home. Clinton became the "substitute father" in the household. To help support the family financially, Clinton dropped out of school at age fifteen. His first job was for the architectural firm of Visscher & Burley. They recognized that he was talented and taught him how to draft.

Another source of encouragement for Clinton was a friend of his father's, neighbor Norman Forte. Forte was one of the first African American members of the Carpenters' Union in New York City. He encouraged Harris to enroll in the General Society of Mechanics and Tradesmen's Mechanics Institute to improve his drafting. Harris finished the course in 1918, and subsequently went to work as a draftsman with Lowinson & Schubert in New York City from 1919 to 1924. Simultaneously, Harris attended evening school at City College School of Technology in New York City. He earned a certificate for courses in building construction and architectural engineering.

Harris worked for a brief time for VERTNER WOODSON TANDY circa 1923 to 1924, until a higher-paying civil service position opened up in New York City. For the next year and a half he worked for the New York City Board of Education. After that he spent three years with the firm of William O. Sommerfeld. Harris returned to local government to work for the Board of Transportation and the Department of Parks until 1932 when the Great Depression took its toll and city payrolls were purged.[2]

On May 29, 1930, Clinton married Helen Anna Lankford, a niece of JOHN ANDERSON LANKFORD and ARTHUR EDWARD LANKFORD and one of the first African American public school teachers in New York City.

Unable to find employment in New York City, Clinton Harris relocated to Washington, D.C., where he worked for ALBERT IRVIN CASSELL at HOWARD UNIVERSITY, preparing construction plans and supervising the construction of Founders Library, the Chemistry Building, and Frederick Douglass Hall.[3] He then went to work for HILYARD ROBERT ROBINSON, preparing working drawings for Langston Terrace Public Housing.

In 1937 the Harrises became parents of a baby girl, whom they named Perre. Clinton Harris was once again working for New York City in the newly formed Department of Public Works. In the early 1940s, Harris joined the New York State Guard, 369th Regiment, where he eventually rose to the rank of major. Harris's personal life was disrupted when he and Helen divorced in 1949. The next year Clinton married Hazel Forte, the daughter of his first mentor. At the time of their marriage, Hazel was an administrative assistant to the director of Bellevue Psychiatric Hospital.

In the late 1940s, with close friend Frank Leslie Thompson, a civil engineer, Clinton Harris designed a number of churches and other buildings in New York City. In 1949 he designed renovations to the first home that Jackie Robinson purchased after being called up from the minor leagues to play with the Brooklyn Dodgers. The house is located in the Saint Albans neighborhood of the borough of Queens, a neighborhood where many of New York's African American celebrities and professionals lived. Although Harris and Thompson collaborated for many years, the identity of the buildings that they designed has eluded discovery.

Around 1950 Harris was appointed head of the Specifications Division in the Department of Public Works and was the only African American on that level in the department. He was in charge of design specifications for courthouses, hospitals, libraries, community health centers, police precincts, firehouses, municipal parking garages, and correctional institutions for about twenty years.

In 1970 Harris retired from the Department of Public Works after forty-two years. His wife retired in 1978 and they relocated to San Diego, California. They lived in California for fourteen years, but returned to New York City in 1992 when at age ninety-two Clinton Harris's health began to fail.

Clinton Harris died of old age at Booth Memorial Hospital in Flushing, New York, on November 4, 1992.[4] He is buried in Evergreen Cemetery, in the borough of Brooklyn.

Notes

1. New York City Department of Records and Information Services, "Certified Birth Record for Clinton Stevens Harris," Certificate no. 1136, 1900, Municipal Archives.
2. "Clinton S. Harris' Resume of Technical Experience, 1916–1940." In possession of the author.
3. Ibid.
4. New York Department of Health, Vital Records, "Clinton S. Harris, Death Certificate," no. 156-92-059309, New York, N.Y., 1992.

PERRE DECLUE SCOTT,
DAUGHTER OF CLINTON STEVENS HARRIS,
CORONA, NEW YORK

BUILDING LIST

Name	Address	City/Borough	State	Year	Comments
Allerton Branch Library	2740 Barnes Ave.	Bronx	NY	1960	
Auburndale-Clearview Branch Library	2555 Francis Lewis Blvd.	Flushing	NY	1967	
Bay Ridge Branch Library	7223 Ridge Blvd.	Brooklyn	NY	1960	
Bayside Branch Library	214 Northern Blvd.	Bayside	NY	1965	
Bedford District Health Center		Brooklyn	NY	1955	
Bellevue Hospital	1st Ave. & 26th St.	New York	NY	1969	
Bellevue Hospital Nurses School & Residence	1st Ave. & 25th St.	New York	NY	1956	
Bloomingdale Branch Library	150 W. 100th St.	New York	NY	1960	
Borough Park Branch Library	1265 43rd St.	Brooklyn	NY		
Broadway-Astoria Branch Library	21 31st St.	Astoria	NY	1958	
Bronx Municipal Hospital Center	Pelham Pkwy. & E. Chester St.	Bronx	NY	1952	
Brooklyn Community College	Tillary & Adams Sts.	Brooklyn	NY	1959	
Brooklyn Domestic Relations Court	Adams & Johnson Sts.	Brooklyn	NY	1956	
Brooklyn Heights Public Library	280 Cadman Plaza West	Brooklyn	NY	1961	
Brooklyn House of Detention for Men	Atlantic Ave. btwn. Boerum & Smith	Brooklyn	NY	1956	
Brooklyn Supreme Court	Adams & Fulton	Brooklyn	NY		
Brooklyn Welfare Center	Jay & Johnson Sts.	Brooklyn	NY	1955	
Bushwick District Health Center	Central Ave. & Grove St.	Brooklyn	NY	1959	
Central Manhattan Repair Headquarters	FDR Dr. btwn. 37th & 38th Sts.	New York	NY	1955	
City Hospital of Brooklyn Laundry	Kingston Ave. & Rutland Rd.	Brooklyn	NY	1961	
Coney Island Branch Library	1901 Mermaid Ave.	Brooklyn	NY	1956	
Coney Island General Hospital	1844 Ocean Pkwy.	Brooklyn	NY	1956	
Criminal Courts Bldg. & Prison	Borough Hall at Queens Blvd.	Kew Gardens	NY	1961	
Crown Heights Health Center	Troy Ave. & Prospect Pl.	Brooklyn	NY	1956	
Cumberland Hospital	100 N. Portland Ave.	Brooklyn	NY	1961	
East Bronx Municipal Hospital Nurses Residence		Bronx	NY	1964	
East Harlem General Hospital	E. 97th to 99th Sts. btwn. 1st & 2nd Aves.	New York	NY	1959	
Elmhurst General Hospital	7901 Broadway	Elmhurst	NY	1956	
Far Rockaway Branch Library	1637 Central Ave.	Queens	NY	1967	

BUILDING LIST (continued)

Name	Address	City/Borough	State	Year	Comments
Firehouse-Engine Company 11 & Ladder Company 11	222 E. 2nd St.	New York	NY	1959	
Firehouse-Engine Company 165 & Ladder Company 85	Richmond Rd. & Summit Ave.	Staten Island	NY	1960	
Firehouse-Engine Company 202 & Ladder Company 101	29 Richards St.	Brooklyn	NY	1960	
Firehouse-Engine Company 209 & Ladder Company 102	Bedford Ave. near Myrtle Ave.	Brooklyn	NY	1965	
Firehouse-Engine Company 214	495 Hancock St.	Brooklyn	NY	1958	
Firehouse-Engine Company 22 & Ladder Company 13	159 E. 85th St.	New York	NY	1961	
Firehouse-Engine Company 246 & Ladder Company 169	E. 11th St. btwn. Banner Ave. & Shore	Brooklyn	NY	1960	
Firehouse-Engine Company 275 & Spare Trucks	Merrick Blvd. & Sayres Ave.	Queens	NY	1960	
Firehouse-Engine Company 298 & Ladder Company 127	Hillside Ave. near Parsons Blvd.	Queens	NY	1964	
Firehouse-Engine Company 299 & Ladder Company 152	Utopia Pkwy. & 64th Ave.	Fresh Meadows	NY	1960	
Firehouse-Engine Company 3 & Ladder Company 12	West 19th St. near 7th Ave.	New York	NY	1966	
Firehouse-Engie Company 330 & Ladder Company 172		Brooklyn	NY	1964	
Firehouse-Engine Company 40 & Ladder Company 35	66th St. & Amsterdam Ave.	New York	NY	1961	
Firehouse-Engine Company 58 & Ladder Company 26	1365 5th Ave.	New York	NY	1960	
Firehouse-Engine Company 59 & Ladder Company 30	Lenox Ave. & W. 133rd St.	New York	NY	1961	
Firehouse-Engine Company 76 & Ladder Company 22	100th St. east of Amsterdam Ave.	New York	NY	1960	
Firehouse-Engine Company 8 & Ladder Company 2	East 51st St. & 3rd Ave.	New York	NY		
Firehouse-Engine Company 96 & Ladder Company 54	Storey & Croes Aves.	Bronx	NY	1965	
Firehouse-Neponsit Section of Queens	Beach at 169th St.	Neponsit	NY	1961	
Flushing Regional Branch Library	Kissena Blvd. & Main St.	Queens	NY	1955	
Fordham Regional & Children's Library	2556 Bainbridge Ave.	Bronx	NY		
Forest Hills Branch Library	108 71st Ave.	Forest Hills	NY	1958	
Gouverneur Hospital	227 Madison St.	New York	NY		
Grand Concourse Branch Library	155 E. 173rd St.	Bronx	NY	1959	
Gravesend District Health Center	Ave. U & West St.	Brooklyn	NY	1953	
Great Kill Branch Library	56 Giffords Ln.	Staten Island	NY	1954	
Hall of Science	Flushing Meadow Park	Queens	NY	1964	
Hamilton Fish Park Branch Library	415 Houston St.	New York	NY		
Harlem Hospital	506 Malcolm X Blvd.	New York	NY	1968	
Harlem Retail Market	8th Ave. & W. 142nd St.	New York	NY	1955	
Harlem River Representative Shop & Engineers' Office	W. 205th St. & Harlem River	New York	NY	1956	
Harlem Welfare Center	Park Ave. btwn. 131st & 132nd Sts.	New York	NY	1952	
Hillcrest Center for Children		Bedford Hills	NY	1963	
Inwood Branch Library	4790 Broadway	New York	NY	1952	
Jackson Heights Branch Library	35 81st St.	Jackson Heights	NY	1954	
Kings Highway Branch Library	2115 Ocean Ave.	Brooklyn	NY	1954	
Laurelton Branch Library	134 225th St.	Springfield Gardens	NY	1954	
Library for the Blind	40 W. 20th St.	New York	NY	1952	
Lincoln Hospital	234 E. 149th St.	Bronx	NY	1956	
Mapleton Branch Library	1702 60th St.	Brooklyn	NY		
Medical Examiner's Bldg.	1st Ave. & E. 30th St.	New York	NY	1960	

BUILDING LIST (continued)

Name	Address	City/Borough	State	Year	Comments
Metropolitan Hospital Nurses Residence & School	1st Ave. & E. 97th St.	New York	NY	1961	
Midwood Branch Library	975 E. 16th St.	Brooklyn	NY	1955	
Morningside Health Center	268 W. 118th St.	New York	NY	1959	
Morrisania District Health Center	Fulton Ave. near E. 169th St.	Bronx	NY	1955	
Mosholu Branch Library	285 E. 205th St.	Bronx	NY	1954	
NYC Community College Academic & Science Bldgs.	Jay, & Johnson Sts.	Brooklyn	NY	1966	
NYC Department of Public Works Repair Shop	Kent Ave. & S. 6th St.	Brooklyn	NY	1955	
NYC Department of Sanitation Central Repair Shop	Betts Ave.	Maspeth	NY	1965	
NYC Department of Sanitation Incinerator	Hamilton Ave.	Brooklyn	NY	1961	
NYC Department of Sanitation Incinerator		Brooklyn	NY	1961	
NYC Department of Sanitation Incinerator	E. 73rd St.	New York	NY	1961	
NYC Fire Department College Training Bldg.	Welfare Island	New York	NY	1964	
NYC Institution for Female Prisoners	Rikers Island	New York	NY		
NYC Municipal Court	111 Centre St.	New York	NY	1960	
NYC Police Academy—13th & 15th Precincts	E. 20th St. btwn. 2nd & 3rd Aves.	New York	NY	1964	
NYC Police Headquarters	Manhattan Civic Center	New York	NY	1964	
NYC Police Station 24th Precinct	100th St. & Amsterdam Ave.	New York	NY	1960	
NYC Public Health Laboratory	1st Ave. & 26th St.	New York	NY	1966	
NYC Terminal Market	Hunts Point Section	Bronx	NY	1964	
Queens Central Library	89 Merrick Blvd.	Jamaica	NY	1965	
Queens General Hospital Nurses Residence	Grand Central Pkwy.	Jamaica	NY	1956	
Queens General Hospital Stores Bldg.	82 164th St.	Jamaica	NY	1958	
Queens Village Regional Branch Library	94 217th St.	Queens Village	NY	1953	
Remand Shelter for Adolescent Boys	Rikers Island	New York	NY	1964	
Richmond Central Fire Alarm Station	Clove Lakes Park	Staten Island	NY	1960	
Riverside Health Center	Amsterdam Ave. & 100th St.	New York	NY	1960	
Rochdale Village Branch Library	169 137th Ave.	Jamaica	NY	1966	
St. George Regional Branch Library	14 Bay St.	Staten Island	NY	1952	
Tuberculosis & Chronic Disease Hospital	Welfare Island	New York	NY	1954	
University Heights Branch Library	2556 Bainbridge Ave.	Bronx	NY	1957	
West Farms Branch Library	2085 Honeywell Ave.	Bronx	NY	1953	
Westchester Square Branch Library	2521 Glebe Ave.	Bronx	NY	1955	
Williamsburg Regional Branch Library	240 Division Ave.	Brooklyn	NY		
Youth House for Girls Temporary Annex	Zerega & Gleason Aves.	Bronx	NY	1960	

Isaiah Truman Hatton
(1883–1921)

Isaiah T. Hatton was the only son of Isaiah and Mary Susan Hatton. He was born on March 1, 1883, in Hagerstown, Maryland, and was thirty-eight years old when he died.[1] His family moved to Washington, D.C., when he was seven years old. He graduated from M Street High School in 1905. After receiving his diploma, he successfully completed courses in steam engineering and mechanical drafting. Having prepared himself for his life's work, he began as a draftsman in the office of WILLIAM SIDNEY PITTMAN.

As early as 1911, *District of Columbia telephone directories* list Hatton as a draftsman.[2] In 1911 and 1912, *District of Columbia directories* list him at 317 6th Street, NW; this was the same address used by JOHN ANDERSON LANKFORD for his architectural office. It is possible that Hatton worked for Lankford and began an independent practice for several years, beginning in 1911 when Lankford left Washington, D.C. From 1912 to 1917, Hatton was listed as an architect in the *District of Columbia telephone directories*.

Hatton launched I. T. Hatton & Architects with an office on the corner of Louisiana Avenue and 5th Street, NW. He later moved to the Knights of Pythias Building, designed by William Pittman, on U Street, NW, where he maintained his office until his early death in 1921.

On November 29, 1911, Hatton married Bertha B. Sayles of Washington, D.C., and soon thereafter became one of the pioneer settlers of the newly established African American suburban community of Lincoln in Prince George's County, Maryland, conveniently located fifteen miles east of Washington, D.C. and twenty-six miles south of Baltimore, Maryland. The Black developer of Lincoln was Thomas J. Calloway, the former compiler of the "Negro Exhibit" at the Exposition Universelle in Paris (1900). Hatton designed a house (1910) for Calloway at 9949 Elm Street. Elsewhere in Lincoln, Hatton designed his own residence at 5502 Center Avenue in 1911 and a house for Dr. Daniel P. Seaton. In 1918 Isaiah and Bertha moved closer to Washington, D.C., to Buena Vista—still in Prince George's County—where he designed and built their new home. They did not have any children.

In 1915 at the age of thirty-two, Hatton was the architect for Industrial Bank, founded by well-known Black developer John Whitelaw Lewis on the corner of 12th and U Streets, NW. The bank was in the heart of the Shaw neighborhood, which during the late 1920s and early 1930s was known as Washington, D.C.'s, "Great Black Way" due to the number of Black musical stars such as Edward "Duke" Ellington and Cab Calloway who performed in the theaters and jazz clubs that lined U Street. Also in 1915, Hatton received a second commission from developer John Whitelaw Lewis to design the Whitelaw Hotel at 13th and T Streets, NW. The building was described as the "first hotel of its size built for the exclusive use of colored people."[3] When it opened in November 1919, the hotel quickly became a gathering place for the "New Negro" *intelligentsia* of Washington, D.C. Hatton's floor plan called for twenty-five one-bedroom apartments for long-term rent and twenty-two hotel rooms. The spacious lobby was crowned with a large skylight. There was a banquet hall suitable for large social gatherings and conventions. The fancy restaurant required patrons to be formally dressed in order to be seated by the hostess. An appointment-only beauty salon took up most of the occupied basement space.

Other commissions by Hatton included the Southern Aid Insurance of Virginia building; inside this building was the Dunbar Theatre, one of the most popular jazz venues, which was designed by Hatton in 1920 at a cost of $60,000. The theater had a seating capacity of 395 with seven-seat rows in the middle and four-seat rows on either side. To the rear was a small balcony where the organist accompanied featured motion pictures. Another entertainment commission that Hatton received was the design of the Murray Palace Casino. The casino was to be Hatton's final work; he took to bed with an undisclosed illness before the building was completed.

Isaiah Truman Hatton was funeralized on May 20, 1921. It was reported in his obituary that Hatton executed commissions in Norfolk, Newport News, and

Whitelaw Hotel, Prints and Photographs Division, Library of Congress

Richmond, Virginia; and Philadelphia, Pennsylvania.[3] The identity of these buildings remain to be discovered.

Notes
1. 14th U.S. Census, "Isaiah T. Hatton," E.D. 88, 1920, Sheet 9, Line 87.
2. Pamela Scott, *A Directory of District of Columbia Architects 1822–1960,* 2nd ed. (D.C. self-published, 2001), p. 129.
3. "I.T. Hatton, Architect, Dead," *Washington Tribune,* 21 May 1921, p. 1.
4. Ibid., p. 2.

Bibliography
Headley, Robert K. *Motion Picture Exhibition in Washington, D.C.: An Illustrated History of Parlors, Palaces and Multiplexes in the Metropolitan Area, 1894–1997.* Jefferson, N.C.: McFarland & Company, 1999.

"National Register of Historic Places Registration Form for Whitelaw Apartment Hotel." Historic American Buildings Survey, National Park Service, no. DC363, 1993.

RONNIE MCGHEE, PRINCIPAL,
R. MCGHEE & ASSOCIATES,
WASHINGTON, D.C.

BUILDING LIST

Name	Address	City	State	Year	Comments
Antioch Baptist Church	9th & Barry Sts., NW	Washington	DC	1913	
Calloway, Thomas J.	9949 Elm St.	Lincoln	MD	1910	
Calvary Baptist Church	2129 Virginia Ave., NW	Washington	DC	1916	
Crown Savings Bank		Newport News	VA	1918	
Dandridge, W. B.	1404 Franklin St., NE	Washington	DC	1911	
Dunbar Theatre	1903 7th St., NW	Washington	DC	1920	Reginald Geare, assoc. architect
Hatton, Isaiah T.	5502 Center Ave.	Lincoln	MD	1911	
Hatton, Isaiah T.	1346 Franklin St., NE	Washington	DC	1905	
Hatton, Isaiah T.		Buena Vista	MD	1914	
House	1441 Alabama Ave., SE	Washington	DC		
Industrial Savings Bank	12th & U Sts., NW	Washington	DC	1915	
Jerusalem Baptist Church	2604 P St., NW	Washington	DC	1922	
Lewis, John W.	2000 11th St., NW	Washington	DC	1917	Demolished
Mechanics Bank	212 E. Clay St.	Richmond	VA		
Murray Palace Casino	918 U St., NW	Washington	DC	1920	
Seaton, Dr. Daniel P.		Lincoln	MD	1918	
Southern Aid Insurance of Virginia Bldg.	1901 7th St., NW	Washington	DC	1920	
Whitelaw Hotel	1839 13th St., NW	Washington	DC	1918	

William Augustus Hazel
(1854–1929)

Louise Daniel Hutchinson

William Hazel was born on September 12, 1854, in Wilmington, North Carolina. He was the eldest child of Benjamin Gillette Hazel and Margaret Ann Kellogg Hazel, both of whom were free persons of color. As a youth, Benjamin Hazel was apprenticed to a free Black, William Kellogg, to learn the trade of carpentry and they developed a close working relationship. Benjamin subsequently married one of Kellogg's daughters. Benjamin and Margaret Hazel moved to Ohio shortly before the Civil War, and moved to Cambridge, Massachusetts, after the Civil War ended. Benjamin Hazel was a carpenter and wheelwright for over twenty years at the Boston Woven Hose Company; his wife, Margaret Ann, took care of the Cambridge home. Eventually William had two brothers and two sisters; one brother died as an infant.

William Hazel completed his public school education in Cambridge by 1870 and attracted attention with his talent in art. For two years, William was a servant in the Cambridge household of Charles Russell Lowell Jr., a Union officer celebrated for his battle exploits leading the Army of the Potomac. By 1872 William Hazel was serving an apprenticeship with France-born stained-glass designer John LaFarge (1835–1910), who at the time was designing the stained-glass windows for Boston's Trinity Church (1873), designed by architect Henry Hobson Richardson (1838–1886). Hazel's formative experience in LaFarge's studio and being tutored by a graduate of the Ecole des Beaux Arts must have motivated him to think that a career as a stained-glass designer was possible—his race notwithstanding. Hazel's later decision to become an architect might have been influenced by his experiences as a stained-glass designer, working as a draftsman alongside architects who were designing churches in which his window designs were to be installed.

By 1875 Hazel was living at 67 Cushing Street in Providence, Rhode Island, and was employed as a draftsman in the office of Samuel J. F. Thayer (1842–1878), the architect for Providence City Hall (1874).

On April 29, 1882, William Hazel married the former Rosa Elizabeth Grosvenor Hazard at Mathewson Street Methodist Church in Providence, Rhode Island. Rosa was two years older than William and was a daughter of an anti-slavery free Black family who fought against the British army during the American Revolutionary War. In a class of thirty-eight female students, she became the first of her race to graduate from the Girl's Department of Providence High School, in 1871. While William Hazel was serving an apprenticeship with Charles Dexter Gambrill (1834–1880), who was the former New York partner of Henry Hobson Richardson, Rosa Hazel was the first Black hired in 1874 to teach at HAMPTON INSTITUTE'S Butler Demonstration school. They had a son, William Hazard, born in 1883; a second son, Robert C., born in 1884; and a daughter, Rosa Dorothea, born in 1885 in Cambridge.

Because Hazel was one of the first African American stained-glass designers in the United States, his arrival in Saint Paul, Minnesota, in January 1887 must have created a buzz in the exclusively White art salons of the Twin Cities. The Black press heralded his arrival with the headline "Tell 'Em We's Risin!"[1]

Hazel arrived as a representative of Tiffany & Company of New York. He had to have been one of few, if not the only, African American designer-salesmen representing the popular Tiffany & Company. On his arrival in Saint Paul, Hazel affiliated with Brown & Haywood Stained Glass Works, a local glass manufacturer. Hazel was invited to read two papers, "Stained Glass in Its Relations to Architecture," before White architecture students at Minnesota State University.[2] Hazel was also invited to speak before the Minnesota chapter of the American Institute of Architects. He, of course, was not a member of the institute and never joined.

The Hazel family resided at 1122 Raymond Avenue in Saint Paul's fashionable Saint Anthony Park, the same neighborhood where architect CLARENCE WESLEY WIGINGTON would later purchase a house. The Hazels had two more children while in Saint Paul: a daughter, Constance Eleanor, born in 1893; and a son, Francis Putnam, born in 1899.

In the spring of 1887, William Hazel was denied accommodations at Saint Paul's Clarendon Hotel and Astoria Hotel for no other reason than his race. The hotel owners were sued for violating the progressive Minnesota Civil Rights Act of 1885[3]; Hazel won the lawsuit. The award of $25 did not even cover his legal fees; however, his moxie and high-profile response to the denial of his civil rights attracted additional Black clients. He went on to win election to the influential position of secretary for the state of Minnesota's Civil Rights Committee in 1881.

William Hazel's first foray as an architect was in association with Saint Paul architect FRANCIS JEFFERSON ROBERSON on Saint Peter's African Methodist Episcopal Church in Minneapolis in 1888. Design attribution for the church is impossible to sort out, but it is known that Hazel contributed to the architectural design of the church.

In 1895 Hazel won a competition to design a $3,000 stained-glass memorial window for a new Catholic church in Austin, Minnesota, eighty miles south of Saint Paul near the Iowa state border.[4] Without a single Black person, the town of fewer than 25,000 was an out-of-the-way locale for Hazel to have gained his first Minnesota stained-glass commission. Frederick L. McGhee, Hazel's lawyer and cofounder of the Afro-American League, was a *confidant* of Catholic archbishop John Ireland. Either McGhee or Archbishop Ireland might have informed Hazel of the competition. Unfortunately, the church, along with its stained-glass windows, was demolished years ago.

Hazel, who was not Catholic, probably felt a closer religious kinship to the African Methodist Episcopal Church, given its celebrated abolitionist history. In 1899 Hazel designed for Saint Paul's African Methodist Episcopal Church in Springfield, Illinois, thirty-four stained-glass Martyrs' windows "containing a full-length portrait of Lincoln... John Brown and Elijah P. Lovejoy and the 'Grand Army' window that will contain a fine bust of General Grant."[5] The church burned to the ground in 1903 and the memorial windows did not survive.

During the winter of 1897, Hazel entered working drawings and a stained-glass window that portrayed a full-length figure of Jesus to the TENNESSEE CENTENNIAL AND INTERNATIONAL EXPOSITION and won a silver medal in decorative arts.

Sometime around 1900, the Hazel family was struck by tragedy. Their middle son Robert, who was almost six years old, died. Rosa Hazel took the remaining four young children, ranging in age from seven to one, back to Cambridge. William Hazel remained alone in Saint Paul until 1904, when he rejoined his family. However, there would be years when William Hazel's career would cause the family to live apart.

In 1909 William Hazel accepted an invitation to join the faculty at TUSKEGEE INSTITUTE. He began teaching in the Mechanical Industries Department in the fall of 1909. Similar to ROBERT ROBINSON TAYLOR and WALTER THOMAS BAILEY, and the other instructors in the department, Hazel not only carried a full teaching workload, but simultaneously was called on to design and supervise construction of five Boys Trade Buildings. Hazel remained at Tuskegee Institute for nearly a decade, a long time for him.

In 1919 Hazel accepted an administrator-teacher position at HOWARD UNIVERSITY's School of Applied Arts and Mechanics following the five-year tenure of WILLIAM JEFFERSON DECATUR. Hazel was charged with establishing a School of Architecture "where especial stress was laid upon the subject of architectural history, covering the field of painting and sculpture."[6] He organized the first library for the School of Architecture, and in 1921 was the architect for the Dining Hall and Home Economics Building (since demolished). One year before the school that he had organized awarded its first two baccalaureate degrees, Hazel resigned.

The Frederick Douglass Home Committee, headed by Judge Robert Huberton Terrell, set out in 1916 to raise $15,000 to save and restore the Douglass home "Cedar Hill" and its fifteen acres in the Anacostia neighborhood of southeast Washington, D.C. The

Dining Hall and Home Economic Building, Howard University, *Moorland-Spingarn Research Center*

chairman of the Douglass Memorial and Historical Association, Reverend Francis Grimke, commissioned William Hazel. It is believed that the restoration of "Cedar Hill," which was completed in 1922, was the first architectural historic preservation project in the nation executed by a Black architect. In addition to his buildings on the campus of Howard University, the restoration of "Cedar Hill" is Hazel's only known project in the nation's capital.

By 1924 William Hazel had moved his studio/home to 1724 Christian Street in south Philadelphia, only two city blocks from another African American architect, JULIAN FRANCIS ABELE. His reason for relocating to Philadelphia is not known, nor is the identity of any of his works during his stay in that city.

His health failing in 1927, William Hazel joined his wife, daughter Constance, and son-in-law at their residence on the grounds of Cardinal Gibbons Institute in Ridge, Maryland. Called the "Catholic Tuskegee," it was the second boarding school for African Americans north of Richmond, Virginia, the first being the National Training School for Women and Girls in Washington, D.C., which boasted several buildings designed by JOHN AYCOCKS MOORE.

William Hazel suffered a fatal heart attack on February 13, 1929.[7] He was buried in the family plot at Cambridge City Cemetery in Massachusetts.

Notes

1. "Tell 'Em We's Risin! [*sic*]," *Appeal (St. Paul)*, 8 February 1890, p. 1.
2. "W.A. Hazel," *Appeal*, 21 November 1891, p. 3.
3. *William A. Hazel v. Michael E. Foley and Thomas J. Foley* (Civil Court of the Second Judicial District, State of Minnesota, Judgment, 17 October 1887).
4. *The College of Life or Practical Self-Educator: A Manual of Self-Improvement for the Colored Race Forming an Educational Emancipator and a Guide to Success Giving Examples and Achievements of Successful Men and Women of the Race as an Incentive and Inspiration to the Rising Generation Including Afro-American Progress Illustrated and the Whole Embracing Business, Social, Domestic, Historical, and Religious Education Embellished with Hundreds of Superb Engravings,* n.p., 1895, p. 158 Library of Congress.
5. "Window for Memorial Church," *Appeal*, 5 March 1898, p. 2.
6. William Hazel, "Architectural Education at Howard University," *Howard University Record*, (April 1920): 317.
7. Maryland State Registrar, "Certificate of Death for William Hazel," no. 287, issued 13 February 1929, Crownsville, Md.

Bibliography

Abajian, James T. *Blacks in Selected Newspapers, Census, and Other Sources.* Boston: G. H. Hall & Company, 1977.

Dyson, Walter. *Howard University, the Capstone of Negro Education—A History, 1867–1940.* D.C.: The Graduate School, 1941.

Hazel, William A. "Pathfinders." *Howard University Record*, (May 1920): 346.

Hutchinson, Louise Daniel. "Ancestral Bridges: A Family History." June 1999, unpublished manuscript, Washington, D.C.

LOUISE DANIEL HUTCHINSON,
GRANDDAUGHTER OF WILLIAM AUGUSTUS HAZEL
AND RETIRED SMITHSONIAN INSTITUTION HISTORIAN

WILLIAM AUGUSTUS HAZEL

BUILDING LIST

Name	Address	City	State	Year	Comments
Austin Catholic Church stained-glass windows		Austin	MN	1895	Demolished
Douglass Memorial and Historical Association "Cedar Hill"	1411 W St., SE	Washington	DC	1922	Restoration
Howard University Dining Hall & Home Economics Bldg.	Campus	Washington	DC	1921	Demolished
St. Paul's African Methodist Episcopal Church Martyrs' windows	6th & Mason Sts.	Springfield	IL	1899	Church destroyed by fire
St. Peter's African Methodist Episcopal Church stained-glass windows	22nd St. btwn. 9th & 10th Aves. South	St. Paul	MN	1888	Demolished
Tennessee Centennial and International Exposition Competition	Fairgrounds	Nashville	TN	1897	Stained-glass window
Tuskegee Institute Boy's Trade Bldgs.	Campus	Tuskegee	AL	1909–19	Five Bldgs.

Cornelius Langston Henderson Sr.
(1888–1976)

Bentley Historical Library, University of Michigan

Cornelius Langston Henderson Sr. was born on December 11, 1888, in Detroit, Michigan. He was one of six children (three girls and three boys) born to the Reverend James M. Henderson and Cornelia Langston Henderson. James Henderson was a native of Evansville, Indiana. He graduated around 1882 from the Theological Department of Oberlin College in Ohio, and became pastor of Bethel African Methodist Episcopal Church in Detroit in the 1880s. Around 1894 he became an administrator for Morris Brown College in Atlanta, Georgia, and was its president by 1897. Next he served as president of Payne University in Selma, Alabama. Cornelius may have attended public schools for two or three years in Detroit, but it is known that he studied in the pre-college section of Morris Brown College and finished the Normal Department of Payne University in Selma, Alabama, in 1906. He then enrolled in the Engineering School at the University of Michigan in Ann Arbor. Cornelius completed the bachelor of science in civil engineering program in 1911.

Racial segregation existed at the University of Michigan during Henderson's student days. African American students were not allowed to stay in university dormitories until the 1940s. One of Henderson's professors remarked that Henderson had a much better knowledge of the subject than did the other thirty-four graduating seniors because, while the other students studied in groups, "Henderson had to learn his work without help."[1] Henderson was the second African American to graduate from the School of Engineering at the University of Michigan; FREDERICK BLACKBURN PELHAM was the first, in 1887.

After graduation, Henderson was unable to find a job. He received an offer to teach at TUSKEGEE INSTITUTE in Alabama, but his mother did not want him to live in the South. Henderson's opportunity came when he encountered a fellow engineering student, B. K. Bash, who had graduated from the University of Michigan a year before Henderson. When learning that Henderson had no job, Bash encouraged him to consider the company where he was employed, the Canadian Bridge Company in Walkerville, Ontario, Canada, just across the Detroit River from Detroit. Bash spoke to supervisor Blakeslee and arranged an interview for Henderson, and Henderson was subsequently hired. The company was owned by Willard Pope of Grosse Pointe, Michigan, who was also an engineering graduate from the University of Michigan. The company was eventually bought by United States Steel Corporation, which controlled it for most of the forty-seven years that Henderson was an employee.

Henderson held a variety of positions with the Canadian Bridge Company. He began as a draftsman from 1911 to 1916, managed the stock department from 1917 to 1919, was a steel cost estimator from 1920 to 1928, and held the position of structural steel designer from 1928 until his retirement in 1958. Henderson achieved registration as an engineer with both the State of Michigan and the Province of Ontario, Canada. He contributed to the design of the Canadian side of the Ambassador Bridge, which connects the United States to Canada; the Thousand Islands and Quebec Bridges over the Saint Lawrence River; and the vertical lift bridges over the Welland Canal. Henderson was the design engineer when the Canadian Bridge Company re-built the Canadian end of the Detroit-Windsor Tunnel, which allows automobiles to travel under the Detroit River between the United States and Canada. He also contributed to the design of numerous railroad and highway bridges in various parts of Canada.

Buildings designed by Henderson include factory buildings for the Dominion Forge & Stamping Company, the Dominion Iron & Steel Company, General Motors Corporation, Ford Motor Company of Canada, and Chrysler Corporation. He made a major innovation in design when he designed the first large-scale all-welded factory for the General Electric Company at Peterborough, Ontario, Canada. Henderson contributed to the structural design of several buildings in Ontario for the Canadian Government, such as the Royal Air Force Hangars at Trenton, the Supreme Court Building in Ottawa, and Royal Canadian Mounted Police headquarters. Because his responsibilities as design engineer required him to travel, Henderson also designed structures around the world. In Great Britain, Australia, New Zealand, Trinidad, Jamaica, and several South American countries he represented the company.

Henderson also designed buildings and structures independently of his employer, the Canadian Bridge Company. The *Michigan Chronicle* credits Henderson with designing "many residences, apartment buildings, stores and other public buildings in Detroit and suburbs."[2]

Starting in 1926, Henderson played a major role in the design and construction of Detroit Memorial Park Cemetery, located at 4280 East 13 Mile Road in Warren, Michigan. It is the first cemetery in Michigan built, owned, and operated by African Americans. As the resident civil engineer, Henderson designed and platted the 85-acre cemetery, determining where roads and graves would be located. From 1926 until his death in 1975, Henderson was both an investor in the cemetery and a member of the Board of Directors.

During his student days at the University of Michigan, Henderson met Gertrude N. Ewing, whose family lived in the Washington, D.C., area. They married in 1914 and had one son, Cornelius Jr., who earned a bachelor's degree in civil engineering from HOWARD UNIVERSITY and became a civil engineer like his father. Cornelius Henderson Jr. worked as a sanitary engineer for thirty-one years with the City of Detroit.

Ambassador Bridge, *Burton Historical Collection, Detroit Public Library*

Henderson Sr. was active socially and professionally. He was a member of the Engineering Society of Detroit and the Michigan Engineering Society. He was also, at different times, national president, and also a regional director of the NATIONAL TECHNICAL ASSOCIATION, an organization of African American engineers and architects. Henderson pledged *Alpha Phi Alpha* Fraternity, *Epilson* chapter, while he was at the University of Michigan. He was a charter member of *Sigma Pi Phi* Fraternity, *Iota Boule* chapter when it was formed on March 23, 1917; and he was a charter member of the *Alpha Phi Alpha* graduate chapter, *Gamma Lambda,* when it was organized on March 22, 1919, in Detroit.

Henderson learned to play classical violin when growing up in Atlanta. He played in Brown's Orchestra in Ann Arbor during his college years and in Cruzet's dance orchestra after graduation. He continued his membership in the Detroit Federation of Musicians and after fifty years was given a life membership. Henderson was also a fifty-year member of the Saint John's United Presbyterian Church in Detroit.

Cornelius Henderson died on July 23, 1976, in Detroit, Michigan.[3] He is buried in the cemetery he designed, Detroit Memorial Park Cemetery.

Notes

1. Cornelius Henderson, "Dear *Archons* and *Archusae*: Address to *Iota Boule* Chapter, Detroit, Michigan," Biography Reading Room File, Burton Historical Collection, Detroit Pubic Library, p. 2.
2. "Bridge Builder Man of Many Accomplishments," *Michigan Chronicle*, 27 September 1975, p. A4.
3. "Rites Set Wednesday for C. L. Henderson, Engineering Pioneer," *Michigan Chronicle*, 31 July 1976, p. A1.

Bibliography

Robinson, Wilhelmena S., ed. *Historical Negro Biographies*. New York: Publishers Company, 1969.
"Technical Group Plans Honor of C. L. Henderson." *Michigan Chronicle*, 23 February 1957, p. A7.
Wright, Roberta Hughes. *Detroit Memorial Park Cemetery*. Southfield, Mich.: Charro Book Company, 1993.

DEWITT SANFORD DYKES JR.,
PROFESSOR OF HISTORY, OAKLAND UNIVERSITY

STRUCTURE LIST

Name	Address	City	State/Province	Year	Comments
Alter Mack Copper Co.			Canada		
Ambassador Bridge	Over Detroit River	Detroit	MI	1929	
Canadian Supreme Court	301 Wellington St.	Ottawa	Canada		Assoc. Engr.
Detroit Memorial Park Cemetery	4280 East 13 Mile Rd.	Warren	MI		
Detroit-Windsor Tunnel	Under Detroit Tunnel	Detroit	MI		
Dominion Forge & Stamping Co.		Windsor	Canada	1910	Demolished
Dominion Iron & Steel Co.		Sydney	Nova Scotia		
Edmonton High Level Bridge	Over N. Saskatchewan River	Edmonton	Canada	1913	
FalconBridge Nickel Co.	Sudbury District	FalconBridge	Canada	1928	
Ford Motor Co. of Canada			Canada	1929	
General Electric Co. Factory		Peterborough	Canada	1929	
International Nickel Co. Mill Bldgs. & Furnance	Sudbury District	Frood	Canada	1917	
Noranda Mines Factory	Rouyn Twnshp.	Rouyn	Canada	1927	
Ontario Refining Co.		Cooper Cliff	Canada	1913	
Quebec Bridge	Over St. Lawrence River	Quebec	Canada	1917	
Royal Air Force Hangars		Trenton	Canada	1917	
Royal Canadian Mounted Police Headquarters		Ottawa	Canada		
Second Narrows Bridge	Over Burrand Inlet	Vancover	British Columbia	1925	
Skeena River Viaduct	Over Frazier River		Canada		
Thousand Islands Bridge	Over St. Lawrence River	Ontario	Canada	1937	
Welland Vertical Lift Bridge	Over Welland ship canal	Welland	Canada	1930	

Joseph E. Hill
(unknown–1892)

Reminiscences of School Life, and Hints on Teaching

Joseph Hill began his primary education being privately tutored by Ada H. Hinton, an opportunity that well-to-do Olde Philadelphians like his parents were able to provide to their children. From being taught in Miss Hinton's home, Joseph enrolled in the Bird School—later renamed James Forten School—which was established in 1822 as the first private school for Blacks in Philadelphia. Joseph was well prepared academically for the entrance examination given by the Institute for Colored Youth, which he entered in 1873. The Institute for Colored Youth was supported by the Orthodox Society of Friends or Quakers and offered a prestigious preparatory education in the classics or vocational training in the trades. The Institute for Colored Youth boasted that its principal, Fanny Jackson, was the first female to head a preparatory school; that one of its teachers, Edward Bouchet, was the first African American to earn a Ph.D.; another teacher, Ishmael Locke, was the father of the first African American Rhodes Scholar; and yet another teacher, Grace Mappe, was one of the first Black females to earn a college degree. Joseph Hill availed himself of these outstanding teachers and was among the largest class of graduating seniors (eighteen) who received their certificates of completion in 1876, the same year the world's fair Centennial Exposition was held in Philadelphia's Fairmount Park.

Joseph Hill was hand-selected by principal Fanny Jackson to continue his education at the newly organized Pennsylvania Museum and School of Industrial Art in 1877. The faculty at the Institute for Colored Youth held fundraisers and pooled their salaries to pay his tuition and thus big things were expected of him. One of the first African Americans to be admitted, it is believed that he was the school's first African American graduate. He furthered his education by taking courses at the Bryant and Stratton Commercial College.

In the meantime, the Institute for Colored Youth had built a plain-looking 2-story, brick building facing Bainbridge Street for the expanding Industrial Department next door to the Institute's Literary Department. Prior to the start of the Industrial Department, "in Philadelphia, the only place at the time where a colored boy could learn a trade," according to Fanny Jackson, "were the House of Refuge, or Penitentiary."[1] In gratitude for paying his tuition, Hill returned to the Institute for Colored Youth in 1875, to teach in the School of Industrial Art. The Quaker Board of Managers appointed Joseph Hill secretary and registrar of the Industrial Department with the aim of "widen[ing] their [Blacks'] field of usefulness by preparing many of the colored people to become good mechanics."[2] The eighty-seven students, sixteen to twenty-five years of age, could choose from mechanical drawing, map reading and map drawing, carpentry, bricklaying, typesetting, plumbing, plastering, and chemistry laboratory; for females, there were dressmaking and millinery courses. Hill visited the New York Trade School and Pratt Institute in Brooklyn, the *alma mater* of RICHARD CASSIUS WHITE, and Drexel Institute, the *alma mater* of WILLIAM SIDNEY

PITTMAN, to gather ideas for the curriculum at the Institute for Colored Youth. Classroom lessons were supplemented with actual projects; for example, five students prepared an estimate of work and helped to build a church (1891) in Camden, New Jersey, that required 75,000 bricks. Two of the Institute's most outstanding graduates—Esther A. Reese, class of 1885, and JULIAN FRANCIS ABELE class of 1897—both advanced to Joseph Hill's *alma mater*, the School of Industrial Arts, to study engineering and architecture and graduated in 1885 and 1897, respectively. Hill directed the department and taught drafting until his death on January 18, 1892.

For twenty-four years, Hill was Sunday school superintendent and Sunday school teacher at Lombard Street Central Presbyterian Church. He possessed an outstanding singing voice, but whether he sung in the choir is not known. He did however sing with the Amphion Singing Society, where he also served as president for eleven successive years.

On his death, John Hill was memorialized, "The loss to the School is a severe one, as he was peculiarly fitted to perform his duties, with which he had made himself thoroughly familiar. His ideas were progressive, and his abilities and energies were all devoted to the end of advancing the best interest of his race."[3]

Notes
1. Fanny Jackson Coppin, *Reminiscences of School Life, and Hints on Teaching* (Philadelphia: African Methodist Episcopal Book Concern, 1913), p. 23.
2. "Institute for Colored Youth Annual Report," 1888; Coppin, p. 296, Swarthmore College Library Archives.
3. "Institute for Colored Youth Annual Report," 1892, Coppin, p. 221. Swarthmore College Library Archives.

Bibliography
Perkins, Linda. "Fanny Jackson Coppin and the Institute for Colored Youth: A Model of Nineteenth Century Black Female Educational and Community Leadership." Ph.D. diss., University of Illinois, 1978.

DRECK SPURLOCK WILSON

Leroy Hilliard
(1903–1992)

Leroy Hilliard was a native of Brownsville, Tennessee. Hilliard's family moved to Chicago during his childhood in 1908. While attending Wendell Phillips High School, he became active in the Reserve Officers Training Corps and band, graduating in 1921. There is no available documentation indicating how he spent his childhood years or what led him to pursue his chosen career.

After graduating from high school, Hilliard set his sights on a career in architecture. Taking advantage of one of the few employment opportunities readily available to African Americans at the time, he worked as a dining car waiter on trains to pay for his college tuition at Armour Institute on Chicago's south side. He added to his income by playing saxophone with Lionel Hampton's dance band. At times, even two sources of income did not prove to be sufficient and his education was interrupted several times for lack of tuition. Hilliard persisted through those tough times and graduated in 1933 from Armour Institute with a bachelor's degree in architecture. Armour Institute merged with Lewis Institute in 1940 to form the Illinois Institute of Technology, an institution with highly regarded curriculums in architecture and engineering and a fine reputation in technical education academic circles that continues to this day.

Hilliard found employment with WALTER THOMAS BAILEY as a junior draftsman from 1930 to 1931, with CHARLES SUMNER DUKE as a draftsman and architectural designer from 1931 to 1933, and with JAMES HOMER GARROTT of Los Angeles as a draftsman and designer from 1937 to 1941. Hilliard was a civilian employee of the U.S. Army Corps of Engineers in California during World War II. Afterward he worked for Holsman, Holsman, Kiekamp & Taylor of Chicago from 1948 until 1950. Hilliard passed the licensing exam, which allowed him to practice architecture in the state of Illinois.[1] Hilliard was living at 6833 South Champlain Avenue on Chicago's south side when he applied for membership with the American Institute of Architects on November 15, 1950. At the time of his employment with Holsman, Holsman, Kiekamp & Taylor they were designing notable International-style apartment high-rises such as 860 North Lakeshore Drive Apartments, Promotory Point Apartments, and Winchester-Hood Garden Apartments. Although Hilliard's contributions to the design of these apartments could not be confirmed, it is probable that he was involved with their design and/or preparation of construction drawings. He ultimately established his own practice in 1951 in Chicago.

Hillard's firm designed projects in the residential, community, and commercial sectors, exemplified by houses and community child- and health-care facilities. He worked on several original design and remodeling projects at the homes, mosques, and offices of Elijah Muhammed, the founder of the Nation of Islam.

Hilliard's views on soliciting work from the Federal Housing Authority were included in an article in the *Inland Architect*.[2] Like the other Black architects interviewed, he expressed discouragement and distrust of a federal agency not noted for giving projects to small firms. Paradoxically, he stated toward the end of the interview that he had "a 45-unit with FHA right now."[3] Of particular note is the description of his office as "Spartan" with whitewashed walls bare save for two certificates proclaiming his graduation from Armour Institute and his architectural registration. The article remarks on his low-key, soft-spoken manner, and the fact that prominently missing from the office decor was any kind of brochure describing his work, or renderings that depicted his work for the visitors to acknowledge. His response was "I just leave that to the younger guys . . . I've been a registered architect for twenty years, with my own office from time to time, and I don't need to prove to anyone that I'm an architect."[4] It is evident from this statement that Hilliard shied away from self-promotion.

Leroy Hilliard was a world traveler who was fluent in Portuguese, Spanish, French, and Italian. He retired in 1975, remaining in Chicago's south-side Jackson Park neighborhood until his death in 1992.

Notes

1. State of Illinois, Department of Professional Registration, "Leroy Hilliard," issued 27 March 1950, No. 1003473.
2. Rob Crusaden, "Black Architects in Chicago: A Thin Piece of the Action," *Inland Architect,* (June 1969): 32.
3. Ibid.
4. Ibid.

Bibliography

Jaques, Alfred M. "Some African-American Alumni of the Illinois Institute of Technology." Winter term paper, 1994. Illinois Institute of Technology Archives, Chicago.

LISA WILLIS, PRINCIPAL,
URBAN WORKS, LTD.,
CHICAGO, ILLINOIS

BUILDING LIST

Name	Address	City	State	Year	Comments
860 N. Lakeshore Drive Apts.	860 N. Lakeshore Dr.	Chicago	IL	1949	
Lunt Lake Apts.	1122 W. Lunt Ave.	Chicago	IL	1949	
Muhammed, Elijah		Chicago	IL		
Promotory Point Apts.	5530 S. Lakeshore Dr.	Chicago	IL	1949	
Winchester-Hood Garden Apts.	6113 N. Winchester Ave.	Chicago	IL	1949	

Stewart Daniel Hoban Sr.
(1928–2002)

Stewart Daniel Hoban was born on February 24, 1928, in Washington, D.C., where he resided and practiced architecture all his life. He was the second son of Nacy Hoban, a native of Colonial Beach, Virginia, and Carrie Lee Stewart, formerly of Spottsylvania County, Virginia. The Hobans, who married in 1924, settled in the District of Columbia, where their two sons were born. Nacy Hoban operated a shoe shine stand for a number of years in the heart of the U Street district, then known as the "Great Black Way." He later became a building engineer, an occupation in which he was employed the remainder of his life. Carrie Stewart Hoban worked most of her adult life as a nurse. The Hobans were keenly interested in the education of their children and fostered a home environment that was nurturing and supportive. Although the family shares the same name as the architect of the White House and the U.S. Capitol, James Hoban, there is no evidence that they are related.

Stewart Hoban attended public schools in Washington, D.C. In 1942 he was enrolled at Garnett-Patterson Junior High School. He continued on to Armstrong Technical High School, the vocational school established for the segregated African American student population of Washington, D.C., where he was first introduced to drafting. Hoban, nicknamed "Bobbie," was a popular student, having been elected vice-president of the Engineering Club, treasurer of the Officer's Club, student manager of the varsity baseball team, and captain of the Boy's Cadet Corps. His leadership in the latter led to the prediction that he would become the first "Negro navy commander!"[1] It was at Armstrong Tech that he became serious about drafting, which was taught variously by architects ROSCOE INGERSOLL VAUGHN and GEORGE ALONZO FERGUSON and Charles Baltimore, an industrial arts instructor. Exposed to both architectural drafting and mechanical drafting, he ultimately chose architectural drafting. By the time he graduated in 1946, Hoban was committed to a career in architecture.

Hoban entered HOWARD UNIVERSITY's School of Engineering and Architecture in January 1947, where his principal professor was LEROY JOHN HENRY BROWN. Brown became Hoban's mentor. Among Hoban's other professors were HOWARD HAMILTON MACKEY SR. and Frank West. All three operated private architectural offices and brought to academia the practical side of architecture, an influence that served Hoban throughout his career. He received his bachelor of science degree in architecture in June 1951.

During his junior year, Stewart Hoban married Helen Adele Turner of Albany, New York, who was a collateral descendent of Black intellectual Dr. William Edward Burghardt DuBois. She graduated from Washington, D.C.'s, prestigious Dunbar High School and Miner Teacher's College, and taught in the D.C. public schools her entire career until she retired in the 1990s. She and Stewart had three children: Stewart Daniel Jr.; Cynthia Lynn Thompson; and Leslie Adele Moreno, also an architect.

After college graduation, Stewart Hoban worked for Stanbern Construction Company. He was employed as a draftsman and prepared working drawings for the South Capitol Street Bridge. This employment was followed by several years as a draftsman for George M. Ewing, a Philadelphia-based firm with a Washington, D.C., office where Hoban prepared working drawings for commercial and industrial buildings and served as the office's liaison to the U.S. Army Corps of Engineers. In 1954 he was a designer for Daniel, Mann, Johnson & Mendenhall on several military projects. In 1956 Lublin, McGaughy & Associates hired Hoban as an architect. He served on the team that designed the German Embassy along Embassy Row in northwest Washington, D.C., and several top-secret federal facilities. Although he would leave the firm three years later to become a consulting architect to the U.S. Postal Service, he would work with them on other projects. Hoban was methodically making a name for himself. Richard Ball, a structural engineer with whom he worked between 1954 and 1958, described Hoban's designs as showing "a definite amount of imagination and ability."[2]

Hoban did not become a registered architect in the District of Columbia until December 1959.[3] He was also registered in Virginia and Maryland. By then Hoban had become reacquainted with LOUIS EDWIN FRY SR. from their days at Howard University, and Fry became a mentor and lifelong friend. They would later work together as part of a collaborative of local African American architects on a feasibility study for the District of Columbia government's only college, Federal City College.

In 1963 Hoban opened his own practice at 6230 3rd Street, NW, near Howard University, and close to his home on 4th Street, NW. He later moved his office to Kennedy Street, NW, within the same neighborhood; to North Capitol Street, NW; and lastly to Florida Avenue, NW, where he continued his practice until he retired in 1993. At various periods, he was in partnership or collaboration with numerous African American architects, including his former professor Frank West.

Hoban's office became a meeting place for Howard University architecture students. He made space available in the drafting room for students to work on school projects and he fostered discussion among them, providing a relaxed forum for questions, ideas, and information exchange that the classroom setting often inhibited. More importantly, Hoban provided students with an opportunity for employment in the field and time to prepare to take the licensing examination. He was noted for his insistence on precision in drafting and neat lettering and the finished quality of presentation drawings.

After opening his office, Hoban set out to make an impact on the built environment. As a result, his projects became increasingly prestigious or high profile. He stated that at the time that he opened his office, available work was more plentiful for Black architects. Social conditions for African Americans had improved and the federal government was investing in local real estate and building construction. In the era of civil rights and "Black power," traditional African American organizations were seeking to keep "money" within the community. Hoban designed single-family houses, churches, public housing, and school additions.

One of his first projects on his own was commissioned by Saint Stephens Episcopal Church. The upper northwest Washington, D.C., church wanted to provide affordable housing for its parishioners. The result was Urban Village, a handsome design with seventy-two apartments cleverly sited on an odd-shaped parcel of land at 16th and Newton Streets, NW. It was completed in 1972 with Conrad Cafritz, a White developer. Other multi-family buildings designed by Hoban include the 77-unit Arlington View Terrace and the 304-unit Oakland Manor, both in northern Virginia.

Among Hoban's works were the design of the Mount Airy Baptist Church addition at 1100 North Capitol, Street, NW, and the Elks Lodge Hall at 3rd and T Streets, NW. Members of the lodge are proud of their building, which is owned and was designed and constructed by African Americans. The Hawkins Manor I and II (1969) in the Modern style, is a public housing project in Glenarden, Maryland. Glenarden Apartments, in the functional Modernist style, was a public housing project in suburban Maryland. It was completed in 1970.

Hoban worked on a number of schools in Washington, D.C., among which were the Edward Kennedy "Duke" Ellington School of the arts in Georgetown and a 1972 addition to Walker-Jones Elementary School, a historic, African American elementary school at 1st and L Streets, NW. The work on the Walker-Jones School, including the Community Service Center, clearly shows the Walter Gropius influence, a style Hoban admired as being less mechanical looking than the Mies van der Rohe trend of the era.

Hoban was the architectural designer on two collaborative projects in the 1970s. The first was the restoration of the Old Post Office, the Romanesque

Urban Village, *Patsy M. Fletcher*

Revival–style building on 12th and Pennsylvania Avenue, NW. When the building, with its prominent clock tower, was originally built in 1902, the neoclassicists considered it "an object of permanent regret."[4] The General Services Administration, its owner, rebuffed calls for its demolition and instead made it the keystone for a master plan to revitalize Pennsylvania Avenue, the "Avenue of the Presidents." Architect Arthur Cotton Moore (1939–1998) is credited with the restoration along with McGaughy, Marshall & McMillan. However, Hoban is the architect of record. The skylight and the soaring atrium were Hoban's designs, for which he won an award.

Hoban stated that if he could do it again, he would not have gone into business for himself—that it was too hard. However hard it may have been for him, he nevertheless inspired a generation of African American architects.

Hoban battled the effects of sickle cell anemia his entire life. Complications and a lengthy illness caused by the disease led to his death on October 30, 2002. He was buried at Harmony Memorial Park in Suitland, Maryland.

Notes
1. *The Reflector* (Armstrong Technical High School Yearbook), D.C.: Armstrong Technical High School, 1946), p. 25.
2. Interview with Richard Ball (co-worker of Stewert Hoban), Washington, D.C., November 2001.
3. D.C. Board of Examiners and Registrars of Architects, "Stewart Hoban," Certificate no. 1712, issued 8 November 1957.
4. Wolf van Eckardt, "A Preservation Victory Saves Washington's Old Post Office," *National Geographic Magazine*, September 1983: 406.

Bibliography
American Institute of Architects. *AIA Guide to the Architecture of Washington, D.C.*, 3rd ed. Baltimore: Johns Hopkins University Press, 1994.

Fitzpatrick, Sandra, and Maria R. Goodwin. *The Guide to Black Washington: Places and Events of Historical and Cultural Significance in the Nation's Capital.* New York: Hippocrene Books, 1999.

PATSY M. FLETCHER, COMMUNITY
DEVELOPMENT RESOURCE CONSULTANT,
WASHINGTON, D.C.

BUILDING LIST

Name	Address	City	State	Year	Comments
Alexandria Housing Authority FHA Housing	Scattered sites	Alexandria	VA		
Arlington View Terrace	1429 S. Rolf St.	Arlington	VA		77 dwelling units (du)
Bill's Friendly Inn		Washington	DC		
Callan Motors Office & Garage		Arlington	VA		
Carpenter Medical Office		Alexandria	VA		
Elks Lodge Hall	1844 3rd St., NW	Washington	DC	1968	
Ellington School of the Arts	1698 35th St,. NW	Washington	DC	c1970	Alterations
Federal City College Feasibility Study		Washington	DC		
Glenarden Apts.	8405 Hamlin St.	Lanham	MD	1970	
Hawkins Manor I & II	8639 Glenarden Pkwy.	Glenarden	MD	1969	60 du
Mt. Airy Baptist Church	1100 N. Capitol St., NW	Washington	DC	1969	
Nauck Heights		Arlington	VA		48 du
New World Laboratory		Washington	DC		Alterations
Oakland Manor Apts.	3710 Columbia Pk.	Fairfax	VA		304 du
Old Post Office Pavilion	12th & Pennsylvania, Ave., NW	Washington	DC	1983	Now Nancy Hanks Center
Third Baptist Church	1546 5th St., NW	Washington	DC		Alterations
Urban Village	3403 16th St., NW	Washington	DC	1972	72 du
Walker-Jones Elementary School	100 L St., NW	Washington	DC	1970	

John Bunyon Holloway Jr.
(1913–1993)

John Holloway was a journeyman architect who was the first African American architect to open an office in Augusta, Georgia, in 1932, and was employed as an architectural draftsman for some of the leading African American architects and architectural engineers of his era, namely ALBERT IRVIN CASSELL, ROMULUS CORNELIUS ARCHER, and GEORGE MACEO JONES.

John Jr. was born in Augusta, Georgia, on September 5, 1913, and was brought home to 1343 Railroad Avenue. His father was a contractor who took him along to job sites. His mother, Marie Holloway, was a native of Augusta. John Sr. and Marie were intent on providing John Jr. and his siblings, Charles, Ruby, and Claudia with the best education they could afford. They enrolled John Jr. in the prestigious Presbyterian-supported Haines Normal and Industrial School, whose principal was the pioneering education reformer Lucy Craft Laney. Lucy Laney led Haines to establish the first *kindergarten* in the South for Black children, organized the first football team at a Black high school in Georgia, and developed a four-year high school curriculum that combined the classics of fine art and science with industrial vocational training. It is speculated that John Holloway took drafting classes during the four years he attended Haines Normal and Industrial School between 1919 and 1923.

He enrolled at TUSKEGEE INSTITUTE during the early 1930s. Under the directorship of ROBERT ROBINSON TAYLOR in the Mechanical Industries Department, Holloway improved his drafting skill and learned to become an architect.

Holloway returned to Augusta, Georgia, in January 1932, where he opened an office that he operated until 1937. His principal designs were for single-family houses and at least one church—Antioch Baptist Church (1934).

Holloway moved to Washington, D.C., in August 1937 and worked a brief four months as an architectural draftsman for Albert Irvin Cassell. Not long thereafter, in April 1938, he switched to Romulus Cornelius Archer's office, again working as a draftsman. After one year with Archer, he journeyed west to Chicago in August 1939, where he found employment with George Maceo Jones as an office manager and draftsman, a situation that was closer in managerial responsibility to the one he'd held when he had operated his own one-man office. He resigned from Jones's office after one year and founded the firm of Holloway & Associates, which lasted until 1942.

Acutely aware of the business advantages of possessing a degree in architecture, Holloway enrolled in June 1942 at the Urbana-Champaign campus of the University of Illinois School of Architecture. He covered his tuition with an Illinois General Assembly Scholarship and a Manerrie Barlow Ware Scholarship. On his registration application he listed architectural engineer WILLIAM FERGUSON THORNTON as his next of kin and boss. (Thornton was neither related to Holloway nor was he his legal guardian. Holloway's parents were probably deceased by then, but he did have a sister, Martha D. Lucie, who was still living.) Holloway lived off campus in Urbana at 1301 Clark Street because Blacks were prohibited from residing in the dormitories. Holloway earned money for his room and board by working for C. E. Palmer, associate dean of the College of Fine and Applied Art. He stated that he withdrew from the university because of World War II, although he did not serve in the armed forces.[1] Deciding to leave the university must have been a bitter pill for Holloway to swallow because he had earned A's for thirty semester hours, which safeguarded his scholarships and earned him a place on the Dean's Honor Roll.[2] Six years would elapse before he resumed his architecture studies, beginning in the winter semester of 1949, this time at The Catholic University of America School of Architecture and Engineering in Washington, D.C. He lasted four semesters before withdrawing at the end of the fall semester of 1951.

Holloway's failure to earn his architecture degree on what proved to be his last attempt may have been due to the four apartment buildings he had on the boards in 1950 and 1951 for builder R. A. Froe plus three single-family houses he was designing for separate clients. Holloway had opened an office at 701 42nd Street, NE, in the same historic Deanwood neighborhood where Black architects LEWIS WENTWORTH GILES SR., ROBERT PRINCE MADISON, and JOHN ALEXANDER MELBY were residentially active. Having

Antioch Baptist Church, *Courtesy of Antioch Missionary Baptist Church*

practiced in Washington, D.C., since 1943, he did not become a registered architect until 1951.[3]

John Holloway died at D.C. General Hospital in May 1993.

Notes
1. University of Illinois, Student Records, "John B. Holloway Jr.," University of Illinois Archives, 1943.
2. Ibid.
3. D.C. Board of Examiners and Registrars of Architects, "John Bunyan Holloway, Jr.," Certificate no. 772, issued 11 June 1951.

DRECK SPURLOCK WILSON

BUILDING LIST

Name	Address	City	State	Year	Comments
Antioch Baptist Church	1454 Florence St.	Augusta	GA	1934	
Benning, H. S.		Augusta	GA	1943	Alterations
Beth-Eden Church		Washington	DC		Plans only
Bowman, Theodore A.		Augusta	GA	1940	
Boyce, Jacob		Augusta	GA	1930	
Burton Store & Apts.		Washington	DC	1948	
Butcher Apartments		Washington	DC	1950	Addition
Christ Presbyterian Church	1136 Ceclia St.	Augusta	GA	1939	
Crawford, Susie		GlenArden	MD	1947	
Danziger, William H.		Aiken	SC	1931	
Eastland Gardens Apts.		Washington	DC	1949	
Federal Housing Administration Housing		Seat Pleasant	MD	1947	
First Church of Christ	2490 Alabama Ave., SE	Washington	DC	1954	
Froe Apartment Bldg.		Washington	DC	1951	
Froe Apartment Bldg.		Washington	DC	1952	
Froe Houses		Washington	DC	1948	3 houses
Froe, R. A.		Washington	DC	1949	
Greater St. John Church	316 S. Kostner Ave.	Chicago	IL		Plans only
Holloway, John B.		Augusta	GA	1930	
Johnson, Fielding		Chicago	IL	1944	

JOHN BUNYON HOLLOWAY JR.

BUILDING LIST *(continued)*

Name	Address	City	State	Year	Comments
Johnson, Walter A.		Augusta	GA	1940	
King, Cornelius		Washington	DC	1951	
Lagana, Josephine		Lanham	MD		
Langley, Howard E.		Aiken	SC	1932	
Lawrence, Phillip		Washington	DC		
Liggio Housing		Arlington	VA		5 rowhouses
Liggio Housing		Arlington	VA		34 houses
McIntosh, Ernest W.		Washington	DC		Plans only
Miller, Charles M.		Washington	DC		Plans only
Mt. Pisgah Church	4622 South Dr.	Chicago	IL		Plans only
Mt. Zion Church	1134 S. San Francisco Ave.	Chicago	IL		Plans only
Perry, L. D.		Augusta	GA	1940	
Plymouth Theatre	1365 H St., NE	Washington	DC	1946	Alterations
Quarles,		Tuskegee	AL	1935	
Quigless Medical Clinic	99 Main St.	Tarboro	NC	1947	
Reed, J. D.		Tuskegee	AL	1935	
Ridgely, Marion		Augusta	GA	1931	
Scioscia, Pete		Lanham	MD	1948	
Scott, M. M.		Augusta	GA	1941	
Settle, R. T		Augusta	GA	1929	
Simms, Edgar R.		Washington	DC		Plans only
Smith, Raymond		Glenarden	MD	1947	
Stillman, Robert		Chicago	IL	1942	
Thornton, William		Chicago	IL	1942	
Village of Robbins Town Hall	3327 W. 137th St.	Robbins	IL	1940	
Whitlock Print Shop		Washington	DC	1946	Alterations
Williams, Dr. J. W.		Robbins	IL	1940	
Winestock, Reba		Washington	DC	1944	Addition
Winston, Leon		Chicago	IL	1944	
Woods, James A.		Washington	DC		Plans only

Howard University, Department of Architecture
(1919)

Several convergent initiatives in the early years gave rise to architecture as a course of study at Howard University. The Building Block Company organized in 1867 with the opening of a manufacturing plant on the hilltop campus to make masonry units for the construction of university buildings. The structural failure of unsound walls erected by the Building Block Company caused its demise. The industrial arts program, which occupied the sheds left behind by the Building Block Company, might have seemed a logical academic and practical environment in which to initiate architectural studies. However, the building and carpentry component of the industrial arts program taught by James Henry Hill paled before increased academic standards and the evolution of architecture as a degree program associated with fine arts.

It is not unique that the Department of Architecture's birth evolved from the teaching of drawing as a fine art in this university. Walter Dyson discussed the close relationship between the development of architecture and fine arts. Writing on the late-nineteenth-century development of Howard University, he recounted the scenario in which architecture asserted itself as a department and degree-offering unit that was incubated in the Department of Art:

> In 1891, drawing was transferred from the Industrial Department to the Normal Department as "drawing" and not "mechanical drawing." This transfer from the Industrial to the Normal Department was epoch-making. It suggested that the emphasis was beginning to be placed upon the educative value of drawing. With this transfer of emphasis in 1891 the second period of the history of drawing at the University began. Fortunately throughout this whole second period drawing at the University was in charge of one teacher, Harry J. Bradford. Much progress was made, especially in mechanical drawing. But it was the appointment of William N. Buckner as instructor of drawing in 1917 that the third period in the history of drawing at the University began. Under Buckner the students in drawing devoted their time "expressing simple forms by lines . . . drawing of historical ornaments; free-hand and mechanical perspective; drawing from objects and casts in light and shade and pencil sketching. Thus Buckner during his six years at the University emphasized the artistic side of drawing. Fortunately for painting, William A. Hazel was appointed in 1919 to teach architecture. Hazel organized a Department of Architecture. In this Department "especial stress laid upon the subject of architectural history, covering the field of painting and sculpture. The study of architectural design emphasized from the standpoint of architecture as a fine art.[1]

The first faculty member appointed in architecture was WILLIAM JEFFERSON DECATUR, who taught from 1908 until 1912. However, it was the appointment of WILLIAM AUGUSTUS HAZEL in 1919 that marked the beginning of architect-educators being appointed to teach architecture. Dyson continues:

> Albert I. Cassell of Cornell University was added to the faculty of the Department of Architecture in 1920, and upon the resignation of Hazel the next year, was placed in charge of the department. The increased number of students and the employment of Cassell by the University in its building program made an assistant necessary. In 1921, James V. Herring, a graduate of Syracuse University, was employed as Instructor in Architecture and to teach the subjects in the field most closely related to the fine arts. For the first time at the University illustrated lectures in the history of architecture, sculpture and painting were given by Herring. And new courses, such as watercolor, painting and drawing from life, were added to the curriculum. By the autumn of 1921, Herring had organized these subjects into the first official Department of Art at the University. With Herring, therefore, the fourth period in the history of drawing at the University began.[2]

In 1923 HILYARD ROBERT ROBINSON was appointed to the faculty. The holder of a professional degree in architecture from Columbia University, he became chairman in 1924, the same year that HOWARD HAMILTON MACKEY SR. was appointed an instructor. Robinson remained on the faculty until 1930 and later returned for a brief period, 1932 to 1934, after receiving a master of arts degree in architecture from Columbia University. His 1934 Department of Architecture *Annual Report* provides a view into his pedagogic philosophy when he writes,

> Our teaching must reflect the fact that the young Negro trained as an architect and handling problems originating essentially among Negro masses, urban and rural, still has the work of a pioneer to do, and that it was especially important that Negro architects be well prepared for the responsibility.[3]

Nineteen twenty-three was also the year that the first two degree recipients in architecture, ARTHUR WILFRED FERGUSON and Julius Gardner, graduated. Ferguson returned to teach the following year and continued on the faculty until 1933. Gardner was appointed to the faculty in 1928 and continued until 1932.

Like ALBERT IRVIN CASSELL, Hilyard Robert Robinson became an esteemed practitioner and contributed to the classic order of the university's campus. George Cook Hall, the men's dormitory, was among the early commissions completed by Robinson in association with PAUL REVERE WILLIAMS, the celebrated southern California architect with impeccable Republican Party credentials. The detailed 1933 Howard University Master Plan of classic proportions and spatial relationships by Albert Irvin Cassell and his firm's designs for Douglas Hall, Founders Library, and the entrance gates and wrought-iron fences enclosing the main yard stand as internationally known symbols of the strength and endurance of Howard University and its place in higher education.

Nineteen thirty-three was a difficult year for architectural education at Howard University. The Board of Trustees voted to drop studies in architecture at the end of academic year 1933 to 1934, and advised undergraduates that only one year of study could be expected. Upon the petition of JOHN ANDERSON LANKFORD, vice-president of the NATIONAL TECHNICAL ASSOCIATION, the Board of Trustees reaffirmed their commitment to continue and reorganize instruction in architecture. Lankford's testimony to the trustees included the following compelling arguments supporting the university's responsibility for educating Negro architects:

> "[in] the usual Negro Communities it is common knowledge that there is a far greater need for the services the well trained and socially minded architect is prepared to give, than in some of the more blighted districts in which white people live. This is the work, even more, the insistent demand for the trained Negro architects. . . . The community that Howard University serves looks to Howard to play a significant part."[4]

The early association of pioneer Negro architects with architecture education at Howard University was to be continued and increased throughout the program's history. The centrality of Howard University's position for people of color in the profession was es-

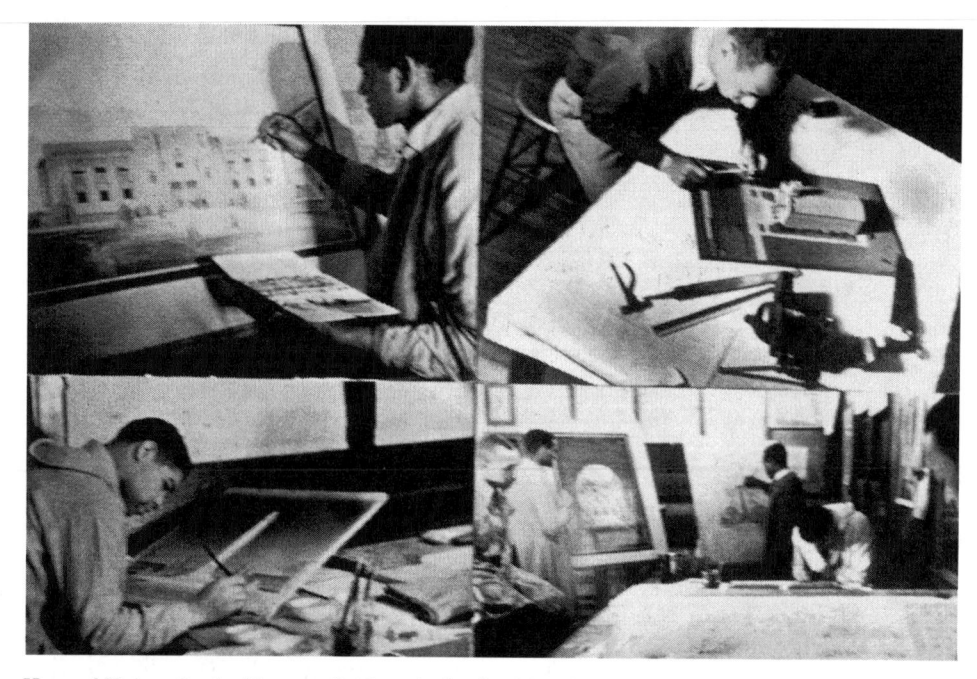

Howard University Architecture Students in Studio, *Moorland-Spingarn Research Center*

tablished with the early efforts of Howard Hamilton Mackey Sr. in organizing the first juried "Exhibition of the Work of Negro Architects," May 12 to 28, 1931, mounted in the Howard University Art Gallery, which brought notoriety to WALTER THOMAS BAILEY of Chicago, Illinois; JOHN EDMONSON BRENT of Buffalo, New York; CURTIS GRAHAM ELLIOT of Cincinnati, Ohio; ROBERT ROBINSON TAYLOR of TUSKEGEE INSTITUTE; CALVIN LUNSFORD MCKISSACK and his brother MOSES MCKISSACK of Nashville, Tennessee; Albert Irvin Cassell; Howard University students JAMES ALONZO PLATER, RALPH AUGUSTINE VAUGHN, CLARENCE BUCHANAN WHEAT SR., and William Winder; and Howard University–educated DAVID AUGUSTUS WILLISTON. This 1931 exhibit set the direction for the school's continuing activist role in support of increasing the numbers of African American architects and making visible and supporting, in general, those in the profession. The importance of Howard University to the surrounding community in which it matured as a great university applied equally to the architecture program's role in the growth of Washington, D.C.'s, architectural community. Although not extensively promoted to the larger community, African American architects have been registered to practice the profession since the District of Columbia registration law was enacted in 1923.

The pedagogical and sociocultural centers of gravity that placed the Howard University architecture program in the position to educate a majority of the mid-20th-century African American architects were generated by Mackey and a *cadre* of educator-architects who brought diverse yet focused views and talents to the educational experience of hundreds of aspiring architects. As with the great collaborations of Martin Luther King Jr., A. Phillip Randolph, and Ralph David Abernathy, as they planned the historic 1963 march on Washington, D.C., and, ultimately, the civil rights movement; and that of George Washington, Thomas Jefferson, Benjamin Franklin, and John Quincy Adams in their forming the philosophic basis for a new nation; LEROY JOHN HENRY BROWN, GRANVILLE HURLEY, and LOUIS FRY SR. as well as others were part of a great collaborative effort with Mackey. If they had chosen to act independently they would not have accomplished their goals and Mackey's vision. Each brought something different to the collaboration and each was absolutely essential. Together they saw the profession come of age.

LEROY JOHN HENRY BROWN and GRANVILLE WARNER HURLEY SR. brought special qualities and experiences to the collaboration and built their individual and collective reputations in doing so. In the years approaching the first accreditation of the program, individual roles sharpened; Mackey was the leader; Fry brought the practitioner's perspective to curriculum planning; Brown was the disciplinarian who developed and taught the core courses in graphics, structures lab, and construction documentation; and Hurley was the history and theory master. The reciprocal relationship between faculty involvement in Howard University's architecture program and the enhancement of personal reputations is symbolized by the Washington, D.C., chapter of the American Institute of Architect's 1991 Centennial Award to Leroy Brown in recognition of, in the main, his association with Howard University, the success of its architectural students who studied with him, and his firm being the first White-owned firm to hire a Negro architect. In 1951 the National Architectural Accrediting Board conveyed full accreditation on the professional degree program that Mackey and his colleagues brought to maturity. This was the first such degree so recognized in a historic and predominantly African American institution of higher education. Forty years after the action of the Board of Trustees to establish architecture as a degree program, Howard University's "capstone" status was enhanced with a level of validation not previously possessed in the African American academic community.

Notes
1. Walter Dyson, *Howard University the Capstone of Negro Education, 1867–1940* (D.C.: Graduate School Howard University, 1941), p. 108.
2. Harry G. Robinson, "Howard Hamilton Mackey Lecture," Howard University, 10 February 1992, Washington, D.C. p. 4.
3. Ibid.
4. Dyson, p. 50.

Bibliography
Robinson, Harry G., and Hazel R. Edwards. *The Long Walk: The Place Making Legacy of Howard University*. D.C.: Moorland-Spingarn Research Center, 1996.

HARRY G. ROBINSON III, FAIA,
PROFESSOR AND DEAN EMERITUS,
HOWARD UNIVERSITY SCHOOL
OF ARCHITECTURE AND DESIGN

Granville Warner Hurley
(1904–1991)

Granville Hurley Jr.

Granville W. Hurley was born on March 10, 1904, to Ethel Peterson and William Granville Hurley of Philadelphia, Pennsylvania. William Hurley worked as a mailman and Ethel Hurley was a housewife. Granville had a younger brother Harry. When Granville was three years old his mother died; his father re-married and had a son William. Granville was the only one of William Sr.'s sons to pursue a career in architecture.

Granville entered the academically rigorous and racially integrated Central High School in center city Philadelphia in 1920. Central High enjoyed a well-deserved reputation for graduating talented students seeking professional careers in the fine arts, including architecture. The year that Granville entered Central High School was the year that HOWARD HAMILTON MACKEY SR. graduated and JULIAN ABELE COOK and WILLIAM HENRY MOSES were in their third years. An accomplished freehand artist, Granville won the highly competitive Senior Art Prize during his fourth year. He graduated in 1924.

Lacking college tuition, he instead went to work as a draftsman for architect Edward A. Crane of Philadelphia for two years beginning in 1926.

In 1928 Hurley enrolled in the University of Pennsylvania School of Architecture, whose curriculum was modeled on that at the *l'Ecole des Beaux-Arts* in Paris. The School of Architecture was led by Dean Corbett Koyl, who tried his best to eliminate the unofficial quota on Jews and women (the number of Blacks being so miniscule as to not warrant attention).

Hurley earned his bachelor of architecture degree in 1933, continued on for another year, and was awarded his master of architecture degree in 1934. Hurley became only the third African American to graduate from the School of Architecture, following JULIAN ABELE (class of 1902) and Howard Hamilton Mackey Sr. (class of 1924).

The year that Hurley graduated from the University of Pennsylvania, fellow alumnus Howard Mackey was director of the DEPARTMENT OF ARCHITECTURE AT HOWARD UNIVERSITY. He hired Hurley as an assistant professor to teach construction details. Full-time employment surely must have been a relief to Hurley, coming when it did during the throes of the Great Depression in 1934. Hurley would remain at Howard University for a total of thirty-eight years. During Howard Mackey's sabbatical, Hurley served as acting director of the Department of Architecture from 1954 to 1957.

Hurley worked summers from 1938 to 1948 in Howard Mackey's private practice as an architectural draftsman. During the summer months from 1949 to 1952 he taught architectural drafting at the Washington School of Drafting at their downtown D.C. northwest location.

Granville Hurley married Catherine Grey in 1932. They had a son, Granville Jr., who became a financial analyst on mass transit projects for the U.S. Department of Transportation. The couple divorced in 1963. Hurley remarried in 1968 to Emmeta Cardozo of

Washington, D.C., and became stepfather to her daughter, Gloria Olney.

Hurley registered as an architect in the District of Columbia in 1950.[1] In 1958 he was hired as a private consultant to the International Cooperation Administration mission in Sudan. He taught building construction at the Khartoum Technical Institute and designed two buildings on the campus. These two international buildings were the only architectural designs attributed to Hurley during his lengthy architectural career. His outstanding contributions to the profession were not as a practitioner but rather as an educator. On his return to Howard University from the Sudan he developed the syllabus and taught one of the first collegiate courses and taught tropical architecture.

Hurley's contributions to the profession of architecture were duly recognized when he was elevated to fellow status by the American Institute of Architects in 1974. He had been a member of the American Institute of Architects since his name first appeared in the *AIA Directory* in 1956.

Granville Hurley Sr. died from a stroke on February 11, 1991. He was cremated.

Notes

1. D.C. Board of Examiners and Registrars of Architects, "Granville Warner Hurley," Certificate no. 1250, issued 31 October 1950.

GRANVILLE HURLEY JR.,
WASHINGTON, D.C.

BUILDING LIST

Name	Address	City	Country	Year	Comments
Khartoum Technical Institute Classroom Bldg.	Campus	Kharutoum	Sudan	1959	Now Sudan University
Khartoum Technical Institute Administration Bldg.	Campus	Kharutoum	Sudan	1958	Now Sudan University

James Edward Hutchins
(1890–1970)

Courtesy Janie Roxwell Robinson

Born on November 25, 1890, in Blakely, Georgia, James Edward Hutchins moved to Jacksonville, Florida, after completing vocational classes at Savannah State College. Identified as living and working in Jacksonville as a carpenter as early as 1918, Hutchins was first associated in different capacities with the Dawkins Building and Supply Company, except for a few years in the mid-1920s when he was employed as a railroad car porter with the Pullman Company.[1] After forming J. E. Hutchins Construction Company & American Builders Service in the 1930s, Hutchins became recognized for the design and construction of numerous churches for African American congregations in Jacksonville, as well as residences in the Durkee Gardens and College Park subdivisions that are located north and west of downtown Jacksonville, where the city's growing African American middle class had settled. Churches in Jacksonville designed and constructed by him include St. Paul African Methodist Episcopal Church, New Bethel African Methodist Episcopal Church, First Born Church of the Living God, Zion Hope Church, Emmanuel Baptist Church, and Triumph the Church.[2]

Hutchins is recognized as one of the few African American architect-builders in Jacksonville. As a result, he became a mentor to many African American builders who sought his counsel and expertise on preparing construction plans. Shortly after World War II, his construction company consulted with the U.S. Veterans Administration to provide training for returning Black veterans. As a result, Hutchins trained a whole generation of African American carpenters, masons, and draftsmen who helped to build the growing Jacksonville of the 1940s and 1950s. Hutchins was elected the first president of the United Craftsmen and Builders Association and was a member of the Jacksonville Chamber of Commerce, the Florida State Business League, and the National Association of Real Estate Brokers.

A long-time resident of the New Town neighborhood of Jacksonville, Hutchins was first married to Luvinia Brown and together they adopted a son, James Edward Hutchins Jr. After the untimely death of his first wife, Hutchins married Mattie Haynes of Walterboro, South Carolina, and together they raised her niece, Janie Robinson.

Active in his community, Hutchins was a long-time member of Saint Paul's African Methodist Episcopal Church, a member of the S. H. Coleman Lodge No. 193, founder of the Gateway Golf Association, and one of the owners of the Lincoln Golf and Country Club. Because racial segregation had limited access to White-owned golf courses, A. L. Lewis, one of the founders of the Afro-American Life Insurance Company, had opened the Lincoln Golf and Country Club in the 1920s.

James E. Hutchins died from a sudden illness on May 16, 1970.

Saint Paul African Methodist Episcopal Church, *Courtesy of Thomas G. Carpenter Library, Eartha M.M. White Collection, University of North Florida*

Notes
1. "Death Notices—James Hutchinson," *Florida Times Union*, 20 May 1970, p. B6.
2. City of Jacksonville, Building Inspection Division, Department of Public Works, Building Permit Records.

JOEL W. MCEACHIN,
SENIOR HISTORIC PRESERVATION PLANNER,
JACKSONVILLE PLANNING
AND DEVELOPMENT DEPARTMENT

BUILDING LIST

Name	Address	City	State	Year	Comments
Emmanuel Baptist Church		Jacksonville	FL		
First Born Church of the Living God	2816 Edison Dr.	Jacksonville	FL		
New Bethel African Methodist Episcopal Church	5031 Halley Dr.	Jacksonville	FL		
St. Paul African Methodist Episcopal Church	6920 New Kings Rd.	Jacksonville	FL		
Triumph the Church	1312 Franklin St.	Jacksonville	FL		
Zion Hope Baptist Church	2803 Edgewood Ave.	Jacksonville	FL		

Percy Costa Ifill
(1913–1973)

Clem Constan

Percy Ifill was a co-founder of Ifill Johnson Architects, which in the late 1960s was one of the best-known and most respected Black-owned architectural firms in the northeast United States.

Percy Ifill was born in Harlem on June 16, 1913. His father, James Percy, was a well-known lawyer from Barbados, British West Indies, and his mother, Louise Costa Ifill, was from Saint Thomas, U.S. Virgin Islands. Ifill grew up in Harlem and attended public schools. He discovered his talent for drawing and sketching early in his life and after graduating from DeWitt Clinton High School he entered Cornell University. Ifill attended Cornell University for one year before transferring in 1935 to New York University, where he attended night school while working during the day.

In 1939, while at New York University, Ifill won third prize in a General Electric National Competition for a "Transmitting Design Studio." In 1943 Ifill graduated from New York University with a bachelor of science in architecture degree. Later in 1945, he won third prize in the General Motors National Dealer Establishment Competition.

While attending New York University, Ifill worked at several drafting jobs. From 1935 to 1940, he worked as a draftsman for a Works Project Administration project with the U.S. Army Corps of Engineers and for the Department of Hospitals. In 1941 he worked for HILYARD ROBERT ROBINSON in Washington, D.C., as an architectural engineer for the 99th Pursuit Squadron Airfield and Training Base at Chehaw, Alabama where the "Tuskegee airmen trained." During 1941 he also worked for the Office of Civilian Defense in New York City. Ifill again worked for Robinson in 1942 on the George Washington Carver dormitory on Howard University's campus and in 1945 as a designer and renderer for the Liberian Centennial. From 1943 to 1945, Ifill worked as a hull structure designer for a naval architect in New York City.

Three years after his graduation from New York University, Percy Ifill began a long working relationship with the interior design firm of Eleanor LeMaire in New York City—a prestigious department store design firm. He was the first Black employee in the twelve-

PERCY COSTA IFILL

person firm. Between 1946 and 1961, Ifill was a staff designer for various department stores and offices.

Percy Ifill was licensed on June 30, 1950, in New York State.[1]

Ifill's retail projects included a Neiman-Marcus department store in Dallas, Texas, and Riches store in Atlanta. Office designs included Comme Investment Trust and Financial Company offices at Madison Avenue and 60th Street in New York City and a brokerage office. Ifill also designed the interiors for a private railroad car, the Studebaker automobile, and cruise ships. During his employment at Eleanor LeMaire's office, he designed desks, store fixtures, and lighting fixtures. Not all of Eleanor LeMaire's clients were pleased to see an African American working as lead designer, but LeMaire was firm in her commitment to employing the best talent available.

During this period at LeMaire's, Ifill met and married Natsu Ikeda, who was an administrative assistant in the office.

New York State Office Building, *Adeniyi Omowaze*

In 1962 Percy Ifill and fellow Harlemite CONRAD ADOLPHUS JOHNSON JR. founded Ifill Johnson Architects. At the time no Black firms in New York City employed more than a few people. The firm took on another partner, George Hanchard, in 1967, and became known as Ifill Johnson Hanchard Architects. Their office, which was located in midtown Manhattan at 49 West 45th Street, had grown to a staff of thirty-five by 1975.

The firm's most notable project was the New York State Office Building in Harlem (originally named the Adam Clayton Powell Jr. State Office Building), which Ifill worked on before his death. The 20-story building was the largest office building designed by Black architects in New York until that time. When construction concluded in 1974, it was a $35-million office building with parking for two hundred vehicles. The office building was also newsworthy at the time because it featured an all-electric heating system that used heat recovered from the building's lights and its occupants.

Before being commissioned as the architects for the State Office Building, Ifill Johnson Hanchard Architects was known for designs of residential and institutional buildings and planning studies. The planning studies included the Saint Nicholas Park Urban Renewal study in 1967 (Harlem), East Harlem North; and a New Communities "Town-in-Town" planning report for the City of Schenectady, New York.

Ifill Johnson Hanchard Architects designed apartment buildings, churches, banks, educational facilities, and airport facilities. Prominent projects included Saint Martin's Tower, a 27-story apartment building in upper Manhattan; the 434-unit Village East Towers (three apartment buildings and townhouses) located the Lower East Side of Manhattan; the Mount Morris Park swimming pool and bathhouse in Harlem; the Chelsea Branch of Carver Savings and Loan Bank; and the Mount Calvary Baptist Church and Community Center in Harlem.

Ifill was active in the *Alpha Phi Alpha* Fraternity, the Sickle Cell Disease Foundation of Greater New York, and the board of the New York Urban League, and was chairman of Harlem Preparatory School from 1969 to 1970.

In 1972 Ifill was diagnosed with terminal cancer. From his hospital bed at Saint Luke's Hospital, he was able to observe the construction of the firm's prized commission, the New York State Office Building.

Percy Ifill died on May 18, 1973, at the age of fifty-nine. His funeral was held in Canaan Baptist Church in Harlem. Reverend Wyatt Tee Walker, who played a pivotal role as state community liaison during the initial discussions about a state office building, officiated. Attendees included Manhattan borough president, Percy Sutton, who described Ifill as a person who "walked among giants but had his foot in the community."[2]

A scholarship was later set up in Percy Costa Ifill's name at Howard University's School of Architecture by his widow.

Notes
1. New York State Board of Education, "Percy C. Ifill," no. 6254, issued 30 June 1950.
2. Simon Anekwe, "Percy Ifill Cancer Victim at Age 59," *New Amsterdam News*, 20 May 1973, p. A1.

Bibliography
"State Building in Harlem Finally Becomes a Reality." *New York Times*, 11 May 1971, p. 41.
"State Office Building: Little Rocky." *Progressive Architecture*, (February 1970): 25.

ROBERTA WASHINGTON, R.A., PRINCIPAL,
ROBERTA WASHINGTON ARCHITECTS, PA,
NEW YORK, NEW YORK

BUILDING LIST

Name	Address	City	State/Country	Year	Comments
20th Precinct Station	120 W. 82nd St.	New York	NY	1964	
American Airlines		New York	NY	1969	LaGuardia Airport
Amsterdam Avenue Housing		New York	NY	1971	1,000 dwelling units (du)
Baber-Daniels Apts.		Baltimore	MD	1967	268 du
Caanan Baptist Church	132 W. 116th St.	New York	NY	1968	Alterations
Carver Savings & Loan	8th Ave.	New York	NY	1962	
Comme Investment Trust Co.	60th & Madison Ave.	New York	NY		Alterations
Freedom National Bank	271 West 125th St.	New York	NY	1963	Demolished
Freedom National Bank	Fulton St.	New York	NY	1966	Fulton St. Branch demolished

PERCY COSTA IFILL

BUILDING LIST (continued)

Name	Address	City	State/Country	Year	Comments
Greater Refuge Temple	2081 Powell Jr. Dr.	New York	NY	1970	
Guinea Government Bldg. Complex		Bissau	Guinea	1962	
Harlem Community Center	231 W. 142nd St.	New York	NY		
M. Edgar Evers State College	Campus	New York	NY	1971	
Milbank-Frawley Urban Renewal Site No. 2	125th St.	New York	NY	1973	146 du
Mt. Morris Park Swimming Pool & Bath House	124th St. & Fifth Ave.	New York	NY	1966	
Neiman-Marcus Department Store	Main & Ervay Sts.	Dallas	TX	1946	Alterations
New York City Public School 13		New York	NY	1969	
New York State Office Bldg.	163 W. 125th St.	New York	NY	1974	
Ojike Memorial Medical Center	Orla Province	Lagos	Nigeria	1962	
Phipps Center Police Athletic League	225 W. 123rd St.	New York	NY	1967	
Riches Department Store		Atlanta	GA		Alterations
Rockdale Park		Atlanta	GA	1967	1,500 du
Salem Methodist Church Community Center	W. 129th St.	New York	NY	1965	
Sherman Creek Project		New York	NY	1973	1,240 du
Southside Committee for Community Improvement		Mt. Vernon	NY	1963	
St. Martin's Towers	65 W. 90th St.	New York	NY	1966	150 du
St. Philip's Church Community Center	204 W. 134th St.	New York	NY	1966	
Swissair	JFK Airport	New York	NY	1963	Addition
Tri-Boro Plaza Complex		New York	NY	1966	
Trinity Baptist Church	250 E. 61st St.	New York	NY	1970	
United Moravian Church	200 E. 127th St.	New York	NY	1973	
U.S. Post Office	434 E. 14th St.	New York	NY	1974	Stuyvesant Station
Varick Community Center	151 W. 136th St.	New York	NY	1970	
Village East Towers	170 Ave. A & 411 E. 10th St.	New York	NY	1964	434 du
Western Union Message Center	1290 Powell Jr. Dr.	New York	NY	1973	
Wynn Center Police Athletic League		New York	NY	1963	Alterations

Leon Quincy Jackson
(1926–1995)

Savannah Jackson Clark

Leon Quincy Jackson was born on January 9, 1926, in Wewoka, Oklahoma, which is approximately sixty miles southeast of Oklahoma City. His natural father abandoned him and his mother soon after his birth. Leon's mother, Roxie Ann Jackson, was a high school principal. Leon was her only child. Subsequently, she attracted the attention of Lonnie Galimore, a pharmacy graduate of MeHarry Medical College in Nashville, Tennessee. He became Leon's stepfather and raised him as if he were his natural son. Roxie Ann Jackson Galimore was one-half Seminole on her mother's side of the family. She owned a two-hundred-acre farm that was rich in oil deposits. By 1949 there were seven to eight pumping oil derricks. Black gold royalties paid for construction of their 20-room house and for Leon's nanny.

Leon Jackson attended Wewoka Public School for Negroes and Indians. He graduated at age sixteen in 1942. He entered the African Methodist Episcopal–affiliated Wilberforce University in Ohio in January 1943, declaring a major in arts and sciences. Wilberforce was the school of choice of Black Oklahoma oil families. He spent two years there before transferring in 1945 to Iowa State College in Ames to study architecture. He left Iowa State at the end of the academic year because the winter was too cold and enrolled at Kansas State College in Manhattan, Kansas, starting in September 1945. He chose Kansas State because of the reputation of its School of Architecure. Interrupting his second year, he was personally recruited in 1947 by Claude L. Wilson, Dean of Engineering of PRAIRIE VIEW AGRICULTURAL & MECHANICAL COLLEGE, to come to Texas to teach architecture. While at Prairie View, Leon met Savannah Marie Vaughn, from Hutchinson, Kansas, who was a sophomore studying dance and gymnastics. They married in 1947. Leon and Savannah did not have any children. In 1949 Leon and Savannah returned to Manhattan, where Leon completed the requirements for a bachelor of science in architecture at Kansas State College that year. He remained an additional year and earned his master of science in architecture, which was conferred on January 27, 1950.

The Jacksons then moved to Oklahoma City, Oklahoma. Leon Jackson worked part-time for the Oklahoma City Board of Education and opened a solo private practice in 1950 with an office on Second Street, becoming the first African American architect to open an office in Oklahoma. He advertised in the *Oklahoma City Directory* as an "architect" relying on his Kansas license, which he had obtained based on being an architecture graduate of the state university.[1] His advertisement attracted the attention of state officials, who made him withdraw the listing because he was not licensed to practice in Oklahoma. In August 1952 Jackson was hired as an architectural engineer for the U.S. Air Force. A civil service employee at Tinker Air Force Base in Oklahoma City, he worked in facilities management doing what he described as "sundry bureaucratic paper shuffling."[2] Although obviously feeling unchallenged, he stayed for eleven months. In the meantime he continued his private practice from an office at 201 Slaughter Street in Oklahoma City designing mostly small houses.

In April 1952 Jackson enrolled in the University of Oklahoma's graduate program in urban planning. At the time, the School of Architecture and Planning was headed by iconoclast architect Bruce Goff (1904–1982), who was dean of the school. Jackson majored in city planning. His terminal planning project was for West Africa involving a radical form of tropical architecture. Jackson received his master of science degree in city planning on August 12, 1954.

Jackson's attempt to register to take the two-day state licensing examination was rejected by state officials because he was a Negro-Seminole. It did not matter to state officials that his application had been endorsed by NATIONAL TECHNICAL ASSOCIATION members, architect Nathan Johnson, principal of his own firm in Detroit, Michigan; Benson L. Dutton, head of the Department of Engineering at HAMPTON INSTITUTE; and James Parsons, professor of engineering at Tennessee Agricultural and Industrial University. Savannah Jackson interceded on her husband's behalf with Governor Johnson, for whom she had worked as a staffer during his successful campaign for the governorship. The governor asked Oklahoma City architects Lee and Thomas Sorey to sponsor Jackson for the examination and ordered state officials to accept his application. The test site was a segregated downtown hotel. Jackson had to enter the hotel through the rear entrance and was made to ride the freight elevator instead of the passenger elevator to the test site on an upper floor. He was then hustled off to an unoccupied room where he took the test all alone except for the proctor. Regrettably he failed the structures section of the test. Again his wife came to his assistance. She had formerly worked as a secretary for architect Ortho McCracken in Hutchinson, Kansas. She asked Mc-Cracken to tutor her husband in structures, which he did. Jackson failed the second time he took the test. In advance of his third attempt, Leonard Bailey, "dean" of Oklahoma architects and secretary-treasurer of the Board of Examiners of Architects for the state of Oklahoma, wrote to the Board, "I can speak authoritatively as to his [Jackson's] persistence and determination to pass the severe test imposed by our Board. Because of his color, he met with many obstacles that White

Saint John Baptist Church Educational Building, *James Gabbert*

applicants never have to contend with...."[3] On his third attempt, on April 3, 1954, L. Quincy Jackson passed the architect licensing examination.[4] A local newspaper hailed Jackson's achievement as the "1st Licensed Seminole and Colored Young Man in OK."

Jackson continued coursework at Oklahoma Agricultural & Mechanical University during the summers. It was during this period that he designed his largest commissions, a Moderne-style, red brick, $100,000 educational building (1951) for Saint John Baptist Church and a $150,000 clinic/office (1952) for Dr. Gravely E. Finley, which was also in the Moderne style but used blonde instead of red bricks. The building is extant in "Deep Deuce," the middle of the Black business corridor of Oklahoma City.

Jackson was a member of the National Technical Association, Architects' League of Oklahoma City, American Institute of Architects, and *Alpha Phi Alpha* fraternity. He was licensed by the National Council of Architectural Registration Boards. In his leisure time he was an oil painter. No doubt because of his previous struggles, he maintained a business listing in the *Oklahoma City Directory* from 1958 to 1959 even though he was living and working in Nashville.

On September 15, 1954, Jackson began teaching at Tennessee Agricultural & Industrial State University in Nashville, Tennessee, at their School of Engineering to fill a position vacated by a professor on sabbatical. He stayed on to start the architectural engineering program, where he taught building construction and specification preparation.

Having been divorced from his first wife for five years, on April 5, 1966, Leon married Marilyn Finley, formerly from Bolivar, Tennessee. Together they had three children: Lillian Qinell, Leon Jr., and Davis Andrew, who became an artist like his father.

L. Quincy Jackson died on July 21, 1995, from a brain aneurysm. He is buried in Greenwood Cemetery in Nashville.

Notes
1. Kansas State Registration and Examination Board of Architects, "L. Quincy Jackson," Certificate no. 223, issued 10 February 1950.
2. State of Tennessee, State Board of Architectural and Engineering Examinations, "Leon Quincy Jackson," no. 383, issued 3 April 1953.
3. Leonard H. Bailey, Fala, Secretary-Treasurer, Board of Governors of Licensed Architects of Oklahoma, Letter to State Board of Architectural and Engineering Examiners, State of Tennessee, 1 August 1995.
4. State of Oklahoma Board of Examiners of Architects, "L. Quincy Jackson," Certificate no. 383, issued 3 April 1953.

JAMES GABBERT, ARCHITECTURAL HISTORIAN,
OKLAHOMA OFFICE OF HISTORIC PRESERVATION

BUILDING LIST

Name	Address	City	State	Year	Comments
18th Avenue Community Center	18th Ave.	Nashville	TN		
Briscoe, Dr. Byron	2516 NE 16th St.	Oklahoma City	OK	1953	
Duncan Ranch		Chickasha	OK	1952	
Finley Clinic	128 NE 2nd St.	Oklahoma City	OK	1952	
First Baptist Church	R. R. 2	Wewoka	OK	1951	
First Baptist Church	225 1st St. SW	Ardmore	OK	1953	
Girls Detention House		Nashville	TN		
Jackson, L. Quincy	2105 NE Grand	Oklahoma City	OK	1951	Destroyed by fire
Jackson, L. Quincy	2026 NE Grand	Oklahoma City	OK		
Kelly Miller Smith Towers	2136 Cliff Dr.	Nashville	TN	1980	
Masonic Hall		Oklahoma City	OK	1954	
Northwest YMCA	3200 Kings Ln.	Nashville	TN		
Perry, Rev. E. W.	507 NE 3rd St.	Oklahoma City	OK	1950	Demolished
Prince Hall Masons Bathhouse		Claremore	OK	1951	
Ridgecrest Country Estates		Midwest City	OK	1950	Subdivision
St. John Baptist Church Education Bldg.	310 N. Phillips	Oklahoma City	OK	1952	
Tabernacle Baptist Church	515 NE 3rd St.	Oklahoma City	OK	1950	Demolished
Tennessee A&I University Health Center	Campus	Nashville	TN		
Tennessee A&I University Music Bldg.	Campus	Nashville	TN		
Third National Bank		Nashville	TN		
Veterans of Foreign War Hall		Guthrie	OK	1952	
Wood, Carl W.	918 Daugherty	Oklahoma City	OK	1950	Demolished

Jamestown Ter-centennial Exposition Negro Building, Virginia
(1907)

The Jamestown Ter-centennial Exposition was organized to honor the 300th anniversary of the landing at Jamestown, Virginia, by the first English settlers. Funds were to be raised by the Jamestown Exposition Company with appropriations from the U.S. Congress. A site was chosen at Hampton Roads to mount a major exposition in honor of the ter-centennial.

The exposition company requested exhibits and buildings from all states and the District of Columbia. All buildings were to be Colonial in style, all work was under the supervision of the Secretary of the Treasury, and all construction was under the direction of the supervising architect of the U.S. Department of the Treasury.[1] Among the features of the exposition, a Negro Exposition Building was planned under the aegis of the Negro Development & Exposition Company. The Jamestown Exposition Company set aside six acres for the Negro Building and it was agreed between the two companies that the Jamestown Exposition Company should receive all gate receipts whereas the Negro Development & Exposition Company should receive all commissions and profits it might provide for on the six-acre reservation. Congress appropriated $100,000 for the Negro Building.

In August 1906 the Jamestown Exposition Company opened competition for the design of the Negro Building, stipulating that the building was to be of Colonial design, 2 stories high, must provide 60,000 square feet of floor space, and should be ornamental and well lighted. The first floor was to have exhibit areas and the second floor was to consist of a post-free auditorium with a platform at one end. Only five architects entered the competition for the design of the Negro Building and all were African American. The supervising architect selected the designs of JOHN ANDERSON LANKFORD and WILLIAM SIDNEY PITTMAN for final review by the Negro Development & Exposition Company, which chose Pittman's entry. Although the competing designs have not survived for comparison, Pittman's design showed exceptional talent and use of classic architectural concepts.[2]

In November 1906 a contract was drawn up with William Sidney Pittman, making him the first African American architect awarded a federal contract; by this contract he was committed not only to providing building plans, but also to supervising construction. Pittman's specifications called for a building 213 × 129 feet, 2 stories high, with a hip roof and central skylight, as well as eighty-six windows; the second story would be supported by 128 pillars. The building was to be of wood-frame construction and its exterior walls were to be covered with pebble dash. It was to be lighted by electricity with approximately four thousand incandescent lamps.

In February 1907 the contract for construction of the Negro Building was awarded to S. H. Bolling and A. J. Everett, Black contractors from Lynchburg, Virginia, who had built the True Reformers Building (1902) in Washington, D.C.

In the months that followed there was a series of problems and delays. When work was begun, there were only eighty days before the exposition was to open on April 26. Delivery of supplies and materials from Norfolk, the closest shipping point nine miles away, was haphazard—everything arrived late. Trolleys from Norfolk were constantly breaking down under the heavy use; this was often disastrous for the more than one hundred mechanics working on the Negro Building because they often arrived hours late at the job site. A complaint was made to Bolling and Everett on April 3, 1907, that no work had been done for the last ten days. They were reminded that they must have the roof on before the end of April. The contractors responded that they had indeed been working for the last ten days, doing odds and ends like bracing, stair risers, and other essentials, but were still waiting for the window frames to be delivered by railroad. The window frames and iron trusses arrived the next day and work proceeded. The Negro Building, however, as well as many other buildings at the exposition, were not completed by the official opening on April 26.

In spite of the problems and delays, it was announced that President Theodore Roosevelt would

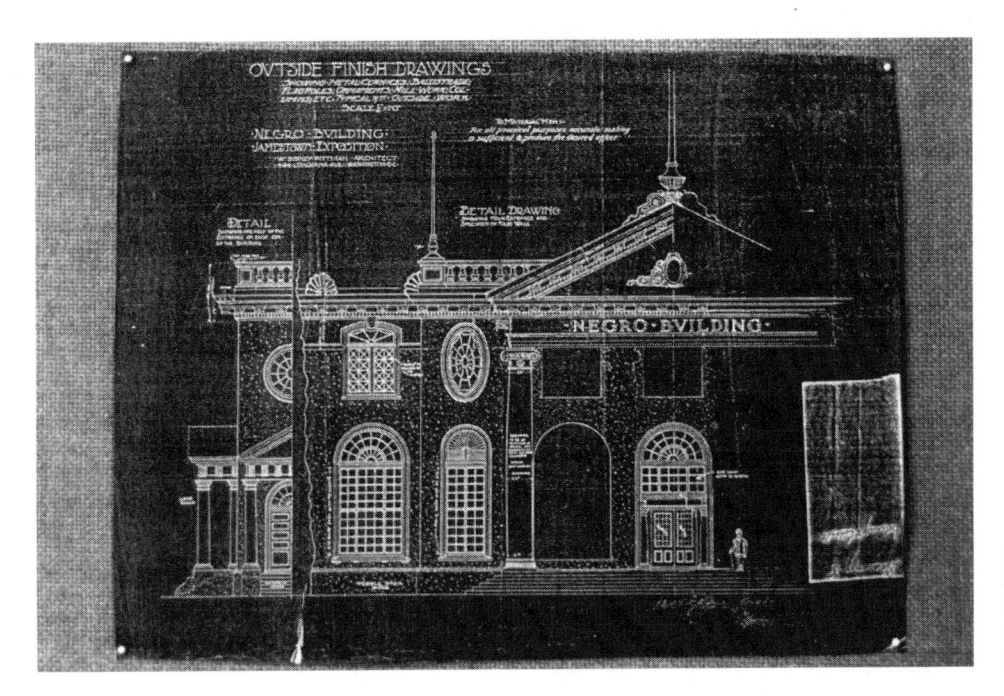

Jamestown Ter-centennial Negro Building (outside finished drawing). *Cartographic Branch, National Archives II.*

visit the Negro Building on June 10. Under this pressure, the roof was finished and interior decorations were completed although only approximately 10 percent of the exhibits had been installed. In his remarks, Roosevelt referred to the Negro Building as "this magnificent building" and described the exhibits as "unmistakable evidences of progress."[3]

The building at the time of President Roosevelt's visit was described as follows:

> Festoons of orange and white conceal the hundreds of columns, the ceiling covered with burlap, flanked by mural trimmings of green and maroon; American flags at frequent intervals. No building on the grounds is more handsomely decorated than the Negro Exposition home. Not a few influential men and women of the other race freely confessed that the Negro Exhibit was a revelation, and left the building fully converted.[4]

The Fourth of July was the official opening of the Negro Building and by that time all of the exhibits were in place. From the beginning of 1907, field agents from thirty-six states and the District of Columbia had been soliciting and collecting exhibits to illustrate the progress of Blacks in America. The exhibits illustrated all varieties of the arts, music, literature, portraiture, and sculpture; displays of machines, patents, and inventions; displays from agricultural, educational, and industrial institutions; kitchen and hospital exhibits in two separate small buildings designed by Pittman; exhibits regarding journalism, photography, and other businesses; and even a functioning bank. In all there were 9,926 exhibits.

The highlight of the Jamestown Ter-centennial Exposition for African Americans occurred August 3, which had been designated by the Jamestown Exposition Company as "Negro Day." BOOKER T. WASHINGTON, principal of TUSKEGEE INSTITUTE, was the day's orator. An estimated ten thousand persons crowded in front of the Negro Building to hear him speak, one of the largest audiences of Blacks ever gathered. "I [am] . . . surprised and pleased at the neat and attractive appearance of the Negro Building. From an architectural point of view it does high credit to Mr. Pittman and all connected with its construction."[5] Praise was heaped on the committee regarding the building and it was estimated that approximately 750,000 people, both Black and White, visited the Negro Building before the Exposition closed on November 30, 1907.

It had been intended after the close of the Exposition for the Negro Development & Exposition Company to buy the Negro Building, move it to Richmond, and convert it into a National Museum for Colored People. The political climate in Richmond, however, was not ready for establishing a Negro History Museum and the relocation never happened. The Exposition site was redeveloped into the Norfolk Naval Station in 1917. Several state Exposition buildings now serve as commanders' residences. The Negro Building, like many other buildings constructed for the Exposition, was demolished. Its design, however, was much praised during the time that it stood; it left a lasting impression and was the springboard for the career of its architect, William Sidney Pittman.

Notes

1. *Final Report of the Jamestown Ter-centennial Commission, Norfolk, Virginia 1907* (Washington, D.C.: Government Printing Office, 1909), p. 138.
2. Giles B. Jackson and D. Webster Davis, *The Industrial History of the Negro Race of the United States* (1908; reprint, Freeport, N.Y.: Books for Libraries Press, 1971), p. 200.
3. Ibid., p. 196.
4. Ibid., p. 177.

Bibliography

Franklin, Lucy B. "The Negro Exhibition of the Jamestown Ter-centennial Exposition of 1907." *Negro History Bulletin* 38, no. 5 (June–July 1975).
Official Blue Book of the Jamestown Ter-centennial Exposition, A.D. 1907. Norfolk: Colonial Publishing Company, 1909.
Pittman, William S. "Architectural Drawings for the Negro Building." Record Group no. 2, Cartographic Branch of the National Archives, Arlington, Va.

SUSAN G. PEARL, ARCHITECTURAL HISTORIAN,
MARYLAND NATIONAL CAPITAL PARK
AND PLANNING COMMISSION,
PRINCE GEORGE'S, MARYLAND COUNTY

Willie Edward Jenkins
(1923–1988)

Samuel J. Hodges III

W. Edward Jenkins, who was known as "Blue" by his many friends and colleagues, was born on November 24, 1923, in Wake County, North Carolina, to Willie and Emmaline Jenkins. His father died when he was still a toddler. His mother was a seamstress.

He received his public school education in the Raleigh, North Carolina, public schools, completing Washington High School. Jenkins served his country in the U.S. Army Corps of Engineers from 1943 until February 19, 1946, when he was honorably discharged. While in the U.S. army, Jenkins married Gladys Rand in 1945. One daughter, Miltrine, was born to this union. Following his military stint, he entered NORTH CAROLINA AGRICULTURAL & TECHNICAL STATE UNIVERSITY, where he received a bachelor of science degree in architectural engineering with high honors in 1949.

Jenkins was a registered architect and practiced architecture for thirty-nine years in North Carolina, South Carolina, Florida, and Virginia. He distinguished himself as an architect, community leader, and public servant in the state of North Carolina. From 1949 to 1961, he served as design and project manager with Loewenstein & Atkinson Architects in Greensboro, North Carolina. During that time of rigid racial separation, it was rare to find a Black architect working for a White firm.

While working at Loewenstein & Atkinson Architects in the late 1950s, Jenkins served as design architect for the Dudley High School gymnasium in Greensboro. His design was innovative because of its intersecting roof arches and many windows. This innovative gymnasium design received accolades from the National Association of School Architects, the local chapter of the American Institute of Architects, and the American Institute of Steel Construction.[1]

Because of pressure by the Dudley High School alumni and historic preservationists, the Guilford County Board of Education spared the gymnasium and main building from demolition. A decision to rebuild the school was replaced with one to renovate it. In 2002 the Dudley High School gymnasium along with the main building (1920) were nominated for listing on the National Register of Historic Places.[2]

In 1962 Jenkins opened his own architectural practice, W. Edward Jenkins, AIA, Architects, in Greensboro. During his architectural career, he designed and supervised the construction of many buildings on the campus of North Carolina Agricultural & Technical State University, including the football stadium and the Ronald McNair School of Engineering. The McNair building was designed in association with J. Hyatt Hammond Associates of Greensboro. His other works included the Saint James Presbyterian and Saint Matthews United Methodist churches and renovation of the Hayes-Taylor Young Men's Christian Association (YMCA) in Greensboro and the Law School Building at North Carolina Central University in Durham. Jenkins also designed the Three College Observatory in Greensboro in 1981, which featured a state-of-the-art telescope for use by students, faculty, and members of the community. He also designed the Modern-style home of Greensboro attorney, J. Kenneth Lee.

White Rock Baptist Church, *Samuel J. Hodges III*

In 1975 Jenkins was appointed by the governor to the North Carolina Board of Architecture. He served on the board until his term expired in April 1980. Some of his other professional and civic memberships included the North Carolina chapter of the American Institute of Architects, North Carolina Board of Architectural Registration, Board of Directors of Greensboro National Bank, board member of the Hayes-Taylor Young Mens Christian Association, City of Greensboro's Clearing House Committee, sustaining member of the Boy Scouts of America, *Kappa Alpha Psi* Fraternity, and the North Carolina Agricultural & Technical State University Sports Hall of Fame. In 1972 he received the Outstanding Achievement Award from the North Carolina Agricultural & Technical State University School of Engineering.

W. Edward Jenkins died on March 18, 1988, at Moses Cone Hospital in Greensboro after a brief illness. Years after his death, Jenkins and his architectural designs are still being recognized. Jim Schlosser wrote,

> The late Greensboro architect Ed Loewenstein said dedicated architects die unhappy. They never get to unleash creative juices because of pressure to please clients. But in at least one instance, architect W. Edward Jenkins,

who worked for Loewenstein, was able to satisfy the urge for innovation and Jenkins likely would have enjoyed a successful career without Loewenstein's help, but the experience and mentoring he received surely made it easier once he went on his own.[3]

Notes
1. Interview with Miltrine Jenkins Barden (daughter of William Jenkins), Greensboro, N.C., 18 May 2002.
2. U.S. Department of Interior, National Park Service and National Register of Historic Places, "Dudley High School Gymnasium," 11 April 2003.
3. Jim Schlosser, "Architectural Buffs Are Impressed with the Gym's Unusual Design and Its Architect W. Edward Jenkins," *Greensboro News & Record*, 3 September 2002, p. A1.
4. "Willie Edward Jenkins," *Neiys-Record* (Greensboro), 21 March 1988, p. A5.

Bibliography
American Institute of Architects. Prospectus for W. Edward Jenkins, n.d. AIA Archives, Washington, D.C.

SAMUEL J. HODGES III, AIA,
U.S. DEPARTMENT OF AGRICULTURE,
RURAL HOUSING SERVICE,
WASHINGTON, D.C.

BUILDING LIST

Name	Address	City/County	State	Year	Comments
American Federal Savings & Loan Association	1913 E. Market St.	Greensboro	NC	1968	
Bethel African Methodist Episcopal Church	200 Reagon St.	Greensboro	NC	1961	Addition
Carolina Nursing Home	107 N. Murrow Blvd.	Greensboro	NC	1968	

BUILDING LIST *(continued)*

Name	Address	City/County	State	Year	Comments
Country Manor		Greensboro	NC	1968	
Cumberland Office Bldg.	107 N. Cumberland Blvd.	Greensboro	NC	1964	
Dudley High School Gym	1200 Lincoln St.	Greensboro	NC	1958	
First Christian Church	158 Rone Ave., SW	Concord	NC	1970	
Gadison, ____		Winston-Salem	NC	1960	
Gillespie Junior High School	King Jr. Dr.	Greensboro	NC	1960	Addition
Goler Metropolitan Apts.	1435 E. 4th St.	Winston-Salem	NC	1972	
Greensboro National Bank	100 Marrow	Greensboro	NC	1976	
Hayes-Taylor YMCA	1101 E. Market St.	Greensboro	NC	1986	Alterations
Heart of Town Motel		Greensboro	NC	1967	
Holley, Edward	1202 Julian St.	Greensboro	NC	1960	
Lee, Atty. J. Kenneth	1021 Broad Ave.	Greensboro	NC	1960	
Mt. Zion Baptist Church	950 File St.	Winston-Salem	NC	1969	
New Bethel Church Homes		Winston-Salem	NC	1969	
North Carolina A&T Univ. Aggie Stadium	Campus	Greensboro	NC	1980	
North Carolina A&T Univ. Classroom Bldg.	Campus	Greensboro	NC	1966	
North Carolina A&T Univ. Communication Bldg.	Campus	Greensboro	NC	1973	
North Carolina A&T Univ. Law School Bldg.	Campus	Greensboro	NC	1978	
North Carolina A&T Univ. School of Engineering	Campus	Greensboro	NC	1984	
North Carolina A&T Univ. Williams Cafeteria	Campus	Greensboro	NC	1974	
Oliver, ____		Winston-Salem	NC	1960	
Palmer Memorial Institute Boys Dormitory	Campus	Sedalia	NC	1967	
Parker Heights	1623 Madison Ave.	Charlotte	NC	1970	
Ritchwood, ____	51 Baldwin Ave.	Newark	NJ	1972	
Shaw University Apts.	Campus	Raleigh	NC	1973	
Shoffner, ____	100 Main St.	Weldon	NC	1967	
Smith Funeral Home	512 King Jr. Dr.	Greensboro	NC	1967	
St. James Presbyterian Church	802 Ross Ave.	Greensboro	NC	1959	
St. Matthews United Methodist Church	600 E. Florida St.	Greensboro	NC	1970	
Thomasville Church Homes	901 Doak St.	Thomasville	NC	1968	
Three College Observatory	Cane Creek Mountain	Almance County	NC	1981	
U.S. Post Office		Ft. Myers	FL	1965	
U.S. Post Office		Henderson	NC	1970	
U.S. Post Office		North Wilkesboro	NC	1965	
U.S. Post Office		Roanoke	VA	1960	
Wells, ____	1201 Benbow Rd.	Greensboro	NC	1960	
White Rock Baptist Church	3400 Fayetteville St.	Durham	NC	1977	Alterations
Zion Hills Apts.	212 W. Liberty St.	Salisbury	NC	1970	

Conrad Adolphus Johnson Jr.
(1919–1991)

Clivetta Johnson

Conrad Johnson was one-half of the founding duo of Ifill & Johnson, an architectural firm that during the 1970s was one of the most successful Black-owned firms in the northeast United States.

Conrad Adolphus Johnson Jr. was born at his parents' home in Harlem. His grandfather had been a contractor in Barbados. His father, Conrad A. Johnson Sr., immigrated to the United States when he was sixteen and became a lawyer and Republican politician who held public office in Harlem and the state of New York. His mother, Ernestine Davis, lived at home in Harlem until she met and married Conrad Sr. They had one daughter, Ernestine Jr.

Conrad Johnson Jr. attended Stuyvesant High School in Manhattan. He planned to pursue a career in commercial art, but a teacher suggested that architecture might prove to be a more lucrative career. Flying was also an early interest. All during high school he built model airplanes. He attended New York University, along with his boyhood friend PERCY COSTA IFILL, who later became their firm's co-founder. Johnson is believed to have worked for a contractor during the day, while attending night school to study architecture until 1942.

Rather than be drafted into the U.S. Army, Johnson left New York University and enlisted because he wanted to be a pilot. He was first stationed in Biloxi, Mississippi, and was later accepted into the pilot training program at Chehaw, Alabama, in 1943. The training was rigorous and also involved being able to withstand racial insults from some of the White flight instructors and air traffic controllers. Johnson earned his wings and joined the 332nd Fighter Group of the 15th U.S. Air Force. He flew forty-four missions over North Africa, Italy, France, and Germany. This group, a famed corps of African American pilots known for never having lost an escorted B-52, later became known as the "Tuskegee Airmen."

When he returned to the United States, Johnson considered becoming a commercial pilot, but due to racism he received no job offers.

Using the GI Bill, which guaranteed college tuition for veterans of World War II, Johnson continued his architecture education at Harvard University starting in 1945. He graduated with a bachelor of architecture degree in 1947 (a later re-calculation of his earned credits resulted in Harvard University awarding him a master of architecture degree in 1976). At that time, the Harvard University School of Architecture was led by one of the founders of the Bauhaus movement, Walter Groupius (1883–1969).

It was while at Harvard University that Johnson met his future wife, Clivetta Stuart. They had one date before he graduated in June 1947, and did not meet again until one year later in New York City. Stuart, who taught piano at HAMPTON INSTITUTE, remembered that Johnson had said to call if she were ever in New York. She did and they were married in 1950.

Johnson became licensed in New York State on June 1, 1948. When Johnson's parents asked him what he wanted as a graduation present, he replied that he wanted to design a home for them. During World War II, Johnson's parents had begun looking for a site and found a suitable one-acre parcel in Purchase, New York, which they presented to him after graduation.

The house that Johnson designed was built in 1950. It featured radiant floor heating and a fieldstone fireplace. The house was based on the Johnson family's lifestyle and exhibited Johnson's fondness for bold colors. "Framed in red brick and glass, the residence blends into the landscape as naturally as the sloping wooded terrain."[1] The house remained in the family until 1977, when it was sold.

One of Johnson's earliest jobs was with the office of HILYARD ROBERT ROBINSON, preparing construction drawings for the 99th Pursuit Squadron Pilot Training and Airfield in Chehaw, Alabama, where Johnson himself would later receive training.

From 1947 to 1953, Johnson worked at the firm of Isadore Rosenfield, a well-known hospital design firm in New York City. By 1950 Johnson was architect for the $45-million Ponce Medical Center in Ponce, Puerto Rico, which was completed in 1953. He advanced to chief planner, senior designer, and office manager of the firm before leaving in 1955. Johnson also contributed to the writing and illustrating of *Hospital-Integrated Design*, which was edited by

Saint Martin's Tower, New York, NY, *Adeniyi Ormowaze*

CONRAD ADOLPHUS JOHNSON JR.

Isadore Rosenfield.[2] Not many principals of White-owned firms were eager to hire Black architects, but Rosenfield was one of the few who did. He employed eight to ten persons, including BEVERLY LORAINE GREENE, who was a family friend of the Johnsons.

From 1953 to 1955, Johnson worked for Oscar Wiggens. From 1955 to 1962, he was employed by Kiff, Colean, Voss & Sonder. During this period, Johnson was project manager for Saint Francis Hospital in Syracuse, built at a cost of $25 million, and an $18-million medical center in Hartford, Connecticut. He led the team that developed and designed nineteen hospitals in Kentucky, West Virginia, and Virginia for the United Mine Workers of America, which received several awards.

When his father died in 1960, Johnson used his inheritance to start his own firm. He said at the time that he wanted to have his own firm rather than be "window dressing" in someone else's firm.[3]

In 1962 he and Percy Costa Ifill started the firm of Ifill & Johnson Architects. In 1967 George Hanchard was made a partner and the firm became known as Ifill Johnson Hanchard Architects. After the death of Ifill in 1973, the firm was known as Johnson-Hanchard PC.

Johnson wanted a firm that designed large commercial buildings rather than single-family houses. Two of the firm's early jobs were for American Airlines and SwissAir. The firm also designed churches for Black congregations.

Although the firm's dominant client became the State of New York, the firm produced a mix of award-winning projects. Johnson was most proud of the New York State Office Building in Harlem, which won a New York Award for Excellence. His design philosophy for the New York State Office Building included paying homage to the "soapbox" sessions for which the block was famous. In these sessions, well-known speakers like Malcolm X and lesser-known persons would attract a crowd of passersby and address current issues and problems. Other projects included the master planning for Saint Nicholas Park Urban Renewal Area, a Harlem community with 55,000 people; Barber Daniels Garden Apartments in Baltimore, Maryland, which won a City of Baltimore Design Award for Excellence; the American Airlines expansion at LaGuardia Airport; Saint Martin's Tower, an apartment building in Manhattan, which won an American Institute of Architects Award for Excellence; and housing for four thousand persons attending the Black Arts Festival held in Lagos, Nigeria.

Unable to collect fees they were owed and without new commissions to sustain the office, Johnson-Hanchard PC closed in 1974. After the closing of his firm, Johnson become chief of construction at Presbyterian Medical Center in New York City.

Johnson took a position as chief of review for Levien, Rich & Company, where he wrote reports on buildings under construction and reports for bank underwriters who were considering financing construction projects. When Johnson reached the age of seventy in 1990, the company forced him into retirement.

After a brief illness, Conrad A. Johnson Jr. died of pancreatic cancer on July 20, 1991, at Columbia Presbyterian Medical Center.

Notes
1. Brooks Peters, "Bauhaus by Southwest," *Architectural Digest* (March 1993): p. 158.
2. Isadore Rosenfield, ed., *Hospital-Integrated Design* (New York: Reinhold Publishing Corp., 1949).
3. Conrad A. Johnson III, interview, New York, New York, 1 April 2000.

Bibliography
"Black Architects Designed Building." *Amsterdam News*, 21 May 1974, p. D2.

ROBERT WASHINGTON, RA, PRINCIPAL,
ROBERTA WASHINGTON ARCHITECTS, PA,
NEW YORK, NEW YORK

BUILDING LIST

Client	Address	City	State/Country	Year	Comments
Badagry Hotel	Badagry Expressway	Lagos	Africa	1975	350 rms & convention center
Black Arts Festival Housing	Fairgrounds	Lagos	Africa	1975	
Franklin Plaza subway station	2nd Ave.	New York	NY	1974	
Johnson, Conrad, Sr.	72 Lincoln Ave.	Purchase	NY	1950	
Ponce Medical Center		Ponce	Puerto Rico	1950	
St. Philip's Church Community Youth Center	204 W. 134th St.	New York	NY	1966	

Harvey Nathaniel Johnson Sr.
(1892–1973)

Harvey N. Johnson Jr.

Harvey Johnson was born in Richmond, Virginia, on September 26, 1892. He was the third son of Ruffin F. and Ellen Johnson. His two brothers were Alpheus and Joseph. Harvey's grandfather was Samuel Johnson of Caroline County, Virginia, a strong character of Native American and African American ancestry who not only purchased his freedom before the Civil War with wages earned as a carpenter but later was a successful builder and casketmaker. Harvey Johnson's maternal great-grandmother was an octoroon and a free person.

According to family oral history, at five years of age Harvey Johnson was classified by his teacher, Nelson Williams, as a second grade student.[1] Later at age fifteen, on the advice of his minister, Reverend Nelson Brown, Johnson enrolled in Wayland Academy, now Virginia Union University, in Richmond. There he met Professor CHARLES THADDEUS RUSSELL, who became his mentor. Johnson ceased his studies at Wayland Academy in 1910 to devote himself full-time to family businesses.

Harvey Johnson was influenced by his father's and grandfather's business experiences. Ruffin Johnson included his sons in his business; however, Joseph died as a youth. *Richmond City Directory* lists Ruffin Johnson as a carpenter and builder in the 1905 and 1910 editions. It also shows that in 1910, the name of the business had become R. F. Johnson & Sons—Architects and Builders. The Johnson firm built many houses and offices for African Americans throughout the Jackson Ward and Fulton Bottom areas of Richmond. Harvey Johnson is listed by himself in the *Richmond City Directory* as a carpenter in 1915.

In 1912 Harvey Johnson married Mary Etta Sharrah, the fourth daughter of Henry and Annie Sharrah of Richmond. They had two children born during that decade: Harvey Jr. and Edith Antoinette.

During World War I, the U.S. government needed architects to work for the Department of the Navy. Harvey Johnson Jr. recalls that his father was interviewed, but was refused a position because of his race.[4] Harvey Johnson was told that the practices of the U.S. Navy would not allow hiring an African American architect. He was instead assigned to Newport News, Virginia, where he became a foreman in warehouse construction at Camp Hill. Johnson was in charge of an all-Negro construction crew. Because several Whites wanted to see him fail and prove his incompetence, they refused to allow him to see the blueprints. One day he sneaked into the foreman's office, memorized the plans, and successfully completed his assignment.

After the war, in 1919, Johnson traveled to Pittsburgh, Pennsylvania, where he enrolled as an architecture student at Carnegie Institute of Technology. One course he took was architectural composition, which was described as follows:

> The first part of this course is given in the first year, and consists of a system of illustrated lectures and exercises in drawing, dealing with the development of

237

J. C. Brooks House. Richard A. Singletary

architectural motives and details. The second part is given in the fourth year and consists of a series of illustrated lectures on advanced composition in plan and elevation.²

To pay for his education, Johnson worked during the day as a carpenter. He was employed by Frank Darrah, a local contractor who was building a school in the Hazelwood section at the time. Johnson broke the color barrier while in Pittsburgh; prior to this, African Americans were only employed as helpers.

On his return to Virginia, Johnson opened an architectural office in Norfolk. He was commissioned to execute several projects throughout Virginia, both alone and in collaboration with his mentor, Charles Thaddeus Russell. His most well-known extant works are the Attucks Theater & Office Building in Norfolk, which was done in collaboration with Russell and the Phoenix Bank of Nansemond in Suffolk.

Most of Johnson's clients were African American. For many of them, he designed distinctive houses in Richmond, Portsmouth, and Norfolk, Virginia. Reputedly, many of the houses he designed in Norfolk were modeled on existing houses of wealthy Whites in the Ghent area of that city. It should be remembered that it was a common practice for architects of the time to copy older buildings, and eclectic architects were adept at observing and synthesizing contemporary styles into a new creative statement.

Ministers were a major client group for Johnson. He designed more than twelve churches over a span of twenty-five years. When his architectural career began to blossom, a deeply religious side of him also blossomed. He studied theology at Virginia Union University from 1920 to 1924, and became an ordained minister; his first pastorate was Mount Olive Baptist Church in Norfolk from 1924 to 1931. He remodeled this structure and installed a pipe organ. Johnson then became pastor of Ebenezer Baptist Church in Portsmouth, Virginia, from 1931 to 1973. Here in 1939 he made a complete renovation of the 1894 brick sanctuary; built an annex with a multi-purpose hall, kitchen, and lounges; and in 1949, rebuilt the facade in white granite. He continued to design churches and alter them up through the 1960s.

Johnson was also active in civic affairs. He became the first African American board member of the Portsmouth Community Chest, served on the Portsmouth School Board from 1961 to 1968, founded Boy Scout Troop No. 72 at Mt. Olive Baptist Church in Norfolk in 1928, and founded Boy Scout Troop No. 82 in Portsmouth in 1935. In 1935 he was also one of the founders of the Norfolk Division of Virginia Union University, which is now Norfolk State University.

Johnson's long and multifaceted career illustrates several patterns shared by many African American architects: they came from families that had experience in construction, their mentors were frequently fellow African Americans, they formed collaborations/partnerships with other African American architects, the majority of their clients were African Americans, and as highly visible professionals they became leaders in their communities. Harvey N. Johnson died in 1973. His architectural, ministerial, and philanthropic contributions to his community were extolled in the eulogy carried in the local newspaper:

> Dr. Johnson's contributions to his city and his people have reached into virtually every community endeavor and have touched the lives of many citizens, black and white. These many accomplishments reflect not only that Dr. Johnson was a man of immense talent and energy, but also that he was a man of immense good will.[3]

Notes
1. Interview with Harvey Johnson Jr., Portsmouth, Va, 10 October 1996.
2. *General Catalog* (Pittsburgh: Carnegie Institute of Technology, 1918–1919), p. 14.
3. "Harvey Johnson," *Ledger Star*, 7 December 1973, p. B4.

Bibliography
Brownell, Charles. "Thomas Jefferson's Architectural Models and the United States Capitol." In *A Republic for the Ages*. Donald Kennon, ed., Charlottesville: University Press of Virginia, 1999.

Bryant, K. G. H. "The Complex Decorative Aesthetic of Virginia's Black Elite during the Gilded Age." Ph.D. diss. Tulane University, 1990.

Kimball, Gregg D. "African-Virginians and the Vernacular Building Tradition in Richmond City, 1890–1860." In *Perspectives in Vernacular Architecture, IV*. Columbia, Missouri: University of Missouri Press for Vernacular Architecture Forum, 1991.

DR. RICHARD A. SINGLETARY,
PROFESSOR OF ART HISTORY,
NORFOLK STATE UNIVERSITY

BUILDING LIST

Name	Address	City	State	Year	Comments
Alston's Esso Service Station	Church St.	Norfolk	VA	c1920	Demolished
Attucks Theatre	10 Wise St.	Norfolk	VA	1919	
Brooks, J. C.	2515 Virginia Beach Blvd.	Norfolk	VA	1921	
Carter, Charles S.	Virginia Beach Blvd.	Norfolk	VA	c1925	
Central Baptist Church	714 Walker Ave.	Norfolk	VA		
Cook, ___	Virginia Beach Blvd.	Norfolk	VA	c1925	
Corprew, Maggie	Chestnut St.	Portsmouth	VA		
Cumberland Street Houses	Various Addresses	Portsmouth	VA		
Diggs, ___	2509 Virginia Beach Blvd.	Norfolk	VA	1921	
Ebenezer Baptist Church Annex	728 Effingham St.	Portsmouth	VA	1936	
Ebenezer Baptist Church Auditorium	728 Effingham St.	Portsmouth	VA	1939	
Ebenezer Plaza Apts.	1140 Chisholm Cr.	Portsmouth	VA	1968	
First Baptist Church	1445 Centre Ave.	South Portsmouth	VA	1919	
First Baptist Church	Turnpike Rd.	Portsmouth	VA	1940	
First Baptist Church	418 Bute St.	Norfolk	VA		Addition
First Baptist Church	236 Harrkon St.	Petersburg	VA		
First Baptist Church Home for the Aged		Norfolk	VA	1951	Demolished
First Church of Christ Holiness	862 Princess Anne Rd.	Norfolk	VA	c1922	Demolished
France, Dr. J. J.	Effingham & London Sts.	Portsmouth	VA	c1918	Demolished
Grove Baptist Church	W. Norfolk Rd.	Portsmouth	VA	c1928	
Hale Funeral Home	905 Princess Anne Rd.	Norfolk	VA	c1933	Demolished
Handy, Dr. James	Virginia Beach Blvd.	Norfolk	VA	1921	
Harrison Street Baptist Church		Petersburg	VA		
Holland, Catherine	2500 Effingham St.	Portsmouth	VA	1956	Demolished
Jackson Cleaners	Effingham St.	Portsmouth	VA	1952	
Jackson Memorial Baptist Church Educational Bldg.	Atlanta & Lincoln Sts.	Portsmouth	VA	1948	Now Centennial Baptist Church
Jackson, Dr. J. A.	3400 Deep Creek Blvd.	Portsmouth	VA	1939	
Kelly, Emma V.	Maltby Ave.	Norfolk	VA	c1925	Demolished
McAdoo, John	Virginia Beach Blvd.	Norfolk	VA	c1920	Demolished
Metompkin Baptist Church		Parksley	VA	1958	
Mother Church of God in Christ	Goff St.	Norfolk	VA	1959	

BUILDING LIST (continued)

Name	Address	City	State	Year	Comments
Mt. Gilead Baptist Church	1057 Kennedy St.	Norfolk	VA	1952	
Mt. Hermon Baptist Temple	2901 London Blvd.	Portsmouth	VA	1924	
Mt. Olive Baptist Church	2401 Ludlow St.	Norfolk	VA	1919	Destroyed by fire
Mt. Olive Baptist Church		Lewiston	NC	1957	
Mt. Pleasant Baptist Church		Norfolk	VA		
New Ahoskie Baptis Church	Catherine Creek Rd.	Ahoskie	NC		
New Bethel Baptist Church	4212 Greenwood Dr.	Portsmouth	VA	1952	
Phoenix Bank of Nansemond	339 E. Washington St.	Suffolk	VA	1936	
Queen Street Baptist Church Annex	413 Brambleton Ave.	Norfolk	VA	1957	
Rich, William	631 Landing St.	Norfolk	VA	1919	Demolished
Riddick, ____	Virginia Beach Blvd.	Norfolk	VA	c1922	
Second Calvary Baptist Church	2940 Corprew Ave.	Norfolk	VA	1919	
Shaw University Roanoke Institute	Campus	Elizabeth City	NC		
St. John African Methodist Episcopal Church Auditorium	545 E. Bute St.	Norfolk	VA	1952	
St. John Baptist Church	2200 Effingham St.	Portsmouth	VA	1919	
St. Mark Reformed Zion United Apostolic Church	1522 W. 44th St.	Norfolk	VA	1919	
St. Paul's Colored Methodist Episcopal Church		Norfolk	VA	1920	Demolished
Tabernacle Baptist Church	418 Halixfax St.	Petersburg	VA	1966	
Thompson, Atty. J. W.	102 W. Jackson St.	Richmond	VA		
Trigg, ____	Virginia Beach Blvd.	Norfolk	VA	1921	
Turpin, ____	Virginia Beach Blvd.	Norfolk	VA	1922	
Tynes Street Church	125 County St.	Suffolk	VA	1936	Now Metropolitan Baptist Church
Union Commercial Bank	County St.	Portsmouth	VA	1919	Demolished
Union Holiness Church	1419 County St.	Portsmouth	VA	1954	Now Twine Memorial Temple
Waters, W. E.	Lincoln St.	Portsmouth	VA		
Wood, J. P.	1115 N. 31st St.	Richmond	VA		
Zion Baptist Church	225 Byrne St.	Petersburg	VA	1959	Addition
Zion Bethel Church	900 Middlesex Rd.	Norfolk	VA	1958	

George Maceo Jones
(1900–1970)

George Maceo Jones, architect, engineer, professor, and public official, was born in Albany, Georgia, on August 25, 1900. George was the son of Richard and Eliza Brown Jones and the brother of Richard L. Jones. He married Beatrice Coles in 1926. No children were born to their union.

George Jones's education began in his native state of Georgia, where he attended Atlanta University High School and began his undergraduate studies at Atlanta University, where he spent two years between 1919 and 1921 before entering the University of Michigan in Ann Arbor. Jones had a distinguished educational experience at the University of Michigan between 1921 and 1934, and he was awarded a bachelor of science in architecture in 1924, a master of science in architecture one year later in 1925, and a doctor of philosophy in civil engineering in 1934. Not allowed to reside in the dormitory, he commuted from Detroit. His doctoral dissertation was titled "Wind Stresses in Tall Buildings: A Comparative Analysis by Successive Approximations and Six Approximate Methods." Jones was the first Black in the United States to earn a doctorate in civil engineering at a time when fewer than twenty-four Whites held such a degree.[1]

Jones had a varied and distinguished professional career that began after receiving his undergraduate and graduate degrees in architecture from the University of Michigan. His first professional experience was as an assistant architect in the office of WILLIAM WILSON COOKE, in Gary, Indiana, from 1925 to 1926. A year later, in 1927, Jones moved to Washington, D.C., and was employed part-time as an architectural draftsman in the office of JOHN ANDERSON LANKFORD, where he remained for six years until 1934, which coincided with the award of his doctoral degree. Jones then accepted a position as dean of the Trade School at FLORIDA AGRICULTURAL & MECHANICAL COLLEGE in Tallahassee in 1927, where he remained until 1929. During his employment with Florida Agricultural & Mechanical College he was affiliated with the Jacksonville office of John Anderson Lankford. Jones resigned his deanship after two years to return to Washington, D.C. Beginning in the winter of 1931, Jones was an assistant professor in the Department of Architecture at HOWARD UNIVERSITY. From 1937 until 1938 he took a sabbatical to attend Armour Institute of Technology (now Illinois Institute of Technology) in Chicago. Jones concluded his tenure with Howard University in 1938 and returned to Chicago, where he entered private practice as an architectural engineer, remaining until 1950.

The year 1950 marked a turning point in Jones's professional career when he entered government service for the first time and served two years as development director for the Cook County, Illinois Housing Authority. In 1952, Jones reentered private practice and remained in the private sector for several years until he was appointed to several successive high-profile positions with the federal government.

In 1954 Jones was appointed architectural advisor to the Government of Liberia by the U.S. Department of State, Foreign Operations Administration.[2] When George Jones's brother Richard was appointed mission director to Monrovia, Liberia, George Jones was reassigned to New Delhi, India, where he advised Indian government officials on the planning and construction of a large-scale five-year housing program. During his posting in India, Jones traveled extensively throughout Egypt, Iran, France, Italy, Greece, China, and Japan. His overseas posting was cut short when his wife became seriously ill and he requested and was granted a transfer back to Chicago. In Chicago, George Jones served as general engineer to the Housing and Home Finance Agency in the Public Housing Administration until his retirement in 1966. He participated in the planning of several urban renewal projects and the master planning of several public housing projects in Chicago.

Jones was a member of the American Institute of Architects and was licensed to practice architecture in Illinois, Indiana, and North Carolina. He was also a registered engineer in Ohio and Illinois. Jones served on the City Planning Advisory Board of the Chicago Plan Commission. In addition he maintained memberships in the Illinois Academy of Science, the American Association for the Advancement of Science, American Mathematical Society, and the National Association of Housing Officials. Jones was also a member of the *Alpha Phi Alpha* Fraternity and the NATIONAL TECHNICAL ASSOCIATION.

George Maceo Jones died on December 24, 1970, at Michael Reese Hospital in Chicago, Illinois.[3] He was interred at Lincoln Cemetery in Worth Township, Illinois.

Notes

1. Harry Washington Green, *Holders of Doctorates among American Negroes* (Boston: Meador Publishing Company, 1946), p. 125.
2. Biographical Data, "George M. Jones," Foreign Operations Administration, National Personnel Records Center, St. Louis, Mo., 22 June 1954.
3. Chicago Board of Health, "George Maceo Jones Death Certificate," Chicago, Ill. issued 28 December 1970, no. 637813.

Bibliography

"Highest Architectural Degree." *Washington Tribune*, 15 February 1934, p. 8.
Sammons, Vivian Ovelton. *Blacks in Science and Medicine.* New York: Hemisphere Publishing Company, 1990.

EDWARD D. DUNSON JR., AIA,
ASSOCIATE PROFESSOR OF
ARCHITECTURE, HOWARD UNIVERSITY
SCHOOL OF ARCHITECTURE AND DESIGN

William Thomas Jones
(c1890–unknown)

William T. Jones, known as W. T., was born circa 1890. The exact date of his birth is not known. Assuming that he was nineteen years old when he graduated from the Normal School at Knoxville College in 1909, that would place his birth year at 1890.

W. T. Jones taught elementary woodworking at Knoxville College and supervised the construction of campus buildings. He designed and supervised construction of a six-room brick faculty house with three basement apartments.

In 1909 Jones took a leave of absence from Knoxville College to pursue a degree in architecture at Carnegie Institute of Technology (now Carnegie Mellon University) in Pittsburgh, Pennsylvania.[1] He showed early promise and proved to be a good student. He was recognized as a skillful architectural draftsman. He apparently withdrew from the institute around 1912 without receiving a degree.

Returning to Knoxville, Tennessee, Jones was asked to design a chapel for Knoxville College. The structure, known as McMillan Chapel, is named for the Reverend W. H. McMillan, president of the Board of Freedmen's Missions. This group provided financial assistance to many Black colleges. Excavation for McMillan Chapel was completed in 1913. On June 7 of the same year, the cornerstone was laid. The exterior is "an imposing Doric structure" 60 × 80 feet with large Doric columns in front.[2] Comments about the chapel were favorable. H. C. Cansler of Knoxville College Industrial Department had this reaction:

> The chapel is a model in every respect. Perfect in design as well as equipment. Dr. McGranahan [president of Knoxville College] has made use of the very latest methods both in the natural and artificial lighting of the building. The ventilating qualities of the building compel admiration and the acoustic properties will [be] found to be as nearly perfect in design as the skill of the architect and builder can well make them.[3]

Although services were held in the chapel by May 1914, it was not dedicated until Sunday, June 7, 1914, during morning worship.

McMillan Chapel, *Knoxville College Archives*

WILLIAM THOMAS JONES

Further details about William Jones' architectural career are not known. The details of his death are also not known.

Notes
1. "William T. Jones," *Aurora* (Knoxville College newspaper), no. 1 October 1909, p. 10.
2. "Chapel," *Aurora*, no. 9 June 1913: 5.
3. "McMillan Chapel," *Aurora*, no. 8 May 1914, p. 7.

Bibliography
Booker, Robert J. *Two Hundred Years of Black Culture in Knoxville, Tennessee, 1791–1991*. Virginia Beach: Donning Company, 1993.

CAROLYN ASHKAR,
REFERENCE LIBRARIAN,
KNOXVILLE COLLEGE

BUILDING LIST

Name	Address	City	State	Year	Comments
Knoxville College Faculty House	Campus	Knoxville	TN		
Knoxville College McMillan Chapel	Campus	Knoxville	TN	1914	

Horace King
(1807–1885)

Theodore Thomas

Horace King was born a slave of African, European, and Native American (Catawba) ancestry in Chesterfield District, South Carolina. He became the most celebrated bridge designer and builder and best-known free Black in much of Georgia and Alabama—a distinction he still retains in the lower Chattahoochee Valley.

King's initial master, about whom little is known, died circa 1829. Horace was then sold twice, becoming the property of John Godwin, a house builder in Cheraw, Alabama. Moving with the frontier, in 1832 Godwin became an early resident of Girard (later Phenix City), Alabama, settling there because he had secured the contract from the nearby City of Columbus, Georgia, to build the first major bridge spanning the Chattahoochee River. Horace probably supervised the construction of the Town Lattice Truss structure. Godwin apparently realized King's intuitive genius as a designer–builder and exploited those skills.

King designed and built bridges over every crossing of the Chattahoochee River from Carroll County to Fort Gaines and over every major river from the Oconee in middle Georgia to the Tombigbee in Mississippi. With Godwin securing the contracts, Horace designed and erected courthouses in Columbus and Russell County, Alabama. The personal relationship between Godwin and his slaves was unique, as was the degree of freedom he allowed Horace. While still a slave, Horace worked on projects without Godwin's supervision. By the mid-1840s, Horace was identified as the architect and superintendent of major bridges in Tuscaloosa, Alabama, and Columbus, Mississippi.

In 1846 Godwin petitioned the Alabama legislature for Horace's freedom, perhaps because Godwin was in debt and wanted to ensure that creditors could not seize his valuable slave. Horace said he bought his freedom and given the magnitude of the bridges he designed and built that was certainly feasible. His new legal status brought few if any changes in his relationship with his former owner and business partner. King, as a freedman, served as a contractor on the Alabama State Capitol (1850), perhaps designing its circular staircase. After Godwin's death in 1859, King erected a monument over his grave that declared "the love and gratitude he [King] felt for his lost friend and former master."[1]

Eufala Covered Bridge, *B.H. Hardaway*

As a freedman, King provided technical advice and formed partnerships with some of the most prominent White entrepreneurs in the lower South. Together with Robert Jemison Jr. (a Tuscaloosa planter, industrialist, and politician), King designed and built bridges, mills, and possibly the insane asylum in Montgomery. Jemison shepherded the 1846 law manumitting King through the Alabama legislature. Later during the hysteria on the eve of the Civil War, Jemison introduced another resolution to ensure King's freedom even if all Alabama free Blacks were re-enslaved.

Nelson Tift, the leading builder of Albany, Georgia, hired King to design a bridge over the Flint River (1858). King used lumber and timbers that had originally been cut for a bridge at Milledgeville, Georgia. When that project ended in a dispute, King simply hauled his materials by railroad to Albany. This action illustrates the portability and universalness of Ithiel Town's utilitarian trusses of redundant triangles: a skilled designer-builder could span any river with standardized beams and braces connected with double tree nails. Such tunnels of timber, designed with the proper camber, would then stand for decades.

In 1855 King accepted stock in Moore's Bridge, which he built over the Chattahoochee River between Newnan and Carrollton, Georgia. Perhaps as early as 1856, and definitely by the 1860s, he moved to this location, where the family worked as bridge keepers and farmed twenty-five acres until 1864, when Union troops torched the bridge. During this period, King frequently visited Moore's Bridge while maintaining a second home in Girard, Alabama, and completing projects in several states.

During the Civil War, in a manner similar to that of other southern builders, King worked for the Confederacy. He had little choice—there were few other sources of income. In addition to his familiar bridge-building tasks, he supplied timbers and knee braces for a gunboat and constructed the structure for a large rolling mill, both for the Naval Iron Works in Columbus, Georgia. The Alabama governor pressed an unwilling King into service placing obstructions in the lower Alabama River to prevent an overriver attack. After the war, King filed for damages inflicted on his personal property by federal troops, arguing that he remained a Unionist throughout the war. Even though his claim was denied, King was a reluctant supporter of the Confederacy and resented the appellation of "Black Confederate."

During Reconstruction, King became a conflicted Republican politician, being elected twice to the Alabama legislature. The legislators chided him for not occupying his seat during the first year of his initial term. Despite his vocal protestations he was elected to a second term. Although he did begin to participate, he was never an active legislator, perhaps because these years were the busiest of his professional life.

The destruction wrought by the war and his reputation as a skilled designer produced numerous opportunities for King. He rebuilt most of his old wagon and railroad bridges in Georgia and Alabama. In the Columbus area, he erected a large cotton warehouse, a gristmill, a textile complex, and numerous undocumented structures in the late 1860s. The newly formed Lee County, Alabama, hired King to design and build its first courthouse and jail in 1867. Despite the surfeit of contracts, King experienced financial reversals during this period, perhaps because he accepted virtually worthless municipal and corporate bonds for his work coupled with the lagging economy of the region.

In 1872, for reasons lost to history, King and his family moved to LaGrange, Georgia, where he continued to design and build bridges, stores, houses, and college buildings. At the cornerstone ceremony for the Southern Female College in 1877, King was called a "venerable architect."

King married twice: his first marriage was to Frances Gould Thomas on April 28, 1839; and the second, to Sarah Jane Jones McManus on June 6, 1866. All of his children (the offspring of his first marriage)—Washington W. (1843–1910), Marshall Ney (1844–1879), John Thomas (1846–1926), Annie Elizabeth (1848–1919), and George (1850–1918)—continued the work of King Bridge Company as they built bridges and various structures in LaGrange, Atlanta; west Georgia; and east Alabama. JOHN THOMAS KING served as a trustee for Clark University from the 1890s until the 1920s and was one of the contractors who built the COTTON STATES AND INTERNATIONAL EXPOSITION NEGRO BUILDING in Atlanta, Georgia, in 1895.

Horace King's death on May 28, 1885, was mourned with obituaries in the Atlanta, LaGrange, and Columbus newspapers. According to the latter, "Probably no . . . man in the south was longer or more generally known than Horace."[2] His skill as a designer and contractor of bridges coupled with his noble character won King recognition and praise not often afforded an African American in the post–Civil War South.

Notes

1. "Robert Jemison Jr. Collection," William Stanley Hoole Special Collections Library, University of Alabama, Tuscaloosa.
2. "Horace King," *Columbus Enquirer—Sun,* 30 May 1885, p. 1.

Bibliography

Cherry, Francis. "The History of Opelika and Her Agricultural Tributary Territory, Embracing More Particularly Lee and Russell Counties from the Earliest Settlement to the Present Date," 1885. Reprint *Alabama Historical Quarterly* 15, no. 2 (1953): 178; and 15 no. 3 (1953): 383.

French, Thomas L., Jr., and Edward L. French. "Horace King, Bridge Builder." *Alabama Heritage,* Winter 1989, p. 35.

French, Thomas L., Jr., and John S. Lupold. *Bridging the Rivers of the Deep South: The Life and Legend of Horace King.* Athens: University of Georgia Press, forthcoming.

"Horace King Interrogatories," Records of the U.S. House of Representatives, Case File of the Southern Claims Commission, Commissioners of Claims, no. 19661, National Archives Record Group, no. 233.

JOHN S. LUPOLD
AND THOMAS L. FRENCH,
LUPOLD & ASSOCIATES, COLUMBUS, GEORGIA

STRUCTURE LIST

Name	Address	City/County	State	Year	Comments
Alabama State Courthouse	Goat Hill	Montgomery	AL	1850	Spiral staircase
Bradfield Bldg.	East Square	LaGrange	GA	1879	
City Mills Co.	18th St. & Chattahoochee River	Columbus	GA	1869	
Clapp's Textile Factory	Site of present Oliver Dam	Columbus	GA	c1866	Burned c1910
Columbus Bridge	Dillingham St. over Chattahoochee River	Columbus	AL	1832	Destroyed by freshet in 1841
Columbus Bridge	Dillingham St. over Chattahoochee River	Columbus	AL	1841	Burned by Union troops
Columbus Bridge	Dillingham St. over Chattahoochee River	Columbus	AL	1865	Demolished
Columbus Bridge	Over Tombigbee River	Columbus	MS	1842	Demolished
Confederate Defensive Obstructions	Lower reaches of rivers		AL	1802–03	Demolished
Confederate Naval Iron Works Rolling Mill	Front Ave.	Columbus	GA	1864–65	Destroyed by Union troops
Factory Bridge	Bryan St.	Columbus	AL	1858	Demolished 1862
Factory Bridge	Franklin St.	Columbus	AL	1862	Destroyed by Union troops
Factory Bridge	Franklin St.	Columbus	AL	1867	Demolished
Florence Bridge	Over Chattahoochee River	Florence	GA	1841	Demolished
Fontaine Warehouse	Front Ave.	Columbus	GA	c1865	Now Bradley Co.
Ft. Gaines Bridge	Over Chattahoochee River	Ft. Gaines	GA	1870	Washed away in 1875
Franklin Bridge	Over Chattahoochee River	Franklin	GA	1873	Demolished

HORACE KING

STRUCTURE LIST *(continued)*

Name	Address	City/County	State	Year	Comments
Glass Bridge	Over Chattahoochee River	West of LaGrange	GA	1873	Demolished
Irwinton Bridge	Over Chattahoochee River	Irwinton	AL	1838	Demolished
Jemison, Robert, Jr.	Over Yellow & Catalpa Creeks	Northeast of Columbus	MS	1845	Small bridges for roads leading to grist mill
Lee County Courthouse & Jail	Courthouse Square	Opelika	AL	1868	Demolished
Loyd, James	East Square	LaGrange	GA	1879	Now Bradfield Drug Store
Miller Factory		Coweta County	GA	1861–64	Demolished
Mobile & Girard Railroad Bridge	Over Chattahoochee River	Columbus	AL		Replaced in 1890s
Moore's Bridge	Over Chattahoochee River	Newnan & Carrolton	GA	1855–56	Burned by Union troops
Muscogee County Courthouse	Courthouse Square	Columbus	GA	1838	Demolished
Render, __	Two miles from Greenville	Meriwether County	GA	1879	
Russell County Bridge	Broad St. at Holland Creek	Girard	AL	1866	Demolished
Russell County Courthouse	Courthouse Square	Crawford	AL	1841	Demolished
Southern Female College Administration Bldg.	Campus	LaGrange	GA	1877	Demolished
Tallassee Bridge	Over Tallapoosa River	Tallassee	AL	1839–41	Demolished
Tift, Nelson Bridge & Keeper's House	Over and next to Flint River	Albany	GA	1858	Destroyed by fire
Tuscaloosa Bridge	Over Black Warrior River	Tuscaloosa	AL	1871–72	Demolished
Tuscaloosa Bridge	Over Black Warrior River	Tuscaloosa	AL	1834	Destroyed during Civil War
Warren Temple Christian Methodist Episcopal Sabbath School		LaGrange	GA	1870s	
Warrior Manufacturing	Next to Black Warrior River	Tuscaloosa	AL	1845–46	
West Point Bridge	Over Chattahoochee River	West Point	GA	1838–39	Demolished
West Point Female College	Campus	West Point	GA	1873	Plans only
Wetumpka Bridge	Over Coosa River	Wetumpka	AL	1844	Destroyed by a flood
White Oak Bridge	Over White Oak Creek	Meriwether County	GA	c1869	Destroyed by fire
Yonge, William Penn C.		Opelika	AL	1850s	

John Thomas King
(1846–1926)

Troup County Archives

John T. King was the son of covered bridge designer and builder HORACE KING. John King carried on the family business by designing and building bridges, houses, and commercial buildings in Georgia and Alabama, and by constructing the COTTON STATES AND INTERNATIONAL EXPOSITION NEGRO BUILDING in Atlanta in 1895. Following his birth in 1846 in Girard (now Phenix City), Alabama, to Horace and his wife Francis Thomas King, John worked with his father and brothers, George and Marshall, in the family construction business. The King family did much to develop West Georgia and East Alabama and open up the area for commerce. John King also served long tenures as a church leader and trustee of Clark College in Atlanta.

King started his career at age fourteen as bridge keeper for the Dillingham Bridge in Columbus, Georgia. He moved to LaGrange in 1872 with other family members. As his father's health began to fail, John became head of King Brothers Bridge Company, a thriving business in western Georgia and eastern Alabama in the late nineteenth century. The company not only built bridges, but also designed and built in the town of LaGrange the Loyd Building on East Court Square, a sash and blind factory operated by the Kings, the Hotel Andrews, numerous houses, and the LaGrange Cotton Oil Factory. The LaGrange Cotton Oil Factory was the town's first "modern" textile mill to be built following the Civil War. Covered bridges that John King designed and constructed included ones in LaGrange, West Point, Columbus, and eastern Alabama.

John King married Julia Sanders on February 8, 1871. They had eight daughters and one son, whom they named Horace after his grandfather. John King served as Sunday school superintendent and trustee of Warren Temple Methodist Church of LaGange from 1874 until his death in 1926. He was a trustee of Clark College from 1893 to 1918, and in 1924 and 1926. King strongly believed in the saying "ignorance breeds poverty" and continually urged Blacks to go to school and to church.

Thanks to business contacts he made through service to Clark College, King was awarded the contract to build the Negro Building (1895) at the COTTON STATES AND INTERNATIONAL EXPOSITION held in Atlanta, which became famous because of Booker T. Washington's "Atlanta Compromise" speech when he repudiated civil agitation for racial equality. The Negro Building's White architect was Bradford Gilbert of New York City. King was joined by another Black contractor, J. W. Smith of Atlanta, in constructing the Negro Building, but Smith's responsibilities during construction are not known. During the exposition, "models of the most useful inventions of colored men" were shown, according to a reporter for the *New York Observer Exposition Supplement*.[1]

John King died on November 9, 1926. He is buried at Eastview Cemetery in LaGrange. His obituary in the *LaGrange Reporter* stated that "he had the confidence of a large circle of white friends. Among his own race, he was a constructive leader and wielded a wholesome influence."[2]

JOHN THOMAS KING

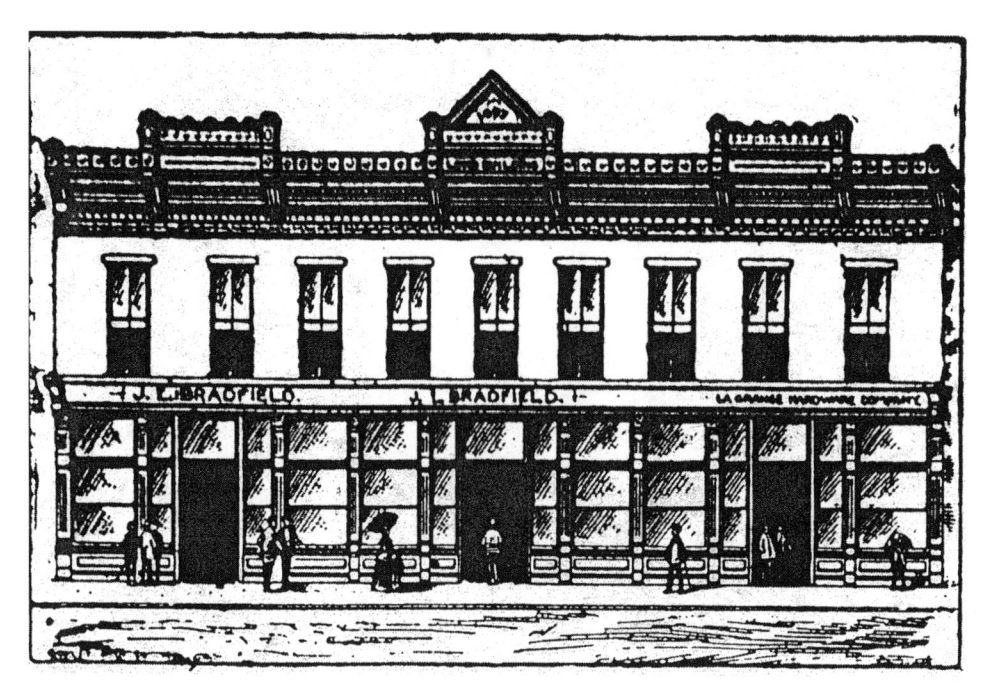

Loyd Building, LaGrange Reporter

Notes
1. John Brown, "Cotton States and International Exposition," *New York Observer,* suppl. 27 June 1895 n. p.
2. "John Thomas King in Memory" *LaGrange Reporter*, 26 November 1926, p. 10.

Bibliography
"King Family Vertical Files." Troup County Archives, LaGrange, Georgia.

KAYE L. MINCHEW, DIRECTOR,
TROUP COUNTY ARCHIVES, LAGRANGE, GEORGIA

STRUCTURE LIST

Name	Address	City	State	Year	Comments
Bradfield, E. R.	East Court Square	LaGrange	GA	1886	
Columbus Bridge	Over Chattahoochee River	Columbus	GA		
Dallis & Edmundson	Greenfield St.	LaGrange	GA	1883	
First Presbyterian Church	118 Church St.	LaGrange	GA	1886	
Flat Shoals Creek Bridge	Salem community	LaGrange	GA	1888	
Hotel Andrews	Main St.	LaGrange	GA	1890	
King, John T.	603 Greenville St.	LaGrange	GA	1888	
LaGrange Cotton Oil Factory	Monroe St.	LaGrange	GA	1890	Demolished
Long Cane Creek Bridge	Sulpher Springs Rd.	LaGrange	GA	1888	
Loyd Bldg.	East Court Square	LaGrange	GA	1897	
Sash and Blind Factory	Greenfield St.	LaGrange	GA		
Smith, Alwyn M.		LaGrange	GA	1890	
Troup County Courthouse	Town Square	LaGrange	GA	1886	Demolished
Unity Methodist Church	Truitt Ave.	LaGrange	GA	1903	
Warren Temple Christian Methodist Church	King St.	LaGrange	GA	1903	Demolished
West Point Bridge	Over Chattahoochee River	LaGrange	GA	1874	

Arthur Edward Lankford
(1879–1908)

Arthur Lankford (3rd from right), *David deClue*

Arthur Edward Lankford was born at the family farm in November 1879, in Potosi, Missouri. Arthur was one of sixteen children of Phillip Anderson Lankford (1837–1907) and Nancy Ella Johnson Lankford (1835–1884) and the younger brother of prominent architect JOHN ANDERSON LANKFORD and cousin of CLINTON STEVENS HARRIS and architect John Thomas Brown.[1] Phillip Lankford, a freedman, owned the small farm and worked in the nearby mines. Nancy Lankford was a devout Christian and dedicated temperance worker.

Arthur Lankford was schooled in the public schools of Washington County, Missouri, in and around Potosi. Arthur Lankford followed his brother's lead and attended TUSKEGEE INSTITUTE, where he studied mechanics. He later took correspondence courses in architecture and engineering from the International Correspondence School located in Scranton, Pennsylvania.

On completion of his educational studies and after gaining experience in managing complex steam plants in St. Louis, Missouri, Arthur Edward established residence in Washington, D.C., where in 1905 he joined his brother's architecture firm, necessitating a name change to J. A. Lankford & Brother. The firm, which was located in the Lewis Building at the corner of 6th and Louisiana Streets, NW, provided comprehensive professional services in architecture, mechanical engineering, and construction. The firm specialized in the installation of steam plants owing to Arthur Lankford's expertise with this large and dangerous machinery. Despite his own noteworthy accomplishments, Arthur Lankford was forever destined to dwell in the professional shadow of his older brother. Arthur Edward Lankford remained in association with the firm until his untimely death in 1908.

In the spring of 1908, Arthur Lankford returned to Missouri to stay with his sister in Ironton because of failing health. He was not yet married and had no children to care for him. Arthur Edward Lankford died of consumption (tuberculosis) on September 21, 1908, at the home of his sister.[2] His remains were transported to Potosi, where he was buried on the family farm.

Notes
1. Twelfth Census of the United States, 1900 Index—Arthur Lankford, U.S. Department of Commerce, Bureau of the Census, 11 June 1900, sheet no. 3, Enumeration District no. 155, Macon, Georgia.
2. "Arthur Edward Lankford Dead," *Richmond Planet*, 26 September 1908, p. 1.

Bibliography
Edwards, Bruce M. *The Lankfords and Lankfords of Virginia*. Baltimore: Gateway Press, 1987.
"A.E. Lankford Dead." *Afro-American Ledger (Baltimore)*, 26 September 1908, p. 1.

EDWARD D. DUNSON JR.,
ARCHITECT AND ASSOCIATE PROFESSOR
OF ARCHITECTURE, HOWARD UNIVERSITY SCHOOL
OF ARCHITECTURE AND DESIGN

John Anderson Lankford
(1874–1946)

District of Columbia Archives

John Lankford was born on the family farm near Potosi, Missouri, on December 4, 1874. Following public schools in Potosi, Lankford pursued education in many venues. He spent 1889 to 1895, ages fifteen to twenty-one, at the State College, Lincoln University in Jefferson City, Missouri, where he took classes in mathematics, natural and chemical sciences, blacksmithing, carpentry, woodworking, and mechanical drawing. He then attended TUSKEGEE INSTITUTE from 1895 to 1896, taking courses in physics and chemistry, but graduating with a certificate in steam fitting. The following year, he took courses in architectural and mechanical drawing from the International Correspondence School in Scranton, Pennsylvania. A year later, in 1898, he received a bachelor of science degree from Shaw University in Raleigh, North Carolina. Lankford served as the university's superintendent of the Industrial Department from 1900 to 1902. In 1901 Lankford secured a master of science degree from Morris Brown College in Atlanta, Georgia, and in 1902 secured another master of science degree from Wilberforce University in Ohio. Lankford also received a master mechanic degree in 1908 from the Agricultural and Mechanical College in Normal, Alabama. In addition to holding teaching positions at each of the schools from which he received a degree, he also taught at Edward Waters College in Jacksonville, Florida.

Sometime after 1896 and prior to 1902, Lankford owned a blacksmith shop in Saint Louis, Missouri, and was superintendent of the Blacksmith Department of the Fulton Cotton Mills in Atlanta, Georgia—one of the largest White-owned cotton mills at the time. He also served as the chief engineer of the National Ice Cream Company, and was a master mechanic for Black-owned Coleman Cotton Mills in Concord, North Carolina.

Lankford married one of his former pupils, Charlotte Josephine Upshaw, in 1901. They had one daughter, Josephine. Lankford and his wife moved to Washington, D.C., in 1902 to complete the design and supervise construction of the United Order of True Reformer Building. An unusually large and complex structure, the building was his first substantial commission, and its design and massing were emulated in his later 1924 design of the proposed People's Federation Bank in Charleston, South Carolina, which was never built. Lankford would throughout his life attend concerts, club meetings, and even twenty years later attend law classes in the True Reformer Building.

Lankford first lived close to the True Reformer Building at 1916 11th Street, NW, but later resided at 1448 Q Street, NW. He initially practiced from his residence, but later opened an office at 1210 W Street, NW, and later still moved his business to 1115 U Street, NW. In a newspaper advertisement in 1904, Lankford noted that his office had received "$500,000 worth of Work in Washington, D.C. in the preceding 32 months."[1]

Most of Lankford's architectural commissions came from within the Black community; however, much of his work was completed outside the District of Columbia. He specialized in church, fraternal, and school designs along with residential commissions.

In August 1906, Lankford entered a competition for the design of the Negro Building for the JAMESTOWN TER-CENTENNIAL EXPOSITION, which was held in Norfolk, Virginia, in 1907. Lankford's design was deemed the second best of the five entrants, behind the winning design of WILLIAM SIDNEY PITTMAN. However, he served as commissioner general representing the District of Columbia. He and ROBERT ROBINSON TAYLOR were selected as supervising architects for the National Negro Fair to be held in Mobile, Alabama in 1908, but fair organizers could not raise the needed funds and the fair was never held.

In 1908 Lankford was appointed supervising architect for the African Methodist Episcopal (AME) denomination, which led to numerous commissions throughout the United States and South Africa. One possible explanation for his appointment was that Lankford's wife was the granddaughter of prominent AME bishop Henry McNeal Turner.

In 1916 the first edition of Lankford's *Artistic Churches and Other Designs* was printed by Black-owned Hamilton Printing Company.[2] It was released again in 1924. The book contained numerous drawings and photographs of his work. Notable commissions included two hundred cottages for the Jonesburg Land Improvement Company, five miles south of Richmond, Virginia, in 1906, which were not built; Saint John's African Methodist Episcopal Church in Norfolk, Virginia (1907); Arnett Hall at Wilberforce University (1910); Big Bethel African Methodist Episcopal Church in Columbia, South Carolina, (1921); and Big Bethel African Methodist Episcopal Church in Atlanta, Georgia, (1924). His Haven African Methodist Episcopal Church (1923) is his only known surviving church in Washington, D.C.

From 1917 to 1919 Lankford attended Frelinghuysen University's John Mercer Langston School of Law. The classes were held in the True Reformers Building, which he designed. In 1921 he was listed as a master of laws graduate and a member of the legal bars in the District of Columbia and Indiana. In 1927 Lankford designed a large administration building for Frelinghuysen University that was not realized.

In the 1920s Lankford was the consulting architect for the Capitol View Realty Company, a suburban Maryland planned development advertised as "America's Finest Colored Community," about which he wrote, "You will find crystallized for colored People a home community that has no equal in America. Here is an opportunity for Colored people to develop living standards on a plane dear to their hearts."[3]

The Commonwealth of Virginia began licensing architects in 1920. The Board of Architects issued Lankford Certificate No. 63 on October 2, 1922.[4] The Board of Architects also issued on the same date Cer-

Masonic Lodge, *Paul Williams*

tificate No. 69 to CHARLES THADDEUS RUSSELL. A conjecture is that the Board of Architects granted a number of certificates on that day, and issued them in alphabetical order. Thus, Lankford is credibly the first African American architect licensed in Virginia.

The District of Columbia began licensing architects in 1924. Lankford became the first registered African American architect in the District of Columbia. He held the distinction of being the city's only Black architect for two years, until ROMULUS CORNELIUS ARCHER JR. was licensed.

In the late 1930s, Lankford was an architectural engineer, housing consultant, and advisor to the U.S. Department of Interior, and during World War II served as a consulting engineer for the U.S. Navy at the Navy Yard on Capitol Hill.

Lankford was a member of many societies and organizations. In 1905 Lankford founded the Colored Men's Business League. In 1905 he organized the Washington, D.C., branch of the National Negro Business League, which had been founded by his former principal, Booker T. Washington, only five years prior. At their 1906 national convention, he delivered a speech titled, "The Negro as an Architect and Builder." He was a life member of the National Negro Business League, and was a very active member of the NATIONAL TECHNICAL ASSOCIATION, serving as its national president from 1941 to 1942. Lankford is also credited with saving the School of Architecture at HOWARD UNIVERSITY after university trustees had voted to close the school. He served as president of the American Technical Institute, and as chairman of the liaison committee, representing the organization before Congress and governmental departments. Lankford was a member of the Independent Order of Saint Luke, the Mu-So-Lit Club, and a 33rd-degree Mason.

Following seven days at Freedman's Hospital in Washington, D.C., Lankford died from heart disease on July 2, 1946. His funeral was officiated by Reverend J. Campbell Beckett, pastor of the Metropolitan African Methodist Episcopal Church, and burial was in Lincoln Memorial Cemetery, in Suitland, Maryland.[5]

Notes

1. "J.A. Lankford, Architect and Builder," *Washington Bee*, 24 December 1904, p. 5.
2. John Lankford, *Artistic Churches and Other Designs* (Washington, D.C.: Hamilton Printing Company, 1916), Library of Congress.
3. "Capitol View Promotional Brochure," Lankford Vertical File, Moorland-Spingarn Research Center, Washington, D.C., n.d.
4. Virginia Board of Architects, Professional Engineers, Land Surveyors, and Landscape Architects, "John Anderson Lankford," no. 63, 2 October 1922, Application Registers, 1921–95. Accession 36313, Book 04AR-03, p. 66.
5. D.C. Health Department, Bureau of Vital Statistics, "John Anderson Lankford, Death Certificate," Record No. 46504, Washington, D.C., 1946.

Bibliography

Ferris, William. "John A. Lankford." *Spokesman* (February 1925): 17.
"John Lankford, Washington's First [*sic*] African-American Architect." *Washington Magazine* (November 1992): 49.
Lankford, John A. "What the Negro Builder Is Doing in D.C." *Alexander's Magazine* (September 1905): 34.
Schulyer, George S. "John A. Lankford: Prominent Negro Architect." *The Messenger* (June 1924): 192.

PAUL KELSEY WILLIAMS,
KELSEY & ASSOCIATES, WASHINGTON, D.C.

BUILDING LIST

Name	Address	City/County	State/Country	Year	Comments
Alabama Agricultural & Mechanical College Palmer Hall	Campus	Huntsville	AL	c1915	
Alabama Agricultural & Mechanical College Saw Mill	Campus	Huntsville	AL	c1899	
Alabama Agricultural & Mechanical College Seay Hall	Campus	Huntsville	AL	c1915	
Alabama Agricultural & Mechanical College Steam Plant	Campus	Huntsville	AL	c1899	
Allen Chapel African Methodist Episcopal Church	921 W. Beverly St.	Stauton	VA	1922	
Allen Chapel Methodist Church		Franktown	VA	1921	
Allen University Chapel	Campus	Columbia	SC		
Allen University Chapelle Administration Bldg.	1530 Harden St.	Columbia	SC	1922	
Apartment Bldg.	1446 Church St., NW	Washington	DC	1921	
Aquilar Cigar Factory	1720 14th St., NW	Washington	DC	1907	
Baptist Academy Master plan	Campus	Jacksonville	FL		
Baptist Seminary	Campus	Washington	DC		
Bethel African Methodist Episcopal Church	Howert Ave.	Deland	FL	c1915	
Bethel African Methodist Episcopal Church		Malvern	AK		
Big Bethel African Methodist Episcopal Church	Butler & Auburn Aves.	Atlanta	GA	1924	

JOHN ANDERSON LANKFORD

BUILDING LIST (continued)

Name	Address	City/County	State/Country	Year	Comments
Big Bethel African Methodist Episcopal Church	819 Woodward St.	Columbia	SC	1921	
Birdville African Methodist Episcopal Zion Church		Washington	DC		
Bower, Mattie	25th & M St., NW	Washington	DC		
Butler Brothers Garage	2009 8th St., NW	Washington	DC	1922	Now Club Y2K
Campbell Chapel African Methodist Episcopal Church		Baldwin	FL	c1911	
Central Heights Normal & Industrial School	Campus	Savannah	GA		
Central Methodist Episcopal Church	1215 5th St., NW	Washington	DC	c1910	Demolished
Coleman, Dr. J.	1234 U St., NW	Washington	DC	1918	
Colonial Church		Pittsburgh	PA	c1931	
Colored Young Mens Christian Association Bldg.		Baltimore	MD	c1915	
Cornerstone Chapel African Methodist Episcopal Church		Lagrange	IL	c1915	
Cosmic Metropolitan African Methodist Episcopal Church		Capetown	South Africa	c1920	
Cosmopolitan Temple Baptist Church	btwn. 9th & 10th Sts., NW	Washington	DC	c1928	Demolished
Davis, D. Webster	908 N. 7th St.	Richmond	VA	c1905	Demolished
Ebenezer African Methodist Episcopal Church		Detroit	MI		
Ebenezer African Methodist Episcopal Church		Indianapolis	IND	1922	
Ebenezer Baptist Church	112 6th St., NW	Charlottesville	VA	c1910	
Emanuel African Methodist Episcopal Church	637 North St.	Portsmouth	VA	c1907	Alteration
Ferguson, ___	1207 25th St., NW	Washington	DC		Alteration
First Baptist Church		Raleigh	NC	c1915	
First Colored Baptist Church	6th St., btwn. G & H Sts.	Washington	DC	1930	
First Presbyterian Church	104 W. Breton St.	Potosi	MO	1909	
Florida Masonic Grand Lodge	410 Broad St.	Jacksonville	FL	1912	
Freeman, Daniel	1334 U St., NW	Washington	DC	c1905	
Frelinghuysen University Administration Bldg.	5th & M Sts., NW	Washington	DC	1927	Plans only
Galbrieth Chapel African Methodist Episcopal Church	1114 6th St., NW	Washington	DC	c1923	
Good Hope Office Bldg.	Lexington & Vine Sts.	Baltimore	MD	1907	Demolished
Grant Memorial African Methodist Episcopal Church	424 W. Orange St.	Jacksonville	FL	1908	
Haven Methodist Episcopal Church	1401 Independence Ave, SE	Washington	DC	1923	
Hotel Golden		Colton	MD		
Independent Order of Odd Fellows Temple		Savannah	GA		
Independent Order of Odd Fellows Temple		Waycross	GA		
Independent Order of Odd Fellows Temple	Anacostia, SE	Washington	DC		
Industrial School	Campus	Falls Church	VA	1909	
John Wesley African Methodist Episcopal Zion Church	18th btwn. L & M Sts., NW	Washington	DC	1902	Demolished
Jonesburg Land Improvement Co.		Ft. Lee	VA	1906	200 cottages; plans only
Larkin's Chapel African Methodist Episcopal Church		Apex	NC		
Lee Chapel African Methodist Episcopal Church		Kenglar	MD	c1915	
Leonard Avenue Baptist Church		St. Louis	MO		
Lomax African Methodist Episcopal Church		Nauck	VA		
Masonic Hall	Bridge St.	Jacksonville	FL	1908	
Morris Brown College Central Heights Industrial Bldg.	Campus	Atlanta	GA		
Mt. Moab Baptist Church	942 26th St.	Washington	DC	1919	
Mt. Zion African Methodist Episcopal Church		Princess Anne Courthouse	VA	c1910	
Mt. Zion Baptist Church		Liberty	MO		
Murray, Daniel	934 S. St., NW	Washington	DC	c1905	
Murray's Ice Cream Factory		Washington	DC		
National Negro Fair	Fairgrounds	Mobile	AL	1908	Plans only
Parnell, William J.	48th St., NE	Washington	DC	1922	
People's Federation Bank	218 St. Philip St.	Charleston	SC	c1921	Plans only
Prince Hall Grand Lodge		Jacksonville	FL	c1944	
Queen Street Baptist Church	413 E. Brambleton St.	Norfolk	VA	1910	
Red Cap Bldg.		Washington	DC	c1920	
Robertson Apts.		Richmond	VA	c1907	
Robertson, Atty, J. C.		Richmond	VA	c1907	

BUILDING LIST *(continued)*

Name	Address	City/County	State/Country	Year	Comments
Robinson, Rev.		Jacksonville	FL	c1915	
Sessoms Drug Store & Office		Waycross	GA		
Shiloh Baptist Church Vestry #1	1628 L St., NW	Washington	DC		Alterations
Society and Business Bldg.		Washington	DC		
Southern Aid Society Bldg.	527 N. 2nd St.	Richmond	VA	1907	Demolished
Southern Appeal Bldg.		Atlanta	GA		
St. John Tabernacle Baptist Church	432 W St., NW	Washington	DC	1920	
St. John's African Methodist Episcopal Church	539 E. Bute St.	Norfolk	VA	c1907	Alterations
St. John's African Methodist Episcopal Church		Indianapolis	IN		
St. John's African Methodist Episcopal Church Parsonage	539 E. Bute St.	Norfolk	VA	1907	
St. John's African Methodist Episcopal Church		Asheville	NC		
St. Phillip's African Methodist Episcopal Church		Savannah	GA	1912	
St. Phillip's African Methodist Episcopal Church Parsonage		Savannah	GA	1912	
St. Stephen's African Methodist Episcopal Church		Detroit	MI		
Stewarts Chapel & Undertaking	30 H St., NE	Washington	DC	c1925	
Sumter Masonic Lodge		Sumter	FL	1919	
Taylor Apts.	520 N. 2nd St.	Richmond	VA	1907	Demolished
Taylor, Rev. W. L.	526 N. 2nd St.	Richmond	VA	1907	Now Elks Club
Thompson, Prof. C. T.		Jacksonville	FL	c1915	
Tooks, Rev. H. Y.		Jacksonville	FL	c1915	
Trinity Baptist Church		Washington	DC		
True Reformers Hall	1200 U St., NW	Washington	DC	1902	
Union Bethel African Methodist Episcopal Church	1518 M St., NW	Washington	DC	1924	Alterations
Walker Memorial Baptist Church		Washington	DC		
Walker, Dr. T. H. B.	Van Buren St.	Palataka	FL	c1915	
Wilberforce University Arnett Hall	Campus	Wilberforce	OH	1910	
Wilberforce University Heating Tunnel	Campus	Wilberforce	OH	c1910	
Wilberforce University Womens Dormitory	Campus	Wilberforce	OH	c1910	
Williams Chapel African Methodist Episcopal Church		Orangeburg	SC	c1915	
Williams Office Bldg.		Savannah	GA		
Williams & Ferguson Industrial Academy	Campus	Abbeville	SC	1909	
Windslow Stable	1700 12th St., NW	Washington	DC	c1915	

Calvin Esau Lightner
(1877–1960)

Lightner Family

Calvin E. Lightner was a native of Winsboro, South Carolina. His father, Frank, was born a slave in 1847, and was a farmer and carpenter who built houses in Chester, South Carolina, during the 1870s. His mother, Daphney Thompson, was free born, the daughter of Joseph and Millie Thompson. Joseph Thompson was a South Carolina state legislator during the Reconstruction era. Frank and Daphney Lightner's union produced nine sons and four daughters (one died as a toddler). In 1881 the family migrated to North Carolina.

Frank and Daphney Lightner instilled in all their children a yearning for education and a determination to become productive citizens. John, the oldest son, became a successful grocery store owner in Atlanta, Georgia. Joseph became a physician in Norfolk, Virginia. Frank Jr. became a cabinetmaker and settled in Richmond, Virginia. Herbert became a master builder who was recruited to help excavate and build the Panama Canal. Preston died during his senior year at Shaw University. Allen became a real estate developer in Atlanta. Lawrence became a mortician in Goldsboro, North Carolina, as did Rayford in Sanford, North Carolina. Ethel, Gladys, and Lethia all became public school teachers.

Calvin Lightner played on Shaw University's first football team in 1906, graduating the following year. He was elected president of the first Shaw University Alumni Association and played an influential role in helping to secure Shaw University's first African American president.

In 1909 he completed embalming school in Nashville, Tennessee, and returned to Raleigh to become the first licensed Black mortician in the city. It took him several years to obtain a charter, but by 1911 he had founded the Lightner Funeral Home, which remains in the family to this day.

In 1909 Calvin married Mamie Blackman. She was a graduate of HAMPTON INSTITUTE and Fayetteville State Normal School. Mamie Lightner taught home economics in the Raleigh public schools. The Lightners had four children: Nicholas (deceased), Lawrence (deceased), Clarence, and Margaret Lightner Hayes.

Without a formal education in architecture, Calvin Lightner designed and constructed his home in Raleigh—a modified Triple A Craftsman, which was a popular style in the Piedmont region of North Carolina. He also designed and constructed commercial buildings on East Hargett Street in downtown Raleigh. Lightner designed the Davie Street Presbyterian Church, where he served as an elder for sixty-two years. The church, located at 300 East Davie Street, is fashioned in the Gothic style and is distinguished by its brick tower and slate roof. The church's rich Gothic architectural details include pointed-arched doors and stained-glass windows with brick hood molds. The original congregation occupied a building on this site in 1875, which was demolished. The present edifice was enlarged in the 1920s.

In 1919 Lightner designed and built the Lightner Building in the 100 block of East Hargett Street. The

Lightner Arcade and Hotel, *University of North Carolina Collection*

mixed-use building contained dental and medical offices, apartments, beauty salons, a barber shop, and a tailoring and dry cleaning business. Encouraged by the successes of the Lightner Building, he completed the Lightner Arcade and Hotel in 1921, in the same block. The arcade also contained dental and medical offices, a barber shop, a drugstore, the first home of *The Carolinian*, an amusement emporium, Harris Barber College, a haberdashery, a store, a ballroom, and the first hotel for Blacks in the state of North Carolina. The Lightner Arcade and Hotel became the jumping-off place for Edward Kennedy, Duke Ellington, Count Basie, and Don Reading's big bands and was the social hub of Black society.

Lightner prepared the blueprints and drawings for many of the outstanding houses located in the Black community. For his houses, he installed wood trusses rather than steel. Many of these houses lasted well into the 1940s.

Calvin Lightner died on May 5, 1960, and is buried in the family plot in Mount Hope Cemetery in Raleigh. His multi-faceted, productive career is a testament that much can be achieved with talent and determination.

Notes
1. Linda Simmons-Henry and Linda Harris-Edmisten, *Culture Town-Life in Raleigh's African American Communities* (Raleigh: Historic Districts Commission, Inc., 1993), p. 60.
2. Phillip N. Henry and Carol M. Speas, *The Heritage of Blacks in North Carolina* (Charlotte: North Carolina African American Heritage Foundation, 1990), p. 327.
3. Alice Eley Jones, *African American Builders and Architects in North Carolina, 1526–1998.* (Raleigh: Preservation North Carolina, 1998), p. 188.

Bibliography
Bishir, Catherine W., Charlotte V. Brown, Carl R. Lounsbert, and Ernest H. Wood. *Architects and Builders in North Carolina: A History of the Practice of Building.* Chapel Hill: University of North Carolina Press, 1990.

Upton, Dell *America's Architectural Roots: Ethnic Groups That Built America.* Washington, D.C.: Preservation Press, 1986.

Wood, Peter H. "Whetting, Setting, and Laying Timbers: Black Builders in the South." *Southern Exposure* (Spring 1980): 3.

ALICE ELEY JONES, AUTHOR AND OWNER
HISTORICALLY SPEAKING, A HISTORY CONSULTING FIRM
SPECIALIZING IN CURRICULUM DESIGN, DIVERSITY
TRAINING, PUBLIC HISTORY,
AND HERITAGE TOURISM,
MURFREESBORO, NORTH CAROLINA

CALVIN ESAU LIGHTNER

BUILDING LIST

Name	Address	City	State	Year	Comments
Capehart, ___	55A Hargett St.	Raleigh	NC		Now YWCA
Davie Street Presbyterian Church	300 E. Davie St.	Raleigh	NC	c1920	Addition
Lightner Arcade & Hotel	129 E. Hargett St.	Raleigh	NC	1921	
Lightner Bldg.	129 E. Hargett St.	Raleigh	NC	1919	
Lightner, Calvin E.	419 S. East St.	Raleigh	NC	c1907	Demolished
Mechanic & Farmers Bank	114 W. Parish St.	Durham	NC	1922	
Taylor Bldg.	Hargett St.	Raleigh	NC		Destroyed by fire

Henry Lewis Livas
(1912–1979)

Courtesy of District of Columbia Archives

Henry L. Livas was born in Hot Springs, Arkansas, on April 20, 1912. In 1916 his father, Harry Thomas Livas, moved his young family to Springfield, Ohio, where Henry attended Woodward Elementary from 1916 to 1922. Harry Livas's trade was tailoring, and he owned a dry cleaners. Henry's mother, Mary Strong Livas, died the same year he entered second grade. His father remarried to Hattie Shivers, his piano teacher.[1] The family then moved to Paris, Kentucky, where Henry attended Western Junior-High School starting in 1923 and graduated in 1929.

In 1930 Henry Livas enrolled in the building construction program at HAMPTON INSTITUTE and graduated in May 1935 with a bachelor of science degree. By July 1944, he was enrolled at the Pennsylvania State College School of Engineering, where he earned a master of science degree in architectural engineering with a minor in architecture in a short eighteen months. His tuition was paid for with a Graduate Stipend Scholarship. Livas made average, not superior, grades. While at Pennsylvania State College he was a teaching assistant for professor of architecture Elliot L. Whittaker. His thesis topic was "Building Code Requirements for Structures Housing Selected Mixed Occupancies," which played to his engineering strengths instead of architectural design.

From 1936 to 1937, Henry Livas was employed by Berry Construction Company in Durham, North Carolina. His duties included drafting, designing, writing specifications, and field supervision on a housing project. His full-time job made it possible for him to marry Cocheeys Smith of Durham, North Carolina in 1940. They had one son, Henry Jr. From 1937 to 1941, Livas taught at Arkansas Mechanical & Normal College in Pine Bluff, Arkansas, and was superintendent of buildings and grounds. From 1942 to 1943, he was a civilian teacher at the U.S. Army Engineering School affiliated with Virginia State College in Ettrick, supervised by White officers. Livas returned to his *alma mater*, Hampton Institute, in 1945 as a newly minted associate professor; he taught there for seven years. In 1952 he opened Livas & Associates in Hampton, Virginia, and simultaneously in Burgaw, North Carolina, where he maintained a second home. The small, rural town of Burgaw was also the home of architect JOHN AYCOCKS MOORE.

Livas was an exceptionally well-credentialed architect, being licensed in at least three states and the District of Columbia. He sat for the four-day North Carolina written examination in 1948 and passed it on his first try, and was licensed in Missouri in 1948, Virginia in 1949, and the District of Columbia in 1950. In addition, he passed the difficult National Council of Architectural Registration Boards examination in 1950.[2]

The same year he gained his license from the state of Missouri, Livas opened Henry L. Livas Architect & Associates in Hampton, Virginia. In 1950 he applied for membership in the Virginia Chapter of the American Institute of Architects and was rejected due to his race. He turned to the District of Columbia of the

HENRY LEWIS LIVAS

Hobson Reynolds Residence Hall, *Alice Ely Jones*

American Institute of Architects and was accepted. He then was able to add "AIA" to his company's title. In 1960 Livas opened an office in Norfolk, Virginia. The architectural office Livas opened in 1950 has been continually in business for fifty-five years and presently operates under the corporate name of the Livas Group, Architects, P.C.

Livas was a member of the American Society for Engineering Education and served as national president of the NATIONAL TECHNICAL ASSOCIATION from 1958 to 1959.

Henry Lewis Livas died on June 10, 1979 from a heart attack. Having taught at Hampton Institute for over three decades it is fitting that he was buried at the landmark Hampton Institute Cemetery.

Notes

1. Interview with Mary Hester Smith (Henry Livas's half-sister), by the author, Durham, N.C., 19 December 2002.
2. National Council of Architectural Registration Boards, "Henry L. Livas," Certificate no. 2861, issued 30 December 1949.

WILLIAM MILLIGAN, SR.
THE LIVAS GROUP, ARCHITECTS, P.C.
NORFOLK, VIRGINIA

BUILDING LIST

Name	Address	City	State	Year	Comments
Berry Construction Co.		Durham	NC	1948	Housing project
Douglas, Dr. ____		Hampton	VA	1955	
Fellowship Christian Church		Chesapeake	VA	1972	
First Baptist Church Annex	540 E. Bute St.	Norfolk	VA	1962	
Gillifield Baptist Church Family Life Center	Pear & Farmer	Petersburg	VA	1976	Addition
Hampton Institute Laundry Bldg.	Campus	Hampton	VA		
Hampton Institute Model House	Campus	Hampton	VA		Student-built
Professional Associate Medical Bldg.		Norfolk	VA	1953	
Reynolds Residence Hall	Colefield & Tuscarora Rds.	Winton	NC	1965	United Order of Elks
St. Augustine Episcopal Church	2515 Marshall Ave.	Newport News	VA	1960	
Suffolk Community Hospital		Suffolk	VA	1952	Plans only
Willow Grove Baptist Church	841 St. Bridges Rd.	Chesapeake	VA	1963	
Wilson Pine Garden Apts.	2525 E. Washington St.	Suffolk	VA	1976	

Howard Hamilton Mackey Sr.
(1901–1987)

Moorland-Spingarn Research Center

Howard H. Mackey was born in Philadelphia, Pennsylvania, on November 25, 1901, the second child of Henry Bardon Mackey and Anna Willis Mackey. His father, although illiterate, improved his station in life by working for decades as a butler to a wealthy White family. His mother, originally from Charlottesville, Virginia, worked outside the home as a domestic.

Howard Mackey attended South Philadelphia High School from 1916 to 1920. The story was told "that while working for an [unnamed] architect he found out how much money the architect was paid for what he felt wasn't very much effort"[1] and it was then that Mackey decided to become an architect. Mackey worked the summer of 1920 as a junior draftsman for WILLIAM AUGUSTUS HAZEL. By the fall semester of 1920, Mackey was a first-year student at the University of Pennsylvania School of Architecture. Mackey was awarded a bachelor of architecture degree during the spring commencement of 1924.

Mackey arrived at HOWARD UNIVERSITY prior to the start of academic year 1924 to 1925 to teach in the fledgling Department of Architecture. Mackey's hiring increased the number of full-time instructors to three: HILYARD ROBERT ROBINSON, ALBERT IRVIN CASSELL, and James Herring, an artist who taught freehand drawing.

In 1924 Mackey's university salary was $2,000 for the nine-month academic year, two-thirds of which was paid by the federal government. It was a well-paying job and predictable enough for him to support a family. On February 2, 1925, Howard Mackey wed Eleanor Matilda Kendrick of Cincinnati, Ohio. One child was born to their union, Howard Jr. Not only would Howard Jr. enroll at Howard University in 1944, but he would take several design studios that were taught by his father and later fashioned a successful career as an architect with the federal government.

In the summers of 1925 thru 1927, Howard Mackey Sr. returned to Philadelphia to serve an unpaid apprenticeship with Henry Horner Jefferson in order to qualify to take the District of Columbia architect registration examination.

In 1929 forty Chicago civic associations including the Illinois Architects' Association jointly announced a design competition to memorialize the sacrifices of all who had served in the Great War. The competition attracted 114 entrants with Mackey being the only known Negro entrant. Mackey's site plan, perspective, and elevation, which featured a 100-foot, monolithic limestone obelisk—reminiscent of H. Van Buren Magonigle's War Memorial (1921) overlooking downtown Kansas City, Missouri—was handsomely rendered in *The Beaux-Arts*, but failed to be judged a prize winner.

At the start of academic year 1929 to 1930, Mackey was appointed acting head *pro tempore* of the Department of Architecture at Howard University. Mackey's elation was short lived when one month later the stock market crashed on Black Friday, October 29. By June 1930, enrollment had dwindled to five students and Mackey was the only instructor. The desperate university board of trustees voted to abolish the Department of Architecture to save money. Mackey rallied the remaining students to sign a petition in opposition of abolishing the department and solicited local architect JOHN ANDERSON LANKFORD, vice president of the NATIONAL TECHNICAL ASSOCIATION and member of the National Business League, to craft a legal argument as to why the department deserved to be spared. The trustees buckled under the lobbying pressure. Not only did they rescind their vote to abolish the department but on June 8, 1931, in a historic action, they created the first School of Engineering and Architecture at a historically Black college or university. Howard Mackey was named acting director.

Mackey had taught for a decade and apprenticed with Henry Horner Jefferson in Philadelphia and White architect John Sohl in Washington, D.C., when he sat for the four-day, thirty-three-hour District of Columbia architect licensing examination in December 1934. On his third attempt, in December 1935, he passed the exam and received Certificate No. 279.[2]

In 1936 Mackey returned to his alma mater to pursue a master of architecture degree. His tuition was covered by a General Education Board Fellowship. He completed his studies in one year, and his terminal project, a "Commercial Door Building," was approved. On June 9, 1937, Mackey received his master's degree in architecture.

Mackey resumed directorship of the School of Engineering and Architecture in the fall semester of 1938, and went on to serve as director for thirty-two years. He was singularly responsible for the School of Architecture becoming the first historically Black college or university to be accredited by the National Architecture Accrediting Board to award a five-year bachelor of architecture degree. Passage of the GI Bill of Rights in 1946 made tuition money plentiful for

Chicago War Memorial, *Moorland-Spingarn Research Center*

veterans, which pushed the School of Architecture's enrollment to an all-time high of 199, one of the largest enrollments at any school or department of architecture in the nation. Mackey was endearingly referred to as "the father of Black architects" for having taught and guided to graduation a majority of the Black architects who were then in practice.

From 1954 to 1957, on sabbatical from Howard University, Mackey was an adjunct instructor in the Civil Engineering Department at the University of Maryland. He provided technical assistance and administered a $900,000 contract with the U.S. Department of State, Foreign Operations Administration, for developing master plans for Lodge Housing and Ruimvledt Housing in Georgetown, British Guiana, and Latourweg Housing in Paramaribo, Surinam.

Howard Mackey gave his professional time to the District of Columbia Board of Examiners and Registrars of Architects, the National Capital Planning Commission's Joint Committee on Fine Arts, and the District of Columbia Committee on Landmarks and was the first Black member of the city of Baltimore Design Advisory Panel.

Howard Mackey taught would-be architects for seven years before he ever designed a building that was actually built, in 1931. The reason for Mackey's delayed entry into private practice was because of Dean Lewis Downing, who discouraged his directors from practicing on the side because he felt it took away time and usurped energy from the students. Mackey's design *oeuvre* ranged from Cape Cod to Colonial to Georgian to International Style for houses, to Art Deco for apartment buildings, to no discernible style for public housing.

On May 2, 1962, Howard Mackey was elevated to fellow status by the American Institute of Architects. In May 1983 Howard Mackey was again honored by the American Institute of Architects as the ninth recipient of the "Whitney M. Young Jr. Citation" (named after the drowned executive director of the National Urban League) for "having influenced the lives and careers of a great majority of this nation's black architects."[3]

Mackey retired from Howard University in 1968. He was called out of retirement one year later to guide the School of Architecture as it added an undergraduate program in city planning that was made possible by a $400,000 grant from the Ford Foundation. Mackey retired a second and final time at the end of academic year 1970 to 1971, placing a capstone on an academic career that had spanned almost half a century.

Howard Mackey entered the eternal *Omega* chapter on August 20, 1987.[4] He died at Holy Cross Hospital in Silver Spring, Maryland, of pneumonia complicated by Parkinson's disease, and was buried in Eden Cemetery in Collinsdale, Pennsylvania, north of Philadelphia.

Notes

1. Interview with Howard Mackey Jr. by the author, Annapolis, Md., 26 April 1988.
2. District Columbia Board of Examiners and Registrars of Architects, "Howard Mackey," Certificate no. 279, issued 4 December 1935.
3. "Whitney M. Young, Jr. Citation," *AIA Journal* (26 January 1983): 5.
4. "Howard Mackey, 85, Dies." *Washington Post*, 21 August 1987, p. D4.

Bibliography

"Howard Mackey." African-American Architects Archive, Moorland-Spingarn Research Center, Washington, D.C.

Dallet, Francis P. "A Century of Black Presence at the University of Pennsylvania" (typescript). University of Pennsylvania Archives, 1981.

DRECK SPURLOCK WILSON

BUILDING LIST

Name	Address	City	State	Year	Comments
Adams, Dr. Charles	1838 13th St., NW	Washington	DC	1939	Alteration
Aiken, Ernest	635 Newton Pl., NW	Washington	DC	1951	Apts.
Aiken, Ernest	944 Eastern Ave., SE	Washington	DC	1950	Apts.
Alexander, John A.	1214 Franklin St., NE	Washington	DC	1937	Alteration
Band, Louis M.	1831 Providence St., NE	Washington	DC	1955	Store/apt., demolished
Cardozo, Dr.	3600 New Hampshire Ave., NW	Washington	DC		Plans only
Cedar Knoll Baptist Church		Cedar Knoll	NC	1930	
Chicago War Memorial Competition	Grant Park	Chicago	IL	1930	
Coleman, Dr. Frank	1232 Girard St., NE	Washington	DC	1940	
Deal Funeral Parlor	4812 Georgia Ave., NW	Washington	DC	1938	Now Independence Bank
Dyson, Dr. Walter	1345 Douglas Ave.	Highland Beach	MD	1931	Summer cottage
First Baptist Church of Georgetown	27th & Dumbarton Ave., NW	Washington	DC		Alterations
Fisher, Robert E.	St. MacArthur Blvd.	Washington	DC	1949	
Golden Grove Church		Golden Grove	CA	1946	
Hamilton, Sara A.	925 48th Pl., NE	Washington	DC	1950	Apts.
House, Christopher C.	2824 14th St., NE	Washington	DC	1939	
Howard University Snack Bar	2400 6th St., NW	Washington	DC	1946	Demolished
Hunter, Edward	Salude Hall Rd. & Hwy. 13	Ahoski	NC	1949	
Industrial Savings Bank	2000 11th St., NW	Washington	DC	1943	Alterations
Jones, J. C.	Arundel Rd.	Oyster Bay	MD	1954	Summer cottage
Kelly, Dr. Charles H.	1217 Hamlin St., NE	Washington	DC	1949	
Kelly, Dr. Charles H.	1509 Newton Pl., NE	Washington	DC	1951	Store/apts.
Kramer		Silver Spring	MD	1950	
Langon, Willenton	2480 Ontario Rd., NW	Washington	DC	1950	

HOWARD HAMILTON MACKEY SR.

BUILDING LIST (continued)

Name	Address	City	State	Year	Comments
Lawe Funeral Parlor		Dundalk	MD	1948	
Lawnside Gardens & Shopping Center		Lawnside	NJ	1946	150 dwelling units
Lewis, Dr. Douglas L.	5006 E. Capitol St., NE	Washington	DC	1950	
Mackey, Howard H.	1023 Fairmont St., NW	Washington	DC	1952	Apts.
Mackey, Howard H.	1512 Marion St., NW	Washington	DC	1950	Apts.
Miskan Tora Community Center	10 Ridge Rd.	Greenbelt	MD	1951	
Morris Furniture Store	3708 Georgia Ave., NW	Washington	DC	1945	Demolished
Mt. Bethel Baptist Church	71 Rhode Island Ave., NW	Washington	DC		Alterations
Mt. Pleasant Baptist Church	215 Rhode Island Ave., NE	Washington	DC		Alterations
Newton, Frontis J.	4101 Meade St., NE	Washington	DC	1954	
Parkside Dwellings Public Housing	Kenilworth Ave & Barnes Ln., NE	Washington	DC	1940	Demolished
Randal United Methodist Church	1002 46th St., NE	Washington	DC	1946	Alterations
Roberts, Dr. James E.	1233 Kearney St., NE	Washington	DC	1945	
Robinson, Dr. Alvin F.	1509 Newton St., NE	Washington	DC	1954	Demolished
Rogers, Madeline P.	1300 Lawrence St., NE	Washington	DC	1948	
Shelton, J. E.	4730 N. 24th St.	Arlington	VA		Apts.
Southern Baptist Church	134 L St., NW	Washington	DC	1950	Addition
Spencer, Dr. A. L.	434 Park Pl., NW	Washington	DC		Plans only
Stoddard Baptist Home for the Aged	1220 Rhode Island Ave., NW	Washington	DC	1952	Plans only
Sullivan, Dr. J. W.	719 N. 43rd St.	Philadelphia	PA	1933	Alterations
Supreme Liberty Life Insurance Co.	3914–3922 Clay Pl., NE	Washington	DC	1938	3 houses
Thurston, Thomas C.	2912 15th St., NE	Washington	DC	1938	
United Grove Disciples Church		Clinton	NC	1945	
Uricolo, Dr. Raphael	4215 Argyle Terr., NW	Washington	DC	1951	
Virginia Seminary & College Dormitory	Campus	Lynchburg	VA		Demolished
Weaver, Dr. Joseph D.	Hwy. 13 North	Ahoski	NC	1949	
Whitted, Dr. Harold L.	1249 Irving St., NW	Washington	DC	1948	
Williams, Dr. Arthur C.	2400 Alabama Ave., SE	Washington	DC	1951	Apt. alterations
Williston, Dr. Thomas	1204 Q St., NW	Washington	DC	1939	Addition
Worther, Edmund C.	3311 Military Rd., NW	Washington	DC	1932	
Young, Col. Lucius	2900 15th St., NE	Washington	DC	1938	

Robert Prince Madison

(1923–   )

Robert Prince Madison was born in Cleveland, Ohio, on July 28, 1923, to Robert James Madison (1899–1951) and Nettie Brown Madison (1900–1974). His father was born in Mobile, Alabama, and graduated from Snowhill Institute in Selma in 1918. His mother was born in Selma and graduated from Morris Brown College in Atlanta. His father was a civil engineering graduate of Howard University and in 1930, the first African American employed as an engineer in the War Department. His mother was an instructor of drama at Selma University and Benedict College.

Robert Prince Madison attended East Technical High School in Cleveland, Ohio, and graduated with honors in mathematics and science at age seventeen in June 1940. Initially he enrolled in the SCHOOL OF ARCHITECTURE AT HOWARD UNIVERSITY, but withdrew to serve in World War II as a second lieutenant in the U.S. Army. He was wounded in action in the Italian campaign and was awarded three combat ribbons and the Purple Heart. Returning to Cleveland after the war in 1946, he applied to Western Reserve University to continue his architectural studies:

> The dean [of architecture] told him, "You can't come here. We don't have black folks here. There's no jobs out there for you" . . . Madison was not giving up that easily. "So, I went home. I put on my uniform, all my ribbons, all this stuff," he said. "I went back up there and asked to see the dean of admissions. I said, 'You know what? I have spent the last two and a half years of my life fighting in Italy. Fighting to make this world free for democracy. Killing people I don't even know to come back home and all I want to do is study and you tell me that I can't because I'm colored?"[1]

His plea convinced the dean, and Madison was admitted, but required to take examinations to be sure he "measured-up." The GI Bill paid his tuition. Voted the "Outstanding Student in His Class," he earned a bachelor of architecture degree in June 1948. He was the first African American to graduate from Case Western Reserve's School of Architecture. After graduating, Madison discovered that the dean's prediction was true. No one would hire him. He made an offer to Robert A. Little, one of his former professors, to work for two weeks without pay to prove himself. Madison remained with Little until 1951. In 1948 Madison joined the Cleveland chapter of the American Institute of Architects. He also took the four-day state of Ohio architectural licensing examination in June 1950 and passed.[2] It is believed that he was the first licensed African American architect in Ohio.

During his undergraduate days at Howard University, Robert Madison met Leatrice Branch. They were married on April 16, 1949, in Washington, D.C. They subsequently had two daughters, Jeanne and Juliette.

Seeking an advanced degree, in 1951 Madison entered Harvard University's Graduate School of Design, which at the time was led by Walter Gropius (1883–1969), famous for his stylized industrial designs and as an educator from the Bauhaus. Madison was a natural leader and war veteran. His mostly younger fellow students elected him class president

267

Church of the Redeemer, Presbyterian, *Dreck Spurlock Wilson*

(1951–52). He completed his coursework in January 1952 and was awarded his master's degree in architecture during the June commencement of 1952.

Howard Hamilton Mackey, Sr. director of the School of Architecture at Howard University, hired Madison in February 1952 to teach architectural design and site planning. However, shortly thereafter, Madison was notified that he had been selected one of 240 Americans awarded a Fulbright Scholarship under the auspices of the U.S. Educational Exchange Program to study abroad. Madison was the first African American selected to study architecture in the Fulbright program. He sailed to Paris, France, in September 1952 and enrolled in the Ecole des Beaux Arts. There for nine months, he studied urban design and pre-stressed concrete construction. When not in the atelier, he spent delightful hours touring French architectural monuments.

Madison returned to his teaching position at Howard University after his study in Paris. He moonlighted in a solo practice to supplement his teaching salary, and designed houses, churches, and a bank. Madison obtained registration in October 1953, being assigned license number 1429 by the D.C. Board of Examiners and Registrars of Architects.[3] In 1954 Madison decided to return to Cleveland. He opened Madison & Madison with his brother Julian, a civil engineer, and with office help from his wife and mother. The firm specialized in architecture, civil engineering, and interior design. The firm grew steadily through the 1960s and then opportunities increased with the election of Carl Stokes as Cleveland's first Black mayor. In the 1970s, the firm expanded to open offices in Detroit, Chicago, Atlanta, Milwaukee, and Trinidad. As the firm prospered into the 1980s and marketed their professional services beyond the metropolitan Cleveland area, the corporate name was changed to Robert P. Madison, International, Inc.

Recognition and honors came to Robert Madison during the 1970s and 1980s as he became active in civic organizations. He was elected to the College of Fellows of the American Institute of Architects in 1974, and in 1985 he was appointed chairman of the prestigious Jury of Fellows, who vetted and admitted candidates to the College of Fellows. In 1982 he founded the Ohio Association of Minority Architects and Engineers. He was awarded an Honorary Doctor of Humane Letters degree from Howard University in 1987. He became a member of the Board of Trustees of his alma mater, Case Western Reserve University. Additionally, he served as a guest lecturer and accrediting visitor to Cornell University, Harvard University, Howard University, Kent State University, Ohio State University, SOUTHERN UNIVERSITY, TUSKEGEE INSTITUTE, University of Cincinnati, and the University of Shanghai. The Ohio chapter of the American Institute of Architects awarded his firm the Gold Medal in 1997. In 2002 he was chosen by the national American Institute of Architects as the recipient of the Whitney M. Young, Jr. Award for meritorious community service.

Robert Madison is a member of Saint John African Methodist Episcopal Church in Cleveland, Ohio where he formerly served as Sunday School Superintendent. He is also a member of the Cleveland Civic Vision 2000 and Beyond. In 2002 Madison was inducted into the Northeast Ohio Business Hall of Fame.

Notes
1. Miriam Smith, "Renaissance Man," *Inside Business*. (December 2002): 16.
2. Architects Board of Ohio License, "Robert P. Madison," no. 1834, issued 10 June 1950.
3. D.C. Board of Examiners and Registrars of Architects, "Robert P. Madison," no. 1429, issued 7 October 1953.

Bibliography
"Madison Design Group, Firm Prospectus." Cleveland: Madison Design Group, 1986. In the possession of the firm.

ROBERT P. MADISON, FAIA,
PRESIDENT AND CHIEF EXECUTIVE OFFICER,
ROBERT P. MADISON INTERNATIONAL, INC.

BUILDING LIST

Name	Address	City	State/Country	Year	Comments
Allen A.M.E. Church	11-54 Merrick Blvd.	Jamica	NY	1963	
Bell Tower, Lady of Fatima	6604 Lexington Ave.	Cleveland	OH	2000	
Bethel A.M.E. Church	2720 Webster Ave.	Pittsburgh	PA	1959	
Bethel A.M.E. Church	815 West 16th St.	Little Rock	AR	1963	
Bethel A.M.E. Church	150 Fairfield Ave.	Stamford	CT	1964	
Bibleway Temple	4451 Benning Rd., S.E.	Washington	DC	1975	
Captain Arthur Roth Elementary School	12523 Woodside Ave.	Cleveland	OH	1965	
Chambers Elementary School	14305 Shaw Ave.	East Cleveland	OH	1978	
Chambers Elementary School	14305 Shaw Ave.	East Cleveland	OH	1998	Addition
Church of the Redeemer, Presbyterian	1423 Girard St., NE	Washington	DC	1960	
Cleveland State University Science & Research Center	2121 Euclid Ave.	Cleveland	OH	1982	
Cleveland Trust Co. Bank	60th & St. Clair Ave.	Cleveland	OH	1961	
Continental Concourse "C" Cleveland-Hopkins	U.S. Route 237	Cleveland	OH	1999	
Cuyahoga Community College East Campus	Campus	Highland Hills	OH	1986	
Cuyahoga Community College Technology Learning Center	Campus	Highland Hills	OH	1994	
Cuyahoga Community College Theatre Complex & Classroom	Campus	Highland Hills	OH	1994	
DeLeon, Charles A.	2333 North Park Blvd.	Cleveland	OH	1960	
E. F. Boyd Funeral Home	2165 East 89th St.	Cleveland	OH	1966	
East Cleveland Municipal Bldg.	14340 Euclid Ave.	East Cleveland	OH	2001	
East Cleveland Municipal Courtrooms	14340 Euclid Ave.	East Cleveland	OH	1999	
East Cleveland Police Station	14340 Euclid Ave.	East Cleveland	OH	2002	
Eliza Bryand Cluster Homes	7201 Wade Park Ave.	Cleveland	OH	2002	
Emmanuel Baptist Church	7901 Quincy Ave.	Cleveland	OH	1958	
Engineering Services Building (N.A.S.A.)	21000 Brookpark Rd.	Cleveland	OH	1989	
Fatima Family Center	6600 Lexington Ave.	Cleveland	OH	1996	
Fire Fighters Memorial	Erieside Ave.	Cleveland	OH	1999	
First Apostolic Faith Institutional Church	40 South Caroline St.	Baltimore	MD	1982	
First Greater New Zion Baptist Church	3824 King Jr. Blvd.	Cleveland	OH	1999	
Golden Rule Shopping Center	901 New Jersey Ave., N.W.	Washington	DC	1979	
Harvard Yard Service Facility	4068 Harvard Ave.	Newburgh Heights	OH	1987	
Hebrew Cultural Garden	East Boulevard & Columbia	Cleveland	OH	2000	
Henley, Stewart	4234 S. Dakota Ave, NE	Washington	DC	1956	

ROBERT PRINCE MADISON

BUILDING LIST *(continued)*

Name	Address	City	State/Country	Year	Comments
Hopkins Airport, Cafe Connection Concession	U.S. Route 237	Cleveland	OH	2001	
House	1501 Girard St., NW	Washington	DC	1956	Spec. House
House	2815 15th St., NE	Washington	DC	1950	Spec. House
Imani Church	1505 East 260th St.	Euclid	OH	1999	
Industrial Bank of Washington	4812 Georgia Ave.	Washington	DC	1962	
Industrial Bank of Washington	4500 Blane Rd., NE	Washington	DC	1963	J. H. Mitchell Branch
Kathryn Tyler Neighborhood Center	900 East 105th St.	Cleveland	OH	1967	
Madison, Robert P.	2339 North Park	Cleveland Heights	OH	1960	
Martin de Porres Center	1274 East 123rd St.	Cleveland	OH	1984	
Martin Luther King Jr. High School	1651 East 71st St.	Cleveland	OH	1973	
Martin Luther King Jr. Shopping Plaza	9300 Wade Park Ave.	Cleveland	OH	1972	
Medical Center Courts	4276 St. Antoine St.	Detroit	MI	1964	
Medical Dental Arts Bldg.	143rd & Kinsman Ave.	Cleveland	OH	1967	
Medic's Medical Bldg.	1464 East 105th St.	Cleveland	OH	1960	
Mt. Hermon Baptist Church	2516 East 40th St.	Cleveland	OH	1958	
Mt. Pleasant Family Center	13890 Kinsman Rd.	Cleveland	OH	1999	
Mt. Pleasant Medical Center	13915 Kinsman Rd.	Cleveland	OH	1957	
Mt. Zion Baptist Church	1501 14th St., NE	Washington	DC	1962	
Naperville Transit Station	Downtown & River	Naperville	IL	1979	
Plymouth Congregational Church	4276 Saint Antoine St.	Detroit	MI	1970	
Plymouth Housing Estate	4276 Saint Antoine St.	Detroit	MI	1970	410 dwelling units
Research Analysis Center, N.A.S.A.	21000 Brookpark Rd.	Cleveland	OH	1978	
Residence Deputy Chief of Mission	LeCorniche	Dakar, Senegal	West Africa	1965	
Second Calvary Baptist Church	12017 Emery Rd.	Cleveland	OH	1978	
Southeast Seventh Day Adventists Church	16602 Tarkington Ave.	Cleveland	OH	1985	
St. Johns A.M.E. Church	917 Garden Ave.	Niagara Falls	NY	1969	
St. Johns Presbyterian Church	3151 Gratiot Ave.	Detroit	MI	1972	
St. Paul A.M.E. Church	1350 Locust St.	McKeesport	PA	1962	
State of Ohio Computer Center	North Star Rd. & Lane Ave.	Columbus	OH	1987	
Tuskegee University Engineering Nuclear Bldg.	Campus	Tuskegee	AL	1966	
U.S. Embassy Office Bldg.	Au Jean XXIII - Rue Kleber	Dakar, Senegal	West Africa	1965, 1977	
U.S. Embassy, Staff Apt.	Rue Jean Mermoz	Dakar, Senegal	West Africa	1965	
Union Commerce Bank Branch	9300 Wade Park Ave.	Cleveland	OH	1972	
Washington Chapel A.M.E. Church	1402 Old Mountain Rd.	Tuskegee	AL	1966	
Wayne County Justice Center	201 West North St.	Wooster	OH	1976	
Wilberforce University, School of Religion	1055 North Bickett Rd.	Xenia	OH	1960	
Zion Baptist Church	1231 Kenilworth Ave.	Washington	DC	1966	

Calvin Lunsford McKissack
(1890–1968)

Harmon Foundation

Calvin McKissack was a co-partner in McKissack & McKissack, the first African American–owned architectural firm in Tennessee. The firm was established in 1905 by Calvin's older brother MOSES MCKISSACK III. The brothers came from a rich history of carpenters and builders that can be traced back to their grandfather, Moses, a West African Ashanti tribesman. Captured and sold into slavery to North Carolina builder William McKissack, Moses acquired carpentry and building skills. His son Gabriel also learned these skills. Following the Civil War, Gabriel relocated his family to Pulaski, Tennessee, where he worked as a builder. He and his wife Dolly Ann raised seven sons, including Calvin, who was born on February 23, 1890.

Growing up in Pulaski, Tennessee, Calvin was exposed to building construction working alongside his father and older brother Moses III. Calvin followed in the footsteps of his older brother and pursued a career in architecture. After studying three years at Barrows School in Springfield, Massachusetts, Calvin McKissack attended Fisk University from 1905 to 1909. He subsequently received a certificate in architecture from the International Correspondence School in Scranton, Pennsylvania.

In 1912 Calvin McKissack struck out on his own and started a practice in Dallas, Texas. He remained in Dallas for three years, during which time he designed numerous churches and schools for the Negro community. After returning to Nashville in 1915, he taught architectural drawing at Tennessee Agricultural and Industrial State Normal School for three years. He then went on to direct the Industrial Arts Department of Pearl High School. Advancing his academic career, Calvin McKissack became the first executive secretary of the Tennessee State Association of Teachers in Colored Schools. He held this post until 1922, when he resigned to join his brother as a partner in the architectural firm. The firm became known as McKissack & McKissack.

Simultaneously, Calvin McKissack and his brother submitted their credentials in 1922 to the recently formed Tennessee Board of Architects and Engineers Examiners. In spite of some racial prejudice by board members, the majority of members affirmed the professional abilities of both Calvin and Moses McKissack and they became among the first architects registered in Tennessee.[1]

Throughout the 1920s, McKissack & McKissack's clientele grew. Calvin McKissack produced designs for numerous Nashville residences and became especially noted for his churches. His designs were typically in the Colonial Revival and Neo-Classical styles, reflecting the period's most popular architecture. Primary among his ecclesiastic designs is the Capers Congressional Methodist Episcopal Church in Nashville, a Neo-Classical structure completed in 1925. Calvin McKissack's and the firm's reputations continued to grow. One of the firm's most prominent commissions came from the National Baptist Convention, U.S.A., Inc., to design the Morris Memorial Building in downtown Nashville. Completed in 1924, the 4-story Neo-Classical-style office building features a limestone exterior and is one of Calvin McKissack's finest designs. In the late 1920s and into the 1930s and 1940s, Calvin McKissack designed numerous educational buildings for the City of Nashville and State of Tennessee, including the Martha M. Brown Library and other Tennessee Agricultural and Industrial State College buildings. As the firm's reputation grew, Calvin McKissack became a leader in the African American business community. He served as president of Nashville's Negro Board of Trade in 1925, and later served as national president of the NATIONAL TECHNICAL ASSOCIATION from 1951 to 1952.

During the 1930s and the Great Depression, the firm struggled financially. Although it slid close to bankruptcy, it managed to survive because of contracts for public schools and a number of Public Works Administration projects. In the 1940s, Calvin McKissack acquired architectural licenses in Alabama, Georgia, South Carolina, Florida, and Mississippi.

Calvin McKissack and his brother garnered national attention in 1942 when McKissack & McKissack was awarded a War Department contract to construct the 99th Pursuit Squadron Training School and Air Field at Chehaw, Alabama, near TUSKEGEE INSTITUTE. The contract amount was $5,700,000, the largest federal construction contract ever awarded to an African American–owned company. HILYARD ROBERT ROBINSON was the project architect for the administration building, barracks, warehouse, training school, and clinic; and DAVID AUGUSTUS WILLISTON was the project landscape architect–site engineer. That same year, McKissack & McKissack received the Spaulding Medal from President Franklin Delanor Roosevelt as the "Outstanding Negro Business" in the United States. The award was named for Charles C. Spaulding, founder and first president of North Carolina Mutal Life Insurance Company, the largest Black-owned insurance company in the United States.

After his brother's death in 1952, Calvin McKissack assumed leadership of the firm and continued to work until his death at age seventy-eight in 1968.

Note
1. State of Tennessee Architectural and Engineering Examiners, "Calvin L. McKissack," no. 73, issued 24 February 1922.

Bibliography
Elmore, Mary Eloise. "McKissack & McKissack Negro Architects and Builders." Tennessee State College, Senior Project, Tennessee State University Library, 1943.

Universal Life Insurance Company, *Hook Brothers Photographers*

CALVIN LUNSFORD McKISSACK

Harris, Mitchell Jerome. "The History of the McKissack Family and McKissack and McKissack Corporation of Nashville, Tennessee." Master's thesis, Fisk University, 1974.

Gallenbeck, Warren, "$2,500,000 College Hill Apartments Will Replace Squalid Housing Conditions Here." *Nashville Banner*, 24 February 1951, p. 3.

PHILIP THOMASON,
PRINCIPAL, THOMASON AND ASSOCIATES,
PRESERVATION PLANNERS, NASHVILLE, TENNESSEE

BUILDING LIST

Name	Address	City	State	Year	Comments
African Methodist Episcopal Publishing House	8th Ave. & Lafayette	Nashville	TN		Demolished
Alabama State Teachers College Science Bldg.	Campus	Montgomery	AL	1938	
AME Sunday School Union Publishing House	8th & Lea Ave.	Nashville	TN	1930	Demolished
Avery Apts.	8th Ave.	Nashville	TN	1930	Demolished
Avoca Apts.	31st Ave. N.	Nashville	TN	c1920	Demolished
Bastian, Nate A.	3722 Central Ave.	Nashville	TN	1921	
Bransfort Realty Co.	Belle Meade area	Nashville	TN	1920	4 houses—demolished
Cameron Junior High School	1034 1st Ave.	Nashville	TN	1940	
Capers Christian Methodist Episcopal Church	319 15th Ave. N.	Nashville	TN	1925	
Colored Methodist Episcopal Publishing Board Office		Jackson	TN	1931	Demolished
Colored Methodist Episcopal Publishing House		Jackson	TN	c1920	Demolished
Comer, Montgomery	1411 Eastland Ave.	Nashville	TN	1920	
Ewing, Edward B.	Central Ave.	Nashville	TN	1919	Demolished
Fairfield Baptist Church	Fain St.	Nashville	TN	1927	
Fisk University Carnegie Library	1720 Meharry Blvd.	Nashville	TN	1908	
Ford Green Public School		Nashville	TN	1939	Demolished
Ft. Valley State College Student Center	Campus	Ft. Valley	GA	1939	Now St. Luke's Episcopal Church
Glenn, Dr. L. C.	2111 Garland Ave.	Nashville	TN	c1920	Demolished
Griswold, Norman W.	2809 W. End Ave.	Nashville	TN	1919	Demolished
House, John	340 Chesterfield	Nashville	TN	1919	
Hubbard, Dr. George	1109 1st Ave. S.	Nashville	TN	1920	Demolished
Lane College Cleaves Womens Dormitory	Campus	Jackson	TN	1920	
Lane College Hamlett Mens Dormitory	Campus	Jackson	TN	1914	Destroyed by fire
Masonic Temple		Nashville	TN	1928	
Meigs Public School	123 Douglas Ave.	Nashville	TN	1933	
Morris Memorial Bldg.	810 18th Ave. N.	Nashville	TN	1924	
Payne Chapel African Methodist Episcopal Church	212 Neill Ave.	Nashville	TN	1921	
Pearcy, G. C.	Long Blvd.	Nashville	TN	1919	Demolished
Pearl High School	601 17th Ave.	Nashville	TN	1935	
Pulaski Public School		Pulaski	TN	1937	
Roberts, Albert	Lebanon Rd.	Nashville	TN	1937	
Roger Williams University Dormitory	Campus	Nashville	TN	c1920	Demolished
Sexton, Daniel P.	3506 Byron Ave.	Nashville	TN	1921	
St. Stephens Baptist Church	3045 Chelsea Ave.	Memphis	TN	1929	
Tennessee A&I College Brown Library	Campus	Nashville	TN	1927	
Tennessee A&I College Admin. Bldg.	Campus	Nashville	TN	1926	
Texas College Carter Womens Dormitory	Campus	Tyler	TX	1937	
Texas College Wiley Mens Dormitory	Campus	Tyler	TX	1913	
Turner Normal & Industrial Institute Admin. Bldg.	Campus	Shelbyville	TN	1912	
Universal Life Insurance Co.	480 Linden St.	Memphis	TN	1930	
Washington Junior High School		Nashville	TN	1927	Demolished

Moses McKissack III
(1879–1952)

Negro History Bulletin

Moses McKissack III was the founder of the first African American–owned architectural firm in the state of Tennessee, established in 1905. Building construction was a part of Moses McKissack's heritage; both his grandfather and father were trained in the trades of carpentry and construction. His grandfather, Moses (his Anglicized name)—an Ashanti tribesman from the gold coast that extends thru Ghana, West Africa—was forced into slavery and sold in 1790 to William McKissack, a builder from Charlotte, North Carolina.[1] Moses and his wife, Miriam (her Anglicized name), a Cherokee slave, produced fourteen children, the ninth of whom was Moses II (also known as Gabriel). After the Civil War, Moses McKissack II settled his second wife and family in Pulaski, Tennessee, where he started McKissack Contractors.

Born on May 8, 1879, Moses McKissack III was one of seven sons of Moses II and Dolly Ann McKissack. While growing up, Moses III gained hands-on construction experience working alongside his namesake father. Moses III dropped out of Pulaski Colored High School in 1890, a year shy of graduation, to apprentice with local White architect James Porter. For the next five years, McKissack prepared construction drawings and was sent to job sites to build what he had drawn. Next he worked as construction supervisor at Vale Rolling and Riverburg Mills and prepared shop drawings for B. F. McGrew and Pitman & Patterson; he also built his own houses in Pulaski, Mount Pleasant, and Columbia, Tennessee; and Athens and Decatur, Alabama.

In 1905 Moses McKissack III relocated to Nashville to work as an architect-builder. His first documented client was Granberry Jackson, dean of architecture and engineering at Vanderbilt University. McKissack designed Jackson's residence and was soon commissioned to design and build stately residences for other Vanderbilt University faculty and Tennessee governor Calvin Brown. Around the same time, he completed an architecture course offered by the International Correspondence School in Scranton, Pennsylvania.

Moses McKissack III received his first large commercial commission in 1908—the Carnegie Library on the campus of Fisk University. The brick building is Neo-Classical in style and one of the first major buildings erected on campus. In 1912 McKissack designed the Administration Building for Turner Normal & Industrial School for Negroes in Shelbyville, Tennessee. He also designed dormitories for Roger Williams University in Nashville and Lane College in Jackson.

As his business prospered, Moses married Miranda P. Winter in 1912. They became the parents of six sons: Lewis Winter, architect; Moses IV, architect; Lemuel, industrial arts teacher; Calvin, construction supervisor; Samuel, industrial arts teacher; and William DeBerry, architect.

During the 1920s, Moses McKissack III produced designs for both African American and White clients. In addition to educational buildings, McKissack designed several Nashville houses including one for Dr.

274

George Hubbard, director of Meharry Medical College. The majority of McKissack's houses were designed in the Anglo-Colonial Revival style.

To solidify their professional standing, both Moses McKissack III and his brother CALVIN LUNSFORD MCKISSACK, who joined the firm in 1922, submitted credentials to be licensed as architects by the Tennessee Board of Architects and Engineers Examiners. The State of Tennessee had effected a registration law only a year earlier in 1921. Moses McKissack received Certificate No. 117 and Calvin McKissack received Certificate No. 118.[2]

Through the 1920s, the McKissack brothers gained statewide recognition. Moses McKissack was a major stockholder in the African American–owned Universal Life Insurance Company of Memphis and Penny Savings Bank in Nashville. President Franklin Delano Roosevelt appointed Moses McKissack to the White House Conference on Housing Problems due to his political clout and experience designing and constructing public housing.

Moses McKissack III died at home December 12, 1952, at age seventy-three, leaving behind his brother as the surviving partner. His funeral service was held at Capers Memorial Christian Methodist Episcopal Church, which he had designed. In addition to his legacy of buildings, Moses McKissack III's contributions to the City of Nashville are remembered by an elementary school and neighborhood park named in his honor.

Begun by Moses McKissack III in 1905 as the first African American–owned architectural firm in Tennessee, McKissack & McKissack is the oldest continually operating architectural firm in the United States, with offices in Nashville and Memphis, Tennessee, and Tuskegee, Alabama.

Notes

1. Anonymous author, "The Family Record of Moses and Miriam McKissack," Nashville, Tennessee, 1969, Fisk University Archives.
2. State of Tennessee, State Board of Architectural and Engineering Examiners, "Moses McKissack" Certificate no. 117, issued 24 February 1922.

Bibliography

Taylor, Tulie W. "National Register of Historic Places Registration Form for "St. John's Baptist Church." U.S. Department of the Interior, National Park Service, 1992.
"Building Tennessee: The Story of the McKissacks." *The Courier* 16, no. 1 (October 1977): 4.
Reed, W. A., Jr. "Pioneer Architect Called by Death." *Pittsburgh Courier*, 27 December 1952, p. 15.

PHILIP THOMASON,
PRINCIPAL, THOMASON & ASSOCIATES,
PRESERVATION PLANNERS, NASHVILLE, TENNESSEE

BUILDING LIST

Name	Address	City	State	Year	Comments
Housing		Miami	FL	1940	
Brown, Gov. John		Nashville	TN		
Boyd Park Community Center		Nashville	TN		
College Hill Housing	37th & Albion Sts.	Nashville	TN	1951	216 dwelling units
Collins Chapel Hospital	409 Ayers St.	Memphis	TN		Addition
Eaton Day Care Home	1708 Pearl St.	Nashville	TN		
First American Bank		Nashville	TN		
Fisk University Burris Music Hall	Campus	Nashville	TN	1945	
Fisk University English Department Bldg.	Campus	Nashville	TN	1952	
Fisk University Henderson-Johnson Gym	Campus.	Nashville	TN	1950	
Fisk University Parker-Johnson Hall	Campus	Nashville	TN	1954	
Jackson Courts Housing	1457 Jackson St.	Nashville	TX		
Jackson, Granberry Sr.	204 24th Ave. S.	Nashville	TN	1905	Demolished
Kayne Avenue Baptist Church	1025 12th Ave. S.	Nashville	TN		
Kings Lane Elementary School	3200 Kings Ln.	Nashville	TN		Addition
Lane College Health Bldg.	Campus	Jackson	TN	1942	
Mammoth Life Insurance Co.	480 Linden St.	Memphis	TN		Now Universal Life Insurance Co.
Meharry Medical College Hubbard Hospital	Campus	Nashville	TN		
Meharry Medical College Mental Health Center	Campus	Nashville	TN		
Meharry Medical College Sciences Center	Campus	Nashville	TN		
North Nashville Community Center	1005 21st Ave. N.	Nashville	TN		
Phillips Chapel Colored Methodist Episcopal Church		Milan	TN		
Riverside Sanitarium & Hospital	800 Young's Ln.	Nashville	TN	1948	
St. John's Baptist Church	1328 NW 3rd Ave.	Miami	FL	1927	
Taborian Hospital	Drawer 169	Mound Bayou	MS	1940	
Tennessee Agricultural & Industrial University Engineering Bldg.	Campus	Nashville	TN	1950	
Tennessee Agricultural & Industrial University Residence Economic Bldg.	Campus	Nashville	TN		
Tennessee Agricultural & Industrial University Library	Campus	Nashville	TN		
Tennessee Agricultural & Industrial University Physical Education Bldg.	33rd Ave. & Centennial Blvd.	Nashville	TN	1951	
Tennessee Agricultural & Industrial University President's Residence	Campus	Nashville	TN		
Tennessee Agricultural & Industrial University School of Business	Campus	Nashville	TN		
Texas College Carter Dormitory	Campus	Tyler	TX	1940	
Texas College Glass Library	Campus	Tyler	TX	1954	
Texas College McKinney Administration Bldg.	Campus	Tyler	TX	1954	
Texas College President's Residence	Campus	Tyler	TX	1954	
Texas College Taylor Gym	Campus	Tyler	TX	1940	
Universal Life Insurance Co.		Dallas	TX	c1940	

John Alexander Melby
(1880–1943)

John Melby (3rd row, center), *Courtesy of the University of Illinois Archives*

John A. Melby was born in Toronto, Canada, on September 20, 1880. John's Canadian mother, Catherine Elizabeth, died during childbirth. His widowed American father, Perry, left Canada and settled in Chicago, Illinois, along with his infant son.

John Melby attended Jones Grammar School in Chicago, Illinois, for eight years. He entered South Division High School (now Wendell Phillips High School) in 1894 and graduated three years later with honor roll–qualifying grades of 90 and higher in his drawing and music classes. By 1898 he was a first-year student at Clark University in Atlanta, Georgia. He spent the summers from 1898 to 1901 working as a draftsman for MacDonald Engineering Company, whose office was in Burnham & Root's skyscraper, Monadnack Building (1892), in Chicago's "Loop." Company president James MacDonald encouraged his only Black staffer to consider a career in architecture, so Melby transferred to the University of Illinois in downstate Urbana-Champaign and started classes in September 1899. John Melby was the second African American admitted to the School of Architecture, following by one year WALTER THOMAS BAILEY. Melby was a member of the Architect's Club, an indicator of acceptance by his peers. After four years of study, Melby withdrew from the university—one year shy of earning a degree.

Melby returned to his former employer, MacDonald Engineering Company, for three years ending in 1906 when he was hired to teach in the MECHANICAL INDUSTRIES DEPARTMENT AT TUSKEGEE INSTITUTE. Although faculty were routinely called on to design institute buildings, there are no known buildings attributed to Melby. He remained at Tuskegee Institute until 1909 and then his whereabouts for six years are unknown. In 1915 he was back at MacDonald Engineering Company and stayed there for two years. Melby relocated thirty miles southeast of Chicago to

Gary, Indiana, in 1918 and opened an office on 16th Avenue. His business card stated that he offered professional services in "practical engineering, house plans, concrete block [construction], contracting, estimating."[1] Melby was unable to attract a sufficient number of clients and thus in order to make ends meet he went to work far from his chosen profession, in the coke-fired, inferno furnace mills of U.S. Steel and then as a mailman.

By 1921 Melby was employed as an architect by SAMUEL M. PLATO in his Walnut Street Louisville, Kentucky, office. He left Plato's office after only one year to make a second attempt at establishing his own architectural office. Melby also tried to turn his hobby of electronics into a business by opening an electronics repair shop, but it did not last long enough to reach its first anniversary.

The commission that probably spurred Melby to consider opening an office in Louisville was a brick church (1922). However, one project does not a practice make. By 1925 Melby had relocated to Washington, D.C., where he hung out his shingle at 13th and U Streets and then at First Street, NW. His first significant commission was the design of an apartment building (1925) for Ab[raham] Leonard. He followed that project with the design of speculative houses for Capitol View Realty Company, which was developing modest, 1-story homes in the southeast neighborhood of the nation's capital. Melby knew premiere Black architect JOHN ANDERSON LANKFORD, who provided a professional reference for him when he applied for a District of Columbia license in 1926.[2]

John Melby met nurse-in-training Ohioian Viola Ragland, and they wed in 1914. She put aside her ambition to become a nurse to stay at home and care for their six children—John Jr., Francis, William, Paul, James, and Catherine—all of whom are now deceased. Only one pursued a career in the fine arts; Paul became a commercial artist.

John Melby died at home from complications caused by a non-medicated bleeding ulcer in 1943. Having practiced in Washington, D.C., for eighteen years, there were many clients and young architects whom he had apprenticed who, when combined with family members, generated an overflow crowd of mourners. His nephew remembered that his homegoing celebration lasted two days.[3] John Melby is buried in Harmony Memorial Cemetery in Suitland, Maryland.

Notes
1. Photocopy of business card which is in the possession of the author.
2. D.C. Board of Examiners and Registrars of Architects, "John Alexander Melby," Certificate no. 199, issued 13 December 1924.
3. Interview with Luther Marshall (nephew of John Melby) by the author, Washington, D.C., 10 October 2002.

DRECK SPURLOCK WILSON

John King Duplex, *Dreck Spurlock Wilson*

BUILDING LIST

Name	Address	City	State	Year	Comments
Antioch Baptist Church	1107 50th St.	Washington	DC	1929	
Capitol View Realty Co.	Various addresses	Washington	DC	1926	Spec houses
Church		Louisville	KY	1922	
Gas Station	9th & O Sts., NW	Washington	DC		Demolished
King, John M.	1416–1418 Kearney St., NE	Washington	DC	1927	Duplex
King, John M.	1422–1424 Kearney St., NE	Washington	DC	1927	Duplex
King, John M.	1426 Kearney St., NE	Washington	DC	1927	
King, John M.	3214 14th St., NE	Washington	DC	1930	
King, John M.	3218 14th St., NE	Washington	DC	1930	
King, John M.	3220 14th St., NE	Washington	DC	1930	
King, John M.	3222 14th St., NE	Washington	DC	1930	
King, John M.	3204 15th St., NE	Washington	DC	1931	
King, John M.	3208 15th St., NE	Washington	DC	1931	
Leonard Apts.		Washington	DC	1925	
Lightbown Store	3924 12th St., NE	Washington	DC	1929	
Marshall, Faith	5225 Ames St., NE	Washington	DC	c1932	
Nite-Club	15th & Massachusetts Ave., NW	Washington	DC		Demolished
Reno Store	2940 12th St., NE	Washington	DC	1932	
Ridell, A. F.	1222 Girard St., NE	Washington	DC	1931	

Amaza Lee Meredith
(1895–1984)

Special Collections, Virginia State University

Amaza Lee Meredith was a highly regarded educator and regionally celebrated landscape and still-life artist who designed buildings for her friends, her church, and her family. She did not receive formal training as an architect nor is there any record of her having apprenticed with an architect.

Amaza Meredith was born in Lynchburg, Virginia, on August 14, 1895, the youngest child of a bi-racial marriage. Her White father, Samuel Peter Meredith, was a master stair builder. In a record of her family's "Historiography" Meredith cites her sister's description of Samuel Meredith: "If ever a saint walked this earth, it was he."[1] Her mother, Emma Pink Kenney Meredith, is described in the same document as the "beautiful black daughter of James and Mary Kenney . . . proud, aggressive, devout baptist."[2]

Amaza was a student in Lynchburg elementary public schools and completed her secondary education at Jackson Street High School. She took on her first teaching position in a one-room schoolhouse in Indian Rock, Virginia. The school had 110 students, including an eighth grader who was older than Amaza. She returned to Lynchburg and taught elementary and high school before attending college. In 1922 she completed a two-year program at Virginia State Normal and Industrial Institute and was valedictorian of her class. She taught for six years at Lynchburg's Dunbar High School before continuing her college education at Columbia University's Teacher College, where she earned a bachelor of arts degree with honors (1930) and a master's degree (1935) in art education. After receiving her first degree from Columbia University in 1930, Meredith was appointed art teacher at Virginia State Normal and Industrial College in Ettrick, Virginia. She founded the Art Department and became its head in 1935. She retired from this position twenty-three years later in 1958.

Meredith's earliest documented architectural effort, and her best known, began in the mid-1930s, when she was in her forties. It was at this time when she designed "Azurest South," a small, 1-story home for herself and Dr. Edna Meade Colson, who headed Virginia State University's School of Education and was Meredith's lifelong companion. Sited in a lush dell at the east edge of campus, the house is a bold investigation of the International style. The exterior has a smooth stucco finish with curved corners and industrial-type windows. Bands of glass block round the corners of the bedroom wing. The copings and rails that line the flat roof as well as the columns and carport roof are painted an eye-catching turquoise. The limited palette of exterior materials explodes on the interior with an unexpected mix of colors and finishes. The multicolor, metal fleck, vinyl tile; Carrara glass; acoustic tile; mosaic tiles; and tile-board finishes specified by Meredith were the most current interior finishes available. "Azurest South" was filled with art and modern furniture that were carefully documented in Meredith's scrapbooks.

Amaza Lee Meredith House "Azurest South," *Virginia Department of Historic Resources.*

Meredith had clearly been exposed to the work of International style architects like Marcel Breuer (1902–1981) and Walter Gropius (1883–1969), who emigrated from Germany to the United States to teach at Harvard University in 1937. The intellectual courage exemplified in the design of her groundbreaking house cannot be overstated. In Virginia, the Anglo-Colonial Revival style, even now, has been consistently reaffirmed as the style of choice, particularly since the 1910s. The mid-1930s expansion of Virginia State University's campus—the immediate setting for "Azurest South"—was completed in the Colonial Revival style. Although Meredith's plans and isometric drawings for her house and for subsequent buildings are not rendered by the experienced hand of a professionally trained architect, the drawings clearly delineate the details of style and construction. The roof drains and wall sections are illustrated with precision, as are the pipe railings and ship's ladder leading to the roof terrace.

"Azurest South" was listed in the National Register of Historic Places in 1993. Judged by architectural historian Richard Guy Wilson as "one of the most advanced residential designs in the state in its day,"[3] the house is one of the commonwealth's few mature examples of the International style and a landmark of African American material culture.[3]

Beginning around 1947, Meredith joined relatives and family friends in developing a 120-lot subdivision named Azurest North in Sag Harbor, a posh all-Black former whaling village in East Hampton, Long Island, New York. She named a road for herself (Meredith Street) and one for her sister Maude Terry (Terry Drive). Amaza Meredith designed two houses in "Azurest North." Drawings for "HIHIL" for her sister, with a dramatic bow front, reapplies the same formal and stylistic devices seen at "Azurest South." "Edendot," the Prairie-style house she designed for Dorothy Spaulding is a simple shed-roof cottage opening onto the dunes. Other architectural drawings in Virginia State University's Meredith Archive include floor plans for "Anndot," a house in Prairie View, Texas; the Reed house; and Gillfield Baptist Church education wing in Petersburg, Virginia.

Throughout her career, Meredith engaged in a wide range of creative community endeavors beyond teaching, painting, and architecture. In 1955 she applied for and received a patent for an accessory to be attached to a golf bag. In 1977 Meredith designed and submitted alternative logos for the National Association for the Advancement of Colored People, which was considering a name change to the National Association for the Advancement of All People. Generous with her work, Meredith donated paintings to Petersburg

General Hospital in appreciation for the care that the doctors and nurses had given her. A room in the education wing that she designed at Gillfield Baptist Church has on exhibit twelve paintings titled "Story of Creation."

When she began designing buildings in the mid-1930s, Amaza Lee Meredith was one of only a handful of female African Americans architects. Like her more prolific contemporary ETHEL MADISON BAILEY FURMAN of nearby Richmond, Amaza Meredith's practice focused on family, friends, and church while her spare time was devoted to the advancement of her race.

Amaza Meredith lived at "Azurest South" during the academic year and vacationed at "Azurest North" from 1939 until her death in 1984. Her remains were cremated and her ashes placed in a crypt in Gillfield Baptist Church in Petersburg, Virginia.

Notes

1. "Amaza Lee Meredith Papers," Special Collections, University Archives, Johnston Memorial Library, Virginia State University, Petersburg, Virginia, nd.
2. Ibid.
3. Charles Brownell et al., *The Making of Virginia Architecture* (Richmond: Virginia Museum of Fine Arts, 1992), p. 104.

Bibliography

Hill, James Christian, Loth Calder, and Mary Harding Sadler. "National Register of Historic Places Registration Form for Azurest South." Virginia Department of Historic Resources, Richmond, 1993.

Kersey, Frederick F. "Speech Honoring Amaza Lee Meredith Presented to President Daniel, Retiring Members of the Faculty, Visitors, Ladies, and Gentlemen." Special Collections, Johnston Memorial Library, Virginia State University, Petersburg, Virginia, n.d.

Meredith, Amaza Lee. "Historiography." Johnston Memorial Library, Virginia State University, Petersburg, Virginia, n.d.

Sadler, Mary Harding. "Amaza Lee Meredith, Out of the Mainstream and into History." *Inform*, no. 2 (1994): 26.

MARY HARDING SADLER, HISTORICAL ARCHITECT,
SADLER & WHITEHEAD ARCHITECTS,
RICHMOND, VIRGINIA

BUILDING LIST

Name	Address	City	State	Year	Comments
Gillfield Baptist Church Education Bldg.	209 Perry St.	Petersburg	VA	1964	
Johnson, Dr. James H.	3rd Ave.	Ettrick	VA	1954	
Meredith, Amaza L. "Azurest South"	2900 Boisseau St.	Ettrick	VA	1938	
Meredith, Amaza L. "Azurest North"		Sag Harbor	NY	1947	Subdivision
Parker, Evelyn L.				1975	Plans only
Preston, Ann C. "Anndot"		Prairie View	TX	1956	
Reed	S. Lawn Dr.	Ettrick	VA	n.d.	Plans only
Richards, Dr. F. F. "Hillside"		Sag Harbor	NY	1946	
Spaulding, Dorothy "Edendot"	Terry Dr.	Sag Harbor	NY	1951	
Terry, Maude "HIHIL"	Terry Dr.	Sag Harbor	NY		
Virginia State University Alumni House	Campus	Ettrick	VA	1949	Plans only

John Merrick
(1859–1919)

John Merrick was born a slave in Clinton, North Carolina, in 1859, on the eastern edge of North Carolina's Black belt. His White father, the plantation owner's son, disavowed any responsibility for John, his brother Richard, or his mother Margaret. In 1871 Margaret Merrick left the plantation and moved her family to Chapel Hill, where she worked as a domestic while John worked in the local brickyard and learned to read and write in one of the Reconstruction-era schools. After six years in Chapel Hill, the family moved to Raleigh. John worked as a hod carrier and later as a brick mason, helping to construct the first large buildings at Shaw University. When this work became uncertain, he worked as a bootblack in a Black-owned barbershop and soon learned barbering.

In 1880 John Merrick married Martha Hunter of Raleigh and they had five children: Geneva B., Mable V., Martha C., Edward R., and John T. Merrick eventually became the favorite barber of Washington Duke, president of W. Duke & Sons, predecessor of the American Tobacco Company, who traveled to Raleigh because of the poor-looking haircuts he received in Durham. Duke persuaded Merrick to relocate to Durham and provide the New South city with the professional tonsorial parlor that wealthy White men wanted. Merrick opened a Durham barbershop in 1880 in partnership with another Black barber. By 1892 Merrick owned five barbershops and for a while as many as nine.

With the barbershops doing turn-away business, Merrick began investing in real estate. He purchased a lot in Durham and designed and constructed two small houses: one for his family and one for his business partner. They were compact, 3-room cottages that faced the railroad tracks on Pettigrew Street in the Black section of town known as Hayti.

After 1892 Merrick's real estate investments grew by leaps and bounds. The profits from his barbershops subsidized his land purchases and the construction of houses for rent. He drew plans for the houses and figured out the bills for lumber and then hauled the lumber from the mill himself in his wagon. He was his own architect, drayman, foreman, and carpenter.

On October 20, 1898, North Carolina Mutual and Provident Association was organized by seven Blacks who had met in the Durham office of Dr. Aaron M. Moore. The newly formed insurance company was incorporated by the General Assembly of the state of North Carolina on February 28, 1899. John Merrick was elected president, a position he held until his death in 1919. Merrick, along with Dr. Aaron M. Moore and Charles C. Spaulding, built the company into the largest Black-owned business in the nation.

Five years after North Carolina Mutual Insurance Company was founded, the directors expanded its operations to include real estate development. In 1903 the company began buying land in the Black sections of Durham and constructing rental housing to satisfy the demand generated by the influx of Black laborers employed in Durham's many tobacco factories. North Carolina Mutual was guided in this enterprise by John Merrick, who had been designing and building rental houses in Hayti for several years and by the first decade of the twentieth century owned more than sixty houses. Merrick was North Carolina Mutual's realtor, architect, and builder. For years Merrick bought dilapidated buildings from the Duke family at bargain prices in exchange for providing crews to demolish them and haul away the debris.

In 1910 North Carolina Mutual formed a real estate subsidiary, the Merrick-Moore-Spaulding Land Company. The company constructed hundreds of low-cost rental houses across southeast Durham up until the 1940s. The majority were 1-story duplexes, one room wide with a rectangular gable or hip roof, centrally placed chimney, front porches, and minimal ornamentation. As North Carolina Mutual consumed more of his time, Merrick hired a full-time construction supervisor and master carpenter.

Of larger significance to Black-owned businesses in Durham was North Carolina Mutual's decision to organize and capitalize the Mechanics and Farmers Bank in 1907. The Black-owned bank complemented the insurance company and land company as a depository for premiums, and mortgages. The bank filled an economic vacuum in Durham's Black economy.

In 1910 Merrick designed and supervised the construction of a large Queen Anne–style house with a wraparound porch and polygonal tower for his family.

In the midst of North Carolina Mutual's spectacular growth and expansion, John Merrick, the company's first and only president, died after a lingering illness on August 6, 1919. His funeral was held at Saint Joseph's African Methodist Episcopal Church and was attended by local, state, and national dignitaries.

In memory of John Merrick, barber, architect, builder, insurance company founder, and bank director, the Liberty Ship S.S. *John Merrick* was christened and launched into wartime service in 1943 and the Merrick-Moore School in Durham was dedicated in 1950.

Merrick House, *Durham Public Library*

Notes
1. William J. Kennedy Jr., *The North Carolina Mutual Story: A Symbol of Progress, 1898–1970* (Durham: North Carolina Mutual Life Insurance Company, 1970), p. 3.
2. Claudia Roberts and Diane E. Lea, *The Durham Architectural and Historic Inventory* (Durham: City of Durham and the Historic Preservation Society of Durham, 1982), p. 114.
3. R. McCants Andrews, *John Merrick: A Biographical Sketch* (Durham: Press of the Seeman Printery, 1920), p. 33.

Bibliography
Jones, Alice Eley. *African American Builders and Architects in North Carolina, 1526–1998*. Raleigh: Preservation North Carolina, 1998.

Weare, Walter B. *Black Business in the New South: A Social History of North Carolina Mutual Life Insurance Company*. Urbana: University of Illinois Press, 1973.

ALICE ELEY JONES, AUTHOR AND PRINCIPAL, HISTORICALLY SPEAKING, A HISTORY CONSULTING FIRM SPECIALIZING IN CURRICULUM DESIGN, DIVERSITY TRAINING, PUBLIC HISTORY AND HERITAGE TOURISM, MURFREESBORO, NORTH CAROLINA

BUILDING LIST

Name	Address	City	State	Year	Comments
Merrick, John	506 Fayetteville St.	Durham	NC	c1910	Demolished
Merrick, John	Pettigrew St. & R.R. tracks	Durham	NC	1881	Demolished

John Henry Michael
(1867–1940)

Helen Michael Patterson

John Henry Michael was born in 1867—most likely in Wilcox County, Alabama—the son of Bob and Martha, former slaves, who were owned by Mary Catherine Michael, a farmer who in the 1870 U.S. Census listed her birthplace as Wuertemberg, Germany.[1] As was customary for former slaves, Bob and Martha took the surname of their former mistress. Bob Michael was a carpenter who built Cameron Presbyterian Church in Wilcox County. He passed down his carpentry know-how to his sons John Henry and Lonnie. Bob and Martha Michael could not read and could barely write their own names, but made sacrifices to send their six children to school.

John Michael graduated from TUSKEGEE INSTITUTE in May 1892 with an elephantine certificate in teaching.[2] He pursued further studies at HAMPTON INSTITUTE, a school founded to educate former slaves and American Indians. It is believed that Michael's training in architecture commenced at Hampton Institute instead of Tuskegee Institute. During Hampton's early years, those who were accepted as students were selected for their potential to teach and lead others like themselves.

On June 22, 1895, John married Leila Bell Walker in the chapel designed by ROBERT ROBINSON TAYLOR on the campus of Tuskegee Institute. She was a native Alabamian and also a graduate of Tuskegee Institute who was a normal school teacher and fearless field organizer for the National Association for the Advancement of Colored People. They established their home in nearby Mount Meigs, Alabama. By the time their first two children were born—Carroll in 1896 and Leslie in 1898—the family was living in Greensboro, North Carolina, and John Michael was an instructor at Greensboro Normal and Industrial School in Greensboro, North Carolina (now NORTH CAROLINA AGRICULTURAL & TECHNICAL STATE UNIVERSITY). He then returned to his *alma mater* Tuskegee Institute as an instructor in the Mechanical Industries Department. The birth of their third and fourth children, Robert and Otis, took place in 1900 and 1903, respectively, while the family was living in Pine Bluff, Arkansas, and John Michael was serving as vice principal of Branch Normal College. Their last two children—Julian in 1905 and Norma in 1909—were born in Mount Meigs during the time their father was superintendent of industries at Mount Meigs Institute.

Michael resigned from Mount Meigs Institute in June 1909 and accepted a teaching position at Knoxville College as the foreman of the Carpentry Department and instructor in mechanical drawing and elementary woodworking. He designed and, using student labor, built the glass greenhouse; a 2-story red brick building of unknown use; and several faculty cottages. He designed and built his own home at 1657 Clinton Street, in a racially integrated Knoxville neighborhood. In addition, Michael designed a 2-story house on Brandau Hill, a neighborhood favored by Knoxville College faculty. In the winter of 1911, Dr. Matthew William Gilbert, pastor of Mount Zion Baptist Church, selected Michael "to design the first church parsonage, a grand 13 room manse"[3] next door to the historic church. Comparison of stylistic similarities suggests that Michael was also the architect for the Community Home and Apartments erected by Dr. J. H. Henderson, who also was affiliated with Mount Zion Baptist Church.

John Michael's most famous building was the Negro Building commissioned for the APPALACHIAN EXHIBITION held in Knoxville in 1910. The 3-story building was 60 × 60 feet and featured a 5,500-square-foot exhibition hall. The structure was intended as a tribute to Blacks in Knoxville, the state of Tennessee, and the entire Appalachian region. To ensure that the Negro Building would come into being, well-known members of Knoxville's Black community formed a Colored Board of Governance headed by Dr. Henry Morgan Green, a graduate of Knoxville College and a prominent physician. This board conceived of, presented to White exposition officials, and supported the construction of a Negro Building designed, supervised, and built by Blacks. It is unclear whether the choice of John Michael as the architect was made by Dr. Green acting alone or in consort with the board, or by J. R. Graf, a local White contractor who played a key behind-the-scenes role in choosing younger-generation architects for all exposition buildings.

For twenty consecutive summers, from 1917 until 1937, John Michael served as director of Winston-Salem Teachers College Summer School held at the Hill Street School in Asheville, North Carolina. He moved his family to Asheville in 1920 when he was appointed principal of Hill Street School. Hill Street School was operated under the auspices of the Winston-Salem Teachers College, with whom Michael had longstanding ties. The architect of the school—located at 125 Hill Street—is not known and there is inconclusive evidence to attribute the school to Michael. He was, however, the architect for the school's auditorium and gymnasium additions and the landscape designer who beautified the school grounds into some of the most colorful in Asheville.

Michael's tenure as principal and the laborious efforts it took to launch a public school system for Blacks in Asheville monopolized his time. The practice of architecture took a backseat to his educational pursuits. He designed the family homestead at 81 Hill Street, within walking distance of the school, complete with a regulation-sized outdoor tennis court to the rear of the house.[4] He also designed the house that was built next door at 83 Hill Street for teacher Mamie Howell as well as a row of six houses behind his own home on Hill Street (now Barfield Street), giving one to each of his children. He sized each house depending on how many were in each family.

Mount Zion Baptist Church, *Mount Zion Baptist Church Archives*

John Henry Michael was still the principal of the Hill Street School when he died on December 26, 1940.[5] He is buried in Asheville.

Notes
1. U.S. Census, 1870, "Mary Catherine Michael," Demopolis, Marengo County, Alabama, 1 June 1870, no. 8, p. 1.
2. Tuskegee Institute Diploma. "John Michael" May 1892. In the possession of granddaughter Helen Patterson, Reistertown, Maryland.
3. "Historical Highlights, the Mount Zion Baptist Church," Mount Zion Baptist Church, 137th Church Anniversary, n.p., p. 2. In the possession of Mount Zion Baptist Church.
4. Interview with Harvey Michael (grandson of John Michael), by the author, Silver Spring, Maryland, 12 October 2002.
5. "The Late Prof. J.H. Michael," *The Church and Southland Advocate*, December 1946, p. 1.

Bibliography
"Negro Building." *Knoxville Sentinel: Appalachian Exposition Extra Edition.* 6 September 1910, p. 45.

DRECK SPURLOCK WILSON

BUILDING LIST

Name	Address	City	State	Year	Comments
Appalachian Exposition Negro Bldg.	Chilhowee Park	Knoxville	TN	1910	Demolished
Henderson Community Home & Apts.		Knoxville	TN	1911	
Hill Street School Auditorium		Asheville	NC	1904	Addition
Hill Street School Gym		Asheville	NC	1904	Addition
Howell, Mamie	83 Hill St.	Asheville	NC	c1921	
Knoxville College Bldg.	Campus	Knoxville	TN		
Knoxville College Faculty Cottages	Campus	Knoxville	TN		
Knoxville College Greenhouse	Campus	Knoxville	TN		
Michael Family Compound	Hill St.	Asheville	NC		6 houses
Michael, John H.	81 Hill St.	Asheville	NC	1920	
Michael, John H.	1657 Clinton St.	Knoxville	TN	1909	
Mt. Zion Baptist Church Parsonage	324 Patton St.	Knoxville	TN	1911	Demolished

Elon Howard Mickels
(1929–1988)

Mickels Family

Elon Howard Mickels was born on December 31, 1929, in Gordon, Alabama, the son of Francis Mickels and Emma Lou Robinson Mickels. Elon attended Alabama Agricultural & Mechanical College in Huntsville, Alabama, from 1948 to 1952 and received a bachelor of science degree with a major in ornamental horticulture. He worked as site planner and superintendent of grounds at Alabama State Teachers College in Montgomery, Alabama, for seven months in 1952. On April 14, 1953, in Dothan, Alabama, Elon Mickels married Mildred Nichols, also a student at Alabama Agricultural & Mechanical College. They were the parents of three daughters: Cheryl, Crescenda, and Gina. After two years of service as an intelligence specialist in the U.S. Army, Mickels enrolled in Michigan State University at East Lansing, Michigan. He received a bachelor of science in landscape architecture and urban planning in March 1957. Concurrently, he worked for the State of Michigan as a supervisor of social welfare at the Boy's Vocational School from 1955 to 1957. In May 1957 Mickels became director of planning and urban renewal for the Village of Inkster, a suburb of Detroit with a sizeable African American population. He also started and operated his own firm, Inkster Landscape Architects & Site Planners. From September 1959 until June 1960, he studied urban planning at Wayne State University in Detroit.

In 1964 Mickels sought registration with the State of Michigan. He appeared before the Board of Landscape Architects in July and was approved based on education and experience. In October 1964 he received registration No. 123, becoming the first African American registered landscape architect in Michigan.[1] Later, he gained registration as a landscape architect in Ohio, Georgia, Louisiana, and Florida. In 1966 Mickels left his position with the Village of Inkster to devote himself full time to his renamed firm, Elon Mickels & Associates, with headquarters in Detroit. Mickels offered professional services in landscape architecture, site planning, housing, urban redevelopment, zoning, and community planning. He was granted registration as a professional community planner in the state of Michigan in 1969.

Mickels was a member of the American Society of Landscape Architects and associate member of the American Institute of Planners. He was a member and eventually an officer of the National Board of Landscape Architect Accreditation, and was an active contributor to the civic life of metropolitan Detroit. Mickels was a member of both the Building Committee and the Housing Corporation of his church, Saint Clement's Episcopal Church, and served one term as president of the *Xi Beta Sigma* chapter of *Phi Beta Sigma* Fraternity. He was also a member of the Jolly Old Timers Club, Young Mens Christian Association, and the Cotillion Club.

Elon Howard Mickels died of cancer on July 20, 1988.[2]

Forest Park and Playground
De Witt Sanford Dykes Jr.

Notes
1. State of Michigan, "Elon H. Mickels," Registration no. 123, Michigan Department of Agriculture, issued October 1964.
2. "Elon H. Mickels, Urban Planner," *Michigan Chronicle*, 20 August 1988, p. 3A.

Bibliography
"The Black Landscape Architect." *American Society of Landscape Architects* (April 1973): 13.
"Elon Howard Mickels." In *Personalities of the South*. Raleigh: American Biographical Institute, 1972.

DEWITT SANFORD DYKES JR.,
PROFESSOR OF HISTORY, OAKLAND UNIVERSITY

LANDSCAPE PROJECT LIST

Name	Address	City	State	Year	Comments
Forest Park & Playground	E. Canfield & Russell Sts.	Detroit	MI		
St. Martins-Griggs Park	8200 St. Martins N.	Detroit	MI		

Edward Charles Miller
(1904–1981)

Pratt Institute Archives

Edward Miller was born in Charleston, South Carolina, on January 1, 1904, the son of Presbyterian minister Lawrence Miller. Following the death of his father, he and his mother moved to College Park, a suburb of Atlanta, Georgia. Miller attended elementary school in College Park and Atlanta University High School from 1920 to 1923. He later enrolled at Lincoln University in Pennsylvania, where he received an undergraduate degree in 1927. Miller attended Pratt Institute between 1927 and 1930. An outstanding athlete, he was a member of the varsity soccer, basketball, and baseball teams. He transferred to New York University and received his bachelor of architecture degree in 1935.

George L. Washington, director of the DEPARTMENT OF MECHANICAL INDUSTRIES AT TUSKEGEE INSTITUTE, convinced Edward Miller to join his staff in 1940. Miller began his professional career there as an architect and instructor and became a registered architect in the state of Alabama on December 2, 1941.[1]

Miller also took charge of the Housing Program at Tuskegee Institute in 1941 and eventually replaced JOHN AUSTIN WELCH as campus architect. While at Tuskegee Institute, Miller designed several building additions, the entrance gates, and additions to Hangars No. 1 and No. 2 at Moton Airfield, owned by Tuskegee Institute. George L. Washington considered Miller an excellent architect and often consulted with him during the construction of Moton Airfield. While at Tuskegee Institute, Miller also designed several school buildings and Greenwood Missionary Baptist Church. Shortly thereafter he moved back to Atlanta.

Upon returning to Atlanta, Miller operated his own architectural firm for several years. He designed several buildings for Morehouse College and the Christian Education Building for Ebenezer Baptist Church.

His wife, Nina King, owned a real estate business in Atlanta, Georgia. The couple had two children.

From 1958 to 1959, Miller was in a partnership known as Miller & Allain. Miller joined the North Georgia chapter of the American Institute of Architects in 1959. In 1967 Miller & Allain was dissolved and Miller went back to a solo practice. That same year, Atlanta Mayor Ivan Allen appointed Miller to the Building Code Advisory Board. Several years later, he was a member of the committee charged with historic preservation of the Reverend Martin Luther King Jr. birth home.

Edward Miller died at the age of seventy-seven on February 12, 1981, in Atlanta, Georgia, and was interred at South View Cemetery.[2] Edward Miller encouraged young African Americans to explore new professions that were previously closed to them and used his influence to help African American architects gain positions in the field. George L. Washington later remarked that Miller was always "ready and willing to serve."[3]

Notes

1. State Board for Registration of Architects, "Edward C. Miller," Alabama, no. 2/3, issued 2 December 1941.
2. "Edward Miller Dies; Rites Held Saturday," *Atlanta Daily News,* 15 February 1981, p. 1.
3. George L. Washington, "The History of Military and Civilian Pilot Training of Negroes at Tuskegee Alabama, 1939–45," photocopy held by Southeast Regional Office, National Park Service, Atlanta, Georgia.

Bibliography

American Institute of Architects. *American Architects Directory,* 3rd ed. New York: R. R. Bower Company, 1970.

Atlanta University Bulletin. Atlanta: Atlanta University, 1918 to 1928. Archives special collections, Woodruff Library, Atlanta University Center.

Bradley, James P. *The Clark College Legacy, An Interpretive History of Relevant Education, 1869–1975.* Atlanta: Clark College 1977.

CHRISTINE TREBELLAS,
ARCHITECTURAL HISTORIAN,
U.S. DEPARTMENT OF INTERIOR,
NATIONAL PARK SERVICE, ATLANTA, GEORGIA

BUILDING LIST

Name	Address	City	State	Year	Comments
Atlanta Life Insurance Co.	953 King Jr. Dr., NW	Atlanta	GA	1974	
Clark College McPheeters-Dennis Hall	Campus	Atlanta	GA	1969	Assoc. architect
Ebenezer Baptist Church Christian Education Bldg.	407 Auburn Ave.	Atlanta	GA	1956	
Greenwood Missionary Baptist Church	Washington Ave.	Tuskegee	AL		
King, Martin Jr.	501 Auburn Ave.	Atlanta	GA	1974	Restoration
Morehouse College Archer Bldg.	Campus	Atlanta	GA	1958	
Morehouse College Bennett Dormitory	Campus	Atlanta	GA	1962	
Morehouse College Chemistry Bldg.	Campus	Atlanta	GA	1953	
Morehouse College Danforth Chapel	Campus	Atlanta	GA	1955	
Price High School Gym Middle School	1670 Bickers Ave.	Atlanta	GA	1970	Assoc. architect
Tuskegee Institute Andrews Hospital	Campus	Tuskegee	AL		Addition
Tuskegee Institute Harvey Hall	Campus	Tuskegee	AL		
Tuskegee Institute Moton Airfield Cadet Classroom		Tuskegee	AL	1942	Demolished
Tuskegee Institute Moton Airfield Entrance Gate		Tuskegee	AL	1943	Demolished
Tuskegee Institute Moton Airfield Hangar No. 1		Tuskegee	AL	1942	Demolished
Tuskegee Institute Moton Airfield Hangar No. 2		Tuskegee	AL	1942	Demolished
Tuskegee Institute Moton Airfield Warehouse		Tuskegee	AL	1943	Demolished

John Aycocks Moore
(1888–1939)

Courtesy of New Hanover County Public Library

John A. Moore was born in 1888 at Rock Hill, North Carolina, a small Black settlement in New Hanover County, located near the Cape Fear River about six miles from downtown Wilmington. The settlement got its name from a former rice plantation named Rock Hill. Moore's father, Joshua, was listed as a farm laborer in the 1880 U.S. Census, as were most of the African Americans in the area. His mother, Sylvia Aycocks Moore, was listed as a homemaker.[1]

To date no information has been found as to how John Moore escaped the life of the son of a tenant farmer to become an architect or where he received his education. He was the only one of his siblings to acquire an education higher than that provided by a small county school. It is possible that his parents sent him to the city of Wilmington, where the schools were better. The city had two very good public schools for African Americans: Peabody Graded School and Williston Industrial School. There was also a good private school, Gregory Normal School, which had been attended by ROBERT ROBINSON TAYLOR, who became a well-known architect.

By 1911 Moore was in Washington, D.C., where he worked for one year as a draftsman for the Supervising Architect's Office, U.S. Treasury Department. His employment there coincided with the years that HOWARD DILWORTH WOODSON and WILLIAM WILSON COOKE were in the Supervising Architect's Office. Beginning in 1912, Moore listed himself as an "architect" in *Boyd's Directory of the District of Columbia*.[2]

He apparently enjoyed marginal business success, because he was able to maintain his private practice until 1917. Moore designed a laundry and model home, and constructed several complicated carpentry projects for the National Training School for Women and Girls. The boarding school was founded in 1909 in Lincoln Heights, Maryland, by headmistress Nannie Helen Burroughs under the auspices of the National Baptist Convention. She referred to the school as the 3B's "Bible, Bath, and Broom."[3] The school offered classes in Bible study, interior decoration, weaving, Black history, gardening, housekeeping, and physical education. Moore also designed a "Jubilee Arch" (1915) for the school to memorialize the passing of fifty years after the assassination of the "Great Emancipator" Abraham Lincoln.

Don Speed Smith Goodloe, the first principal of the Maryland Normal and Industrial School (now Bowie State University), commissioned Moore to design a single-family house (1915) close to the school. Goodloe was a graduate of Knoxville College in Tennessee, which was the *alma mater* of architects JOHN HENRY MICHAEL and WILLIAM THOMAS JONES. He was also a former teacher-principal at Manassas Industrial School in Virginia, which was the *alma mater* of architect WILLIAM JEFFERSON DECATUR. Knowing Black architects and holding the high-profile position of principal of the only Black vocational school supported by the state of Maryland, he no doubt felt an obligation to his race to commission a Black architect

Dr Frank Avant House and Office, *Courtesy of New Hanover County Public Library*

to design his personal residence. The house and six-bay storage shed still exist northwest of the campus. A 2,000-gallon water tower that provided potable water has been demolished.

On May 16, 1918, from Washington, D.C., Moore enlisted in the U.S. Army. He was a sergeant first class with the 28th Construction Company Air Services Aeronautics stationed at Langley Field in Virginia. His honorable discharge states that he was thirty years of age when he joined and his occupation was a carpenter. He left the service in April 1919 and returned to Washington D.C.[4]

Beginning in 1918 and running through 1921—the last year he was listed—Moore dropped his listing in *Boyd's Directory* as an architect and instead listed himself as a carpenter under his company's name, J. A. Moore & Co.

On April 15, 1920, at age thirty-two, John Moore married twenty-one-year-old Susan Brown. They were married by a Catholic priest at her parents' home in Wilmington. Her father, William A. Brown, was the proprietor of the Plaza, a popular restaurant catering to African Americans. It was probably marriage that brought Moore back to Wilmington. Shortly after the wedding, he left Washington, D.C., and they moved in with his in-laws. The next year the newlyweds moved to 19 South 12th Street, where Moore lived until his death.

From 1922 through 1924, John Moore is listed as an architect in the *Wilmington, North Carolina City Directory*. From 1926 until 1938, he is listed as a carpenter. When a son, John Houston Moore, was born in 1927, his birth certificate listed his father as a contractor. Listed variously as an architect, contractor, and carpenter, Moore undoubtedly worked on many buildings during the seventeen years he lived in Wilmington. Working with his brother Joshua, who was also a carpenter, he is credited with designing and building Dr. Frank W. Avant's house. Built in 1929 and located at 813 Red Cross Street, the 2-story brick Colonial Revival–style house matched the prominent African American physician. A 1-story office was constructed with similar brick next door. According to oral family history, the Moore brothers were responsible for the design and construction of many houses in Wilmington's Forest Hills neighborhood. Perhaps the Great Depression had an impact on Moore's practice, because he is listed in city directories as a carpenter during the 1930s. In the *1938 Wilmington City Directory*, he is listed as a recreation worker at the Wilmington–New Hanover County Recreation Office.

It may be that poor health was the reason that Moore took an indoor job at the County Recreation Office, because he died the next year. A newspaper obituary stated that John Aycocks Moore died on October 31, 1939, in the William Jennings Bryan Dorn Veterans Hospital at Columbia, South Carolina. His funeral was held at Gregory Congregational Church. He was buried in the Moore family plot in the cemetery at Rock Hill.

JOHN AYCOCKS MOORE

Notes

1. US Fifteenth Census, New Hanover County, Wilmington Township, North Carolina, 1880, Cape Fear Township, p. 184B.
2. As listed in Pam Scott's "A Directory of District of Columbia Architects, 1822–1960," D.C.: n.p., p. 199.
3. "Discovering Hidden Washington, A Journey Through the Alley Communities of the Nation's Capital," http:/loc.gov/loc/kids.
4. "Moore Rights [sic]," *Wilmington News,* 1 November 1939, n.p.

Bibliography

"Dr. Frank Avant House and Office," Historic Buildings Collection, New Hanover County Public Library, Wilmington, North Carolina.

"John Aycocks Moore, Honorable Discharge from the U.S. Army," 22 April 1927, Book No. 1, p. 93. New Hanover County, Register of Deeds Office, Wilmington, North Carolina, 1919.

Moore Family File, William M. Reaves Collection, New Hanover County Public Library, Wilmington, North Carolina.

BEVERLY TETTERTON,
SPECIAL COLLECTIONS LIBRARIAN,
NEW HANOVER COUNTY PUBLIC LIBRARY

BUILDING LIST

Name	Address	City	State	Year	Comments
Avant, Dr. Frank W.	813 Red Cross St.	Wilmington	NC	1929	
Goodloe, Don S.	13809 Jericho Park Rd.	Bowie	MD	1915	
National Training School for Women and Girls Laundry	50th & Grant Sts., NE	Washington	DC	1917	
National Training School for Women and Girls Model House	50th & Grant Sts., NE	Washington	DC	1917	
National Training School for Women and Girls Jubilee Arch	50th & Grant Sts., NE	Washington	DC	1915	Demolished

William Henry Moses Jr.
(1901–1991)

Hampton University Archives and Museum Collection

William Moses Jr. was born on August 20, 1901, in Cumberland County, Virginia, one of six children of William Moses Sr. and Julia Trent Moses. His father, a Baptist minister, moved the family many times as he was growing up: to Staunton, Virginia, to Washington, D.C., to Newberry, South Carolina, to Knoxville, Tennessee, to Seguin, Texas, to New York City, and to Philadelphia, Pennsylvania. His mother was a homemaker who concentrated on raising six children.

William Moses Jr. won an architectural drawing award his senior year at Central High School in Philadelphia. He graduated in 1922 and enrolled that fall at Pennsylvania State University. A lack of money forced him to withdraw after two years. He spent the next seven years in New York City working as a draftsman for VERTNER WOODSON TANDY, as a field superintendent for Landscape Engineers Company, as a draftsman for architect Louis E. Jallade, and finally as a freelance draftsman. Moses returned to Penn State in 1931 and received his bachelor of science degree in architecture in 1933. He worked the next year as a draftsman on "Columbia University Housing Studies," a Public Works Administration project in New York City.

In 1934 Moses joined the faculty at HAMPTON INSTITUTE to teach architectural drafting. With his degree from Penn State he was the first formally educated African American architect to join the faculty. He soon became the driving force behind the development of a professional curriculum in architecture.

On August 15, 1935, William Moses Jr. married Julia Anne Mason, a native of Petersburg, Virginia, and a graduate of Virginia State College. At the time they met, she was living in Newport News, Virginia, with her sister and teaching elementary school students in the Newport News Public Schools. The school system at that time would not hire married females, so the marriage was kept a secret. Julia Moses resigned her teaching position in May 1937. A "second wedding" was held in the Hampton Institute Chapel later that month. The marriage produced two children.

William Moses Jr. had an abiding interest in housing and designed Dixie Cottage, on the Hampton Institute campus. Between 1936 and 1939, he designed residences, schools, and commercial building such as renovations to classroom buildings at the Bricks Rural Life School (1937) in Enfield, North Carolina, and the Peoples Building and Loan Association Bank (1937) and the Colonial Tavern (1938), both in Hampton, Virginia.

In 1938 Moses wrote to the state of Virginia requesting the rules for the design competition to select Virginia's exhibit at the upcoming New York World's Fair. He received the rules just five days before the competition submission deadline. For the next five days and nights he developed his design and submitted it just at the deadline. On November 17, 1938, it was announced that William Moses' photo *montage* and Williamsburg scale model had won. However, when it was discovered that Moses was a Negro, Virginia Art Commission officials turned to Leslie Cheek Jr., a White professor from the College of William of Mary, to design a more "appropriate state entry."[1] Moses was given the $350 prize, but his winning design was discarded.

In 1939 Moses was awarded a General Education Board Fellowship for one semester of advanced study at New York University School of Architecture followed by four months of travel and investigation of public housing in the South.

For the next thirty-five years Moses had dual careers as an educator and practicing architect. His efforts at Hampton Institute led to the initiation of a four-year curriculum in architectural design, a five-year curriculum in architecture, and a five-year curriculum in building construction and engineering. William Moses was appointed acting chairman of the program in 1945 and served as chairman from 1947 to 1965. He saw the architecture program that he had initiated and guided for many years achieve accreditation in 1969.

Although he never achieved registration as an architect, Moses enjoyed a prolific career as an architect. In 1942 he collaborated with Benson L. Dutton and CHARLES THADDEUS RUSSELL, a collaboration that lasted decades. Dutton was a Black civil engineer and fellow faculty member at Hampton Institute. The Moses-Dutton-Russell collaboration produced the Whittaker Memorial Hospital (1942), the Madeline Foreman residence (1943), the Uganda Ballroom (1943), the Butler Oak Park War Housing (1944), the Earl Wilson residence (1944), the Dr. John A. Singleton residence (1945), the First Baptist Church Home for the Aged (1948), and the Robert Jones residence (1949). Moses was a versatile designer who was skilled at building design, landscape design, and interior design. He designed the Hampton Institute exhibit at the American Negro Exposition held in Chicago in 1940 and the book plates and pictorial maps for *The Negro in Virginia*.[2]

In 1954 Moses was associate architect to HILYARD ROBERT ROBINSON on Harkness Hall Men's Dormitory on the Hampton Institute campus. In 1956 in addition to his teaching duties he became campus architect responsible for coordinating the Hampton Institute Building Program.

Moses retired from full-time teaching at the end of the 1967 academic year, but continued as an adjunct professor until 1971. Beginning in 1968, he wrote a weekly newspaper column under the byline "A Dark Point of View," which appeared in *The New Observer* and *The Carolinian*. He contributed an essay in *Newsweek*'s "My Turn" about the startling changes he

Whittaker Memorial Hospital, *Gill Commercial Photography*

had observed in White Americans' attitudes about Black Americans.³ Moses was an active member of the NATIONAL TECHNICAL ASSOCIATION; the National Builders Association; the Elks Miszpah Lodge in Phoebus, Virginia; and the *Omega Psi Phi* Fraternity, and was president of the Hampton chapter of the National Association for the Advancement of Colored People.

The early setback of the World's Fair entry did not stop Moses from achieving a distinguished career in education and architecture. He was listed in the *Dictionary of International Biography*, *Who's Who in the South and Southwest*, and *Personalities of the South*.⁴ He received a Distinguished Alumni Award from Pennsylvania State University in 1980. The citation read, "To William H. Moses, architect and teacher, for overcoming obstacles to achieve distinction in two professions, for opening doors to opportunity for countless young people, and for promoting social change for the good of all."³

William Moses, best known as the father of the program in architecture at Hampton Institute, died on October 19, 1991, at age ninety. He is buried in the historic Hampton University Cemetery.

Notes

1. Mentor A. Howe, "Come to the Fair," *Phylon* 1 (Fourth Quarter, 1940): 314.
2. *The Negro in Virginia* (Historical Guide Series, Federal Writer's Project) (Richmond: Hastings House, 1940).
3. "Pennsylvania State University Program," Distinguished Alumni Award, "William H. Moses," 1980.

Bibliography

"Negro Winner of the Art Award." *The Southern Workman*. (November 1938): 18.
Potterfield, Thomas, Jr. "Charles T. Russell, Virginia's Pioneer African-American Architect, 1875–1953." In the possession of Thomas Tyler Potterfield, Richmond, Virginia.

JOHN H. SPENCER, FAIA, ASLA,
FORMER CHAIRPERSON DEPARTMENT
OF ARCHITECTURE, HAMPTON UNIVERSITY
THE LIVAS GROUP
NORFOLK, VIRGINIA

BUILDING LIST

Name	Address	City	State	Year	Comments
American Negro Exposition		Chicago	IL	1940	Hampton Institute exhibit
Blue, Alllie Congregational	152 Rip Rap Rd.	Hampton	VA		Charles Russell, assoc. architect
Bricks Rural Life School		Enfield	NC	1937	Alterations
Bridges, James L.	509 Vaughn Ave.			1959	Alterations
Burke, Dr.	707 Wood St.	Norfolk	VA	1946	Addition
Butler Oak Park War Housing		Hampton	VA	1944	Plans only
Carter, W. H., Jr.		Hampton	VA		Addition
Chicago Tribune House Competition		Chicago	IL	1945	Single-family house
Colonial Tavern		Hampton	VA	1938	
Cooper, Lajoie	Gayle St.	Hampton	VA	1955	
Federated Colored Women's Club		Portsmouth	VA		Demonstration model home
First Baptist Church Home for the Aged	Butte St.	Norfolk	VA	1948	Charles Russell, assoc. architect
Foreman, Madeline	624 25th St.	Newport News	VA	1943	now USO Bldg.
Frazier, Dr. Maurice	303 Woodland Rd.	Hampton	VA	1956	
Hampton Institute Dixie Cottage	Campus	Hampton	VA	1936	
Hampton Institute Harkness Hall Men's Dormitory	Campus	Hampton	VA	1954	Assoc. architect
Hampton Institute Holley Tree Inn & Monestery	Campus	Hampton	VA	1964	Alterations
Hampton Institute Laundry & Dry Cleaning Plant	Campus	Hampton	VA	1951	
Hampton Institute Long Range Plan		Hampton	VA	1963	
Hampton Institute President's Residence	Campus	Hampton	VA		Alterations
Hampton Institute Tuskegee Memorial Sun Dial	Outside Harkness Dorm.	Hampton	VA	1957	
Harris, Lemuel	S. Stewart St.	Hampton	VA		
Hayes, Ernest H.	Locust St.	Hampton	VA	1939	
Horne, Dr. W. L.		Weldon	NC	1937	
Johnson Office Bldg. & Apts.	202 Walnut St.	Covington	VA	1957	
Jones, Edward N.	Langley Field Rd.	Hampton	VA	1939	
Jones, Robert	21st St.	Newport News	VA	1949	Charles Russell, assoc. architect

WILLIAM HENRY MOSES JR.

BUILDING LIST *(continued)*

Name	Address	City	State	Year	Comments
Lewis Clinic	Church & Iowa Sts.	Uniontown	PA		Plans only
McAlister, Dr. H. A.		Hampton	VA	1941	Plans only
Miller, Alfred Z.	826 4th St.	Newport News	VA		Plans only
Patterson Laundry Bldg.	615–617 Hampton Ave.	Newport News	VA	1951	
Peoples Building & Loan Association Bank		Hampton	VA	1937	
Progressive Architecture Rich Competition				1946	4-family dwelling
Reynolds, T. A.	Blunt Point Rd.	Warrick	VA	1953	Alterations
Robbins, Dr. C. A.	Rome St.	Petersburg	VA	1949	Charles Russell, assoc. architect
Rooks, Rev. Shelby		Yorktown	VA	1948	Addition
Scott, Dr. A. J.		Hampton	VA	1941	Alterations
Scott, Dr. Anderson T.	226 W. Queen St.	Hampton	VA	1950	Alterations
Singleton, Dr. John A.	163 South Rd.	Jamaica	NY	1945	Addition
Uganda Ballroom		Newport News	VA	1943	Charles Russell, assoc. architect
Virginia Pavilion Competition	Fairgrounds	Queens	NY	1938	New York World's Fair exhibit
Virginia School for Colored Deaf & Blind	700 Shell Rd.	Hampton	VA	1945	Charles Russell, assoc. architect
Watts, Dr. Irvin		Portsmouth	VA	1953	
White, George L.	Langley Field Rd.	Hampton	VA	1948	Plans only
Whittaker Memorial Hospital	28th St. & Orcutt Ave.	Newport News	VA	1942	Now Newport News General Hospital
Williams, L. Anthony	239 W. Queen St.	Hampton	VA		Charles Russell, assoc. architect
Williams, Paul	E. Queen St.	Hampton	VA		
Wilson, Earl		Hampton	VA	1944	Plans only
Wren, Fred D.		Smithfield	VA	1946	

National Technical Association
(1925)

The National Technical Association has withstood the test of time since its inception in 1925 to the present. The National Technical Association was conceived when Samuel R. Cheevers, a civil engineer renting a room at the Wabash Avenue Young Mens Christian Association (YMCA) in Chicago, conferred with George Arthur, branch secretary at the YMCA, about the advisability of calling together all the "colored men" in the city trained by technical schools.[1] As a result, nine men met for dinner at the YMCA on November 12, 1925, and discussed forming an organization of technical men that would be national in scope.

Those present at the meeting included Samuel R. Cheevers, junior engineer, Illinois Highway Department; F. C. Downs, instructor, Department of Industrial Arts, Chicago Public Schools; CHARLES SUMNER DUKE, architectural engineer; W. I. Gough, draftsman, Pullman Car Company; Oscar Randall, assistant engineer, Chicago Suburban Sanitary District; Howard D. Shaw, chief electrician, Pullman Car Company; WILLIAM FERGUSON THORNTON, junior engineer, Illinois Highway Department; August D. Watson, electrician, Pullman Car Company; and A. T. Weathers, senior chemist, Chicago Suburban Sanitary District. The purpose of the meeting was to discuss the formation of a permanent organization that would foster exchanges of information and ideas among African Americans in technologic fields including architecture, engineering, and applied sciences.

A second meeting was held one week later. Joining the original nine members were E. M. Akin, American Maze Company; ROBERT LESTER BUFFINS, architect; Dr. E. M. A. Chandler, research chemist, Abbott Laboratories; L. A. Hall, consulting chemist; Henry R. Lewis, electrical engineering draftsman, Commonwealth Edison Company; Thomas B. Mayo, chief chemist, Heller & Company; and C. W. Pierce, physics teacher, Wendell Phillips High School.

On December 10, 1925, a draft of the constitution was adopted, a committee was appointed to prepare the bylaws, and the first election of officers was held. Charles Duke was elected president; A. T. Weathers, vice president; F. C. Downs, secretary; and August D. Watson, treasurer. On January 14, 1926, the constitution was adopted. The National Technical Association was incorporated as a domestic nonprofit corporation in the state of Illinois, August 26, 1926.

The foreword from the *First Annual Report* read,

> At the present time, economic considerations seem to be uppermost in the minds of the ruling classes of the world. Economic advantage is won and maintained through the operation of efficient organization and mass action. The physical resources of the entire world are divided-up and parceled-out geographically to the more favored groups of humanity. If through force of circumstance a group must maintain its racial identity, it will be only through effective mass organization directed by the most efficient apostles of applied science: that group will be able to maintain its place in the sun. The other alternative is commercial and economic servitude. In a society where he happens to constitute the minority group, the person of color will be able to impress himself favorably upon that society only through the reaction of the brains and character of its men of the applied sciences.
>
> In recognition of the foregoing statements, the National Technical Association is presenting its First Annual Report merely as a gesture in the hope that it will provoke consideration of these things on the part of the thinking member of the darker races.[2]

In 1928 delegates from the Chicago chapter; the American Negro Technical Society in Dayton, Ohio;

NATIONAL TECHNICAL ASSOCIATION

Members attending National Technical Association Convention, *Moorland-Spingarn Research Center*

and Howard University Engineering Society met in Chicago to organize a national body of Black technicians. Delegates elected officers, adopted a constitution, and voted to officially name the national organization the "National Technical Association."

Subsequently, the first National Technical Association convention was held at the Appomattox Club in Chicago in 1929.[3] Charles Sumner Duke was elected national president. The convention lasted three days, which included business sessions, inspection trips of engineering interest, a movie, and closing banquet. The second convention, in 1930, held in Dayton, Ohio, included presentations of technical papers, business sessions, and social activities. In 1931 the third annual convention was held in Washington, D.C., where HOWARD DILWORTH WOODSON was the keynote speaker. In addition to the presentation of technical papers and business sessions, a public forum was convened at the historic Metropolitan African Methodist Episcopal Church.

Since that first convention, there have been seventy-two consecutive conventions held in twenty-six cities and one foreign country. Initially, the convention site was chosen according to the chronologic date that the chapter joined the National Technical Association, and in the formative years conventions often convened at historically Black colleges and universities. In later years conventions were held in the resident city of the current president.

Women were minor participants in the early years of the National Technical Association. The wives of National Technical Association members met and formed the Ladies Auxiliary in 1940 at the Chicago annual convention. Even though the auxiliary was socially oriented, their mission was to increase National Technical Association membership. After a name change to the National Women's Auxiliary in 1958, the group became more involved with mainstream National Technical Association activities. For their dedication, the organization was officially accepted as the National Technical Association Auxiliary (men included) by the parent body August 3, 1969, at the 41st National Technical Association convention, held in Washington, D.C. Lyla M. Washington was the founding president.

During the intervening years, the National Technical Association has endeavored to build and maintain its image as a professional and respected technical association. For over seventy-five years the National Technical Association has persevered, due to the dedicated leadership of its national presidents:

CHARLES S. DUKE (1929–34)
James A. Parsons (1935–36)
CORNELIUS LANGSTON HENDERSON SR. (1937–38)
Lewis K. Downing (1938–39)
Paul E. Johnson (1939–40)
RICHARD CASSIUS WHITE (1940–41)
JOHN ANDERSON LANKFORD (1941–42)

James A. Dunn (1942–43)
Damely E. Howard (1943–45)
WILLIAM FERGUSON THORNTON (1945–46)
William C. Holly (1947–48)
DONALD FRANK WHITE (1949–50)
CALVIN LUNSFORD MCKISSACK (1951–52)
James C. Evans (1953–54)
Heilbron B. Love (1954–55)
James C. Evans (1956–57)
HENRY LEWIS LIVAS (1958–59)
David R. Byrd (1960–61)
James A. Davis (1962–64)
Samuel R. Cheevers (1965–66)
George F. Washington (1967–68)
Woodrow B. Dolphin (1969–71)
Edward W. Taylor (1972–74)
Louis Stevenson (1974–75)
James A. Davis (1975–76)
Julian M. Earls (1976–77)
Leonard E. Thomas (1977–79)
Lester Clemons Jr. (1979–80)
Eugene M. Bentley III (1980–81)
Willard O. Williamson (1981–82)
Clyde Foster (1982–83)
James J. Jennings (1983–84)
Valerie L. Thomas (1984–85)
Gilbert A. Haynes (1985–86)
Lawrence P. King (1986–87)
Kevin Greenbaugh (1987–88)
Patricia Richardson (1988–89)
Kathye E. Lewis (1989–91)
Carrington H. Stewart (1991–93)
Jimmy King (1993–95)
Michael A. Chapman (1995–97)
Garry A. Harris (1997–2000)
Katherine W. Coleman (2000–01)

National Technical Association members have continually built on the goals and objectives established by the nine founders. This has been accomplished through the growth of the association, which now includes sixty chapters and more than thirty student chapters; the National Technical Association Auxiliary; the Career Awareness Program, which provides motivation for minority students in science and technology; the 3-T Mentor Program—technicians who mentor teachers who mentor students; the National Technical Association annual national convention; local chapter activities during which professional members serve as role models, guest speakers, and panelists at high school and college Career Day programs; the National Technical Association Resource Center, which includes videotapes, books, and instructional materials; the National Technical Association Speakers Bureau, a cadre of one hundred volunteer speakers; and National Technical Association Board Luncheons hosted by a corporation in the city where quarterly board of directors meetings are held.

The National Technical Association nationally presents Awards for Excellence to National Technical Association members, community leaders, and students; the Top Women in Science and Technology Award; the Crystal Image Award for the Technical Achiever of the Year, Engineer of the Year, Scientist of the Year, Computer Engineer of the Year, Outstanding Academic Support Achievement of the Year, Science Educator of the Year, and Engineering School of the Year; and the Corporate-Government-Institution Technical Excellence Award of the Year. The National Technical Association sponsors a Charles S. Duke Distinguished Lecture Series and Regional Science/Technology Symposia. It also publishes quarterly the *Journal of the NTA*, and a "Membership Newsletter." In addition, the National Technical Association established its archives at the Moorland-Spingarn Research Center to preserve its illustrious history.

The National Technical Association has received a transfusion of new members who have accepted the gauntlet and are eager to maintain the continuity and vision of the association. Their presence has resulted in renewed efforts to break down barriers of race, creed, sex, and religion that stand in the way of achievement in the technical professions. They carry on the tradition of monitoring new developments in science and technology to ensure that the impact on the quality of life and on the African American community is positive. The National Technical Association's challenge is to ensure that African American males, females, and youth, in particular, will be skilled in the sciences and technologies that are required of the workforce in the new millennium.

Notes
1. Jeane Elliot, "The National Technical Association: An Account of Its Activities" master's thesis, Howard University, 1958, p. 31.
2. National Technical Association (NTA), *Annual Report* (Chicago: NTA, 1927), p. 17.
3. "Technicians Hold First Convention," *Chicago Defender*, 24 August 1929, p. 1.

JOHN H. THOMPSON,
NATIONAL TECHNICAL ASSOCIATION
HISTORICAL PUBLICIST
BALTIMORE, MARYLAND

John Clavon Norman Sr.
(1892–1967)

John C. Norman Sr. was born in Bloomfield, New Jersey, on October 23, 1892. His parents were Sandy and Sally Hunt Norman. Both parents died during his early adolescence and he and his sister were raised by their grandmother, Lucy Hunt, in Oxford, North Carolina. He attended the Mary Potter and San Augustine Schools and was inspired to become an architect by his principal, Lucy Craft Laney, who would later mold the educational career of architect-to-be JOHN BUNYON HOLLOWAY.

Norman attended NORTH CAROLINA AGRICULTURAL & TECHNICAL STATE INSTITUTE in Greensboro, financially aided by his sister. He subsequently enlisted with the U.S. Army Cavalry Engineers during World War I and trained at Fort Meade, Maryland, and Camp Chillicothe, Ohio, before being shipped to France along with the Rainbow Division commanded by General John "Black Jack" Pershing. In 1918 Norman was mustered out as a first lieutenant.

Norman completed postgraduate studies in architecture and structural engineering at Carnegie Technical Institute (now Carnegie-Mellon University) in Pittsburgh, Pennsylvania, without earning a degree. In 1919 he moved to the state capital in Charleston, West Virginia, to begin what was to become a life's work in architecture. He took up bachelor quarters at a local lodging house, ate meals at Mrs. Buster's family restaurant, and opened his office on the second floor of the Knights of Pythias building on the corner of Washington and Dickinson Streets. In 1919 he designed and supervised construction of the Ferguson Business Complex, which consisted of a hotel, cinema, pharmacy, and several offices along East Washington Street.

In 1922 John Clavon Norman became the seventh licensed architect in West Virginia—Black or White—which had begun licensing architects only a year earlier. He maintained Certificate No. 7 throughout his forty-eight-year career.[1]

Charleston, including Kanawha County and central West Virginia, experienced a post–World War I economic expansion fueled by returning veterans. This enabled Norman to expand his practice. After establishing a steady stream of revenue, John courted Ruth Lydia Stephenson, a young English teacher, who was Charleston's first graduate of Howard University in 1919. John and Ruth were married in June 1924, at the First Baptist Church by Dr. Mordecai Wyatt Johnson, who later was appointed the first African American president of Howard University. After their honeymoon in Niagra Falls the couple returned to a new home John designed for his bride at 1118 2nd Avenue in West Charleston. John C. and Ruth Norman had one child, John Jr., born on May 11, 1929.

In 1925 John Norman was recruited by Dr. John W. Davis and Dr. Harrison Farrell, then president and dean of West Virginia State College, respectively, to establish a department of architecture and engineering. He did this while establishing a satellite office of his own on campus in the Technical Building. Norman designed and supervised the construction of twelve faculty houses. The houses, which were built by Nabigaul & Leech of Huntington, West Virginia, are classics of the period. They were built on acreage that was formerly an apple orchard. Each has its own distinctive English Tudor style individuality of form that came to represent Norman's residential signature. The sunlight-filled houses feature intricate brick detailing; native stone foundations; and the finest of cedar, walnut, mahogany, and cherry hardwoods handcrafted into unique domestic gems that have been enjoyed by faculty family members for seven decades and counting.

Norman also designed residences in exclusive White neighborhoods around Elizabeth and Quarrier Streets adjacent to the State Capitol, including a home for Dr. and Mrs. Gamble and a carriage house for their daughter, Katherine. He designed similar houses in the fashionable South Hills neighborhood, including houses for Dr. Ira J. K. Wells, superintendent of Charleston Public Schools; W. W. Saunders, deputy superintendent of schools; and for Saunders's closest friend, Dr. Joseph R. Jones Sr., occupied to this day by Jones' widow and son. All of these houses embody Norman's aesthetics of view, economy of space, elegance of function, and efficiency of use. Each house was meticulously constructed by skilled artisans who were known for their craftsmanship and attention to detail.

Norman's residences were metaphors for his attention to detail. His commercial buildings likewise were metaphors for his belief in minimalism, permanence, and timelessness. His commercial buildings reflect his educational background in structural engineering. He had a preference for reinforced concrete, cantilevered steel, and expansive glass fenestration. Norman's sturdy design principles can be seen in the Washington Manor Complex along the the Elk River, just before it enters the Kanawha River; Staats Hospital Complex above West Washington Street on the west side of the Elk River; Faulkner Hardware Store and Pfizer Chemical Store, also on West Washington Street; Frankel's Men's Apparel Store on Virginia Street in downtown Charleston; and an office complex for Don Catalina Sr., father of the future mayor, at the corner of Capitol and Donnelly Streets.

As Norman's practice grew, so did his collaborations with Kuhn Construction Company; Pfaff & Smith Concrete; Goldfarb Electrical Contractors; Alfred Sayer Carpenters; Swacker Plumbing; Homer Davis Decorators; Ted Gallion Plastering; Martens & Associates, Architects; and Louis Smoot Contracting. Norman's reputation for precise, economic, and utilitarian buildings led to a succession of commissions for the Community Center at Wilson Place, Cabell Junior High School and the Municipal Auditorium on East Virginia Street, and the Greenbriar Theater on Lee Street.

At the same time, within what was becoming "the greater Charleston area," Norman began a commuting practice to near and far communities of Sissonville, Cedar Grove, Cabin Creek, Saint Albans, Malden (birthplace of Booker T. Washington), Montgomery, Marmet, Beckley, Huntington, Gauley Bridge, Logan, London, Ronceverte, New River Gorge, Parkersburg, Clarksburg, Whitesville, and Summersville, all in West Virginia; and Ashland, Kentucky; and Xenia, Ohio.

Some of the more memorable designs were the hotel, cinema, and business complex for Sheriff Connelly at Gauley Bridge, made of reinforced concrete cantilevered over the Kanawha River; the handsome native stone winter home on the banks of the Kanawha River for Mr. and Mrs. Shanklin, owners of the Greenbriar Theater; and Brown Payne Business Complex in Beckley. Many of Norman's buildings, now classified as Art Deco, were *avant garde* for their time. Over four decades he designed and supervised construction for more than five hundred buildings.

Norman's penchant for accuracy and promptness in business matters qualified several of his female secretaries to become executive assistants to the governor. His insistence on quality construction is best exemplified by the nationally successful Black-owned firm of Lewis Smoot Jr. of Columbus, Ohio, whose father was one of Norman's students.

Norman carried himself like the military officer he once was. He was soft-spoken, even-tempered, reserved, and self-assured. His upbringing by his grandmother formed his character. He loved Smithfield

West Virgina State University Fleming Hall, *West Virginia State College Archives*

JOHN CLAVON NORMAN SR.

Country cured hams nearly a century before they became gourmet collectibles. He learned to hunt upland game, bobwhite quail, pheasant, and grouse, accompanied by Irish setter bird dogs. He smoked Dry Slitz stogies until age forty-five, but did not drink alcohol. He was a fiscal conservative, believing that a man should own his home before purchasing a car. He tithed to his church and supported the integration efforts of Walter White and the National Association for the Advancement of Colored People. He enjoyed the sermons of Dr. Mordecai W. Johnson, Robert J. Hill, Vernon Johns, Moses Newsome, Reverend Adam Clayton Powell Jr., Bishop Fulton J. Sheen, and Norman Vincent Peale. He voted for Wilson, Coolidge, Hoover, Roosevelt, Dewey, and Eisenhower. His drafting instruments were German and Swiss state-of-the-art with individually numbered Eberhard-Faber sketching pencils, Munroe adding machines, Ditto copiers, Royal manual typewriters, and Keuffel & Essen duplex slide rules.

Norman's social activities took a distant second to his business. He found time, however, to serve as archon of the regional chapter of the *Boule*, and Marian Anderson, Paul Robeson, and Roland Hayes gave recitals in his home *en route* to concerts at nearby segregated colleges.

Norman was listening to the afternoon radio broadcast of Father Coughlin, the isolationist in Detroit on December 7, 1941, when the Japanese bombed Pearl Harbor. As World War II escalated, civilian construction slowed. He spent nearly three years in Langley, Virginia, in the wooded area now dominated by the Central Intelligence Agency, working on classified construction projects related to the invasion of North Africa and the D-Day invasion of Europe. Following World War II, Norman resumed his architectural practice back in Charleston.

A neurologic disorder slowly progressed until John C. Norman died on July 11, 1967. He is buried in Spring Hill, West Virginia, on a lovely knoll overlooking the Kanawha Valley with an expansive view of the State Capitol.

Note

1. West Virginia State Board of Architects "John Clavon Norman," Certificate no. 7, issued 19 February 1922.

JOHN C. NORMAN JR., M.D., D.SCI.
CONCORD, MASSACHUSETTS.

BUILDING LIST

Name	Address	City	State	Year	Comments
Community Center	Wilson Pl.	Charleston	WV		
Municipal Auditorium	224 E. Virginia St.	Charleston	WV	1938	
Brown-Payne Business Complex		Beckley	WV	1939	Demolished
Cabell Junior High School		Charleston	WV	1940	
Catalina Business Complex	Capitol & Donnelly Sts.	Charleston	WV	1941	
Connelly Business Complex		Gauley Bridge	WV	1937	Hotel, cinema, & offices
Faulkner Hardware Store	W. Washington St.	Charleston	WV	1938	
Ferguson Business Complex	Shrewsbury & Washington St.	Charleston	WV	1919	
Fisher, Brothers Homes	300 Blk Park Ave.	Charleston	WV	1935	
Frankel's Men's Apparel Store	Arcade & Virginia St.	Charleston	WV	1936	
Gamble, Dr. Howard	Elizabeth St.	Charleston	WV	1920	
Gamble, Katherine	Elizabeth St.	Charleston	WV	1940	Carriage house
Garnet High School	Shrewsbury & Dickinson	Charleston	WV	1941	Mechanical Arts addition
Greenbriar Theater	Summers & Lee Sts.	Charleston	WV	1941	
Jones, Dr. Joseph R.	Oakmont Rd., S. H.	Charleston	WV	1939	
London High School		London	WV	1940	
Norman, John C.	1118 2nd Ave.	Charleston	WV	1924	
Pfizer Chemical Store	W. Washington St.	Charleston	WV	1941	
Saunders, W. W.	1026 Oakmont Rd.	Charleston	WV	1929	
Shanklin		Charleston	WV	1934	
Simmons High School		Montgomery	WV	1938	
Staats Hospital Complex	West Washington St.	Charleston	WV	1939	
Washington Manor Complex	Elk River & Glendenin Sts.	Charleston	WV	1938	
Wells, Dr. Ira J. K.		Charleston	WV	1935	
West Virginia State College Auditorium	Campus	Charleston	WV	1941	
West Virginia State College Houses	Campus	Charleston	WV	1933	12 faculty houses
West Virginia State College Library	Campus	Charleston	WV	1937	

North Carolina Agricultural & Technical State University School of Mechanical Arts (1926)

North Carolina Agricultural & Technical State University was founded in Greensboro, North Carolina, in 1891. The initial name of the institution was the Agricultural and Mechanical College for the Colored Race. It was a land-grant college for African Americans founded in tandem with the Agricultural & Mechanical College of North Carolina at Raleigh, now North Carolina State University, which was for Whites. There were two initial divisions: Agriculture and Mechanic Arts. The Mechanic Arts Division offered classes in blacksmithing, carpentry, drawing, masonry, mathematics, woodworking, and industrial/vocational education.

In 1915 the institution's name changed to the Agricultural and Technical College of North Carolina. The Mechanic Arts Division was subdivided and from it came the Department of Mechanic Arts. In 1918 this department began offering courses in architecture and architectural drawing. In 1921 the department organized a four-year program in architectural engineering that led to a bachelor of science degree. In 1925 a program for a bachelor of science in building construction began.

Another reorganization occurred in 1926, which resulted in a School of Mechanic Arts, and within that was a Department of Architecture. A four-year program in architecture was initiated, leading to a bachelor of science degree. ARTHUR WILFRED FERGUSON directed the program. In 1929 the College of Architecture and Engineering was established, and it included a Department of Contracting and Building. Professor F. A. Mayfield joined the faculty in 1930, succeeding Professor Ferguson as head.

In 1941 the Department of Architecture became the Department of Architectural Engineering. Professor Mayfield remained as head until 1947, when he was succeeded by H. W. Carter. H. P. Holloman was the next head in 1948. In 1949 WILLIAM ALFRED STREAT JR. joined the faculty and became chairman of the Architectural Engineering Department, remaining so until 1985.

In 1952 the College of Architecture and Engineering was renamed the School of Engineering and within that was the Department of Architectural Engineering. The four-year program changed to a five-year program in 1964. The program in architectural engineering was first accredited by the Engineers' Council for Professional Development in 1969, and the program has remained accredited to this day, although the accrediting agency has changed its name to the Accrediting Board for Engineering and Technology. In response to a changing societal context, the North Carolina legislators in 1971 combined governance of all sixteen degree-granting, state-supported colleges in North Carolina into one board and changed the institution's name to its current configuration.

Prior to Professor Streat's retirement, he prepared the proposal to offer a master of science in architectural engineering degree, which was approved in 1985. Reginald C. Whitsett then became interim chairman until 1986. Peter Rojeski Jr. was chairman from 1986 to 1993. Ronald N. Helms became chairman in 1993 and served until 2000. Ronnie Bailey served as interim chairman from January to August 2000. Professor Rojeski then resumed chairmanship and currently serves in this position.

RONALD N. HELMS,
PROFESSOR OF HISTORY,
NORTH CAROLINA AGRICULTURAL
& TECHNICAL STATE UNIVERSITY

Kenneth Roderick O'Neal
(1908–1989)

Brian D. O'Neal

Kenneth Roderick O'Neal was born in Union, Missouri, on July 30, 1908. His parents, Oscar and Bessie O'Neal, both taught school in what was then Indian Territory near Union, Missouri, west of Saint Louis. Kenneth had an older sister and brother and younger sister. The family moved the seventy-five or so miles from Union to the big city of Saint Louis, Missouri, where O'Neal attended Saint Louis public schools. O'Neal was acknowledged as a talented artist as a teenager. His high school art teacher recommended him for an art scholarship.[1] He graduated from Sumner High School.

Art was offered by the University of Missouri at Columbia, but the state university did not admit African American students. Lincoln University in Jefferson City, the state Black university, did not offer art courses. Rather than allow O'Neal to attend the University of Missouri, the state of Missouri paid his tuition and that of other Black students to study art at an out-of-state school. O'Neal chose the State University of Iowa in Iowa City.

While going to college, he worked for Shorts, a well-known Black owner of a shoe shop where he swept up at night in exchange for a room above the shop. O'Neal, who was married three times, met his first wife, who was from Des Moines, while at the State University of Iowa. She died while he was in the U.S. Army.

O'Neal studied graphic arts and received a bachelor of arts in graphic arts in 1931. His paintings were shown in exhibitions at the State University of Iowa Memorial Union in 1929, 1930, and again in 1934; and at the Harmon Foundation Exhibit in New York City in 1933. In the Harmon-sponsored "Exhibit of the Work of Negro Artists," O'Neal's charcoal and pencil portrait of a young Black girl titled "Portrait of a Child" was displayed.[2]

O'Neal also studied structural engineering, for which he received a bachelor of science degree in 1935. He worked as a draftsman for the State University of Iowa and later at the Civilian Works Administration on a mapping project of Johnson County, Iowa.

Around 1935, Kenneth O'Neal moved to Chicago, where one of his sisters already lived. At the time of O'Neal's arrival, WILLIAM THOMAS BAILEY was the most prominent Black architect in Chicago. O'Neal returned to school, studying at night at the Armour Institute (now Illinois Institute of Technology). There he studied city planning and principles of architecture from Ludwig Mies van der Rohe (1886–1969) and eventually completed the requirements for a degree in architecture.

In 1940 O'Neal passed all the requirements for licensure as an architect in the state of Illinois.[3] Later he became certified by the National Council of Architectural Registration Boards and during his career was registered in Illinois, Iowa, Montana, and North Dakota.

O'Neal earlier joined the NATIONAL TECHNICAL ASSOCIATION, which was an all-Black organization composed of architects, engineers, and scientists. In 1940 he joined the American Institute of Architects. He was also a member of the Architects Association of Illinois.

Prior to enlisting in the U.S. Army to fight in World War II, O'Neal worked at the Illinois Highway Department and for the U.S. Army Corps of Engineers. From 1943 to 1945 he served in an engineering unit. O'Neal was stationed in England and France. At Normandy, he dug trenches, built bridges, and buried corpses. Before returning stateside, he studied English architecture by auditing a series of evening lectures at the University of Liverpool.

Arriving back in Chicago, O'Neal began his architectural practice working out of his home. He experienced the usual difficulties renting office space in downtown Chicago due to racism. He opened his downtown office in 1946. The same year he married Geraldine Teater from Wheeling, West Virginia.

In the beginning, getting work was difficult. O'Neal's projects include a police station, churches, and public works projects. Although he once stated in an interview that he had little private work, he was the architect of record for Coppin Chapel at 56th Street and Michigan Avenue in Chicago and a Credit Union in the Morgan Park Community. As a designer, O'Neal considered himself a Miesian.

O'Neal was professionally acquainted with the first Black licensed female architect, BEVERLY LORAINE GREENE, who worked at the Chicago Housing Authority, and he employed the second Black licensed female architect, GEORGIA LOUISE HARRIS BROWN. Brown worked in O'Neal's office from 1945 to 1949, before immigrating to Brazil.

In 1949 O'Neal published *A Portfolio of Modern Homes*.[4] This slender volume of thirty-one pages included renderings drawn by O'Neal and offered commentary on single-family houses he had designed. The book's short introduction gave no hint of the architect's race except to state that he was a member of the National Technical Association, an organization that many of the book's readers had probably never heard of. The book also contained instructions on

Saint Edmund's School, *Chicago Architectural Photographing Company*

how readers could mail order house plans from the author.

Kenneth Roderick O'Neal met and later married his third wife, Margaret, in 1954.

O'Neal closed his downtown office in 1956, at the nadir of a dispiriting recession, and returned to his home office. He shuttered his home office and went to work for various Chicago-based firms including Schmidt, Gassonion & Erickson, where he worked on hospital projects; and Skidmore, Owings & Merrill.

In 1958 he accepted a professional position with the City of Chicago Architect's Office. He was hired at Level 4 and had great difficulty advancing from that grade due to racism. Over time his persistence and undeniable talent won out and O'Neal was promoted to the highest level. He became coordinating architect for municipal-run airports: O'Hare, Midway and Miegs Field where he worked until 1983, then he retired.

In 1980 O'Neal published his second book, *A Volume of Contemporary Homes*.[5] O'Neal and his wife Margaret moved to Tucson, Arizona, where they lived for a year. They then moved to Honolulu, Hawaii. O'Neal, who was in excellent physical condition, jogged, played tennis, and even rode his bicycle to work. During this time, O'Neal was a contributing author to *Modern Building Magazine*.

The O'Neals and their three children lived in Honolulu for three years. In March 1989, he developed an aneurism which erupted. After surgery, complications set in and Kenneth O'Neal died in the hospital ten days later. He is buried in Punchbowl, the National Cemetery of the Pacific.

Notes

1. Interview with Margaret O'Neal (wife of Kenneth O'Neal) Honolulu, Hawaii, 16 July 2001.
2. Harmon Foundation, "Exhibition of the Work of Negro Artists," February 20–March 4, 1933, New York City. Portrait held by National Archives II, College Park, Md.
3. Illinois Records of Architects and License Applications, "Kenneth R. O'Neal," no. 2944, issued 1 July 1941. State of Illinois Archives.
4. Kenneth R. O'Neal, *A Portfolio of Modern Homes* (Chicago: Architectural Drafting Bureau, 1949).
5. Kenneth R. O'Neal, *A Volume of Contemporary Homes*, Ork Enterprises, 1980.

Bibliography

Fleming, G. James ed. *Who's Who in Colored America.* "O'Neal, K. R." Yonkers on Hudson, New York: Burckel & Associates 1950.

Chicago Tribune. "Credit Union Opens Building in Morgan Park." 27 November 1955, p. 8.

Chicago American, The Daily Gothic. "Island of Culture Proposal for Chicago." 12 May 1952, p. 23.

ROBERTA WASHINGTON, R.A., PRINCIPAL,
ROBERTA WASHINGTON & ASSOCIATES, P.C.,
NEW YORK, NEW YORK

BUILDING LIST

Name	Address	City	State	Year	Comments
Coppin Chapel	56th St. & Michigan Ave.	Chicago	IL	c1948	
Credit Union	11043 Vincennes Ave.	Morgan Park	IL	1955	
Princess Kaiulani Hotel	120 Kaiulani	Honolulu	HW	c1948	Alterations

Helen Eugenia Parker
(1909–unknown)

Courtesy of Detroit Chapter, American Institute of Architects

Helen Parker was born in Pine Bluff, Arkansas, on November 17, 1909. Her father, Walter Eugene Parker, from Pulaski County, was for many years a leading building contractor in the central Arkansas area. Her mother, Willie Parker, maintained the household and helped to raise Helen, the oldest child, and Sidney, Alfred, Willie, and Laurette.[1] The family lived at 1874 Cross Street in the historic Dunbar High School neighborhood located in "Center City" Little Rock, where many Black professionals made their homes.

Helen Parker attended segregated public elementary school in Little Rock, and in 1922 she began her high school education at Wiley High School-College in Marshall, Texas. Wiley High School-College, founded in 1873 by the Methodist Episcopal Church, offered teacher training to the "newly freed men." The school was chartered by the Freedmen's Aid and Southern Education Society. A top student, Helen Parker excelled in mathematics, science, geometry, English, American history, and Negro history.[2] She graduated in 1926.

After returning to Little Rock, Helen Parker taught mathematics in the segregated public school system and also served for a time as librarian in the Little Rock Colored Library. In addition, Parker acted as technical consultant to the Southern Tenant Farmers Union.

It is believed that Helen Parker studied architecture at Howard University, but records to confirm this could not be located. She stopped short of earning her degree and moved to Detroit, Michigan.

During the Great Depression, Parker worked as an instructor in the Shop Drafting Training Program of the Works Progress Administration's National Youth Administration, which provided work and training to unemployed youth.

By 1930 Parker was employed as a draftswoman by Detroit architect Alfonso R. Feliciano (1883–1940), a graduate of the *Universidad de Barcelona*.[3] Feliciano, originally from Puerto Rico, was noted as one of two registered architects of color in Detroit. Eventually, when Feliciano died, the other registered architect of color, DONALD FRANK WHITE, took over Feliciano's workload and added Helen Parker as a draftswoman.

As a woman and a Negro, Helen Parker had met with much opposition on her quest to becoming an architect. The state of Michigan began licensing architects in 1916, but there is no record that she obtained her license. Nevertheless, Helen Parker is recognized for her tenacity and for her contributions as a successful draftswoman and educator.

Helen Parker was a member of *Alpha Kappa Alpha* Sorority, the NATIONAL TECHNICAL ASSOCIATION, and the Detroit Youth Assembly, and served as board member of the Peter Pan Nursery.

Notes

1. U.S. Census, "Walter E. Parker," Enumeration District No. 115, 2 January 1920, Sheet 1, Line 92.
2. "Helen Parker's Grading Card," *Registrar's Office, Wiley University,* Marshall, Tex., 1922–1926.
3. "Architecture 'A La Femme,'" *Michigan Chronicle*, 17 August 1940, p. 1.

CONSTANCE E. SARTO,
MAPPING THE LEGACY OF AFRICAN AMERICAN HISTORY, INC., LITTLE ROCK, ARKANSAS

BUILDING LIST

Name	Address	City	State	Year	Comments
Trinity Hospital	681 Vernor Highway	Detroit	MI		Assoc. architect

Joseph Lincoln Parker
(1898–1959)

MIT Museum

Joseph Lincoln Parker was an architectural engineer associated with large public transportation projects in New York. He was born in Cooksville, Maryland, on April 6, 1898, into a family of four sisters. Information about his mother and father was not found. It is believed that Parker attended the Maryland Normal and Industrial School in Bowie and then he advanced to the Baptist-supported Storer College, the first Negro teacher's college in the state of West Virginia at Harper's Ferry. By 1918, he was enrolled at the small, private Bates College in Lewiston, Maine. In 1920, Parker transferred to the Massachusetts Institute of Technology in Cambridge, majoring in engineering. He was enrolled in Course II, which encompassed urban design instead of individual building design. Parker was a member of the student chapters of the Civil Engineering Society and American Society of Civil Engineers and he found time away from his studies to pledge *Omega Psi Phi* Fraternity. Parker's undergraduate thesis, "A Study of the Vernon Power Development of the New England Power System," examined the hydroelectric power dam on the Connecticut River and its impact on regional development along with the specifics of heavy concrete construction and hydraulics, all of which combined to chart the path of his professional career.[1] Joseph Parker graduated from the Massachusetts Institute of Technology with a bachelor of science in engineering in 1923.[2]

After receiving his degree, Joseph wed Cecil B. Higgins of Boston, Massachusetts. The Parkers set up a household in Mount Vernon, New York. Cecil Parker was a housewife. The family grew with the addition of two sons: Joseph Jr. and John Wesley. Joseph Parker gained his engineer registration in the state of New York on February 26, 1932. He was issued license number 011974 by the New York State Licensing Board. He was a design engineer with the New York City Transit Authority and New York City Tunnel Division of the Board of Transportation on large public works projects that defined the regional growth of New York City. It is believed that Parker was employed by a private contractor for these transit agencies from the late 1920s until the 1930s. He supplemented his technical training and kept current with industry trends by attending graduate courses in engineering at New York University from 1931 to 1933.

By 1940, it is believed Parker was employed by the Triborough Bridge and Tunnel Authority, which was responsible for constructing huge public infrastructure projects orchestrated by legendary public works czar Robert Moses.

Parker left the public sector for the private sector to work for the Manhattan office of Parsons, Brinckerhoff, Hall & MacDonald, where he remained through the 1950s.

At the age of sixty-one, Joseph Parker died of natural causes on August 11, 1959, at Mount Vernon Hospital.[3]

JOSEPH LINCOLN PARKER

Holland Tunnel Opening Day, November 12, 1927, *Courtesy of Port Authority of New York and New Jersey*

Notes

1. Joseph L. Parker, "A Study of the Vernon Power Development of the New England Power System," bachelor of science thesis, Massachusetts Institute of Technology, 1923.
2. *A Great History of the Great Class of 1923, Massachusetts Institute of Technology: 50th Reunion Book* (Boston: n.p., 1973), p. 274.
3. "Joseph L. Parker, Dies," *New York Times*, 12 August 1959, p. 29.

Bibliography

"Joseph L. Parker." *Technique: Yearbook of the Class of 1923.* Boston: Perry & Elliott, 1924.

Wharton, David E. *A Struggle Worthy of Note: The Engineering and Technological Education of Black Americans.* Westport, Conn.: Greenwood Press, 1992.

LESLIE SMITH (PSUEDONYM)
WELLESLEY, MASSACHUSETTS

STRUCTURE LIST

Name	Address	City	State	Year	Comments
Triborough Bridge	Over East River	New York	NY	1940	
Triborough Tunnel	Under East River	New York	NY	1942	

Frederick Blackburn Pelham
(1864–1895)

Bentley Historical Library, University of Michigan

Frederick Blackburn Pelham was born on November 7, 1864, in Detroit, Michigan, the son of Robert Pelham and Frances Butcher Pelham. In a family of three girls and four boys, Frederick was the seventh and youngest child of a remarkable family. The family's origins were in Virginia, where both Robert Pelham and Frances Butcher were free persons and landowners in the 1850s, but chafing under the legal restrictions placed on even free Blacks as well as the widespread racial discrimination. Robert Pelham Sr. not only operated his own farm, but also worked as a bricklayer and masonry contractor. Robert and Frances desired greater opportunities and education for their children. However, it was illegal for free Blacks in Virginia to receive an education. In the late 1850s, the Pelham family left Virginia and migrated to several cities before settling permanently in Detroit, Michigan, in 1862, where their two youngest sons, Benjamin and Frederick, were born. In Detroit Frances concentrated on homemaking while Robert Sr. was employed as a mechanic and masonry contractor—skills that Robert undoubtedly shared with his son Frederick.

Five of the Pelham children became professionals and played significant public roles in the late nineteenth century and first half of the twentieth century. Robert H. Pelham Jr. and Benjamin B. Pelham were co-editors along with two other African American men of the *Detroit Plaindealer* newspaper from 1883 to 1893; sister Meta Pelham worked on the *Detroit Plaindealer* also. Robert Pelham Jr. became an employee of the federal government in Washington, D.C., serving longest (thirty years) in the Census Bureau of the U.S. Department of Commerce and Labor. To lessen the manual labor used in recording statistics, he patented a tabulation device and later a tallying machine. Benjamin Pelham served in several high-level administrator positions in the Wayne County, Michigan, government for forty-seven years. Joseph Pelham was a school teacher and principal for over thirty-five years in Missouri, and Meta Pelham also worked as a teacher in Missouri and in Detroit

Following the high standards set by his older siblings, in 1882 Frederick Pelham graduated from Detroit High School with highest honors. He became the fifth of the seven children to finish high school at a time when few Americans of any race did so. He enrolled in the University of Michigan Engineering School, graduating with a degree in civil engineering in 1887 "at the head of his class."[1] Pelham was the first African American to graduate from the University of Michigan School of Engineering; CORNELIUS LANGSTON HENDERSON SR. in 1911 was the second to do so. As graduation was approaching, officers of the Michigan Central Railroad asked the faculty of the School of Engineering to recommend two graduating students for employment. Frederick Pelham was one of the students recommended and was hired. His employment with the Michigan Central Railroad lasted from 1887 until his death in 1895. He is credited with

Michigan Central Railroad Arch Bridge, *Post Card Collection, Bentley Historical Library, University of Michigan*

designing and building approximately eighteen bridges for the Michigan Central Railroad as assistant engineer. A photograph of one of his bridges—a skew arch bridge at Dexter, Michigan—was featured in Michigan Central literature and is reproduced in the *Michigan Manual of Freedmen's Progress*.[2] Although Pelham only worked for the company for slightly longer than seven years, he was promoted more than once and was "acting 1st Assistant Engineer" at the time of his death.[3]

He also did some civil engineering work for the Detroit Citizens Railway Company. A quote from the *Michigan Manual* stated that "Ex-Manager J. D. Hawks [spoke] very highly of Mr. Pelham's assistance in changing some of the curves of the tracks."[4]

Pelham was described as being quiet and gentlemanly. He was a member of the Michigan Engineering Society, the Michigan Central Branch of the Young Mens Christian Association, and the Maccabees. He also taught Sunday school at Bethel African Methodist Episcopal Church in Detroit. He never married.

Frederick Pelham died on February 2, 1895, from acute pneumonia.[5] He is buried in the family plot in Elmwood Cemetery located in Detroit, Michigan.

Notes
1. Francis H. Warren, compiler, *Michigan Manual of Freedmen's Progress* (John M. Green, Detroit: 1915), p. 217.
2. Ibid., p. 273.
3. "Pelham Family Papers," Burton Historical Collection, Detroit Public Library.
4. *Michigan Manual*, p. 275.
5. City of Detroit, Department of Health, Vital Records, "Frederick B. Pelham Death Certificate, no. 1143980" 1895.

Bibliography
"Familiar and Famous." *Ann Arbor News,* 17 March 1938, p. 17.
Mallas, Aris A., Rea McCain, and Margaret K. Hadden. *Forty Years in Politics: The Story of Ben Pelham.* Detroit: Wayne State University, 1957.

DE WITT SANFORD DYKES JR.,
PROFESSOR OF HISTORY, OAKLAND UNIVERSITY

STRUCTURE LIST

Name	Address	City	State	Year	Comments
Dexter Skew Arch Bridge	Over Huron River	Dexter	MI		
Michigan Central Railroad Arch Bridge	Over Huron River	Dexter	MI	1890	
Michigan Central Railroad Arch Bridge	Over Portage Lake Rd.	Dexter	MI	1890	

Louis Hudison Persley
(1890–1932)

Vinson E. McKenzie

In 1890, during the emergence of modern America, Louis Hudison Persley was born. His father, T. K. Persley, was a prestigious member of the African American community in their hometown of Macon, Georgia. Louis Persley was born, raised, and eventually buried in Macon. His early education was spent in Macon public schools and after commencement he ventured out to attend Lincoln University in Pennsylvania. He later attended Carnegie Institute of Technology, from which he graduated with an architecture degree in 1914.[1]

After graduating from Carnegie Institute of Technology, Persley was offered a teaching position at TUSKEGEE INSTITUTE. When Persley joined the staff, ROBERT ROBINSON TAYLOR was director of the Mechanical Industries Department. Persley taught mechanical drawing until 1917, when he volunteered to serve in World War I. In addition to teaching, Persley designed several buildings that were built by students even before he was registered to practice architecture.

Like many African American architects of his era, Persley worked in the realm of church architecture. In 1916, one of his early church designs—the First African Methodist Episcopal Church of Athens, Georgia—was made into reality by the state's first African American builder, R. F. Walker.[2]

The war ended on November 11, 1918. When Louis Persley returned to the states, he was promoted to head of the division of architecture at Tuskegee Institute. Robert Robinson Taylor was now vice-president of Tuskegee Institute and soon became vice-president of the firm to be named Taylor & Persley Architects. The two completed their first building for the campus, James Hall, in 1921. It was only one year before, on

Colored Masonic Temple, *Courtesy of Birmingham Public Library Archives*

April 5, 1920, that Persley had become the twentieth architect and first African American architect registered in the state of Georgia.[3]

The firm of Taylor & Persley Architects may have been the first formal partnership of two African American architects. In the beginning, most of their commissions came from Tuskegee Institute. Because of this, Persley spent most of his time in Alabama and in 1924, he briefly lost his license because he was not at his Georgia address to receive the renewal notice. The situation was quickly remedied and Persley was reinstated in August of the same year.

Persley married twice. His first wife was Elnora G. Lockett, whom he married in 1921. After her death he wed Phala Harper in 1927, and adopted her daughter Gwendolyn.

Louis Persley died on July 23, 1932.[4] He completed his final design, his family home, only months before his death, but did not live long enough to see it built.

Notes

1. Georgia State Historic Preservation Office, "Biographical Information on Louis Persley," Atlanta, Georgia, 2001.
2. Cara Donlon, "First African Methodist Church," Athens Newspapers, *Online Athens*, website 1998.
3. Georgia Department of Archives and History, "Original Documents: Registered Architects: Louis Hudson Persley," Folder no. 20, Atlanta, Georgia, 1920.
4. "Tuskegee Architect L.H. Persley Dead," *The New York Age*, 23 July 1932, p. 1.

Bibliography

Athens-Clarke County Online. "Virtual Tour of Athens Landmarks." Athens, Ga.: Unified Government of Athens-Clarke County, 2001.

McKenzie, Vinson E. "Louis Hudson Persley: Georgia's First Registered African American Architect." *The Atlanta Metro*, February 1996, p. 12.

KIRA MICHELE ALSTON,
JUNIOR ARCHITECT-RESEARCHER,
RESTON, VIRGINIA

BUILDING LIST

Name	Address	City	State	Year	Comments
Campbell Chapel Church	503 N. Jackson St.	Americus	GA		
Colored Masonic Temple	1630 4th Ave. N.	Birmingham	AL	1924	
First African Methodist Episcopal Church	521 N. Hull St.	Athens	GA	1916	
Persley, Louis H.	1202 Clark St.	Tuskegee	AL	1927	
Samaritan Order Bldg.	Lumpkins & Washington Sts.	Athens	GA	1916	
Selma University Dinkins Memorial Chapel	Campus	Selma	AL	1921	
Tuskegee Institute Carnegie Library	Campus	Tuskegee	AL		Alterations
Tuskegee Institute James Hall	Campus	Tuskegee	AL	1921	
Tuskegee Institute Logan Hall Gym	Campus	Tuskegee	AL		
Tuskegee Institute Sage Hall	Campus	Tuskegee	AL	1927	
Tuskegee Institute Science Hall	Campus	Tuskegee	AL		

William Sidney Pittman
(1875–1958)

Ruth Ann Stewart

William Sidney Pittman was born in Montgomery, Alabama, on April 21, 1875, and was educated in the segregated public schools of Montgomery. In 1892, at age seventeen, he enrolled at TUSKEGEE INSTITUTE. He completed his studies in mechanical and architectural drawing in 1897. With financial support from Tuskegee Institute's principal, Booker Taliferro Washington, Pittman continued his education at Drexel Institute in Philadelphia, and earned a diploma in architectural drawing in 1900. Returning to Tuskegee Institute as assistant in the Division of Architectural and Mechanical Drawing, he supplied blueprints for several buildings on the Tuskegee campus.[1]

In May 1905 Pittman left Tuskegee Institute for Washington, D.C. He began work as a draftsman in the office of JOHN ANDERSON LANKFORD, and within a year opened his own office. In the fall of 1906, he entered and won the competition for the design of the Negro Building at the JAMESTOWN TER-CENTENNIAL EXPOSITION. The exposition was partially supported by appropriations from the U.S. Congress and work was under the supervision of the secretary of the treasury; Pittman was contracted to supervise construction of the building, which marked the first federal contract with a Black architect. Open for six months in 1907, the Negro Building was a significant success and launched the career of its architect.[2]

In 1907 Pittman married Portia Marshall Washington, daughter of Booker T. Washington. Portia was a professional pianist who had been educated in Europe and taught music for much of her adult life. The newlyweds made their home in the African American community of Fairmount Heights, Maryland, just outside the District of Columbia boundary. The Pittmans' three children were all born during their residence in Fairmount Heights. Sidney Pittman was involved in the planning of Fairmount Heights, where he designed not only his family home, but also the town meeting hall and the first elementary school.

During these years, Pittman was commissioned to design several important buildings in Washington, D.C., including the Garfield Elementary Public School (1909) and the 12th Street Young Mens Christian Association Building. The Young Mens Christian Association cornerstone was placed in November 1908 by President Theodore Roosevelt and the building opened with ceremonies on May 19, 1912. The 4-story Young Mens Christian Association building was constructed of brick with decorative quoins, a modillioned cornice, and a portico with polished stone columns; it included a swimming pool, showers and lockers, a bowling alley, a billiard room, and fifty-four sleeping rooms.[3] During the same period, Pittman designed institutional buildings in several southern states and in 1912 received several commissions in Texas. At the end of that year, he moved his family to Dallas, Texas, where he designed several churches and institutional buildings, of which the Pythian Temple was the most notable. Finished in 1916, this 5-story, classically inspired brick building

12th Street colored YMCA, *Dreck Spurlock Wilson*

was erected as the Texas state headquarters of the Knights of Pythias, a Black fraternal organization.[4]

Pittman's architectural career began to wane in the 1920s. Always critical and difficult to satisfy, he was, by the late 1920s, unable to secure contracts from either Blacks or Whites. He became increasingly bitter and in 1931 published *Brotherhood Eyes*, a local tabloid that railed against the employment of Whites by some Blacks who had proclaimed their commitment to Black civil rights.

Portia Pittman separated from her husband in 1928 and returned to Tuskegee, Alabama. William Sidney Pittman remained in Dallas, supporting himself by performing carpentry work. In his last years, nearly blind and destitute, he was considered eccentric, but treated with some deference. Pittman died of coronary thrombosis on March 14, 1958, and was buried in an unmarked paupers grave in Glen Oaks Cemetery in South Dallas. In 1985, through the efforts of the Dallas Historical Society and several architects and admirers of his work, a granite memorial stone was erected at his grave site.

The design and construction of the Negro Building at the Jamestown Exposition was the springboard for the architectural career of William Sidney Pittman. His career, although illustrious, was relatively brief, hampered by a combination of arrogance and personal frustration. Because of his talent, ambition, and industry, however, William Pittman made a place for himself.

Notes
1. W. S. Pittman to B. T. Washington, 11 November 1897, "Report of William Sidney Pittman, Second Year—First Term: Papers of Booker T. Washington," Manuscripts Division, School of Architecture, Drexel Institute of Art, Science and Industry, Philadelphia, Pa.
2. *Jamestown Ter-centennial Commission, Jamestown Exposition, Norfolk, Virginia, 1907* (D.C.: Government Printing Office, 1909). General Records of the U.S. Department of Treasury, Series no. 644.
3. Antoinette J. Lee, "Garfield Elementary School Building Survey Form," District of Columbia Public Schools, August 1986. Historic American Buildings Survey DC-361, Prints and Photographs Division, Library of Congress, Washington, D.C.
4. "National Historic Landmark Nomination Form for Knights of Pythias Building," U.S. Department of the Interior, June 1984.

Bibliography
Hill, Roy L. *Booker T.'s Child*. Newark: McDaniel Press, 1974.
Stewart, Ruth Ann. *Portia*. Garden City, N.J.: Doubleday & Company, 1977.

SUSAN G. PEARL, ARCHITECTURAL HISTORIAN,
MARYLAND NATIONAL PARK AND PLANNING
COMMISSION, PRINCE GEORGE'S COUNTY, MARYLAND

BUILDING LIST

Name	Address	City	State	Year	Comments
12th Street Colored YMCA	1816 12th St., NW	Washington	DC	1908	Now Thurgood Marshall Ctr.
Allen Chapel African Methodist Episcopal Church	116 Elm St.	Ft. Worth	TX	1914	
Brown, R. W.	1629 12th St., NW	Washington	DC	1909	
Colored Carnegie Branch Library	1112 Frederick St.	Houston	TX	1913	Demolished
Colored State Normal School Library	Campus	Montgomery	AL	1910	Now Alabama State University
Fairmount Heights Mutual Improvement Corp.	715 61st Ave.	Fairmount Heights	MD	1908	Now private residence
Fairmount Heights Public School	737 61st Ave.	Fairmount Heights	MD	1912	Now Mt. Zion Apostolic Faith Church
Fairmount Heights Village Hall		Fairmount Heights	MD		
Garfield Elementary Public School	Irving & Alabama Ave., SE	Washington	DC	1909	
Jamestown Ter-centennial Negro Bldg.	Hampton Roads	Hampton Roads	VA	1907	Demolished
Joshua Chapel African Methodist Episcopal Church	110 N. Aiken St.	Waxahachie	TX	1917	
Kentucky Normal & Industrial Institute Hume Hall	Campus	Frankfort	KY	1909	Now Kentucky State University
Kentucky Normal & Industrial Institute Trade School	Campus	Frankfort	KY	1909	Now Kentucky State University
Knights of Pythias Temple	2551 Elm St.	Dallas	TX	1915	Now Union Bankers Insurance Co.
Laborers Bldg. & Loan Office	2002 11th St., NW	Washington	DC	1908	
Lincoln Memorial Theatre & Office Bldg.	1000 U St., NW	Washington	DC	1910	Plans only
Marshall, Clement		Fairmount Heights	MD	1911	Store/residence
Mission Church	4318 Sheriff Rd., SE	Washington	DC	1908	
Moore Drug Store	1904 L St., NW	Washington	DC	1911	
National Religious Training School Avery Auditorium	Campus	Durham	NC	1910	Now North Carolina Central Univ.
National Religious Training School Dining Hall	Campus	Durham	NC	1910	Now North Carolina Central Univ.
National Religious Training School Dormitory	Campus	Durham	NC	1910	Now North Carolina Central Univ.
National Religious Training School President's Residence	Campus	Durham	NC	1910	
National Religious Training School Theology Hall	Campus	Durham	NC	1910	Now North Carolina Central Univ.
Paul Quinn College Grant Hall Dormitory	Campus	Waco	TX	1921	Destroyed by fire
Pittman, William S. "Little White Tops"	505 Eastern Ave.	Fairmount Heights	MD	1907	
Rounds, T. S.	2622 P St., NW	Washington	DC	1908	
St. James African Methodist Episcopal Temple	624 N. Good-Latimer Expwy.	Dallas	TX	1918	Now office bldg.
Stowe, Thomas H.	4322 Sheriff Rd., SE	Washington	DC	1907	
Temple of Gailean Fisherman	320 F St., SW	Washington	DC	1890	Addition
Trinity North Washington Church	771 Morton St., NW	Washington	DC	1905	
Tuskegee Institute Huntington Memorial Bldg.	Campus	Tuskegee	AL	1907	
Tuskegee Institute Rockefellar Hall	Campus	Tuskegee	AL	1907	
United Brothers of Friendship Lodge	Commerce St.	San Antonio	TX	1915	Demolished
United Order of Odd Fellows Lodge	Louisiana St. & Prairie Ave.	Houston	TX	1924	Demolished
United Order of Odd Fellows Lodge No. 1	228 Auburn Ave.	Atlanta	GA	1912	
Voorhees Industrial School Admin./Classroom Bldg.	Campus	Denmark	SC	1914	
Wesley Chapel African Methodist Episcopal Church	2209 Dowling St.	Houston	TX	1926	Alterations
White Rock Baptist Church	3400 Fayetteville St.	Durham	NC	1910	
Williams & Ferguson College	Campus	Abbeville	SC	1910	Demolished
Zion Baptist Church	4316 Sheriff Rd., NE	Washington	DC	1908	

James Alonzo Plater
(1908–1965)

Plater Family

J. Alonzo Plater was born to James and Mary Florence Thomas Plater on December 15, 1908, in the Deanwood section of northeast Washington, D.C. He graduated from Armstrong Technical High School in 1927 and enrolled in HOWARD UNIVERSITY'S SCHOOL OF ARCHITECTURE that same year, receiving his degree in 1932.

Plater began his architectural career working for ROMULUS CORNELIUS ARCHER JR. from 1932 to 1934, preparing plans and specifications for several houses, apartments, and a funeral parlor. He then worked as a draftsman and architectural detailer for HILYARD ROBERT ROBINSON from 1934 to 1936 and as a designer for HOWARD HAMILTON MACKEY SR. from 1936 to 1937.

J. Alonzo Plater practiced mainly in Philadelphia and Washington, D.C., his work ranging from residential to commercial. He was a founder of the Philadelphia chapter of the NATIONAL TECHNICAL ASSOCIATION and member of the Philadelphia chapter of the American Institute of Architects and Pennsylvania Society of Architects.

Plater accepted a three-month position in 1937 as an engineer draftsman at the Frankford Arsenal in Philadelphia. From this modest beginning, he advanced to chief of the Engineer and Planning Division at the arsenal, holding that position until his death in 1965. As division chief, he was responsible for supervising the design and development of all projects for the operating departments and support for the arsenal's missions.

With a slackening of work at the arsenal following World War II, Plater registered as an architect with the State of Pennsylvania in July 1947 and opened his own practice at 1611 North Broad Street the next month. During the next two years he designed several houses as well as a beauty school and the Supreme Liberty Insurance Building, both in Philadelphia. In the 1950s and 1960s, he designed churches, a motel, U.S. Post Offices, and a masonic lodge.

Although Plater continued to live and work in the Philadelphia area, he was registered to practice architecture in the District of Columbia and New Jersey.[1] He designed more than twelve houses in the Deanwood and Eastland Gardens neighborhoods of northeast Washington, D.C. By the end of World War II, he was an associate of his former employer Howard Hamilton Mackey Sr., who was then chairman of the Department of Architecture at Howard University. In 1946 Plater, along with Mackey, were recommended as proposed architects for the new federally funded Architecture and Engineering Building at Howard University. Senator Joseph Guffey of Pennsylvania wrote to Howard University's president, Dr. Mordecai Johnson, that

> J. Alonzo Plater, Howard Mackey and George G. Billinslia, each with many years of experience, are architectural alumni of Howard University. It would make a fine demonstration of faith in the educational work of your Department of Architecture, and it would stimulate the interest of prospective students of architecture if the fact could be pointed to that a faculty member and

Rosa Plater House, *Caroline Hickman*

two of the alumni of the Department . . . had been selected by the University to participate in its building program.[2]

Plater married Florence Greene, a public school teacher, on January 1, 1941, in Washington, D.C. They had two daughters, Carol and Terry. Terry Plater followed her father into architecture when she received her master of arts in architecture from Columbia University in New York.

As a professional reference for Plater in his application for registration in the District of Columbia, his former employer, Romulus Cornelius Archer, characterized him as "a gentleman of fine Christian character, good habits, capable, and trustworthy in addition to his qualifications as an architect."[3]

James Alonzo Plater died in Philadelphia from a heart attack on December 22, 1965.

Notes

1. District of Columbia Board of Examiners and Registrars of Architects, "J. Alonzo Plater," Certificate no. 798, issued October 1951.
2. Joseph Guffy to Dr. Mordacai Johnson, 29 July 1946, "Howard Mackey Papers," Moorland-Spingarn Research Center, Washington, D.C. The commission instead was awarded to the joint venture of HILYARD ROBERT ROBINSON and PAUL REVERE WILLIAMS.
3. District of Columbia Board of Examiners and Registrars files, "J. Alonzo Plater," Box 48, October 1951.

Bibliography

Lee, J. V. "Deanwood Historic Study: The Role of Black Architects in the Development of Deanwood." August 1987. D.C. Historic Preservation Office.

"Plater Family Papers." In the possession of daughters Carol Plater Restifo, Bryn Mawr, Pa., and Terry Plater, Ithaca, N.Y.

CAROLINE MESROBIAN HICKMAN,
ART AND ARCHITECTURAL HISTORIAN,
WASHINGTON, D.C.

BUILDING LIST

Name	Address	City	State	Year	Comments
Apex Beauty School	521 S. Broad St.	Philadelphia	PA	1948	
Bell Masonic Lodge		Havertown	PA		
Bright Hope Baptist Church	11th & Oxford Sts.	Philadelphia	PA	1951	Alterations
Cornell, Harry W.	1310 Irving St., NE	Washington	DC	1938	
Grady, James	4615 Aubrey St.	Philadelphia	PA	1948	
Harris, Rose P.	4008 Meade St., NE	Washington	DC		

JAMES ALONZO PLATER

BUILDING LIST (continued)

Name	Address	City	State	Year	Comments
Central Union Baptist Church	4401 Foote St., NE	Washington	DC	1935	
Glenside Baptist Church	4504 Gault Pl., NE	Washington	DC	1931	
Henderson, Douglass		Germantown	PA		
House	926 45th Pl., NE	Washington	DC		
Jessup, Cedric	1120 42nd St., NE	Washington	DC	1932	
Livingston, W. R.	Kay Ave. & Walnut St.	Linconia Park	PA	1949	
New Apostolic Church of North America	K & Cayuga Sts.	Philadelphia	PA		
Otis, Clyde		Englewood	NJ		
Savoy, Archie	4700 Blaine St., NE	Washington	DC	1949	
Smith, William G.	Pershing Rd.	Pennlyn	PA	1951	
Star of Hope Baptist Church	443 N. 60th St.	Philadelphia	PA	1962	
Supreme Liberty Life Insurance Office	1637 N. Broad St.	Philadelphia	PA	1949	
U.S. Post Office	Germantown Ave. & Luzerne St.	Philadelphia	PA		
United Sports Club	22nd & Clearfield Sts.	Philadelphia	PA	1940	

Samuel M. Plato
(1882–1957)

Oil by James Porter, c. 1960. Howard University Gallery of Art

Samuel Plato was born in Waugh, Montgomery County, Alabama, on January 10, 1882, to James and Katie Hendrick Plato. At the time, his parents were living in a cabin on a large plantation where his father worked as a sharecropper and carpenter. James Plato had been an apprentice to Samuel Carter, a noted artisan and former slave. At his death, Carter willed his tools to James Plato, who named his second son in Carter's honor.

At an early age, Samuel showed an aptitude for learning and for mechanics. He learned to use his father's tools, and handcrafted displays for his school, Mount Meigs. The school was built on the grounds of his boyhood home when the plantation was purchased by White philanthropists from Plainfield, Connecticut. They established a school that was organized by Booker T. Washington. Plato spent seven years at Mount Meigs and another year in school in Winston-Salem, North Carolina. He was unable to enter TUSKEGEE INSTITUTE due to lack of money, but was accepted at the State University in Louisville, Kentucky, in 1898. Plato cut down trees and carved washboards to sell at 25¢ each to earn the $12 train fare.[1]

At State University, Plato earned his room and board and tuition by repairing campus buildings. He came under the wing of school president, Dr. C. L. Purce, for whom Plato is believed to have built a farmhouse near Bardstown, Kentucky. After completing the normal course, Plato went to Alabama and taught school; however, he desired to return to Louisville to become a lawyer, despite encouragement to consider developing his mechanic talent. He continued to work his way through State University in Louisville. Two years later, Plato read an advertisement for the International Correspondence School of Scranton, Pennsylvania, which offered a course in architecture. Although still enrolled in school, Plato soon gave up his other studies to focus on the architectural course.

Plato moved to Marion, Indiana, in 1905. Northeastern Indiana was still experiencing a financial boom following the discovery of natural gas in 1887, although the gas ran out soon after his arrival. His search for a job was frustrating because local building contractors refused to hire him; however, small finish carpentry work eventually led to larger building contracts.

One of Plato's early projects was the design and construction of the Second Baptist Church (1905) in Marion. The plain, wood-sided church is a vernacular building with stained-glass windows. He designed and built a number of small houses in Marion, including a row of five cottages (c1906) along Pennsylvania Avenue next to the railroad tracks at 10th and Boots Streets. The compact worker houses were carpenter-builder in style and were probably occupied by employees of the nearby United States Glove Factory located across the tracks.

In the *Centennial History of Grant County, Indiana* of which Marion is the county seat, Rolland Whitson identifies Plato as the architect and contractor for No. 2 School, a one-room elementary school near the rural Black community of Weaver.[2] The small rectangular

325

brick building had a corner, pyramidal capped tower with a round arch doorway. Located near County Roads 600 South and 300 West, the school was razed in 1977.

After his arrival in Marion, Plato formed a partnership with Black contractor Jasper Burden. His son, Everett Burden, described Plato "as a solemn, slow-talking man who dressed plainly and shunned publicity."[3]

Samuel Plato's first wife, Nettie, is buried in Marion. His second wife, Elnora Davis Lucas, was from Alexandria, Indiana. She had training in textile design and was operating a one-woman dress shop when they married. Elnora Plato worked alongside her husband serving as part of the office staff and traveling with him to out-of-town assignments.

Plato began to grow in his design sensibility after 1910, and began to adopt the popular early-twentieth-century Anglo-Colonial Revival style that rippled across the country. His use of classical details is evident in the Platonian Apartments (1910) that he designed and named after himself, but is expanded in the Neo-Classical house he designed and built for businessman J. Woodrow Wilson (1912) and the First Baptist Church (1913). The church design is repeated by Plato in six other churches including Broadway Temple African Methodist Episcopal Zion Church (1915) and James Lee Memorial Church (1928) in Louisville, Kentucky. He continued to design and build houses including his own American Foursquare style house (1915) and a Mission-style bungalow for David Lavengood (1920). The latter is brick with a tile roof and attached garage.

Leaving Marion circa 1919, Plato returned to Louisville and was busy designing and building churches, banks, Virginia Avenue School (c1925), and William H. Stewart Hall (c1930) at Simmons University. A residential neighborhood that Plato designed and built was named Plato Terrace (date unknown) in his honor. In 1945 Plato was the architect and contractor for Westover subdivision; located on South Western Parkway, opposite Chickasaw Park. The two-bedroom houses were marketed to Blacks who received mortgage financing from Black-owned Mammoth Life Insurance Company.

Plato increasingly worked on federal projects after 1940, including designing and constructing over thirty-nine U.S. Post Offices. One of Plato's largest federal commissions was the eighty-eight-unit housing project constructed as part of a larger 250-unit complex of civilian housing for Curtis Wright Defense Plant (c1942) in Louisville. After World War II, the complex was converted into public housing and in the 1950s became cooperative housing known as Fincastle Apartments. Other public housing projects included constructing the 304-unit complex in Sparrows Point, Maryland, near Baltimore (c1943), designed by HILYARD ROBERT ROBINSON, and being the architect and contractor for dormitories Midway and Wake (c1948) in Washington, D.C.

Samuel Plato died of a brain blood clot while in Jewish Hospital in Louisville on May 13, 1957.[4] He was buried in the Louisville Cemetery. His extant buildings are the legacy of his work, ideas, and architectural talent.

Notes

1. Amalia Ray, "Samuel Plato," *Negro History Bulletin* (December 1946): 52.
2. Rolland Whitson, *Centennial History of Grant County, Indiana, 1812–1912*, 2 vols. (Chicago: Lewis Publishing Company, 1914), p. 354.
3. Jerry Miller, "People of Color: Grant County's Black Heritage," *Marion Chronicle Tribune Magazine*, 9 July 1978.
4. "Samuel Plato, Death Certificate," Department of Vital Statistics, no. 116–57–10214, Jefferson County, Kentucky, issued 13 May 1957.

Bibliography

Guidero, Miriam. "Looking Back, Samuel Plato, Architect." *Architecture* (November 1989): 24.
Jourdan, Katherine. "The Architecture of Samuel M. Plato." *Black History News and Notes,* August 1989, p. 4.
"Samuel Plato Papers." Filson Historical Society. Louisville, Kentucky.
Smith, Jon. "The Architecture of Samuel M. Plato, the Marion Years, 1902 to 1921." master's thesis, Ball State University, 1998.

KATHERINE M. JOURDAN,
FORMER NATIONAL REGISTER COORDINATOR,
WEST VIRGINIA DIVISION OF CULTURE AND HISTORY

J. Woodrow Wilson Residence, *Katherine M. Jourdan*

BUILDING LIST

Name	Address	City	State	Year	Comments
Broadway Temple African Methodist Episcopal Zion Church	662 S. 13th Street	Louisville	KY	1915	
Curtis Wright Defense Plant Housing	Popular Level Rd.	Louisville	KY	c1942	Now Fincastle Apts.
First Baptist Church	4th & Nebraska Sts.	Marion	IN	1913	
House	2306 S. Boots St.	Marion	IN	c1915	
Lavengood, David	722 S. Washington	Marion	IN	c1920	
Lee Memorial Church	1754 Frankfort	Louisville	KY	c1928	
Midway & Wake Dormitories		Washington	DC	c1948	
Plato, Samuel M.	2308 S. Boots St.	Marion	IN	c1915	
Platonian Apts.	Adams & 15th St.	Marion	IN	1910	
Purce Store & Post Office	Bardstown Rd.	Bardstown	KY	c1900	
School No. 2	Roads 600 South & 300 West	Weaver	IN	1908	Demolished
Second Baptist Church	1824 S. Branston St.	Marion	IN	1905	Now Full Gospel Church
Simmons University Stewart Hall	Campus	Louisville	KY		
Soldier's Home	West Bank of Missinena River	Marion	IN	c1905	Demolished
Sparrows Pt. Defense Housing		Sparrows Pt.	MD	1941	Assoc. architect
U.S. Post Office	230 E. Chestnut St.	Coatesville	PA		
U.S. Post Office	400 Well St., NE	Decatur	AL		
U.S. Post Office	130 E. Main St.	Frankfort	NY		
U.S. Post Office	202 W. Main St.	Marion	IN	1907	
U.S. Post Office	524 Main St.	Morgantown	WV	1931	Addition
U.S. Post Office	121 Valley St.	New Philadelphia	PA		
U.S. Post Office	301 Memorial Pkwy.	Phillipsburg	NJ		
U.S. Post Office	189 E. Main St.	Xenia	OH		
Virginia Avenue School		Louisville	KY		
Westover Subdivision	S. Western Pkwy. opp. Chickasaw Park	Louisville	KY	1945	Demolished
Wilson, J. Woodrow	723 W. Adams St.	Marion	IN	1912	Now Hostess House Women's Club
Workers' Housing	10th & Boots Sts.	Marion	IN	c1906	5 cottages (4 demolished)

Prairie View Agricultural & Mechanical College School of Architecture, Texas

Prairie View Agricultural & Mechanical University is the second oldest public institution of higher education in the state of Texas. The Fifteenth Texas Legislature on August 14, 1876, authorized the establishment of the Agricultural and Mechanical College of Texas for Colored Youths in Waller County, approximately fifty miles northwest of Houston. The legislators used provisions of the federal Morrill Act of 1862 for initial funding, making Prairie View Agricultural & Mechanical College a land-grant institution whose mission was teaching, research, and public service. The legislators stipulated that Prairie View Agricultural & Mechanical College would be a component of what has evolved into the Texas Agricultural & Mechanical University System. The college system was initially segregated, and this arrangement had its genesis in the Texas Constitution of 1876, which stated that "separate schools shall be provided for white and colored children, and impartial provisions shall be made for both."[1] However, in the day-to-day operations of the two universities, there was never parity in funding, until the Texas Constitution was amended in 1984, designating Prairie View Agricultural & Mechanical University as one of only three "institutions of the first class" in Texas.

Classes began at Prairie View Agricultural & Mechanical College in 1878. Architectural drawing and building construction classes began in the 1920s as adjuncts to the mechanic arts program. In the 1920s, the faculty included Claude L. Wilson and LOUIS EDWIN FRY SR. Fry was the first Prairie View Agricultural & Mechanical College graduate to become a licensed architect. Wilson, Fry, and Frederick E. Giesecke, a faculty member at Texas Agricultural & Mechanical College, collaborated to help shape Prairie View's built environment in the early twentieth century. The campus buildings that they designed were generally Collegiate Gothic in style.

During the 1930s and 1940s, many graduates pursued careers as teachers in high school industrial arts programs and in construction-related occupations. ROY ANTHONY SEALEY, who had a successful architectural practice in Los Angeles, California, attended Prairie View Agricultural & Mechanical College in the 1930s.

In 1947 the Texas Legislature formalized the name of Prairie View Agricultural & Mechanical College of Texas, and the Board of Regents approved the creation of the School of Engineering. The first dean was Dr. Claude L. Wilson, who became the first African American to receive an engineer's license in Texas. At that time, a four-year degree program in architectural engineering was initiated. Architectural engineering faculty included LEON QUINCY JACKSON and H. S. Houston, who was a structural engineer. The first graduates were Lidge D. Green and Grover Colton.

In 1952 the School of Engineering moved into the new Gibb Gilchrist Engineering Building, which had space allocated for architectural design studios, offices, and laboratories. Austin E. Greaux became the first department head for Architectural Engineering in 1951 and served until 1968. Another faculty member in the early 1950s was Lawrence A. Collins, a practicing architect based in Houston. Distinguished graduates in the 1950s included Otis Anderson, Doyle Carrington, Ben Franklin, Charles Kellum, Nathelyne Archie Kennedy (who was the first female graduate), and Leroy Woodson.

In the 1960s, the faculty expanded to include Christian K. Andoh, Norcell D. Haywood, and Rubin Sherman. More studio design classes were added and more emphasis was placed on architectural design. Distinguished graduates in this decade included Marshall V. Brown Jr., Randolph Clark, O'Neil Gregory, George Gibson, Willie North, Clyde Porter, and Raymond Wright. In 1968 Dr. Claude L. Wilson became vice president of Prairie View Agricultural & Mechanical College and Austin E. Greaux became dean of the College of Engineering.

In the early 1970s, the college was elevated to university status and became a self-governing unit of the Texas Agricultural & Mechanical University System. In 1972 the university's Board of Regents changed the curriculum from architectural engineering to a five-year program leading to a bachelor of architecture degree. Christian K. Andoh became the department head,

Prairie View Agricultural & Mechanical College Mechanical Drawing Class, *Praire View Agricultural & Mechanical University Archives*

and faculty included Wesley H. Henderson, Rubin Sherman, Jimmy Walker, and Percy Williams. Outstanding graduates in this decade included Michael Buster, Lincoln Calhoun, Ben S. McMillian III, and Christus Powell.

In the 1980s a reorganization resulted in a renamed College of Engineering and Architecture. Alumnus Marshall V. Brown Jr. became department head for Architecture and associate dean. A new building named for Dr. Claude L. Wilson allowed the Department of Architecture to expand into over 11,000 square feet of new design studios, offices, laboratories, photography laboratories, a model shop, and a slide library. A number of honor and professional societies were added during this decade.

In 1984 the curriculum was revised to meet the National Architectural Accrediting Board Standards, and the Department of Architecture applied for "Candidacy" status for accreditation. In 1986 the department gained membership in the Association of Collegiate Schools of Architecture. Faculty included Don B. Kerl, Ikhlas Saboui, Chuka Ugochukwu, Simon R. Wiltz, and His Chi Yang. Outstanding graduates included Regina Blair, Thomas H. Carroll, Verna R. Hunter, Kevin Smith, and Tyrone R. Williams.

In 1992 the department received accreditation from the National Architectural Accrediting Board. During this time, Marshall V. Brown Jr. served as interim dean of the College of Engineering and Architecture, and Simon R. Wiltz was interim department head for Architecture. In 1993 Dr. Ikhlas Sabouni became the first female department head. In 1995 there was another reorganization. Dr. Sabouni became the first Dean of the School of Architecture. Faculty during this decade included Jonti Bolles, Jamie Crawley, Richard Ferrier, James Griffin, Brad McCorkle, Barry Norwood, Unsik Song, Major Stewart, Tyrone R. Williams, and Peter Wood. Outstanding graduates included Kelvin B. Hall, Terry Smith, and Verrick D. Walker.

The School of Architecture currently offers a bachelor of science degree in architecture and master of architecture degree, a bachelor of science in construction science, and a master of community development degree. Upon the recommendation of President Charles Hines, the university Board of Regents has authorized the expenditure of $28 million for the design and construction of a new building for the exclusive use by the School of Architecture.

Prairie View's existence for 126 years stands as a testament to the struggle by African Americans for advancement and quality education. The School of Architecture has always accepted students without regard to race, and has students and faculty of various ethnicities and nationalities. The current enrollment is about 120 students, with fifteen faculty. Prairie View Agricultural & Mechanical University is now in the position to offer a high-quality architectural education for all Texans.

Note

1. *Prairie View A&M Catalog* (Prairie View: Texas A&M University System, 2002), p. 21. College Station, Texas.

MARSHALL V. BROWN JR.,
ASSOCIATE DEAN, PRAIRIE VIEW
AGRICULTURAL & MECHANICAL UNIVERSITY

Henry James Price
(1858–c1930)

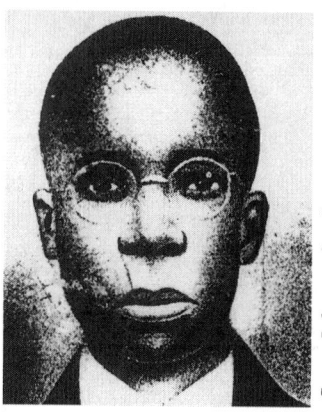

Steve Johnson Studio

Henry James Price was born in Meridian, Mississippi, in 1858. His approximate birth year was 1858, based on the 1880 U.S. Census for Lauderdale County.[1] His race was listed as "other" and his age was given as twenty-two while living in the household of Rufus and Anice Ellis along with their two minor children. No information could be found about Henry's parents or his early years.

No documents were found to confirm Henry Price's primary and secondary education experiences in Meridian, Mississippi. Family oral history claims that he graduated from the School of Architecture at Howard University with academic honors of summa cum laude. However, university officials could not find any records to confirm that Price was either a student or a graduate of Howard University. A Howard University records department staffer further stated, "I am skeptical that Price graduated *summa cum laude*, because I don't think they had such an honor back in the 1900s and especially not in architecture."

It is speculated that Henry James Price was trained as an architect after serving an apprenticeship with a skilled architect.

Dr. Elias Camp Morris (1879–1922), pastor of Centennial Missionary Baptist Church of Helena, Arkansas and founding president of the National Baptist Convention, the largest African American organization in America during the latter decades of the nineteenth century, asked Price to design a Gothic Revival–style church like the ones he had seen during his travels to Europe. Price, a member of Centennial, collaborated with Morris to design the 1,000-seat church, which was completed in 1905. The church is a 1-story, brick edifice with Gothic Revival–style elements such as "tower entries, double-hung lancet windows with hood molds of soldier bricks, buttresses, and brick corbels on the tower cornices and the central gable."[2] One outstanding feature of Centennial Missionary Baptist Church is its "great height," high ceilings, built to accommodate the hot Arkansas summers. Centennial is located on York and Columbia Streets. It served as the headquarters for the National Baptist Convention during Morris's presidency from 1899 to 1919, in addition to being the center for civil rights and community events. This church is the only known structure designed by Price in the state of Arkansas.

In August 1906, Price purchased property in Old Helena, Arkansas, from Henry Avant for $939, which he paid in cash. On September 30, 1907, he married Pearl M. Jackson, the only child of Henry Jackson of Helena, and to this union were born two daughters: Louise, who preceded both of them in death, and Katie Elizabeth, who lived to age eighty-seven and died on October 1, 1999.

Pearl Jackson received degrees from TUSKEGEE INSTITUTE, Philander Smith College in Little Rock, and Agricultural, Mechanical & Normal College in Pine Bluff, Arkansas. She was a prominent educator and religious and civic leader in Helena until her death on November 3, 1979, at the age of ninety-two.

Henry's marriage to Pearl ended on March 27, 1916, after nine years. She divorced him after suffer-

Centennial Missionary Baptist Church, *Steve Johnson Studio*

ing years of mental cruelty. After his divorce, Henry Price moved to Gary, Indiana. Along with being an accomplished architect, Price became a successful businessman and owner of a dry goods store in Gary, where he manufactured and sold custom-crafted furniture while touting his skills as a cabinetmaker. According to Harold Jefferson Price, his grandmother seldom spoke of her marriage to his grandfather. When the grandson learned of his grandfather's success as a businessman in Gary, Indiana, he asked his grandmother, "why didn't our family share in grandpa's wealth?"[3] Pearl Price replied, "Sometimes peace of mind is better than all the money in the world."[4] Price suffered "fits" for a short time and suddenly died in 1930. The cause of death is unknown.

Henry Price's architectural career remains to be discovered. His only known architectural design, Centennial Missionary Baptist Church, is listed on the National Register of Historic Places for its architectural significance and connection with a national figure, Dr. E. C. Morris, and a national event, the founding of the National Baptist Convention. Centennial Missionary Baptist Church is the only African American church in Arkansas designed by an African American architect and built by African Americans for an African American congregation. The church designed by Henry Price "has stood the test of time" for nearly one hundred years.

Notes

1. Interview with Dr. Clifford Muse (Howard University Archivist) 10 August 2002, Washington, D.C.
2. U.S. Department of the Interior, National Park Service. "National Register of Historic Places Nomination Form, Centennial Baptist Church." March 1987.
3. Interview with Harold Jefferson Price (Henry Price's grandson) 14 August 2002, Helena, Arkansas.
4. Harold Price interview.

Bibliography

"A Land Given: 19th Century African Americans in the Arkansas Delta Exhibit." Department of Arkansas Heritage, Delta Cultural Center. Helena, Ark., 1993.

PHYLIS HAMMOND, PRESIDENT,
ARKANSAS DELTA AFRICAN AMERICAN
HISTORICAL SOCIETY
HELENA, ARKANSAS

BUILDING LIST

Name	Address	City	State	Year	Comments
Centennial Missionary Baptist Church	York & Columbia Sts.	Helena	AK	1905	

Edward Lyons Pryce
(1914–)

Hawkins Studio, Inc

Edward Pryce, landscape architect, horticulturalist, educator, and artist, has left an indelible stamp on the landscape design of Tuskegee University (formerly TUSKEGEE INSTITUTE), where he served from 1948 until 1977 as superintendent of buildings and grounds and professor in the School of Architecture, and from 1977 to 1990 as consulting landscape architect. Using his industry and creative abilities, Pryce made a name for himself in the profession of landscape architecture during a period when there were few practitioners and even fewer Black practitioners.

Edward Pryce was born in Lake Charles, Louisiana, in 1914, the son of George Codrington Pryce, who owned a pharmacy there, and Dora Raymond, a housewife. His father, who was an 1898 graduate of Meharry Medical College in Nashville, Tennessee, moved his family to Los Angeles, California, when the cost of educating his eight children in a private high school in New Orleans became too expensive. African Americans were prohibited from attending the public high school in Lake Charles back then.

Pryce attended the public schools of Los Angeles and then in 1932 entered the pre-medicine program at the University of California at Los Angeles, where he was one of only five Black students. After a year and a half, he changed from medicine to horticulture when he met a Black plant specialist who persuaded him to go study with the preeminent agricultural scientist Dr. George Washington Carver at Tuskegee Institute. Arriving at Tuskegee Institute, Pryce signed on as an assistant to Dr. Carver, who was on sabbatical from teaching, but was continuing to conduct his now-famous agricultural experiments. As his assistant, Pryce collected mushrooms for Carver's mycologic studies. He also collected edible weeds, such as wild lettuce and dandelions, which Dr. Carver used to demonstrate to Black subsistence farmers the nutritional value.

After earning his bachelor of science degree in agriculture from Tuskegee Institute in 1937, Pryce's interest in landscape architecture took hold when he worked as landscape foreman on the "*San Marino*" estate of the president of the Southern Pacific Railroad, Collis P. Huntington, in San Marino, California, from 1937 until 1939. During World War II, Pryce was a park maintenance foreman for the City of Los Angeles. After earning the bachelor of science degree in landscape architecture from Ohio State University in 1948, Pryce, who was married with two children by then, returned to Tuskegee Institute, where from 1948 until 1955 he was head of the Department of Ornamental Horticulture and in charge of campus landscape maintenance. In 1953 he earned the master of landscape architecture degree from the University of California at Berkeley.

At Tuskegee Institute, Pryce collaborated closely with DAVID AUGUSTUS WILLISTON, one of the first African American landscape architects who was integrally involved in the master planning and planting of the campus. From 1955 to 1969, Pryce was superintendent of buildings and grounds and was responsible for 72 buildings and 140 housing units. He faced the challenge of inadequate funding to maintain the his-

Tuskegee Institute Campus, *Prints and Photographs Division, Library of Congress*

toric buildings on Tuskegee's campus, which in 1965 had been designated a National Historic Landmark. Pryce was the first Black to be licensed as a landscape architect when he received his state of Alabama license in 1972.¹ Also in 1972, he wrote the grant proposal that resulted in the campus being nominated as a National Historic Site two years later.² From 1969 to 1977, Pryce was a part-time instructor in the Department of Architecture and part-time campus planner.

Pryce's landscape architecture projects reached far beyond Tuskegee Institute. He served as a consultant in facilities planning and maintenance for two higher-education facilities in Liberia, West Africa: Zorzor College and Kakata Teacher Training College. As consultant for campus and grounds planning and maintenance with the Robert R. Moton Memorial Institute, Plant Management Program, he worked with eight historically Black colleges and universities in the South from 1976 through 1982. He also served as consultant landscape architect for two Mass Area Rapid Transit Authority stations in Atlanta, Georgia. Pryce retired from private practice in 1990.

Throughout his career, Pryce relied on nature to guide his landscape designs. He maintained that a landscape that required minimal maintenance was more ecologically sound because it required less water and less polluting chemicals. He believed that grass and trees are the basis of a landscape; that there is little need for flower beds, which not only impede pedestrian flow, but are also labor intensive. He was particularly disdainful of drastically pruning shrubs with electric shears, preferring a naturally formed shrub over an artificially sculptured one.³

In honor of his distinguished career in landscape architecture, Pryce was elected a fellow in the American Society of Landscape Architecture (ASLA) in 1984. He was the first African American to receive this honor, and the first landscape architect, White or Black, from the state of Alabama. Becoming a fellow carried with it a tinge of irony—because of his race he had been denied membership in the southeastern chapter of ASLA when he returned to Tuskegee, Alabama, in the late 1940s. Years later, however, when state chapters were formed, he was elected by his peers vice-president of the Alabama chapter and served from 1977 to 1978.

After his retirement from Tuskegee Institute, Pryce devoted much of his time to painting Afro-centric themes and carving wood sculptures. His works of art can be found in buildings on the campus of Tuskegee Institute, including the mural and copper bas-relief in Tuskegee Chapel. Two 45-foot-long murals depicting African American history are on display in the local Booker T. Washington High School. His paintings, which incorporate copper, are the dominant artworks for the newly renovated Hollis Burke Frissell Library.

In 1940 Pryce married Woodia B. Smith, who was born in Tuskegee, Alabama, when her father, the Reverend Woodford S. Smith, was pastor of the Greenwood Missionary Baptist Church. The Pryces, who met as students at Tuskegee Institute, have two daughters: Marilyn and Joellen.

Edward Pryce resides in Tuskegee, Alabama, where he continues to paint and sculpt and tend a large vegetable garden.

Notes

1. Alabama Board of Examiners of Landscape Architects, "Edward Pryce," no. 19, issued 11 April 1972.
2. U.S. Department of Interior, National Park Service, "Tuskegee Institute National Historic Site," 23 June 1965.
3. Elizabeth Brown, "Designing Beauty, Retired Architect Sculpts Landscapes into Pieces of Art," *Montgomery Advertiser*, 22 February 1997, p. 1C.

Bibliography

Guy Rhodes, "At Age 82, Tuskegee Artist, Edward Pryce Isn't Slowing Down." *Inside East Alabama and Auburn-Opelika.* 2, no. 3 (March 1997): 17.

JOELLEN ELBASHIR, DAUGHTER OF EDWARD PRYCE AND ARCHIVIST, MOORLAND-SPINGARN RESEARCH CENTER, WASHINGTON, D.C.

LANDSCAPE PROJECT LIST

Name	Address	City	State/Country	Year	Comments
Adams Elementary School	1133 W. Old Montgomery Rd.	Tuskegee	AL	1966	
Alabama Christian College	Campus	Montgomery	AL	1980	
Lakewood Transit Center	59th Ave. & 108th St. SW	Atlanta	GA	1976	William, Russell & Johnson, assoc. LAs
Lenvox Transit Station	955 E. Pages Ferry Rd.	Atlanta	GA	1976	William, Russell & Johnson, assoc. LAs
Njala University Master Plan	Campus	Njala	Sierra Leone	1976	
Tuskegee Institute Middle School	1809 Franklin Rd.	Tuskegee	AL	1968	Now Tuskegee Middle School
Tuskegee University Andrews Hospital	Campus	Tuskegee	AL	1974	
Tuskegee University Carver Bldg.	Campus	Tuskegee	AL	1951	
Tuskegee University Carver Dormitory	Campus	Tuskegee	AL	1961	
Tuskegee University Chapel	Campus	Tuskegee	AL	1969	
Tuskegee University Dresge Center	Campus	Tuskegee	AL	1982	
Tuskegee University Drew Dormitory	Campus	Tuskegee	AL	1960	
Tuskegee University James Center	Campus	Tuskegee	AL	1982	
Tuskegee University Landscape Plan	Campus	Tuskegee	AL	1972	Ehrenkrantz Group, assoc. LAs
Tuskegee University Moton Hall	Campus	Tuskegee	AL	1965	
Tuskegee University Roberts Housing	Campus	Tuskegee	AL	1950	
Tuskegee University School of Engineering	Campus	Tuskegee	AL	1965	
Tuskegee University School of Nursing	Campus	Tuskegee	AL	1960	
Tuskegee University School of Veterinary Medicine	Campus	Tuskegee	AL	1950	
Tuskegee University Tantum Dormitory	Campus	Tuskegee	AL	1961	
Tuskegee University Thrasher Dormitory	Campus	Tuskegee	AL	1962	
Tuskegee University Tree Inventory	Campus	Tuskegee	AL	1998	
Tuskegee University Tubman Dormitory	Campus	Tuskegee	AL	1960	
Tuskegee University Woodruff Food Plant	Campus	Tuskegee	AL	1962	
Tuskegee Veterans Hospital		Tuskegee	AL	1967	
Vine City Transit Station	561 Rhodes St.	Atlanta	GA	1976	Harris Associates, assoc. LAs
Washington High School	204 Cedar St.	Tuskegee	AL	1955	

Leon Andrew Ransom Jr.
(1929–1971)

Diane Ransom

The first African American architect of prominence from Columbus, Ohio, Leon Ransom Jr., was born in Columbus on April 30, 1929, to attorney Leon A. Ransom Sr. and Willa C. Ransom. In 1931 the Ransoms moved to Washington, D.C., where the elder Ransom taught at Howard University's trailblazing Law School from 1931 until 1946. Homemaker Willa Ransom later worked in her husband's law firm. Raised in the nation's capital, Leon Jr. attended Mott Elementary School, Banneker Junior High School, and Dunbar High School, graduating in 1946. Leon's sister, Mary Jean Hunter, reminisced, "we always knew that some day Leon was going to build something. As a child he spent hours putting together model airplanes; elaborate structures with his Erector sets; and intricate systems of dams, pools, and bridges in our backyard."[1] At the Catholic University of America in Washington, D.C., he majored in geography and was a member of *Kappa Alpha Psi* Fraternity. After obtaining his bachelor's degree in 1950, he married Delores Collins of the District of Columbia on June 17, 1950. Returning to The Catholic University of America, he received his master's degree in architecture in 1953.

Hired as a draftsman by Peter Kiewett & Sons, a firm involved in constructing the Portsmouth nuclear enrichment facility in Piketon about twenty-five miles south of Chillicothe, Ransom returned to Ohio. In 1954 he found employment as a draftsman for Columbus architectural firm Louis Karlsberger & Associates, which specialized in health care facilities. Following the requisite three years of work under the supervision of a licensed architect, he passed the state licensing examination and became a registered architect in 1957.[2] Ransom remained with Karlsberger & Associates until 1963. For the next several years he was in partnership with Sylvester C. Angel—Columbus's only other Black architect—as Angel & Ransom, with an office in the Urlin Building at 36 West Gay Street in downtown Columbus. The younger Angel recalls Ransom as very practical, not idealistic, and as having people skills—perhaps acquired through a stint as a Washington, D.C., taxi driver while in college—to break through social barriers, meet prospective clients,

Bethel Apartments, *Thomas M. Wolfe*

and obtain commissions.[3] In 1966 Ransom launched a solo practice, Leon A. Ransom & Associates, Architects–Planners–Designers, with an office in the historic Firestone mansion at 1266 East Broad Street in Columbus. He continued as a sole proprietor until failing health forced him to shutter the office in 1970.

In the 1960s, as a member of the American Institute of Architects, Ransom traveled to Sweden with a delegation to study congregate housing. He also served on the Columbus Board of Zoning Adjustment from 1963 until 1970. He worshipped at Saint Thomas the Apostle Roman Catholic Church, where he was active in the Society of Saint Vincent de Paul, which provided social services to the indigent.

Leon Ransom and his wife, Delores C. Ransom, had four children: Leon C., Michael L., Dolores B., and Denise M. Ransom. For most of his career, Ransom and his family lived at 210 Sherbourne Drive in Eastgate, an early-twentieth-century suburban look-alike development of curvilinear streets and period Revival-style houses characterized by a reporter for the *Columbus Citizen*, a local African American newspaper, "as proud, respectable Eastgate . . . the show place of Negro neighborhoods."[4]

Leon Ransom designed the No. 47 Miami Apartments in Columbus, a symmetrical 2-story apartment house with the lower story faced in brick and an overhanging Mansard second story faced in wood-shake shingles, typical of small apartment houses of the era. He designed the No. 8 Fire Station in Columbus, a 1-story, three-bay Wrightonian-influenced firehouse. Because the No. 15 Fire Station resembles the No. 8 Fire Station, it is likely that the former was also designed by Ranson. While employed by Karlsberger & Associates and later in his own practice, Ransom designed two round buildings: the Christopher Inn, a 16-story hotel; and Saint Anthony Hospital, which was inspired by the Christopher Inn. He designed the 1-story, International-style Martin Luther King Jr. Branch Public Library. However, the library that he was most proud of is the Hallie Q. Brown Library at Central State University in Wilberforce, possibly because of the storied historic significance of Central State University to African Americans.

Following a year-long illness, Leon Ransom died on May 11, 1971, at age forty-two.[5] His unmarked grave is in the Miraculous Medal section at Saint Joseph Cemetery south of Columbus.

Notes

1. Interview with Mary Jean Ransom Hunter (sister of Leon Ransom Jr.), by the author, Carrboro, N.C., 17 November 2002.
2. Ohio Board of Examiners of Architects, "Leon A. Ransom," 21 January 1957, no. 2697.
3. Interview with Sylvester Angel (partner of Leon Ransom Jr.), by the author, Columbus, Ohio, 3 November 2002.
4. "Ranson," *Columbus Citizen Journal*, 13 May 1971, p. 34.
5. "Leon Ransom," *Columbus Dispatch,* 13 May 1971, p. 7A (Deaths) and p. B13 (Obituary).

Bibliography

"47 Main Apartments." *Columbus Challenger,* November 1967, p. 13.

THOMAS M. WOLFE,
PUBLIC EDUCATION MANAGER,
OHIO HISTORIC PRESERVATION OFFICE,
AND TOM WISEMILLER, INTERN

BUILDING LIST

Name	Address	City	State	Year	Comments
Bell, Atty. Napoleon	1975 Sunbury Rd.	Columbus	OH	c1967	Assoc. architect
Bethel Apts.	Kenmore & Bancroft	Columbus	OH	1968	
Bolivar Arms Apts.	Bolvar Arms Urban Renewal Area	Columbus	OH		Alterations
Central State University Brown Library	Campus	Wilberforce	OH	1969	Destroyed by tornado
Church of Christ Apostolic Faith	1200 Brentnell Ave.	Columbus	OH	1965	
Christopher Inn—Round Hotel	300 E. Broad St.	Columbus	OH	1963	Demolished
City of Columbus Single-Family Housing	Various addresses	Columbus	OH		
Columbus Fire Station No. 8	1240 E. Long St.	Columbus	OH	1968	
Franklin Park Medical Center	1829 E. Long St.	Columbus	OH	c1962	Staff architect
Grant Hospital	111 S. Grant St.	Columbus	OH	1961	Staff architect
IGA Food Liner	1315 Mt. Vernon Ave.	Columbus	OH	c1968	
Martin Luther King Jr. Public Library	1600 E. Long St.	Columbus	OH	1969	
Mock Road Senior Citizens Housing	2295 Mock Rd.	Columbus	OH	1969	Demolished
No. 47 Miami Apts.	47 Miami Ave.	Columbus	OH	1966	
Ohio State University Hospitals	Campus	Columbus	OH	c1961	Staff architect
Ransom, Leon A.	210 Sherbourne Dr.	Columbus	OH	1957	Alterations
St. Anthony Hospital	1450 Hawthorne Ave.	Columbus	OH	c1960	
St. Augustine Roman Catholic Church Parish	1569 Loretta Ave.	Columbus	OH	1954	Alterations
St. Paul African Methodist Episcopal Church	628 E. Long St.	Columbus	OH		Annex alterations
St. Vincent's Orphanage	1490 E. Main St.	Columbus	OH	c1950	
Waddington, Dr. Harold	5800 Sunbury Rd.	Columbus	OH	c1969	

Wallace Augustus Rayfield
(1874–1941)

Prints and Photographs Division, Library of Congress

Wallace A. Rayfield was born on May 10, 1874, in Bibb County, near Macon, Georgia. His father was a railroad porter and accounts refer to his mother as having attended Atlanta University, but elsewhere state that she worked as a maid.[1] While in Macon, Wallace was a student of the noted African American educator Lucy G. Laney for seven years.

After the death of his mother when Rayfield was twelve years old, he lived with his aunt in Washington, D.C., and attended the preparatory department of Howard University. He continued his studies at Howard University and received a diploma of graduation from the Classical Department with the degree of bachelor of science in 1896. While a student at Howard University, Rayfield received lessons in art for two years at the home of Miss D. L. Mussey. Through her father, who was a lawyer representing the architectural firm of A. B. Mullett & Company of Washington, D.C., Rayfield obtained employment with the firm for two years. In 1896, upon graduating from Howard University, Rayfield moved to Brooklyn, New York, to receive formal architectural training. He studied architecture at Pratt Institute and received a certificate of graduation in 1898. He then entered the Department of Architecture of Columbia University and received a bachelor of architecture degree in 1899.

While at Columbia University, Rayfield met Booker T. Washington, who offered him a position teaching mechanical and architectural drawing at TUSKEGEE INSTITUTE. Rayfield remained at Tuskegee Institute for eight years. He resigned following a disagreement over the publication of a set of drawing plates he had created and after failing to receive an anticipated raise.

Rayfield moved to Birmingham, Alabama, and established the first Black-owned architectural office in Alabama. Registration laws did not come into effect in Alabama until 1931, and Rayfield never sought state registration. During his early career, he collaborated with Black contractor Thomas C. Windham. This collaboration designed and constructed buildings for the growing Black population of Birmingham and produced at least five houses, as well as the Sixteenth Street Baptist Church; the Sixth Avenue Baptist Church (old); Trinity Baptist Church; and Saint Paul's Church of Batesville, Arkansas. The African Methodist Episcopal Zion Church denomination appointed Rayfield as their "official architect" in charge of designing all churches and parsonages throughout the United States and Africa.

During his career, Rayfield served as a mentor for younger men either through his teaching at Tuskegee Institute or through training in his office. Among his better-known students and employees were WILLIAM SIDNEY PITTMAN and VERTNER WOODSON TANDY. Rayfield was also secretary of Birmingham's branch of the National Negro Business League.

Wallace Rayfield died on February 28, 1941. Two of his Birmingham buildings are listed on the National Register of Historic Places: Dr. Arthur McKim-

16th Street Baptist Church, *Hollis Burke Frissell Library, Tuskegee University*

mon Brown's residence and the Sixteenth Street Baptist Church.[2]

Notes

1. Interview with Allen Durough (Wallace Rayfield Biographer) 29 April 2001, Centre, Alabama and G. P. Hamilton, *Beacon Light's of the Race*, Memphis: Clark & Brothers, 1911, p. 452.
2. U.S. Department of Interior, National Park Service, "Dr. Arthur McKimmon Brown House," 20 June 1974; and Sixteenth Street Baptist Church, 17 September 1980.

Bibliography

Brown, Charles A. *W.A. Rayfield: Pioneer Black Architect of Birmingham, Alabama*. Birmingham: Gray Printing Company, 1972.

Feldman, Lynne B. *A Sense of Place: Birmingham's Black Middle-Class Community, 1890–1930*. Tuscaloosa: University of Alabama Press, 1999.

McKenzie, Vinson E. "A Pioneering African-American Architect in Alabama: Wallace A. Rayfield, 1874–1941." *Preservation Report* (Alabama Historical Commission) 21, no. 1 (Jan./Feb. 1994).

Rabiroff, Jon. "Historic Find Printing Plates Discovered About Birmingham's First Black Architect, His Work." *Birmingham News*, 11 June 1993, p. 1.

Satterfield, Carolyn Green. *Historic Sites of Jefferson County, Alabama*. Birmingham: Jefferson County Historical Commission, 1985.

ELIZABETH MEREDITH DOWLING,
ASSOCIATE PROFESSOR,
GEORGIA INSTITUTE OF TECHNOLOGY

BUILDING LIST

Name	Address	City	State	Year	Comments
Antioch Baptist Church	956 W. 9th St.	Cincinnatti	OH		
Birmingham Art Club		Birmingham	AL	1908	
Blount, R. A.	322 6th Ave., N.	Birmingham	AL	1914	
Brown, Dr. Arthur M.	319 4th Terr.	Birmingham	AL	1908	Demolished
Brown, R. T.	470 1st St., N.	Birmingham	AL	1928	Now Mt. Pilgrim Baptist Church
Coar, John M.	812 Center St.	Birmingham	AL	c1907	
Dobbins, A. G.	424 1st St., N.	Birmingham	AL	1926	
Dunbar Hotel		Birmingham	AL		
Ebenezer Baptist Church		Chicago	IL		
First Congregational Church	Campus	Talladega	AL		Talladega College
French Cleaners	1721 4th Ave., N.	Birmingham	AL		
Haven Institute Dormitory	Campus	Meridian	MS		
Independent Benevolent Order Lodge No. 1	512 S. Broad St.	Atlanta	GA		Now 8th Ave. YMCA
Jackson, Bishop T. S.	500 8th Ave., N.	Birmingham	AL	1912	
Knights of Pythias Temple	310 18th St., N.	Birmingham	AL	1913	

WALLACE AUGUSTUS RAYFIELD

BUILDING LIST *(continued)*

Name	Address	City	State	Year	Comments
Metropolitan African Methodist Episcopal Zion Church	1530 4th St., N.	Birmingham	AL		
Mt. Pilgrim African Baptist Church	Clara & Alice Sts.	Milton	FL	1916	
Parker, Arthur H.	522 5th St., N.	Birmingham	AL	1908	
Penny Savings Bank	310 18th St. N.	Birmingham	AL	1913	
Pharrow, Ed	309 4th Terr.	Birmingham	AL	1908	
Rayfield, Wallace A.	105 1st Ave., S.	Birmingham	AL	1908	
Seymour, R. W.		Birmingham	AL		
Sixteenth Street Baptist Church	1530 6th Ave., N.	Birmingham	AL	1909	
Sixth Avenue Baptist Church	1531 6th Ave., S.	Birmingham	AL	1909	
Smith-Gaston "Hill Top"	60 Ave. D	Fairfield	AL		
South Elyton Baptist Church	102 1st St., S.	Birmingham	AL		
St. Paul's Parish Church	5th & Main Sts.	Batesville	AR	1924	
Strawbridge, T. S.		Birmingham	AL		
Strong Undertaking Co.		Birmingham	AL		
Thirty-Second Avenue Baptist Church	32nd Ave.	Birmingham	AL		
Thomas Public School	3400 2nd Ave., S.	Birmingham	AL		
Trinity African Methodist Episcopal Church	400 Evins St.	Spartanburg	SC	1922	
Trinity Baptist Church	328 4th St., N.	Birmingham	AL	c1920	
Tuggle Institute	Campus	Birmingham	AL		
Walton's Cafe		Birmingham	AL		

Lawrence Reese
(1865–1915)

Audrey L. Reese Jones

Lawrence Reese was a master craftsman and gentleman architect. He was the youngest son of nine, born in 1864 to Richard and Fannie Reese in Marlboro County, South Carolina. His family farmed and engaged in building and carpentry work in an area called Sand Hills.

As a teen, Lawrence learned the rudiments of basic carpentry from the males of his immediate family and extended family. He decided early on that he preferred carpentry to farming. Lawrence had no formal education, but realized that he needed to learn to read, write, count, and measure. He was self-taught and managed to acquire those needed skills. He left the farm and traveled to Darlington, South Carolina, around 1887.

In Darlington, Reece was hired to perform small carpentry jobs. As he gained experience and expertise in his trade, he became more confident of his talents and his projects became larger. He was a dedicated hard worker.

Later, he met a young Cherokee girl, Lula Aiken, who was being raised in the household of Dr. and Mrs. McGirt, along with their natural children. Lawrence asked Dr. McGirt for Lula's hand in marriage. Dr. McGirt asked Reece how he expected to support her, to which Reece replied that he was a carpenter. At that point, Dr. McGirt used a stick to mark off a small plot on his property and said "build me a house here."[1] When the small house was completed, Dr. McGirt approved the results and granted Reece permission to marry Lula. Eight children who lived to adulthood were born to their union: four sons and four daughters.

Reece trained his sons in the skill of the trade. Two of his sons became master carpenters in Darlington; one son became a master carpenter in Boston, Massachusetts; and the other son served in the U.S. Army in the Philippines. Three daughters became public school teachers and one a nurse.

Reece was an entrepreneur who owned a neighborhood store and undertaking business. Being a carpenter, he also built caskets for his business and for White undertakers in the area. His sons helped, but preferred carpentry to undertaking.

As his reputation as a talented craftsman and builder grew, he received numerous contracts from prominent citizens. He educated himself about emerging architectural trends by buying books such as *House Patterns and Plans*, and learned to apply and modify the styles to replicate and alter plans, and to include his own signature detailing. His houses are known for their intricate woodwork and elaborate Gothic-style architectural elements.

Most of the houses designed and built by Reese were 2-story with double porches. All contain high ceilings, hardwood floors, and signature fireplaces. Some have original stained-glass front windows. The houses are sited on deep lots with tall trees and a variety of shrubs.

Historic records indicate that fourteen extant residences are attributed to Lawrence Reese. They were listed on the National Register of Historic Places in 1988 as the West Broad Street Historic District,[2] and

Western Railroad Station, *Audrey L. Jones*

are all located on the same street. In the early 1900s, the area was colloquially known as "Reese's Row."

Two other buildings outside "Reece's Row" were also designed and built by Lawrence Reese: the Edward Sanders House on South Main Street and the Western Railway Station. Both are listed on the National Register of Historic Places.

Lawrence Reese was fifty years old when he died in 1915 of a heart attack at his home, which he had designed and built in the late 1800s. His architectural achievements spanned a period of thirty years. On May 6, 2001, a marker was unveiled and dedicated, honoring Lawrence Reese for his outstanding architectural achievements. His legacy is richly evidenced in the city of Darlington, South Carolina.

Note
1. Jim Faile, "The Architectural Achievements of Lawrence Reese," *The Darlington News and Press*, 25 June 1998, p. 1.
2. U.S. Department of Interior, National Park Service "West Broad Street Historic District," 10 February 1988.

AUDREY L. REESE JONES, GRANDDAUGHTER AND RETIRED EDUCATOR, D.C. PUBLIC SCHOOLS

BUILDING LIST

Name	Address	City	State	Year	Comments
Bonnoit, M.	235 W. Broad St.	Darlington	SC	c1890	
Early, W. F.	368 W. Broad St.	Darlington	SC	c1890	
Hart, M. S.	393 W. Broad St.	Darlington	SC	c1895	
Hennig, Henry	379 W. Broad St.	Darlington	SC	c1895	
Hyman, Abraham	229 W. Broad St.	Darlington	SC	c1900	Now Belk Funeral Home
Kirven, J. K.	389 W. Broad St.	Darlington	SC	c1893	
Lucas, C. L.	245 W. Broad St.	Darlington	SC	c1895	
Lunn, E. E.	232 W. Broad St.	Darlington	SC	c1895	
Lunney, Dr. John	242 W. Broad St.	Darlington	SC	c1895	
Mertz, G. O.	395 W. Broad St.	Darlington	SC	c1895	
Muldrow, J. O.	375 W. Broad St.	Darlington	SC	c1895	
Reese, Lawrence	434 W. Broad St.	Darlington	SC	c1890	
Sanders, Edward	818 S. Main St.	Darlington	SC	c1900	
Spears, J. Monroe	241 W. Broad St.	Darlington	SC	c1890	
West, E. J.	237 W. Broad St.	Darlington	SC	c1890	
Western Railway Station	Russell St.	Darlington	SC	1911	Now Bella Durnoni Salon
Wilson, J. F.	258 W. Broad St.	Darlington	SC	c1895	

Francis Jefferson Roberson
(1862–1944)

Francis Jefferson Roberson with son Francis Rassieur, Nick Woods

Francis Jefferson Roberson was born in Saint Louis, Missouri, the son of William A. Roberson and Lucy Jefferson Roberson. His father, a free person of color before the Civil War, was the proprietor of a prosperous barbershop and massage parlor housed in one of Saint Louis' premier hotels until his death in 1878.[1] Francis's mother was born in slavery in Mississippi. Her father, also a slave, was, according to family oral history, a natural son of Thomas Jefferson.

After his father's death, Francis and his family moved to Oberlin, Ohio, where Francis Roberson attended preparatory classes at Oberlin College from 1878 to 1885. He then sailed to Germany, where he enrolled at the Technische Hochschule at Karlsruhe University from 1885 until 1887, studying art and architecture.[2]

Returning from Germany, Roberson settled in Saint Paul, Minnesota, joining his mother and siblings. He obtained a position as a draftsman with the Minneapolis architectural firm of J. W. Haley & Sons. Roberson was assigned to draw the plans for Saint Peter's African Methodist Episcopal church in Minneapolis and presumably contributed to or was the author of its design. The church, which is no longer extant, was a 40-foot × 74-foot Gothic style-edifice. African American stained-glass designer WILLIAM AUGUSTUS HAZEL designed the church's memorial windows.[3] After several years with Haley & Sons, Roberson went to work for the Saint Paul architectural firm of A. F. Gauger & Company as a draftsman. Which, if any, building designs can be attributed to Roberson are unknown. At various times during the 1890s, he intermittently attended the University of Minnesota and the Normal Art School in Chicago.[4]

After marrying Jessie Eudora Watson of Saint Louis, Missouri, around 1895, Roberson and his bride moved to Zanesville, Ohio, where he was employed as draftsman by the firm of H. C. Lindsay until mid-1897, when he received an appointment as art instructor at Charles Sumner High School in Saint Louis, the first high school for Black students west of the Mississippi River. He taught at Sumner High School and then at Vashon High School, which opened in 1927, into his seventies. His wife was one of the first *kindergarten* teachers in the Saint Louis public schools. As a part of Sumner High School's 100th anniversary celebration in 1975, Roberson was named "one of the 100 most outstanding teachers."[5] Francis and Jessie Roberson had four children: Laura, Francis, William, and Leroy.

Around 1920 Roberson opened an architectural office with his architect son FRANCIS RASSIEUR ROBERSON and civil engineer son William Artrudoe Roberson, which he maintained into the 1930s. Buildings designed by them include the sanctuary of the Antioch Baptist Church in Saint Louis's historic Ville neighborhood as well as other unidentified houses, hotels, and churches. Throughout his adult life, Rober-

FRANCIS JEFFERSON ROBERSON

Saint Peters American Methodist Episcopal Church, *Saint Paul Appeal Paper*

son painted using oils. The whereabouts of his paintings are unknown.

Francis Jefferson Roberson died in 1944 in Saint Louis at age eighty-two after an illness of several weeks. He is buried in the Roberson family plot in Bellefontaine Cemetery in Saint Louis.

Francis Roberson's opportunities as an architect, like those of many others, were circumscribed by his race and the pervasive segregation and discrimination of his lifetime. Although trained at an academically demanding German institute, he was underemployed as a "draftsman" in White-owned architectural firms. His later, independent work in Saint Louis and elsewhere for African American clients is not yet a part of the public record and remains to be discovered.

Notes
1. "The Freedmen of Missouri," *New York Tribune*, 6 July 1871, n.p.
2. *Technische Hochschule au Karlsruhe, Generallandesarchiv Karlsruhe,* Student Records, Winter Semester 1887, "Frank Roberson, St. Louis," Karlsruhe, Germany.
3. "Minneapolis Matters," *St. Paul Appeal*, 11 August 1888, p. 4.
4. *Sumner High School Yearbook*, "Western Historical Manuscript Collection," Jefferson Library, University of Missouri–St. Louis.
5. "Down Memory Lane," *50th Anniversary Celebration, Class of 1909* (St. Louis: St. Louis Public Schools, 1959), p. 22.

Bibliography
Christensen, Lawrence O. "Black St. Louis: A Study in Race Relations." Ph.D. diss., University of Missouri, 1972.
"Negroes—Their Gift to St. Louis, Mo." St. Louis: Employees Loan Company, 1964.
Young, Nathan B. ed. "Your St. Louis and Mine." St. Louis: N. B. Young, 1937.

DAVID RIEHLE, RESEARCHER AND WRITER ABOUT LOCAL LABOR RELATIONS AND AFRICAN AMERICAN HISTORY, SAINT PAUL, MINNESOTA

BUILDING LIST

Name	Address	City	State	Year	Comments
Antioch Baptist Church Sanctuary	4213 N. Market St.	St. Louis	MO	1907	
Roberson, Francis J.	3412 Humphrey St.	St. Louis	MO		
St. Louis Botanical Garden Greenhouse	4344 Shaw Blvd.	St. Louis	MO		
St. Louis Union Station Canopies	1820 Market St.	St. Louis	MO		
St. Peter's African Methodist Episcopal Church	22nd St. btwn. 9th & 10th Aves. South	Minneapolis	MN	1888	

Francis Rassieur Roberson
(1898–1979)

Francis Rassieur Roberson was born in Saint Louis, Missouri on January 31, 1898, the son of FRANCIS JEFFERSON ROBERSON and Jessie Eudora Watson Roberson, a public school teacher. Family oral history claims that Francis Jefferson was a descendant of Thomas Jefferson.[1] Francis's unusual middle name "Rassieur" came from prominent Saint Louis civic leader and jurist Leo Rassieur, who was admired as an "uncompromising abolitionist."[2] Francis Rassieur was the second oldest of four siblings. His sister, Laura Belle, was a longtime Saint Louis public school teacher. his brother, William Artudoe was a civil engineer. A third sibling died before reaching adulthood.

Francis Rassieur Roberson graduated in 1916 from Sumner High School in Saint Louis, the first high school for Black students west of the Mississippi River, where his father taught. After graduating from high school, he joined the U.S. Navy, where he spent his tour of duty aboard a submarine chaser. It was during his navy stint that he acquired the nickname "Skipper." After being honorably discharged he worked as a draftsman for his father in the firm that his father maintained well into the 1930s. In 1925 Francis Rassieur was awarded a second place medal from the Beaux-Arts Institute of Design based in Manhattan. From 1926 to 1933, he was employed by the Saint Louis architectural firm of W. P. Manske & Associates, advancing to become vice president and treasurer.

Francis Rassieur Roberson received a bachelor of science degree in architecture from the University of Illinois in June 1928. While at the university he pledged or in other words "crossed the burning sands" of *Kappa Alpha Psi* fraternity.

During the Great Depression, Francis Rassieur Roberson found steady work with the Civilian Conservation Corps (CCC) managing the Cuivre River Camp in northeast Missouri. He supervised crews constructing roads, dams, and bridges and fabricating road signs when not fighting floods and clearing fire breaks. About 1946, Roberson went to work for the U.S. Department of Interior, National Park Service regional office in Omaha, Nebraska, as a regional architect. After nineteen years he retired from the National Park Service and opened a private practice in 1965 from his home on 91st Street in Omaha.

Roberson was married to Edna W. Miller for over forty years. She worked as a secretary for her husband

Fort Laramie Officers Quarters, *Fort Laramie National Park Archives*

after he opened his own office. They had one daughter, Frances JoRay Roberson Dale.

Francis Rassieur Roberson died from a stroke on July 5, 1979. He is buried in Forest Lawn Cemetery in Omaha.

Notes
1. Interview with Nick Woods, grandson of Francis Rassieur Roberson, 1 April 2003, Troy, Ohio.
2. Douglas R. Niemeyer, "Leo Rassieur Biography," Military Order of the Loyal Legion of the United States (n.p.: 2001), n.p.

Bibliography
MacVaugh, Fred. *National Park Service Records and Archives in the National Archives of the United States: A Collection and Repository Guide*. Omaha: National Park Service, 2002.
Mattes, Merrill J. *Fort Laramie Park History, 1834–1977*. Omaha: National Parks Service, 1980.

DAVE RIEHLE, RESEARCHER AND WRITES
ABOUT LOCAL LABOR RELATIONS
AND AFRICAN AMERICAN HISTORY,
SAINT PAUL, MINNESOTA

BUILDING LIST

Name	Address	City	State	Year	Comments
Badlands National Park Museum	Badlands National Park		SD	1939	
Bryce Canyon National Park Museum	Bryce Canyon National Park	Bryce Canyon	UT	1929	
Camp David Trader Center	Camp David	Thurmont	MD	1964	Restoration
Carter Lake School	1105 Redick Blvd.	Carter Lake	IA		
Carver National Monument Visitor Center	Carver National Monument	Diamond	MO	1964	
Custer National Park Museum	Custer National Park	Custer	SD		
Custer National Park Visitor Center	Custer National Park	Custer	SD		
Devils Tower National Monument Visitor Center	Devils Tower Monument	Devils Tower	WY	1956	
Dinosaur National Monument Trader Center	Dinosaur National Monument	Dinosaur	CO		
Effigy Mounds National Monument Visitor Center	Effigy Mounds Monument	Harpers Ferry	IA	1949	
Ft. Laramie Cavalry Barracks	Ft. Laramie Park	Laramie	WY	1953	Restoration
Ft. Laramie Commissary Store	Ft. Laramie Park	Laramie	WY	1952	Restoration
Ft. Laramie Guardhouse	Ft. Laramie Park	Laramie	WY	1955	Restoration
Ft. Laramie Officers Quarters	Ft. Laramie Park	Laramie	WY	1954	Restoration
Ft. Laramie Old Bedlam Bachelor Quarters	Ft. Laramie Park	Laramie	WY	1957	Restoration
Ft. Laramie Sutlers Store	Ft. Laramie Park	Laramie	WY	1951	Restoration
Ft. Laramie Visitors Center	Ft. Laramie Park	Laramie	WY		
Ft. Larned National Historic Site Trader Center	Ft. Larned Site	Ft. Larned	KS	1964	
Glacier National Park Trader Center	Glacier National Park, Nr. Lake MacDonald		MT	1932	
Grand Portage National Monument Trader Center	Grand Portage Monument	Grand Portage	MN	1951	Restoration
Grand Teton National Park Trader Center	Grand Teton National Park	Moose	WY	1950	
Homestead National Park Visitor Center	Homestead National Park	Beatrice	NE		
Jefferson Expansion Memorial Visitor Center	Jefferson Expansion Memorial	St. Louis	MO		
Mt. Rushmore National Monument Visitor Center	Mt. Rushmore National Monument	Keystone	SD	1925	
Pipestone National Monument Visitor Center	Pipestone National Monument	Pipestone	MN	1937	
Salvage Bldg.		Omaha	NE	1966	
St. Louis Courthouse	11 N. 4th St.	St. Louis	MO		Alterations
Wind Caves National Park Visitor Center	Wind Caves National Park	Hot Springs	SD		
Yellowstone National Park Ranger Museum	Yellowstone National Park	Norris Junction	WY		

Walter Lenox Roberts Jr.
(1908–1982)

Courtesy of Massachusetts College of Art

Walter Lenox Roberts Jr. was born on July 24, 1908, in Cambridge, Massachusetts, the son of postal clerk Walter Roberts Sr. (1880–1949) and Mabel Foster Roberts (1882–1979). He was the fifth of eleven children and a great-grandson of John Telemachus Hilton (1801–1864), a barber who was prominent in the antislavery movement in Massachusetts. The family moved within the city several times before settling by 1930 at 154 Fayerweather Street in the heart of one of Cambridge's African American neighborhoods.

Roberts attended local public schools and graduated from Cambridge High and Latin School in June 1931. He was accepted into the four-year art and handwork course at the Massachusetts School of Art (now Massachusetts College of Art) in Boston. The nation's first public college of art and design, the Massachusetts Normal Art School was founded in 1873 to train students in drawing and to teach art. Although early institutional records did not record students' racial background, there is photographic evidence of at least one African American student enrolled at MassArt as early as 1903.[1]

Roberts majored in design, a concentration that prepared students for careers in theater, film, advertising, and industry, as well as for work in glass and textiles. His course of study included classes in architecture, drawing, painting, anatomy, art history, and psychology. The 1935 *Massachusetts School of Art Annual* published a sketch by Roberts for a "battery box" decorated with geometric, abstract forms—among more pictorial graphics by his classmates.[2] It is no wonder that in the senior yearbook his portrait is accompanied by the following limerick,

R is for Walter Roberts,
Whose modern designs we think;
Abstract, esoteric symbolic, hysteric-
Drive conventional-minded to drink.[3]

Roberts served as the senior class treasurer. He earned a diploma in general design from the Massachusetts School of Art in June 1935.

That fall Roberts enrolled at the College of Fine Arts at the Carnegie Institute of Technology (now Carnegie Mellon University) in Pittsburgh. While a student at Carnegie, Roberts lived at the Young Men's Christian Association on Centre Avenue in the Hill District, a largely African American neighborhood that would be the location of many of his professional projects. In 1937 Roberts received a bachelor of arts degree in industrial design. His senior thesis, a welded metal gate with a flashing stoplight, was installed on a campus road between the College of Fine Arts and Margaret Morrison College.

The December 1938 issue of *Opportunity Magazine* ran a profile of the young architect who was then employed by the New York World's Fair Corporation.[4] According to the article, Roberts had won a competition to represent Carnegie Institute at the 1939 New York World's Fair. His thoroughly modern composition featured the products of Pittsburgh factories, a circular arrangement of steel beams encircled near the top by a wide, extending band of aluminum bearing the name of the institute. Between the columns, rising for a part of their height, were glass panels etched with figures and symbols representing the various departments. According to *Opportunity Magazine*, the World's Fair Corporation had hired Roberts and sculptor Augusta Savage after the Urban League protested discrimination against African Americans.[4]

Walter Roberts married Margaret Lee Hughes of Louisville, Kentucky, in the early 1940s. She worked as a secretary. Their only child, Gregory, was born in 1956.

Less is known about Roberts's professional activities during the 1940s and 1950s. According to his son, his father moved to Washington, D.C., to work on the design of airfields and military bases for the U.S. Army during World War II.[5] Perhaps he was part of an emerging trend that saw African American architects employed on federal projects. After the war, Roberts returned to Pittsburgh to work as an architect for at least one firm. Gregory Roberts remembers his father describing his work on designs for the East Hills Shopping Center in Penn Hills, just outside Pittsburgh. Around 1959 Roberts established his own architectural firm in Pittsburgh, Walter Roberts Associates. He became a registered architect on October 5, 1953.[6] He joined the American Institute of Architects and the Pennsylvania Society of Architects in 1967. A promotional brochure from 1973 announced Walter Roberts Associates's specialty in institutional, industrial, and public works structures for the inner city. The extensive list of clients included nonprofit agencies such as the Selma Burke Art Center and Three Rivers Youth, Inc.; and African American–owned businesses such as All-Pro Chicken and West Funeral Home. Walter Roberts Associates's mainstays, however, were public clients, including a Brutalist-style, concrete-and-brick classroom building for Pennsylvania State University's McKeesport campus, East End Middle School (1976); and work for several housing and development corporations. The firm's reliance on public projects reflected a nationwide movement for state and municipal agencies to hire minority-owned architectural firms in the 1960s and 1970s. In Pittsburgh, Roberts forged an alliance with Louis Mason Jr., the first African American to serve as city council president (1970–77). Mason appointed Roberts to the City Planning Commission. Another explanation for Walter Roberts Associates's long list of public clients comes from Gregory Roberts, who claims that his father "hated houses" and preferred to work on large-scale public and institutional buildings.[7]

In 1971 Roberts's work was featured in two *Architectural Record* articles. One article on modern workplaces showcased the Westinghouse Electric Vehicle Plant in Homewood, which is a neighborhood in Pittsburgh. The project included two low-slung steel structures—one to house offices and the other to contain

Westinghouse Electric Vehicle Plant, *Courtesy of Architectural Record*

the plant. Located within walking distance of an African American workforce, the factory was a triumph for the community: it was designed by an African American architect, developed by an African American local development corporation, and managed and staffed by African Americans. Editor James D. Morgan emphasized that the Westinghouse plant solved a critical problem. If Blacks were going to continue to be denied free access to housing near suburban industries, perhaps it was up to industry to build new factories on appropriate sites in the inner city. An article on low-income housing featured Roberts's innovative design for Reed-Roberts Street Housing, five buildings located in the Hill District. Roberts collaborated with architect Lewis Downing of Jal-Donn Modular Buildings to create a series of 20,000-pound prefab modules that were delivered to the site with kitchen, baths, carpeting, and mechanical systems pre-installed. With nine modules stacked on a masonry foundation containing two apartments, each building contained eighteen units of low- and moderate-income housing. The buildings were developed by the Allegheny Housing Rehabilitation Corporation and operated by Hill House Housing Development Corporation.

Probably Roberts's most enduring project was the Hill House Center located at 1835 Centre Avenue in the Hill District. The Hill House Association was established in 1964 as a modern settlement house offering extensive health, welfare, recreation, and community programs. Walter Roberts designed the agency's new headquarters. Anchored by a series of tapered double piers of laminated wood, the horizontal building appears to hover above the recessed first story. The construction of Hill House Center was like dropping a stone in a quiet lake—it caused ripples of reinvestment and pride throughout the neighborhood.

By the mid- to late 1970s, the firm of Walter Roberts Associates had dissolved. An ongoing conflict with the general contractor during the construction of East End Middle School hastened the firm's demise. Roberts entered a new phase of his career, teaching architecture and mechanical engineering at Pittsburgh Technical Institute and at his *alma mater*, Carnegie Mellon University.

Walter Roberts died in his downtown apartment at the age of sixty-seven on February 9, 1982.[8] He was survived by his brother George Roberts and sisters Helen Jeffreys and Louise M. Jones, and his son Gregory Roberts.

As a student, Walter Lenox Roberts Jr. identified with the Modernist movement, which propelled him into work on the nation's ultimate modern showcase, the 1939 New York World's Fair. In his career, Roberts established himself as one of Pittsburgh's premier African American architects. His innovative designs kept pace with technical possibilities and responded to social conditions. When Walter Roberts Associates disbanded, he made the transition into teaching. For Roberts, a sense of self-reliance guided both his own professional development and his projects for Pittsburgh's African American community.

Notes
1. Massachusetts School of Art Archives. "Class of 1903."
2. "Walter L. Roberts," *Massachusetts School of Art Catalog*, 1935–1937, n.p.
3. Ibid., n.p.
4. "The News Column," *Opportunity Magazine*, (December 1938), p. 359.
5. Interview with Gregory Roberts (son of Walter Roberts), Pittsburgh, Pennyslvania, 2 August 2002.
6. Commonwealth of Pennsylvania, architects licensing board, "Walter Robersts" no. 2886, issued 5 October 1953.
7. Gregory Roberts interview.
8. "Walter L. Roberts, Jr.," *Pittsburgh Press*, 10 February 1982, p. B4.

Bibliography
Dorman, Franklin A. *Twenty Families of Color in Massachusetts, 1742–1998*. Boston: New England Historic Genealogy, 1998.

SARAH H. ZURIER, HISTORIAN,
RHODE ISLAND HISTORICAL PRESERVATION
AND HERITAGE COMMISSION

WALTER LENOX ROBERTS JR.

BUILDING LIST

Name	Address	City	State	Year	Comments
Allegheny County Community College	Campus	Pittsburgh	PA	c1973	
Allegheny County Housing Authority		Pittsburgh	PA	c1973	
Allegheny Housing Rehabilitation Corp.		Pittsburgh	PA	c1973	
All-Pro Chicken		Pittsburgh	PA	c1973	
Business and Jobs Development Corp.		Pittsburgh	PA	c1973	
Carnegie Institute Gate	Campus	Pittsburgh	PA	c1937	Demolished
Carnegie Library of Pittsburgh	4400 Forbes Ave.	Pittsburgh	PA	c1973	Alternations
East End Middle School	129 Denniston Ave.	Pittsburgh	PA	1976	Now Reizenstein M.S.
East Hills Shopping Center	Robinson Blvd. & Frankstown Rd.	Penn Hills	PA	pre-1960	Partially demolished
Hill House Center	1835 Centre Ave.	Pittsburgh	PA	c1974	
Hiram Masonic Lodge	1117 Woods St.	Pittsburgh	PA	c1973	
Keystone Park Multi-family Housing		Pittsburgh	PA	c1973	
Lincoln Avenue Church of God	404 Lincoln Ave.	Pittsburgh	PA	c1973	
Lovell, Robert		Oakland	PA	c1955	
Mathews/Phillips, Inc.				c1973	
Opportunities Industrialization Center				c1973	
Pennsylvania General State Authority		Harrisburg	PA	c1973	
Pennsylvania State University Classroom Bldg.	Campus	McKeesport	PA	c1973	
Pittsburgh Board of Public Education		Pittsburgh	PA	c1973	
Pittsburgh Housing Authority		Pittsburgh	PA	c1973	
Pittsburgh Presbytery	801 Union St.	Pittsburgh	PA	c1973	
Pittsburgh, City of		Pittsburgh	PA	c1973	
PPG Industries		Pittsburgh	PA	c1973	
Reed-Roberts Street Housing	Reed-Roberts Pl.	Pittsburgh	PA	c1971	
Selma Burke Art Center		Pittsburgh	PA	c1968	Now Kingsley Association
Three Rivers Youth, Inc.		Pittsburgh	PA	c1973	
Urban Redevelopment Authority of Pittsburgh		Pittsburgh	PA	c1973	
West Funeral Home	215 Wylie St.	Pittsburgh	PA	c1973	
Westinghouse Electric Vehicle Plant		Homewood	PA	c1971	
World's Fair Corp.	Fairgrounds	New York	NY	c1939	
Youth Opportunities Unlimited		Pittsburgh	PA	c1973	

Hilyard Robert Robinson
(1899–1986)

Harmon Foundation

Hilyard Robinson was a native of Washington, D.C., and became one of the District's most prolific and successful African American architects of the first half of the twentieth century. His commissions included buildings at historically Black colleges and universities, wartime public housing projects, and residences in a range of styles.

Robinson graduated from Washington, D.C.'s, M Street High School in 1916, and entered the Pennsylvania Museum and School of Industrial Arts in Philadelphia, which he left in 1917. He enlisted in the U.S. Army Field Artillery Corps, 167th Brigade, in 1917, and as a second lieutenant served in France during World War I. Robinson was in Paris for the Armistice and was so profoundly impressed by that city's Haussmann-era architecture that on his return to the United States in 1919 he transferred to the University of Pennsylvania and began architectural studies under Ecole des Beaux Arts–trained Paul Philippe Cret (1876–1945).

During the summers of 1921 and 1922, while working as a draftsman for VERTNER WOODSON TANDY in Harlem, Robinson met the Swiss-born Ecole des Beaux Arts–trained Paul B. LaVelle (unknown–1942), a friend of Tandy's and practicing architect and professor of architecture at Columbia University. LaVelle assisted Robinson's transfer to Columbia University in 1922 and employed him as an architectural draftsman from 1922 to 1924. Robinson assisted with LaVelle's entry to the *Chicago Tribune* competition for a new headquarters building and received from LaVelle an unselfish "guiding hand in [his] student days."[1]

Prior to receiving his bachelor of architecture degree from Columbia University in 1924, Robinson initiated what would become a long relationship with HOWARD UNIVERSITY with part-time teaching at its nascent School of Architecture. Subsequently, Robinson served as instructor and department chairman until 1937, and designed eleven campus buildings that helped to establish a distinct and Modernist sensibility to the hilltop campus.

During the late 1920s, while he taught and completed modest residential remodeling jobs mined from his Howard University contacts, Robinson explored the woeful slums and decrepit alley dwellings occupied by Washington, D.C.'s, poorest Blacks. In 1920 Robinson obtained architectural registration in the District of Columbia and soon thereafter took a leave of absence from Howard University to complete graduate studies and his thesis on congregate housing at Columbia University in New York City.[2] When Robinson received his master's degree in 1931, he and his new (White) wife, Helena Rooks Robinson, embarked on an eighteen-month subsidized tour of Europe as a Kinne Fellow. A daughter born to their union died before reaching her teens.

From his base in Berlin, Robinson attended Dr Ausland Insitut and traveled extensively to examine and photograph post–World War I bomb-resistant construction techniques and government-sponsored housing solutions throughout Europe and Scandinavia, as well as the Soviet commissions of the Bauhaus Brigade. He returned frequently to Paris and toured the 1931 exposition. He was most impressed, however, by the pioneering concept for the reconstruction of Rotterdam and contemporary Scandinavian architecture, which he found to possess an obvious freedom from timid compromise. Robinson returned to Washington, D.C., with a comprehensive understanding of housing solutions and resumed teaching at Howard University in 1932.

From his survey of the housing needs of the poor in the District of Columbia, Robinson became known at the newly established Public Works Administration, the agency empowered to address the ill-housed "one-third of the nation," which statutorily required "Negro participation" in its mission. Robinson's desire to apply his trenchant understanding of seminal European low-cost housing efforts to the benefit of his race led to a second leave of absence from Howard University and employment by the Public Works Administration in 1935 as chief architect of a partnership composed of the politically well-connected PAUL REVERE WILLIAMS, Vertner Tandy; and two local White architects, Irwin Porter and Alexander Trowbridge. This team was charged with designing the first federally sponsored public housing project in Washington, D.C., and one of the first in the nation.

Situated not far from the U.S. Capitol, Langston Terrace became the most conspicuous of the fifty-one federal housing projects sponsored by the Public Works Administration. The series of modestly scaled dwellings, which enclose a central common designed by DAVID AUGUSTUS WILLISTON, and their unadorned cast-stone features established Robinson as a leading designer of public housing and remained his favorite project. Architectural critic Lewis Mumford noted, "it looks better than the best modern work in Hamburg or Vienna."[3] The success of Langston Terrace was critical to the passage of the first national Housing Act of 1937. Robinson went on to design the New Deal prototypical Aberdeen Gardens in Newport News, Virginia (1935), and housing for Black defense workers.

Even during the Great Depression, Robinson never lacked for work. Robinson's office was at 1927 11th Street, NW, in a small building that he designed, and Robinson maintained a staff of six to seven through 1962. Aside from the nominal partnerships that Robinson formed with non-participating, politically well-connected architects to secure commissions, he never elevated any of his approximately forty associates to partner. Although numerous architects were in his employ, Robinson alone deserves attribution for the firm's buildings.

For the residence of Dr. Ralph Johnson Bunche—former director of the Department of Political Science at Howard University—in the Brooklyn neighborhood of Washington, D.C., Robinson created a distinctive hip-roof house with subtle International-style references in 1941.

On the eve of the United States' entry into World War II, as a result of a successful National Association for the Advancement of Colored People lawsuit, the War Department was obligated to solicit bids for the design of a new segregated airfield to train African American pilots in 1941. The entire undertaking, however, was almost sabotaged by erroneous quantities of excavation, dredging, filling, and grading specified in the War Department Request for Proposal. Robinson arranged for a private flight over the flood plain, creeks, and mounds of the selected site and confirmed that the earthwork requirements stipulated in the RFP were, in fact, approximately ten percent of the actual amount needed. The realization that the airfield as well as his professional practice could so easily have met "certain doom" only served to increase Robinson's commitment to the project. Robinson entrusted his chief draftsman, JOHN DENNIS SULTON, with the completion of the Bunche house and took up quarters on the TUSKEGEE INSTITUTE campus in June 1941 in order to supervise his most challenging wartime project, the design and construction of the Tuskegee Army Airfield in Chehaw. With a staff of twenty-one architects, engineers, and administrative personnel, Robinson produced "in about half the normal designing time" a topographic survey, finished grading plans, scale models, and construction drawings for an airfield, landing strips, barracks, hangars, control tower, and a curvilinear administration building by mid-1941. The project was constructed by MCKISSACK & MCKISSACK. Despite the enormous challenges, Robinson successfully fulfilled "the first Defense contract given to a Negro" and pilot training of the legendary Tuskegee Airmen began in December 1941.[4] Within the larger Washington, D.C., architectural community, Robinson was active and involved with his White peers. He served on the National Capital Planning Commission from 1950 to 1955 and was director of the Washington Housing Association. Following the war, Robinson served as a planning consultant to the Republic of Liberia (1946–49) and was architect for that country's 1947 Centennial Exposition (plans only). Campus projects such as Howard University's School of Engineering and Architecture (1952) account for a significant portion of his later oeuvre. From 1962 when he went into semi-retirement until his death in 1986, Robinson main-

Langston Terrace Public Housing, *Hilyard Robinson*

tained his office and completed a 272-bed wing to Provident Hospital as well as Southern Baptist Church in East Baltimore.

Hilyard Robinson died at Howard University Hospital on July 2, 1986. Reflecting on his successful career as an African American architect, Robinson noted the lack of bias he had encountered. Rather, he believed, his race may have better qualified him for the "demands of housing needed and programmed for low-income Black occupancy and a wide range of facilities for Black colleges."[5] In addition, he speculated that "the small number of professionally well-trained and experienced Black architects conditioned to effectively operate the business of Architectural Practice probably accounts for the activities of the few who meet these qualifications."[6] Robinson enjoyed a prolific practice, held several design patents for lighting devices, designed important housing and campus buildings, was responsible for numerous wartime commissions, was an educator, and participated in professional affairs. His enduring contribution is a significant body of architecture that conveys his distinctly rational and human interpretation of Modernism.

Notes
1. Interview with Hilyard Robinson by Dreck Wilson, Washington, D.C., 18 May 1983.
2. D.C. Board of Examiners and Registrars of Architects, "Hilyard Robinson," no. 217 issued 30 April 1930.
3. Lewis Mumford, "The Skyline," *New Yorker*, 29 April 1938, p. 66.
4. Letter from Hilyard Robinson to Calvin McKissack, 23 December 1941, Moorland-Spingarn Research Center, Washington, D.C.
5. Robinson interview.
6. Ibid.

Bibliography
Ethridge, Harrison M. "The Black Architects of Washington, D.C., 1900–Present." Ph.D. diss., The Catholic University of America, 1979.
Historic American Building Survey. "Ralph J. Bunche House." no. DC 360, Library of Congress, 1980.
Leiner, Glen B. "The Langston Terrace Dwellings." In *Trans Lux*. Art Deco Society of Washington, 1984.

GLEN B. LEINER,
ARCHITECTURAL HISTORIAN,
NEW YORK, NEW YORK

BUILDING LIST

Name	Address	City	State/Country	Year	Comments
99th Pursuit Squadron Training School	Airfield	Chehaw	AL	1941	
Aberdeen Gardens		Newport News	VA	1935	
Arthur Capper Public Dwellings	M St., SE	Washington	DC	1952	159 Houses

HILYARD ROBERT ROBINSON

BUILDING LIST *(continued)*

Name	Address	City	State/Country	Year	Comments
Atkins, Louise	1253 Girard St., NE	Washington	DC	1937	
Bunche, Dr. Ralph J.	1510 Jackson St., NE	Washington	DC	1941	
Cherry Hill Public Housing	2700 Spelman Rd.	Baltimore	MD		Addition
Cherry Hill Public Housing	2700 Spelman Rd.	Baltimore	MD	1945	
Chester Recreation Center	9th St.	Chester	PA	1953	
Davis, Don	Pembroke Ave.	Hampton	VA	1955	
Fabcrete Demountable Housing			VA	1940	12 dwelling units (plans only)
Flanner House Social Center	2424 King Jr. Dr.	Indianapolis	IN	1943	
Fowler, Dr.	1305 Hamilin Ave., NE	Washington	DC	1948	
Frederick Douglass Public Dwellings	1200 Alabama Ave., SE	Washington	DC	1941	
George Washington Carver Public Housing	211 Elm St., NW	Washington	DC	1942	Now Howard Univ. Carver Dormitory
Hampton University Armstong Hall	Campus	Hampton	VA	1964	
Hampton University Davidson Dormitory	Campus	Hampton	VA	1954	Assoc. architect
Hampton University Harkness Dormitory	Campus	Hampton	VA	1954	Assoc. architect
Harris, Mortimer	1726 U St., NW	Washington	DC	1927	Alterations
Holabird Public Housing		Dundalk	MD	1941	Demolished
Howard University Aldridge Theatre	Campus	Washington	DC	1948	
Howard University Bethune Dormitory	Campus	Washington	DC	1948	
Howard University Biology Bldg.	Campus	Washington	DC	1954	
Howard University Cook Dormitory	Campus	Washington	DC	1938	Assoc. architect
Howard University Cramton Auditorium	Campus	Washington	DC	1948	Assoc. architect
Howard University Drew Dormitory	Campus	Washington	DC	1951	Assoc. architect
Howard University Engineering & Architecture Bldg.	Campus	Washington	DC	1952	Assoc. architect
Howard University Fine Arts Bldg.	Campus	Washington	DC	1951	Assoc. architect
Howard University School of Dentistry	Campus	Washington	DC	1954	
Howard University School of Human Ecology	Campus	Washington	DC	1960	
Howard University School of Pharmacy	Campus	Washington	DC	1955	Assoc. architect
Howard University Slowe Dormitory	Campus	Washington	DC	1942	Assoc. architect
Hudson Hotel Dining Room		Troy	NY	1922	
Jarvis Christian College Dining Hall	Campus	Hawkins	TX		Destroyed by fire
Johnson, Dr. Joseph	1830 16th St., NW	Washington	DC		Apts.
Langston Terrace Public Housing	2100 Benning Rd., NE	Washington	DC	1935	274 d.u.
Lawson, Belford		Washington	DC		Alterations
Lewis, S. W.	456 N. St., NW	Washington	DC	1976	Alterations
Livingston College Aggrey Student Union	Campus	Salisbury	NC	1962	
Livingston College Harris Dormitory	Campus	Salisbury	NC	1955	
Livingston College Moore Faculty House	Campus	Salisbury	NC	1948	
Livingston College Varrick Auditorium	Campus	Salisbury	NC	1963	
Logan, Dr. Rayford	1519 Jackson St., NE	Washington	DC	1943	
Lyon Village Defense Housing		Turner Station	MD	1941	
Provident Hospital	1418 Division St.	Baltimore	MD	1927	Alterations
Provident Hospital	Liberty Heights Ave.	Baltimore	MD	1968	Assoc. architect
Provident Hospital	1418 Division St.	Baltimore	MD	1928	Addition
Roberts Airfield	Medaster River Basin	Harbel	Liberia	1941	
Scott, Dr. Armond	1927 11th St., NW	Washington	DC	1927	Apts.
Soller's Homes		Soller's Pt.	MD	1941	Demolished
Southern Baptist Church	1701 N. Chester St.	Baltimore	MD	1972	Addition
Sparrows Pt. Defense Housing		Sparrows Pt.	MD	1941	
St. Luke's Church	P St., NW	Washington	DC	1955	Parish house
Virginia Union University Hartshorn Dormitory	Campus	Richmond	VA	1928	Assoc. architect
Williston, Dr. Thomas	1204 Q St., NW	Washington	DC	1944	Alterations
Ypsilanti Public Housing	601 Armstrong Dr.	Ypsilanti	MI	1943	Now Armstrong Drive Apts.

Robert L. Robinson
(1870–1942)

Robert L. Robinson was born on July 12, 1870, in King William County, Virginia, the son of Jonah and Jane Robinson. Both of his parents were native Virginians. Little, however, is known about his early life, such as his primary and secondary education. No record has yet been found of any collegiate-level education or apprenticeship. Indeed, no record could be found to ascertain what name his middle initial "L" stood for.

Robinson first appears on the rolls of New Jersey architects in 1902, with registration number A387, where he is listed in the state directory as practicing in Westfield at 112 Broad Street.[1] New Jersey began licensing architects in 1902. State archivists who are familiar with the registration records believe that his registration number is a low one, indicating that he probably had been admitted through a "grandfather"-type procedure. This was done for many architects who had been practicing for some time prior to enactment of the registration laws. Robinson was probably one of the first African Americans to be registered in New Jersey, because he obtained licensure so soon after the law's enactment.

He was a sole practitioner, working in the town's central area for mostly Black clients. In 1916 Robinson moved his office from 112 Broad Street to his home at 502 West Broad Street in Westfield, New Jersey. He maintained an active practice in Westfield until 1934. Following his retirement as an architect, he served as a trustee at Bethel Baptist Church—although its design is not attributed to him—and as a Baptist minister without a pastorate.

Robert L. Robinson was seventy-two years old when he died from a heart attack on April 20, 1942.[2] He was buried in the family plot at Fairview Cemetery in Westfield. His wife, Martha, predeceased him. He was survived by a daughter, Viola Robinson Hamilton, a son, Carl Robinson, and four grandchildren.

Notes
1. State of New Jersey, Certificate to Practice Architecture, "Robert L. Robinson," Certificate no. 389, issued 25 July 1902.
2. "Rev. R.L. Robinson Also Architect, Is Dead at 72," *Plainfield Courier-News*, 21 April 1942, p. 10.

MARK HEWITT, PRINCIPAL,
HEWITT & ASSOCIATES,
BERNARDSVILLE, NEW JERSEY

Humphrey Hall,
Dreck Spurlock Wilson

ROBERT L. ROBINSON

BUILDING LIST

Name	Address	City	State	Year	Comments
House		Plainfield	NJ	1922	Permit #12936
House		Plainfield	NJ	1925	Permit #13920
Church		Plainfield	NJ	1930	Permit #9216
Church		Plainfield	NJ	1921	Permit #1459
Duplex	68–70 Raymond Ave.	Plainfield	NJ	1928	
House		Plainfield	NJ	1903	Permit #1402
House		Plainfield	NJ	1903	Permit #5922
House		Plainfield	NJ	1919	Permit #1903
House		Plainfield	NJ	1926	Permit #1920
House		Plainfield	NJ	1930	Permit #17074
House		Plainfield	NJ	1926	Permit #14174
House		Plainfield	NJ	1923	Permit #11374
House		Plainfield	NJ	1923	Permit #9929
House	127 Wachung Ave.	Plainfield	NJ	1927	
House		Plainfield	NJ	1926	Permit #13316
Shed		Plainfield	NJ	1918	Permit #5891
Humphrey Hall	601 W. 4th St.	Plainfield	NJ	1928	

William J. Robinson
(unknown–unknown)

Courtesy of Philadelphia African-American Archives

William J. Robinson hailed from Virginia, where he apprenticed on a farm with an unnamed Kent County carpenter before moving to Richmond around 1880 to work for a contractor with jobs at Virginia Union University. Within the decade, Robinson allegedly worked for Standard Oil tycoon John David Rockefeller Jr. Robinson was chosen to build an upstate New York barn for Rockefeller; successive projects included a building at the University of Chicago paid for by Rockefeller, and the family's mansion and hall at Bryn Mawr College.[1] Robinson moved to Philadelphia around 1898, residing at 1520 South 19th Street. He was engaged in building Pennsylvania Hall and Chapel at Downingtown Industrial and Agricultural School and several alteration projects, including the Keystone Aid Building, the Market Building, and the People's Bank Building. The Downingtown Industrial and Agricultural School, founded as a trade school for African Americans, opened in 1904. It seems likely that the school—which advertised in the 1910 *Philadelphia Colored Directory: A Handbook of the Religious, Social, Political, and Other Activities of the Negroes of Philadelphia, Philadelphia*—would have employed a Black contractor.[2] The Keystone Bank, designed by Willis G. Hale and continuously under construction from 1880 until 1899, was enlarged in the 1890s, but not by Robinson. Allegedly he worked on the addition to the Citizen's Republican Club and several church and house renovations and additions.[2]

Robinson wrote to John D. Rockefeller Jr. while staying at a Young Men's Christian Association

People's Savings Bank, *Historical Society of Pennsylvania*

(YMCA) in Manhattan in October 1909, September 1911, and again in May 1914, seeking employment and was told on all three occasions that no vacancies existed.[3] His stay at the YMCA suggests that he was not married, because only single Black men were permitted to rent rooms.

The information gap in William Robinson's biography is an example of a larger issue in the documentation of African American architect-builders—too often records were kept only sporadically, if at all. In order to bridge the information void, the reader can accept oral history, but not as accredited.

Notes

1. The University of Chicago and Bryn Mawr College buildings designed respectively by well-known architects Henry Ives Cobb and Cope & Stewardson, were indeed built in the 1890s, but no record of Robinson's involvement could be found at either school's archive. The construction of the Rockefeller mansion "Kykuit" is well documented, but Robinson's name does not appear in any records. City directories published between 1895 and 1911 do not list William Robinson. *Philadelphia Colored Directories* for 1908, 1910, and 1914, published to promote local Black-owned businesses, do not list Robinson.

2. Richard Dozier, *Philadelphia's African American Architects, 1995* (Philadelphia: The Afro-American Historical and Cultural Museum, 1995), p. 4.

3. William J. Robinson to John D. Rockefeller Jr., "John David Rockefeller Letterbooks," Record Group 1, vols. 128, 297, and 147, Rockefeller Archives. Sleepy Hollow, New York.

LAUREN JACOBI,
VENTURI, SCOTT BROWN & ASSOCIATES,
PHILADELPHIA, PENNSYLVANIA

BUILDING LIST

Name	Address	City	State	Year	Comments
Rockefeller Barn		Pocantico Hills	NY	c1890	

John Henry Rosemond
(c1876–1958)

Janie Madry

John H. Rosemond has the distinction of being one of two African American builders in pre–World War II Jacksonville, Florida, who identified himself as an architect. Little has been documented about Rosemond's early life, education, or work experiences before arriving in Jacksonville between 1910 and 1915. Initially identified as a contractor, Rosemond, a South Carolina native, was first listed in the *Jacksonville City Directory* in 1916. In that year, he and his wife, Ida, resided in the historic Oakland neighborhood of East Jacksonville. By 1918 they had moved to 1442 Florida Avenue, where the Rosemonds lived until 1947, eventually leaving Oakland and moving to the west side of Jacksonville.[1]

With construction jobs limited mainly to within his own community, Rosemond was known for his church designs. One of his earliest and most notable churches was Simpson Memorial United Methodist Church, completed in 1923. In his design of Simpson Church, which was later gutted by fire and rebuilt in 1945, Rosemond was able to incorporate elements of the late Gothic Revival style to create a strong visual presence along Old Kings Road immediately west of downtown Jacksonville. A longtime member of First

Simpson Memorial United Methodist Church, *Jacksonville Historical Society*

JOHN HENRY ROSEMOND

Baptist Church of Oakland, Rosemond was also responsible for the design and construction of their new sanctuary in 1944.[2]

After the death of his first wife, Rosemond married Marion J. Reynolds in 1950, and moved to a new residence at 1137 West 20th Street. Unfortunately, Rosemond was only to enjoy his new home for a few years, passing away on June 24, 1958, while visiting his home state of South Carolina.[3]

Notes

1. "John H. Rosemond," *Polk City Directory of Jacksonville* (Jacksonville: R.L. Polk & Co., 1916–56).
2. City of Jacksonville, Fla., "Building Permit Records," Permit nos. 223-1923 and nos. 318-1944. Building Inspection Division, Jacksonville Public Works Department.
3. "John H. Rosemond," *Florida Times Union, Star Edition*, 25 June 1958, p. 38.

JOEL W. MCEACHIN,
SENIOR HISTORIC PRESERVATION PLANNER,
JACKSONVILLE PLANNING
AND DEVELOPMENT DEPARTMENT

BUILDING LIST

Name	Address	City	State	Year	Comments
First Baptist Church of Oakland Sanctuary	1025 Jessie St.	Jacksonville	FL	1944	
Rosemond, John H.	1137 W. 20th St.	Jacksonvile	FL	1956	
Simpson Memorial United Methodist Church	1114 Cleveland St.	Jacksonvile	FL	1923	Destroyed by fire

Ferdinand Lucien Rousseve

(1904–1965)

John J. Burns Library, Boston College Archives

Ferdinand Rousseve was born on July 18, 1904, in New Orleans, Louisiana, into a devout Catholic household headed by his Creole father, Bartholomew, who was a postman, and his mother, Valentine Marie, who was a housewife. Ferdinand had three brothers and four sisters including twins, Leonie and Leona. His father faithfully recited the Rosary every morning and raised his children to have devotion for the Virgin Mary. Ferdinand's sister, Theresa, married Jesus Christ by becoming a nun, and one brother, Maurice, ordained his soul to the Catholic Church by becoming a priest. One brother, Rene, was a social worker. Two brothers, Numa and Charles, who were gifted artists, became a professional landscape painter and university professor of fine arts, respectively. Ferdinand, like two of his brothers, chose a profession in the fine arts, but his *oeuvre* was forever ecclesiastically influenced.

Ferdinand's father enrolled him in Saint Louis Elementary, a private school in New Orleans, and then successive New Orleans parochial schools—Holy Family Boys' Middle School and Xavier Preparatory High School. Ferdinand Rousseve was inspired to study architecture by his Xavier drafting and industrial arts teacher, William Lewis. He graduated with academic honors third in his class in June 1922.

Rousseve was a smart and determined student who advanced his station in life by seeking out and conquering the educational opportunities that presented themselves to him. Following his graduation from high school, he enrolled at Guillaume College in New Orleans in 1924 and received a diploma from the commercial course. Also in 1924, he attended Coyne Trade and Engineering School in Chicago, Illinois, earning a certificate in mechanical drawing and elementary machine design. The latter was a discipline in which patternmaker RICHARD MASON HANCOCK had excelled. Rousseve returned to New Orleans and worked as a draftsman for Louis J. Charbonnett, a family friend, mechanical engineer, and mentor and owner of one of the leading millwright companies in the lower Mississippi Delta. After Charbonnett died in 1924, Rousseve left for Cambridge, Massachusetts, intending to enter the Massachusetts Institute of Technology. To prepare for the entrance examination, Rousseve enrolled at Rindge Technical High School in Cambridge. It was a worthwhile investment of a year of study. He won a Gold Medal in oratory and qualified for a four-year, full-tuition Cambridge scholarship. The summer before he started college, he worked as a draftsman for Maginnis, Walsh & Kennedy Architects, who specialized in church architecture. Rousseve entered Massachusetts Institute of Technology in the fall of 1925. His matriculation was highlighted by many honors, such as receiving a $1,000 scholarship grant from the Cambridge Rotary Club. He was the only African American member of the Architectural Society and he was a dependable member of the Catholic Club. He spent the summer of 1926 working as a draftsman in the Boston office of Edward T. P. Graham (1871–1964). The summer of

Greater Tulane Baptist Church, *Neil Alexander Photography*

1929 he worked as a draftsman for the nonprofit Architectural Bureau of the Young Men's Christian Association in Chicago. His terminal thesis was "The Hall of Fame of a National Capital Building in Design." In his fifth year, Rousseve graduated from MIT with a bachelor of science in architecture in 1930.

Not since ROBERT ROBINSON TAYLOR in 1892 had the Massachusetts Institute of Technology graduated a Black architect. Rousseve was a hot commodity and he quickly found employment as an instructor in the School of Architecture at HOWARD UNIVERSITY. He taught at the university from 1930 to 1933. During the two summers he taught at Howard he took classes in interior decoration, arts, and ornamental decoration in New York City, probably offered by the popular *Beaux-Arts* Institute of Design.

In April 1934 he sat for and passed the state licensing examination for architects, becoming the first licensed Black architect in Louisiana.[1]

Rousseve was an architect-academician with a strong preference for classical styles. His interest motivated him to attend the University of Chicago during the summers from 1936 to 1939 in a specialized field of the history of art, concentrating on twelfth-century French architecture. For his terminal thesis he wrote "The *Majestas Domini* in the Tympanum of the Twelfth Century French Church—A Study in Iconography."[2] It was an iconographic analysis of the "Majesty of the Lord" decoration theme found in the tympana of medieval church portals. Rousseve received his master of art degree during commencement ceremonies held in the summer of 1940.

Rousseve added a capital to his record of scholarship in 1948 when he was awarded a doctoral degree in architecture from Harvard University. He made A's in all his courses, completed his foreign (French) language requirement, and passed his oral comprehensive examination all within two semesters. His thesis, supplemented by a detailed scale model that he built, was a critical assessment of one of the last churches along the great Pilgrimage Road, "The Romanesque Abbey—Church of St. Martial at Limoges, France."

Ferdinand married Elise Mirault Clarke of Augusta, Georgia, in the fall of 1930. They were parents to Yvonne Elise, Angela Rose, and Marie Valentine.

Rousseve, in the vein of ALBERT IRVIN CASSELL and HOWARD HAMILTON MACKEY SR., was a successful architect-administrator. In the fall of 1933, he was appointed assistant to the university president and business manager for SOUTHERN UNIVERSITY at Baton Rouge. In 1940 Rousseve received a dual appointment as head of the Department of Fine Arts at Xavier University in New Orleans and university architect. He managed the department, taught design classes, and was responsible for supervising the Facilities Department as well as the construction of university buildings.

When Rousseve returned to New Orleans in 1940, he opened a solo private practice to supplement the salary he received from Xavier University. Rousseve maintained his architectural practice until 1948.

Rousseve designed many buildings in the Gulf region of Louisiana, Mississippi, Alabama, and Texas. His commissions ranged from Catholic high schools to Catholic churches to houses. Among the most noteworthy were greater Tulane Baptist Church in New Orleans and St. Jude's Catholic Hospital in Montgomery, Alabama.

Rousseve was quoted as saying, "I have a strong conviction that it is our individual and collective duty to make our communities better places in which to live."[3] His civic commitment was demonstrated by board memberships in the New Orleans Family Services Society and New Orleans Council of Social Agencies and in Boston by board memberships in the Cambridge Planning Board, Catholic Inter-racial Council of Boston, National Council of Christians and Jews, and more than a dozen other groups.

In 1961 Rousseve returned to Massachusetts to accept the directorship of the Fine Arts Department at Boston College in Chestnut Hill. He was once again a trailblazer by being one of the few African Americans to head an Art Department at a predominately White college and being one of the few architects to head an Art Department at a college or university.

Ferdinand Rousseve died on July 18, 1965, at Saint Elizabeth's Hospital in Brighton, Massachusetts.[4] He is interred at Newton Cemetery in Newton Centre, Massachusetts.

Notes

1. Louisiana State Board of Architectural Examiners, "Ferdinand Rousseve," no. (unknown), issued 23 April 1934.
2. Ferdinand Rousseve, "The *Majestas Domini* in the Tympanum of the Twelfth Century French Church—A Study in Iconography," (master's thesis, University of Chicago, 1939).
3. Clarence Laws, "Ferdinand L. Rousseve-Architect and Citizen," *Opportunity*. (September 1947): 95.
4. "Dr. Ferdinand Rousseve, B.C. Fine Arts Chairman," *Traveler* (Boston), 19 July 1965, p. 30.

Bibliography

"Rousseve, Ferdinand Lucien." In *Who Was Who in America*. A. N. Marquis, ed., vol. 33. New York: Marquis Company, 1964.

"Rousseve, Ferdinand." In *Directory of American Scholars*. Lancaster, Pennsylvania: Science Press, 1951.

DRECK SPURLOCK WILSON

BUILDING LIST

Name	Address	City	State	Year	Comments
House	1436 Pauger St.	New Orleans	LA		
House	1428 Bourbon St.	New Orleans	LA		
House	1625 Pauger St.	New Orleans	LA		
Twin House	1455–1457 Pauger St.	New Orleans	LA		
5th African Baptist Church	3419 S. Robinson St.	New Orleans	LA		Michael D'Orsi, assoc. architect
Ashton Theatre		New Orleans	LA		Michael D'Orsi, assoc. architect
Beecher Memorial Congregational Church	1914 N. Miro St.	New Orleans	LA		
Central Congregational Church of Christ	2401 Bienville Ave.	New Orleans	LA		
Cherrie-Segue Medical Clinic		New Orleans	LA		Michael D'Orsi, assoc. architect
Convents Holy Ghost Catholic Church Rectory	2015 Louisiana Ave.	New Orleans	LA		Addition
Dryades Street YMCA	Dryades St.	New Orleans	LA		Destroyed by fire
Greater Tulane Baptist Church	214 N. Johnston St.	New Orleans	LA		
Le Rendezvous Restaurant					Michael D'Orsi, assoc. architect
Louisiana Colored Teachers Association Bldg.	Campus	Baton Rogue	LA		Now Southern Univ. Archives Bldg.
McDonald Dental Office		New Orleans	LA		
People's United Methodist Church Community Center		New Orleans	LA		Michael D'Orsi, assoc. architect
Rhodes Funeral Home	1716 N. Claiborne Ave.	New Orleans	LA		
Rose Hill Baptist Church	4520 Willow Rd.	New Orleans	LA		Michael D'Orsi, assoc. architect
Rousseve, Ferdinand L.	4636 Willow St.	Cambridge	MA		
St. Claver's Catholic Elementary School	1020 N. Prieur St.	New Orleans	LA	1921	Michael D'Orsi, assoc. architect
St. Jude's Catholic Hospital	2048 W. Fairview Ave.	Montgomery	AL	1951	Now Apts.
St. Raymond's Catholic Church	3738 Paris Ave.	New Orleans	LA		

Charles Thaddeus Russell
(1875–1952)

Courtesy of Sixth Mount Zion Baptist Church

Charles Thaddeus Russell, a native of Richmond, Virginia, was born in 1875 and grew up in Richmond's Jackson Ward neighborhood. At that time, Jackson Ward was Richmond's primary African American neighborhood and the site of considerable construction activity by and for African Americans. Russell apparently attended Richmond Public Schools and in 1893 began his training at HAMPTON INSTITUTE.[1] Russell received a trade certificate in carpentry in 1899, for which he had taken shop instruction, participated in campus construction projects, and learned mechanical drawing.

In 1901 Russell became supervisor of the Carpentry Division at TUSKEGEE INSTITUTE. During his tenure, Russell worked on the largest African American building project in the country, the Tuskegee campus. The ambitious building program of Tuskegee Institute principal Booker T. Washington was proudly referred to as "Mr. Washington's City." Russell taught carpentry and supervised the carpentry work on all the campus buildings. He collaborated with the architects on the institute's staff and honed his mechanical drawing skills, essentially serving an architectural apprenticeship.

In 1907 Russell received a dual appointment as an instructor in manual training and superintendent of grounds at Virginia Union University in Richmond. With the permission of the Virginia Union president, Professor Russell began a career in architecture in 1909. The design of the Saint Luke Penny Savings Bank in Richmond, completed in 1910, was Russell's first commission. A city building inspector approved Russell's permit drawings.[2] This commission distinguished Russell as the first African American to maintain an architectural practice in Richmond and probably the first to do so in the Commonwealth of Virginia.

In 1909 Richmond boasted an African American community of 50,000. Richmond is credited with being one of the largest African American business centers in the country. The city has a long tradition of African American builders and in 1909 there were a number of Black contractors for Russell to work with. The business, professional, and religious leaders of Richmond's African American community were willing and financially able to hire Russell to design renovations and new buildings.

Russell's largest corpus of work was the group of commercial buildings located in Jackson Ward. Two buildings of comparable size and style to the Saint Luke Penny Savings Bank are Johnson's Hall (a funeral parlor, Masonic lodge, and auditorium) and the Richmond Beneficial Insurance Company headquarters designed in 1910. Russell also designed a variety of smaller insurance, banking, funerary, and commercial buildings. In 1919 Russell saw construction completed for two major commissions: the Saint Luke Hall expansion and Attucks Theater. The former involved the expansion and fireproofing of the headquarters and auditorium of the International Order of Saint Luke. Outside of Richmond, he designed the At-

Riverside Baptist Church, *Tyler Potterfield Jr.*

tucks Theater in Norfolk in collaboration with his former student HARVEY NATHANIEL JOHNSON.

Russell was a deacon at Ebenezer Baptist Church and a significant component of his practice was planning and designing the expansion or construction of churches. He designed the expansion of Ebenezer Baptist Church and alterations to other Baptist churches in Richmond over the years. Russell was the architect for the Neo-Classical Riverside Baptist Church and Rectory in Richmond in 1914. In 1919 he collaborated again with Harvey Nathaniel Johnson on the Gothic-style First Baptist Church in Portsmouth. In 1925 Russell's renovation of Sixth Mount Zion Baptist successfully enlarged the sanctuary, added a new facade and main entrance, and attached an education wing.

Russell received several opportunities to design houses. He prepared the construction drawings for an expansion to banker Maggie Walker's house in the 1920s and designed four faculty houses at Virginia Union University. Russell also designed the large Georgian Revival–style house for Dr. W. H. Hughes in 1915. His largest residential commission was the combination residence and apartment building of attorney J. Thomas Hewen.

By 1930 Russell had designed construction projects worth more than $1 million. In 1942 Russell completed his last major architectural project—the Belgian Friendship Complex.[3] This International-style *tour de force* was designed by a collaboration of Belgian architects for the New York World's Fair (1939). Russell served as assistant architect to Hugo Van-Kuyck, the supervising architect in charge of literally moving the building to Richmond after the fair closed. Charles Russell retired after the Belgian project was completed, concluding a thirty-three-year career as an architect.

Russell died in 1952, not far from where he was born in Jackson Ward.[4]

Notes

1. Thomas Tyler Potterfield Jr., "Professor Charles T. Russell, 1875–1952: Virginia's Pioneer African American Architect," In . . . *And the Walls Came Tumbling Down: the Early African American Architects of the District of Columbia and Tidewater Virginia,* unpublished manuscript 1995, p. 129. In the possession of the author.
2. City of Richmond, "Building Permit Records" (microfilm), Permit No. 53, The Library of Virginia, Richmond.
3. "A Bit of Belgium Comes Here," *Richmond Times Dispatch*, 25 January 1942, p. 3.
4. "C.T. Russell Buried with Simple Ceremonies," *Norfolk Journal and Guide*, 30 August 1952, p. 3.

Bibliography

Hampton University, Student File. "C.T. Russell Practical and Professional Experience," Hampton University Archives, Hampton, Virginia.

THOMAS TYLER POTTERFIELD JR.,
HISTORIC PRESERVATION PLANNER,
CITY OF RICHMOND, VIRGINIA,
AND INSTRUCTOR IN ARCHITECTURAL HISTORY,
VIRGINIA COMMONWEALTH UNIVERSITY

CHARLES THADDEUS RUSSELL

BUILDING LIST

Name	Address	City	State	Year	Comments
Attucks Theater		Richmond	VA	1919	
Attucks Theater	1008 Church St.	Norfolk	VA		Assoc. architect
Belgian Friendship Complex	Campus	Richmond	VA	1939	Assoc. architect, Virginia Union Univ.
Ebenezer Baptist Church	216 W. Leigh St.	Richmond	VA		Alterations
First Baptist Church	1445 Central Ave.	Portsmouth	VA	1919	Assoc. architect
Hewen, Atty, J. Thomas		Richmond	VA		House/apt.
Hughes, Dr. W. H.	508 St. James St.	Richmond	VA	1915	
Johnson's Hall	10 E. Leigh St.	Richmond	VA	1910	Funeral parlor, lodge, & audtiorium
Richmond Beneficial Insurance Co.		Richmond	VA	1911	
Riverside Baptist Church	Lombardy St.	Richmond	VA	1914	
Sixth Mt. Zion Baptist Church	114 W. Duval St.	Richmond	VA	1925	Alterations
St. Luke's Hall	Franklin St.	Richmond	VA	1919	Addition
St. Luke's Penny Savings Bank	2nd St.	Richmond	VA	1910	Now Consolidated Bank
Virginia Union University	Campus	Richmond	VA		4 faculty houses
Virginia Union University Huntley Hall	Campus	Richmond	VA		
Walker, Maggie L.	110A Leigh St.	Richmond	VA	c1920	Alterations

Roy Anthony Sealey
(1917–   )

Halycon O. Watkins

Roy Anthony Sealey is the second of four children born to Dr. Samuel Joseph Sealey and Ethel Blanche McPherson Sealey. His mother was born in 1893 in Dutch Guiana (now Surinam). His father was born in 1888 in Georgetown, British Guiana (now Guyana). The countries are adjacent on the northern Caribbean coast of South America. His father was employed by a steamship company and his mother was a homemaker.

Roy Sealey was born in Gatun, Panama, on July 3, 1917. Shortly thereafter his father received a Methodist missionary scholarship to study medicine in the United States. While his father was a student at Meharry Medical College in Nashville, Roy, his sister, and his mother lived in Kingston, Jamaica. Later on they immigrated to the United States, disembarking at Ellis Island on June 26, 1924, when Roy was seven years old, having arrived aboard the steamship *Carrillo*. After reuniting in New York City, the family lived with Roy Sealey's maternal grandfather. Subsequently, Roy was enrolled in Saint Emma Military Academy in Rock Castle, Virginia.

After graduating from Meharry Medical College and short stays in Memphis, Tennessee, and Waco, Texas, Dr. Samuel Sealey established a medical practice in Cameron, Texas, and moved the family to the nearby town of Bryan. Approximately thirty-five miles from Bryan was Prairie View Agricultural & Mechanical College, where Roy Sealey enrolled in 1936 to study architecture. He left in the fall semester of 1939 to accept an academic scholarship to the University of Southern California at Los Angeles and studied architecture there from 1939 to 1941.

Another reason Roy Sealey migrated to southern California was his interest in jazz. Although his father tried to discourage him, Sealey played trumpet in a jazz band at Prairie View Agricultural & Mechanical College and several members of the band had moved to southern California. Sealey remained in Los Angeles and began his architectural career.

Sealey received a huge public relations bonanza when he was profiled in the August 1950 edition of *Ebony* magazine.[1] The magazine included a photo of him, photographs of several buildings he had designed, and speculated about his income. Sealey was quoted as saying that he had worked for the noted Los Angeles architect PAUL REVERE WILLIAMS, starting in 1939 while a student at USC, and left in 1945 to open his own office in the same Wilshire Boulevard building adjacent to Williams's office. Also in the *Ebony* article, Sealey described how happy he was that Paul Williams's book, *Small Homes of Tomorrow*, had sold over one million copies because he had drawn many of the floor plans and renderings in it.[2]

Sealey obtained his California architect's license in 1957.[3] His office address was 7966 Beverly Boulevard in the mid-Wilshire area of Los Angeles and he employed three draftsmen. In 1975 he was admitted to the American Institute of Architects based on having designed six commercial buildings, five industrial buildings, four houses, three laboratories, two public schools, two municipal parking garages, and one hospital. Sealey was a consulting architect to Arthur Froehlich, designer of the Los Angeles County/University of Southern California Medical Center; Marvin A. Hornstein, structural engineer; Cornell Bridgers & Troller, landscape architects; B. L. Engineering, Inc., civil engineers; Samuel L. Kaye & Associates, mechanical engineers; and Tedd Darby, building specification writer.[4]

In 1971 L. P. Vander Haeghen, president of Vanlar Construction, Inc., wrote to the director of the Los Angeles County Engineering Office,

> After recently completing the $2,330,000.00 North End Parking Structure at the [Los Angeles County] University of Southern California Medical Center facilities, I have some feelings which I'd like to share with you.
>
> One of the primary concerns we have on projects as a contractor is the clarity and accuracy of the contract drawings. Also "on the job" service we obtain from the architect is extremely important.
>
> Having never worked with, or known, Mr. Roy Sealey, Architect prior to this job, it was a pleasant surprise to find a clear, accurate, well coordinated set of drawings. We were appreciative of the prompt constructive job-site counciling [sic] we received during the construction period.
>
> Having constructed seven parking structures we found that the per square foot cost and the per car stall cost of this structure was one of the most economical, and yet the most attractive and functional, of the structures we have completed. In checking the change order file we find this job had the fewest number of change orders on it, and involved the least amount of change order monies.
>
> You may be assured that in preparing any bid on a project on which Roy Sealey is the architect, we will very definately [sic] take these facts into consideration in our bids.[5]

Los Angeles in the 1940s and 1950s was the "hot" place to be for architects. The modern, casual California lifestyle was being formulated and built by adventurous architects. Sealey's work placed him among those adventurous architects. He seems to have assimilated influences from noted architects PAUL REVERE WILLIAMS, Richard Neutra (1892–1970), and Frank Lloyd Wright (1867–1959) and mixed them into a personal statement of modernism. Sealey developed several architectural specialties, one of which was veterinarian offices and clinics.

Department of Social Services-Metro North, *Halcyon O. Watkins*

Roy Sealey had no children with his first wife, Katherine. However, with his second wife, Lois, he has a son, Anthony John Sealey, born in 1957, who also became an architect.

Roy Sealey currently resides in Los Angeles and although his practice has slowed, fellow architects report that he is still active.

Notes

1. "Architect for the Wealthy," *Ebony* (August 1950): 32.
2. Paul Williams, *Small Homes of Tomorrow* (Hollywood: Murray & Gee, 1945).
3. California Architects Board, "Roy Sealey," Certificate no. C2312, issued 7 April 1957.
4. U.S. Form 251, *Professional Qualifications Statement for Roy Sealey*, D.C.: U.S. Government Printing Office, 1975. In the possession of Belle Sealey, St. Louis, MO.
5. L. P. Vander Haeghen to Los Angeles County Engineering Department, 1971. Letter in the possession of Belle Sealey, St. Louis, Missouri.

Bibliography

Pradling, Mary, ed. *In Black & White*. vol. 2. Detroit: Gale Research Company, 1980.

WESLEY HOWARD HENDERSON,
DALLAS, TEXAS

BUILDING LIST

Name	Address	City	State	Year	Comments
Apartment Bldg.		Los Angeles	CA	c1950	40 dwelling units (du)
Bank of America—Vermont/Slauson Branch	5700 S. Vermont Ave.	Los Angeles	CA	1971	
Belvedere Department of Social Services	5445 Whittier Blvd.	East Los Angeles	CA	1967	
Belvedere Department of Social Services Garage	5445 Whittier Blvd.	East Los Angeles	CA	1967	
Cockatoo Hotel Restaurant & Garage	4334 West Imperial Hwy.	Hawthorne	CA	1968	
Edgewater Hyatt House Hotel	6400 E. Pacific Coast Hwy.	Long Beach	CA	1966	
Fine, Maurice T.		Beverly Hills	CA	c1950	
LA County/USC Medical Admitting and Minor Trauma	1200 State St.	Los Angeles	CA	1972	
LA County/USC Medical Center North Parking Garage	1200 State St.	Los Angeles	CA	1971	
LA County/USC Medical Diagnostic and Evaluation	1200 State St.	Los Angeles	CA	1974	
LA County/USC Medical Employee's Cafeteria and Kitchen	1200 State St.	Los Angeles	CA	1975	
LA County/USC Medical Premature Nurseries	1200 State St.	Los Angeles	CA	1975	
Metro-North Department of Social Services	2910 Beverly Blvd.	Los Angeles	CA	1970	
Metro-North Department of Social Services Garage	2910 Beverly Blvd.	Los Angeles	CA	1970	
Mount Gleason Junior High School	10965 Mount Gleason Ave.	Sunland	CA	1970	
Rosenthal, J.		Los Angeles	CA	c1950	4 du
Stein, Ben		Beverly Hills	CA	c1950	
Thirty-Second Street Elementary School	822 West 32nd St.	Los Angeles	CA	1975	

William W. Smith
(1862–1937)

Livingston College, Heritage Hall Collection

William Smith, the son of Robert C. Smith, was born in Mecklenburg County, North Carolina. William Smith lived in Mecklenburg County all his life and perhaps gained his first construction experience serving as an apprentice with William Houser, an older, Black brick mason and contractor. Smith never received a formal education.

Charlotte, the industrial hub of Mecklenburg County, came to represent one of the booming towns of the New South in post–Civil War North Carolina. Smith's name first appeared in the *Charlotte City Directory* as a brick mason in the early 1890s and at the end of the decade he was briefly a partner with Houser in a brickmaking yard.[1] By the 1900s, he had emerged as a busy brick mason, contractor, and architect in Charlotte and Salisbury, North Carolina, and Rock Hill, South Carolina.

The New South decades saw development of a range of African American neighborhoods in Charlotte's Second Ward, which became almost exclusively Black, including the section known as Brooklyn. In west Charlotte, Blacks developed Biddleville near Biddle Institute (1867; now Johnson C. Smith University), which expanded Charlotte's Black professional sector. By the 1910s, Brooklyn boasted the Colored Young Men's Christian Association and public library, a "main street" with Black-run businesses, a hotel, and the African Methodist Episcopal Zion Publishing House, which made Charlotte a hub of the denomination—second only to New York City.

Smith advanced as mason, contractor, and architect and emerged as a leader of the city's African American community. In 1886 he and his wife were instrumental in founding Grace African Methodist Episcopal Zion Church. In 1902, Smith designed and built a handsome sanctuary for the church at 223 South Brevard Street, the most elegant avenue in the Brooklyn neighborhood of Charlotte. The Victorian Gothic–style Grace Church is the earliest known example of Smith's churches. According to stepson Arthur Anderson, "Mr. Smith, being a contractor, told the trustee board of Grace Church, 'if you get the material I'll have my men to build the church.' And that's the church that's standing today. He paid his own men; he built that church from the foundation up.'"[2] Smith was not the designer, but was the on-site architect. The plans were probably prepared by the African Methodist Episcopal Zion denomination's own architects in their New York City headquarters. Smith, however, was responsible for the elaborate brickwork on the front facade. His favorite technique was "corbelling"—stepping brick out from the wall plane. Even the sides and rear of the church have corbel Gothic arches, corbel bands under the eaves, and unique chimneylike pinnacles that rise above the roofline. On the two corner towers that flank the front facade, Smith displayed all his craft: buttresses, lancet windows, castlelike parapets, and extensive corbelling.

About the same time, Smith began his association with Livingstone College, fifty miles away in Salisbury, which was financially supported by the African Methodist Episcopal Zion denomination. Grace Church member Ed Cathey recalls that Smith taught masonry: "He'd take up the young men that wanted to learn bricklaying and work them on these jobs so that they could earn money as they went to school." In 1906 Smith designed and built Hood Hall (named for Bishop James W. Hood, himself once a brick mason). Smith approached the design of a building with the mind-set of a mason. His designs all have boxy massing, accentuated by flat parapet roofs. The brick pattern is either basket weave, mouse-tooth, or checkerboard. Rough brick, smooth brick, pressed brick, common brick, and even enameled brick are utilized for decorative effect. Most unusual and striking was Smith's use of polychrome. This decorative use of color brick had reached its zenith of popularity in the Victorian era of the late nineteenth century and then the technique declined. Smith incorporated polychrome in his buildings well into the 1920s. His combinations of red and yellow brick radiate an exuberance that seems to go beyond the Victorian, perhaps drawing on African aesthetic traditions.

It is believed that Smith was the architect for the renovations to Ballard Hall, which was damaged in a 1905 storm. Ballard Hall displays an elaborate cornice of red brick with diamonds, crosses, and checkerboards in yellow. Smith was also the architect and contractor for Goler Hall (1917), the college's largest building. Goler Hall served as a womens dormitory with ninety sleeping rooms, a dining room, post office, and staff quarters. Smith chose a T-shaped floor plan for the 3-story, red brick building and topped it with a familiar parapet roof. The long, symmetrical front facade is broken into five "pavilions" that step forward or back for visual effect. Corbel quoins and double cornices emphasize each pavilion. The center pavilion is a tapestry of polychrome pilasters, quoins, basket-weave brick, checkerboard diamonds, and arches.

The best example of Smith's design work in Charlotte is the Mecklenburg Investment Company Building (1922) on South Brevard at 3rd Street. The building was funded by a group of Black professionals who wanted to rent office space downtown, but were denied by White building owners due to their race. The ground floor held shops, the second floor held offices flanking a central corridor, and the third floor held a doctor's office and a large lodge hall with a coffered wooden ceiling. Smith used cream-colored brick for the front facade with yellow brick quoins and a double cornice of corbel red brick. Red brick

Afro-American Mutual Insurance Company, *Museum of the New South*

headers form a diamond pattern above the third-story windows and a checkerboard pattern above the second-story windows. Side walls are red brick with yellow brick detailing.

Two other commercial buildings that stood near the Mecklenburg Investment Company Building were the African Methodist Episcopal Zion Publishing House (1911) and the Afro-American Mutual Insurance Company building (1912). The Afro-American Mutual Insurance Company was organized by a group of Charlotte's Black leaders and was listed in the National Register of Historic Places. Both buildings were 2 stories tall with massing and lively polychrome that stamped them as Smith designs. They were demolished during the city's urban renewal activities.

In Rock Hill, South Carolina, Smith designed and constructed a 2-story branch office of the Afro-American Mutual Insurance Company in 1909. The building has red brick sides and an elaborate yellow brick facade, characteristic of Smith's designs. Quoin-like pilasters and a wide corbel cornice frames the front facade. A large arched panel in the cornice once held the building's name. Front windows have Roman-style arches with sashes, springers, and keystones in contrasting red sandstone.

William W. Smith died on May 23, 1937. At the time of his death he was one of the most highly regarded men in the Charlotte area. He is buried in a mausoleum that he designed in Charlotte's all-Black Pinewood Cemetery, joining his father, first wife, and his sister Mayme J. Smith Hargrove. The mausoleum, one of two inside the cemetery designed by Smith, takes its form from a Roman temple. It is a virtuoso exercise in brick masonry, incorporating red and yellow brick, plain and textured brick, and glazed white brick. A pair of locally fabricated cast-iron columns frame the entry.

Notes
1. William H. Huffman, "Grace A. M. E. Zion Church, Survey, and Report," Charlotte: Charlotte-Mecklenburg Historic Properties Commission, 1980, p. 93.

2. Thomas W. Hancett, "W. W. Smith, Black Designer and Builder." *Raleigh: North Carolina Preservation*, no. 67 (Spring 1987): 7.

Bibliography
Bishir, Catherine W. *North Carolina Architecture*. Chapel Hill: University of North Carolina Press, 1994.

Bishir, Catherine W., and Lawrence S. Early. *Early Twentieth-Century Suburbs in North Carolina*. Raleigh: North Carolina Department of Cultural Resources, 1985.

Jones, Alice Eley. *African American Builders and Architects in North Carolina, 1526–1998*. Raleigh: Preservation North Carolina, 1998.

ALICE ELEY JONES, AUTHOR AND OWNER OF HISTORICALLY SPEAKING, A HISTORY CONSULTING FIRM THAT SPECIALIZES IN CURRICULUM DESIGN, DIVERSITY TRAINING, PUBLIC HISTORY AND HERITAGE TOURISM, MURFREESBORO, NORTH CAROLINA

BUILDING LIST

Name	Address	City	State	Year	Comments
African Methodist Episcopal Zion Publishing House	2nd & Brevard Sts.	Charlotte	NC	c1912	Demolished
Afro-American Mutual Insurance Co.	412 E. 2nd St.	Charlotte	NC	1912	Demolished
Afro-American Mutual Insurance Co.	Dave Lyle Blvd.	Rock Hill	NC	c1909	
Grace African Methodist Episcopal Zion Church	223 S. Brevard St.	Charlotte	NC	c1902	
Livingston College Ballard Hall	Campus	Salisbury	NC	1905	
Livingston College Goler Hall	Campus	Salisbury	NC	c1917	
Livingston College Hood Hall	Campus	Salisbury	NC	c1906	
Mecklenbug Investment Co. Bldg.	223 S. Brevard St.	Charlotte	NC	c1922	

South Carolina Interstate and West Indian Exposition Negro Building, Charleston
(1901)

Located on the banks of Charleston's beautiful Ashley River and constructed in less than twelve months, the South Carolina Interstate and West Indian Exposition was the epitome of southern charm and elegance. The exposition, which opened with great fanfare on December 1, 1901, and operated through the end of May of the following year, was planned to showcase South Carolina's commercial advantages to the entire country and the world. By playing up Charleston's superior seaport facilities and geographic closeness to the West Indies, exposition planners hoped to foster an increase in trade with their island neighbors to the south. Although the fair was a modest success in drawing attention to the state's industrial and agricultural base, it failed to attract enough visitors to return a profit to its investors and ended in bankruptcy.

The majority of the official buildings on the grounds were designed by Bradford L. Gilbert (1859–1934) of New York City, who also had been chief architect of the COTTON STATES AND INTERNATIONAL EXPOSITION Atlanta in 1895. Gilbert divided the 250-acre site into two sections. The Natural Section, closest to the river, took advantage of the low-country landscape and featured smaller buildings and meandering walkways winding amid moss-covered oaks and palmettos. The Art Section, farthest from the river, was dominated by the main palaces that were arranged around a large courtyard and nearby formal gardens. The exposition's architectural theme consisted of a melding of two seemingly disparate styles with buildings of Anglo-Colonial style interspersed among those with a decidedly Spanish motif. Gilbert in-

South Carolina Interstate and West Indian Exposition Negro Building, *Abertype Company/Tony Chibbaro*

tended that this distinctly odd combination should be reflective of the region's early colonial heritage as well as its links to the Spanish Caribbean. The Iberian theme prevailed, however, because all of the main buildings were Spanish Renaissance style with elaborate cornices, embrasures, moldings, finials, and other ornamentation.

The Negro Building was located in the Natural Section, along with the Palace of Fine Arts, the Woman's Building, and many of the city- and state-sponsored buildings. It was designed in an elegantly Spanish Mission style compatible with nearby buildings. Gilbert had originally planned that it would "carry out in typical style some well known Southern homestead, possibly surrounded by Negro quarters, the whole so designed as to show the natural development of the Negro within the last twenty-five years."[1] Apparently the plan was modified prior to construction, however, and the Negro Building's style came to resemble that of the Spanish Mission style, albeit with less ornamentation.

Funds for construction of the Negro Building had been provided by the exposition's Board of Directors, which had also appointed Booker Taliferro Washington, principal of TUSKEGEE INSTITUTE, as chairman of the Negro Department. Washington was joined by Dr. W. D. Crum, a respected physician in Charleston and Thomas E. Miller, president of South Carolina State Colored College at Orangeburg. The latter two individuals were charged with managing the day-to-day affairs of the department while Washington supervised matters from afar. Washington considered the Negro Department's participation in the exposition to be "a most important event in the history of the South and took full advantage of the opportunity to show the world the progress African Americans had made since Emancipation."[2]

Ground was broken for construction of the Negro Building in mid-1901 and the cornerstone was laid during an elaborate ceremony on July 4. A large parade was organized in downtown Charleston and culminated at the construction site where it was met by exposition president F. W. Wagener and director-general J. H. Averill. Both men addressed their comments to the positive effects that the Negro Building would have in demonstrating the advances made by the Black man in the South.

Completed just in time for the opening ceremonies, the 1-story building featured a hip roof and large arch windows. Exterior ornamentation was minimal compared with other official buildings, but did exist around the front entrance and front windows. Exterior walls, as well as all the building ornaments, were made of staff—stucco made from plaster, cement, and jute fibers. The building was painted off-white, which matched the other buildings in the "Ivory City," as the exposition was nicknamed. The floor plan of the Negro Building resembled the letter "U" with the two wings connected by a central hall. The main entrance was in the middle of the central hall with a rear entrance in the opposite wall. The plan provided ample floor space for the many exhibits.

Although open to fairgoers beginning on December 1, 1901, the dedication of the Negro Building did not occur until a month later. It was decided to delay the dedication ceremonies until January 1, 1902, as that day had been chosen as the exposition's "Negro Day." On that date, which was celebrated by African Americans throughout the South as Emancipation Day, the Negro Building and all exhibits were ceremoniously turned over to the Board of Directors.

The exhibits covered a broad range of subjects pertaining to African Americans, including many that featured educational, historical, industrial, or artistic content. Perhaps the most prominent was the U.S. Negro Exhibit, which had been on display at the Paris Expo of 1900 and the Buffalo, New York, Pan-American Expo of 1901. It had received many accolades at these two fairs, including a total of seventeen medals. The U.S. Negro Exhibit presented demographic data that illustrated by way of hard data the progress made by African Americans since the end of slavery. Also featured was a display of silk manufacturing put together by T. W. Thurston of North Carolina. Thurston owned and operated a large silk mill that employed only Black workers. He handpicked a few employees and sent some of his most expensive machines to Charleston to provide a working demonstration of modern industrial machinery in the capable hands of Black mill operators. Other exhibits showcased dairy and poultry raising, broom manufacturing, mechanics, and several inventions by Black inventors, including Eugene Burkin's machine gun, L. C. Bailey's truss, and A. C. Bailey's railroad car coupler. An entire wing was devoted to educational exhibits and a large amount of floor space was also dedicated to the Woman's Bureau.

The Negro Building closed its doors on May 31, 1902, along with the exposition. All of the exposition buildings including the Negro Building, as planned, were demolished soon after the exposition closed. The site is now home to Hampton City Park, the Citadel Military College, and a single-family subdivision. The legacy of the Negro Building lives on, however, as an integral part of the story of South Carolina's only World's Fair.

SOUTH CAROLINA INTERSTATE AND WEST INDIAN EXPOSITION NEGRO BUILDING

Notes

1. Bradford L. Gilbert, "Letter to Col. Jno. H. Averill, 18 October 1900," *The Exposition*, vol. 1, (July 1901): 26. South Caroliniana Library.
2. Booker T. Washington, "The Negro Department of the Exposition," *The Exposition*, vol. 1 (July 1901) 200. South Caroliniana Library.

Bibliography

Chibbaro, Anthony. *Images of America: The Charleston Exposition.* Charleston: Arcadia Publishing Company, 2001.

Gilbert, Bradford L. "The Buildings and the Builders." *The Exposition* vol. 1, no. 9. (1 July 1901): 287, South Caroliniana Library.

Harvey, Bruce G. "World's Fairs in a Southern Accent: Atlanta, Nashville, Charleston, 1895–1902." Ph.D. diss., Vanderbilt University, 1998.

Smyth, William D. "Blacks and the South Carolina Interstate and West Indian Exposition." *South Carolina Historical Magazine* vol. 88, (October 1987): 211.

ANTHONY CHIBBARO, AUTHOR AND HISTORIAN,
PROSPERITY, SOUTH CAROLINA

Southern University School of Architecture, Louisiana
(1946)

Southern University is part of the Southern University System, which operates campuses in Shreveport and New Orleans, Louisiana. The campus at Baton Rouge is the flagship of the system.

Colored delegates Pinckney Benton Steward Pinchback, Theophile T. Allain, T. B. Stamps, and Henry Demas championed the idea of a Southern University during the Louisiana Constitutional Convention of 1879, arguing persuasively for the necessity of an equal-opportunity institution of higher learning in the state for persons of color. Their efforts were rewarded with Legislative Act 87, which authorized the creation of Southern University's inaugural campus in New Orleans in April 1880. Initially, Southern University opened with twelve students. In 1890 the university was reorganized to receive land-grant funds and in 1912 the state legislature closed the New Orleans campus and authorized its reestablishment north of Baton Rouge at a place locally referred to as Scott's Bluff in Scotlandville. The newly chartered Southern University opened in 1914 with Joseph S. Clark as its first president, a position he was to hold until 1938.

Succeeding his father as president, Felton G. Clark served from 1938 to 1968. He began what was known as the "Greater Southern University Expansion Program."[1] President Clark's program addressed not only the physical infrastructure but the curriculum as well. As a result, the Division of Mechanical Arts was established in 1939 and by the 1942 to 1943 academic year there were fifteen four-year degree programs and several two-year nondegree trade programs including mechanical arts. In 1941 the Division of Mechanical Arts, with Robert Lee Shade as acting director, offered a bachelor of science degree in mechanical arts, with a two-year mechanical drawing requirement. The prerequisite courses included mechanical drawing, orthographic projection and pictorial sketches, and applied mechanical drawing. In 1945, under the direction of Jeremiah William McLeod, the division offered a two-year curriculum leading to a certificate in a trade. Four-year majors working toward the bachelor of science degree in trade and industrial education were encouraged to work in their particular trade for ten forty-hour weeks during the summer to develop their skills, and new courses including working drawings and layout work were added.

Arguably the seeds of what is now the School of Architecture were planted in 1946, with the creation of the Division of Vocational and Industrial Education and its emphasis on training in the building trades. The educational objective for this newly formed division was to prepare its graduates for careers in the construction trades and as manual arts instructors throughout the South's segregated public schools. Faculty members J. B. Moore and James L. Hunt taught the building construction courses and for completing this two-year program students were awarded a vocational education certificate. The division program was described as follows:

> The program of this department is designed to contribute to the efforts of Southern University to achieve its purpose—preparing Negro Leaders and citizens in general for wholesome participation in the "American Way of Life.". . . Toward this end, the Industrial Education Department provides opportunities for individuals to acquire the necessary technical knowledge and skills for participation in some technical vocation or occupation and to be able to help others to acquire similar competency.[2]

In 1948, while completing his master's degree at the University of Illinois (a degree he was to receive in 1949), Henry L. Thurman Jr. was recruited to join the faculty. The appointment of Professor Thurman—"Dean" Thurman as he would come to be respectfully called—marked the initiation of a new educational philosophy within the division. Primarily based on his immersion in the "Tuskegee Model" of education while receiving his undergraduate degree from HAMPTON INSTITUTE in 1947, Professor Thurman brought a commitment that would serve as the fire by which the program and its students would be forged over the next forty-plus years.

Under Elton C. Harrison, who would continue as head until 1953, the Division of Technical and Industrial Education offered a bachelor of science in industrial education degree that focused on building construction, expanding the course offerings to include mechanical drafting, foundation, framing and roofing, architectural drafting and design, building construction, and construction problems. In addition, all students were required to receive at least eight hundred hours of work experience in their respective major.

The year 1954 proved to be a seminal one for the architectural program. The Division of Industrial Technology was established with Professor Thurman as its director. Thurman was the second African American to pass the architectural professional practice examination in Louisiana, following FERDINAND LUCIEN ROUSSEVE, who passed the exam in 1934.[3] It was during his tenure that the division offered a four-year program leading to a bachelor of science degree in industrial technology with an emphasis on architectural construction. In that same year, the state legislature approved the inauguration of a series of four-year programs in architecture, and civil, electrical, and mechanical engineering. In the 1955 to 1956 academic year, the division began offering courses in freehand drawing, architectural perspective, architectural history, structures, accounting, and architectural practice, leading to a bachelor of science in architectural construction degree. Recognizing the need to provide balance between the additional level of mastery that these courses required and the responsibility to provide students with marketable skills, the eight hundred hours of practical work was reduced to four hundred. In 1956 instruction in the newly instituted College of Engineering began. The founding of the College of Engineering was an integral component in the university's effort to keep pace with the technological advances of the time. More importantly, placing the architectural program within the College of Engineering signaled a clear preference for the professional education model for its architectural students instead of the vocational model of the past. With the establishment of this more contemporary educational paradigm, the foundation for a professional program had been laid. At its creation, the college had five faculty members and twenty students. Professor Thurman was named the first dean of the college, a position he was to hold intermittently for thirteen years.

The College of Engineering awarded its first bachelor's degree in 1960 and granted its first bachelor of science degree in architectural engineering in 1961. However, one year later the four-year architectural engineering degree program was expanded to a five-year bachelor of architecture degree. The architectural degree program was housed in the newly created Department of Architecture within the College of Engineering.

Courses required in the five-year professional program included sociology, political science, materials and methods of construction, watercolors, analytical mechanics, principles of city planning, sculpture, working drawings, theory, and professional ethics and practice. The first five-year bachelor of architecture degree was awarded in May 1963 to Ernest Ray Blow.

The high level of achievement by faculty and students was recognized and rewarded both externally and internally to the university when accreditation of the professional degree program was granted by the National Architectural Accreditation Board in 1970 and the department was granted divisional status by the university in 1972.

Under President Jesse N. Stone, who served from 1974 to 1985, Southern University faced one of the most formidable challenges in its history from the federal government's efforts to desegregate public education in Louisiana. The U.S. Justice Department stipulated that by the fall of 1978, Louisiana's dual system of education had to end. Unfortunately for Southern University this had the effect of halting any expansion of departments or programs for several years. Eventually a settlement between the state and the U.S. Justice Department put to rest the threat of consolidating campuses, leaving the mission of Southern University intact, but not before the years of skepticism and inertia had taken its toll on the architecture program.

The Louisiana Board of Regents granted independent status to the division, creating the School of Architecture in 1985, and course offerings were expanded to include design processes, graphic presentation, computer programming and applications, site planning, construction management and cost controls, and professional registration preparation. The school's mission was revised to reflect its position as an autonomous, accredited professional school of architecture and it received a five-year accreditation in 1990.

With the establishment of an independent school of architecture, the program had reached the institutional zenith of its long-unfolding teleology. Unfortunately, overcoming the lingering effects of the period of dormancy that began in the latter half of the decade proved difficult. As a result, the School of Architecture experienced administrative instability.

In its prime, the School of Architecture produced high-quality, dedicated, and creative African American professionals who have gone on to become successful and influential practitioners and educators.[4]

In 1997 the School of Architecture faculty instituted a School Advisory Board whose initiatives included selective admissions after the second year, a mandatory co-op program supported by a grant from the U.S. Department of Education, a study-abroad program to Mexico, and the establishment of a Community Design Center providing design assistance to communities in Louisiana supported by funding from U.S. Department of Housing and Urban Development.

Although it remains to be seen whether the infusion of new faculty, funds, and initiatives will be sufficient to revive the once-formidable architecture program, what is clear is that through the graduates and educators who have passed through its corridors in all of its manifestations over the past fifty years, the influence of the School of Architecture will remain very much alive in the field of architecture for some time to come.

Division of Mechanical Arts Directors

Robert Lee Shade (acting) (1941–42)
Dr. Walter T. Daniels (1942–43)
Jeremiah William McLeod (1943–46)

Division of Technical and Industrial Education Directors

Elton C. Harrison (1946–53)

Division of Industrial Technology/Division of Architecture, College of Architecture Directors

Henry L. Thurman Jr. (1953–59)

Division of Architecture, College of Engineering Directors

Leon Daughtry (1959–63)
Julian White (1963–67)
Robert "Skip" Perkins (1967–70)
E. Donald Van Purnell (1970–72)
Henry L. Thurman Jr. (1972–74)
E. Donald Van Purnell (1974–78)
Henry L. Thurman Jr. (1978–81)
Dr. Arthur Symes (1981–85)

School of Architecture Deans

Dr. Arthur Symes (1985–90)
Henry L. Thurman Jr. (interim) (1990–92)
E. Donald Van Purnell (interim) (1992–95)
Lonnie Wilkinson (interim) (1995)
Mohammed Uddin, Brian Lafleur, and Reginald Verret (interim committee) (1996)
Frank M. Bosworth III (1997–99)
Dr. Adenrele A. Awotona (1999–present)

Notes

1. Charles Vincent, *A Centennial History of Southern University and A & M College, 1880–1980* (Baton Rouge, La.: Southern University Press, 1981), p. 153.
2. *Southern University Bulletin* (Baton Rouge, La.: Southern University Press, 1947), p. 104.
3. Interview with Henry L. Thurman Jr. (former director of the School of Architecture), by the author, Baton Rouge, La., 13 October 2000.
4. Distinguished graduates include Jude Paten (1962), past director of transportation and development for the State of Louisiana; Dr. James Chaffers (1964), professor, University of Michigan; Sir James L. Robinson (1964), principal, Robinson Architects, New York City; Paul Devrouax (1966), principal, Devrouax & Purnell Architects, Washington, D.C.; Lonnie Hewitt (1969), principal, Hewitt-Washington Associates, New Orleans, Louisiana; James Washington (1970), principal, Hewitt-Washington Associates, New Orleans, Louisiana; William Raymond Manning (1974), principal, Billes/Manning Architects, New Orleans, Louisiana; Mary Calvin Wells (1975), facilities planner, Southern University; and Lolalisa King (1982), principal, Lolalisa King Architect, Greensboro, North Carolina.

Bibliography

"2000 Architectural Program Report on the Five Year Bachelor of Architecture Program: Southern University and A&M College School of Architecture." School of Architecture, Baton Rouge, La., May 2000.

CRAIG L. WILKINS,
ADJUNCT ASSOCIATE PROFESSOR OF ARCHITECTURE,
UNIVERSITY OF MINNESOTA, COLLEGE OF
ARCHITECTURE AND LANDSCAPE ARCHITECTURE

Prince W. Spears
(c1879–unknown)

Prince Spears—a Georgia-born mulatto architect, builder, and brick mason—fashioned a career for himself not in his native Georgia, but in Sanford, Florida.[1] Little is known about his family background or schooling. What is known about Spears comes from his documented buildings in the predominately African American communities of Georgetown and Goldsboro near Sanford. The community of Georgetown existed before the town was named after land speculator Henry Sanford, around 1871, decided he would designate Georgetown as Sanford's "Black Community."[2] Georgetown was thriving, made up of mostly working-class Blacks who either farmed or worked on the railroad. Spears's arrival in Sanford between 1906 and 1910 was of critical importance to his career. On their way to Florida from Georgia with Spears and another brick mason, Neal Lofton of Milledgeville, detoured to TUSKEGEE INSTITUTE, where they enrolled but did not stay long enough to receive certificates. When Spears arrived in central Florida, he lived modestly as a boarder in the home of the Muses at R1023 West 12th Street.[3] Shortly after his arrival in town, he was commissioned by Reverend W. H. Brown to design and build the third version of Saint James African Methodist Episcopal Church (1910). It took three years to design and build the church. Given its surroundings of early American vernacular, Spears copied a style prevalent throughout the region, which was

Saint James African Methodist Episcopal Church, *Monica L. Walker*

Gothic Revival style. The interior is similar to that of a Roman baptistery with short transepts and nave proportions. Spears's talent as an architect was displayed for all to see. His reputation established, he became Sanford's "church architect." While Saint James African Methodist Episcopal Church was still on the boards, he was commissioned to design and build Saint John Missionary Baptist Church. This church is located only one block from Saint James, yet it is more modest in scale, details, and design. Saint John followed the style of an early American vernacular church, which was common to the area. Spears designed and built two more churches in Sanford: New Mount Calvary Missionary Baptist Church in Goldsboro and Trinity Methodist Baptist Church in Georgetown.

In 1920 at age forty-one Spears married Theodocia Purcell in Sanford on March 25. Their vows were witnessed by Herman Refoe and Italy Littles, for whom Spears had designed houses.

By the latter half of the 1920s, Spears was designing more houses than churches. He was the architect for single-family residences for Dr. George Brewer and David C. Brock, as well as his own home.[4]

In the 1940s his wife moved to Texas. There is no documented evidence of any buildings in Sanford designed by Spears during the 1940s so it is speculated that he must have accompanied her.

Notes

1. U.S. Census, "Prince Spears," Seminole County, Florida, West Sanford Precinct, 1920, p. 200
2. Nolan Pitts, "Church Files/Church History, St. James African Methodist Episcopal Church," n.d., Sanford Museum, Sanford, Florida.
3. Altremese Bentley, *Black American Series Seminole County* (Charleston: Arcadia Publishing, 2000), p. 20.
4. "Spears, Prince," *Polk's Sanford City Directory*, vol. 5 (Jacksonville, Florida: Polk & Co., 1924–25), p. 261.

Bibliography

Robison, Jim. "Church Has Place in History," *Orlando Sentinel*, 21 June 1992, p. K15.

MONICA L. WALKER,
DESIGNER AND HISTORIAN, ORLANDO, FLORIDA

BUILDING LIST

Name	Address	City	State	Year	Comments
Brewer, Dr. George	612 Sanford Ave.	Sanford	FL	c1920	
Brock, David C.	620 Sanford Ave.	Sanford	FL	c1920	
Duhart, Harry L.	Sanford Ave. btwn. 3rd & 4th Sts.	Sanford	FL	1912	Destroyed by fire
Green, William O.	611 Sanford Ave.	Sanford	FL	c1920	
Littles, Italy	614 Sanford Ave.	Sanford	FL	c1920	
New Mt. Calvary Missionary Baptist Church	1109 W. 12th St.	Goldsboro	FL	1918	
Refoe, Herman L.	612 Sanford Ave.	Sanford	FL	c1920	
Spears, Prince	W. 12th St.	Goldsboro	FL	c1930	Demolished
St. James African Methodist Episcopal Church	819 Cypress Ave.	Sanford	FL	1910	
St. John Missionary Baptist Church	920 Cypress Ave.	Sanford	FL	c1910	
Strickland, Dr. Edwin D.	511 Sanford Ave.	Sanford	FL	c1920	
Trinity Methodist Baptist Church	526 Sanford Ave.	Sanford	FL	c1920	Demolished

William Alfred Streat Jr.
(1920–1994)

Samual J. Hodges III

William A. Streat Jr. was born on July 15, 1920, in Clover, Virginia, and spent his childhood on the campus of Saint Paul's College in Lawrenceville, Virginia, where his parents William A. Streat Sr. and Marie Green Streat were teachers. He was the grandson of William Munford Streat, landowner and planter, and Bettie Streat of Victoria, Virginia; and James Edward Green, merchant and landowner, and Ellen Coleman Green of Clover, Virginia.

Streat completed Saint Paul's High School in 1937. He received a bachelor of science degree in building construction from HAMPTON INSTITUTE in 1941 and a bachelor of science degree in architecture from the University of Illinois in 1948. He earned the master of science degree in architectural engineering from the Massachusetts Institute of Technology in 1949. Streat completed additional study in civil engineering at Duke University and the University of California at Berkeley; and attended the jointly offered program in architectural criticism at Harvard University/Massachusetts Institute of Technology, and city and regional planning at Columbia University.

During World War II, Streat served in the U.S. Corps of Engineers and in the Army Air Corps as a B-25 twin-engine bomber pilot with the 99th U.S. Pursuit Squadron, better known as the "Tuskegee Airmen."[1]

In 1951 Streat married Louise Guenveur of Charleston, South Carolina, who served as professor and chair of the Department of Home Economics at Bennett College in Greensboro, North Carolina.

Streat was a registered architect and practiced for forty-two years in North Carolina, South Carolina, and Virginia.[2] In 1952 he became the second African American licensed to practice architecture in the state of North Carolina. He maintained a practice in North Carolina and surrounding states from 1952 until his death in 1994. Churches, houses, and historic restorations were predominant among his designs. He was also certified by the Department of Defense to design buildings protected against natural and nuclear disasters.

As an educator, Streat served as professor and chair of the Architectural Engineering Department at NORTH CAROLINA AGRICULTURAL & TECHNICAL STATE UNIVERSITY from 1949 until his retirement in 1985. The department grew from twenty students to 200 under his leadership and included a tenfold increase in faculty and the addition of a master's program in architectural engineering.

Professor Streat served on numerous committees to aid North Carolina A&T University. He was chair of the Building Committee for the new engineering building (1981–86), and in collaboration with two other faculty from the School of Engineering, he planned and established the Transportation Institute at the university. The Institute initiated research in other university departments as well as in the Department of Architectural Engineering.

During the early 1970s, through the combined efforts of Streat and the chairs of other historically Black college and university engineering departments, the

Searborough Nursery, *Samuel J. Hodges III*

Department of Architectural Engineering at North Carolina A&T State University secured a two-year U.S. Department of Education Development Grant. The grant provided funds for architectural engineering student scholarships, enrichment programs, and field trips. The grant funds also provided for faculty development and research, and faculty and secretarial positions.

Streat's involvement in research at the university included the "Effects of Building Structures on Transportation," sponsored by the U.S. Department of Transportation; "Solar Energy Application and Energy Conservation for Low-Income Rural Families," sponsored by the U.S. Department of Agriculture; and "Elements of Structures" (graphical and numerical solutions), sponsored by the U.S. Department of Health, Education, and Welfare.[1]

Streat served a six-year term on the Engineering Accrediting Committee, which reviewed architectural engineering programs. This committee became the Accrediting Board for Engineering and Technology. He also served as chair and vice chair of the Architectural Engineering Division of the American Society for Engineering Education and served as chair and vice-chair of the Civil Defense Committee.

Streat was a member of the Episcopal Church of the Redeemer in Greensboro and served on the vestry. He was a life member of the *Alpha Phi Alpha* Fraternity. His other affiliations included the American Institute of Architects, the American Society for Engineering Education, and the NATIONAL TECHNICAL ASSOCIATION. He was a member of the Gargoyle Architectural Honor Society in recognition of proficiency in architecture and the *Beta Kappa Chi* Honor Society.

After his retirement from teaching, he continued a limited architectural practice. With his wife, he became actively involved as a benefactor to the United Negro College Fund and fund-raising development for college scholarships at Saint Paul's College, Hampton University, and North Carolina Agricultural and Technical State University. He served on the board of the J. M. Marteena Loan-Grant Scholarship fund at North Carolina Agricultural and Technical State University, and also served on the board of the Greensboro Cerebral Palsy School and the Canterbury School in Greensboro established by the Episcopal Church.[2]

Since her husband's death in 1994, Louise Streat has endowed scholarships in her husband's name at North Carolina Agricultural and Technical State University, Saint Paul's College, and Bennett College.[3]

Notes
1. "Professor Streat Will Retire," *Architectural Engineering News* Greensboro: Architectural Engineering Department, North Carolina A&T State University (April–July 1985) 1.
2. North Carolina Board of Architecture, "William A. Streat, Jr.," no. 748, 10 September 1952.
3. Interview with Louise Guenveur Streat (wife of William Streat), Greensboro, N.C., 12 October 2001.

Bibliography
Streat, William A. "Effects of Building Structures on Transportation. 1 July 1972. North Carolina Agricultural & Technical University, Bluford Library Archives.

SAMUEL J. HODGES III, AIA,
U.S. DEPARTMENT OF AGRICULTURE,
RURAL HOUSING SERVICE, WASHINGTON, D.C.

BUILDING LIST

Name	Address	City	State	Year	Comments
Alexander, Judge ___	Salem St.	Greensboro	NC	1957	
Baptist Church		Trinity	NC	1987	
Bennett College Dett Cottage	Campus	Greensboro	NC	1975	Restoration
Bruce, Dr. ___	2021 New Walkertown Rd.	Winston-Salem	NC	1963	
Coleman, Dr. ___		Winston-Salem	NC	1961	
Coley, Dr. ___	1901 Circle View Dr.	Greensboro	NC	1971	
Davis, Dr. Earl F.	1103 S. Benbow Rd.	Greensboro	NC	1966	
Episcopal Church of the Redeemer	901 E. Friendly Ave.	Greensboro	NC	1956	
First Baptist Church	302 Monroe St.	Fayetteville	NC	1958	
Gore, Dr. ___	Eastside Dr.	Greensboro	NC	1987	
Guenveur, E .L.	Hariestown Village	Charleston	SC	1973	
John Wesley Methodist Church	616 Cumberland St.	Fayetteville	NC	1958	
Johnson G. Smith Univ. Mens Dorm.	Campus	Charlotte	NC	1968	Restoration
North Carolina Mutual Insurance Co.	501 Williard St.	Durham	NC	1969	Now Baines Bldg.
Quick, Dr.	Cumberland Rd.	Winston-Salem	NC	1961	
Reed, Dr. ___	2711 McConnell Rd.	Greensboro	NC	1959	
Russell Funeral Home	Russell Ave.	Winston-Salem	NC	1957	
St. Paul's College President's Residence	Campus	Lawrenceville	VA	1953	Restoration
St. Paul's College Saul Bldg.	Campus	Lawrenceville	VA	1993	Restoration
St. Paul's College Student Center	Campus	Lawrenceville	VA	1952	Restoration
Searborough Nursery	Queen St.	Durham	NC	1972	
Seventh Day Adventist Educ. Bldg.	1800 E. Market St.	Greensboro	NC	1986	
Streat, William A.	1507 Tuscaloosa St.	Greensboro	NC	1962	
Trader, Dr. ___	323 Willough St.		NC	1970	
United Durham, Inc.		Durham	NC		
Watkins, Dr. ___	4601 Splitrail Rd.	Greensboro	NC	1967	
White, Dr. Frank	Eastside Dr.	Greensboro	NC	1976	
Women's Clinic	Walkerton Rd.	Winston-Salem	NC	1957	

John Dennis Sulton
(1912–1994)

Sulton, Campbell, Britt & Associates

John D. Sulton, founding partner of Sulton Campbell & Associates, was born on August 18, 1912, in Saint George, South Carolina. He was the second son of three children of John J. and Daisy Hume Sulton. He was reared in Orangeburg, South Carolina, where his father was a second-generation operator of the first Negro-owned lumber yard in the state, Sulton & Sons, established in 1825, which offered John an early education about building materials. He completed his elementary and high school education at CLAFLIN UNIVERSITY in Orangeburg, South Carolina, and went on to receive his bachelor of science degree in mechanical arts from South Carolina State College. Upon graduation in 1934, he worked in the family lumber yard until he was able to matriculate to Kansas State College in Manhattan as an architecture major.

To meet college expenses, Sulton worked as a dining car waiter on the Union Pacific Railroad during the summer. One year he had to drop out of college and work full time on the railroad to enable him to make tuition. Through his personal perseverance, he graduated from Kansas State College in 1941 with a bachelor of science degree in architecture, and an American Institute of Architects (AIA) Achievement Award.

Despite having graduated with honors, Sulton was not able to find employment in his profession—a not unusual occurrence for African Americans. He continued to work for the railroad until he was offered a position with the Federal Housing Authority (FHA) in Washington, D.C., in 1942.

Sulton stayed with the Federal Housing Authority for two years. After being passed over for several promotions, he decided to join the architectural firm of HILYARD ROBERT ROBINSON and ALBERT IRVIN CASSELL, where he remained from 1944 to 1964. While working for Robinson & Cassell he managed many notable projects including the International-style house of Ralph Johnson Bunche, U.S. undersecretary at the United Nations, and the Ira Aldridge Theatre on the campus of Howard University. It was during this affiliation that he met architect Leroy Campbell (1927–1957), who would later become his partner.

In 1964 John Sulton left Robinson & Cassell to work full time on the *Omega Psi Phi* Fraternity house for his fraternity. Leroy Campbell worked with him part time on this project and several others over the next two years. In 1966 Sulton and Campbell formed a partnership, hanging out the Sulton & Campbell shingle in Washington, D.C.

As part of its continued growth, in 1968 Sulton Campbell & Associates established an office in Baltimore, Maryland, relying on a contract to design Oswego Mall Public Housing for the Baltimore City Housing Authority. In 1982 the firm grew into Sulton, Campbell, Britt, Owens & Associates with John Sulton as chairman of the board and chief executive officer.

Sulton was actively involved with various communities in Washington, D.C. He believed that it was his

7th District Police Station, Washington, D.C. *Ronald N. Anderson*

civic responsibility to give something back to the community. He had a particular passion for youth causes. In the 1970s Sulton was a member of the District of Columbia Citizens for Better Public Education, which sponsored a program called "Project Men." The objective of this program was to introduce public school students to a variety of Black-owned professional firms, making them aware of what each firm did. Sulton Campbell & Associates was the only architectural firm represented. Regularly two or three students from various junior and senior public high schools would spend an afternoon or day at the firm talking with the principals and associates about what it "took" to be an architect.

In addition to wanting to reach out to youth, Sulton believed that it was important for Black professionals to work together. He insisted that Black engineers work on his projects. In the vernacular of the 1970s, Sulton believed that true "Black Power" was about helping and giving back to the community on a variety of levels. This commitment made him greatly admired and respected in his community.

After successfully completing an "Existing Conditions Survey" of buildings in the Shaw Urban Renewal Area, the firm received its first multimillion-dollar contract to design Shaw Junior High School in 1969, with a $7.7-million construction budget. Sulton & Campbell immediately engaged two Black engineering firms—George Worsley & Associates, a mechanical and electrical engineering firm, and Jackson Tull, a structural engineering firm—to consult with them on the school.

Other buildings designed under Sulton's guidance included the Seeley G. Mudd School of Medicine at Howard University, Howard University School of Business and Public Administration, Howard Inn, Addison Road Metro Station, Mount Sinai Baptist Church, 7th District Police Station, and Francis Bathhouse and Swimming Pool.

In 1981 his *alma mater*, Kansas State University, awarded Sulton the "Distinguished Service in Architecture and Design Award." In 1982 he was elected to the College of Fellows of the American Institute of Architects.

Sulton also was active in a number of professional associations. He was treasurer of the NATIONAL TECHNICAL ASSOCIATION and a member of the Washington chapter of the American Institute of Architects and the National Organization of Minority Architects. He was also appointed to the D.C. Historic Preservation Review Board and the D.C. Code and Zoning Committee, which he chaired.

In keeping with his roots in the community, Sulton was also a lifelong member of the National Association for the Advancement of Colored People. He served as an elder and member of the Trustee Board of the 15th Street Presbyterian Church, and was also a member of the Black Friars Social Club and the

JOHN DENNIS SULTON

Commissioners Regional Hospital Advisory Committee.

In 1944 Sulton married Kathleen Hunter of Washington, D.C., a teacher in the District of Columbia public school system. They were married for fifty years and blessed with a daughter, Linda Sulton Nwosu.

On February 25, 1994, at the age of eighty-one, John Sulton died at his desk doing what he most loved, practicing architecture.[1] District of Columbia Mayor Marion S. Barry Jr. declared March 4, 1994, "John D. Sulton Day" in recognition of his tireless support and civic and professional contributions to the District. A memorial scholarship fund was established in his name at HOWARD UNIVERSITY SCHOOL OF ARCHITECTURE AND PLANNING.

Notes

1. "John D. Sulton Dies; Washington Architect," *Washington Post,* 3 March 1994, p. D5.

STANFORD R. BRITT, FAIA,
PRINCIPAL,
SULTON, CAMPBELL, BRITT & ASSOCIATES
WASHINGTON, D.C.

BUILDING LIST

Name	Address	City	State	Year	Comments
7th District Police Station	2455 Alabama Ave., SE	Washington	DC		
10th Street Baptist Church	1000 R St., NW	Washington	DC	1975	Plans only
13th & M Streets Office Bldg.	13th & M Streets, NW	Washington	DC	1981	Alterations
15th Street Presbyterian Church	1701 15th St., NW	Washington	DC	1967	
Addison Road Metro Station	Central Ave. East of Addison Rd.	Capitol Hts.	MD		
Barry Farm Public Housing	1230 Summer Rd., SE	Washington	DC	1983	Demolished
Brown Memorial African Methodist Episcopal Church Annex	1400 Constitution Ave., NE	Washington	DC	1986	
Brown Memorial Church		Baltimore	MD	1988	Addition
Brummel Manor	520 Brummel Ct., NW	Washington	DC	1979	Alterations
Campbell Heights Elderly Housing	2001 15th St., NW	Washington	DC	1979	
Capitol View Public Housing	5901 E. Capitol St., SE	Washington	DC	1972	
Carolina Missionary Baptist Church		Washington	DC	1990	
Congress Heights Recreation Center	Alabama Ave. & Randle Pl., SE	Washington	DC	1991	Alterations
Congress Park Homes	1313 Savannah St., SE	Washington	DC	1982	Alterations
Faith Temple No. 2 Baptist Church	211 Maryland Pk. Dr.	Capitol Hts.	MD	1988	
First Rising Baptist Church		Washington	DC	1987	
First Rising Education Building		Washington	DC	1978	
First Rising Mt. Zion Baptist Church Adult Center	600 N. St., NW	Washington	DC	1978	Addition
First Rising Mt. Zion Baptist Church Education Bldg.	602 N. St., NW	Washington	DC	1978	Plans only
Friendship Baptist Church	900 Delaware Ave., SW	Washington	DC	1964	
Hardy Recreation Center	45th & Q Sts., NW	Washington	DC	1991	
House of Prayer Housing		Macon	GA	1976	
Howard Inn	2041 Georgia Ave., NW	Washington	DC	1976	Demolished
Howard University East of the River Health Clinic	123 45th St.	Washington	DC	1977	
Howard University Hospital Parking Structure	Campus	Washington	DC	1983	560 cars
Howard University Mudd Medical Research Bldg.	Campus	Washington	DC	1977	
Howard University Mudd Medical Research Bldg.	Campus	Washington	DC	1979	Alterations
Howard University School of Business	Campus	Washington	DC	1983	
Hughes Memorial United Methodist Church	25 53rd St., NW	Washington	DC		
Iowa Condominiums	7 Iowa Cir., NW	Washington	DC	1978	Alterations
Kimball Elementary School	3375 Minnesota Ave., SE	Washington	DC	1964	
Knox Hill Elderly Housing	2700 Jasper St., SE	Washington	DC	1984	
Knox Hill Recretion Center		Washington	DC	1990	
Missouri Mews		Washington	DC	1980	
Morning Star Baptist Church	1063 W. Fayettville St.	Baltimore	MD	1970	
Mt. Sinai Baptist Church	1615 3rd St., NW	Washington	DC	1986	Alterations
Omega Psi Phi Fraternity National Headquarters		Washington	DC	1973	Alterations
Oswego Mall Public Housing	717 Druid Park Lake Dr.	Baltimore	MD	1968	Alterations
Randall Memorial United Methodist Church	1002 46th St., NE	Washington	DC	1981	Plans only
RCA Educational Laboratory Animal Facility		Beltsville	MD	1978	
Rhines Funeral Home	3015 12th St., NE	Washington	DC	1985	Alterations

BUILDING LIST *(continued)*

Name	Address	City	State	Year	Comments
Sargent Memorial Presbyterian Church Multipurpose Bldg.	5109 Burroughs Ave., NE	Washington	DC	1970	Alterations
Seaton Elementary School	1503 10th St., NW	Washington	DC	1974	
Sharpe Health Center	4300 13th St., NW	Washington	DC	1974	
Shaw Junior High School	925 Rhode Island Ave., NW	Washington	DC	1975	
U.S. Dept. of Agricultural Animal Research Facility	10300 Baltimore Ave.	Beltsville	MD	1980	
United National Bank	3940 Minnesota Ave., NW	Washington	DC	1977	

Vertner Woodson Tandy
(1885–1949)

Cornell University Archives

Vertner Woodson Tandy was the foremost African American architect practicing in New York City during the first half of the twentieth century.[1] His design output over the course of a forty-year career represents one of the most dynamic periods in domestic architectural history and, in particular, the emergence of Harlem as a majority African American community and cultural capital of Black America. Tandy embodied a number of important attributes that helped to ensure his success as an architect. He was appropriately trained in professional terms to practice in a large, sophisticated city of the caliber of New York; he was self-assured; his affiliations with influential fraternal organizations in Harlem (for example, the Elks and *Alpha Phi Alpha* Fraternity) provided strategic business contacts; he established a professional rapport with White architect, engineer, and contractor colleagues; and last, but not least, he cultivated important patrons at an early point in his career, securing high-profile commissions from African Americans for several key buildings in Harlem. Because of his entry into a profession that was considered at the time an anomaly for African Americans, being one of six founders of *Alpha Phi Alpha* Fraternity, and his rank of major in the "Hell Fighters," the all-Negro U.S. 369th Infantry, 15th New York Regiment of the National Guard, Tandy was held in high esteem and considered Harlem's architect. Yet, despite being lionized in Harlem for his civic and architecture achievements, Tandy's career reveals how tenuous an African American architect's success could be.

Vertner Tandy was born in Lexington, Kentucky, the son of Henry A. and Emma Brice Tandy. Henry Tandy (1854–1918) was a successful brick contractor. A prominent building in Lexington built by Tandy & Bird, Builders, was the Fayette County Courthouse (1898). The elder Tandy was the single most important inspiration for both the choice and patterning of his son's career.

Coming of age just after the turn of the twentieth century, Vertner Tandy's education reflects the increasing professionalization of architecture. In 1900 he matriculated from Chandler Normal School in Lexington, Kentucky, a first-rate academic institution established under the auspices of the American Missionary Association. Upon graduation, Tandy began

389

his professional training at TUSKEGEE INSTITUTE in 1902. Tuskegee Institute, under the leadership of Booker T. Washington, had become one the foremost African American institutions for training of architects and building trades professionals. With a presumed major in architectural drawing and design, Tandy gained not only drawing and design instruction, but also practical training in the building trades and hands-on construction experience.

In the fall of 1905, Tandy continued his architectural training by enrolling as a special student at Cornell University, receiving the certificate granted upon completion of those studies in 1907. Cornell University's architectural curriculum emphasized artistic training and design in an atmosphere modeled after The Ecole des Beaux-Arts in Paris. Tandy was a roommate of Eugene Kinckle Jones (1885–1954), who went on to be a staunch civil rights activist and New Deal advisor to President Franklin Delano Roosevelt; and Gordon Jones, an outstanding mechanical engineer with the New York Department of Public Works. After graduation Tandy was associated with the Julius Kessler whiskey company and after that with the H. M. Miller Company in Toronto, Canada. By mid-1908, Tandy appears to have begun an architectural practice in New York City.

By his own account in a speech given at a National Negro Business League luncheon in 1918, Tandy's first commission was from Julius Kessler for a horse stable and garage in an unidentified location in New Jersey in 1908.[2] He next designed a series of stables, small houses, and three public schools for the New Jersey State Board of Education, all between 1908 and 1910. By 1918, Tandy claimed, he had designed forty-three schools throughout the United States.[3]

During his first year in practice, Tandy formed a partnership with GEORGE WASHINGTON FOSTER JR. under the firm name of Tandy & Foster, Architects. The partnership was dissolved in early 1915 for reasons that are not known. During this same period (beginning approximately 1912) Tandy took on another associate, William E. Young (1861–1922), an Ohio-born White architect who continued working with Tandy until his death circa 1922.

Having achieved financial prosperity and increasingly confident in his business, Tandy wed Sadie Hale Dorsette on June 3, 1912. Sadie Dorsette, a graduate of Barnard and Columbia Teacher's College, was the daughter of Dr. Cornelius Nathaniel Dorsette, considered by many to have been Alabama's first formally trained African American physician. Nine years later their son Vertner Jr. was born.

Less than two years after forming Tandy & Foster, Architects, the firm obtained a commission for Saint Philip's Protestant Episcopal Church. The church was not only Tandy's seminal work designed in collaboration with Foster, but would commemorate symbolically the transformation of Harlem from a predominately White to predominately Black community. Saint Philip's Protestant Episcopal Church,

Madame C. J. Walker Mansion, "Villa le Waro," *Carson Anderson*

which had a reputation as the "wealthiest Negro church in the country," was also Tandy's first commission from an African American client. The $100,000 English Gothic Revival-style church was dedicated in April 1911. The project raised Tandy from anonymity to being one of the best-known Black architects in the city. The church was described by the African American press and published in *Architecture and Building*, a mainstream building trade periodical.[4] It is conjectured that after being published in *Architecture and Building*, Tandy & Foster, Architects, found a larger market outside metropolitan New York that led to a series of church commissions during the 1910s reaching from Alaska to Arkansas to Puerto Rico.

From 1915 to 1916, Tandy obtained three high-profile commissions. The first was for hair-care millionairess Madame C. J. Walker's Harlem townhouse. Completed in August 1916, the townhouse was a large and opulent remodeling of two side-by-side row houses into a Federal/Regency Revival-style *hotel de ville*. Later in 1916, when Madame Walker pressed forward with her dream to build a suburban home she turned again to Tandy. He produced a $250,000 Italian Renaissance Revival style mansion, "Villa le Waro," in Irvington-on-the-Hudson, New York. Even as late as 1956, "Villa le Waro" was regarded as the "finest home ever owned by an American Negro."[5] Next Tandy secured a commission from the Montgomery Munitions Corporation for a 25,000-square foot manufacturing factory, which was possibly the first defense industry commission awarded to a Black architect.

Tandy's practice flourished during the 1920s. He received a large number of building alteration contracts from African American individuals, churches, and clubs moving to Harlem. His most noteworthy commission was the Imperial Elks Lodge (1922). During that same time, he was directing a significant amount of work outside of Manhattan and kept a staff of six German and Swiss draftsmen busy.[6]

Tandy's good fortune ended in the local economic downturn that preceded the Great Depression. He did not secure any new commissions in the borough of Manhattan between 1927 and 1945 and had virtually no new work outside the borough. He continued in practice by accepting small fees to correct building code violations, doing architectural engineering consulting for other architects, and teaching evening courses on the *New York City Zoning Code* and *Building Code*. Sadie Tandy, who had retired, resumed teaching in the New York public school system to supplement the family income.

The end of World War II brought renewed opportunities for Vertner Tandy. He applied for and was accepted for membership in the American Institute of Architects in 1945, presumably in anticipation of joining a joint venture for the design of the Abraham Lincoln Houses, a massive urban renewal project being master planned under the direction of the New York State Housing Authority. Tandy served as associate architect along with Edwin Forbes and Skidmore Owings & Merrill, on the $8.5-million project (1945).

Beginning with the Abraham Lincoln Houses commission, through the time of his illness in the fall of 1949, Tandy maintained a vigorous practice, but not of the same magnitude as earlier in his career. He secured the majority of his commissions from White business owners who desired building alterations and additions. His key work during the last year of his life, however, was one of the largest commissions of his career, the Ivey Terrace Apartments (1948). It was one the first, multi-family developments commissioned by an African American client in New York and one of the earliest African American developments financed by the Federal Housing Administration in the state of New York.

Tandy achieved remarkable success during an era when the social and economic life of New York City was segregated. His success, however, was uneven, a fact shown by the almost total absence of commissions for new buildings between 1927 and 1945. Although he had a vigorous practice the last four years of his life, it was essentially local and consisted primarily of rehabilitations. His professional advantages with regard to education, social contacts, and memberships served him well, but only intermittently.

Vertner Tandy died on November 7, 1949. Coincidentally, considering his tour of duty in the New York National Guard, his funeral was held on Armistice Day, November 11th at Saint Philip's Protestant Episcopal Church, which he had co-designed.

Notes

1. It is possible that Vertner Tandy was the first Black architect licensed in the state of New York even though the New York Department of Education, Office of the Professions was unable to verify this because pertinent records dating back to circa 1910 have been lost.
2. Report of the National Negro Business League, (22 August 1918): 313.
3. Excluding Lincoln Ridge Colored Institute, Simpsonville, Kentucky, research has not confirmed the location or dates of most of these schools.
4. "St. Phillips [sic] Church, New York," *Architecture and Building* (June 1911): 394.
5. "Hall of Fame," *Ebony Magazine*, February 1956, 25.
6. Interview with Vertner Tandy Jr. Nyack, New York, 22 January 1980.

VERTNER WOODSON TANDY

Bibliography

Anderson, Carson A. "The Architectural Practice of Vertner W. Tandy: An Evaluation of the Professional and Social Position of a Black Architect." Master's thesis, University of Virginia, 1982.

"Cornerstone Laid Despite Rain." *New York Age.* 23 June 1919, p. 1.

Graves, Lynne G. "National Register of Historic Places Registration Form for *Villa Le Waro*. National Park Service. October 1975. New York.

Withey, Henry, and Elsie R. Withey. "Vertner Tandy Sr." In *Biographical Dictionary of American Architects (deceased).* Los Angeles: New Day Press, 1956.

CARSON A. ANDERSON,
ARCHITECTURAL HISTORIAN,
SIGNAL HILL, CALIFORNIA

BUILDING LIST

Name	Address	City	State	Year	Comments
Abraham Lincoln Houses	132nd & 135th Sts.	New York	NY	1945	Assoc. architect
Chandler Normal School Webster Hall	548 Georgetown St.	Lexington	KY	c1914	
Children's Aid Society Bldg.	105 E. 22nd St.	New York	NY	c1922	
Cotton Bldg.		Newark	NJ	c1920	Demolished
Cotton, Dr. Norman F.	139th St.	New York	NY		Alterations
Globe National Bank	135th & 7th Ave.	New York	NY		Demolished
Highview Avenue Elementary School	24 Highview Ave.	Nanuet	NY	1908	Addition
Imperial Elks Lodge	160 W. 129th St.	New York	NY	1922	
Ivey Terrace Apts.	19 Hamilton Terrace	New York	NY	1948	
Lewissohn Garage and Shop	3793 Broadway	Nanuet	NY	1911	
Lincoln Hospital	141st St. & Wales Ave.	New York	NY		Alterations
Lincoln Ridge Colored Institute Belknap Dormitory	Campus	Simpsonville	KY	1922	
Lincoln Ridge Colored Institute Berea Hall	Campus	Simpsonville	KY	1911	
Lincoln Ridge Colored Institute Industrial Bldg	Campus	Simpsonville	KY	1922	
Lincoln Ridge Colored Institute North Dormitory	Campus	Simpsonville	KY	1922	
Morosco, Oliver	150 Hicks Ln.	Great Neck	NY	1929	Demolished
Mt. Moriah Baptist Church	45 W. 134th St.	New York	NY	1924	
Paducah Junior College Anderson Hall	Campus	Paducah	KY		
Penny Savings Bank	Oak St.	Waycross	GA		
Presbyterian Hospital		Humacao	PR	c1920	Demolished
Small's Paradise *Cabaret*	7th Ave & 135th St.	New York	NY	1925	
St. David's Protestant Episcopal Church	387 E. 160th St.	New York	NY	c1922	
St. Philip's Protestant Episcopal Church	208 W. 134th St.	New York	NY	1910	Assoc. architect
St. Philip's Protestant Episcopal Church Parish Hall	213 W. 134th St.	New York	NY	1910	Assoc. architect
Tillotson Institute	Campus	Austin	TX		
Walker, Madame C. J.	109 W. 136th St.	New York	NY	1917	Demolished
Walker, Madame C. J. *Villa Le Waro*	N. Broadway nr. Fargo Ln.	Irvington-on-the Hudson	NY	1917	

Robert Robinson Taylor
(1868–1942)

Francis Benjamin Johnston Collection, Library of Congress

Robert R. Taylor was the first African American to earn a bachelor of science degree in architecture, on May 31, 1892, from the Massachusetts Institute of Technology.

Robert Taylor was born on June 8, 1868, the second son of Henry and Emily Taylor of Wilmington, North Carolina. Henry Taylor was "the son of a White man who was at the same time his master."[1] Henry Taylor was a carpenter who was hired out by his master to fix cargo ships along the Wilmington docks.

Robert Taylor's normal school education was obtained from the abolitionist American Missionary Association's all-Black Gregory Institute in Wilmington. From there, after graduating and without attending any sort of preparatory school, Robert Taylor passed the entrance exams given in algebra, geography, literature, French, and English, and was admitted to the Massachusetts Institute of Technology on September 23, 1888.

Taylor was the first Negro admitted to the MIT School of Architecture and the only Negro among the nineteen first-year students in the architecture *atelier* of the first school of architecture in the United States that had adopted the Parisian-inspired *techniques de Beaux Arts*. In his fourth year, as a terminal project required for graduation, Taylor wrote "Description and Design of a Soldier's Home."[2] This fourteen-page thesis, written in longhand and supplemented with rendered floor plan and building elevation, captured in detail his knowledge of architecture and patriotic compassion for Civil War veterans.

Booker Taliaferro Washington, the principal of TUSKEGEE INSTITUTE, had heard about Robert Taylor and during one of his countless trips north to woo White philanthropists, captains of industry, and robber barons for donations to Tuskegee Institute, he recruited Taylor to join his fledgling faculty.

Robert Taylor's dual careers as an educator and architect and the expansion of Tuskegee Institute's physical infrastructure are inextricably interwoven. From 1893 to 1933, with only a four-year interruption, Taylor taught, designed buildings, and supervised the construction of student-built buildings at Tuskegee Institute. From the womb of Tuskegee Institute came a phalanx of the next generation of African American architects, including JOHN ANDERSON LANKFORD, WILLIAM SIDNEY PITTMAN, WALLACE AUGUSTUS RAYFIELD, LOUIS HUDSON PERSLEY, VERTNER WOODSON TANDY, CHARLES SUMNER BOWMAN, and many others.

In addition to his full-time teaching duties in the Mechanical Industries Department, Taylor was Tuskegee Institute's campus architect, campus planner, and construction supervisor. The first building that Taylor designed for Tuskegee Institute was Thrasher Hall, completed in 1893. It was his second building, however—Butler Chapel—whose appearance surpassed the other ten buildings he subsequently designed for the campus. The chapel featured a dominate gable tower at one corner with a projecting triangular portico identifying the main entrance. Taylor defused the massive longitudinal facade and steep

Booker T. Washington Residence "The Oaks," *Helen Taylor Dibble*

slate roof, which was the primary facade seen by approaching worshipers, with a projecting chancel and Norman-style buttresses. He enlivened the chancel's facade with varying window shapes. A wheel-shaped window was used to naturally light the clerestory; below it were three squat, Norman-style windows; and below them four elongated lancet windows. The floor plan was cruciform with a 154-foot nave and 106-foot transept. Taylor designed a complicated-to-build hammer-beam wood roof truss, which must have posed a challenge for the students to erect. The 63-foot clear span of the nave could accommodate 2,400 congregants and the apse could fit a 150-member choir. Taylor chose yellow pine for the molding, trim, chancel, pews, and gallery because it was plentiful on land owned by Tuskegee Institute and could be felled and milled by students.

From 1900 to 1902, Taylor was employed as an architectural draftsman in the Cleveland, Ohio, office of Charles W. Hopkinson. It is believed that while there, Taylor contributed to the design of Alta Settlement House (1901).[3] The following two years, Taylor is listed as a "builder" in the *Cleveland Telephone Directory*.[4] Apparently, he no longer was employed by Hopkinson and, not being registered to practice architecture in Ohio, was not allowed to advertise himself as an "architect."

In 1904 Booker T. Washington convinced his prized recruit to return to Tuskegee Institute by offering Taylor the directorship of the Mechanical Industries Department and its 778 students dispersed among twenty-five trades. Taylor was kept busy teaching architectural and mechanical drafting, performing administrative duties, and supervising construction. The demands on his time were such that he did not pursue any private commissions for seventeen years. In 1921 Taylor was promoted to general superintendent of industries. Four years later, he was promoted again to vice-principal of Tuskegee Institute.

Robert and his first wife, Beatrice, were the parents of ROBERT ROCHON, Helen, Edward, and Beatrice Jr. He was a strict father to his first four children. To his only child, Henry, with his second wife, Nellie Chestnut Taylor, he was noticeably more relaxed and given to windy reminiscences about his friendship with the scruffy and brilliant agriculturist/horticulturist George Washington Carver.[5]

In 1921 Taylor was commissioned by the trustees of Selma University to design Dinkins Memorial Building. The building was designed 3 stories above grade with offices for the president, dean, registrar, admissions, and alumni. In addition, the building housed classrooms and a chapel.

In 1924 Taylor received the coveted commission to design the Most Wonderful Prince Hall Northern Jurisdiction Ancient Accepted Scottish Rite of Freemasonry Lodge Free & Accepted Masons in downtown Birmingham, Alabama. The original 4-story building (three upper floors were added by others) is an unsatisfying mix of Corinthian, Doric, and Ionic details.

Taylor was chairman of the Tuskegee, Alabama, chapter of the American Red Cross (the only all-Negro chapter in the United States), when the devastating flood of 1927 inundated the Mississippi delta. Taylor was appointed to the Colored Advisory Commission to the American Red Cross. The commission was organized to investigate relief efforts aimed at the more than 400,000 rural colored refugee victims of the flood. The commission's scathing report concluded that the efforts of the American Red Cross had largely been ineffective, minuscule, corrupt, and biased.[6] The report was transmitted to the U.S. Secretary of Commerce, Herbert H. Hoover, later to become United States President, who accepted the report, thanked the commission, drawered the report, and took no action.

In 1933, after serving Tuskegee Institute for thirty-seven years, Taylor retired to Wilmington, North Carolina. He attended Chestnut Street Presbyterian Church almost every Sunday morning, was a trustee of Fayetteville State Teachers College appointed by three successive governors, and remained a staunch "race" man by actively participating in local civil rights organizations.

In a manner befitting an architect who had fashioned a productive professional career and led an upstanding life, on December 20, 1942, Robert Taylor died from a heart attack suffered while visiting Tuskegee Institute and praying in a pew in Butler Chapel, his favorite building.

Notes

1. Booker T. Washington, *The Story of the Negro, the Rise of the Race from Slavery* (New York: Doubleday, Page & Co., 1909), p. 81.

2. Robert R. Taylor, "Description and Design of a Soldier's Home," senior thesis, course IV, Massachusetts Institute of Technology, 1892). This document is housed in the MIT Archives. The Soldier's Home was 494 feet × 250 feet with rooms axially balanced. It featured an octagonal, 3-story hall in the center with a split-level vestibule flanked on either side by 2-story wings—one for officers and one for non-commissioned officers. There were separate parlors, libraries, toilets, dormitories, and dining rooms. The officers shared an entertainment hall, dispensary, operating room, convalescence room, chapel, and laundry.

3. Interview with Eric Johannessen (author of *The Architecture of Cleveland, 1876–1976*), Cleveland, Ohio, 12 February 1981.

4. "Taylor, Robert," *Cleveland Directory,* Cleveland: Cleveland Directory Company, 1902, n.p.

5. Interview with Henry Taylor (son of Robert Taylor Sr.) Three Rivers, Mich., 12 November 1980.

6. American Red Cross, "Report of Colored Advisory Commission—Mississippi Valley Flood Relief," Herbert Hoover Presidential Library, West Branch, Iowa, 13 December 1927.

Bibliography

Birmingham Alabama Regional Planning Commission. *Historic Site Survey Jefferson County—Black Masonic Temple.* Birmingham: Regional Planning Commission, 1972.

Imes, G. Lake. "Race Lost Great Figure in Taylor Death." *Chicago Bee*, 17 January 1943, p. 1.

Weiss, Ellen. "Robert R. Taylor of Tuskegee: An Early Black American Architect." *Journal of the Southeast Chapter of the Society of Architectural Historians.* vol. 2, 1991.

Williams, Clarence G. "From 'Tech' to Tuskegee: The Life of Robert Robinson Taylor, 1868–1942." http://libraries.mit.edu/archives/taylor.html.

DRECK SPURLOCK WILSON

BUILDING LIST

Name	Address	City	State	Year	Comments
Alabama Agricultural Fair Negro Bldg.	Fairgrounds	Montgomery	AL	1906	Assoc. Architect
Alta Settlement House	Mayfield Rd. & E. 125th St.	Cleveland	OH	1901	Office of Charles Hopkinson
Elk's Rest Home	1830 8th Ave.	Birmingham	AL	1926	Destroyed by fire
Johnson, Dr. Frank		Tuskegee	AL		
Johnson, Dr. Luther		Tuskegee	AL		
Livingston College Carnegie Library	Campus	Salisbury	NC	1905	
Mississippi Industrial College Dining Hall	Campus	Holly Springs	MS	c1910	
Mississippi Industrial College Dormitory	Campus	Holly Springs	MS	c1910	
Odd Fellows Office Bldg.	Louisiana St. & Prairie Ave.	Houston	TX	1924	
Prince Hall Masonic Temple	1630 4th Ave. North	Birmingham	AL	1924	Assoc. Architect
Selma University Dinkins Memorial Bldg.	Campus	Selma	AL	1921	
Tuskegee Institute Administration Bldg.	Campus	Tuskegee	AL	1902	
Tuskegee Institute Andrews Hospital	Campus	Tuskegee	AL	1913	Demolished
Tuskegee Institute Armstrong Science Bldg.	Campus	Tuskegee	AL	1932	
Tuskegee Institute Butler Chapel	Campus	Tuskegee	AL	1896	Destroyed by fire
Tuskegee Institute Carnegie Library	Campus	Tuskegee	AL	1901	
Tuskegee Institute Cassedy Hall	Campus	Tuskegee	AL		Demolished
Tuskegee Institute Davidson Hall	Campus	Tuskegee	AL		Demolished

ROBERT ROBINSON TAYLOR

BUILDING LIST (continued)

Name	Address	City	State	Year	Comments
Tuskegee Institute Dorothy Hall	Campus	Tuskegee	AL	1901	
Tuskegee Institute Douglass Dormitory	Campus	Tuskegee	AL	1904	
Tuskegee Institute Emery Dormitories	Campus	Tuskegee	AL	1897	4 bldgs.
Tuskegee Institute Hollis Burke Frissell Library	Campus	Tuskegee	AL	1932	
Tuskegee Institute Huntington Memorial Bldg.	Campus	Tuskegee	AL	1902	
Tuskegee Institute James Hall	Campus	Tuskegee	AL	1921	
Tuskegee Institute Laundry Bldg.	Campus	Tuskegee	AL	1915	Now Carver Museum
Tuskegee Institute Logan Hall	Campus	Tuskegee	AL	1931	
Tuskegee Institute Millbank Bldg.	Campus	Tuskegee	AL	1909	
Tuskegee Institute Rockefeller Hall	Campus	Tuskegee	AL	1903	
Tuskegee Institute Sage Dormitory	Campus	Tuskegee	AL	1926	
Tuskegee Institute Science Hall	Campus	Tuskegee	AL	1893	Now Thrasher Hall
Tuskegee Institute Tantum Hall	Campus	Tuskegee	AL	1907	
Tuskegee Institute Thrasher Hall	Campus	Tuskegee	AL	1893	
Tuskegee Institute Tompkins Dining Hall	Campus	Tuskegee	AL	1910	Assoc. architect
Tuskegee Institute White Dormitory	Campus	Tuskegee	AL	1909	
Washington, Booker T. "The Oaks"	Campus	Tuskegee	AL	1898	
Wiley College Bldg.	Campus	Marshall	TX	1920	Now King Administration Bldg.

Robert Rochon Taylor
(1899–1957)

University of Illinois Archives

Robert Rochon Taylor was born in Tuskegee, Alabama, on April 12, 1899, the son of ROBERT ROBINSON TAYLOR, director of Mechanical Industries at TUSKEGEE INSTITUTE, and Beatrice Rochon Taylor. Prior to marrying, Beatrice Taylor was a music teacher. After marrying, she stayed at home and cared for Robert, the oldest, and Helen, Edward, and Beatrice.[1]

Robert Rochon's elementary schooling was provided by Tuskegee public schools. He entered the daytime architectural program at his father's institute, where he not only had his father as a teacher, but was also taught by WALTER THOMAS BAILEY. Robert Rochon received his certificate of completion in 1916.

Taylor followed Tuskegee Institute architects WILLIAM AUGUSTUS HAZEL and ALBERT IRVIN CASSELL and landscape architect DAVID AUGUSTUS WILLISTON to HOWARD UNIVERSITY. From 1916 until 1919, he was enrolled in the School of Architecture, and lived off campus with family friend David Williston and his wife. Although he was within a year of graduation, Taylor did not return to Howard University for the start of academic year 1920–21.

No longer in school, Taylor was placed by his father in charge of operating the sawmill that he had designed and built in Opelika, Alabama. Attending college was more fun, however, and after gaining practical business experience for three years operating the sawmill, Robert Rochon transferred to the University of Illinois in Urbana-Champaign; and graduated in 1925 with a bachelor of science in business administration. Later, in 1932, he took graduate courses at in the School of Economics at Northwestern University in Evanston, Illinois, but did not complete the requirements for his master's degree.

A career demarcation had been crossed. Taylor decided not to practice architecture and instead chose a career in business. Frank L. Gillespie, president of the Chicago-based Liberty Life Insurance Company of America, the second largest minority-owned insurance company in the United States, hired him as an assistant. As the company's dollar amount of insurance in force rose, so did Taylor's responsibilities and salary. By 1928 Taylor was secretary and general manager of Liberty Life Insurance Company of America. His position catapulted him into becoming a force in the insurance industry—at least within the minority faction—and recognized as a corporate leader within Chicago's Black business community, which was prosperous. That same year he contributed to the design of the 500-unit Michigan Boulevard Garden Apartments, one of the first luxury apartment buildings constructed on the segregated near-southside of Chicago at 54 East 47th Street that was marketed to middle-class Negroes. The apartments were developed in partnership with Julius Rosenwald, Sears, Roebuck & Company president, who was closely affiliated with Tuskegee Institute by virtue of his philanthropy, which built one-room schools for Negroes throughout the South. Taylor maintained his connection to the Michigan Boulevard Garden Apartments by serving on its board of managers and becoming vice-president of the corporation that owned it. Recognizing that there was money to be made in issuing private mortgage insurance to aggressive Black real estate dealers such as Jesse Binga—all of whom were profiting handsomely and, in some cases, illegally from the great migration of southern Blacks to Chicago following World War I—Taylor started a mortgage insurance company that by 1928 became profitable. A decade later he would return to his training as an architect and combine that training with his experience in developing multi-family housing to fashion a successful career as a housing consultant to federal agencies.

Robert Rochon married Dorothy Vaughn—formerly from Louisville, Kentucky—in a Roman Catholic ceremony on February 10, 1926. Dorothy Taylor was a government employee. They had two daughters: Lauranita Taylor Dugas and Barbara Taylor Bowman.

In 1933 Taylor sailed to Germany and then to Holland, France, and Belgium to study government-subsidized congregate housing, a Grand Tour that was similar to the one taken by HILYARD ROBERT ROBINSON. One year later, Taylor was appointed secretary and general manager of the Illinois Federal Savings and Loan Association, the largest minority-owned mortgagor in Illinois. Taylor leveraged his top managerial position with Illinois Federal Savings and Loan to take an ownership percentage as majority or minority partner in scores of development projects.

In 1935 Taylor was appointed by Mayor Edward Joseph Kelly as vice chairman of the Chicago Housing Authority and succeeded to chairman in 1939, where he remained through three different mayoral administrations until 1950. During his tenure, $150 million worth of publicly subsidized housing was built throughout Chicago's "Black Belt," the segregated south and westside neighborhoods. Taylor has been credited with having produced public housing for over 50,000 Blacks and financially assisting another 7,000 to achieve home ownership. The nation's densest and largest public housing project—twenty-eight monotonous-looking, 16-story concrete buildings for 28,000 tenants, the Robert Taylor Homes (1962)—were named after him. Taylor's chairmanship atop the Chicago Housing Authority and the hundreds of patronage positions he controlled arguably made him the most powerful non-elected African American inside the most politically powerful Democratic "machine" in the country.

During World War II, from 1941 to 1943, Taylor served as a consultant to the federal government, spe-

Michigan Boulevard Garden Apartments, *Chicago Historical Society*

cializing in defense housing for Blacks. In this position, he was influential in getting Chicagoan CHARLES SUMNER DUKE as well as Hilyard Robinson hired by the Public Works Administration. Taylor was also associate architect for Altgeld Gardens Public Housing (1944), a Public Works Administration project at 130th Street and Langley Avenue in Altgeld, Illinois.

In 1945 Mayor Kelley turned to Taylor again, this time naming him to the Executive Board of the Chicago Planning Commission, which was the all-powerful arbiter for local governmental decisions on the zoning and development of publicly owned land and which developer would be selected to develop the city-owned land. A year later he received another mayoral appointment to the Commission on Human Relations. He remained on the Commission for twelve years. In 1952 he was named by President Harry Simpson Truman as a delegate to the Large-Scale Housing Conference convened by the federal government. Yet another mayoral appointment placed him on the Chicago Conservation Board as commissioner, where he served until 1950. The mandate of the board was to develop housing policies and draft Building Code regulations to conserve the housing stock of Black neighborhoods and arrest the spread of slums. For one term, 1945 to 1946, he was a member of the Board of Governors of the National Association of Housing Officials. He was also a director of Hull House, a community-based social service settlement organization made famous by social reformer Jane Addams; and was treasurer and trustee of the all-Black Provident Hospital from 1950 to 1955, which was one of the leading Black teaching hospitals.

Taylor was the recipient of the Service Award in Housing from the Citizens Committee of Chicago in 1943 and received a Citation for Public Service in 1950 from the Illinois Welfare Association, the statewide social workers' organization. He was also a member of the 47th Street Businessmen's Association, *Kappa Alpha Psi* Fraternity, and the Catholic Inter-Racial Council.

Robert Rochon Taylor died in Chicago from a heart attack on March 1, 1957.

Note

1. Interview with Dorothy Vaughn Taylor (daughter of Robert Rochon Taylor), interview by author, Washington, D.C., 3 October 1980.

Bibliography

Altgeld-Carver Alumni Association. *History of Altgeld Gardens (1944–60)*. Chicago: Newberry Library, 1993.

CHYLA DIBBLE EVANS,
GREAT GRANDDAUGHTER OF ROBERT ROCHON TAYLOR,
POTOMAC, MARYLAND

BUILDING LIST

Name	Address	City	State	Year	Comments
Altgeld Gardens Public Housing	130th St. & Langley Ave.	Altgeld	IL	1944	Assoc. architect
Michigan Boulevard Garden Apts.	54 E. 47th St.	Chicago	IL	1928	

Tennessee Centennial and International Exposition Negro Building, Nashville
(1897)

The Negro Building for the Tennessee Centennial and International Exposition of 1897 in Nashville was located on the northern bank of Lake Watauga in what was to become Centennial Park. The building housed exhibits that illustrated the past achievements of the Negro race from the time of plantations up to the 1890s. The Negro Building was a 3-story structure with a footprint of 250 feet × 100 feet. It was described as Spanish Renaissance in style. Flanking its main entrance were two 90-foot towers. In addition to containing exhibits, there was an auditorium, a roof garden, and a restaurant in the cellar. The building's collections, prepared by Negroes from "all walks of life," were considered to be some of the most comprehensive displays of Negro achievements ever assembled.[1] Included were individual and group displays from a variety of social, professional, and academic organizations and institutions. Although the building was not completed in time for the exposition's opening ceremonies on May 1, 1987, fairgoers recognized the Negro Building as being one of the most beautiful on the exposition grounds.

Like those of other southern fairs, the White leaders of the Tennessee Centennial established a Negro Department to manage exhibits that focused on Negro contributions in agriculture and industry throughout Tennessee and the South. James Carroll Napier (1845–1940), Nashville's most powerful politician, was tapped to head the Negro Department and was assisted by a Women's Board Executive Committee, preachers, teachers, and successful local business owners. The Negro Department put forth the idea of having a Negro Building, which was accepted by Centennial officials.

The designer of the Negro Building was a White architect, Frederick Thompson (1872–1919). His effort earned him an Architectural Design Medal and $2,500 award. Thompson was born in Ironton, Ohio, to Fred "Casey" Thompson, a steel manufacturer, and Martha Williams Thompson, a housewife. After dropping out of school at age fourteen, Thompson worked as a clerk in a pump factory and then as a building materials broker. Between 1890 and 1897, he apprenticed as a draftsman in his uncle's firm. Thompson's uncle, George W. Thompson, co-owned one of Nashville's leading architectural offices, Thompson & Zwicker. Frederick Thompson also studied at the Ecole des Beaux Arts in Paris.

By the age of twenty-one, Thompson was a manager of exhibits for Manning, Maxwell & Moore at the Columbia World's Fair Exposition in Chicago held in 1893. Four years later he teamed up with a Nashville builder and his uncle to pursue contracts for the Tennessee Centennial as both an independent architect and a member of the team representing his uncle's firm.

Following his success at the Tennessee Centennial, Thompson went on to design the Exposition Auditorium Building and Transportation and Machinery Building. He also designed and operated amusement concessions at the Trans-Mississippi Exposition held in Omaha, Nebraska, in 1898. After that he formed a partnership with Elmer "Skip" Dundy and designed several novelty attractions for the Pan-American Exposition held in Buffalo in 1901 including "A Trip to the Moon." Later he collaborated with New York architect Jay Morgan and designed Coney Island's famously popular Luna Park and the Hippodrome in New York City. Frederick Thompson died in 1919.

Inside the Negro Building were educational exhibits sent by TUSKEGEE INSTITUTE; Roger Williams University; Lincoln University in Pennsylvania; Central Tennessee College; Fisk University; Nashville's Fireside School; Hamilton County's public school; Chattanooga's city school; and a Cincinnati, Ohio, public school. There were displays representing Minneapolis and New York City; the states of Massachusetts, Maryland, and Indiana; and the Tennessee counties of Maury, Gibson, Shelby, Davidson, and Williamson. The building housed the General Exhibit of Woman's Board and its art gallery. The gallery showcased the art of Nashville's Clarence Jones and Susie Williams, a student from the Cincinnati Art School. Exhibits in the categories of education, his-

TENNESSEE CENTENNIAL AND INTERNATIONAL EXPOSITION NEGRO BUILDING, NASHVILLE

Tennessee Centennial Negro Building, *The Parthenon, Nashville, Tennessee*

tory, literature, and decorative arts were awarded medals by White jurors.

The total cost of the Negro Building recorded in the auditor's report was $12,759.77, which included architectural fees and construction costs. The Tennessee Centennial ran for six months and closed in November 1897. The Negro Building was demolished two years later as were all but two Centennial buildings. A scaled-down replica of the Parthenon, built for the Exposition in 1897 and restored in the 1920s, is the only remaining structure on the former Exposition site. All that remains of the Negro Building is its cornerstone, which was laid by the Ancient Order of Free & Accepted Masons and can be found on display at Fisk University Library.

Notes
1. Tennessee Centennial and International Exposition, *Tennessee Centennial and International Exposition Opens at Nashville, May 1, 1897 and Continues Six Months*, (Nashville: Brandon Printing Co., 1897), p. 20.

Bibliography
Lovett, Bobby L. *The African American History of Nashville, Tennessee, 1780–1930*. Fayetteville: University of Arkansas Press, 1999.

Rydell, Robert W. "The New Orleans, Atlanta, and Nashville Expositions: New Markets, 'New Negroes,' and a New South." In *All the World's a Fair: Visions of Empire at American International Expositions, 1876–1916*. Chicago: University of Chicago Press, 1984.

DIANE DAVIS, ASSISTANT PROFESSOR,
ARCHITECTURE AND ENVIRONMENTAL DESIGN,
KENT STATE UNIVERSITY

Texas Centennial Exposition, Hall of Negro Life, Dallas
(1936)

In 1936 the State of Texas celebrated one hundred years of independence from Mexico by having the Texas Centennial Exposition in Dallas, which showcased the state's products, people, and entertainment attractions. It was also a time when the Great Depression gripped the nation, and Texas counted heavily on the Centennial's entertainment value as an economic stimulus to give the state economy a shot in the arm. The aims of the Texas Centennial Exposition were achieved; many visitors attended the Exposition and 1936 was the year that "America discovered Texas."[1]

As plans for the exposition were being developed, local civic leaders such as A. Maceo Smith (1903–1977), executive secretary of the Dallas Negro Chamber of Commerce, lobbied for state and municipal funding to create "a Negro display at the main exposition in Dallas and for the creation of a special advisory committee on Negro affairs to represent the state's Negroes during the centennial preparation."[2]

Smith hoped to have an African American architect design the building and for the hall to be staffed by and house exhibits by African Americans. However, fund raising fell victim to political wrangling. It was not until October 1935 that a $100,000 appropriation for "Negro participation" was finally announced, and the exposition was due to open in June 1936. The money came from federal—not state or municipal—funds and it was not made available for spending until March 1936. Of the $100,000, $50,000 was earmarked for constructing the hall and the remaining $50,000 was for the exhibits.

Plans for the Centennial buildings and grounds were well under way by the time money became available for the Hall of Negro Life and supporters had to abandon their hopes to have an African American architect design the building. Dallas architect George L. Dahl (1894–1987) was in charge of the Centennial project and he hired a number of assistants

Texas Centennial Hall of Negro Life, *Texas/Dallas History and Archives Division, Dallas Public Library*

to design various buildings. Among them was Donald S. Nelson (1907–1992), who was the architect for the Hall of Negro Life. Nelson studied at Ecole des Beaux Arts in Paris and was an architecture graduate of the Massachusetts Institute of Technology. He designed a number of buildings for the Century of Progress Exposition in Chicago in 1933 to 1934, which brought him to Dahl's attention. Dahl appointed Nelson chief designer for the Texas Centennial Exposition.

Nelson's design for the Hall of Negro Life followed the Moderne and Art Deco styles that were used for other Centennial buildings. The building was a 1-story, stucco-clad structure with an L-shaped floor plan measuring approximately 106 feet × 102 feet. Over the main entrance was a seal sculpted by French-born staff artist Raoul Josset, depicting a figure with broken chains. Inside was an octagonal lobby flanked by two exhibit wings. The lobby contained four murals by the well-known Harlem Renaissance artist Aaron Douglas (1898–1979). One of the murals depicted Estevan, an African who accompanied Spanish explorer Cabeza de Vaca on his 1527 to 1535 expedition into some of the lands that would become Texas.

An open-air amphitheater with seating for two thousand was sheltered in the wings of the building. It was used for film, drama, and musical performances. "Little Harlem," an open-air dining area and dance pavilion, was located north of the east wing, and contained the "only negro concessions on the grounds."[3] Cross Construction Company, a firm that built many of the other Centennial structures, began construction of the hall on March 9, 1936.

By June 6, the opening day for the Centennial, the structure was largely complete, but the contractor had failed to install the required fire suppression system. The federal government refused to approve the building for occupancy and allow access. It took another thirteen days for the situation to be resolved. Therefore, the opening day for the Hall of Negro Life took place on June 19, after the exposition had opened and on a traditional holiday known as Juneteenth, which celebrated the date African Americans in Texas learned about the Emancipation Proclamation.

The exhibits in the Hall of Negro Life had African Americans as curators. Jesse O. Thomas, who was from the National Urban League and was general manager for Negro participation in the Centennial, helped to design the guidelines for exhibit materials, which were grouped into six categories: education, fine arts, health, agriculture, mechanic arts, and business. There were exhibits from thirty-two states, mostly from the South and the District of Columbia. Among the exhibit highlights were five hundred books said to be

> [t]he largest number of books written by and about Negroes ever assembled; models of school buildings, businesses, and farms; two rooms of original paintings, prints, and sculpture loaned by the Harmon Foundation of New York; a display of one hundred twenty six Negro newspapers; photographs of buildings designed by California architect Paul R. Williams; and a section devoted to the scientific discoveries of George Washington Carver.[4]

Several brochures were available, including one by Booker T. Washington entitled *The Negro in the Field of Education*, another by Dr. W. E. B. DuBois, *What the Negro Has Done for the United States and Texas*, and a bibliography of the book display.[5] Among the artists displayed were Laura Wheeler Waring, Aaron Douglas, Henry Ossawa Tanner, Richmond Barthe, Malvin Gray Johnson, Sam Brown, Hilda Wilkinson Brown, Sargent Johnson, Hale Woodruff, and J. Lesene Wells.

In addition to June 19, Emancipation Day, two other dates were reserved especially for "Negro participation" in the Centennial. August 19 was "Church and Music Day" and October 19 was "Negro Education Day." The big bands of Cab Calloway and "Duke" Ellington each played the Fair Park Band Shell as part of these special celebrations, and the Harlem Unit of the Works Progress Administration Theater Project of New York City presented a well-attended and well-received production of *Macbeth*.

By the time the Texas Centennial Exposition closed on November 29, 1936, attendance was almost 6.5 million people; of those, 403,227 had visited the Hall of Negro Life. According to statistics that Thomas and his staff kept, approximately 60 percent of the visitors were White.[6] The reviews had been good and there was every expectation that the Hall of Negro Life would re-open in June 1937 just like all the other exposition buildings in what would be renamed the Pan American Exposition. However, the Texas Centennial Exposition Corporation directors decided otherwise. On December 30, 1936, they passed a resolution that stated, "it seems best, in light of the circumstances [racism], that the Negro building be abolished."[7] The Hall of Negro Life had opened nearly two weeks after all the other buildings of the exposition and it was the first to be demolished. It was gone by the time the Pan American Exposition opened in 1937. (The Pan American Exposition did not have a

Negro Building.) The land where the Hall of Negro Life stood remained vacant until November 1993, when it was chosen as the site for a new African American Museum.

Notes
1. Cited in *The Year America Discovered Texas*, Kenneth B. Ragsdale (College Station: Texas A&M University Press, 1987), p. vii (frontispiece).
2. Ibid., p. 65.
3. "History of Negro from Jungles to Now to Be Shown," *Dallas Morning News*, 14 May 1936, p. 15.
4. "Negro Art Works Being Displayed at Fair Exhibit," *Dallas Morning News*, 28 June 1936, p. 4.
5. W. E. B. DuBois, "What the Negro Has Done for the United States and Texas" (Washington, D.C.: Government Printing Office, 1936). University of Texas at Austin, Center for American History.
6. Jesse O. Thomas, *Negro Participation in the Texas Centennial* (Boston: Christopher Publishing House, 1930), p. 36.
7. Ibid., p. 122.

Bibliography
Aden, Alonzo J. "Educational Tour through the Hall of Negro Life." *The Southern Workman* (November 1936): 331.
"Centennial Negro Hall Accepted by Federal Officials." *Dallas Evening Journal*, 12 May 1936, p. 3.
"Negroes' Participation in Centennial Set Precedent for Future World Fairs." *Dallas Evening Journal*, 20 November 1936.

CAROL ROARK,
TEXAS/DALLAS HISTORY AND ARCHIVES DIVISION,
DALLAS PUBLIC LIBRARY

Martha Ann Cassell Thompson
(1925–1968)

Charles Irwin Cassell

Martha Cassell was born on September 26, 1925, into a Washington, D.C., family with the largest number of known family members who became architects.[1] Martha was the second child of Albert and Martha Ann Mason. Her mother, who was originally from Baltimore, was a public school teacher. Her father graduated from Cornell University's College of Architecture in 1919. He sent four of his children to Cornell University, two of whom graduated from the College of Architecture: Martha Ann, class of 1947; and Alberta Jeanette, class of 1948. Martha's uncle, Oliver, attended Cornell University, but instead of becoming an architect became a successful building contractor. Martha was a straight-A student beginning at James Monroe Elementary School and straight through Garnet Patterson Middle School, Banneker Junior High School, and Dunbar High School. She was valedictorian of the graduating class of 1943, and entered Cornell University in 1943. Martha received her bachelor of architecture degree four years later, becoming the first African American female to graduate from the College of Architecture, in 1947.

By 1949 she was working for an unidentified White-owned architectural office in Saint Louis, Missouri. She remained in their employ until 1951.

Martha married Dr. Victor Thompson, a medical student at Meharry in 1948. One child, Karen, born in 1949, completed their family. She became the third generation of the extended family to become an architect after graduating from the Illinois Institute of Technology in Chicago.

Martha Thompson's renderings of European cathedrals and her in-depth knowledge of Gothic-style ecclesiastic architecture were instrumental in her being hired by Philip Hubert Frohman (1887–1972), principal of Frohman, Robb & Little and chief restoration architect of the Cathedral of Saint Peter and Saint Paul (1907)—also known as the Washington National Cathedral, by Bodley & Vaughn. Martha Thompson's detailed renderings of French Gothic-style cathedrals so impressed Frohman that he assigned her to produce drawings and renderings for the cathedral, even though Frohman's vision for the renovations were Neo-Gothic in style. Frohman, who was trained in France, recognized Martha Thompson's mastery of eighteenth-century Gothic style. Similar to the medieval cathedral architects who labored for decades on a single cathedral, Martha Thompson spent almost a decade—1959 to 1968—preparing perspective drawings and creating clay mock-ups of sculptural figures and ornamental details that were passed on to European stone masons to guide them as they cut and carved marble. During the last years of her life Martha Thompson was a special assistant to Frohman.

Martha Cassell Thompson was an accomplished pianist. Her father would listen to her play for hours seemingly lost in the pleasure of hearing his daughter play.

Martha Thompson's leadership qualities were reflected in her organizing a Social Service Committee at the Young Womens Christian Association of the

Washington National Cathedral, *Dreck Spurlock Wilson*

District of Columbia. This committee succeeded the one formed by her mother years earlier.

Martha Thompson died in 1968. She is interred in Lincoln Memorial Cemetery in Suitland, Maryland.

Notes
1. See ALBERT IRVIN CASSELL, CHARLES IRVIN CASSEL, and ALBERTA JEANETTE CASSELL BUTLER.

Bibliography
Feller, Richard T. *For Thy Great Glory.* Culpepper, Va.: Community Press, 1965.
Scott, Pamela, and Antoinete Lee. *Buildings of the District of Columbia.* New York: Oxford University Press, 1993.

CHARLES IRVIN CASSELL, FAIA,
WASHINGTON, D.C.

William Ferguson Thornton
(1901–1981)

William Thornton Family

William F. Thornton was born in Chicago, Illinois, on January 31, 1901, to William E. Thornton and Eva Wilson Thornton. His father was a caterer who owned his own business. His mother was active in civic causes with the League of Woman Voters and the Recreation Commission in Chicago. Raised in a middle-class family, he graduated from Englewood High School, and then enrolled at the University of Illinois at Urbana-Champaign.[1]

Thornton thoroughly enjoyed his time as an undergraduate. He pledged *Alpha Phi Alpha* fraternity and lived in the fraternity's campus house, forging friendships that would last a lifetime. He enrolled in the university Reserve Officers Training Corps, but was never called to active duty. Thornton graduated in 1923 with a bachelor of science degree in structural engineering, and found employment with the Illinois Department of Transportation's Chicago office as a resident engineer, designing roads throughout Elgin, Monmouth, and McHenry Counties. As a result of his hard work he was promoted to resident engineer in charge of concrete and bridge design.

Thornton was one of the founders of the NATIONAL TECHNICAL ASSOCIATION, an organization dedicated to confronting racial discrimination and unequal opportunity for minorities in technical fields. He served as national president in 1946.

After working in Chicago, Thornton moved to Hampton, Virginia, and was employed as the construction engineer for the U.S. Resettlement Administration in Hampton and Newport News, Virginia. While living in the South, he worked on many projects, including student housing at TUSKEGEE INSTITUTE. During the summer of 1936, while living in Washington, D.C., he met Urath Peters, the woman he would marry two years later on June 12, 1938. Shortly after their marriage they moved to Chicago, where William Thornton opened his own office, William F. Thornton & Associates. Urath Thornton taught foods and nutrition at Dunbar Vocational High School and became the first Black cafeteria manager in the Chicago public schools, assigned to DuSable High School.

William Thornton shared office space in the "Loop" with several Black attorneys. His firm typically employed two draftsmen, and during busy times employed up to six. During the Great Depression, with very little work, he operated his own auto repair garage. He was also known as the neighborhood "handyman" who would earn pocket money installing residential hot water heaters and repairing wood furniture. Residential work kept his firm busy throughout the 1960s and 1970s, mostly preparing permit drawings to comply with the building code and for multi-family buildings.

Throughout his professional career, Thornton wore different hats and was actively involved with the Chicago community. Thornton served as the treasurer of the Structural Engineers Association of Illinois. On several occasions he served as an expert witness in civil trials involving building collapses. His testimonies in court sparked an interest in the law, which led him to take law classes at Loyola University

State Street subway station concourse, *Courtesy Chicago Transit Authority*

School of Law. As president of the Property Conservation Commission, Thornton led efforts to prevent African American homeowners' land from being condemned by the City of Chicago and sold to speculative developers who intended to demolish their houses and replace them with condominiums. He marched in protest against housing discrimination in the all-White western Chicago suburb of Cicero, Illinois, as well as in the Chicago civil rights march led by Dr. Martin Luther King Jr. of the Southern Christian Leadership Conference in 1965. Thornton was a volunteer with the Florence Crittinton Anchorage service organization, a home for pregnant, unwed women; and was a board member of the Randall House, an Episcopal-sponsored orphanage for boys. In addition, he volunteered with Saint Edmunds Episcopal Church, where he served as the secretary of the church's credit union.

Thornton found time to be a dedicated husband and father. A carefree spirit, he and his wife traveled all over the United States, oftentimes getting in their car and driving without planning where they would end up. He was a steady fatherly presence to his natural son, William Jr., and to his foster daughter, Syrena Antoinette. She described him as being "a very compassionate and hard-working man, who spent time with the kids first when arriving home from work before retiring to his home office to draft drawings late into the night."[2]

William Thornton died on June 25, 1981, in Chicago at the age of eighty and was laid to rest in Oak Hill Cemetery. His legacy can be seen today at Chicago's Dearborn and State Street subway stations. He was one of the six architectural engineers who designed and supervised construction that was completed in a record seven years. Thornton's unwavering commitment to his profession, love for his family, and dedication to the community are the traits of the consummate professional.

Notes

1. William Thornton Jr., "Funeral Program for William Thornton, Sr.," Harris Funeral Home, Chicago, 1981, p. 2.
2. Interview with Syrena Antoinette Thornton Bradford (foster daughter of William Thornton Sr.), by the author, Ill., 2002.

Bibliography

Taylor, Pat, ed. *Chicago Chapter Update*. Chicago: National Technical Association, 1981.

Washington, Audrey, ed. "In Rembrance," *Chicago Chapter National Technical Association Newsletter*. Chicago: NTA, 1981, p. 3.

CURTIS CLAY, ASSOCIATE AIA,
CHICAGO, ILLINOIS

STRUCTURE LIST

Name	Address	City	State	Year	Comments
Dearborn Street Subway Station	Washington & Dearborn Sts.	Chicago	IL	1951	Assoc. engineer
State Street Subway Station	State St.	Chicago	IL	1944	Assoc. engineer
Tuskegee Institute Student Housing	Campus	Tuskegee	AL		Supervising engineer

Tuskegee Normal & Industrial Institute, Mechanical Industries Department
(1892)

The architecture program at Tuskegee Normal & Industrial Institute (renamed University in 1985) has a rich and enduring history. Booker Taliaferro Washington (1856–1915) founded the institute on July 4, 1881, in a school rented from Butler African Methodist Episcopal Zion Church in the rural town of Tuskegee, Alabama. The original concept for the institute was that it would teach a "normal" curriculum to train teachers. The state of Alabama provided an annual appropriation of $2,000, but use of the appropriation was restricted to paying salaries and could not be spent to buy land or construct buildings. By November 1881, with a loan from friends from Washington's *alma mater* HAMPTON INSTITUTE, he was able to purchase a one-hundred-acre former plantation two miles outside of town. The site initially had only utility farm buildings on it. By 1915, the year of Washington's death, thirty-four years later, Tuskegee Institute had grown to 2,500 acres and eighty-six buildings and boasted the most impressive physical facilities of any predominately Black school of that time.

Because Washington started with essentially nothing and wanted to be self-sufficient, he had to create an infrastructure to support his ambitious building plans, which translated into starting brickyards, lumberyards, and shops for carpentry, electricity, blacksmithing, tinmaking, and masonry; starting farms to grow their own food and produce their own lard; and starting dairies so that they would have their own milk. The shops evolved into manual training divisions that later became the institute's hallmark. This "up-by-the-bootstraps" system also provided job opportunities for students. Self-sufficiency, however, was not just an expedient due to circumstance. Washington saw positive moral benefits in having students construct campus buildings. It taught the dignity of labor, the efficiency of teamwork, and the wisdom of planning ahead for construction, with the end result being deeper student pride and respect for the campus. Washington had a vision for his buildings and how Black architects should be educated. The simplistic perception is that Washington only wanted to educate his students in manual training devoid of aesthetic and intellectual content. Quotations from Washington himself, however, yield a more complex view. "We must," he said, "have not only carpenters, but also architects: we must not only have persons who can do the work with the hand, but persons at the same time who plan the work with the brain. Not only were colored horticulturalists and landscape gardeners needed," he offered, "but also mechanical and civil engineers, architects, and brick makers."[1]

Although some scholars debate the exact year when the architecture program officially began at Tuskegee Institute, an important threshold year is 1892, when Washington recruited ROBERT ROBINSON TAYLOR, a recent graduate of the Massachusetts Institute of Technology, to head the Mechanical Industries Department. Taylor made dramatic changes to the curriculum, adding history and design to what was a vocational drafting and industrial arts program. The institute's 1892 catalog gave the following description of the four-year architecture course:

> Strictly speaking the work in architectural drawing begins in the second year with the study of materials and of construction in wood and brick. Considerable time is devoted to the study of the more common materials used in building, and to detail and working drawings. Special stress is laid on designing. In the last three years, a great amount of time has been given to the study of strength of materials, estimates, specifications, etc. A brief review is taken of the history of architecture, to give the student a better knowledge of building as carried on today. Throughout the course, students are required to spend a good deal of time in free-hand drawing, to give them skill and facility with the pencil, which are essential to good drafting. In addition to the time spent in the drawing room, students must spend some time in the work shops, to give them a more intimate knowledge of the materials with which they will deal, and to supervise work intelligently.
>
> The amount of time required depends on the knowledge the student already has of materials and construction. The amount of building constantly in operation on the school grounds and in the vicinity, gives students an

excellent opportunity to study work in progress of erection under the careful supervision of the heads of the different divisions, and to enter competitions for buildings which are to be erected.[2]

The architectural program at Tuskegee Institute initially had thirty-five students and was located in one 8 × 12-foot room on the third floor of Cassedy Hall. By the fall of 1899, the program had 320 students and had moved into the student-built Slater Armstrong Memorial Trades Building designed by Taylor, with a drawing room that was 37 × 80 feet and seven large windows that provided the preferred morning light. It was described as "one of the most beautiful places in which a visitor can linger."[3]

The architecture faculty at Tuskegee Institute was one of its strengths. Many outstanding Black architects were attracted to Tuskegee Institute because teaching opportunities elsewhere were limited and because the institute provided them with the opportunity to not only practice their profession, but to see their designs built. Washington sought out talented Black graduates of prestigious White universities for his teaching posts, and it is credible that outstanding Tuskegee Institute students were given financial aid to attend leading White universities, obtain degrees, and return to teach at Tuskegee Institute. During Washington's era, from 1881 until 1915, eighteen faculty were listed in the catalogs as teachers in the Architectural and Mechanical Drawing Division. From 1893 to 1920, five architects served as head of the architectural division: ROBERT ROBINSON TAYLOR, who served from 1893 to 1898; WALLACE AUGUSTUS RAYFIELD, who served from 1898 to 1901; WILLIAM SIDNEY PITTMAN, who served from 1901 to 1905; WALTER THOMAS BAILEY, who served from 1905 to 1914; and WILLIAM AUGUSTUS HAZEL, who served from 1914 to 1919. Hazel resigned from Tuskegee Institute in 1920 to become the first head of the architecture program at HOWARD UNIVERSITY.

Robert Robinson Taylor (1869–1942) was the Tuskegee architectural faculty member who had the greatest impact, due to his longevity of nearly forty years at Tuskegee Institute. His first campus buildings included Thrasher Hall (1893) and the impressive Butler Chapel (1894). Wallace Augustus Rayfield (1874–1941) did not have any campus buildings to his credit, but was kept busy altering and remodeling to keep up with the rapid increase of students. William Sidney Pittman (1875–1958) was alternately called the most gifted and the most eccentric. Notably in 1907 Pittman became Booker T. Washington's son-in-law by marrying his daughter, Portia. He was the architect of Carnegie Library (1901) and Huntington Memorial Academic Building (1902). Walter Thomas Bailey (1882–1941), like Rayfield, did not have any campus buildings to his

Tuskegee Institute Drawing Class (Wallace Rayfield Standing), *Prints and Photographs Division, Library of Congress*

credit during the time he headed up the Mechanical Industries Department.

Students were a diverse group. Between 1881 and 1890, six thousand students had passed through the institute, but only three hundred had stayed long enough to obtain a prized certificate. Reasons for this were many, but tuition—even though it was relatively low—was a major obstacle. In response to this issue, starting in 1884 two divisions were formed: day school and night school. Day students had to be fourteen years old and pass a written exam. In addition to their required academic work, day students were involved in some trade. Day students worked from 7:00 A.M. to 5:00 P.M. on alternate days with their class studies and a half-day on Saturday. Students sixteen years old and older who were unable to pass the written exam and/or unable to pay their tuition and board were considered for night school. Night students worked from 7:00 A.M. to 5:00 P.M. six days a week and attended class from 7:00 P.M. to 9:00 P.M. Every effort was made to have the trade be compatible with the student's interests.

Over 75 percent of Tuskegee's student body during Booker T. Washington's era was from the South. Of this group, students from Alabama dominated, making up 35 percent of the student body, with Georgia and Mississippi students averaging 12 percent each. The remaining 16 percent represented nine other southern states. Although the latter percentage fluctuated considerably during these years, the southern states with the largest number of students were Texas, Louisiana, and Kentucky. The remaining 25 percent of the student body came from northern and eastern states. The states of Illinois, New York, Oklahoma, and Pennsylvania, with an average of 11 percent, were the most consistently represented. Less than 5 percent, or approximately seventy students, represented twenty-three foreign countries. The largest groups of foreign students were from the West Indies, Central America, South America, and Africa. Between 1904 and 1913, Cuba, Jamaica, and Puerto Rico dominated this group with an average of seventeen students.

Tuskegee's architecture program graduated many outstanding architects. A select few included: VERTNER WOODSON TANDY, JOHN ANDERSON LANKFORD, ALBERT IRVIN CASSELL, JOHN EDMONSON BRENT, CHARLES SUMNER BOWMAN, and Puerto Ricans Angel Whatts Echavarria, Alphonso Reverson, and Jose Zarzulela Falu. Echavarria and Reverson, after graduating, went to work in the Birmingham office of Wallace Rayfield. Echavarria later returned to Puerto Rico and became a teacher of mechanical drawing. Reverson also returned to Puerto Rico and became a building inspector for the City of Yabucoa, Falu opened his own architecture office on the island.

The impact of Tuskegee Institute's architecture program on the "Black Belt" of the South and on the careers of Black architects was immense. It was a major patron of Black architects, second only to the Black church. As an awe-inspiring college campus, Tuskegee Institute made an indelible impression on students and visitors alike, which translated into a deeper appreciation of the built environment. Tuskegee's architectural faculty were involved in designing buildings throughout the South. Each faculty member designed at least one commercial or institutional building in the Tuskegee-Montgomery area. Tuskegee's graduates fanned out to various Black communities, and solicitations were constantly received from Black communities in need of architects, contractors, carpenters, brick masons, and the like.

Notes
1. Richard Dozier, "Tuskegee: Booker T. Washington's Contributions to the Education of Black Architects," (Ph.D. diss., University of Michigan, 1990), p. 38.
2. *Tuskegee Institute Bulletin, Annual Catalog, 1892* (Tuskegee: Tuskegee Institute Press, 1892), n.p.
3. Dozier, p. 59.

Bibliography
Grandison, Kenrick Ian. "From Plantation to Campus: Progress, Community, and the Lay of the Land in Shaping the Early Tuskegee Campus." *Landscape Journal* (Spring 1996): 6.
Harlan, Louis R. *Booker T. Washington, the Wizard of Tuskegee, 1901–1915*. New York: Oxford University Press, 1983.
Johnston, Frances Benjamin. "Tuskegee Institute, Tuskegee, Alabama, 1918." Prints and Photographs Division, Lot 2962, Library of Congress.

DR. WESLEY HOWARD HENDERSON,
DALLAS, TEXAS

Ralph Augustine Vaughn
(1907–2000)

Ronald Vaughn

Ralph A. Vaughn was the eldest of four children, born to ROSCOE INGERSOLL VAUGHN and Mary Elizabeth Waring Vaughn on April 24, 1907, in Washington, D.C. Ralph Vaughn grew up in the nation's capital attending its public schools and graduating from Armstrong Technical High School in 1925. His father taught mechanical drafting at Armstrong Tech for forty-seven years.

Ralph Vaughn pursued undergraduate studies at HOWARD UNIVERSITY'S School of Architecture from 1926 to 1927. However, he took a year off to work and his experiences crystallized his desire to continue his education. Starting in 1928, he was a student at the University of Illinois at Urbana-Champaign, where he was a founder of the *Pi Psi* chapter of *Omega Psi Phi* Fraternity in 1929.[1] He earned a bachelor of science in architecture degree on June 13, 1932 from the University of Illinois.[2] Vaughn then pursued graduate study during the summer at the University of Michigan in 1932.

In 1933 Vaughn returned to the District of Columbia and became a draftsman in the office of ALBERT IRVIN CASSELL. While in Cassell's office, Vaughn contributed to the design of a science laboratory and Howard University Founders Library. Sometime during the early 1930s, he also worked for two years with the U.S. Department of Agriculture Resettlement Administration as a draftsman. Also working for the Resettlement Administration at that time as a consultant was HILYARD ROBERT ROBINSON, who became a mentor to Vaughn. Around 1935 Vaughn became an employee in Robinson's firm.

During the 1935 to 1936 school year, Vaughn returned to Howard University to teach architectural rendering. Vaughn met Los Angeles architect PAUL REVERE WILLIAMS when the latter came to the university as a guest lecturer. Williams was the Republican stalwart in a joint venture with Hilyard Robert Robinson and Irving Porter for the design of Langston Terrace Public Housing in Washington, D.C. Williams recruited Vaughn and he became the chief draftsman for the groundbreaking project.

Williams subsequently offered to employ Vaughn if he ever came to Los Angeles, where Williams' main office was located. Vaughn accepted Williams' offer and relocated to Los Angeles in 1937. Vaughn brought with him a new bride, Elizabeth Estelle Christmas Fry, whom he had met while teaching at Howard, and wed in 1935. They had one son, Ronald Fry Vaughn, born on March 7, 1940. After moving to Los Angeles, Elizabeth Vaughn became a librarian with the Los Angeles Unified School District and Ronald Vaughn became an architect like his father.

Ralph Vaughn worked four and a half years for Paul Revere Williams. Projects that Vaughn worked on included an eighteen-car garage for Everet Lebaron Cord; Music Corporation of America headquarters; a Saks Fifth Avenue Department Store addition; a project in Columbia, South America; and residences for movie stars including Charles Correll (Amos on the radio show *Amos 'n Andy*), Bert Lahr (the cowardly lion in the *Wizard of Oz*), actor Tyrone Power, comedian Grace Moore, and tap dancer Bill "Bojangles" Robinson.

A significant threshold was crossed in Vaughn's career when a house that he had designed was published in *California Arts and Architecture* magazine in 1941.[3] The clients, the Smiths, had also commissioned a recently arrived Swedish interior designer, Gretta Grossman. She asked well-known architectural photographer Julius Shulman to photograph the house. This collaboration put Vaughn into the mainstream of the progressive architectural community in southern California. Regrettably, the house was demolished in 1949 to make way for the Hollywood Freeway.

When the United States entered World War II in 1941, most civilian construction ceased. Vaughn was laid off from Williams's firm, but they kept in contact afterward for many years. Possibly because Vaughn met various people in the movie business while working for Williams, Vaughn began moonlighting as a movie set designer for Metro-Goldwyn-Mayer studio in Culver City, California, which eventually became his full-time job. Vaughn worked for noted set designer Cedric Gibbons. In addition to war movies, he also worked on *The Last Time I Saw Paris*, *Thirty Seconds over Tokyo*, *A Guy Named Joe*, and *Kismet*.

Vaughn believed that the movie industry was a strong influence on architects in Los Angeles. In addition to providing work on movie sets, the movie industry was both a creative outlet and a technology stimulus—plus it provided wealthy clients that appreciated sophisticated designs. Vaughn speculated that movie star clients employed African American architects for several reasons: they did not care what others said about their choice of an architect, many appreciated talent regardless of race, and many movie stars were liberals and wanted to make a "statement" about race relations. Vaughn speculated that not only did he benefit from this social climate, but so did Paul Williams and JAMES HOMER GARROTT.

After World War II ended and civilian construction resumed, Vaughn began an independent architectural practice. In addition to residential and commercial projects, he executed interior design projects and continued to design movie sets. His practice received a boost in 1952 when he received an award from a newspaper in Chicago for his home that he designed, and the story was published in the Los Angeles *Herald Examiner* newspaper.

One of Vaughn's best-known extant projects is Lincoln Place Apartments in Venice, California, which was completed around 1951. It has 795 units in fifty-two buildings and covers thirty-five acres. The crisply geometric buildings are Modern in style and the site is lushly landscaped. Attesting to its popularity, tenant turnover was very low. In support of a nomination to the California office of historic preservation which was not approved, builder Gerald Blake wrote:

> My father, Sam Bialac acquired the land in 1945 and decided to build a large garden style apartment complex under the section 608 of the National Housing Act. He teamed up with the Myers Brothers Contractors for the project and I joined my father in early 1946 after being discharged from the air force.... We looked at garden style apartments throughout the Southland in order to find the very best architect.... Ralph Vaughn was far and away the best. He had not only the best footprints but had an incredible flair for design and an ability to deliver affordable housing that looked and felt like luxury housing.... We did not know at that time that Ralph was African American but it would not have mattered to us. We later received death threats for working with a black architect but that did not stop us ... we were committed to creating the finest project in the country.... The FHA was so impressed with Lincoln Place, that throughout the '50s, ... when a developer submitted lackluster plans complaining of FHA budget and design restrictions, he would be sent to take a look at Lincoln Place.[4]

Because Vaughn was not licensed at that time, he teamed up with a White architect who was—Heth Wharton. They had met while they were coworkers at Metro-Goldwyn-Mayer and formed the firm Wharton & Vaughn Associates. Wharton (1892–1958) had

Lincoln Place Apartments, *Hans Adamson*

been a student at Harvard University from 1915 to 1917 and had clients who were in the film industry. He had liberal political views and welcomed having a Black partner. Many of the staff in the firm were licensed architects but had also been movie set designers. Vaughn believed that his experiences with the movie industry had increased his creative imagination. Vaughn designed North Hollywood Manor and Chase Knolls Apartments. However, the Korean War caused the cancellation of many of their subsequent projects, and, additionally, Wharton became ill. They closed their firm in the mid-1950s and Vaughn began working from his home. He dabbled with alternate careers as a realtor, contractor, and inventor.

Ralph A. Vaughn received his state of California architect's license in 1963.[5] His practice expanded to include clients in Arizona, Arkansas, and Oregon. In addition to residences, Vaughn designed hotels, restaurants, bars, stores, bowling alleys, and churches, as well as additions and alterations to projects that others had designed. He was the architect for Congregation Beth Am Synagogue (1959) in Los Angeles, for which he received an award from the Society of American Registered Architects in 1967. Vaughn's career received another boost when he became the architect for the Biff's chain of coffee shops. He specialized in restaurants and nightclubs, and designed many, including the Rubiyat, King's "X," Mardi Gras Room in the Park Wilshire Hotel, Melody Cocktail Bar, Hi-Hat Club and Bar, and the Oyster House Restaurant. It can be easily surmised that his experience in designing movie sets helped him to design these specialized theme environments.

Ralph Vaughn divorced his first wife and entered a second marriage to Jeanne Arnold Mason around 1971. From this union, there was a daughter, Arianna Vaughn. However, this second marriage also ended in divorce seven years later.

Vaughn's design philosophy emphasized abstraction of form and clarity of structure, but also affordability and context. He was a committed Modernist who distilled influences from Cassell, Robinson, and Williams; however, he adapted Modernism to the warm climate of southern California, emphasizing an easy transition for occupants from exterior to interior with patios, balconies, and generous fenestration. Vaughn was influenced by the Garden City movement and incorporated many of its tenets, including the integration of landscaping with buildings. His dwellings were cost effective, primarily due to his experience with the Federal Housing Authority.

Vaughn's work was solidly part of the architectural vanguard in southern California during the 1950s and 1960s, when the region experienced explosive growth and also when its imagery came to represent to the rest of the nation an ideal of casual, affordable modern living. Vaughn liked the openness, newness, climate, and culture of southern California and this fostered in him a freedom of expression that was in harmony with his innovative and explorative way of designing.

Vaughn was a founding member of the Los Angeles chapter of the Society of American Registered Architects; a member of the Archaeological Institute of America, the National Society of Interior Decorators, the American Association for the Advancement of Science, and the Smithsonian Institute Association; and founder of the Magna Carta Foundation, which was dedicated to the research and development of consumer products, particularly shelter.

Ralph Augustine Vaughn lived in Los Angeles from 1937 to 1998, and then moved in with his son in Stockton, California. He continued to paint, sketch, and invent. He was alert and walking the evening before he died in his sleep on October 20, 2000. He was cremated and his ashes were scattered over the Pacific Ocean.

Notes

1. Interview with Ralph Augustine Vaughn grandson, 16 February 1992, Los Angeles, Calif.
2. University of Illinois, "Ralph Vaughn," degree awarded 13 June 1932.
3. "Bermuda House: House for Mr. & Mrs. Darr Smith—Ralph Vaughn Designer." *California Arts and Architecture*, (September 1941): 32.
4. Gerald Bialac, President of Bialac Group to Marilyn Lortie in support of nomination of Lincoln Place to California Register of Historic Places, 14 September 2002, project files, Office of Historic Preservation, Sacramento, CA.
5. California Architects Board Records, "Ralph Augustine Vaughn," Certificate no. C3998, issued 30 September 1963.

Dr. Wesley Howard Henderson,
Dallas, Texas

BUILDING LIST

Name	Address	City	State	Year	Comments
Apartment Bldg.	27th St. at Arlington Ave.	Los Angeles	CA		45 (dwelling units) du
Biff's Coffee Shop	Cahuenga Blvd. & Yucca St.	Hollywood	CA		
Chase Knolls Apts.	1301 Riverside Dr.	Van Nuys	CA	1949	260 du
Cherry Cove Night Club	Wilshire Blvd	Hollywood	CA		
Congregation Beth Am Synagogue	1039 S. La Cienega Blvd.	Los Angeles	CA	1959	
Congregation Mogen David	9600 Pico Blvd.	Los Angeles	CA	1960	12-classroom addition
Congregation Mogen David	9600 Pico Blvd.	Los Angeles	CA	1959	
Drake Hotel	1121 E. 7th St.	Los Angeles	CA		
Dunbar Hotel	Central Ave. at 42nd St.	Los Angeles	CA	1966	Alterations
Fon-Ri Bowling Alley	1175 W. Foothill Blvd.	Rialto	CA		Now Bethlehem Church
Good Wife Restaurant	16800 Ventura Blvd. at Balboa	Encino	CA	1958	
Hi-Hat Club & Bar		Los Angeles	CA		
Holiday Lanes Bowling Alley		Santa Ana	CA		
House		Washington	DC	1932	Roscoe Vaughn, assoc. architect
Houses	Various addresses	Southgate	CA	1937	5 houses
Housing	Various addresses	Pacoima	CA		95 houses
Independence Square	St. Andrews Pl. at Adams Blvd.	Los Angeles	CA	1966	
King's "X" Restaurant & Bar	6600 LaTijera Blvd.	Inglewood	CA	1961	
Lahr, Bert		Beverly Hills	CA	1941	
Lincoln Place Apartments	1064 Elkgrove Ave.	Venice	CA	1949	795 du
Malibu Inn	22969 Pacific Coast Hwy.	Malibu	CA		Alterations
Melody Cocktail Bar		Los Angeles	CA		
Metzler, I. S.		Beverly Hills	CA	1938	
Nikki's Dress Shop		Hollywood	CA	1961	
North Hollywood Manor Apts.	6724 Tujunga Ave.	North Hollywood	CA	1949	501 du
Orange Lanes Bowling Alley		Fullerton	CA		
Oyster House Restaurant	666 N. La Cienega Blvd.	Los Angeles	CA	1956	
Park Wilshire Hotel Mardi Gras Room	2424 Wilshire Blvd.	Los Angeles	CA		
Power, Tyrone	139 Saltair Ave.	Brentwood	CA	1937	Assoc. Architect
San Marcos Hotel Golf Club House	100 N. Dakota St.	Chandler	AZ		Now Sheraton Hotel
Schwab Drug Store		Hollywood	CA	1961	4 stores
Second Baptist Church	2nd & Baker	Santa Ana	CA	1966	
Sherman Shopping Center		Los Angeles	CA	1962	
Sherman Shopping Center	Pico Blvd. at Cardiff Ave.	Los Angeles	CA		

BUILDING LIST (continued)

Name	Address	City	State	Year	Comments
Sherman Shopping Center	Robertson Blvd. & Cahio St.	Los Angeles	CA		
Smith, Darr	2116 Fairfield Ave.	Hollywood	CA	1941	Demolished
Vaughn, Ralph A.	2171 W. 26th Pl.	Los Angeles	CA	1952	Alterations
Veterans Administration Housing	Various addresses	Ontario	CA		55 houses
Watkins Hotel	3109 S. Western Ave.	Los Angeles	CA		
West Los Angeles Synagogue	Westwood Blvd. at National Blvd.	Westwood	CA	1960	
Wilcox Hotel		Los Angeles	CA		
Wineburg, C.		Bel Air	CA	1938	

Roscoe Ingersoll Vaughn
(1884–1971)

Ronald Vaughn

Roscoe I. Vaughn is best known for his many years of teaching architectural and mechanical drafting at Armstrong Technical High School in Washington, D.C. He was a member of the faculty for forty-seven years and served as the head of the Department of Manual Arts from 1919 to 1951. He also was a practicing architect in partnership with HOWARD DILWORTH WOODSON and GEORGE ALONZO FERGUSON intermittently from the 1920s to the 1950s. Vaughn was the constant as the partners changed over thirty years from Woodson, Vaughn & Company to Woodson, Vaughn, & Ferguson to Vaughn, Ferguson & Company.

Roscoe Vaughn was born on December 24, 1884, in Washington, D.C. His father Rudolph changed his first name to Henry after the much admired auto industrialist, Henry Ford and the spelling of his last name from Vaughan to Vaughn. Rudolph (nee Henry) Vaughan was originally from Richmond Virginia and worked as a waiter in New York City. His mother Jenny was a domestic in New York City. Roscoe graduated from Armstrong Technical High School in 1904. Although he never earned an architectural degree, Vaughn studied three consecutive summers from 1907 to 1910 at the University of Pennsylvania School of Architecture in Philadelphia. He undertook education extension work at Columbia University in New York City and the University of Wisconsin at Madison. Vaughn was privately tutored in architectural design and structural engineering by WILLIAM WILSON COOKE and Howard Dilworth Woodson while each was employed by the U.S. Treasury, Office of Supervising Architect.

Vaughn returned to his *alma mater*, Armstrong Technical High School, on July 1, 1904 (one month after graduating) to teach mechanical drawing. He was appointed head of the Department of Mechanical Arts in 1919 and served in that capacity until he retired in 1951. His architectural knowledge was used by the school system for new buildings and alterations before the creation of the centrally headquartered Office of Buildings and Grounds. Vaughn supervised mechanical arts departments at fifteen schools and over fifty teachers. During his near half-century career at Armstrong Tech, he served as acting principal and principal of its night school and proudly let it be known that he never missed a class he taught in over forty years. Vaughn was quoted as saying that he owed everything to that school.[1]

Vaughn began his own practice in Washington, D.C., at 506 T St., NW in 1918. He was in partnership with Howard Dilworth Woodson beginning in 1922, with Woodson and George Ferguson from 1922 to 1924, and with Ferguson from 1924 to 1931. Vaughn and Ferguson formed a partnership again starting in 1938, and after World War II, Woodson joined them. Within the partnerships, Vaughn was responsible for preparing construction drawings and specifications whereas George Ferguson was the office's senior architectural designer and Woodson was the senior engineer.

Mount Bethel Baptist Church, *Caroline Hickman*

Vaughn saw himself as a specialist in church architecture.² His designs for Mount Bethel Baptist Church (1921) and Meridian Hill Baptist Church (1948) feature simplified elements of Gothic style with limestone or brick facades. Houses such as the one he designed for Frank Young (1949) were typically Colonial style with a center hall, and faced with red brick or cut stone.

Vaughn received his architect registration in the District of Columbia in May 1951 by exemption, having supplied an affidavit certifying five years of professional practice preceding 1950. His references were ALBERT IRVIN CASSELL, HILYARD ROBERT ROBINSON and HOWARD HAMILTON MACKEY.³

Vaughn was active in the American Vocational Association, the National Education Association, the American Teachers Association, the Columbian Educational Association, the National Capital Vocational Association, and the School Club of Washington—the latter of which he served as president from 1942 to 1945.

Roscoe and his wife, Mamie Waring Vaughn, had four children; one RALPH AUGUSTINE VAUGHN became an architect in Los Angeles. The daughters were: Lorraine, Mildred, and Imogene.

Roscoe Vaughn died from cancer on December 9, 1971. He is interred at Mount Olivet Cemetery in Washington, D.C.

Notes

1. "Roscoe Vaughn Retires After 47 Years of School Service," *Washington Pittsburg Courier*, 6 October 1951, p. 3.
2. Ibid.
3. District of Columbia Board of Examiners and Registrars for Architects, "Roscoe Ingersoll Vaughn," no. 1299, 31 May 1951. D.C. Archives. They did not consider Vaughn's knowledge up to standard. Collectively, they gave a "qualified" recommendation in the areas of structural engineering, specification writing, and mechanical systems design.

Bibliography

Comer, Elizabeth A. *Archaeological Investigation for Rite-Aid Pharmacy*. D.C.: Comer/Archaeology, 1999. Fomer site of Elks Lodge.

CAROLINE MESROBIAN HICKMAN,
ART AND ARCHITECTURAL HISTORIAN,
WASHINGTON, D.C.

BUILDING LIST

Name	Address	City	State	Year	Comments
Ambler, George M.	1350 Franklin St., NE	Washington	DC	1914	student built
Barker Electrical Appliance Store	725 Florida Ave., NW	Washington	DC	1945	
Brookland Union Baptist Church	3101 14th St., NE	Washington	DC	1963	George Ferguson, assoc. architect
Clewman, Nelson		Washington	DC	1939	
Cole, Laura P.	2905 14th St., NE	Washington	DC	1956	
Elks Lodge No. 85	301 Rhode Island Ave.	Washington	DC	1931	Demolished
First Baptist Church	1038 Wittingham Pl., NE	Washington	DC	1929	
Gregory, F. A.	4015 Massachusetts Ave., SE	Washington	DC	1940	
Hersh, Ben	1340 Newton St., NE	Washington	DC	1957	
Holy Trinity Church	709 4th St., NE	Washington	DC	1948	Alterations
House		Washington	DC	1932	Ralph Vaughn, assoc. architect
Iowa Apts.	7 Iowa Circle, NW	Washington	DC	c1924	Alterations

ROSCOE INGERSOLL VAUGHN

BUILDING LIST (continued)

Name	Address	City	State	Year	Comments
Israel Baptist Church	11th & G Sts., NE	Washington	DC	c1925	
Jones, Dr. W. W.	409 58th St., NE	Washington	DC	c1925	
Knox, Ellis O.	1530 Jackson St., NE	Washington	DC	1940	
Marilynn Apts.	1414 V St., NW	Washington	DC	c1925	Demolished
McCulloch Apts.	305 P St., NW	Washington	DC	1940	12 dwelling units
Meridian Hill Baptist Church	1725 Kalorama Rd., NW	Washington	DC	1948	
Metropolitan Baptist Church Service Bldg.	1225 R St., NW	Washington	DC	1950	
Moorer, A. A.	1600 Monroe St, NE	Washington	DC	1923	
Mt. Airy Baptist Church	110 N. Capitol St. NW	Washington	DC	1926	
Mt. Bethel Baptist Church	205 V St., NW	Washington	DC	1921	
Mt. Moriah Baptist Church	1033 3rd St., SW	Washington	DC	1924	
Mt. Olive Baptist Church	1136 6th St., NE	Washington	DC	1916	Alterations
Mt. Zion Baptist Church	258 13th St., NE	Washington	DC	1924	Demolished
National Benefit Bldg.	1209 U St., NW	Washington	DC	c1925	
Newman, Nelson	1513 Jackson St., NE	Washington	DC	1939	
Northeast Baptist Church	424 3rd St., NE	Washington	DC	1919	
Parks, James B.	1346 Irving St., NE	Washington	DC	1936	
Pilgrim Baptist Church	1243 3rd St., SW	Washington	DC	1924	Demolished
Powell Apts.	1807 8th St., NW	Washington	DC	1938	
Prudential Bank	715 Florida Ave., NW	Washington	DC	c1925	
Rivers, Dr. W. N.	4011 Massachusetts Ave., SE	Washington	DC	1940	
Rouse, Charles C.	1325 Franklin St., NE	Washington	DC	1935	
Stoddard Baptist Home	324 Bryant St., NW	Washington	DC	c1925	Demolished
Turner Memorial African Methodist Episcopal Church	501 P St., NW	Washington	DC	1950	Addition
Union Baptist Church	3101 14th St., NW	Washington	DC	1963	
Walker Memorial Baptist Church	2019 13th St., NW	Washington	DC	1950	Addition
Washington Store & Apts.	1738 Kenilworth Ave., NE	Washington	DC	1954	
Willis, Rev. M. J.	4501 Sheriff Rd., NE	Washington	DC	1916	
Young, Frank M.	4256 Meade St., NE	Washington	DC	1949	
Young, John L.	3212 21st St., SE	Washington	DC	1941	

Josiah Joshua Walker
(1860–1923)

Archival Collection of the Kansas African-American Museum

Josiah Walker is credited with the design and construction of numerous churches, but only one can be documented. However, it can be verified that Walker was the architect for two historic structures in Wichita, Kansas, for groups to which he belonged—Calvary Baptist Church and Arkansas Valley Lodge No. 21. He was recognized as an architect, brick mason, and plasterer. He also operated a boarding house and owned a real estate business.

Calvary Baptist Church (1917) is located at 601 North Water Street on the corner of Elm and Water Streets in downtown Wichita and is regarded as one of only a few surviving structures of Wichita's early African American community.[1] The 2-story red brick church features a large portico with four columns topped by Doric capitals. The structure rises above a raised basement with a flat roof and a pyramid-shaped skylight in the center of the roof. It is Neo-Classic Revival in style, typical of Protestant churches. The sanctuary's original "Akron-plan" arrangement consists of a round main sanctuary space with separate adjoining spaces that can be closed off for Sunday school or opened for worship. There is a three-tier balcony that wraps around the sanctuary. The interior has maple woodwork throughout, including the gently sloped floor of the sanctuary. There is a 496-pipe organ that was installed in 1920, and stained-glass windows imported from Germany surround the building.

The Arkansas Valley Lodge (c1910) is located at 615 North Main Street in Wichita, Kansas.[2] It is a 2-story red brick building and was the headquarters of the Arkansas Valley Lodge no. 21, Free & Accepted Masons of the national Prince Hall Masons. It is one of the few remaining institutional buildings from Wichita's early-twentieth-century African American business district, and was used as a meeting, banquet, and dance hall. On April 3, 1910, the cornerstone for the lodge was laid. The architect and contractor was Josiah Walker.

Josiah Walker lived at 529 North Wichita Street in Wichita, Kansas, when he died at Saint Francis Hospital on July 24 1923, at the age of sixty-three. According to his obituary, he was born in the West Indies. His death record fixes his birth year as 1860, which means he came to Wichita at the age of twenty-five.[3] Josiah

Calvary Baptist Church, Archival Collection of the Kansas African-American Museum

Walker's surviving sons were Richard, Reuben, and Edward Walker—all of whom are now deceased.

Notes
1. "History of Calvary Baptist Church," Wichita: Calvary Baptist Church, n.d., p. 1. Kansas African American Museum.
2. "Ark Valley Lodge," in *Historic Wichita: A Listing of Wichita's Registered Historic Landmarks*, Wichita: Historic Preservation Alliance of Wichita & Sedgwick County, 1997, http:/members.cox.net/wichitahpa.
3. "Walker-Joshua," *Wichita Daily Eagle*, 24 July 1923, p. 3.

Bibliography
Alford, Robert. "U.S. Department of Interior, National Register of Historic Places Registration Form for Calvary Baptist Church." 1 June 1988.

Carol M. Ratledge, "The Brothers of the Ark Valley" (typescript), 1975, p. 3. Kansas African American Museum.

"Walker, Joshia." *Wichita Negro Year Book, 1922–23*. Wichita: Negro Star Publishing Co., 1923.

Wyma, Cornelia. "U.S. Department of Interior, National Register of Historic Places Inventory-Nomination Form for Arkansas Valley Lodge No. 21." 6 August 1976.

Wichita Negro Yearbook, 1922–1923. "J. Walker." Wichita: Neely & Simms, 1922–23, p. 16.

ERIC KEYS, PRESIDENT,
KANSAS AFRICAN-AMERICAN MUSEUM,
WICHITA, KANSAS

BUILDING LIST

Name	Address	City	State	Year	Comments
Arkansas Valley Lodge No. 21	615 N. Main St.	Wichita	KS	c1910	
Calvary Baptist Church	601 N. Water St.	Wichita	KS	1917	

Booker Taliaferro Washington III
(1915–1994)

Joyce Dodson Washington

Booker Taliaferro Washington III was born on January 10, 1915, in Greenwood, Alabama, the faculty village for nearby TUSKEGEE INSTITUTE. His paternal grandfather, Booker Taliaferro Washington (1858–1915), was the founder and principal of Tuskegee Institute from its opening in 1881 to his death. Booker III was the eldest of two children born to Nettie Hancock Washington and Booker Taliaferro Washington Jr. Their second child was a daughter named Nettie, born two years after their son. Booker III was the nephew of WILLIAM SIDNEY PITTMAN, who was married to his father's half-sister, Portia Murray Washington.

In Booker T. Washington III's early childhood, the family moved to Los Angeles, California. His mother, a graduate of Fisk University, taught at the California School for the Deaf. His father had studied carpentry at Wellesley School in Wellesley Hills, Massachusetts, and finished the Normal School at Tuskegee Institute. He became a real estate broker and eventually fashioned a successful career in this field. Booker III graduated from the Manual Arts High School in Los Angeles. He returned to Alabama and enrolled in Tuskegee Institute, where he graduated in 1938 with a diploma in architecture.

Drawn by publicity about the New York World's Fair, Washington moved to New York City in 1939. He pursued graduate studies in architecture at Columbia University, New York University, and the Institute of Design and Construction. Washington served in the U.S. Army during World War II. He was a member of the New York chapter of the Tuskegee Institute Alumni Club.

Washington's skills as a designer were recognized when he was selected to exhibit in only the second juried exhibition of minority architects, "The Negro in American Architecture," held April 21 to May 2, 1958, sponsored by the Architectural League of New York. A description of what he lent to the exhibit was not found.

Washington found employment in New York City with several prestigious majority-White firms. With Harrison & Abramovitz, he was an architectural draftsman, construction field supervisor, and assistant director of building.[1] Projects he worked on there include Rockefeller University (c1957) and the Metropolitan Opera House at Lincoln Center (c1966). At Emery Roth & Sons, he worked on the Pan Am Building (c1963) near Grand Central Station. At Rogers Butler & Bergun, he may have worked on Columbia-Presbyterian Medical Center (c1964) in Manhattan, the Harkness House renovation (c1965) also in Manhattan, and the Brooklyn Hospital expansion (c1967) near Fort Green Park in Brooklyn.[2]

Booker T. Washington III married Joyce Dodson in 1967. She was a native of Norfolk, Virginia, and was a public school principal. They lived on Harlem's Striver's Row, an exlusive community of elegant townhouses designed by the noted architect Stanford White (1853–1906). Architect VERTNER WOODSON TANDY also lived on Striver's Row.

423

BOOKER TALIAFERRO WASHINGTON III

Booker T. Washington III was an avid reader who collected a 350-volume personal library. He wrote the introduction to a limited-edition reprint of his grandfather's popular autobiography *Up from Slavery*.[3]

In failing health for several years, Washington died on November 13, 1994 at New York Hospital. He is entombed in a mausoleum inside Trinity Cemetery in Manhattan.

Notes

1. "Booker T. Washington III," Memorial Celebration and Exhibit, Schomberg Center for Research in Black Culture, 10 December 1994.
2. Dates and addresses of buildings came from Elliott Willensky and Norval White, eds., *New York Chapter, American Institute of Architects Guide to New York City*, 3rd ed.: New York: Harcourt Brace Jovanovich, 1988.
3. "Booker Washington, Architect, 79 Dies," *New York Times*, 17 November 1994, p. D23.

JOYCE DODSON WASHINGTON,
RIVERDALE, NEW YORK

Metropolitan Opera, *Metropolitan Opera Archives*

BUILDING LIST

Name	Address	City	State	Year	Comments
Brooklyn Hospital	Dekalb Ave. & Willoughby St.	New York	NY	c1967	Alterations
Calvary Hospital	1740 E. Chester Rd.	New York	NY	c1978	Alterations
Columbian Presbyterian Medical Center	W. 165th St. & Broadway	New York	NY	c1964	Alterations
Harkness House for Ballet Arts	4 E. 75th St.	New York	NY	c1965	
Metropolitan Opera House Grand stair	Lincoln Center	New York	NY	c1966	
Pan American Bldg.	200 Park Ave.	New York	NY	c1963	Now Metropolitan Life Bldg.
Rockefeller University	Campus	New York	NY	c1957	Alterations

Robert Edward Lee Washington
(1883–1971)

Robbin Edwin Lee Washington Jr.

Robert E. L. Washington was the first African American architect licensed in West Virginia, in 1921.[1] He was born on August 23, 1883, in Charles Town, West Virginia. Robert was one of five children born to a Black father, Charles Henry Washington, who had been among the enslaved of Bushrod Washington, a first cousin of President George Washington; and a Cherokee mother, Rebecca Washington, a dressmaker. Robert grew up in Towson, Maryland, and then moved to Baltimore. He attended Brick Academy in North Carolina and Saint Paul's Normal and Industrial School in Lawrenceville, Virginia.

Settling in Huntington, West Virginia, in 1901, Washington met a Huntington teacher, Sara Wilkins. Washington relocated to Eugene, Oregon, in 1909 and was joined by Sara a year later. The couple married in Oregon and remained in the far northwest until 1917, when they returned to Huntington, where they spent the rest of their lives. They were parents to five children.

Washington was the architect for the Brown Brothers and Company building in downtown Huntington and for the C. S. McClain Funeral Home, also in Huntington. Family oral history claims he designed a house for Caroline Callie Barnett, the mother of architect CARL EUGENE BARNETT; a pharmacy; and additions to the Barnett Elementary School for Negroes.[2] Doubtless Washington designed other buildings, but information about them has not been found.

In addition to his architectural fees, Washington supplemented his income by becoming a real estate broker.

Brown Brothers Confectionery, *Ancella R. Bickley*

425

ROBERT EDWARD LEE WASHINGTON

Robert E. L. Washington died in Huntington on September 18, 1971.[3] He is buried in Spring Hill Cemetery there.

Notes

1. West Virginia State Board of Examiners and Registrars of Architects, "Robert E.L. Washington," Certificate no. 10, issued 3 November 1921.
2. Interview with Alice Washington Robinson (daughter of Robert Washington), Cleveland, Ohio, 1 June 1976.
3. "Robert E.L. Washington," *The Herald Advertiser,* 19 September 1971, p. 4.

ANCELLA R. BICKLEY, RESEARCHER
THE VILLAGES, FLORIDA

BUILDING LIST

Name	Address	City	State	Year	Comments
Barnett, Caroline C.	810 7th Ave.	Huntington	WV		
Barnett Elementary School for Negroes	8th Ave. & 16th St.	Huntington	WV		Addition
Brown Brothers & Co.	1123 3rd Ave.	Huntington	WV	1921	Demolished
Commercial Bldg.	4th Ave. & 12th St.	Huntington	WV		
McClain, C. S.	1644–9th Ave.	Huntington	WV	1921	
McClain's Funeral Home	1644 9th Ave.	Huntington	WV	1921	
White Pharmacy	8th Ave. above Greer Blvd.	Huntington	WV		

John Austin Welch
(1906–   )

John Austin Welch was born on October 29, 1906, in Tuskegee, Alabama, to William Marion Welch and Mamie Rivers Welch. From 1920 to 1923, Welch attended TUSKEGEE INSTITUTE, where he obtained a certificate in plumbing. He continued his high school studies at Dunbar Senior High School in Washington, D.C. In 1926 Welch entered HOWARD UNIVERSITY to study architecture. He obtained a bachelor of science in architecture in 1930. That same year, Welch was commissioned a captain in the U.S. Army Reserve Officer Training Corps.

Welch began his architectural career in the Department of Buildings and Grounds at Howard University directed by ALBERT IRVIN CASSELL. Welch worked at Howard University for five years. In 1935 Welch joined the office of Washington, D.C., architects HILYARD ROBERT ROBINSON, Ervin Porter, and PAUL REVERE WILLIAMS as a draftsman. Welch worked on Langston Terrace Public Housing (1935) and Cook Hall at Howard University (1936), on which he was also the construction supervisor. Welch also worked on the Frederick Douglass Public Housing for the District of Columbia Public Housing Authority (1939).

In 1936, while employed at Howard University, Welch met and married Margaret Davis, a secretary to the treasurer at Howard University.

In 1940 Welch returned to Tuskegee Institute as campus architect and director of the Department of Architecture and Mechanical Drawing. In March 1941 he was called to active duty by the U.S. Army. From September 1941 until July 1946, Welch was professor of military science and tactics for the institute's Senior Infantry, Reserve Officer Training Corps unit. From July 1946 until October 1947, he served with the Allied Occupation Forces stationed in Korea. In October 1947, Welch was deactivated and returned to the Reserve Officer Training Corps with the rank of lieutenant colonel.

Welch returned to Washington, D.C., and joined the firm of LOUIS EDWIN FRY SR. as senior designer. John Welch and Louis Fry first met in 1930, when both were employed by Albert Irvin Cassell. While working full time, Welch attended The Catholic University of America, where he received the master of architecture degree in 1952. He passed the District of Columbia architectural license examination on his first try, in 1954. Welch also held architectural registrations in the state of Alabama. Soon thereafter he became a partner in the newly re-named firm of Fry & Welch, Architects. Taking on a partner allowed Louis Fry, who was also a professor of architecture at Howard University, to share office administration and supervision of draftsmen with Welch. In 1954 Welch also joined the faculty of Howard University as an associate professor of architecture.

The firm of Fry & Welch, Architects, designed seven dormitories for men and women at Tuskegee Institute; Tuskegee Chapel, in association with architect Paul Rudolph; Montana Terrace Public Housing Project; Takoma Elementary School; and the United House of Prayer, all in Washington, D.C. Welch's partnership with Fry resulted in their most significant

JOHN AUSTIN WELCH

Chapel Sanctuary, *Tuskegee University Office of Marketing and Communications*

work, Lincoln University Library in Jefferson City, Missouri. Completed in 1947, Lincoln University Library—a Georgian style, 2-story building—was one of the first libraries to open the stacks for easy access by the students.[1] In 1983 Lincoln University Library was placed on the National Register of Historic Places as part of the Lincoln University Hilltop Campus Historic District.[2]

In 1957 Welch returned to Tuskegee Institute as dean of the School of Mechanical Industries. In 1968, when the Schools of Agriculture, Architecture, Business Management, Home Economics, and Mechanical Industries were merged, John Welch was named dean of the School of Applied Sciences. During his tenure as dean, he was instrumental in elevating the architectural program to accredited status. Despite the distance, Welch maintained his partnership with Fry. They practiced together until they both retired in 1972, leaving the firm in the hands of Fry's son, Louis Jr., who was also a graduate of Howard University.

John Welch retired from Tuskegee Institute on May 31, 1972.

Throughout his long career as an architect and an educator, Welch received many awards including the Outstanding Alumnus Award from the School of Engineering and Architecture, Howard University; the Howard University Alumni Federation Meritorious Award for Conspicuous Service to Architecture and Education; and the Tuskegee Institute Architectural Alumni Association Award for Untiring and Devoted Service to the Architectural Profession and Tuskegee Institute's Department of Architecture, Its Students, and Alumni.

Welch was named a fellow of the American Institute of Architects in 1985 for notable contributions to the advancement of the profession in the area of education. Welch was a charter member of the Auburn chapter, and the Tuskegee Planning Commission from 1965 to 1994. He is also a member of *Kappa Alpha Psi* Fraternity; *Tau Beta Pi*, national engineering honor society; *Kappa Delta Pi*, national honor society in education; the NATIONAL TECHNICAL ASSOCIATION; and the National Association for the Advancement of Colored People.

Note
1. Louis Fry Sr., "Louis Edwin Fry Sr.: His Life and His Architecture" (typescript), D.C., n.p., 1980), p. 178. In the possession of Fry & Welch, Architects & Planners, Washington, D.C.
2. U.S. Department of Interior, National Park Service, "Lincoln University Hilltop Campus," National Register of Historic Places, 1983.

Bibliography
Goodwin, Robert. *Biographies, Professional Records and Architectural Work of Louis Edwin Fry and John Austin Welch*. Tuskegee Institute, Architecture 452, May 1974. Martin Luther King, Jr. Memorial Library, Washington, D.C., 3.

Phillips, Joyce. "Farewell Dean Welch." In *Campus Digest*, Tuskegee: Tuskegee Institute, 25 March 1972.

ANNETTE K. CARTER,
ARCHITECTURAL DESIGN GROUP,
ALEXANDRIA, VIRGINIA

BUILDING LIST

Name	Address	City	State	Year	Comments
Alabama State College Library	Campus	Montgomery	AL	1962	Assoc. architect
Alabama State College Classroom Bldg.	Campus	Mobile	AL		Assoc. architect
Alabama State College Dining Hall	Campus	Montgomery	AL		Assoc. architect
Alabama State College Mens Dormitory	Campus	Montgomery	AL	1960	Assoc. architect
Alabama State College Womens Dormitory	Campus	Montgomery	AL		Assoc. architect
Davis, Dr. Stephen		Washington	DC	1962	Assoc. architect

BUILDING LIST *(continued)*

Name	Address	City	State	Year	Comments
Frederick Douglass Public Housing	2001 Stanton Rd., SE	Washington	DC	1939	Assoc. architect
Gray, Dr. James C.		Washington	DC	1962	Assoc. architect
Lincoln University Library	Campus	Jefferson City	MO	1947	Assoc. architect
Montana Terrace Public Housing	1625 Montana Terr.	Washington	DC	1965	Assoc. architect
Phelps High School Greenhouse	704 26th St., NE	Washington	DC	1965	Assoc. architect
Tuskegee Institute Andrews Hospital	Campus	Tuskegee	AL	1962	Assoc. architect
Tuskegee Institute Chapel	Campus	Tuskegee	AL	1960	Assoc. architect
Tuskegee Institute Mens Dormitory	Campus	Tuskegee	AL	1962	Assoc. architect
Tuskegee Institute Nurses Home	Campus	Tuskegee	AL	1962	Assoc. architect
Tuskegee Institute Womens Dormitory	Campus	Tuskegee	AL	1962	Assoc. architect
United House of Prayer	1117 7th St., NW	Washington	DC	1964	Assoc. architect

Clarence Buchanan Wheat Sr.
(1909–2000)

Jane Ellen Wheat Bettistea

Clarence Buchanan "Zack" Wheat Sr. was born in Montgomery, Alabama, on April 27, 1909. His father, Hugh Thompson Wheat, was a masonry contractor and his mother, Emma Lena Buchanan, was a normal school teacher. Clarence gained his first experience in building construction as a teenager working alongside his father.

Clarence Wheat graduated from Troy High School in Troy, Ohio, on June 9, 1927. While still in high school he worked enough to receive his journeyman's card as a brick mason. The first building he contributed to architecturally was a single-family dwelling (1931) for a family friend in Troy, Ohio.

In 1928 Wheat entered HOWARD UNIVERSITY School of Architecture. His most memorable professors were WILLIAM AUGUSTUS HAZEL and ALBERT IRVIN CASSELL. While a student he joined *Alpha Phi Alpha* Fraternity and the NATIONAL TECHNICAL ASSOCIATION. He received a bachelor of science in architecture in June 1932. A year later he was hired by Howard University's Department of Buildings and Grounds as a grass cutter, a job considerably below his education and training but reflective of the scarcity of well-paying jobs. It took him less than one year to work his way up to an indoor position as an architectural draftsman.

On September 24, 1935, Clarence married Mable Olga Neal of Charles County, Maryland. Together they raised four children: Jane Ellen, Clarence (also an architect), Reginald, and Phyllis. They were married for fifty-eight years, parted only by her death.

In 1941 Wheat was drafted into the U.S. Army and served a five-year tour of duty during World War II. He received a field promotion to the rank of captain while a member of the Headquarters and Service Company, 266th Engineers Regiment, which supported the Allied troops fighting in the North Apennines, Arno River, and Rome. Honorably discharged in 1946, he returned to Howard University's Department of Buildings and Grounds, where he remained for the next twenty-nine years. As a member of the largest contingent of Black architects anywhere in America,[1] Wheat drafted drawings, wrote specifications, and supervised alterations and renovations to campus buildings. During the summer of 1951, Wheat was promoted to university architect with supervisory responsibility for seventeen architects, engineers, draftsmen, and specification writers who designed and detailed renovations and alterations to most of the university's forty-four buildings. The last building Wheat contributed to was an addition to Howard University Hospital, which was completed in the early 1970s.

In 1959 Wheat became a partner with ROBERT LIONEL FIELDS in a private practice known as Wheat-Fields Architects & Engineers. Having been denied registration in the District of Columbia, he became registered in Ohio in April 1947.[2] Wheat designed at least two houses that are extant: one in Arlington, Virginia, for Pearl and Jeff Cherry; and one in Muskogee, Oklahoma, for Dr. Jesse Chandler. The partnership was dissolved in 1966.

Dr. Jesse Chandler House, *Jane Ellen Bettistea*

Clarence Wheat was called to serve his country again from 1968 to 1973 as a member of Selective Service Board No. 7, activated during the Vietnam War.

Wheat retired from Howard University in 1975 after a combined thirty-seven years on the payroll. After retiring he was a loyal alumnus, joining and then serving as president of the Howard University Retirees' Association.

Clarence Wheat died at Howard University Hospital on November 25, 2000.[3] He is buried in Fort Lincoln Cemetery in Washington, D.C.

Notes

1. Staff of the Buildings and Grounds Department at various times during his employment included JOHN EDMONSON BRENT, Oliver Cassell, I. D. Fannin, ARTHUR WILFRED FERGUSON, LOUIS EDWIN FRY SR., Julius Gardner, CLINTON STEVENS HARRIS, RALPH AUGUSTINE VAUGHN, and JOHN AUSTIN WELCH.
2. State of Ohio, State Board of Registration for Professional Engineers and Surveyors in the Branch of Architecture, "Clarence B. Wheat," Certificate no. 14437, issued 21 April 1947.
3. "Clarence Wheat Dies; Architect for Howard," *Washington Post,* 27 November 2000, p. T20.

JANE ELLEN BETTISTEA, DAUGHTER,
WASHINGTON, D.C.

BUILDING LIST

Name	Address	City	State	Year	Comments
Chandler, Dr. Jesse	2301 Dennison St.	Muskogee	OK	1950	
Cherry, Jeff	2012 S. Kenmore St.	Arlington	VA	1950	
House	903 E. Main St.	Troy	OH	1931	
Howard University Bethune Hall Dormitory	Campus	Washington	DC	1964	Alterations
Howard University Blackburn Student Center	Campus	Washington	DC	1979	Alterations
Howard University Burr Gym	Campus	Washington	DC	1964	Alterations
Howard University Cancer Research Bldg.	2041 Georgia Ave., NW	Washington	DC	1980	Addition
Howard University Chemistry Bldg.	Campus	Washington	DC	1977	Alterations
Howard University Classroom Bldg.	Campus	Washington	DC	1975	Alterations
Howard University Classroom Bldg.	Campus	Washington	DC	1975	Alterations
Howard University Dental Bldg.	Campus	Washington	DC		Alterations
Howard University Faculty Office	Campus	Washington	DC		Alterations
Howard University Faculty Office	Campus	Washington	DC		Alterations
Howard University Founders Library	Campus	Washington	DC	1984	Alterations

CLARENCE BUCHANAN WHEAT SR.

BUILDING LIST (continued)

Name	Address	City	State	Year	Comments
Howard University Hospital	Campus	Washington	DC	1970s	Addition
Howard University Human Ecology Bldg.	Campus	Washington	DC	1960	Alterations
Howard University Locke Hall	Campus	Washington	DC	1964	Demolished
Howard University Medical/Dental Library	Campus	Washington	DC		Demolished
Howard University School of Business	Campus	Washington	DC	1984	Demolished
Howard University School of Communication	Campus	Washington	DC		
Howard University Seley Mudd Bldg.	Campus	Washington	DC	1979	Alterations

Columbus Bob White
(1855–1912)

Thomasina White Murphy

Columbus White was born into slavery in January 1855, in Laurens County, South Carolina. The surname "White" came from his owners, who took a liking to him and trained him to work in the "big" house. As he grew older, he worked as a joiner and carpenter.

Columbus and Sarah Byrd White wed in 1882 and had eight children (in order of birth): Jodie, who worked for his father as a stonemason; Judson, who was also a stonemason working for his father; Casper, a Railroad Pullman porter; Carrie, a housewife; William, a state education leader; Green, a U.S. Army chaplain; Sarah, a school teacher; and Isaac, an elementary school principal.[1] The parents made sure they attended Sunday-morning worship at Bethel African Methodist Episcopal Church, where Columbus White was treasurer, and they saw to it that all

Bethel African Methodist Episcopal Church, *M. Sara Lenahan*

their children received a college education at AME-supported Allen University, where Columbus White was a trustee. Family oral history contends that Columbus White designed and Jodie and Judson built the family home at 400 Green Street (1908).

After establishing his own construction company, Columbus White began to design the buildings he built. A body of his residential work can be found along Main Street in downtown Laurens.[3] Within the Laurens Historic District, White was the architect for three contributing buildings that exemplify his architectural versatility. The Mary Whitner house (c1896) is a minimally ornamented Victorian-style 1½-story frame house with imbricated shingles on a gable roof and two projecting dormers with bargeboard trim. St. Paul First Baptist Church (1912) was designed in the Romanesque Revival style with deftly proportional, asymmetrical towers, one taller than the other. White also designed his home church, Bethel African Methodist Episcopal Church (c1910), which was also Romanesque Revival in style. The brick, 1-story structure has flanking towers that bracket the facade. The facade is enlivened with brick buttresses with stone caps, segmented brick arches, raked corbelling, and a simple brick balustrade. During World War I, Columbus White ran a crew of twenty-two, constructing barracks at Camp Jackson in Columbia, South Carolina.

Columbus Bob White died on October 19, 1912, of yellow fever. He is buried in the family plot in the Laurens Cemetery on Cemetery Street.

Notes

1. "U.S. Twelfth Census, Laurens County" (Laurens Township., South Carolina) (Washington, D.C.: Government Printing Office, 7 June 1900), line 51; and interview with Thomasina White Murphy, granddaughter, 28 January 2003, Southern Pine, N.C.
2. "National Register of Historic Places Inventory Registration Form for Laurens Historic District," U.S. Department of Interior," National Park Service, 10 October 1980.
3. "White: Born a Slave, Became a County Leader," *Laurens Advertiser*, 30 January 1991, p. 9A.

Bibliography

Caldwell, A. B., ed. *History of the American Negro*. Atlanta: Caldwell Publishing Co., 1919.

M. SARAH LENAHAN, RESEARCHER
LAURENS, SOUTH CAROLINA

BUILDING LIST

Name	Address	City	State	Year	Comments
Bethel African Methodist Episcopal Church	234 Caroline St.	Laurens	SC	c1910	
Camp Jackson Barracks	Camp	Columbia	SC	1914	
St. Paul First Baptist Church	Caroline & Hampton Sts.	Laurens	SC	1912	
White, Columbus B.	400 Green St.	Laurens	SC	1908	
Whitner, Mary	225 Caroline St.	Laurens	SC	c1896	

Donald Frank White
(1908–2002)

Courtesy of the Detroit Chapter American Institute of Architects

Donald F. White was born in Canada on May 28, 1908, but grew up in Cicero, Illinois, a close-in western suburb of Chicago. Along with brothers Louis and Frank, Perry was the son of Ferry and Ada Perry White. His father, a patternmaker, operated a gray iron foundry in Cicero. Donald attended grammar school in Cicero. The family moved to Pontiac, Michigan, where he graduated from Pontiac High School in 1927. He was married to Susie Taylor of Sparta, Georgia for more than sixty years until her death in 1999. The couple had no children.

On September 30, 1932, White received his bachelor's degree in architecture from the University of Michigan in Ann Arbor, making him the school's first Black graduate. White interned from 1931 to 1933 as a field assistant to Dr. Frederick E. Giesecke, who was the Department Head at Texas Agricultural & Mechanical college, which was the White school that governed PRAIRIE VIEW AGRICULTURAL & MECHANICAL COLLEGE. In 1934 Donald White received a master's degree in architecture from the Rackham School of Graduate Studies at the University of Michigan. After receiving his degree, Donald White joined the staff of TUSKEGEE INSTITUTE as an instructor who was supervised by Black engineer George L. Washington.

During his tenure at Tuskegee Institute, Donald White became the first African American architect registered in the state of Alabama, in 1935.[1] He remained at Tuskegee Institute until 1938. At the time White was at Tuskegee Institute he collaborated with LOUIS EDWIN FRY SR. and assisted in the design of educational buildings near Tuskegee, including Alabama State Teachers College in Montgomery and the School for the Deaf in Mount Meigs, Alabama. White returned to Detroit, where he opened an office in the Michigan Chronicle Building located at 268 Eliot Street in 1939. His office had a well-deserved reputation for hiring Black architects, engineers, and draftsmen. Among many others, he provided a drafting job to HELEN EUGENIA PARKER when the firm she was with closed due to the death of the principal owner. In the same year, White became the first registered African American architect in the state of Michigan.[2]

White's professional affiliations included the Detroit chapter of the American Institute of Architects, which he joined in 1944 as its first Negro member; the National Society of Professional Engineers; the National Association for the Advancement of Colored People; and the Albany Inter-Racial Council. In 1944 he became only the third African American member of the national organization of American Institute of Architects and in that same year, became a registered professional civil and structural engineer in the state of Michigan.[3] Between 1946 and 1968, Donald White was a partner with FRANCIS EUGENE GRIFFIN, the firm White & Griffin Architect-Engineer Associates, and worked from an office in the Lawyers Building at 139 Cadillac Square. Later, he was with the firm of Giffels & Vallet and after that, with the Black-owned Nathan Johnson & Associates, all in Detroit.

Between 1953 and 1958, White worked in Harbel, Liberia, where he was the deputy educational project

Saint Stephen African Methodist Episcopal Church, *DeWitt Sanford Dykes Jr. Collection*

chief under an agreement between the U.S. government and the Liberian government to assist Prairie View Agricultural & Mechanical College in developing the Booker T. Washington Institute into an industrial vocational school patterned after the land-grant college system in the United States.

Between 1949 and 1951, Donald White was president of the NATIONAL TECHNICAL ASSOCIATION, an organization of African American engineers, scientists, architects, and others involved in the technical fields. One of the founders and past national president of the National Technical Association, CHARLES SUMNER DUKE, was the one who influenced Donald White to pursue a career in architecture. While in Detroit, White was a member of the Economic Club of Detroit and the Booker T. Washington Business Association.

In 1958 Donald and Susie White moved to Troy, New York, where his sister-in-law and her parents were then living. Donald White commuted to nearby Albany, where he took a position as architect in the New York State Department of Public Works. He received his license to practice architecture and engineering in the state of New York in 1958.[4] During the time he was employed by the Department of Public Works, White assisted young architects in preparing for their licensing examinations during his lunch hour. He retired from state government in 1968. In 1980 White came out of retirement at age seventy-two to become staff architect for the City of Albany Community Development Department. He was chosen as the city's Employee of the Month in January 1988 and Employee of the Year in 1989. In 1995 he retired from city government.

Donald White died on April 23, 2002.[5] His funeral was held at the Fifth Avenue African Methodist Episcopal Zion Church in Troy, where he had been a member for forty years.

Notes
1. Alabama Board for Registration of Architects, "Donald F. White," no. 68, issued 4 December 1934.
2. State of Michigan, Board of Registration for Architects, Professional Engineers and Land Surveyors, "Donald F. White," Certificate no. 2990. 4 June 1938.
3. American Institute of Architects Application for Membership, Donald F. White," Washington, D.C. American Institute of Architects Archives. 27 December 1943.
4. State of New York Department of Education, Office of the Professions, "Donald F. White," no. 7418, issued June 1958.
5. "Reflections Commemorating the Beautiful Life of the Late Donald F. White," *Albany Times Union*, 24 April 2002, p. B10.

Bibliography
"Member's File." Detroit Chapter, American Institute of Architects. *Who's Who Among African Americans*, Farmington Hills, Mich.: Gale Group, 2000.

ANTHONY OPALKA,
STATE OF NEW YORK,
OFFICE OF PRESERVATION RESOURCES
AND HISTORIC PRESERVATION

BUILDING LIST

Name	Address	City	State	Year	Comments
Alabama State Teachers College Dormitory	Campus	Montgomery	AL		Assoc. architect
Alabama State Teachers College Community Center	Campus	Montgomery	AL	1938	
Alabama State Teachers College Extension Service Bldg.	Campus	Montgomery	AL	1937	Assoc. architect
Alabama State Teachers College Gym	Campus	Montgomery	AL	1937	Assoc. architect
Alabama State Teachers College Science Bldg.	Campus	Montgomery	AL	1938	
Bainbridge, Dr. Griffin		Waycross	GA	1938	
Bethel African Methodist Episcopal Church		Detroit	MI	1944	Alterations
Booker T. Washington Institute Trade School	Campus	Harbel	Liberia	1950	
Friend Baptist Church Auditorium		Detroit	MI	1944	
House		Hempstead	TX	1933	
House		Brandon	TX	1931	
House		Ft. Worth	TX	1932	
Lincoln University Library	Campus	Jefferson City	MO	1954	Assoc. architect
Milton Medical Clinic		Detroit	MI	1944	
Mt. Meigs School for the Deaf	Campus	Mt. Meigs	AL	1938	Assoc. architect
Paradise Bowling Alley & Amusement Center		Detroit	MI	1944	
Prairie View A&M College duplex	Campus	Prairie View	TX	1933	
Prairie View A&M College Registrar's Office	Campus	Prairie View	TX	1931	
Prairie View A&M College Unmarried Mens Dormitory	Campus	Prairie View	TX	1932	
Sanitarium		Selma	AL	1938	
St. Stephen African Methodist Episcopal Church	6000 Stanford Ave.	Detroit	MI	1940	Addition
Store		Waycross	AL	1938	
Tuskegee Institute Chambliss Hotel	Campus	Tuskegee	AL	1934	Alterations
Tuskegee Institute Cottage No. 34	Campus	Tuskegee	AL	1934	
Tuskegee Institute Fire-Safe Model House	Campus	Tuskegee	AL	1934	
Tuskegee Institute Kay Barn	Campus	Tuskegee	AL		
Tuskegee Institute Laundry Bldg.	Campus	Tuskegee	AL		Alterations
Tuskegee Institute Russell Barn	Campus	Tuskegee	AL		
Tuskegee Institute Tompkins Dining Hall	Campus	Tuskegee	AL		Alterations
Wayne County Better Homes	Various sites	Detroit	MI	1944	

Richard Cassius White
(1891–1977)

Richard C. White was an architect who practiced in New York City during the 1920s and into the 1940s. Little is known about his family or his life prior to entering college. What is known about him, however, is that beginning in 1920 and for approximately twenty-five years, Richard White was active in the architectural arena locally and nationally, in both the private and public sectors.

White resided in Brooklyn at 97 Bainbridge Street in the historically Black neighborhood of Bedford-Stuyvesant. For college he chose to attend Pratt Institute in Brooklyn, a school that "emphasized applied knowledge and the teaching of skills to meet the needs of an emerging industrial economy."[1] White's yearbook entry noted that he was "most liable to succeed."[2] In June 1920 he completed his classes at Pratt Institute and received a certificate in architectural design. White furthered his education by attending Atlanta University and Columbia University Extension from 1924 to 1925, where he studied structural engineering.

By 1923 White was identified as a junior partner in the firm of (Vertner) Tandy & (Frank) Bissel, Architects, with an office at 1931 Broadway in New York City. He joined his fellow Pratt classmate in the office, Black architect Alonzo J. Brown. While in Tandy's office, White obtained his New York State architect registration on September 17, 1925.[3] In 1930 he left Tandy's office and went to work for the New York City Public School, Bureau of Construction as an assistant architect.

White was an active member of the New York chapter of the newly founded NATIONAL TECHNICAL ASSOCIATION, a professional organization of architects, engineers, mathematicians, natural scientists, and other technicians devoted to the encouragement and advancement of Negroes in the scientific and technical fields, and to the breaking down of barriers within the technical professions. It is highly likely that Richard White was one of the original fifteen who attended the first New York chapter meeting in Brooklyn in April 1935. White's participation in the National Technical Association rapidly increased and by 1936 he was chairman of the Liaison and Program Committee while simultaneously serving as secretary of the New York chapter. During this same time period, Alonzo H. Browne was Housing Committee chair, and VERTNER WOODSON TANDY held the presidency of the New York chapter. JOHN ANDERSON LANKFORD—the prominent Washington, D.C., architect—was the eastern district vice president. White served on the National Technical Association's national Constitution Committee and was nominated by the National Technical Association nominating committee along with John Anderson Lankford as president-elect of the national organization. Richard C. White was elected by unanimous vote and served as the National Technical Association's thirteenth president in 1941. During his tenure as president, the National Technical Association held their annual conference at TUSKEGEE INSTITUTE, the *alma mater* of many of the early Black architects. After his term as

Brooklyn Technical High School, *Wesley Springer*

president, White continued to participate in the National Technical Association at the national level and became more involved politically at the local level. He was one of the five members of the National Technical Association's Post-War Planning Committee, which included PAUL REVERE WILLIAMS of Los Angeles, California, and WILLIAM FERGUSON THORNTON of Chicago, Illinois. This group produced a report that, mindful of the poor economy following World War II, endeavored to address the "peculiar and specialized problems in the American economy" likely to be faced by the National Technical Association membership following the end of World War II.[4] Particular attention was given to the inclusion of African Americans on policy-forming bodies and to employment opportunities for the younger technical members.

In keeping with his civic interests, White was elected in 1943 by the Brooklyn Bureau of Charities to its Board of Directors, becoming the first Black named to the thirty-six member directorate of the bureau.

The circumstances of Richard Cassius White's death are not known. It is known that he died on May 18, 1977 and his funeral was held at Nazarene Congregational Church in Brooklyn.

Notes

1. Pratt Institute did not award a four-year bachelor of science degree in architecture until 1938 (after White's matriculation), when its architecture curriculum was expanded. *Pratt Graduate Bulletin* (2001–2002): 6.
2. "Richard White," *Prattonia* (New York: Pratt Institute, 1920), p. 84.
3. New York State Education Department, Office of the Professions, "Richard C. White," License no. 2936, issued 17 September 1925, Albany, N.Y.
4. Charles Duke, "National Technical Association Report of Its Post-War Planning Committee to the Fifteenth Annual Convention of the NTA," Pittsburgh, NTA, 4 September 1943.

WESLEY SPRINGER, ASSISTANT ARCHITECT,
NEW YORK CITY HOUSING AUTHORITY

BUILDING LIST

Name	Address	City	State	Year	Comments
Brooklyn Technical High School	29 Fort Greene Pl.	New York	NY	1933	
Midwood High School	2839 Bedford Ave.	New York	NY	c1940	
Ridder Junior High School	1619 Boston Rd.	New York	NY	1931	

Miller Fulton Whittaker
(1892–1949)

Miller F. Whittaker was born on December 30, 1892, in Sumter, South Carolina. His father, Johnson C. Whittaker, was a lawyer, high school principal, and college administrator; and his mother, Page Harrison Whittaker, was a housewife. Miller attended elementary school in Sumter and then enrolled in the primary school on the campus of the State Agricultural and Mechanical College in Orangeburg. (Until 1954, the rarely used official name of the institution was the Colored Normal, Industrial, Agricultural & Mechanical College of South Carolina.) The Whittaker family moved to Orangeburg in 1900 after Johnson Whittaker accepted an appointment to serve on the faculty. In 1908 the Whittakers moved to Oklahoma City when the elder Whittaker took a teaching position at all-Black Douglass High School. Miller F. Whittaker graduated from high school in Oklahoma City in 1909, and enrolled in the architecture program at Kansas State College in Manhattan.

Whittaker established an excellent academic record at Kansas State and graduated in 1913 as one of nine students who earned a bachelor's degree in architecture. He promptly returned to Orangeburg to teach physics and mechanical drawing at the State Agricultural and Mechanical College. With the exception of military service, he spent the remainder of his life at the institution. The land-grant college, founded in 1896, provided training in agriculture and trades including carpentry, masonry, plumbing, drafting, and electricity. Whittaker quickly assumed a major role in designing campus buildings as well as supervising the students who built the structures. The college was thus able to offer students instruction and experience in construction skills while conserving the very limited financial resources allocated to the institution.

During World War I, Whittaker earned a commission as a second lieutenant and served in France with the 371st and the 368th infantry regiments, which were part of the all-Black 92nd Division. He resumed his teaching duties after the war. In 1921 he attended summer school at Harvard University, and in 1925 became the dean of State Agricultural and Mechanical College's mechanical arts program while continuing to devote time to architecture. Whittaker designed Hodge Hall, completed in 1928, to house the science and agricultural programs. It contained eight classrooms, five biology and chemistry laboratories, and administrative offices for the deans of agriculture and home economics. It also housed the agricultural extension work and home demonstration agent programs.

In 1928 Kansas State College awarded Whittaker a professional degree in architecture. Kansas State permitted students in architecture to earn an advanced degree without additional coursework if they had been engaged in their profession for at least five years and submitted a thesis involving some phase of their work. Whittaker provided his drawings of Hodge Hall to earn the degree. In the meantime, he designed several other campus buildings, including the Young

Women's Christian Association Hut and Dukes Gymnasium. Aspiring architect JOHN HENRY BLANCHE assisted Whittaker in designing the gymnasium, which was finished in 1929.

In May 1932, Miller F. Whittaker was named the third president of South Carolina State College following the death of Robert Shaw Wilkinson. Whittaker played a pivotal role in leading the underfunded and neglected Black school through the grim days of the Great Depression. State appropriations were slashed and faculty salaries reduced by nearly 40 percent. Whittaker helped to secure federal funds through the Works Progress Administration, which led to the construction of the Mechanical Industries Building in 1938. The drawings of that facility indicate that Whittaker was the principal architect; however, the bronze plaque on the building credits its design to two of Whittaker's faculty colleagues, John Henry Blanche and P. V. Jewell. Whittaker also obtained funds from the General Education Board of the Rockefeller Foundation that were matched by state funds, which led to the construction of the college's first library building, Wilkinson Hall. Although Whittaker was not the architect, he paid very close attention to the design and construction of the building, which was finished in 1938.

Whittaker's interests extended beyond the campus. He was a member of the African Methodist Episcopal Church, and *Omega Psi Phi* Fraternity, and was a Thirty-Second Degree Mason. In 1933 he attended a summer program with seven other land-grant college presidents at Cornell University in Ithaca, New York and served as the president of the National Council of Land-Grant Colleges from 1936 to 1937. He remained active in his profession even after becoming a college president.

Whittaker was also a registered architect in South Carolina and Georgia. He designed houses, offices, and churches, including the Orangeburg Lutheran Church, a project that he and John H. Blanche collaborated on and which was not finished until after Whittaker's death.

As the civil rights movement emerged following World War II, Whittaker—as the head of a state institution—found himself caught between White politicians who vigorously defended segregation and National Association for the Advancement of Colored People officials who were working diligently to eradicate Jim Crow facilities. When a South Carolina State student and World War II veteran, John Wrighten, applied for admission in 1946 to the University of South Carolina Law School, he was rejected because he was a Negro. State authorities proposed building a separate law school at South Carolina State College for Black law students. Whittaker was called to testify in

Hodge Hall, South Carolina State University, *Historical Collection, Whittaker Library, South Carolina State University*

federal court in 1947 to support the state's efforts to perpetuate segregation. Plaintiff attorney Thurgood Marshall pointedly asked Whittaker if the proposed Black law school would be equal to the school already established at the university. Whittaker replied, "I don't think so."[1] Nevertheless, the federal district judge ruled that the state could establish the separate law school. Whittaker hurriedly hired a law faculty and the school was hastily opened in 1947.

The legal and political pressures took their toll on the amiable and soft-spoken Whittaker. He complained in 1947, "They are putting me in the middle between the plaintiff and the defendants in this law school business."[2] In March 1949 he suffered a serious heart attack. Eight months later on November 14, at the age of fifty-six, he died of congestive heart failure. He had never married. Dr. Benjamin Elijah Mays, president of Morehouse College, delivered the eulogy at his funeral that was attended by Governor Strom Thurmond and other state dignitaries both Black and White.

In 1969 a new college library was named in his honor. Although Miller Fulton Whittaker died over half a century ago, he left a legacy that survives through the many buildings he designed, especially those that still grace the campus of South Carolina State University.

Notes

1. *John H. Wrighten v. Board of Trustees,* District Court of the United States for the Eastern District of South Carolina, Civil Action no. 1670, Record Group 21, 1949, p. 7.
2. Miller Whittaker to J. B. Felton, 27 May 1947, "President's Papers Folder," Historical Collection, State Department of Education, Miller F. Whittaker Library, South Carolina State University.

Bibliography

Hine, William C. "South Carolina State College: A Legacy of Education and Public Service." *Agricultural History,* (Summer 1991): 149.

Potts, John F. *The History of South Carolina State College.* Orangeburg: South Carolina State College, 1978.

WILLIAM C. HINE, PROFESSOR OF HISTORY,
SOUTH CAROLINA STATE UNIVERSITY

BUILDING LIST

Name	Address	City	State	Year	Comments
Daniels, Harry	1220 Russell St.	Orangeburg	SC		
Horne Ford Dealership	Russell & Magnolia Sts.	Orangeburg	SC	1949	Now East End Motors
House	1540 Amelia St.	Orangeburg	SC	1930	
Limehouse, Frank	921 Russell St.	Orangeburg	SC	c1930	
Orangeburg Lutheran Church	610 Ellis Ave.	Orangeburg	SC	1949	Assoc. architect
South Carolina State College Bradham Hall	Campus	Orangeburg	SC	1916	
South Carolina State College Creamery Bldg.	Campus	Orangeburg	SC	c1929	
South Carolina State College Dukes Gym	Campus	Orangeburg	SC	c1929	
South Carolina State College Felton Training School	Campus	Orangeburg	SC	1920	
South Carolina State College Floyd Dining Hall	Campus	Orangeburg	SC	1932	
South Carolina State College Hodge Hall	Campus	Orangeburg	SC	1928	
South Carolina State College Home Economics Home	Campus	Orangeburg	SC	1925	
South Carolina State College Lowman Hospital	Campus	Orangeburg	SC	1920	
South Carolina State College Lowman Men's Dormitory	Campus	Orangeburg	SC	1917	
South Carolina State College Manning Hall	Campus	Orangeburg	SC	1016	
South Carolina State College Mechanical Industries Bldg.	Campus	Orangeburg	SC	1938	Assoc. architect
South Carolina State College Poultry Plant	Campus	Orangeburg	SC	c1929	
South Carolina State College White Hall	Campus	Orangeburg	SC	1920	Demolished
South Carolina State College Wilkinson Hall	Campus	Orangeburg	SC	1937	
South Carolina State College Wilkinson YWCA Hut	Campus	Orangeburg	SC	1924	
St. Michael's Methodist Church	116 Cheraw St.	Bennettsville	SC	1918	
Staley, Frank M.	121 Wilkinson Ave.	Orangeburg	SC		
Trinity United Methodist Episcopal Church	185 Boulevard St., NE	Orangeburg	SC	1928	
Wilkinson, Robert S.	1308 Russell St.	Orangeburg	SC	c1930	
Williams Chapel African Methodist Episcopal Church	1908 Glover St.	Orangeburg	SC	1915	

Clarence Wesley Wigington
(1883–1967)

Minnesota Historical Society

On June 25, 1915, Clarence Wesley Wigington was appointed senior architectural draftsman in the St. Paul City Architect's office. The office of city architect was relatively new, created by a new city charter establishing a "commission" form of government. Although the city architect was a political appointment, subordinate positions were subject to civil service examination. Wigington placed first out of a field of eight applicants with a score of 84.78 points on a 100-point scale. He was offered the position that he occupied, off and on, for the next thirty-five years, becoming the first registered Black architect in the state of Minnesota, the first Black municipal architect in the state, and possibly the first Black municipal architect in the United States.[1]

Wigington came to St. Paul from Omaha, Nebraska, in 1914. He was born in Lawrence, Kansas, in 1883 and moved with his parents, Wesley and Jennie, to Omaha. His formal education began at Long Elementary School in 1893, and continued through his graduation from Omaha High School in 1902. His artistic talents were recognized when he won three first place prizes for his work in charcoal, pencil, and ink at the Trans-Mississippi World's Fair in Saint Louis, Missouri, in 1898. Between 1900 and 1904, he was enrolled in evening art classes taught by Professor Alfred Juergens (1866–1934), a still-life and landscape painter, and Professor J. Laurie Wallace (1864–1953), a renowned portrait painter. After graduating from high school, he secured a position of clerk and later cub draftsman in the office of Thomas R. Kimball (1862–1934), whose national profile soared after his participation in the Trans-Mississippi World's Fair. He remained with Kimball's office until 1908. During that time Wigington was promoted from junior draftsman to senior draftsman and then architectural designer. He also holds the distinction of being Nebraska's first Black architect.

Wigington's career can be divided into three distinct periods: early (1908–21), middle (1922–42), and late (1943–60). Wigington left Kimball in 1908 to establish his own office. Between 1908 and 1921, he is credited with designing a potato chip factory in Sheridan, Wyoming; nine houses; a set of duplexes (Broomfield-Crutchfield apartments); Zion Baptist Church; and the remodeling of St. John's African Methodist Episcopal Church in Omaha, Nebraska. He also designed an administration building and two dormitories for the National Religious Training School in Durham, North Carolina. For a brief period of time between 1917 and 1922, he created single-family designs for Gordon Van Dyne Company of Davenport, Iowa, and T. D. McAnulty, builder of houses in St. Paul, Minnesota.

During his middle career years, Wigington is credited with designing seven schools, nineteen municipal buildings, ten renovations to existing public buildings, ten outdoor recreational facilities in St. Paul, and seven ice palaces for the St. Paul Winter Carnival (four of which were actually built).[2] Three of these buildings—the Highland Park Tower (1928), the Harriet Island Pavilion (1940), and the Holman Field

Harriett Island Pavilion. *Don Wong Photography*

Administration Building (1938)—are listed on the National Register of Historic Places.[3] Most of these buildings were funded by the Works Progress Administration. In addition to his municipal work, Wigington maintained a limited private practice designing houses and fraternal, religious, and business buildings. Municipal construction slowed to a standstill during World War II, and no significant municipal structure is credited to Wigington. However, with the cessation of warfare and the return of soldiers from active duty the demand for single-family houses increased dramatically. Taking unpaid leaves from office during the winters of 1947 and 1948 for health reasons, Wigington studied house designs in California. These designs were incorporated into two houses that were built for businessmen in St. Paul. Wigington retired from office in 1949 and moved to Los Angeles, California, where he focused on the construction of private residences; commercial buildings; and facilities for social, religious, and fraternal organizations. While living in Los Angeles he is credited with revitalizing the West Coast chapter of the NATIONAL TECHNICAL ASSOCIATION with the assistance of nationally known architect PAUL REVERE WILLIAMS.

Although living in California between 1949 and 1958, Wigington continued to maintain an architectural office in St. Paul under the management of his brother Paul Wigington, who was also an architect. He and his wife returned to live in St. Paul briefly in 1958. Advancing in age, they relocated to Kansas City, Missouri, in 1962 to live with their daughter Muriel. Clarence Wigington died in Kansas City of cancer on July 7, 1967, at the age of eighty-four.[4] At the time of his death, Wigington was survived by his wife of fifty-nine years, Viola; two daughters, Muriel Pemberton and Mildred Bohanan; three grandchildren; and several brothers and sisters.

His wife, has been described as a very bright woman, an excellent homemaker, and an influential socialite. His spacious home on Saint Anthony Avenue was a site for many social gatherings. A recognized leader in the St. Paul Black community, he was the founder of the Minnesota "Colored" Home Guard; executive secretary of the St. Paul Urban League; chairman of the Urban League Board; member of the National Association for the Advancement of Colored People; charter member and officer of the Sterling Club, the Forty Club, Exalted Ruler of Gopher Lodge No. 105, and Improved Benevolent Protective Order of the Elks of the World; and member of Saint Philip's Episcopal Church. Wigington was professionally acquainted with three Minnesota governors, served on the federal Selective Service Board, was an examiner for the Civil Service Architecture Examination in St. Paul and the state of Minneapolis, and was a member of American Institute of Architects and its local Minnesota chapter.

Notes
1. "Civil Service Bureau Notice of Examination," 25 May 1915, Personnel Archives, City of Saint Paul; "Annual Report," Bureau of Civil Service, City of Saint Paul, 1915.

2. Paul Larson, "St. Paul City Building Projects Attributed to Clarence Wigington," 5 October 1999, n.p., p. 1. Northwest Architectural Archives, University of Minnesota Libraries.

3. "National Register of Historic Places: Nomination Form for Highland Park Tower," June 1984; "National Register of Historic Places Registration Form for Holman Field Administration Building," 28 June 1991; "National Register of Historic Places Registration Form for Harriet Island Pavilion," 12 May 1992; all three are listed in *the National Register of Historic Places: Minnesota Checklist* (St. Paul: Minnesota Historical Society State History Preservation Office), p. 71.

4. Interview with Carolyn Pemberton (granddaughter) 18 October 1983, Chicago, Ill.

Bibliography

Olson, Robert. "Architect to the Kings of the Carnivals: Wigington and His Ice Palace Babies," *Ramsey County History*, (Winter 2000): 12.

Pemberton, Gayle. *Hottest Water in Chicago: Notes of a Native Daughter.* New York: Anchor Books, 1992.

Taylor, David V. "Clarence Wigington." *Architecture Minnesota* (January–February 1999): 30.

———. "A Water Tower, a Pavilion and Three National Historic Sites: Clarence Wigington and the Architectural Legacy He Left to the People of St. Paul." *Ramsey County History*, Winter 2000, p. 4.

———. *Clarence "Cap" Wigington: An Architectural Legacy in Ice and Stone.* St. Paul: St. Paul Foundation, 2000.

"The Man of the Month: Clarence Wesley Wigington." *Eyes Magazine* (May 1946): 4.

DAVID V. TAYLOR,
PROFESSOR OF HISTORY,
UNIVERSITY OF MINNESOTA

BUILDING LIST

Name	Address	City	State	Year	Comments
3rd Street *Esplanda* & Tourist Bldg.	3rd & Robert Sts.	St. Paul	MN	1930	
11th St. Flats	1232 S. 11th St.	Omaha	NE	1914	
40 & 8 Memorial Park		St. Paul	MN		
Bailey, Isaac	2816 Pratt St.	Omaha	NE	1913	
Baker Playground Shelter	209 W. Page	St. Paul	MN	1938	
Belvidere Shelter House	301 E. Belvidere	Sts. Paul	MN	1936	Demolished
Britt, Leonard	E. 2519 Maple St.	Omaha	NE	1912	
Broomfield Crutchfield Apts.	2402 Lake St.	Omaha	NE	1913	
Butwin, J. G.	357 Woodlawn Ave.	St. Paul	MN	1948	
Chelsea Heights Elementary School	Hoyt Ave. & Chelsea St.	St. Paul	MN	1939	Addition
Cleveland Junior High School	1000 Walsh St.	St. Paul	MN	1936	
Como Park Elementary School Entrance	780 W. Wheelock Pkwy.	St. Paul	MN	1915	
Dayton's Bluff Playground Shelter	Euclid St. & Hudson Rd.			1936	Demolished
Edgcumbe Elementary School	1287 Ford Pkwy.	St. Paul	MN	1939	Now Talmund Torah Academy
Edgcumbe Playground Shelter	320 S. Griggs	St. Paul	MN	1934	Demolished
Elk River Creamery	Jefferson Hwy. & Elk River	Elk River	MN	1921	Demolished
Ft. Snelling	Downtown	Minneapolis	MN	c1950	
Gopher Lodge No. 105		St. Paul	MN	1925	
Griffin, James	1592 Western Ave.	St. Paul	MN	1958	
Hamline Playground Shelter	Snelling Ave. & LaFond St.	St. Paul	MN	1938	
Harriet Island Pavilion	75 Water St.	St. Paul	MN	1940	Re-named Wigington Pavilion
Harrison Elementary School	1809 Cypress St.	St. Paul	MN	1923	Now Phalen Lake Elementary School
Hazel Park Playground Shelter	952 Hazel St.	St. Paul	MN	1935	Demolished
Highland Park Monument, Fountain & Flag Staff	Hamline & Ford Pkwy.	St. Paul	MN	1926	
Highland Park Pavilion	Hamline & Ford Pkwy.	St. Paul	MN	1932	
Highland Park Water Tower	Snelling & Ford Pkwy.	St. Paul	MN	1928	
Holman Airfield Administration Bldg.	644 Payfield St.	St. Paul	MN	1938	
Homecroft Elementary School	1845 Sherman Ave.	St. Paul	MN	1918	
Johnson, Hollis M.	1826 Lothrop St.	Omaha	NE	1914	
Keller Golf Course Clubhouse	2166 Maplewood Dr.	St. Paul	MN	1929	
Klein, Simon	2110 Edgcumbe Rd.	St. Paul	MN	1949	
MacAlester Junior High School	1700 Summit Ave.	St. Paul	MN	1926	Now Ramsey Junior High School
Mann Elementary School	2001 W. Eleanor Ave.	St. Paul	MN	1939	Addition
Marshall Junior High School	62 N. Grotto Ave.	St. Paul	MN	1925	
McVay, Catherine	1988 Princeton Ave.	St. Paul	MN	1917	

CLARENCE WESLEY WIGINGTON

BUILDING LIST (continued)

Name	Address	City	State	Year	Comments
Monroe Junior High School	810 Palace Ave.	St. Paul	MN	1924	
Monroe Junior High School Auditorium	810 Palace Ave.	St. Paul	MN	1938	
Moss, Harvey		St. Paul	MN	1959	
National Religious Training School Administration Bldg.	Campus	Durham	NC	1910	Now North Carolina A&T University
National Religious Training School Mens Dormitory	Campus	Durham	NC	1910	Now North Carolina A&T University
National Religious Training School Womens Domitory	Campus	Durham	NC	1910	Now North Carolina A&T University
Northfield Creamery	100 N. Hgwy. 3	Northfield	MN	1920	Now a holiday convenience store
Obee, G. Wade	2518 Lake St.	Omaha	NE	1913	
Orr Duplex	125–27 S. 38th St.	Omaha	NE	1914	
Park Elementary School	1450 Grantham	St. Paul	MN	1938	Now Murray Junior High School
Peterson, Thosmas	3908 N. 18th St.	Omaha	NE	1912	
Potato Chip Factory		Sheridan	WY	1908	Demolished
Pyramid Realty & Investment Co.		St. Paul	MN	1923	
Ramsey County School for Boys	753 E. 7th St.	St. Paul	MN	1928	Destroyed by fire
Rice & Lawson Playground Shelter	225 Rices St.	St. Paul	MN	1935	Demolished
Scheffer Playground Shelter	224 LaFond Ave.	St. Paul	MN	1934	Demolished
Smith Memorial Arch	Rice St. under Banford	St. Paul	MN	1932	
South St. Anthony Playground Shelter	890 Cromwell	St. Paul	MN	1935	Demolished
St. Anthony's Park Branch Library	2245 Como Ave.	St. Paul	MN	1920	
St. Claire Playground Shelter	265 Oneida	St. Paul	MN	1935	Demolished
St. George Greek Orthodox Church	W St.	St. Paul	MN	1947	Alterations
St. James African Methodist Episcopal Church	624 Central Ave. W.	St. Paul	MN	1948	
St. Johns African Methodist Episcopal Church	2402 N. 22nd St.	Omaha	NB	1908	Demolished
St. Paul Fire Station No. 5	860 Ashland Ave.	St. Paul	MN	1929	
St. Paul Fire Station No. 10	750 Randolph Ave.	St. Paul	MN	1940	
St. Paul Fire Station No. 17	1226 Payne Ave.	St. Paul	MN	1929	
St. Paul Public Safety Bldg.	101 E. 10th St.	St. Paul	MN	1929	
St. Paul Winter Carnival Ice Palace	Como Park	St. Paul	MN	1942	Melted
St. Paul Winter Carnival Ice Palace	Como Park	St. Paul	MN	1940	Melted
St. Paul Winter Carnival Ice Palace	State Capitol grounds	St. Paul	MN	1937	Melted
St. Paul Winter Carnival Ice Palace	Como Park	St. Paul	MN	1941	Melted
Sterling Clubhouse		St. Paul	MN	1925	
Sylvan Shelter House	77 W. Rose Ave.	St. Paul	MN	1936	Demolished
Van Buren Elementary School		St. Paul	MN	1924	Demolished
Veterans Hospital		St. Paul	MN		
Washington High School	1041 Marion St.	St. Paul	MN	1924	
West Minnehaha Playground Bldg.	685 W. Minnehaha Ave.	St. Paul	MN	1937	
Wilder Playground Community Bldg.	958 Jessie St.	St. Paul	MN	1940	
Wilkins Auditorium Facade	West 5th St.	St. Paul	MN	1931	
Wilson Junior High School	631 N. Albert St.	St. Paul	MN	1925	
Zion Baptist Church	2215 Grant St.	Omaha	NE	1909	

Paul Revere Williams
(1894–1980)

Moorland-Spingarn Research Center

Paul Revere Williams was born in Los Angeles on February 18, 1894, and died there on January 23, 1980. His biological parents were Chester Stanley Williams and Lila Churchill Williams. Paul was orphaned by age four and raised by foster parents. His foster father, Charles Clarkson, was a bank janitor. During an interview later in life Williams is quoted as saying,

> I determined, when I was still in high school, to become an architect. When I announced that intention to my instructor, he stared at me with as much astonishment as he would have displayed had I proposed a rocket flight to Mars. "Who ever heard of a Negro being an architect?" he demanded. . . . He pointed-out that I would . . . be obliged to depend entirely upon white clients for my livelihood. "You have ability—but use it some other way. Don't butt your head futilely against the stone wall of race prejudice."[1]

Paul Williams graduated from Los Angeles Polytechnic High School in 1912.

From 1916 to 1919, Williams attended the University of Southern California (USC) at Los Angeles, but left before graduating. During the evenings from 1915 until 1920 he attended the West Coast *atelier* of the New York City–based Beaux Arts Institute of Design, where he distinguished himself by winning a commemorative medal for excellence in design.

Before Williams began at the University of Southern California, he obtained a position with landscape architect Wilbur Cook in 1913. Next he worked for noted Pasadena architect Reginald Davis Johnson (1882–1952) in 1914. Johnson specialized in luxury residences. Williams left Johnson's office in 1918 to work for Hollywood architect Arthur Kelly. Kelly's practice was diverse and included designing hotels, residences, and businesses. Williams left Kelly's office in 1921 to work for the architecture firm of John C. Austin. Austin's practice included public, institutional, and commercial clients. Williams remained with Austin's office until 1924, working his way up to chief designer. Williams passed the state of California architect licensing examination in 1923, becoming the first African American architect to be licensed in California.[2] That same year, Williams started his own office and was accepted for membership in the American Institute of Architects (AIA), becoming the first African American member of the AIA.

Williams married Della Mae Givens of Los Angeles on June 27, 1917. To their union were born Marilyn Francis and Norma Lucille, who became an interior designer and worked occassionally with her father.

Over Williams's lengthy career—from 1913 until 1974—he employed various styles—from "traditional" to Art Deco and Streamline Moderne to "contemporary"—in designing more than three thousand buildings, including houses, schools, churches, hospitals, hotels, office buildings, stores, and U.S. Navy bases. Williams's designs were in the main considered beautiful and notable by clients, fellow professionals, critics, and the general public. His aesthetic skill in handling a range of idioms can be seen as one of the major points that attracted clients. Often prospective

447

White clients who had seen only his buildings were shocked when they learned his race.

Although he designed projects all over the United States and in Paris, France, and Colombia, South America, the preponderance of his works are in the Los Angeles region. Williams began his practice with small residential commissions but by the late 1920s his practice grew to include designing luxury homes for movie stars, corporations, and government institutions. Notable projects from this decade include the 28th Street Young Men's Christian Association (YMCA) (1925) for the South Central Los Angeles African American community, an even larger YMCA (1926) for Hollywood, a large church for the African American congregation of Second Baptist (1924), a large residence (1929) for Jack P. Akins in Pasadena, a residence for movie actor Lon Chaney in Beverly Hills (1930), a group house (1926) for the University of California–Los Angeles (UCLA) chapter of *Kappa Sigma* fraternity, and the design of speculative houses in the affluent suburb of Flintridge near Pasadena. Williams's career peaked in the 1930s—many of his most memorable buildings were completed in this decade. Although the Great Depression slowed work for many architects, Williams's office remained busy. The 1930s were the "golden age" of Hollywood, and movie stars were a significant client group for him. Hollywood clients included silent screen star Corinne Griffith (1930), yodeling cowboy Will Hays (1934), zany actress ZaSu Pitts (1936), matinee swashbuckler Tyrone Power (1937), and comedian Grace Moore (1937). Williams continued designing homes for Hollywood stars well into the 1950s.

A breakthrough project for Williams was the Everett Lobban Cord mansion (1930) in Beverly Hills. The client was a self-made millionaire manufacturer of the Cord and Duesenberg automobiles. Although not Williams's first project in Beverly Hills, nor his first "large" commission, it was a significant project because it received widespread publicity in national magazines such as *Architect and Engineer*, a rarity for a Negro architect.[3]

Other residences designed in this period include ones for Black tap dancer Bill "Bojangles" Robinson in South Central Los Angeles; White actor Charles Correll, who was the voice of the Black character 'Andy' in *Amos 'n Andy*, a popular radio show on the airwaves, in Holmby Hills; and CBS television executive Jay Paley in Bel Air.

Williams's expertise in residential design for the affluent led to other types of commissions in the 1930s, especially those in which clients wanted a residential atmosphere. The most significant building of this genre was the headquarters for Music Corporation of America (1938) in Beverly Hills. Williams received an Award of Merit in 1939 from the Southern California chapter of the American Institute of Architects for this building. Another commercial project designed with a residential ambience was the Saks Fifth Avenue Department Store (1936), also in Beverly

Los Angeles International Airport Theme Building, *Wesley Howard Henderson*

Hills. For a building for an African American client—the Angelus Funeral Home (1934)—Williams again utilized a residential "look" for a commercial building.

Williams's project range expanded in the 1930s to include the Sunset Plaza Apartments (1938) and Arrowhead Springs Hotel (1939). Arrowhead Springs Hotel is located in the foothills above San Bernardino. Designed in partnership with noted architect Gordon Kaufmann and landscape architect Edward Huntsman Trout, it was a health resort featuring warm mineral-water baths. The site was arranged as a campus of several substantial buildings, the main one 6 stories in height. The hotel received substantial publicity when it opened. Sunset Plaza Apartments was designed for residents to stay for extended periods with maid service and all the amenities of a hotel.

In the 1930s Williams received national publicity for an autobiographical article he wrote and for articles written about him. His autobiographical essay in *American Magazine* generated considerable controversy in the African American community nationwide because Williams expressed what some considered to be *retardaire* social and political views.[4] More publicity and notice came with a second article, published in *Life* magazine in 1938, naming him one of "20 of America's most distinguished Negroes."[5]

The Great Depression exposed the need for federally subsidized public housing. Williams opened an office in Washington, D.C., and in partnership with HILYARD ROBERT ROBINSON they won the commission to design Langston Terrace Public Housing (1937). Williams brought to the partnership his Republican political contacts, and Robinson contributed his public housing design expertise. Williams forged partnerships with other architects, including Richard Neutra (1892–1970), Walter Wurdeman, and Welton Becket (1902–1969), and designed more public housing projects—*Pueblo del Rio* in 1941 and Nickerson Gardens in 1953, both in Los Angeles.

After World War II, Williams continued to design for the affluent. Major projects included the Palm Springs Tennis Club (1947), an addition to the Beverly Hills Hotel (1947), and Perino's Restaurant (1949) in the Wilshire area of Los Angeles. A new market for mass-produced housing emerged, fueled by returning war veterans. Williams marketed to this audience by authoring two books of house plans: *The Small Homes of Tomorrow* and *New Homes for Today*.[6]

The most significant project that Williams designed in the 1940s was the headquarters for the Golden State Mutual Life Insurance Company in Los Angeles. One of the largest Black-owned companies in the nation, the client desired a landmark building. Their desire was satisfied in 1981 when the City of Los Angeles and State of California designated the building a historic landmark.[7]

In the 1950s, Williams's career reached a plateau—he was elected a fellow in the American Institute of Architects in 1957, the first African American to obtain this high honor. Further evidence of the esteem in which Williams was held was shown when he was awarded honorary degrees by three historically Black universities: a doctor of science from Lincoln University in Missouri in 1941, a doctor of architecture from HOWARD UNIVERSITY in 1952, and a doctor of fine arts from TUSKEGEE INSTITUTE in 1956.

Williams's projects in the 1950s included the Los Angeles County Courthouse and Hall of Administration (1958), Franz Hall addition (1958) and Botany Building (1956) for University of California Los Angeles; Hillside Memorial Mausoleum (1951) in Culver City; and a house for crooner Frank Sinatra (1956) in Hollywood Hills.

Williams's most recognizable project in the 1960s was a collaboration with Pereira & Luckman on the "Theme" Building at the Los Angeles International Airport, completed in 1964. Resembling a futuristic spaceship, it has become a familiar cultural sight because movie and television producers use it as a signature building for Los Angeles.

In 1974 Williams was nominated and received emeritus status with the American Institute of Architects. Williams' career has long fascinated architectural historians because his visible successes early in the twentieth century came at a time when racial discrimination against Negroes was pandemic.

> The weight of my racial handicap forced me, willy-nilly, to develop salesmanship. The average, well-established white architect, secure in his social connections, might be able to rest his hopes on his final plans; I, on the contrary, had to devote as much thought and ingenuity to winning an adequate first hearing as to the execution of the detailed drawings. Some of my simple ruses proved surprisingly effective. For example—I spent hours learning to draw upside down. Then, with a client seated across the desk from me, I would rapidly begin to sketch the living room of his house.[8]

Paul Revere Williams died on January 23, 1980, in Los Angeles. His funeral was held at the First African Methodist Episcopal Church (1963), which he had designed and where he was a lifelong member.

Notes
1. Paul Williams, "I Am a Negro," *Ebony* (November 1986): 161.

PAUL REVERE WILLIAMS

2. California Architects Board, "Paul R. Williams," no. B1086 issued 21 May 1923.
3. Anita Morris, "Recent Work of Paul R. Williams, Architect," *Architect & Engineer* (June 1940): 25.
4. "I Am a Negro," *American Magazine*, vol. 124, no. 1 (July 1937): 59.
5. "20 Most Distinguished Negroes in the United States," *Life* (3 October 1938): 48.
6. Paul Williams, *The Small Homes of Tomorrow*, (Los Angeles: Murray & Gee, 1945); Paul Williams, *New Homes for Today* (Los Angeles: Murray & Gee, 1946).
7. State of California, Ethnic Minority Cultural Resource Study, Sacramento: Office of Historic Preservation, 1989.
8. Williams, "I Am a Negro," p. 162.

Bibliography

Gebhard, David, and Robert Winter. *A Guide to Architecture in Los Angeles and Southern California*. Santa Barbara: Peregrine Smith, Inc. 1975.

Hudson, Karen E. *Paul R. Williams, Architect, A Legacy of Style*, New York: Rizzoli, 1993.

DR. WESLEY HOWARD HENDERSON,
DALLAS, TEXAS

BUILDING LIST

Name	Address	City	State/Country	Year	Comments
28th Street Colored YMCA	1006 E. 28th St.	Los Angeles	CA	1926	
Al Jolson Memorial	6001 W. Centinela Ave.	Culver City	CA	1954	
Anderson, Eddie "Rochester"	3700 Cimarron St.	Los Angeles	CA	1937	
Angelus Funeral Home	1030 E. Jefferson Blvd.	Los Angeles	CA	1934	
Arrowhead Springs Hotel	24600 Arrowhead Springs Rd.	San Bernardino	CA	1939	Assoc. architect
Atkin, Jack P.	160 S. San Rafael Ave.	Pasadena	CA	1929	
Beverly Hills Hotel Polo Lounge	9641 Sunset Blvd.	Beverly Hills	CA	1959	
Blodgett, Louis M.	1102 S. Serrano Ave.	Los Angeles	CA	1922	
Blodgett, Louis M.	1704 Wellington Rd.	Los Angeles	CA	1953	
Bogota Country Club	Diag. 129	Bogota	Columbia	1945	
Cass, Louis	4236 Woodleigh Ave.	Pasadena	CA	1922	
Chaney, Lon	806 Whittier Dr.	Beverly Hills	CA	1930	
Chasen's Restaurant	9039 Beverly Blvd.	Beverly Hills	CA	1936	Now Bristol Market Farms
Collins, William	601 WS. Lorraine Blvd.	Los Angeles	CA	1932	
Cord, Everett L.	400 Doheny Rd.	Beverly Hills	CA	1931	Demolished
Correll, Charles	10250 Sunset Blvd.	Holmby Hills	CA	1937	
Cuerin, Dr. Leon G.	2555 Divisadero St.	San Francisco	CA	1939	
Decotah Elementary School	Decotah & Glenn Sts.	Los Angeles	CA	1925	
Edward, Dr. Joseph T.	3718 Chevy Chase	Pasadena	CA	1928	
El Mirador Hotel	E. Tahquite Canyon Valley	Palm Springs	CA	1928	Demolished
El Reno Housing		Reno	NV	1939	15 bungalows
First African Methodist Episcopal Church	2270 S. Harvard St.	Los Angeles	CA	1963	
First African Methodist Episcopal Church	Vernon Ave. & Kensington Pl.	Pasadena	CA	1925	
First Church of Christ, Scientist	501 Riverside Dr.	Reno	NV	1939	
Flint, Katherine	524 Dartmouth Pl.	Pasadena	CA	1929	
Founders Church of Religious Science	3821 W. 6th St.	Los Angeles	CA	1960	
Fox West Coast Theatre	Zoe & Pacific Blvd.	Huntington	CA		
Fulton, Robert J.	227 S. Roxbury Dr.	Beverly Hills	CA	1938	
Gibbey-Simon	101 Loring Dr.	Holmby Hills	CA	1939	
Golden State Elks Lodge	26th & Central Ave.	Los Angeles	CA	1930	
Golden State Mutual Lite Insurance Co.	1999 W. Adams Blvd.	Los Angeles	CA	1949	
Grave of the Unknown Sailor	Pearl Harbor	Honolulu	HW	1953	
Griffith, Corrine	910 Rexford Dr.	Beverly Hills	CA	1930	
Hamilton, Thomas "Hamiltair"		Arrowhead Springs	CA	1936	
Hays, Will H.		Santa Barbara	CA	1934	
Hillside Memorial Mausoleum	6001 W. Centinela Ave.	Culver City	CA	1951	
Holden, Robert		Hollywood	CA	1939	
Hollywood YMCA	1553 N. Hudson Ave.	Hollywood	CA	1927	Addition
Hostetter Elementary School		Los Angeles	CA	1924	Demolished
Hotel Granada		Bogota	Columbia	1946	
Howard University Cook Hall	Campus	Washington	DC		Assoc. architect
Howard, Opie	630 Sierra Dr.	Beverly Hills	CA	1936	

BUILDING LIST (continued)

Name	Address	City	State/Country	Year	Comments
Hudson Ledell Medical Office Bldg.	4230 S. Central Ave.	Los Angeles	CA	1928	
Imperial-Compton Hotel		Los Angeles	CA	1954	
Isaacs, Hart	425 Parkwood Dr.	Bel Air	CA	1935	
King, Stuart	841 Inverness Dr.	Pasadena	CA	1930	
Landis, John	1001 N. Crescent Dr.	Beverly Hills	CA	1955	
Langston Terrace Public Housing	21st & Benning Rd., NE	Washington	DC	1937	Assoc. architect
Los Angeles County Courthouse	111 N. Hill St.	Los Angeles	CA	1958	Assoc. architect
Los Angeles County Psychiatric Hospital		Los Angeles	CA	1947	
London, Julie P.		Encino	CA	1958	
Macedonia Baptist Church	1755 E. 114th St.	Los Angeles	CA	1952	
Marina Del Ray Junior High School	12500 Braddock Dr.	Los Angeles	CA	1960	
Matteson, Ralph E.	1040 Manhattan Ave.	Hermosa	CA	1921	
McMartin, Pauline Scott	1162 Tower Rd.	Beverly Hills	CA	1933	
Menuhin, Moshe		Santa Clara	CA	1935	
Miles, William	1715 Ambassador Way	Beverly Hills	CA	1930	
Music Corporation of America Bldg.	9370 Burton Way	Beverly Hills	CA	1938	
New Hope Baptist Church	5201 S. Central Ave.	Los Angeles	CA	1954	
Newmark, Robert	617 Arden Dr.	Beverly Hills	CA	1927	
Nickerson Gardens Public Housing	11400 Compton Ave.	Los Angeles	CA	1953	
Nutibara Hotel	Calle 52 A., No. 50	Medelin	Columbia	1955	
Paley, William "Jay"	1056 Brooklawn Dr.	Bel Air	CA	1934	
Palm Springs Tennis Club	701 W. Baristo Rd.	Palm Springs	CA	1947	Assoc. architect
Peachy, Katherine	325 N. Las Palmas Ave.	Los Angeles	CA	1929	
Perino's Restaurant	4101 Wilshire Blvd.	Los Angeles	CA	1949	
Petitfils, Anna S.	1201 Park Way	Beverly Hills	CA	1930	
Pierce, Dr. V. Mott	200 Fern Dr.	Pasadena	CA	1928	
Pitts, Zasu		Brentwood	CA	1936	
Power, Tyrone	139 N. Saltair Ave.	Brentwood	CA	1937	
Preminger, Otto "Rock House"		Los Angeles	CA	c1940	
Pueblo Del Rio Public Housing	1801 E. 53rd St.	Los Angeles	CA	1941	
Pueblo Gardens Subdivision	Scattered sites	Tucson	AZ	1949	Assoc. architect
Ribon Apts.		Bogota	Columbia	1948	
Ridgeway, Edwin	232 S. Rimpau Blvd.	Los Angeles	CA	1966	
Robinson, Bill "Bojangles"	1194 36th Pl.	Los Angeles	CA	1937	
Saks Fifth Avenue	9600 Wilshire Blvd.	Beverly Hills	CA	1936	Assoc. architect
Sanchon Beerup	808 Whittier Dr.	Beverly Hills	CA	1929	
Second Baptist Church	2414 Griffith St.	Los Angeles	CA	1924	
Sensenbrenner, August	703 Arden Dr.	Beverly Hills	CA	1933	
Sheppard, John J.	111 Linda Vista Ave.	Pasadena	CA	1926	
Smith, Colin H.	4121 Pembury Pl.	Holmby Hills	CA	1935	
St. Jude Children's Hospital	332 N. Lauderdale	Memphis	TN	1962	
St. Nicholas Orthodox Church	2300 W. 3rd St.	Los Angeles	CA	1948	
Shuwarger	333 S. Beverly Glen Blvd.	Holmby Hills	CA	1936	Purchased by actor Ronald Reagan
Sinatra, Frank A.	2666 Bowmont Dr.	Beverly Hills	CA	1956	
Stanwyck, Barbara S.	718 Hillcrest Dr.	Beverly Hills	CA	1936	
Sunset Plaza Apts.	1220 Sunset Plaza Rd.	West Hollywood	CA	1938	Demolished
Taylor, Van	1337 Talmadge St.	Los Angeles	CA	1921	
Tex's Sporting Goods Store	910 Wilshire Blvd.	Santa Monica	CA	1939	
Trinity Baptist Church	2040 W. Jefferson Blvd.	Los Angeles	CA	1965	
Tubercular Hospital		Husyswuil	Ecuador	1948	
Tucker, Dr. M. O.	1958 20th St.	Santa Monica	CA	1937	
U.S. Naval Reserve Air Base	Naval Station	Los Alamitos	CA	1947	Assoc. architect
U.S. Navy Foundation Exploration Destroyer Baset	Naval Station	San Diego	CA	1947	Assoc. architect
U.S. Navy Roosevelt Fleet Base	Naval Station	Long Beach	CA	1947	Assoc. architect
U.S. Post Office	Holt Blvd.	Ontario	CA	—	
U.S. Post Office	1555 Holt Ave. E.	Ontario	CA	1925	

PAUL REVERE WILLIAMS

BUILDING LIST (continued)

Name	Address	City	State/Country	Year	Comments
UCLA Botany Bldg.	Campus	Westwood	CA	1956	
UCLA *Chi Omega* Sorority House	Campus	Westwood	CA	1929	
UCLA Franz Hall	Campus	Westwood	CA	1958	
UCLA *Kappa Sigma* Fraternity House	Campus	Westwood	CA	1926	
United Nations Bldg.	125 de Suffren	Paris	France	c1953	Alterations
United Pacific Insurance Co.		Los Angeles	CA		
Villegas, Don Luis Toro		Bogota	Columbia	1948	
W. J. Sloane Department Store	9560 Wilshire Blvd.	Beverly Hills	CA	1949	
Westwood Medical Bldg.	10921 Wilshire Blvd.	Westwood	CA	1963	
Will Rogers Park Community House	Sunset Blvd.	Pacific Palisades	CA	1948	
Williams, Paul R.	1690 Victoria Ave.	Los Angeles	CA	1951	
Wilson High School	4500 Multnomah St.	Los Angeles	CA	1969	
Winberg, Charles	100 N. Delfern Dr.	Bel Air	CA	1938	

David Augustus Williston
(1868–1962)

David Williston (top row right) with brothers and sisters in front of family home in Fayetteville, North Carolina, c1903

David Augustus "Gus" Williston was born three years after the Civil War on a Fayetteville, North Carolina, farm. He was the second child of Frank and Henrietta Williston. While his brothers and sisters grew corn, cotton, and rice, young David grew the most attractive garden among his twelve siblings.[1]

The Willistons were educated beyond normal school, financially well off, and respected members of Evans African Methodist Episcopal Church. David's oldest brother, Edward, led the way educationally by becoming the head of Pediatrics at the all-Negro Freedman's Hospital in Washington, D.C. David's sisters all became teachers. David followed his brother to Washington, D.C., based on his brother's promise to pay his tuition to Howard Normal School.

David Williston attended Howard Normal School from 1893 to 1895, earning a normal diploma when he was twenty-seven years old. Following graduation he enrolled at Cornell University in Ithaca, New York. His intensive preparation at Howard Normal School made it possible for him to place out of a semester's worth of classes at Cornell University. With well-known agricultural scientist and director of the Agricultural Department Liberty Hyde Bailey as his mentor, Williston earned a bachelor of science in agriculture in 1898, the first of his race to graduate from the College of Agriculture. He later completed municipal engineering courses offered by the International Correspondence School in Scranton, Pennsylvania.

Returning to his home state in 1898, Williston began his teaching career at the State College of North Carolina at Greensboro. From 1901 to 1902, he was professor of horticulture at Lincoln Institute in Jefferson City, Missouri. In 1902 Booker Taliaferro Washington, principal of TUSKEGEE INSTITUTE, recruited Williston to join the agricultural science faculty—which included the multi-talented scientist, agriculturist, and floriculturist George Washington

453

DAVID AUGUSTUS WILLISTON

Carver—and serve as superintendent of grounds working in collaboration with campus architect ROBERT ROBINSON TAYLOR. Williston taught intermittently at Tuskegee Institute for twenty-seven years. From 1907 to 1909, Williston taught horticulture and agriculture at Fisk University.

In 1906, at the age of thirty-eight, David married Sue Bell Thomas of Springfield, Ohio, who had been Booker T. Washington's secretary prior to their marriage. Being a new husband may explain David Williston's absence from teaching between 1906 and 1907. David and Sue later became the parents of Thomas Augustus.

The Great Depression marked a period of difficult economic struggle for the nation. Enrollment at Black colleges dropped, unpaid tuition mounted, and gifts and scholarships shrank or disappeared at the schools where Williston taught. After completing his teaching duty at Tennessee Agricultural & Industrial State College in 1930, Williston moved to Washington, D.C., and opened the first African American–owned landscape architecture firm in the nation. From his home office not far from HOWARD UNIVERSITY he exploited his teaching relationships with Black colleges to offer his professional services as a landscape architect. Client schools included Fisk University, Tennessee Agricultural & Industrial, Clark University, Alcorn State University, Howard University, Lane College, and Philander Smith College.[2]

Williston's relationships with Black schools provided a conduit to private commissions from faculty. The Public Works Administration financed many of the landscape designs that Williston created for buildings on the campus of Howard University in collaboration with ALBERT IRVIN CASSELL, as well as his terrace site design for Langston Terrace Public Housing in collaboration with HILYARD ROBERT ROBINSON. Robinson offered that "Williston was a superb horticulturist ... his principle professional interest."[3] The War Department, similar to the PWA, financed Tuskegee's Airmen's Training Airfield at Chehaw, Alabama, where Williston prepared the excavation and grading plans for the swampy 1,700-acre site, again in collaboration with Hilyard Robert Robinson.

Residential landscape design was a large portion of Williston's practice. His earliest residential landscape design was Booker T. Washington's home "The Oaks" (1898) on the campus of Tuskegee Institute designed by ROBERT ROBINSON TAYLOR. Williston was landscape architect for the residence (1932) of Dr. John Hope, president of Atlanta University and undersecretary general of the United Nations, and Dr. Ralph Johnson Bunche's residence (1941) in the northeast

Tuskegee Institute Campus (gazebo also designed by Williston), *Prints and Photographs Division, Library of Congress*

Brookland neighborhood of Washington, D.C., designed by HILYARD ROBERT ROBINSON.

Williston's horticulture knowledge enabled him to propagate an attractive red berry "*Pyracantha Tuskegee.*"4 Williston set a prominent professional standard among his White peers such as Alanson Phelps Wyman (1870–1947) and Bryant Fleming (1877–1946), who were also designing campuses and government projects.

Williston's designs demonstrated his multi-faceted proficiency for creating spaces that were topographically engineered, embraced conservation principles, and utilized durable construction materials. An example is the amphitheater he designed for Alcorn State University in Mississippi, which incorporates the various facets of landscape architecture by blending terracing, planting, and hardscaping into a popular student gathering spot. Williston's planting designs were not only cost effective but practical, considering the hot climate where many of his projects were located.

David Williston continued to practice landscape architecture until he died on July 28, 1962, from a protracted illness at the age of ninety-four. At the time of his death, he was collaborating with Arkansas governor Winthrop Rockefeller on landscape projects throughout the state. Williston's work survives as his landscapes grow and mature. Williston was, in the words of Booker T. Washington, "a sticker, never a quitter."3

Notes

1. Kirk Muckle and Dreck Wilson, "David Augustus Williston: Pioneering Black Professional," *Landscape Architecture Magazine,* (February, 1982): 82.
2. "David Williston Papers," African American Architects Archives, Moorland-Spingarn Research Center, Washington, D.C.
3. Hilyard Robinson to Dreck Wilson, 1 May 1979, p. 1. In the possession of Dreck Wilson, Washington, D.C.
4. Mordaci Johnson, "Charter Day Program," Howard University, 2 March 1946, p. 1. Editor's note: A check of the *Standardized Plant Names* did not disclose the existence of such a cultivar.

Bibliography

Eppse, Merl R. *The Negro Too in American History.* Nashville: Publication Company 1943.

Muckle, Kirk. "Landscape Architecture's Need for Black Professionals" (typescript). January 1981. Syracuse College of Environmental Science and Forestry.

DOUGLAS A. WILLIAMS, INSTRUCTOR,
INSTITUTE FOR ARCHITECTURE, URBAN PLANNING
AND LANDSCAPE ARCHITECTURE,
MORGAN STATE UNIVERSITY

LANDSCAPE PROJECT LIST

Name	Address	City	State/Country	Year	Comments
99th Pursuit Squadron Airfield	Airfield	Chehaw	AL	1941	Re-named Moto Field
Alcorn State University	Campus	Alcorn	MS	1950	
Alpha Phi Alpha Fraternity House	1800 New Hampshire Ave., NW	Washington	DC	1950	
Atlanta University President's Residence	Campus	Atlanta	GA	c1932	
Bunch, Dr. Ralph J.	1510 Jackson St., NE	Washington	DC	1941	
Catholic University of America	Campus	Washington	DC	1940	
Centennial Victory Exposition Center	Fairgrounds	Monrovia	Liberia	1946	
Clark University	Campus	Atlanta	GA	1926	
U.S. Customs Court	717 Madison Pl., NW	Washington	DC	1960	Now U.S. Court of Appeals
Fisk University	Campus	Nashville	TN	1900	
Flanner House Social Center	333 W. 16th St.	Indianapolis	IN	1943	
Holabird Homes		Dundalk	MD	1941	Demolished
Lane College	545 Lane Ave.	Jackson	TN	1045	
Langston Terrace Public Housing	2100 Benning Rd., NE	Washington	DC	1937	
Lyon Village	1920 N. Highland St.	Arlington	VA		
Parkside Dwellings Public Housing	Barnes Ln. & Kenilworth Ave., NE	Washington	DC	1940	Demolished
Philander Smith College	812 W. 13th St.	Little Rock	AR	1958	
Roberts Airfield	Medaster River basin	Harbel	Liberia	1941	
Seton High School	5715 Emerson St.	Bladensburg	MD	1950	
Tennessee State University	Campus	Nashville	TN	1948	
Tuskegee Institute	Campus	Tuskegee	AL	1900	
Veterans Administration Hospital	2400 Hospital Rd.	Tuskegee	AL	1923	
Washington, Booker T. "The Oaks"	Campus	Tuskegee	AL	1898	
Ypsilanti Public Housing	601 Armstrong Dr.	Ypsilanti	MI	1943	Now Armstrong Drive Apts.

John Louis Wilson Jr.
(1899–1989)

Harmon Foundation

John Louis Wilson Jr. was born on January 24, 1899, in Meridian, Mississippi, to a family that traced its lineage back to the American Revolutionary War. His maternal grandfather labored as a blacksmith and although born into slavery, sent his five children to college. His grandmother was one of the first public school music teachers in Mississippi. Wilson's father was a minister. His mother was a pianist and music teacher. Both were graduates of Rust College in Holly Springs, Mississippi.

Wilson's formal education began in elementary school in Meridian. In 1911, at age twelve, he entered Gilbert Academy in New Orleans and graduated in 1915. Next, Wilson attended New Orleans University (now Dillard University), where he received a bachelor of art degree in 1919. From 1920 to 1923, Wilson was employed as a mathematics instructor and football coach at Philander Smith College in Little Rock, Arkansas.

In 1924 Wilson moved to New York City and entered the School of Architecture at Columbia University. For a while financial difficulties forced him to temporarily withdraw from college and work full time. After securing a part-time position as a draftsman in the office of VERTNER WOODSON TANDY, where he worked from 1924 to 1926, Wilson returned to Columbia University and completed his studies and received his bachelor of architecture degree in 1928.

Wilson began his career as an architect in 1929 with the New York City Board of Transportation. He was registered as an architect in New York State on September 24, 1930, and in 1933 he left the Board of Transportation to set up his own office in Harlem.[1] Wilson maintained a private practice until 1980, when he retired at the age of eighty-one. He made his office at 209 West 125th Street into a center for aspiring architects of color—advising and encouraging students and young draftsman from Africa and South and Central America, as well as the United States. Over the span of his fifty-year career, Wilson worked in an urban setting. His designs were primarily for modest apartments, senior citizen housing, and public schools. His work includes the Mount Morris Park Senior Citizen's Housing Project in East Harlem, a federally funded housing program for the elderly completed in 1960; Throgs Neck Branch of the New York Public Library (1972) in the Bronx; an Early Childhood Center (1975) for the New York City Board of Education in Brooklyn; and several high-rise apartments in joint ventures with Ginsbern & Wilson. In the 1950s and 1960s, while still maintaining his private practice, Wilson served as consulting architect for the New York City Department of Parks and Recreation. He designed the Alice and Edward Kerbs Memorial Boathouse in Central Park at East 73rd Street.

Wilson is celebrated for his work on the highly acclaimed Harlem River Houses (1936), New York's first federally funded housing. Constructed during President Franklin Delano Roosevelt's New Deal, the project was a collaboration between the Public Works

Harlem River Houses, *Schomberg Center for Research in Black Culture*

Administration and the New York City Housing Authority. Wilson was the only African American on a team of six associate architects led by Archibald Manning Brown.

Harlem River Houses were built on the garden apartment model with three groups of 4- and 5-story red brick buildings, situated on nine acres, stretching from West 151st to 153rd Streets, between Macombs Place and the Harlem River. Extensive landscaping enhanced the plan, which incorporated a fountain in the center of a large plaza, a natural amphitheater, playgrounds, and outdoor sculpture. The 574 units featured modern kitchens, tile bathrooms, steam heat, and cross-ventilation. A sense of community was achieved by the inclusion of a nursery school and children's indoor recreational space, a health clinic, and several social rooms for adults. Ground-floor space for stores along Seventh Avenue was incorporated into the design. Harlem River Houses were granted landmark status in 1975 by the New York City Landmarks Preservation Commission. The designation report stated that the development "set a precedent for public housing across the country."[2]

Wilson was recognized as a leader in the struggle to eliminate racial barriers in the architectural profession and building trades. In 1953 he helped to organize the Council for the Advancement of the Negro in Architecture (CANA), an organization of architects, draftsmen, teachers, and students dedicated to combating discrimination. The Council led to the founding of the Equal Opportunities Committee of the American Institute of Architects in 1964. The committee, which Wilson chaired from 1967 to 1970, encouraged minority students to enter the architectural profession and raised funds for scholarships. In 1972 Wilson was elected to membership in the prestigious College of Fellows. The citation read in part:

> The truly unique nature of John Wilson's contribution to the practice of architecture is in the important changes that have resulted from it. Now, for the first time, the inner city black areas are the direct clients and participants in the architectural process and talented young people in those areas are entering the profession of architecture.... He is, and has been for many years, the central generating force in the Metropolitan region. The profession is indebted to him for this outstanding achievement.[3]

Other honors bestowed on Wilson include the Andrew J. Thomas Award, a tribute sponsored by the New York Coalition of Black Architects in 1972; an honorary doctor of humane letters from Dillard University conferred in 1986; and two exhibits of his work (1980 and 1990) mounted at Columbia University School of Architecture and Planning.

Wilson lived for many years in an apartment at 156 Riverside Drive in Manhattan and died at age ninety on October 31, 1989.

JOHN LOUIS WILSON JR.

Notes

1. New York State Department of Education, Office of the Professions, "John L. Wilson," issued 24 September 1930, No. 004109.
2. New York City Landmarks Commission, *Harlem River Houses Designation Report* (New York: New York Landmarks Commission, 1975), p. 5.
3. American Institute of Architects, New York Region, *Empire State Architect*, June 1972, p. 20.

Bibliography

Columbia University Graduate School of Architecture, Planning and Preservation. "John Louis Wilson, Columbia University's First African American Graduate of Architecture." Columbia University, 1990. Exhibit Inventory.

Schomburg Center for Research in Black Culture. "John L. Wilson Papers, 1928–1989." Manuscripts, Archives and Rare Books Division, New York City Public Library.

JOYCE MENDELSOHN,
ARCHITECTURAL HISTORIAN AND AUTHOR,
NEW YORK, NEW YORK

BUILDING LIST

Name	Address	City	State	Year	Comments
Apts.	Dumont St.	New York	NY	1972	Alterations
Apts.	193rd St. & Bailey Ave.	New York	NY		Assoc. architect
Apts.	17 E. 124th St.	New York	NY		
Apts.	147th & 7th Ave.	New York	NY		
Apts.	115 E. 122nd St.	New York	NY		
Apts.	120 E. 123rd St.	New York	NY		
Boys and Girls High School	1700 Fulton St.	New York	NY	1975	
East River Park Amphitheatre	East River Park	New York	NY		
Harlem River Houses	W. 151st St. & Macombs Pl.	New York	NY	1936	Assoc. architect
House		Tuckahoe	NY	1935	Restoration
Kerbs Memorial Boathouse	Central Park	New York	NY	1954	
Mt. Morris Park Senior Citizen's Housing	15 E. 124th St.	New York	NY	1960	
NYC Board of Education Early Childhood Center	3rd & Keap Sts.	New York	NY	1975	
Public School	22 E. 128th St.	New York	NY	1971	Modernization
Senior Citizen Housing	Dean & Pacific Sts.	New York	NY		
Propect Park Boathouse	Prospect Park	New York	NY		
St. Philips Episcopal Church	134th & 7th Ave.	New York	NY		Alterations
Throgs Neck Public Library	3025 Cross Bronx Expwy.	New York	NY	1972	

Howard Dilworth Woodson
(1876–1962)

Harris & Ewing, 1955

Howard D. Woodson enjoyed a distinguished career as an architectural engineer and civic leader in Washington, D.C., for over a half century. He was one of the first Negro professionals in the Office of Supervising Architect, U.S. Treasury starting in 1907, designed buildings independently and in partnership with ROSCOE INGERSOLL VAUGHN and GEORGE ALONZO FERGUSON, and worked tirelessly to improve conditions in his community of far northeast Washington, D.C. His numerous contributions were acknowledged in 1972 when Woodson Senior High School (the first high-rise high school in Washington, D.C.) was named after him.[1]

Woodson was born in Pittsburgh, Pennsylvania, on April 26, 1876, to Granville Sharp Woodson, who owned two barbershops, and Catherine Powell Woodson, a homemaker. Howard Woodson attended Central High School from 1892 to 1897, being one of the few African American students in an otherwise ethnically integrated school. There he "showed ability in mathematics and won respect of both students and faculty."[2] He graduated from Western College of Pennsylvania (now University of Pittsburgh) in 1899 with a bachelor of science degree in civil engineering.

After a graduation trip to the South and West, Woodson held a number of positions. He worked for the Pittsburgh Plate Glass Company in 1900 and was an assistant engineer for the Pittsburgh Coal Company and Orient Coal & Coke Company in Uniontown, Pennsylvania. In 1904 he was a draftsman for Cambria Steel Company in Johnstown, Pennsylvania. In 1905 he was a structural engineer for the American Bridge Company in Chicago, Illinois. Afterward he found employment in the office of architect Daniel Hudson Burnham (1846–1912) just as his firm began work on Union Station (1903) in Washington, D.C. Woodson's contribution to the design of the railroad station was the design of the roof. He earned $1,664 per year while working in Burnham's office.

Woodson moved to Washington, D.C., in 1907 and began working in the Office of Supervising Architect, U.S. Treasury, as a structural engineer. He remained with the office until 1943, as a design engineer for U.S. post offices and other federal buildings throughout the nation. He then served as a consultant to the office.

Woodson was in partnership with Roscoe I. Vaughn and George A. Ferguson from 1922 to 1950. Woodson, Vaughn & Company was formed in 1922. When Ferguson joined the partnership later that same year, it became Woodson, Vaughn & Ferguson. Woodson left the partnership in 1924 and rejoined it after World War II.

Woodson was the architectural engineer for a number of buildings in Washington, D.C., including Metropolitan Baptist Church, Prudential Bank Building, Vermont Avenue Baptist Church, and renovations to a building he knew well, Union Station. He was the architect of record for houses along 49th Place, NE, in the Deanwood community of Washington, D.C.[3]

Mesrobian-Mounsey House, *Caroline Hickman*

Woodson was active in District of Columbia civic groups for more than fifty years. After moving to the far northeast section of the District of Columbia in 1913, he helped to organize the Northeast Boundary Civic Association, the Far Northeast Council, and the Far Northeast Business and Professional Association. He was a leader in the civic efforts to build public schools, extend the combined water and sewer system, pave and light streets, build bridges, and create parks for the area. He successfully advocated for a bridge over the Anacostia River at East Capitol Street, NE, instead of Massachusetts Avenue, NE; and lobbied for flood control of the Watts Branch tributary of the Anacostia River. He led the petition drive to widen Benning Road, NE; and vociferously advocated for the Deane Avenue and Grant Street Project, a highway from Kenilworth Avenue east to the District of Columbia boundary line. Woodson was chairman of the Employment Committee, NATIONAL TECHNICAL ASSOCIATION D.C. chapter, which succeeded in getting the first African American appointed to the District of Columbia Alley Dwelling Authority. In 1929 he was a participant along with HILYARD ROBERT ROBINSON and ETHEL MADISON BAILEY FURMAN in the historic Hampton Institute Colored Builders' Conference.

Howard Woodson was married twice and had four sons and one stepson. His first wife, Paulina, died in 1924. His second wife, Audrey, was a housewife. She died in 1958. He was a Sunday school superintendent at Metropolitan African Methodist Episcopal Church in Washington, D.C., and later became a member of Sargent Memorial Presbyterian Church.

Howard Woodson died, after a brief illness, in Freedman's Hospital on March 2, 1962, and is buried in Lincoln Cemetery in Suitland, Maryland.[4]

Notes
1. Christopher Weeks, *AIA Guide to the Architecture of Washington, D.C.* (Baltimore: Johns Hopkins University Press, 1994), p. 292.
2. Howard Woodson is the great great-grandson of Thomas Woodson, whom Mamie Shumate Woodson in *The Sable Curtain* claims was the son of Thomas Jefferson by his slave Sally Hemmings.
3. J. V. Lee, "Deanwood Historic Study: The Role of Black Architects in the Development of Deanwood," Martin Luther King Jr. Public Library, Washington, D.C. August 1987, p. 7.
4. "Howard D. Woodson," *Evening Star,* 4 March 1962, p. B5.

Bibliography
D.C. District Court, Probate Division. "Last Will and Testament: Howard D. Woodson." 18 October 1960.
"Howard Architects at Hampton Conference," *Washington Tribune,* 22 February 1929, p. 2.

CAROLINE MESROBIAN HICKMAN,
ART AND ARCHITECTURAL HISTORIAN,
WASHINGTON, D.C.

BUILDING LIST

Name	Address	City	State	Year	Comments
Allen, Joseph R.	1501 Hamlin St., NE	Washington	DC	1912	
Brandon, Julia B.	1503 Hamlin St., NE	Washington	DC	1912	
Church of God	1206 3rd St., NW	Washington	DC	1926	
Federal Life Bldg.	715 Florida Ave., NW	Washington	DC	c1924	
House	503 49th St., NE	Washington	DC	1912	
House	506 49th St., NE	Washington	DC	1912	
House	4832 Deane Ave., NE	Washington	DC	1923	
House	4834 Deane Ave., NE	Washington	DC	1923	
Jones Memorial Methodist Episcopal Church	4270 Benning Rd., NE	Washington	DC	1923	
Jordan, Isaiah	806 46th St., NE	Washington	DC	1922	
Mounsey, Dr. Ethel N.	2915 University Terr., NW	Washington	DC	1949	
Peace Baptist Church	712 18th St., NE	Washington	DC	c1947	
Third Church of God	1204 3rd St., NW	Washington	DC	1926	
White, George H.	806 49th St., NE	Washington	DC	1922	

Edward Walter Owen Young
(1874–unknown)

Francis Jackson

Edward Young was a cousin of CALVIN THOMAS STOWE BRENT—Washington, D.C.'s, first African American architect—and his son, JOHN EDMONSON BRENT, who was also an architect. Capitalizing on this family connection, Edward W. O. Young was probably instructed in drafting by the elder Brent while he was still a teenager. No information has yet been found about the schools that Young may have attended. He may have been home schooled or attended one of the private academies that sprang up to teach the children of the city's old Black families who had enjoyed their freedom for decades and were financially well off.

Young's name and claim to being a draftsman first appears in print in *Boyd's District of Columbia Directory* in 1891.[1] Four years later, in the same directory, he claims to be an architect. For much of the 1890s the local economy was in the doldrums. The recession slowed building construction and softened the demand for architects. From 1895 to 1899, Young found alternative employment as a waiter, bellman, and valet, probably working for his cousins, the Wormleys, who owned Wormley House, a hotel that catered to wealthy Whites and congressmen. The century year, 1900, after Calvin Brent's death, Young once again advertised himself in *Boyd's City Directory* as an architect. For the next nine years, Young made a living as an architect, although the names of his clients and locations of buildings that he designed are not known except for two houses (1903) that he designed for John W. Becket, which were located in Georgetown at 2914 and 2916 O Street, NW. Being a collateral descendant of the Brent family—whose relatives Mary and Emily Edmondson in 1848 boldly attempted to sail away aboard the schooner *Pearl* seeking freedom, were captured, and became a cause *célèbre* to abolitionists—and a family who were founders of John Wesley African Methodist Episcopal Church in Washington, D.C., should have placed Edward Young in the position to be the architect of choice for Washington, D.C.'s, Black society. However, evidence of buildings he may have designed could not be found.

In January 1909, Young was doing well enough to consider joining the American Institute of Architects,

Edward Young lived with his widowed mother, Josephine Johnson Young; wife, Isabelle Stevens Young; and their children, Dorothy, Elizabeth, Edward Jr., and Isabelle, at 1013 18th Street, NW, on the corner of 18th and L Streets, NW—the family homestead since before the Civil War. He lived across 18th Street from the home office of Calvin Brent. His father, Edward Owen Young, a Civil War veteran who served on the steamer *Bibb*, was a livery driver for Baron von Jeroltz, the Prussian ambassador to the United States.[3] Edward's father died before Edward became an architect.

Beginning in 1919 and lasting six years, Edward Young held a plum federal patronage job—a good position, especially for a Negro—as a civil service messenger for the U.S. Department of Labor.

Edward Young's name did not appear in *Boyd's City Directory* after 1930, which suggests that he may have died before then or left Washington, D.C.

John Beckett Rowhouses, *Dreck Spurlock Wilson*

although he never did. By the decade year, however, he was listed in the U.S. Census as an "out-of-work architect."[2]

Notes

1. *Boyd's District of Columbia Directory,* "Edward Young" (Washington, D.C., 1891), and Pamela Scott, *Directory of District of Columbia Architects, 1822–1960* (Washington, D.C.: Self-published, 2001), p. 321.
2. U.S. Census 1910, "[Edward] Walter Young" (Washington, D.C.: Government Printing Service), 1910.
3. Edward Owen Young, "Diary" (handwritten). In the possession of Cousin Diana Tardd, Washington, D.C., 2 March 1873, n.p.

Bibliography

Paynter, John H. *Fugitives of the Pearl.* Washington, D.C.: The Associated Publishers, 1971.

DRECK SPURLOCK WILSON

BUILDING LIST

Name	Address	City	State	Year	Comments
Becket, John W.	2914 O St., NW	Washington	DC	1903	
Becket, John W.	2916 O St., NW	Washington	DC	1903	
Young, Edward W.O.	1013 18th St., NW	Washington	DC	c1916	Demolished

Golden Joseph Zenon Jr.
(1929–   )

Golden Zenon (first row, second from right) with Architectural Club, *University of Nebraska-Lincoln Libraries*

Golden Zenon was born on March 13, 1929, in Abbeville, Louisiana. His father barely scraped by as a sharecropper, subsistence farming on the outskirts of Abbeville. Golden Jr. walked five miles each way to get to the 1-room parish schoolhouse for Blacks. At the beginning of World War II, his two brothers went off to war. Needed back on the farm, Golden dropped out of elementary school. It took almost three years, but he finally talked his father into letting him go live with a well-off aunt in Houston, Texas. His aunt enrolled him at Jack Yates High School. While at Yates, Golden took mechanical drawing classes and liked them so much that he decided to try for college and earn a degree in something that would involve drafting. After three years, Golden graduated from high school with honors in 1949. Following graduation, Zenon entered Louisiana's SOUTHERN UNIVERSITY'S DEPARTMENT OF VOCATIONAL AND INDUSTRIAL EDUCATION. Disappointed in the course offerings because he was interested in studying architecture as a fine art rather than as an industrial art and encouraged by professor Dr. George Brooks, he transferred to the University of Nebraska at Lincoln. By 1951 Zenon was enrolled in the College of Architecture. With miniscule financial support from home, he was eligible for a minority academic scholarship from the State of Louisiana because the segregation laws of Louisiana prohibited the enrollment of Negroes in the state's flagship university and instead paid for Negroes who wanted to study architecture to attend an out-of-state university. Zenon augmented his scholarship by working as an assistant instructor in the College of Architecture and as a master planner for the Nebraska State Fair Grounds, which was an influential position in a state whose primary industry is agriculture. His matriculation at the University of Nebraska was filled with honors. He placed first out of thirty-eight entries for his design of a model house that was to be built by the Nebraska Home Builder's Association, placed first in the Indiana Limestone Association design contest, received faculty recognition as "Student of the Year," and received the Medal of Honor given to the graduating senior whose overall work exemplified "General Excellence in Architecture." Zenon completed the requirements for graduation in 1956, becoming the College of Architecture's first Black graduate.

After graduating from the University of Nebraska, Zenon returned to Leo Daly Company in Omaha as senior designer, where he had previously been employed as a summer intern. Occupying a lead designer position within a large, otherwise all-White firm was a significant accomplishment for an inexperienced architect, which attests to his talent as a designer.

Zenon's employment with Leo Daly Company must have been professionally rewarding because he remained with them for ten years, until 1966—a relatively long time within the profession.

For the next ten years, Zenon was director of design and senior partner with Dana Larson Roubal Associates, with offices in Omaha and Pierre, South Dakota. The firm specialized in institutional buildings. Zenon's tenure with Roubal Associates was unique because there were few African Americans in upper-management echelons of White-owned firms, and even fewer senior partners.

Zenon married Willie Mae Robinson, formerly from Abbeville. Together they had four children: Golden III, Gerald, Terry, and Wendy Ann.

Golden Zenon passed the thirty-six-hour national Council of Architecture Registration Board examination in 1962.[1] He was licensed to practice in Nebraska, Iowa, and Kansas.

The ease with which Golden Zenon maneuvered through the overwhelming White environs of the profession of architecture as practiced in the Midwest virtually ensured that he would seek membership in the American Institute of Architects, which he joined in 1965. He was elevated to fellow status in 1985, "based on his notable contributions to the advancement of the profession based on exemplary Design and Public Service."[2]

Zenon's favorite building type is schools. He designed over twenty, including elementary schools;

Father Flanagan Alternative High School, *Zenon-Beringer & Associates*

junior high schools; high schools; special-needs schools; vocational schools; and college science, music, nursing, and law buildings.

Public service minded, he served as secretary of the archdiocesan of the Omaha Board of Education, which was responsible for educating a student population of 48,000. He co-founded and in 1983 designed the Dominican Sisters High School (now Father Flanagan Alternative High School) and served as president of his *alma mater's* College of Architecture Alumni Association from 1982 to 1984.

Zenon was a founding partner of Zenon-Beringer & Associates in 1976, a rare, Black-White partnership headquartered in Omaha. The firm specializes in schools, public libraries, and medical facilities. Because of failing health, Golden Zenon retired from the firm in 2000.

Notes

1. State of Nebraska Board of Engineers and Architects, "Golden Zenon, Jr.," Certificate no. A558, issued 15 December 1962.
2. American Institute of Architects Fellowship Nomination Application, "Golden Zenon, Jr.," 1985. American Institute of Architects Archives, Washington, D.C.

DRECK SPURLOCK WILSON

BUILDING LIST

Name	Address	City	State	Year	Comments
Bergan-Mercy Hospital	800 Mercy Dr.	Council Bluffs	IA		
Boy's Town High School	25th & Franklin Sts.	Omaha	NE		
Boy's Town Visitor Center	13628 Flanagan Blvd.	Ohama	NE		
Brandeis Crossroads Shopping Center	7300 Dodge St.	Omaha	NE		
Bryan Senior High School	4700 Giles Rd.	Bellevue	NE	1969	
College of St. Mary's Science Bldg.	Campus	Omaha	NE		
Creighton University Mens Dormitory	Campus	Omaha	NE		
Creighton University Science Bldg.	Campus	Omaha	NE	1965	
Creighton University Swanson Library	Campus	Omaha	NE	1966	
Creighton University Womens Dormitory	Campus	Omaha	NE		
Dominican High School	28th St. & Larimore Ave.	Omaha	NE		Demolished
Edmonson Memorial Hospital	933 E. Pierce St.	Council Bluffs	IA		
Eppley Airfield Terminal	Abbott Dr.	Omaha	NE		
Dominican Sister High School	2606 Hamilton St.	Omaha	NE	1983	
Gilder Elementary School	3705 Chandler Rd.	Omaha	NE		
Hale Junior High School	6143 Whitmore St.	Omaha	NE		
Jefferson High School	2501 Broadway	Council Bluffs	IA	1984	
Johnson Medical Center	29th & Manderson Sts.	Omaha	NE		
Kellom Knoll Apts.	Hamilton & Cummings Sts.	Omaha	NE	1983	132 dwelling units
Marrs Junior High School	5619 S. 19th St.	Omaha	NE		
Lutheran Community Hospital	2700 W. Norfolk Ave.	Norfolk	VA		Now Faith Regional Health
North Branch Public Library	2808 Ames Ave.	Omaha	NE	1972	
Salem Manor Housing		Omaha	NE	1983	
St. Elizabeth Ann Catholic Church	5419 N. 114th St.	Omaha	NE	1984	
St. John's Hospital	2727 McClleand Blvd.	Joplin	MO	1963	
Strategic Air Command Composite Hospital	Offutt Air Base	Bellevue	NE	1962	
U.S. Post Office	909 N. Adams St.	Papillion	NE		
University of Nebraska College of Law	Campus	Lincoln	NE	1969	
University of Nebraska Performing Arts Bldg.	Campus	Lincoln	NE	1973	
West Point Public Library	330 N. Colfax	West Point	NE		

General Bibliography

Locating documentation on late nineteenth century and early twentieth century African American architects is a challenge. This bibliography, a research truss of materials and resources, provides a starting point. A close perusal of this rich tome of references to books, journals, and collections will increase the reader's understanding and knowledge of African American architects and their contributions to American architectural history.

General References

Abajian, James. *Blacks in Selected Newspapers, Censuses, and Other Sources: An Index to Names and Subjects.* Boston: G. K. Hall, 1977.

"African-American Architects Archive." Howard University, Moorland-Spingarn Research Center, Washington, D.C.

"African-American National Register Sites and Historical Markers in South Carolina." South Carolina Archives and History Center, Columbia, South Carolina. 2000.

Hilyer, Andrew. *A Directory of the Colored Mechanics, Business and Professional Men and Women of the District of Columbia.* D.C.: Union League, 1892, 1894, and 1901.

Schomberg Center for Research in Black Culture. *Kaiser Index to Black Resources, 1948–1986.* New York: Carlson Publishing Company, 1992.

Koyl, George S., ed. *American Architects Directory.* New York: R. R. Bowker Company, 1955, 1962, and 1970.

Logan, Rayford, T., and Michael R. Winston, eds. *Dictionary of American Negro Biography.* New York: W. W. Norton & Company, 1982.

Low, Augustus, ed. *Encyclopedia of Black America.* New York: McGraw Hill, 1981

Salzman, Jack, David L. Smith, and Cornel West, eds. *Encyclopedia of African American Culture and History.* New York: MacMillan Library Reference, 1996.

Spralding, Mary Mace, ed. *In Black and White, a Guide to Magazine Articles, Newspaper Articles and Books Concerning more than 15,000 Black Individuals and Groups.* vols. 1 and 2. Detroit: Gale Research Company, 1980.

Sternburg, George M. *Report of Committee on Building of Model Houses.* D.C.: President's Homes Commission, 1908.

Thornton, William. *International Dictionary of Architecture.* Detroit: St. James Press, 1993.

Books

Adams, Michael H., *Harlem Lost and Found, an Architectural and Social History, 1765–1915.* New York: Monacelli Press, 2002.

Alexander, Lois K., ed. *Dee Cee Directory: A Business, Professional and Social Directory of Negro Washington.* D.C.: n.p., 1948.

Baker Associates. *Baker Handbook of Negro Owned Businesses, Professional Persons, Churches and Organizations of the District of Columbia, 1947–1948.* D.C.: Metro Publishers, 1948.

Bauchum, Rosalind G., and James W. A. Bauchum. *The Black Architect.* Monticello, Illinois: Vance Bibliographies, 1982.

Bird, Betty, and Nancy Schwartz. *Thematic Study of African-American Architects, Builders and Developers in Washington, D.C.* D.C.: United Planning Organization and D.C. Historic Preservation Office, 1994.

Brawley, Benjamin G. *The Negro Genius: A New Appraisal of the Achievement of the American Negro in Literature and the Fine Arts.* New York: Biblo & Tannen, 1937.

Brown, T. Robins. *The Architecture of Bergen County, New Jersey: Colonial Period to the Twentieth Century.* New Brunswick, New Jersey: Rutgers University Press, 2000.

Brownell, Charles, Calder Loth, William Rasmussen, and Guy Wilson. *The Making of Virginia Architecture.* Richmond: Virginia Museum of Fine Arts, 1992.

Burrell, G. W., and D. E. Johnson. *Twenty-Five Years-[sic] History of the Grand Fountain of the United Order of True Reformers, 1881–1905.* Richmond: n.p., 1909.

Cederholm, Theresa. *Afro-American Artists.* Boston: Boston Public Library, 1979.

———. *Afro-American Artists: A Bio-Bibliography Directory.* Boston: Boston Public Library, 1973.

Craven, Wayne. *American Art: History and Culture.* New York: H. N. Abrams, 1994.

Dozier, Richard K. *Spaces and Places: A Photographic Exhibit Conveying the Contributions, Aspirations and Aesthetic Values of Afro-Americans As Reflected in Architecture.* {s1. sn}, 1982.

Fleming, James, and Christian Burckel. *An Illustrated Biographical Directory of Notable Living Persons of African Descent in the United States.* Yonkers, New York: Burckel & Associates, 1950.

———. *Who's Who in Colored America* Yonkers-on-Hudson, New York: Burckel & Associates, 1950.

Furer, Howard B. *Washington, A Chronological and Documentary History, 1790–1970.* Dobbs Ferry, New York: Oceana Publications, 1975.

Glasco, Lawrence. *A Legacy in Bricks and Mortar: African American Landmarks in Allegheny County.* Pittsburgh: Pittsburgh History and Landmarks Foundation, 1995.

Guzman, Jessie, ed. *Negro Yearbook—A Review of Events Affecting Negro Life, 1941–46.* Tuskegee, Ala.: Tuskegee Institute, 1947.

Hood, Walter. *Urban Diaries.* D.C.: Spacemaker Press, 1994.

Mather, Frank Lincoln, ed. *Who's Who of the Colored Race: A General Biographical Dictionary of Men and Women of*

GENERAL BIBLIOGRAPHY

African Descent (1915). Detroit: Gale Research Company, 1976.
McDaniel, George, and John Pearce. *Images of Brookland: The History and Architects of a Washington Suburb*. D.C.: George Washington University, 1982.
Mitchell, Melvin. L. *The Crisis of the African-American Architect*. San Jose: Writer's Club Press, 2001.
Newton, John E., and Ronald Lewis. *The Other Slaves: Mechanics, Artisans, and Craftsmen*. Boston: G. K. Hall, 1978.
Olson, Elizabeth. *Registration Indices of District of Columbia Architects 1925 to 1965*. Arlington, Virginia: n.p., 1998. Martin Luther King Jr. Library, Washington, D.C.
Richardson, Clement. *National Cyclopedia of the Colored Race*. Montgomery: National Publishing Company, 1928
Robinson, Harry, and Hazel Edwards. *The Long Walk: The Placemaking Legacy of Howard University*. D.C.: Howard University, 1996.
Robinson, Wilhelmenia. *Historical Negro Biographies*. New York: Publishers Company, 1967.
Russell, Dick. *Black Genius and the American Experience*. New York: Carroll & Graf, 1998.
Savage, Beth, ed. *African American Historic Places*. D.C.: Preservation Press, 1994.
Scott, Pamela. *A Directory of District of Columbia Architects, 1822–1960*. D.C.: n.p., 2001. Martin Luther King Jr. Library, Washington, D.C.
———. *Places of Worship in D.C.* D.C.: District of Columbia Historic Preservation Office, 2003.
Stern, Gail, and Bette Lawrence. *Philadelphia African-Americans: Color, Class and Style, 1840–1940*. Philadelphia: Balch Institute for Ethnic Studies, 1988.
Thompson, Dolphin G. *A Picture Guide to Black America in Washington, D.C.* D.C.: Brownson House, 1976.
Travis, Jack. *African American Architects in Current Practice*. New York: Princeton Architectural Press, 1991.
Wells, John E., and Robert E. Dalton. *The Virginia Architects, 1835–1955: A Biographical Dictionary*. Richmond: New South Architectural Press, 1997.
———. *The South Carolina Architects*. Richmond: New South Architectural Press, 1992.
Withey, Henry, and Elsie Withey. *Biographical Dictionary of American Architects Deceased*. Los Angeles: Hennessey & Ingalls, 1970.
Woods, Mary N. *From Craft to Profession: the Practice of Architecture in Nineteenth Century America*. Berkeley: University of California Press, 1999.
Works Progress Administration Writer's Program. "Negro Architects, Inventors and Engineers, 1936–38." Microfilm 6544, Reel 3. Schomberg Center for Research in Black Culture. New York, New York.

Newspapers, Magazines, and Journals
Adams, Hunter Havelin III. "Hidden Dimensions of Ancient Black Architecture." *Journal of American Civilization*, April 1982, p. 110–117.
Adams, Michael. "A Legacy of Shadows." *Progressive Architecture* (February 1991): 85–87.
Afro-American Historical and Cultural Museum. "Philadelphia's African-American Architects." Philadelphia: Afro-American Historical and Cultural Museum, 1995.
"Architecture Among Negroes in America." *Negro History Bulletin*, no. 7 (April 1940): 99.
"Architecture's Legacy Still Stands Tall." *The Courier Journal*, 26 December 1999, p. 1.
Barnes, William. "The Battle for Washington: Ideology, Racism and Self-Interest in the Controversy Over Public Housing." *Records of the Columbia Historical Society*, 1980, p. 452. Washington, D.C.
Bishir, Catherine W. "Black Builders in Antebellum North Carolina." *North Carolina Historical Review*, no. 61 (1984): 423.
Bond, Max. "Still Here: Three Architects of Afro-America: Julian Abele, Hilyard Robinson, and Paul R. Williams." *Harvard Design Magazine* (summer 1997): 46.
Calloway, Thomas J. "The American Negro Artisan." *Cassier's Magazine* (1901): 435.
Downing, Lewis K. "Contributions of Negro Scientists." *Crisis*, (June 1939): 167.
———. "The Negro in the Professions of Engineering and Architecture." *Journal of Negro Education*, vol. 4 (January 1935): 60–70.
Dozier, Richard K. "African-American Architects in the Art Deco Era." *New America News Service*, 16 July 1997.
———. "From Humble Beginnings to National Shrine: Tuskegee Institute." *Historic Preservation*, no. 1 (1981): 40.
———. "A Historical Survey of Black Architects and Craftsmen." *Black World* (May 1974): 4.
———. "The Black Architecture Experience in America." *AIA Journal* (July 1976): 162.
Drury, Felix. "Yale Events Sound Call for Change." *Architectural Record*, (January 1992): 18.
Hutchinson, Louise D. "Building on a Heritage." *American Visions*, no. 4 (August 1989): 11.
Kay, Jane Holtz. "Invisible Architects." *Architecture*, no. 80 (April 1991): 106.
Kliment, Stephen A. "Upbeat Mood Marks Minority Architects." *Architectural Record*, (December 1992): 13.
Majekodunmi, Olufemi. "Afro-centric Architecture: Myth and Reality." *Architectural Record* January 1994, p. 16.
Murphy, Anthony C. "Architects from the Diaspora." *American Visions*, no. 4 (August–September 1993): 11.
"Negro Architects of Today in Action." *Negro History Bulletin*, no. 7 (May 1940): 115.
"The Negro Nevertheless a Factor in Architecture." *Negro History Bulletin*, no. 7 (April 1940): 101.
Scott, Emmett. "The New South Again [Pittman, Rayfield and Taylor]." *The Colored American*, no. 6 (April 1901): 5.
Simmons-Hodo, Simmona E. "Silent Builders: A Selected Bibliography on African-American Architects." *Bulletin of Bibliography*, no. 3 (1993): 207.
"Successful Architect." *The Colored American Magazine*, no. 13 (December 1906): 424.
Taylor, Joseph. "Architecture with Respect to Africa." *Negro History Bulletin*, no. 7 (1940): 96.
Vlach, John Michael. "African Americans." *America's Architectural Roots*, 1986, p. 43.
Weiss, Ellen. *An Annotated Bibliography of African-American Architects and Builders*. Philadelphia: Society of Architectural Historians, 1993.

Unpublished Papers/Manuscripts/Dissertations
Alston, John C. "An Ecological Study of the Negro Population in the District of Columbia." Master's thesis, Howard University, 1940.

Dozier, Richard K. "Tuskegee: Booker T. Washington's Contribution to the Education of Black Architects." Ph.D. dissertation, University of Michigan, 1990.

Etheridge, Harrison M. "The Black Architects of Washington D.C., 1900–Present." Master's thesis, The Catholic University of America, 1979.

"Exhibition of Work of Negro Architects Presented by the Department of Architecture at Howard University Art Gallery." Howard University, 12 May–28 May 1931 (pamphlet). Moorland-Spingarn Research Center, Washington, D.C.

Harmon Foundation, Inc. "Biographical Files of Negro Artists." Manuscript Division, Library of Congress.

Henderson, Wesley Howard. "African-American Architects of Los Angeles: Oral History Transcripts." Brancroft Library Archive/Manuscript, University of California, 1992.

———. "Two Case Studies of African-American Architects' Careers in Los Angeles, 1890–1945: Paul Williams, FAIA and James H. Garrott, AIA." Ph.D. dissertation, University of California, 1992.

Larson, Judy L. "Creating Self-Portraits at Southern Expositions, Atlanta, Nashville, Charleston." Ph.D. dissertation, Emory University, 1998.

McLoud, Melissa. "Craftsmen and Entrepreneurs: Builders in Late Nineteenth Century Washington, D.C." Ph.D. dissertation, George Washington University, 1988.

Wilson, Dreck. S. "The Negro in Architecture." Master's thesis, University of Chicago, 1975.

SIMMONA E. SIMMONS-HODO,
BIBLIOGRAPHER AND
ASSOCIATE PROFESSOR OF LIBRARY SCIENCES,
UNIVERSITY OF MARYLAND AT COLLEGE PARK AND
UNIVERSITY OF MARYLAND AT BALTIMORE COUNTY

Appendix—Buildings Sorted by State

State	City/County	Name[1]	Year	A/AE/LA[2]
AK	Batesville	St. Paul's Parish Church	1924	Wallace Rayfield
AK	Helena	Centennial Missionary Baptist Church	1905	Henry Price
AK	Hot Springs	Knights of Pythias Bathhouse & Sanitarium	1923	Walter Bailey
AK	Hot Springs	Woodmen of Union Bathhouse	1924	Walter Bailey
AK	Little Rock	Bethel African Methodist Episcopal Church	1963	Robert Madison
AK	Little Rock	Mosaic State Temple Bldg.	1922	Walter Bailey
AK	Little Rock	Philander Smith College Campus Plan	1958	David Williston
AK	Malvern	Bethel African Methodist Episcopal Church	x	John Lankford
AL	Birmingham	Birmingham Art Club	1908	Wallace Rayfield
AL	Birmingham	Blount, R.A.	1914	Wallace Rayfield
AL	Birmingham	Brown, Dr. Arthur M.	1908	Wallace Rayfield
AL	Birmingham	Brown, R.T.	1928	Hilyard Robinson
AL	Birmingham	Coar, John M.	c1907	Wallace Rayfield
AL	Birmingham	Dobbins, A.G.	1926	Wallace Rayfield
AL	Birmingham	Dunbar Hotel	x	Wallace Rayfield
AL	Birmingham	Elk's Rest Home	1926	Robert Robinson Taylor
AL	Birmingham	French Cleaners	x	Wallace Rayfield
AL	Birmingham	Jackson, Bishop T.S.	1912	Wallace Rayfield
AL	Birmingham	Knights of Phythias Temple	1913	Wallace Rayfield
AL	Birmingham	Colored Masonic Temple	1924	Louis Persley
AL	Birmingham	Metropolitan African Methodist Episcopal Zion Church	x	Wallace Rayfield
AL	Birmingham	Parker, Arthur H.	1908	Wallace Rayfield
AL	Birmingham	Penny Savings Bank	1913	Wallace Rayfield
AL	Birmingham	Pharrow, Ed	1908	Wallace Rayfield
AL	Birmingham	Prince Hall Masonic Temple	1924	Robert Robinson Taylor
AL	Birmingham	Rayfield, Wallace A.	1908	Wallace Rayfield
AL	Birmingham	Seymour, R.W.	x	Wallace Rayfield
AL	Birmingham	Sixteenth Street Baptist Church	1909	Wallace Rayfield
AL	Birmingham	Sixth Avenue Baptist Church	1909	Wallace Rayfield
AL	Birmingham	South Elyton Baptist Church	x	Wallace Rayfield
AL	Birmingham	St. James Methodist Church	1960	De Witt Dykes
AL	Birmingham	Strawbridge, T.S.	x	Wallace Rayfield
AL	Birmingham	Strong Undertaking Co.	x	Wallace Rayfield
AL	Birmingham	Thirty Second Avenue Baptist Church	x	Wallace Rayfield
AL	Birmingham	Thomas Public School	x	Wallace Rayfield
AL	Birmingham	Trinity Baptist Church	c1920	Wallace Rayfield
AL	Birmingham	Tuggle Institute	x	Wallace Rayfield
AL	Birmingham	Walton's Cafe	x	Wallace Rayfield
AL	Birmingham	Wright's Chapel Methodist Church	1962	De Witt Dykes
AL	Columbus	Columbus Bridge	1865	Horace King
AL	Columbus	Columbus Bridge	1832	Horace King
AL	Columbus	Columbus Bridge	1841	Horace King
AL	Columbus	Factory Bridge	1867	Horace King
AL	Columbus	Factory Bridge	1858	Horace King
AL	Columbus	Factory Bridge	1862	Horace King
AL	Columbus	Mobile & Girard Railroad Bridge	x	Horace King
AL	Centre	Tiller's Chapel Methodist Church	1959	De Witt Dykes
AL	Chehaw	99th Pursuit Squadron Airfield	1941	David Williston
AL	Chehaw	99th Pursuit Squadron Training School	1941	Hilyard Robinson
AL	Crawford	Russell County Courthouse	1841	Horace King
AL	Decatur	U. S. Post Office	x	Samuel Plato

[1] Surname followed by first name represents single family house.
[2] Architect/Architectural Engineer/Landscape Architect

APPENDIX

State	City/County	Name	Year	A/AE/LA
AL	Eutaw	St. Paul Methodist Church	1960	De Witt Dykes
AL	Fairfield	Smith-Gaston "Hill Top"	x	Wallace Rayfield
AL	Girard	Russell County Bridge	1866	Horace King
AL	Huntsville	Alabama Agricultural & Mechanical College Palmer Hall	c1915	John Lankford
AL	Huntsville	Alabama Agricultural & Mechanical College Saw Mill	c1899	John Lankford
AL	Huntsville	Alabama Agricultural & Mechanical College Seay Hall	c1915	John Lankford
AL	Huntsville	Alabama Agricultural & Mechanical College Steam Plant	c1899	John Lankford
AL	Irwinton	Irwinton Bridge	1838	Horace King
AL	Macon County	Adams Elementary School	1966	Edward Pryce
AL	Macon County	Tuskegee High School	1968	Edward Pryce
AL	Macon County	Washington High School	1955	Edward Pryce
AL	Mobile	Alabama State College Classroom Bldg.	x	Louis Fry
AL	Montgomery	Alabama Agricultural Fair Negro Bldg.	1907	Walter Bailey
AL	Montgomery	Alabama Christian College	1980	Edward Pryce
AL	Montgomery	Alabama State College Arena-Auditorium	1954	Louis Fry
AL	Montgomery	Alabama State College Classroom Bldg.	1954	Louis Fry
AL	Montgomery	Alabama State College Dining Hall	x	John Welch
AL	Montgomery	Alabama State College Library	1962	John Welch
AL	Montgomery	Alabama State College Mens Dormitory	1960	Louis Fry
AL	Montgomery	Alabama State College Science Bldg.	1962	Louis Fry
AL	Montgomery	Alabama State College Swimming Pool Bldg.	1962	Louis Fry
AL	Montgomery	Alabama State College Womens Dormitory	x	Louis Fry
AL	Montgomery	Alabama State Courthouse	1850	Horace King
AL	Montgomery	Alabama State Teachers College Science Bldg.	1938	Donald White
AL	Montgomery	Colored State Normal School Library	1910	William Pittman
AL	Montgomery	Prairie View Agricultural & Mechanical College Gym	1929	Edward Miller
AL	Montgomery	St. Jude's Catholic Hospital	x	Ferdinand Rousseve
AL	Mt. Miegs	Mt. Miegs School for the Deaf	x	Donald White
AL	Opelika	Yonge, William P. C.	c1850	Horace King
AL	Opelika	Lee County Courthouse & Jail	1868	Horace King
AL	Sayreton	Mt. Pleasant Methodist Church	1964	De Witt Dykes
AL	Selma	Brown Chapel African Methodist Episcopal Church	1908	A.J. Farley
AL	Selma	Dinkins Memorial Chapel	1921	Louis Persley
AL	Selma	First Colored Baptist Church	1894	David West
AL	Selma	Selma University Dinkins Memorial Chapel	1921	Louis Persley
AL	Stevenson	St. Paul Methodist Church	1962	De Witt Dykes
AL	Talladega	First Congregational Church	x	Wallace Rayfield
AL	Tallassee	Tallassee Bridge	1839	Horace King
AL	Tuscaloosa	Tuscaloosa Bridge	1871	Horace King
AL	Tuscaloosa	Tuscaloosa Bridge	1834	Horace King
AL	Tuscaloosa	Warrior Manufacturing Co.	1845	Horace King
AL	Tuskegee	Greenwood Missionary Baptist Church	x	Edward Miller
AL	Tuskegee	Johnson, Dr. Frank	x	Robert Robinson Taylor
AL	Tuskegee	Johnson, Dr. Luther	x	Robert Robinson Taylor
AL	Tuskegee	Moton Air Field	c1941	?
AL	Tuskegee	Persley, Louis H.	1927	Louis Persley
AL	Tuskegee	Quarles, _____	1935	John Holloway
AL	Tuskegee	Reed, J.D.	1935	John Holloway
AL	Tuskegee	Tuskegee Institute Administration Bldg.	1902	Robert Robinson Taylor
AL	Tuskegee	Tuskegee Institute Andrews Hospital	1962	Louis Fry
AL	Tuskegee	Tuskegee Institute Andrews Hospital	1913	Robert Robinson Taylor
AL	Tuskegee	Tuskegee Institute Andrews Hospital	x	Edward Miller
AL	Tuskegee	Tuskegee Institute Andrews Hospital	1974	Edward Pryce
AL	Tuskegee	Tuskegee Institute Armstrong Science Bldg.	1932	Robert Robinson Taylor
AL	Tuskegee	Tuskegee Institute Boys Trade Bldgs.	1909	William Hazel
AL	Tuskegee	Tuskegee Institute Carnegie Library	1901	Robert Robinson Taylor
AL	Tuskegee	Tuskegee Institute Cassedy Hall	x	Robert Robinson Taylor
AL	Tuskegee	Tuskegee Institute Chapel	1960	Louis Fry
AL	Tuskegee	Tuskegee Institute Chapel	1896	Robert Robinson Taylor
AL	Tuskegee	Tuskegee Institute Davidson Hall	x	Robert Robinson Taylor
AL	Tuskegee	Tuskegee Institute Dorothy Hall	1901	Robert Robinson Taylor
AL	Tuskegee	Tuskegee Institute Douglass Dormitory	1904	Robert Robinson Taylor

APPENDIX

State	City/County	Name	Year	A/AE/LA
AL	Tuskegee	Tuskegee Institute Emery Dormitories	1897	Robert Robinson Taylor
AL	Tuskegee	Tuskegee Institute Food Processing Plant	1954	Louis Fry
AL	Tuskegee	Tuskegee Institute Harvey Hall	x	Edward Miller
AL	Tuskegee	Tuskegee Institute Hollis Burke Frissell Library	1932	Robert Robinson Taylor
AL	Tuskegee	Tuskegee Institute Huntington Memorial Bldg.	1907	William Pittman
AL	Tuskegee	Tuskegee Institute Huntington Memorial Bldg.	1902	Robert Robinson Taylor
AL	Tuskegee	Tuskegee Institute Infantile Paralysis Hospital	1940	Louis Fry
AL	Tuskegee	Tuskegee Institute James Hall	1921	Robert Robinson Taylor
AL	Tuskegee	Tuskegee Institute Landscape Plan	1900	David Williston
AL	Tuskegee	Tuskegee Institute Laundry Bldg.	1915	Robert Robinson Taylor
AL	Tuskegee	Tuskegee Institute Logan Hall	1931	Robert Robinson Taylor
AL	Tuskegee	Tuskegee Institute Mens Dormitory	1962	Louis Fry
AL	Tuskegee	Tuskegee Institute Millbank Bldg.	1909	Robert Robinson Taylor
AL	Tuskegee	Tuskegee Institute Moton Airfield Cadet Classroom	1942	Edward Miller
AL	Tuskegee	Tuskegee Institute Moton Airfield Entrance Gate	1943	Edward Miller
AL	Tuskegee	Tuskegee Institute Moton Airfield Hangar No. 1	1942	Edward Miller
AL	Tuskegee	Tuskegee Institute Moton Airfield Hangar No. 2	1942	Edward Miller
AL	Tuskegee	Tuskegee Institute Moton Airfield Warehouse	1943	Edward Miller
AL	Tuskegee	Tuskegee Institute Moton Hall	x	Louis Fry
AL	Tuskegee	Tuskegee Institute Nurses Home	1962	John Welch
AL	Tuskegee	Tuskegee Institute Rockefeller Hall	1903	Robert Robinson Taylor
AL	Tuskegee	Tuskegee Institute Rockfellar Hall	1907	Edward Miller
AL	Tuskegee	Tuskegee Institute Sage Hall	1926	Robert Robinson Taylor
AL	Tuskegee	Tuskegee Institute School of Nursing	1962	Louis Fry
AL	Tuskegee	Tuskegee Institute Science Hall	1893	Robert Robinson Taylor
AL	Tuskegee	Tuskegee Institute Student Housing	x	William Thornton
AL	Tuskegee	Tuskegee Institute Tantum Hall	1907	Robert Robinson Taylor
AL	Tuskegee	Tuskegee Institute Tompkins Dining Hall	1910	Robert Robinson Taylor
AL	Tuskegee	Tuskegee Institute Vocational Bldg.	x	Louis Fry
AL	Tuskegee	Tuskegee Institute White Dormitory	1909	Robert Robinson Taylor
AL	Tuskegee	Tuskegee Institute Womens Dormitory	1962	Louis Fry
AL	Tuskegee	Tuskegee University Andrews Hospital	1974	Wallace Rayfield
AL	Tuskegee	Tuskegee University Carver Bldg.	1951	Edward Pryce
AL	Tuskegee	Tuskegee University Carver Dormitory	1961	Edward Pryce
AL	Tuskegee	Tuskegee University Chapel	1969	Wallace Rayfield
AL	Tuskegee	Tuskegee University Kresge Ctr.	1982	Edward Pryce
AL	Tuskegee	Tuskegee University Drew Dormitory	1960	Edward Pryce
AL	Tuskegee	Tuskegee University James Ctr.	1982	Edward Pryce
AL	Tuskegee	Tuskegee University Landscape Plan	1972	Edward Pryce
AL	Tuskegee	Tuskegee University Moton Hall	1965	Edward Pryce
AL	Tuskegee	Tuskegee University Nuclear Engr. Bldg.	1966	Robert Madison
AL	Tuskegee	Tuskegee University Roberts Housing	1950	Edward Pryce
AL	Tuskegee	Tuskegee University School of Engineering	1965	Edward Pryce
AL	Tuskegee	Tuskegee University School of Nursing	1960	Edward Pryce
AL	Tuskegee	Tuskegee University School of Veterinary Medicine	1950	Edward Pryce
AL	Tuskegee	Tuskegee University Tantum Dormitory	1961	Edward Pryce
AL	Tuskegee	Tuskegee University Thrasher Dormitory	1962	Edward Pryce
AL	Tuskegee	Tuskegee University Tubman Dormitory	1960	Edward Pryce
AL	Tuskegee	Tuskegee University Woodruff Food Plant	1962	Edward Pryce
AL	Tuskegee	Tuskegee Veterans Hospital	1967	Edward Pryce
AL	Tuskegee	Veterans Administration Hospital	c1923	David Williston
AL	Tuskegee	Washington, Booker T. "The Oaks"	1898	Robert Robinson Taylor
AL	Tuskegee	Washington Chapel African Methodist Episcopal Church	1966	Robert Madison
AL	Village Springs	Hopewell Methodist Church	1963	De Witt Dykes
AL	Warrior	St. James Methodist Church	1967	De Witt Dykes
AL	Wetumpka	Wetumpka Bridge	1844	Horace King
AZ	Chandler	San Marcos Hotel Golf Clubhouse	x	Ralph Vaughn
AZ	Tucson	Pueblo Gardens Subdivision	1949	Paul Williams
CA	Alameda County	Clinton Mound Tract	x	Grafton Brown
CA	Alameda County	Map of Jones Tract	x	Grafton Brown
CA	Arrowhead Springs	Hamilton, Thomas "Hamiltair"	1936	Paul Williams
CA	Bel Air	Isaacs, Hart	1935	Paul Williams

475

APPENDIX

State	City/County	Name	Year	A/AE/LA
CA	Bel Air	Paley, William "Jay"	1934	Paul Williams
CA	Bel Air	Winberg, Charles	1938	Paul Williams
CA	Bel Air	Wineburg, C.	1938	Ralph Vaughn
CA	Berkeley	Map of the Leonard Tract	1875	Grafton Brown
CA	Beverly Hills	Beverly Hills Hotel Polo Lounge	1959	Paul Williams
CA	Beverly Hills	Chaney, Lon	1930	Paul Williams
CA	Beverly Hills	Chasen's Restaurant	1936	Paul Williams
CA	Beverly Hills	Cord, Everett L.	1931	Paul Williams
CA	Beverly Hills	Fine, Maurice T.	c1950	Roy Sealey
CA	Beverly Hills	Fulton, Robert J.	1938	Paul Williams
CA	Beverly Hills	Griffith, Corrine	1930	Paul Williams
CA	Beverly Hills	Howard, Opie	1936	Paul Williams
CA	Beverly Hills	Landis, John	1955	Paul Williams
CA	Beverly Hills	McMartin, Pauline S.	1933	Paul Williams
CA	Beverly Hills	Metzler, I.S.	1938	Ralph Vaughn
CA	Beverly Hills	Miles, William	1930	Paul Williams
CA	Beverly Hills	Music Corporation of America Bldg.	1938	Paul Williams
CA	Beverly Hills	Newmark, Robert	1927	Paul Williams
CA	Beverly Hills	Petitfils, Anna S.	1930	Paul Williams
CA	Beverly Hills	Saks Fifth Avenue	1936	Paul Williams
CA	Beverly Hills	Sanchon Beerup	1929	Paul Williams
CA	Beverly Hills	Schwab Drug Store	x	Ralph Vaughn
CA	Beverly Hills	Sensenbrenner, August	1933	Paul Williams
CA	Beverly Hills	Sinatra, Frank A.	1956	Paul Williams
CA	Beverly Hills	Sloane Department Store	1949	Paul Williams
CA	Beverly Hills	Stein, Ben	c1950	Roy Sealey
CA	Bodie	Map of the Bodie Mining District	1877	Grafton Brown
CA	Brentwood	Pitts, Zasu	1936	Paul Williams
CA	Brentwood	Power, Tyrone	1937	Paul Williams
CA	Buena Vista	Map of Buena Vista Homestead	1868	Grafton Brown
CA	Calistoga	Calistoga Hotel	1947	James Garrott
CA	Carson	Carson County Public Library	1969	James Garrott
CA	Carson	Victoria County Park Director's Bldg.	1960	James Garrott
CA	Central Valley	Community Valley Methodist Church	1959	De Witt Dykes
CA	Culver City	Hillside Memorial Mausoleum	1951	Paul Williams
CA	Culver City	Al Jolson Memorial	1954	Paul Williams
CA	East Los Angeles	Laguna Park Senior Citizen Bldg.	1967	James Garrott
CA	East Los Angeles	Terrace Park Pavilion & Pool	1962	James Garrott
CA	East Los Angeles	Belvedere Department of Social Services & Garage	1967	Roy Sealey
CA	Encino	Good Wife Restaurant	1958	Ralph Vaughn
CA	Encino	London, Julie P.	1958	Paul Williams
CA	Fullerton	Orange Lanes Bowling Alley	x	Ralph Vaughn
CA	Golden Grove	Golden Grove Church	1946	Howard Mackey
CA	Hawthorne	Bodger County Park Director's Bldg.	1960	James Garrott
CA	Hawthorne	Del Aire County Park Director's Bldg.	1960	James Garrott
CA	Hawthorne	Cockatoo Hotel Restaurant & Garage	1968	Roy Sealey
CA	Hermosa	Matteson, Ralph E.	1921	Paul Williams
CA	Hollywood	Biff's Coffee Shop	x	Ralph Vaughn
CA	Hollywood	Cherry Cove Night Club	x	Ralph Vaughn
CA	Hollywood	Hollywood YMCA	1927	Paul Williams
CA	Hollywood	Holden, Robert	1939	Paul Williams
CA	Hollywood	Margolis, Ben	1961	James Garrott
CA	Hollywood	Nikki's Dress Shop	1961	Ralph Vaughn
CA	Hollywood	Park Wilshire Hotel Mardi Gras Room	x	Ralph Vaughn
CA	Hollywood	Smith, Darr	1941	Ralph Vaughn
CA	Hollywood	Schwab Drug Store	1961	Ralph Vaughn
CA	Holmby Hills	Correll, Charles	1937	Paul Williams
CA	Holmby Hills	Gibbey-Simon	1939	Paul Williams
CA	Holmby Hills	Shuwarger, __	1936	Paul Williams
CA	Holmby Hills	Smith, Colin H.	1935	Paul Williams
CA	Huntington	Fox West Coast Theatre	x	Paul Williams
CA	Inglewood	King's "X" Restaurant & Bar	1961	Ralph Vaughn

APPENDIX

State	City/County	Name	Year	A/AE/LA
CA	Inyo County	Cerro Gordo Ranch	1874	Grafton Brown
CA	Lake Tahoe	Lake Tahoe	x	Grafton Brown
CA	Long Beach	U. S. Navy Roosevelt Fleet Base	1947	Paul Williams
CA	Long Beach	Edgewater Hyatt House Hotel	1966	Roy Sealey
CA	Los Alamitos	U. S. Naval Reserve Air Base	1947	Paul Williams
CA	Los Angeles	Apartment Bldg.	1927	James Garrott
CA	Los Angeles	Apartment Bldg.	1947	James Garrott
CA	Los Angeles	Florence-Firestone Health Clinic	1952	James Garrott
CA	Los Angeles	Florence-Firestone Sheriff's Station	1952	James Garrott
CA	Los Angeles	Garrott Office Bldg.	1951	James Garrott
CA	Los Angeles	Garrott, James H.	1951	James Garrott
CA	Los Angeles	Golden State Mutual Insurance Company	1928	James Garrott
CA	Los Angeles	Hamilton Methodist Church	1950	James Garrott
CA	Los Angeles	Lawndale Administrative Center Health Clinic	1957	James Garrott
CA	Los Angeles	Lawndale Administrative Center Library	1957	James Garrott
CA	Los Angeles	Tufeld, Richard	1959	James Garrott
CA	Los Angeles	Westchester Municipal Bldg.	1960	James Garrott
CA	Los Angeles	Apartment Bldg.	c1950	Roy Sealey
CA	Los Angeles	Bank of America—Vermont/Slauson Branch	1971	Roy Sealey
CA	Los Angeles	LA County/USC Medical Employee's Cafeteria & Kitchen	1975	Roy Sealey
CA	Los Angeles	LA County/USC Medical Admitting & Minor Trauma	1972	Roy Sealey
CA	Los Angeles	LA County/USC Medical North Parking Garage	1971	Roy Sealey
CA	Los Angeles	LA County/USC Medical Diagnostic & Evaluation	1974	Roy Sealey
CA	Los Angeles	LA County/USC Medical Pre-Mature Nurseries	1975	Roy Sealey
CA	Los Angeles	Metro-North Department of Social Services & Garage	1970	Roy Sealey
CA	Los Angeles	Rosenthal, J.	c1950	Roy Sealey
CA	Los Angeles	32nd Street Elementary School	1975	Roy Sealey
CA	Los Angeles	28th Street Colored YMCA	1926	Paul Williams
CA	Los Angeles	Anderson, Eddie "Rochester"	1937	Paul Williams
CA	Los Angeles	Angelus Funeral Home	1934	Paul Williams
CA	Los Angeles	Blodgett, Louis M.	1953	Paul Williams
CA	Los Angeles	Blodgett, Louis M.	1922	Paul Williams
CA	Los Angeles	Collins, William	1932	Paul Williams
CA	Los Angeles	Decotah Elementary School	1925	Paul Williams
CA	Los Angeles	Founders Church of Religious Science	1960	Paul Williams
CA	Los Angeles	Golden State Elks Lodge	1930	Paul Williams
CA	Los Angeles	Golden State Mutual Insurance Co.	1949	Paul Williams
CA	Los Angeles	Hostetter Elementary School	1924	Paul Williams
CA	Los Angeles	Hudson-Ledell Medical Office Bldg.	1928	Paul Williams
CA	Los Angeles	Imperial-Compton Hotel	1954	Paul Williams
CA	Los Angeles	Los Angeles County Courthouse	1958	Paul Williams
CA	Los Angeles	Los Angeles County Psychiatric Hospital	1947	Paul Williams
CA	Los Angeles	Los Angeles International Airport Theme Bldg.	1964	Paul Williams
CA	Los Angeles	Macedonia Baptist Church	1952	Paul Williams
CA	Los Angeles	Marina Del Ray Junior High School	1960	Paul Williams
CA	Los Angeles	New Hope Baptist Church	1954	Paul Williams
CA	Los Angeles	Peachy, Katherine	1929	Paul Williams
CA	Los Angeles	Perino's Restaurant	1949	Paul Williams
CA	Los Angeles	Prominger, Otto "Rock House"	c1949	Paul Williams
CA	Los Angeles	Pueblo Del Rio Public Housing	1941	Paul Williams
CA	Los Angeles	Ridgeway, Edwin	1966	Paul Williams
CA	Los Angeles	Robinson, Bill "Bojangles"	1937	Paul Williams
CA	Los Angeles	Second Baptist Church	1924	Paul Williams
CA	Los Angeles	St. Nicholas Orthodox Church	1948	Paul Williams
CA	Los Angeles	Taylor, Van	1921	Paul Williams
CA	Los Angeles	Trinity Baptist Church	1965	Paul Williams
CA	Los Angeles	United Pacific Insurance Co.	x	Paul Williams
CA	Los Angeles	Williams, Paul R.	1951	Paul Williams
CA	Los Angeles	Wilson High School	1969	Paul Williams
CA	Los Angeles	Apartment Bldg.	x	Lester Bankhead
CA	Los Angeles	New Jerusalem Missionary Baptist Church	x	Lester Bankhead
CA	Los Angeles	Congregation Beth Am	1959	Ralph Vaughn

APPENDIX

State	City/County	Name	Year	A/AE/LA
CA	Los Angeles	Congregation Mogen David	1959	Ralph Vaughn
CA	Los Angeles	Cosmopolitan Hotel	x	Ralph Vaughn
CA	Los Angeles	Drake Hotel	x	Ralph Vaughn
CA	Los Angeles	Hi-Hat Club & Bar	x	Ralph Vaughn
CA	Los Angeles	Melody Cocktail Bar	x	Ralph Vaughn
CA	Los Angeles	Oyster House Restaurant	1956	Ralph Vaughn
CA	Los Angeles	Park Wilshire Hotel	x	Ralph Vaughn
CA	Los Angeles	Vaughn, Ralph I.	1952	Ralph Vaughn
CA	Los Angeles	Watkins Hotel	x	Ralph Vaughn
CA	Los Angeles	Wilcox Hotel	x	Ralph Vaughn
CA	Los Angeles	Apartment Bldg.	x	Ralph Vaughn
CA	Los Angeles	Sherman Shopping Ctr.	1962	Ralph Vaughn
CA	Los Angeles	Dunbar Hotel	1966	Ralph Vaughn
CA	Los Angeles	Independence Square	1966	Ralph Vaughn
CA	Los Angelses	Nickerson Gardens Public Housing	1953	Paul Williams
CA	Los Angles	First African Methodist Episcopal Church	1963	Paul Williams
CA	Malibu	Malibu Inn	x	Ralph Vaughn
CA	North Hollywood	North Hollywood Manor Apts.	1949	Ralph Vaughn
CA	Oakland	Important Auction on 100 Lots in Oakland	1875	Grafton Brown
CA	Oakland	Iron Clad Mine	c1875	Grafton Brown
CA	Oakland	Map of Highland Park	1878	Grafton Brown
CA	Oakland	Map of Oakland	c1875	Grafton Brown
CA	Oakland	Map of the Central Land Company	x	Grafton Brown
CA	Ontario	U. S. Post Office	1925	Paul Williams
CA	Ontario	Veterans Administration Housing	x	Ralph Vaughn
CA	Pacific Palisaides	Will Rogers Park Community House	1948	Paul Williams
CA	Palm Springs	El Mirador Hotel	1928	Paul Williams
CA	Palm Springs	Palm Springs Tennis Club	1947	Paul Williams
CA	Pasadena	Atkin, Jack P.	1929	Paul Williams
CA	Pasadena	Cass, Louis	1922	Paul Williams
CA	Pasadena	Edward, Dr. Joseph T.	1928	Paul Williams
CA	Pasadena	First African Methodist Episcopal Church	1925	Paul Williams
CA	Pasadena	Flint, Katherine	1929	Paul Williams
CA	Pasadena	Jones, Clarence A.	1930	James Garrott
CA	Pasadena	King, Stuart	1930	Paul Williams
CA	Pasadena	Pierce, Dr. V. Mott	1928	Paul Williams
CA	Pasadena	Sheppard, John J.	1926	Paul Williams
CA	Placerville	Comstock Lode Map	1860	Grafton Brown
CA	Redwood City	Map of the Town of Redwood City	x	Grafton Brown
CA	Rialto	Fon-Ri Bowling Alley	x	Ralph Vaughn
CA	San Bernardino	Arrowhead Springs Hotel	1939	Paul Williams
CA	San Diego	Map of Horton's Addition	c1868	Grafton Brown
CA	San Diego	U. S. Navy Foundation Exploration Destroyer Base	1947	Paul Williams
CA	San Diego	View of San Diego	c1857	Grafton Brown
CA	San Francisco	Cuerin, Dr. Leon G.	1939	Paul Williams
CA	San Francisco	Firk's View	1868	Grafton Brown
CA	San Francisco	San Francico View	1869	Grafton Brown
CA	San Francisco	San Francisco Looking South from North Point	1877	Grafton Brown
CA	San Francisco	Sunny Vale Homestead	x	Grafton Brown
CA	San Mateo	Illustrated History of San Mateo County	1878	Grafton Brown
CA	San Mateo	Lake Ranch	1878	Grafton Brown
CA	San Mateo	Ocean View Ranch	1878	Grafton Brown
CA	San Mateo	Ranch and Dairy of V. Guerrero	1878	Grafton Brown
CA	San Mateo	San Felix Station	1878	Grafton Brown
CA	Santa Ana	Holiday Lanes Bowling Alley	x	Ralph Vaughn
CA	Santa Ana	Second Baptist Church	1966	Ralph Vaughn
CA	Santa Clara	Menuhin, Moshe	1935	Paul Williams
CA	Santa Monica	Tex's Sporting Goods Store	1939	Paul Williams
CA	Santa Monica	Tucker, Dr. M.O.	1937	Paul Williams
CA	Santa Rosa	View of Santa Rosa	1855	Grafton Brown
CA	Santa Ynez	Santa Ynez Inn	1941	Ralph Vaughn
CA	Sausalito	Map of the Sausalito Land & Ferry Company	x	Grafton Brown

APPENDIX

State	City/County	Name	Year	A/AE/LA
CA	Simpson's Station	Late Collison Between the Trains	1869	Grafton Brown
CA	Southgate	Single-family Houses	1937	Ralph Vaughn
CA	Stockton	Stockton Fire Department	x	Grafton Brown
CA	Sunland	Mt. Gleason Junior High School	1970	Roy Sealey
CA	Van Nuys	Chase Knolls Apts.	x	Ralph Vaughn
CA	Venice	Lincoln Place Apts.	1949	Ralph Vaughn
CA	West Hollywood	Sunset Plaza Apts.	1938	Paul Williams
CA	Westwood	UCLA Botany Bldg.	1956	Paul Williams
CA	Westwood	UCLA Chi Omega Sorority House	1929	Paul Williams
CA	Westwood	UCLA Franz Hall	1958	Paul Williams
CA	Westwood	UCLA Kappa Sigma Fraternity House	1926	Paul Williams
CA	Westwood	Westwood Medical Bldg.	1963	Paul Williams
CA	Westwood	West Los Angeles Synagogue	1960	Ralph Vaughn
CA	Westwood Hills	Moss, Chester M.	1955	James Garrott
CA	Yolo County	Map of Yolo County	1870	Grafton Brown
CO	Dinosaur	Dinosaur National Monument Trader Center	x	Francis Rassieur Roberson
CT	Danbury	Marian Anderson Studio	c1942	Orpheus Fischer
CT	Danbury	Anderson, Marian "Mariana"	1953	Orpheus Fischer
CT	Danbury	New Hope Baptist Church	1977	Orpheus Fischer
CT	Stamford	Bethel African Methodist Episcopal Church	1964	Robert Madison
CT	Stamford	Reynolds, Libby H. "Treetops"	1947	William Coleman
DC	Washington	Gas Station	x	John Melby
DC	Washington	Nite-Club	x	John Melby
DC	Washington	Shop	1908	William Pittman
DC	Washington	Apartment Bldg.	1939	Cyril Bow
DC	Washington	Baptist Church	1954	Romulus Archer
DC	Washington	Baptist Church	1926	Romulus Archer
DC	Washington	House	x	J. Alonzo Plater
DC	Washington	House	1912	Howard Woodson
DC	Washington	House	1923	Howard Woodson
DC	Washington	House	1908	William Cooke
DC	Washington	House	c1960	Lewis Giles Jr.
DC	Washington	House	c1950	Lewis Giles Sr.
DC	Washington	House	c1924	Lewis Giles Sr.
DC	Washington	House	1936	Lewis Giles Sr.
DC	Washington	House	1923	Lewis Giles Sr.
DC	Washington	House	1945	Lewis Giles Sr.
DC	Washington	House	1956	Robert Madison
DC	Washington	House	c1950	Robert Madison
DC	Washington	House	1928	Horace Turner
DC	Washington	House	1927	Horace Turner
DC	Washington	Apartment Bldg.	1921	John Lankford
DC	Washington	10th Street Baptist Church	1975	John Sulton
DC	Washington	12th Street Colored YMCA	1908	William Pittman
DC	Washington	13th & M Streets Office Bldg.	1981	John Sulton
DC	Washington	15th Street Presbyterian Church	1967	John Sulton
DC	Washington	Ackiss, Dr. Smallwood	1947	David Byrd
DC	Washington	Adams, Dr. Charles	1939	Howard Mackey
DC	Washington	Addison, Willie	1929	James Turner
DC	Washington	Aiken, Ernest	1950	Howard Mackey
DC	Washington	Alabama Court Apts.	1936	Lewis Giles Sr.
DC	Washington	Alexander, John A.	1937	Howard Mackey
DC	Washington	Allen, Joseph R.	1912	Howard Woodson
DC	Washington	Alpha Phi Alpha Fraternity Hqtrs.	1950	David Williston
DC	Washington	Ambler, George M.	1914	Roscoe Vaughn
DC	Washington	Anchor Apts.	1934	Romulus Archer
DC	Washington	Antioch Baptist Church	1913	Isaiah Hatton
DC	Washington	Antioch Baptist Church	1929	John Melby
DC	Washington	Aquilar Cigar Factory	1907	John Lankford
DC	Washington	Archer, Romulus C.	x	Romulus Archer
DC	Washington	Asbury Methodist Church	1950	Romulus Archer
DC	Washington	Asbury United Methodist Church	1978	Leroy Brown

APPENDIX

State	City/County	Name	Year	A/AE/LA
DC	Washington	Atkins, Louise	1937	Hilyard Robinson
DC	Washington	Augusta, Dr. A.T.	1886	Calvin Brent
DC	Washington	Baker, Raymond T. "Marly"	1931	Julian Abele
DC	Washington	Band, Louis M.	1955	Howard Mackey
DC	Washington	Bannister, C.C.	1924	George Ferguson
DC	Washington	Baptist Seminary	x	John Lankford
DC	Washington	Barker Electrical Appliance Store	1945	Roscoe Vaughn
DC	Washington	Barry Farm Public Housing	1983	John Sulton
DC	Washington	Beason, J.T.	1897	Calvin Brent
DC	Washington	Becket, John W.	1903	Edward Young
DC	Washington	Becket, L.M.	1893	Calvin Brent
DC	Washington	Beckley, M.D.	1892	Calvin Brent
DC	Washington	Bennett, Helen Z.	1935	Lewis Giles Sr.
DC	Washington	Bernheimer, L.	1942	Lewis Giles Sr.
DC	Washington	Beta Mu Lambda Clubhouse	1928	Julius Gardner
DC	Washington	Beth-Eden Church	x	John Holloway
DC	Washington	Bethlehem Baptist Church	1954	Clyde Drayton
DC	Washington	Beulah Baptist Church	1967	Lewis Giles Jr.
DC	Washington	Bibleway Temple	1975	Robert Madison
DC	Washington	Bill's Friendly Inn	x	Stewart Hoban
DC	Washington	Birdville African Methodist Episcopal Zion Church	x	John Lankford
DC	Washington	Birney Elementary School	1969	Albert Cassell
DC	Washington	Bivins, L.M.	1954	Clyde Drayton
DC	Washington	Booker, Nelson	1890	Calvin Brent
DC	Washington	Bower, Mattie	x	John Lankford
DC	Washington	Brandon, Julia B.	1912	Howard Woodson
DC	Washington	Branson, Stephen	1893	Calvin Brent
DC	Washington	Brent, Calvin T.S.	1893	Calvin Brent
DC	Washington	Brent, Calvin T.S.	1892	Calvin Brent
DC	Washington	Brent, John E.	1892	Calvin Brent
DC	Washington	Brent, John E.	1889	Calvin Brent
DC	Washington	Brookland Union Baptist Church	1963	Roscoe Vaughn
DC	Washington	Brooks, E.	c1960	Lewis Giles Jr.
DC	Washington	Brooks, J.R.	1957	Romulus Archer
DC	Washington	Brown Memorial African Methodist Episcopal Church Annex	1986	John Sulton
DC	Washington	Brown, Grace A.	1934	Lewis Giles Sr.
DC	Washington	Brown, Laurelia	1891	Calvin Brent
DC	Washington	Brown, R.W.	1909	William Pittman
DC	Washington	Brown, Sterling	1934	Lewis Giles Sr.
DC	Washington	Brown, W. T.	1950	Clyde Drayton
DC	Washington	Brummel Manor	1979	John Sulton
DC	Washington	Bryan, Julius D.	1949	Clyde Drayton
DC	Washington	Bunche, Dr. Ralph J.	1941	Hilyard Robinson
DC	Washington	Bunche, Dr. Ralph J.	1941	David Williston
DC	Washington	Burton Store & Apts.	1948	John Holloway
DC	Washington	Butcher Apts.	1950	John Holloway
DC	Washington	Butler Brothers Garage	1922	John Lankford
DC	Washington	Butler, _____	x	Albert Cassell
DC	Washington	Byrd, David R.	1946	David Byrd
DC	Washington	Calvary Baptist Church	1916	Isaiah Hatton
DC	Washington	Campbell African Methodist Episcopal Church	1917	Albert Cassell
DC	Washington	Campbell Heights Elderly Housing	1979	John Sulton
DC	Washington	Canaanland Apts.	1976	John Sulton
DC	Washington	Capitol View Baptist Church	1947	Romulus Archer
DC	Washington	Capitol View Public Housing	1972	John Sulton
DC	Washington	Capitol View Realty Co. Houses	1926	John Melby
DC	Washington	Arthur Capper Public Dwellings	1941	Hilyard Robinson
DC	Washington	Cardozo, Dr. _____	x	Howard Mackey
DC	Washington	Carolina Missionary Baptist Church	1990	John Sulton
DC	Washington	Carver Public Housing	1952	Hilyard Robinson
DC	Washington	Catholic University of America Landscape Plan	1940	David Williston
DC	Washington	Caton Apts.	1939	Lewis Giles Sr.

APPENDIX

State	City/County	Name	Year	A/AE/LA
DC	Washington	Central Methodist Episcopal Church	c1910	John Lankford
DC	Washington	Central Union Baptist Church	1935	Alonzo Plater
DC	Washington	Chamberlain Vocational High School	1966	Leroy Brown
DC	Washington	Chandler, George M.	1955	Romulus Archer
DC	Washington	Church of God	1926	Howard Woodson
DC	Washington	Church of God	1948	Romulus Archer
DC	Washington	Church of God	1932	Lewis Giles Sr.
DC	Washington	Church of the Redeemer, Presbyterian	1960	Robert Madison
DC	Washington	Church for David Smith	1944	Lewis Giles Sr.
DC	Washington	Clandny Apts.	1944	Lewis Giles Sr.
DC	Washington	Clark, Michael	1890	Calvin Brent
DC	Washington	Clarke, Thomas H.	1892	Calvin Brent
DC	Washington	Clewman, Nelson	1935	Roscoe Vaughn
DC	Washington	Cohen, Samuel L.	1938	Lewis Giles Sr.
DC	Washington	Cohen, Samuel L.	1927	Lewis Giles Sr.
DC	Washington	Colbert, Robert R.	1881	Calvin Brent
DC	Washington	Cole, Laura P.	1956	Roscoe Vaughn
DC	Washington	Coleman, Dr. Frank	1940	Howard Mackey
DC	Washington	Coleman, Dr. J.	1918	John Lankford
DC	Washington	Collins, Dr. William K.	x	Lewis Giles Jr.
DC	Washington	Collins, Lawrence	1939	Thomas Boyde
DC	Washington	Congress Heights Recreation Ctr.	1991	John Sulton
DC	Washington	Congress Park Homes	1982	John Sulton
DC	Washington	Conter African Methodist Episcopal Church	1963	Lewis Giles Sr.
DC	Washington	Corinthian Baptist Church	x	Albert Cassell
DC	Washington	Cornell, Harry W.	1938	J. Alonzo Plater
DC	Washington	Cosmopolitan Temple Baptist Church	c1928	John Lankford
DC	Washington	Crockett, Edward	x	Albert Cassell
DC	Washington	Curtis, J.S.	1935	Romulus Archer
DC	Washington	Dandridge, W.B.	1911	Isaiah Hatton
DC	Washington	Davis Apts.	1933	Lewis Giles Sr.
DC	Washington	Davis, Dr. Stephen	1962	Louis Fry
DC	Washington	Davis, Elizabeth	1891	Calvin Brent
DC	Washington	Deal Funeral Parlor	1938	Howard Mackey
DC	Washington	Deanwood Professional Arts Bldg.	1955	Lewis Giles Jr.
DC	Washington	Delaware Avenue Baptist Church	1950	Robert Fields
DC	Washington	Dillard Apts.	c1925	Romulus Archer
DC	Washington	Dixon, J.A.	1927	Lewis Giles Sr.
DC	Washington	Dodd, Randolph	1928	Lewis Giles Sr.
DC	Washington	Douglas, Walter	1929	James Turner
DC	Washington	Douglass Memorial Estates	1955	Archie Alexander
DC	Washington	Douglass, Frederick "Cedar Hill"	1922	William Hazel
DC	Washington	Dunbar Theatre	1920	Isaiah Hatton
DC	Washington	Duvall, Malcolm	1927	Lewis Giles Sr.
DC	Washington	East Capitol Church of Christ	1968	Lewis Giles Jr.
DC	Washington	Eastland Gardens Apts.	1949	John Holloway
DC	Washington	Ebenezer Methodist Episcopal Church	1891	Calvin Brent
DC	Washington	Edmondson, Gladys	1939	Lewis Giles Sr.
DC	Washington	Eisinger, Jane	x	Lewis Giles Sr.
DC	Washington	Elks Lodge Hall	1968	Stewart Hoban
DC	Washington	Ellis, Lacy B.	1926	Lewis Giles Sr.
DC	Washington	Ephesus 7th Day Adventist Church	1956	Romulus Archer
DC	Washington	Executive Motel	1957	Romulus Archer
DC	Washington	Fairview Apts.	1936	Lewis Giles Sr.
DC	Washington	Federal Life Bldg.	c1924	George Ferguson
DC	Washington	Ferguson, _____	x	John Lankford
DC	Washington	Fides Settlement House	x	Clyde Drayton
DC	Washington	Files, Herbert	1944	Clyde Drayton
DC	Washington	Fire Engine Company No. 6	1977	Leroy Brown
DC	Washington	First Baptist Church	1924	Romulus Archer
DC	Washington	First Baptist Church	1929	Roscoe Vaughn
DC	Washington	First Baptist Church of Georgetown	x	Howard Mackey

APPENDIX

State	City/County	Name	Year	A/AE/LA
DC	Washington	First Church of Christ	1954	John Holloway
DC	Washington	First Church of Christ, Holiness	1958	Lewis Giles Sr.
DC	Washington	First Colored Baptist Church	1930	John Lankford
DC	Washington	First Rising Baptist Church	1987	John Sulton
DC	Washington	First Rising Education Bldg.	1978	John Sulton
DC	Washington	First Rising Mt. Zion Baptist Church Adult Ctr.	1978	John Sulton
DC	Washington	First Rising Mt. Zion Baptist Church Education Bldg.	1978	John Sulton
DC	Washington	Fisher, Robert E.	1949	Howard Mackey
DC	Washington	Ft. Lincoln Elementary School	1967	Louis Fry
DC	Washington	Fourth Baptist Church	1882	Calvin Brent
DC	Washington	Fowler, Dr. _____	1943	Hilyard Robinson
DC	Washington	Francis Scott Key Bridge	x	Archie Alexander
DC	Washington	Francis, John R.	1889	Calvin Brent
DC	Washington	Francis, John R.	1885	Calvin Brent
DC	Washington	Franklin, Homer	1938	Romulus Archer
DC	Washington	Frederick Douglass Public Dwellings	1941	Archie Alexander
DC	Washington	Freeman, Daniel	c1905	John Lankford
DC	Washington	Freeman, Frank	1954	Lewis Giles, Sr.
DC	Washington	Freeman, William L.	1890	Calvin Brent
DC	Washington	Frelinghuysen University Administration Bldg.	1927	John Lankford
DC	Washington	French, Alfred	1887	Calvin Brent
DC	Washington	Friendship Baptist Church	1964	John Sulton
DC	Washington	Froe Apts.	1951	John Holloway
DC	Washington	Froe Houses	1948	John Holloway
DC	Washington	Froe, R.A.	1949	John Holloway
DC	Washington	Froe, U.M.	1937	Romulus Archer
DC	Washington	Gaililee Baptist Church	1938	Romulus Archer
DC	Washington	Galbrieth Chapel African Methodist Episcopal Church	c1923	John Lankford
DC	Washington	Garfield Elementary Public School	1909	William Pittman
DC	Washington	Geiman Apts.	1928	Lewis Giles Sr.
DC	Washington	Georgetown University Theatre	x	Robert Fields
DC	Washington	Georgetown Visitation Prepatory School for Girls	1978	Robert Fields
DC	Washington	Gibson, T. J.	1950	Clyde Drayton
DC	Washington	Giles, Gladys W.	1929	Lewis Giles, Sr.
DC	Washington	Glenside Baptist Church	1931	Alonzo Plater
DC	Washington	Golden Rule Shopping Ctr.	1979	Robert Madison
DC	Washington	Goodloe, Dr. William	1951	David Byrd
DC	Washington	Gott, Howard S.	1926	Lewis Giles, Sr.
DC	Washington	Grady, Washington	1892	Calvin Brent
DC	Washington	Gray, Dr. James C.	1962	Louis Fry
DC	Washington	Gregg, William H.	1950	Clyde Drayton
DC	Washington	Gregory, Francis A.	1940	Roscoe Vaughn
DC	Washington	Gross, William E.	1926	Lewis Giles Sr.
DC	Washington	Guildford Baptist Church	1945	Cyril Bow
DC	Washington	Hall, Alvin C.	1938	Lewis Giles Sr.
DC	Washington	Hamilton Printing Co.	1932	George Ferguson
DC	Washington	Hamilton, Sara A.	1950	Howard Mackey
DC	Washington	Hamline Methodist Episcopal Church	1946	Romulus Archer
DC	Washington	Hardy Recretion Ctr.	1991	John Sulton
DC	Washington	Harris, Mortimer	1927	Hilyard Robinson
DC	Washington	Harris, Rose P.	x	J. Alonzo Plater
DC	Washington	Hatton, Isaiah T.	1905	Isaiah Hatton
DC	Washington	Haven Methodist Episcopal Church	1923	John Lankford
DC	Washington	Henley, Stewart	1956	Robert Madison
DC	Washington	Hersh, Ben	1957	Roscoe Vaughn
DC	Washington	Hirsch Apts.	1940	Lewis Giles Sr.
DC	Washington	Hite, Ronald T.	1957	Lewis Giles Sr.
DC	Washington	Hoffman, Jarrett F.	1890	Calvin Brent
DC	Washington	Holy Trinity Apostolic Church	1955	Romulus Archer
DC	Washington	Holy Trinity Church	1948	Roscoe Vaughn
DC	Washington	House, Christopher C.	1939	Howard Mackey
DC	Washington	Howard Inn	1976	John Sulton

APPENDIX

State	City/County	Name	Year	A/AE/LA
DC	Washington	Howard University Chemistry Bldg.	1973	Leroy Brown
DC	Washington	Howard University Aldridge Theatre	1948	Hilyard Robinson
DC	Washington	Howard University Cook Dormitory	1938	Hilyard Robinson
DC	Washington	Howard University Dental Bldg.	x	Clarence Wheat
DC	Washington	Howard University Drew Dormitory	1951	Hilyard Robinson
DC	Washington	Howard University Engineering & Architecture Bldg.	1952	Hilyard Robinson
DC	Washington	Howard University Fine Arts Bldg.	1951	Hilyard Robinson
DC	Washington	Howard University Slowe Dormitory	1942	Hilyard Robinson
DC	Washington	Howard University Classroom Bldg.	1975	Clarence Wheat
DC	Washington	Howard University Armory	1925	Albert Cassell
DC	Washington	Howard University Baldwin Hall	1951	Albert Cassell
DC	Washington	Howard University Bethune Dormitory	1948	Hilyard Robinson
DC	Washington	Howard University Biology Bldg.	1954	Hilyard Robinson
DC	Washington	Howard University Blackburn Student Ctr.	1979	Clarence Wheat
DC	Washington	Howard University Burr Gym	1964	Clarence Wheat
DC	Washington	Howard University Cancer Research Bldg.	1980	Clarence Wheat
DC	Washington	Howard University Carnegie Library	1932	Julian Cooke
DC	Washington	Howard University Chemistry Bldg.	1977	Clarence Wheat
DC	Washington	Howard University Chemistry Bldg.	1936	Albert Cassell
DC	Washington	Howard University Clark Hall	1933	Julian Cooke
DC	Washington	Howard University College of Medicine	1927	Albert Cassell
DC	Washington	Howard University Cramton Auditorium	1954	Hilyard Robinson
DC	Washington	Howard University Crandall Womens Dormitory	1931	Albert Cassell
DC	Washington	Howard University Dining Hall & Home Economics Bldg.	1921	William Hazel
DC	Washington	Howard University Douglas Mens Dormitory	1936	Albert Cassell
DC	Washington	Howard University East of the River Health Clinic	1977	John Sulton
DC	Washington	Howard University Faculty Office	x	Clarence Wheat
DC	Washington	Howard University Founders Library	1984	Clarence Wheat
DC	Washington	Howard University Founders Library	1937	Albert Cassell
DC	Washington	Howard University Frazier Womens Dormitory	1931	Albert Cassell
DC	Washington	Howard University Greene Stadium	1926	Albert Cassell
DC	Washington	Howard University Gym	1925	Albert Cassell
DC	Washington	Howard University Hospital	1970s	Clarence Wheat
DC	Washington	Howard University Hospital Parking Structure	1983	John Sulton
DC	Washington	Howard University Human Ecology Bldg.	1960	Clarence Wheat
DC	Washington	Howard University Locke Hall	1964	Clarence Wheat
DC	Washington	Howard University Medical/Dental Library	x	Clarence Wheat
DC	Washington	Howard University Mudd Medical Research Bldg.	1979	Clarence Wheat
DC	Washington	Howard University Mudd Medical Research Bldg.	1977	John Sulton
DC	Washington	Howard University Museum	x	Robert Fields
DC	Washington	Howard University Power Plant	1934	Albert Cassell
DC	Washington	Howard University President's Residence	x	Albert Cassell
DC	Washington	Howard University School of Business	1983	John Sulton
DC	Washington	Howard University School of Communication	x	Clarence Wheat
DC	Washington	Howard University School of Dentistry	1954	Hilyard Robinson
DC	Washington	Howard University School of Human Ecology	1960	Hilyard Robinson
DC	Washington	Howard University School of Pharmacy	1955	Hilyard Robinson
DC	Washington	Howard University Slowe Hall	x	Robert Fields
DC	Washington	Howard University Snack Bar	1946	Howard Mackey
DC	Washington	Howard University Student Book Store	x	Robert Fields
DC	Washington	Howard University Truth Womens Dormitory	1931	Albert Cassell
DC	Washington	Howard University Wheatley Hall	1951	Albert Cassell
DC	Washington	Howard University Womens Gym	1922	Albert Cassell
DC	Washington	Howard University Bethune Dormitory	1964	Clarence Wheat
DC	Washington	Howard, J.H.	1886	Calvin Brent
DC	Washington	Huff, George	1906	Julian Abele
DC	Washington	Hughes Memorial United Methodist Church	x	John Sulton
DC	Washington	Independence Avenue Bridge	x	Archie Alexander
DC	Washington	Independent Order of Odd Fellows Temple	x	John Lankford
DC	Washington	Industrial Bank of Washington	1963	Robert Madison
DC	Washington	Industrial Savings Bank	1943	Howard Mackey
DC	Washington	Industrial Savings Bank	1915	Isaiah Hatton

APPENDIX

State	City/County	Name	Year	A/AE/LA
DC	Washington	Iowa Apts.	c1924	Roscoe Vaughn
DC	Washington	Iowa Condominiums	1978	John Sulton
DC	Washington	Israel Baptist Church	1932	George Ferguson
DC	Washington	Israel Baptist Church	c1925	Roscoe Vaughn
DC	Washington	Jackson, F.	1950	Romulus Archer
DC	Washington	James Creek Public Housing	1942	Albert Cassell
DC	Washington	Jarvis Funeral Home	1929	Julius Gardner
DC	Washington	Jason, Robert S.	1937	Lewis Giles Sr.
DC	Washington	Jerusalem Baptist Church	1922	Isaiah Hatton
DC	Washington	Jessup, Cedric	1932	J. Alonzo Plater
DC	Washington	John Wesley African Methodist Episcopal Zion Church	1902	John Lankford
DC	Washington	Johnson, Catherine W	1941	Lewis Giles Sr.
DC	Washington	Johnson, George	1945	David Byrd
DC	Washington	Johnson, Dr. Joseph	x	Hilyard Robinson
DC	Washington	Johnson, Morris	1950	Romulus Archer
DC	Washington	Jones Memorial Methodist Episcopal Church Education Bldg.	1952	Romulus Archer
DC	Washington	Jones Memorial Methodist Episcopal Church	1923	Howard Woodson
DC	Washington	Jones, Cleo	1891	Calvin Brent
DC	Washington	Jones, Dr. W.W.	c1924	George Ferguson
DC	Washington	Jordan, Isaiah	1922	Howard Woodson
DC	Washington	Kapnick Apts.	1945	Romulus Archer
DC	Washington	Kaufman Store & Apts.	1941	Lewis Giles Sr.
DC	Washington	Keith, John	1890	Calvin Brent
DC	Washington	Kelly, Dr. Charles H.	1949	Howard Mackey
DC	Washington	Kimball Elementary School	1964	Albert Cassell
DC	Washington	King, Cornelius	1951	John Holloway
DC	Washington	King, Frank	c1924	Julius Gardner
DC	Washington	King, John M.	1930	John Melby
DC	Washington	King, John M.	1927	John Melby
DC	Washington	King, John M.	1931	John Melby
DC	Washington	Knox Hill Elderly Housing	1984	John Sulton
DC	Washington	Knox Hill Recretion Ctr.	1990	John Sulton
DC	Washington	Knox, Ellis O.	1940	Roscoe Vaughn
DC	Washington	Laborers Building & Loan Office	1908	William Pittman
DC	Washington	Landis, Sylvia	1940	Cyril Bow
DC	Washington	Langon, Willenton	1950	Howard Mackey
DC	Washington	Langston Terrace Pubic Housing	1937	David Williston
DC	Washington	Langston Terrace Public Housing	1964	Leroy Brown
DC	Washington	Langston Terrace Public Housing	1935	Hilyard Robinson
DC	Washington	Langston Terrace Public Housing	1937	Paul Williams
DC	Washington	Lawrence, Phillip	x	John Holloway
DC	Washington	Lawson, Belford	x	Hilyard Robinson
DC	Washington	Lee, Robert	1939	Cyril Bow
DC	Washington	Leonard Apts.	1925	John Melby
DC	Washington	Letcher, Henry	c1950	James Turner
DC	Washington	Lewis Bldg.	1922	Lewis Giles Sr.
DC	Washington	Lewis, Dr. Douglas L.	1950	Howard Mackey
DC	Washington	Lewis, John W.	1917	Isaiah Hatton
DC	Washington	Lewis, R.A.	1927	Lewis Giles Sr.
DC	Washington	Lewis, S.W.	1976	Hilyard Robinson
DC	Washington	Liberty Colored Baptist Church	c1879	Calvin Brent
DC	Washington	Lightbown Store	1929	John Melby
DC	Washington	Logan, Dr. Rayford T.	1943	Hilyard Robinson
DC	Washington	Lucas, William E.	1889	Calvin Brent
DC	Washington	Lunduer Apts.	1936	Lewis Giles Sr.
DC	Washington	Lutes, Bertie M.	1965	Lewis Giles Sr.
DC	Washington	Macedonia Baptist Church	1946	Romulus Archer
DC	Washington	Mackey, Howard H.	1952	Howard Mackey
DC	Washington	Madison, James G.	1893	Calvin Brent
DC	Washington	Malcolm X Elementary School	1970	Leroy Brown
DC	Washington	Marilynn Apts.	c1925	Roscoe Vaughn
DC	Washington	Marshall, Faith	c1932	John Melby

APPENDIX

State	City/County	Name	Year	A/AE/LA
DC	Washington	Martin, George W.	c1924	George Ferguson
DC	Washington	Masonic Temple	1932	Albert Cassell
DC	Washington	Mattingly, Robert	1928	George Ferguson
DC	Washington	Mayfair Gardens	1946	Albert Cassell
DC	Washington	Mazique, Dr. Edward C.	x	Howard Mackey
DC	Washington	McCulloch Apts.	1940	Roscoe Vaughn
DC	Washington	McDuffie, Clyde	1941	Cyril Bow
DC	Washington	McIntosh, Ernest W.	x	John Holloway
DC	Washington	Meridian Hill Baptist Church	1948	Roscoe Vaughn
DC	Washington	Metropolitan Baptist Church Ctr.	x	George Ferguson
DC	Washington	Metropolitan Baptist Church Monument Hall	1950	George Ferguson
DC	Washington	Metropolitan Baptist Church Service Bldg.	1950	Roscoe Vaughn
DC	Washington	Metrotone Baptist Church	1955	Romulus Archer
DC	Washington	Metrotone Baptist Church	1945	Lewis Giles Sr.
DC	Washington	Midway & Wake Dormitories	c1948	Samuel Plato
DC	Washington	Miles Memorial Colored Methodist Episcopal Church	1890	Calvin Brent
DC	Washington	Miller, Charles M.	x	John Holloway
DC	Washington	Minter, Sylvester	1960	Clyde Drayton
DC	Washington	Minton, Theophilus J.	1886	Calvin Brent
DC	Washington	Missouri Mews	1980	John Sulton
DC	Washington	Mitchell, Frank P.	1912	Julian Abele
DC	Washington	Montana Terrace Public Housing	1965	Louis Fry
DC	Washington	Moore Drug Store	1911	William Pittman
DC	Washington	Moorer, A.A.	1923	Roscoe Vaughn
DC	Washington	Morris Furniture Store	1945	Howard Mackey
DC	Washington	Mounsey, Dr. Ethel N.	1949	Howard Woodson
DC	Washington	Mt. Airy Baptist Church	1926	Roscoe Vaughn
DC	Washington	Mt. Airy Baptist Church	1924	George Ferguson
DC	Washington	Mt. Airy Baptist Church	1969	Stewart Hoban
DC	Washington	Mt. Bethel Baptist Church	x	George Ferguson
DC	Washington	Mt. Bethel Baptist Church	1921	Roscoe Vaughn
DC	Washington	Mt. Carmel Baptist Church	x	Robert Fields
DC	Washington	Mt. Carmel Housing	1960	Louis Fry
DC	Washington	Mt. Jezreel Baptist Church	1891	Calvin Brent
DC	Washington	Mt. Moab Baptist Church	1919	John Lankford
DC	Washington	Mt. Moriah Baptist Church	1924	George Ferguson
DC	Washington	Mt. Olive Baptist Church	1916	Roscoe Vaughn
DC	Washington	Mt. Pleasant Baptist Church	x	Howard Mackey
DC	Washington	Mt. Sinai Baptist Church	1986	John Sulton
DC	Washington	Mt. Zion Baptist Church	1924	Roscoe Vaughn
DC	Washington	Mt. Zion Baptist Church Parsonage	1896	Calvin Brent
DC	Washington	Mt. Zion Baptist Church	1962	Robert Madison
DC	Washington	Murray Palace Casino	1920	Isaiah Hatton
DC	Washington	Murray, Daniel	1878	Calvin Brent
DC	Washington	Murray, Daniel	c1905	John Lankford
DC	Washington	Murray's Ice Cream Factory	x	John Lankford
DC	Washington	National Benefit Bldg.	c1924	George Ferguson
DC	Washington	National Training School for Women & Girls Chapel	x	George Ferguson
DC	Washington	National Training School for Women & Girls Dormitory	x	George Ferguson
DC	Washington	National Training School for Women & Girls Jubilee Arch	1915	John Moore
DC	Washington	National Training School for Women & Girls Laundry	1917	John Moore
DC	Washington	National Training School for Women & Girls Model House	1917	John Moore
DC	Washington	Naylor, William T.	1890	Calvin Brent
DC	Washington	Nazareth Baptist Church	1956	Leroy Brown
DC	Washington	New Hope Free Church Parsonage	1938	Lewis Giles Sr.
DC	Washington	New Mt. Olive Baptist Church	1936	Lewis Giles Sr.
DC	Washington	New World Laboratory	x	Stewart Hoban
DC	Washington	Newman Club	1951	Clyde Drayton
DC	Washington	Newman, Nelson	1939	Roscoe Vaughn
DC	Washington	Newton, Frontis J.	1954	Howard Mackey
DC	Washington	Northeast Baptist Church	1919	Roscoe Vaughn
DC	Washington	Odd Fellows Temple	1932	Albert Cassell

APPENDIX

State	City/County	Name	Year	A/AE/LA
DC	Washington	Old Post Office Pavillion	1983	Stewart Hoban
DC	Washington	Omega Psi Phi Fraternity	x	Albert Cassell
DC	Washington	Omega Psi Phi Fraternity National Hqtrs.	1973	John Sulton
DC	Washington	Our Lady Queen of Peace Church	1951	Robert Fields
DC	Washington	Parks, James B.	1936	Roscoe Vaughn
DC	Washington	Parks, Thomas W.	1944	David Byrd
DC	Washington	Parkside Dwellings	1964	Leroy Brown
DC	Washington	Parkside Dwellings	1940	David Williston
DC	Washington	Parkside Dwellings	1940	Howard Mackey
DC	Washington	Parnell, William J.	1922	John Lankford
DC	Washington	Peace Baptist Church	1947	Howard Woodson
DC	Washington	Pemberton, Stafford	x	Albert Cassell
DC	Washington	Pendleton, William H.	1949	Clyde Drayton
DC	Washington	Penn, Garfield A.	1923	George Ferguson
DC	Washington	Phelps High School Greenhouse	1965	Louis Fry
DC	Washington	Phylis Apts.	1939	Lewis Giles Sr.
DC	Washington	Pierre, William	1886	Calvin Brent
DC	Washington	Pilgrim African Methodist Episcopal Church	c1941	Lewis Giles Sr.
DC	Washington	Pilgrim Baptist Church	1924	Roscoe Vaughn
DC	Washington	Pilgrim Baptist Church	c1924	George Ferguson
DC	Washington	Pilgrim Baptist Church	1968	Leroy Brown
DC	Washington	Pincus Apts.	1937	Lewis Giles Sr.
DC	Washington	Plummer, Robert	x	Albert Cassell
DC	Washington	Plummer, Roy U.	1941	Lewis Giles Sr.
DC	Washington	Plymouth Theatre	1946	John Holloway
DC	Washington	Powell Apts.	1938	Roscoe Vaughn
DC	Washington	Prohaska Apts.	1939	Lewis Giles Sr.
DC	Washington	Prudential Bank	c1925	Roscoe Vaughn
DC	Washington	Purity Baptist Church	c1970	Lewis Giles Jr.
DC	Washington	Rahn, Joseph	1959	Lewis Giles Sr.
DC	Washington	Randal United Memorial Church	1946	Howard Mackey
DC	Washington	Randall Memorial United Methodist Church	1981	John Sulton
DC	Washington	Randall Memorial United Methodist Church	1948	Robert Fields
DC	Washington	Randall, John	1936	Lewis Giles Sr.
DC	Washington	Red Cap Bldg.	c1920	John Lankford
DC	Washington	Reed Elementary School	x	Louis Fry
DC	Washington	Reno Store	1932	John Melby
DC	Washington	Rhines Funeral Home	1985	John Sulton
DC	Washington	Rhines, John T.	1938	Lewis Giles Sr.
DC	Washington	Ridell, A.F.	1931	John Melby
DC	Washington	Rivers, Dr. W.N.	1940	Roscoe Vaughn
DC	Washington	Roberts, Dr. James E.	1945	Howard Mackey
DC	Washington	Robinson, Dr. Alvin F.	1954	Howard Mackey
DC	Washington	Robinson, H.J.	1941	Romulus Archer
DC	Washington	Rock Creek Baptist Church	1955	Lewis Giles Sr.
DC	Washington	Rockburne Condominiums	1986	John Sulton
DC	Washington	Rogers, J.L.	1892	Calvin Brent
DC	Washington	Rogers, Madeline P.	1948	Howard Mackey
DC	Washington	Rouse, Charles C.	1935	Roscoe Vaughn
DC	Washington	Rubbert, M. Frank	1930	Lewis Giles Sr.
DC	Washington	Sargent Memorial Presbyterian Church Multi-Purpose Bldg.	1970	John Sulton
DC	Washington	Saterwhite Store	1922	Romulus Archer
DC	Washington	Saunders Apts.	c1924	George Ferguson
DC	Washington	Savoy, Archie	1949	J. Alonzo Plater
DC	Washington	Scott, Dr. Armond	1927	Hilyard Robinson
DC	Washington	Seaton Elementary School	1974	John Sulton
DC	Washington	Seaton Elementary School	1965	Albert Cassell
DC	Washington	Settle, Clay	1929	James Turner
DC	Washington	Seventh District Police Station	1972	Leroy Brown
DC	Washington	Sharpe Health Ctr.	1974	John Sulton
DC	Washington	Shaw Junior High School	1975	John Sulton
DC	Washington	Shaw United Methodist Church	1954	Romulus Archer

APPENDIX

State	City/County	Name	Year	A/AE/LA
DC	Washington	Shephard, Dr. O'Donnel	x	George Ferguson
DC	Washington	Shiloh Baptist Church	x	John Lankford
DC	Washington	Short, Clarence	1939	Cyril Bow
DC	Washington	Simms, Edgar R.	x	John Holloway
DC	Washington	Simon Apts.	1935	Lewis Giles Sr.
DC	Washington	Society & Business Bldg.	x	John Lankford
DC	Washington	Southern Aid Insurance Bldg.	1920	Isaiah Hatton
DC	Washington	Southern Baptist Church	1950	Howard Mackey
DC	Washington	Southern Baptist Church	1938	Romulus Archer
DC	Washington	House	1932	Ralph Vaughn
DC	Washington	Spencer, Dr. A.L.	x	Howard Mackey
DC	Washington	St. John Baptist Church	1945	Lewis Giles Sr.
DC	Washington	St. Luke's Baptist Church	1890	Calvin Brent
DC	Washington	St. Luke Episcopal Church Parish	1960	Albert Cassell
DC	Washington	St. Luke's Church	1955	Hilyard Robinson
DC	Washington	St. Luke's Protestant Episcopal Church	1876	Calvin Brent
DC	Washington	St. Luke's Protestant Episcopal Church	1924	Romulus Archer
DC	Washington	St. Paul Colored Methodist Church	1892	Calvin Brent
DC	Washington	Stewart, Edward	1889	Calvin Brent
DC	Washington	Stewart, William A.	c1925	John Lankford
DC	Washington	Stewarts Chapel & Undertaking	c1925	Roscoe Vaughn
DC	Washington	Stoddard Baptist Home	1952	Howard Mackey
DC	Washington	Stoddard Baptist Home for the Aged	1907	William Pittman
DC	Washington	Stowe, Thomas H.	1942	Lewis Giles Sr.
DC	Washington	Striner, Benjamin	1938	Howard Mackey
DC	Washington	Supreme Liberty Life Insurance Co.	1891	Calvin Brent
DC	Washington	Syphax, Douglass P.	1936	Romulus Archer
DC	Washington	Tabernacle Baptist Church	1953	Lewis Giles Jr.
DC	Washington	Tabernacle Baptist Church	1972	Louis Fry
DC	Washington	Takoma Elementary School	1936	Lewis Giles Sr.
DC	Washington	Talbert, Ella M.	1941	Lewis Giles Sr.
DC	Washington	Talbert, Ella M.	1925	Lewis Giles Sr.
DC	Washington	Tater, William	1925	George Ferguson
DC	Washington	Temple, J.F.	1890	William Pittman
DC	Washington	Temple of Gailean Fisherman	1926	Lewis Giles Sr.
DC	Washington	Tepper, Joseph L.	1923	Lewis Giles Sr.
DC	Washington	Tepper, Joseph L.	1892	Calvin Brent
DC	Washington	Third Baptist Church	x	Stewart Hoban
DC	Washington	Third Baptist Church	1926	Howard Woodson
DC	Washington	Third Church of God	x	Albert Cassell
DC	Washington	Thomas, Edward	1939	Lewis Giles Sr.
DC	Washington	Thomas, George	1938	Howard Mackey
DC	Washington	Thurston, Thomas C.	1938	James Turner
DC	Washington	Toyer, Rosa	x	John Lankford
DC	Washington	Trinity Baptist Church	1905	William Pittman
DC	Washington	Trinity North Baptist Church	1950	Roscoe Vaughn
DC	Washington	Turner Memorial African Methodist Episcopal Church	1960	David Williston
DC	Washington	U. S. Customs Courthouse	1963	Roscoe Vaughn
DC	Washington	Union Baptist Church	1924	John Lankford
DC	Washington	Union Bethel African Methodist Epicsopal Church	1884	Calvin Brent
DC	Washington	Union Wesley African Methodist Episcopal Zion Church	1964	Louis Fry
DC	Washington	United House of Prayer	1977	John Sulton
DC	Washington	United National Bank	1902	John Lankford
DC	Washington	United Order of True Reformers Hall	1972	Stewart Hoban
DC	Washington	Urban Village	1951	Howard Mackey
DC	Washington	Uricolo, Dr. Raphael	1890	Calvin Brent
DC	Washington	Wales, S.S.	1949	David Byrd
DC	Washington	Walker, Dr. James E.	x	John Lankford
DC	Washington	Walker Memorial Baptist Church	1950	Roscoe Vaughn
DC	Washington	Walker Memorial Baptist Church	1970	Stewart Hoban
DC	Washington	Walker-Jones Elementary School	1949	Roscoe Vaughn
DC	Washington	Washington Store & Apts.	1938	Albert Cassell
DC	Washington	Washington Vocational School		

APPENDIX

State	City/County	Name	Year	A/AE/LA
DC	Washington	Wells, Samuel	1888	Calvin Brent
DC	Washington	Wesley African Methodist Episcopal Zion Church	1884	Calvin Brent
DC	Washington	Wesley Zion Church	1893	Calvin Brent
DC	Washington	Wheately YWCA	x	Albert Cassell
DC	Washington	White, George H.	1922	Howard Woodson
DC	Washington	Whitelaw Hotel	1918	Isaiah Hatton
DC	Washington	Whitlock Print Shop	1946	John Holloway
DC	Washington	Whitted, Dr. Harold L.	1948	Howard Mackey
DC	Washington	Wiggins, Elsie C.	1939	Lewis Giles Sr.
DC	Washington	Williams, Dr. Arthur C.	1951	Howard Mackey
DC	Washington	Williamson, Alphonso	1934	Lewis Giles Sr.
DC	Washington	Williamson, Alphonso	1956	Lewis Giles Sr.
DC	Washington	Willis, Rev. M.J.	1916	Roscoe Vaughn
DC	Washington	Williston, Dr. Thomas	1944	Hilyard Robinson
DC	Washington	Williston, Dr. Thomas	1939	Howard Mackey
DC	Washington	Wilma Gardens Apts.	1938	Lewis Giles Sr.
DC	Washington	Wilson Manor Apts.	1940	Lewis Giles Sr.
DC	Washington	Wineland, Lloyd G.	1939	Lewis Giles Sr.
DC	Washington	Winestock, Reba	1944	John Holloway
DC	Washington	Winslow Stable	c1915	John Lankford
DC	Washington	Woods, James A.	x	John Holloway
DC	Washington	Woods, Lawrence	1948	Clyde Drayton
DC	Washington	Wormley, Garrett	1890	Calvin Brent
DC	Washington	Worther, Edmund C.	1932	Howard Mackey
DC	Washington	Yenching Palace Restaurant	1945	Romulus Archer
DC	Washington	Young, Col. Lucius	1938	Howard Mackey
DC	Washington	Young, Edward W.O.	c1916	Edward Young
DC	Washington	Young, Frank M.	1949	Roscoe Vaughn
DC	Washington	Young, John L.	1941	Roscoe Vaughn
DC	Washington	Zion Baptist Church	1908	William Pittman
DC	Washington	Zion Baptist Church	1891	Calvin Brent
DC	Washington	Zion Baptist Church	1966	Robert Madison
DE	Clarksville	Union Wesley Methodist Church	1958	De Witt Dykes
DE	Dover	Delaware State University Boundary Wall	1995	Calvin Hamilton
DE	Dover	Delaware State University Washington Herbarium	1999	Calvin Hamilton
DE	Dover	Delaware Technical Community College Terry Bldg.	1975	Calvin Hamilton
DE	Millsboro	Brandywine Village I	x	Calvin Hamilton
DE	Wilmington	Anderson Community Center	1972	Calvin Hamilton
DE	Wilmington	Asbury Gardens Apts.	x	Calvin Hamilton
DE	Wilmington	Bethlehem Eighth Street Baptist Church	x	Calvin Hamilton
DE	Wilmington	City of Wilmington Housing	1969	Calvin Hamilton
DE	Wilmington	Ebenezer Baptist Church	x	Calvin Hamilton
DE	Wilmington	Ezion United Methodist Church	x	Calvin Hamilton
DE	Wilmington	Ezion-Mt. Carmel United Methodist Church	1972	Calvin Hamilton
DE	Wilmington	Gray Funeral Home	x	Calvin Hamilton
DE	Wilmington	Haven United Methodist Chruch	x	Calvin Hamilton
DE	Wilmington	House	x	Calvin Hamilton
DE	Wilmington	Howard High School	x	Calvin Hamilton
DE	Wilmington	Lockett, Jesse	x	Calvin Hamilton
DE	Wilmington	Mt. Joy United Methodist Church	x	Calvin Hamilton
DE	Wilmington	Nix, Theopholis	x	Calvin Hamilton
DE	Wilmington	Peoples Settlement	x	Calvin Hamilton
DE	Wilmington	Talbert, E.	x	Calvin Hamilton
DE	Wilmington	Westown Square	1972	Calvin Hamilton
DE	Wilmington	Westtown Village	1970	Calvin Hamilton
FL	Alachua	Mt. Nebo Methodist Church	1967	De Witt Dykes
FL	Amelia Island	Brookins, Sanford A.	1936	Sanford Brookins
FL	Baldwin	Campbell Chapel African Methodist Episcopal Church	c1911	John Lankford
FL	Bradford County	Florida Home Improvement Co.	x	John Lankford
FL	Deland	Bethel Afrrican Methodist Episcopal Church	c1915	John Lankford
FL	Ft. Meyers	Trinity Methodist Church	1962	De Witt Dykes
FL	Ft. Myers	U. S. Post Office	1965	Willie Jenkins

APPENDIX

State	City/County	Name	Year	A/AE/LA
FL	Goldsboro	New Mt. Cavalry Missionary Baptist Church	1918	Prince Spears
FL	Goldsboro	Spears, Prince W.	c1930	Prince Spears
FL	Hastings	St. Stephens Methodist Church	1967	De Witt Dykes
FL	Hawthorne	New Hope Methodist Church	1964	De Witt Dykes
FL	Jacksonville	Apartment Bldg.	x	Richard Brown
FL	Jacksonville	Baptist Academy Master Plan	x	John Lankford
FL	Jacksonville	Blodgett, Joseph H.	1919	Louis Blodgett
FL	Jacksonville	Brookins, Sanford A.	1924	Sanford Brookins
FL	Jacksonville	Cookman Institute Dinning Hall & Girls Home	1901	William Cooke
FL	Jacksonville	Cookman Institute Main Bldg.	1905	William Cooke
FL	Jacksonville	Durkee Gardens Single-family Housing	1920s	Sanford Brookins
FL	Jacksonville	Edward Waters College Centennial Hall	1916	Richard Brown
FL	Jacksonville	Emmanuel Baptist Church	x	James Hutchinson
FL	Jacksonville	First Born Church of the Living God	x	James Hutchinson
FL	Jacksonville	Florida Masonic Grand Lodge	1912	John Lankford
FL	Jacksonville	Grant Memorial African Methodist Episcopal Church	1908	John Lankford
FL	Jacksonville	Lawton-Pratt Funeral Home	1915	Louis Blodgett
FL	Jacksonville	Masonic Hall	1908	John Lankford
FL	Jacksonville	Mt. Olive African Methodist Episcopal Church	1921	Richard Brown
FL	Jacksonville	New Bethel African Methodist Episcopal Church	x	James Hutchinson
FL	Jacksonville	Prince Hall Grand Lodge	c1944	John Lankford
FL	Jacksonville	Robinson, Rev.	c1915	John Lankford
FL	Jacksonvile	Rosemond, John H.	1956	John Rosemond
FL	Jacksonvile	Simpson Memorial United Methodist Church	1923	John Rosemond
FL	Jacksonville	St. Paul African Methodist Episcopal Church	x	James Hutchinson
FL	Jacksonville	Sugar Hill Single-family Housing	1920s	Louis Blodgett
FL	Jacksonville	Thompson, Prof. C.T.	c1915	John Lankford
FL	Jacksonville	Tooks, Rev. H. Y.	c1915	John Lankford
FL	Jacksonville	Triumph the Church	x	James Hutchinson
FL	Jacksonville	Zion Baptist Hope Church	x	James Hutchinson
FL	Miami	Housing	1940	Moses McKissack
FL	Miami	St. John's Baptist Church	1927	Moses McKissack
FL	Milton	Mt. Pilgrim African Baptist Church	1916	Wallace Rayfield
FL	Oakland	First Baptist Church of Oakland	1944	John Rosemond
FL	Ocala	Howard Academy	x	Levi Alexander, Sr.
FL	Ocala	Marion Hardware Bldg.	x	Levi Alexander, Sr.
FL	Ocala	Mt. Zion African Methodist Episcopal Church	1891	Levi Alexander, Sr.
FL	Ocala	Rheinauers Store	x	Levi Alexander, Sr.
FL	Opa Locka	Mt. Pleasant Methodist Church	1959	De Witt Dykes
FL	Palataka	Walker, Dr. T. H. B.	c1915	John Lankford
FL	Riveria Beach	Simpson Memorial Methodist Church	1960	De Witt Dykes
FL	Sanford	Brewer, Dr. George	c1920	Prince Spears
FL	Sanford	Brock, David C.	c1920	Prince Spears
FL	Sanford	Duhart, Harry L.	1912	Prince Spears
FL	Sanford	Green, William O.	c1920	Prince Spears
FL	Sanford	Little, Italy	c1920	Prince Spears
FL	Sanford	Refoe, Herman L.	c1920	Prince Spears
FL	Sanford	St. James African Methodist Episcopal Church	1910	Prince Spears
FL	Sanford	St. John Missionary Baptist Church	c1910	Prince Spears
FL	Sanford	Strickland, Dr. Edwin D.	c1920	Prince Spears
FL	Sanford	Trinity Methodist Baptist Church	c1920	Prince Spears
FL	Sanford	Trinity Methodist Church	1967	De Witt Dykes
FL	Sumter	Sumter Masonic Bldg.	1919	John Lankford
FL	Tampa	Harris Temple Methodist Church	1962	De Witt Dykes
FL	West Palm Beach	First Church of Christ, Scientist	1927	Julian Abele
GA	Albany	Tift, Nelson Bridge & Keeper's House	1858	Horace King
GA	Americus	Campbell Chapel	x	Louis Persley
GA	Athens	First African Methodist Episcopal Church	1916	Louis Persley
GA	Athens	Samaritan Order Bldg.	1916	Louis Persley
GA	Atlanta	Aiken Low-Income Housing	x	John Blanche
GA	Atlanta	Atlanta Life Insuance Co.	1974	Edward Miller
GA	Atlanta	Atlanta University President's House	c1932	David Williston

APPENDIX

State	City/County	Name	Year	A/AE/LA
GA	Atlanta	Big Bethel African Methodist Episcopal Church	1924	John Lankford
GA	Atlanta	Clark College McPheeters-Dennis Hall	1969	Edward Miller
GA	Atlanta	Clark University Landscape Plan	1926	David Williston
GA	Atlanta	Ebenezer Baptist Church Education Bldg.	1956	Edward Miller
GA	Atlanta	Independent Benevolent Order Lodge No. 1	x	Wallace Rayfield
GA	Atlanta	King, Martin L. Jr.	1974	Edward Miller
GA	Atlanta	Lakewood Transit Station	1976	Edward Pryce
GA	Atlanta	Lennox Transit Station	1976	Edward Pryce
GA	Atlanta	Morehouse College Archer Bldg.	1958	Edward Miller
GA	Atlanta	Morehouse College Bennett Dormitory	1962	Edward Miller
GA	Atlanta	Morehouse College Chemistry Bldg.	1953	Edward Miller
GA	Atlanta	Morehouse College Danforth Chapel	1955	Edward Miller
GA	Atlanta	Morris Brown College Central Heights Industrial Bldg.	x	John Lankford
GA	Atlanta	Price Middle School Gym	1970	Edward Miller
GA	Atlanta	Rockdale Park	1967	Percy Ifill
GA	Atlanta	Rucker Bldg.	1906	William Decatur
GA	Atlanta	Southern Appeal Bldg.	x	John Lankford
GA	Atlanta	United Order of Odd Fellows Lodge No. 1	1912	William Pittman
GA	Atlanta	Vine City Transit Station	1976	Edward Pryce
GA	Augusta	Antioch Baptist Church	1934	John Holloway
GA	Augusta	Benning, H.S.	1943	John Holloway
GA	Augusta	Bowman, Theodore A.	1940	John Holloway
GA	Augusta	Boyce, Jacob	1930	John Holloway
GA	Augusta	Christ Presbyterian Church	1939	John Holloway
GA	Augusta	Holloway, John B.	1930	John Holloway
GA	Augusta	Johnson, Walter A.	1940	John Holloway
GA	Augusta	Perry, L.D.	1940	John Holloway
GA	Augusta	Ridgely, Marion	1931	John Holloway
GA	Augusta	Scott, M.M.	1941	John Holloway
GA	Augusta	Settle, R.T	1929	John Holloway
GA	Austell	Smith Chapel Methodist Church	1962	De Witt Dykes
GA	Brunswick	Grace Methodist Church	1963	De Witt Dykes
GA	btwn. Newnan & Carrolton	Moore's Bridge	1855–56	Horace King
GA	Cartersville	Alexander Methodist Church	1962	De Witt Dykes
GA	Columbus	City Mills Company	1869	Horace King
GA	Columbus	Clapp's Textile Factory	c1866	Horace King
GA	Columbus	Columbus Bridge	x	John King
GA	Columbus	Confederate Naval Iron Works Rolling Mill	1864	Horace King
GA	Columbus	Fontaine Warehouse	c1865	Horace King
GA	Columbus	Harris Methodist Church	1963	De Witt Dykes
GA	Columbus	Muscogee County Courthouse	1838	Horace King
GA	County Line	County Line Methodist Church	1962	De Witt Dykes
GA	Covington	Grace Methodist Church	1966	De Witt Dykes
GA	Coweta County	Miller Factory	1861	Horace King
GA	Dublin	Howard's Chapel Methodist Church	1967	De Witt Dykes
GA	Florence	Florence Bridge	1841	Horace King
GA	Fort Gaines	Fort Gaines Bridge	1870	Horace King
GA	Fort Valley	Fort Valley State College Student Ctr.	1939	Calvin McKissack
GA	Franklin	Franklin Bridge	1873	Horace King
GA	LaGrange	Andrews Hotel	1890	John King
GA	LaGrange	Bradfield Bldg.	1879	Horace King
GA	LaGrange	Bradfield, E.R.	1886	John King
GA	LaGrange	Dallis & Edmundson	1883	John King
GA	LaGrange	First Presbyterian Church	1886	John King
GA	LaGrange	Flat Shoals Creek Bridge	1888	John King
GA	LaGrange	King, John T.	1888	John King
GA	LaGrange	LaGrange Oil Mill	1890	John King
GA	LaGrange	Long Cane Creek Bridge	1888	John King
GA	LaGrange	Loyd Bldg.	1897	John King
GA	LaGrange	Loyd, James	1879	Horace King
GA	LaGrange	Sash & Blind Factory	x	John King
GA	LaGrange	Smith, Alwyn M.	1890	John King

APPENDIX

State	City/County	Name	Year	A/AE/LA
GA	LaGrange	Southern Female College Administration Bldg.	1877	Horace King
GA	LaGrange	Troup County Courthouse	1886	John King
GA	LaGrange	Warren Temple Christian Methodist Episcopal Church School	1870s	Horace King
GA	Lithhonia	Flat Rock Methodist Church	1966	De Witt Dykes
GA	Macon	House of Prayer Housing	1976	John Sulton
GA	Meriwether County	Render, _____	1879	Horace King
GA	Meriwether County	White Oak Bridge	c1869	Horace King
GA	Savannah	Central Heights Normal & Industrial School	x	John Lankford
GA	Savannah	Georgia Industrial College for Colored Youth Meldrim Hall	1896	William Cooke
GA	Savannah	Independent Order of Odd Fellows Temple	x	John Lankford
GA	Savannah	St. Phillip's African Methodist Episcopal Church & Parsonage	1912	John Lankford
GA	Savannah	Williams Office Bldg.	x	John Lankford
GA	Unionville	Unionville Methodist Church	1961	De Witt Dykes
GA	Villa Rica	Pleasant Hill Methodist Church	1963	De Witt Dykes
GA	Waycross	Independent Order of Odd Fellows Temple	x	John Lankford
GA	Waycross	Penny Savings Bank	x	Vertner Tandy
GA	Waycross	Sessoms Drug Store & Office	x	John Lankford
GA	west of LaGrange	Glass Bridge	1873	Horace King
GA	LaGrange	West Point Bridge	1838	Horace King
GA	LaGrange	West Point Bridge	1874	John King
GA	West Point	West Point Female College	1873	Horace King
HW	Lihue Kauai	House	1931	Robert Buffins
HW	Honolulu	Buffins, Robert L.	x	Robert Buffins
HW	Honolulu	Grave of the Unknown Sailor	1953	Paul Williams
IA	Carter Lake	Carter Lake School	x	Francis Rassieur Roberson
IA	Des Moines	4th Avenue Viaduct	x	Archie Alexander
IA	Des Moines	Alexander, Archie A.	1913	Archie Alexander
IA	Des Moines	Des Moines Sewage Disposal Plant	x	Archie Alexander
IA	Des Moines	East 14th Street Viaduct	1937	Archie Alexander
IA	Des Moines	Fluer Drive Bridge	1937	Archie Alexander
IA	Harpers Ferry	Effigy Mounds National Monument Visitor Center	x	Francis Rassieur Roberson
IA	Iowa City	College Street Viaduct	x	Archie Alexander
IA	Iowa City	University of Iowa Heating Plant	1927	Archie Alexander
IA	Mt. Pleasant	Des Moines River Highway Bridge	x	Archie Alexander
IL	Altgeld	Altgeld Gardens	1944	Robert Rochon Taylor
IL	Brookfield	Bungalow	x	Robert Buffins
IL	Brookfield	House	x	Robert Buffins
IL	Chicago	Apartment Bldg.	x	Robert Buffins
IL	Chicago	Tri-Plex	x	Robert Buffins
IL	Chicago	92nd Street Bridge	1914	Charles Duke
IL	Chicago	Becker Brothers Photographic Studio	x	Charles Duke
IL	Chicago	Century of Progress Du Saible Log Cabin Replica	1951	Charles Duke
IL	Chicago	Chicago Avenue Bridge	1914	Charles Duke
IL	Chicago	Chicago Tribune House Competition	1945	William Moses
IL	Chicago	Chicago War Memorial Competition	1930	Howard Mackey
IL	Chicago	Coastline Apts.	x	Charles Duke
IL	Chicago	Coppin Chapel	x	Kenneth O'Neal
IL	Chicago	Dearborn Street Subway Station	1943	William Thornton
IL	Chicago	Duchess Apts.	x	Robert Buffins
IL	Chicago	Ebenezer Baptist Church	x	Wallace Rayfield
IL	Chicago	Grand Avenue Bridge	1913	Charles Duke
IL	Chicago	Greater St. John Church	x	John Holloway
IL	Chicago	Hedges-Rayfield Motor Co.	1933	Charles Duke
IL	Chicago	Ida B. Wells Homes	1940	Walter Bailey
IL	Chicago	Jackson Boulevard Bridge	1916	Charles Duke
IL	Chicago	Johnson, Fielding	1944	John Holloway
IL	Chicago	Lake Shore Drive Apts.	1950	Georgia Brown
IL	Chicago	Lake Street Bridge	1916	Charles Duke
IL	Chicago	Lunt Lake Apts.	1950	Georgia Brown
IL	Chicago	Michigan Boulevard Garden Apts.	1928	Robert Rochon Taylor
IL	Chicago	Mt. Pisgah Church	x	John Holloway

APPENDIX

State	City/County	Name	Year	A/AE/LA
IL	Chicago	Mt. Zion Church	x	John Holloway
IL	Chicago	Muhammed, Elihjah	x	Leroy Hilliard
IL	Chicago	Oakhaven Old People's Home	1922	Charles Duke
IL	Chicago	Parker House Sausage Co.	x	Robert Buffins
IL	Chicago	People's Church & Metropolitan Ctr.	x	Charles Duke
IL	Chicago	Prairie Court Apts.	1950	Georgia Brown
IL	Chicago	Promotory Apts.	1950	Georgia Brown
IL	Chicago	Sheridan Beach Hotel	1922	Charles Duke
IL	Chicago	Shiloh Seventh Day Adventist Church	1925	Charles Duke
IL	Chicago	Southwest Land & Lake Tunnel	1914	Charles Duke
IL	Chicago	State Street Subway Station	1944	William Thornton
IL	Chicago	Stillman, Robert	1942	John Holloway
IL	Chicago	Thornton, William F.	1942	John Holloway
IL	Chicago	Tudor Apts.	1921	Charles Duke
IL	Chicago	Walters African Methodist Episcopal Zion Church	1914	Charles Duke
IL	Chicago	Washington Boulevard Apts.	x	Charles Duke
IL	Chicago	Washington Street Bridge	1913	Charles Duke
IL	Chicago	Webster Avenue Bridge	1916	Charles Duke
IL	Chicago	Winston, Leon	1944	John Holloway
IL	LaGrange	Cornerstone Chapel African Methodist Episcopal Church	c1915	John Lankford
IL	Peoria	Pere Marquette Hotel	1923	Julian Abele
IL	Robbins	Village of Robbins Town Hall	1940	John Holloway
IL	Robbins	Williams, Dr. J.W.	1940	John Holloway
IN	Gary	Campbell Friendship House	x	William Cooke
IN	Gary	Stewart Settlement House	1925	William Cooke
IN	Gary	Trinity Methodist Episcopal Church	1925	William Cooke
IN	Indianapolis	Ebenezer African Methodist Episcopal Church	1922	John Lankford
IN	Indianapolis	Flanner House Social Center	1943	Hilyard Robinson
IN	Indianapolis	St. John's African Methodist Episcopal Church	x	John Lankford
IN	Marion	First Baptist Church	1913	Samuel Plato
IN	Marion	House	c1915	Samuel Plato
IN	Marion	Lavengood, David	c1920	Samuel Plato
IN	Marion	Plato, Samuel M.	c1915	Samuel Plato
IN	Marion	Platonian Apts.	1910	Samuel Plato
IN	Marion	Second Baptist Church	1905	Samuel Plato
IN	Marion	Soldier's Home	c1905	Samuel Plato
IN	Marion	U. S. Post Office	1907	Samuel Plato
IN	Marion	Wilson, J. Woodrow	1912	Samuel Plato
IN	Marion	Worker's Housing	c1906	Samuel Plato
IN	Weaver	School No. 2	1908	Samuel Plato
KS	Kansas City	Anthony, Dr. Isham H. Apts.	c1904	Charles Bowman
KS	Larned	Ft. Larned National Historic Site Trader Ctr.	x	Francis Rassieur Roberson
KS	Quindaro	Western University Stanley Hall	1900	Charles Bowman
KS	Wichita	Arkansas Valley Lodge	c1910	Josiah Walker
KS	Wichita	Calvary Baptist Church	1917	Josiah Walker
KY	Bardstown	Purce Store & Post Office	c1900	Samuel Plato
KY	Covington	Lyons Hospital	c1940	Edward Birch
KY	Fayette County	Elmendorf Farm	1911	Julian Abele
KY	Frakes	Frakes Fire Station	1967	De Witt Dykes
KY	Frankfort	Kentucky Normal & Industrial Insitute Trade School	1909	William Pittman
KY	Lexington	Chandler Normal School Webster Hall	c1914	Vertner Tandy
KY	Lincoln Ridge	Lincoln Ridge Colored Institute Belknap Dormitory	1922	Vertner Tandy
KY	Lincoln Ridge	Lincoln Ridge Colored Institute Berea Hall	1922	Vertner Tandy
KY	Lincoln Ridge	Lincoln Ridge Colored Institute Industrial Bldg.	1922	Vertner Tandy
KY	Lincoln Ridge	Lincoln Ridge Colored Institute North Dormitory	1922	Vertner Tandy
KY	Louisville	Broadway Temple African Methdist Episcopal Church	1915	Samuel Plato
KY	Louisville	Curtis Wright Defense Housing	c1942	Samuel Plato
KY	Louisville	Lee Memorial Church	c1928	Samuel Plato
KY	Louisville	Simmons University Stewart Hall	x	Samuel Plato
KY	Louisville	Virginia Avenue School	x	Samuel Plato
KY	Louisville	Westover Subdivision	1945	Samuel Plato
KY	Paducah	Paducah Junior College Anderson Hall	x	Vertner Tandy

APPENDIX

State	City/County	Name	Year	A/AE/LA
LA	Abita Springs	Abita Springs Golf Course	x	Joseph Bartholomew
LA	Baton Rogue	Louisiana Colored Teachers Association Bldg.	x	Ferdinand Rousseve
LA	Baton Rouge	Web Park Golf Course	1926	Joseph Bartholomew
LA	Covington	Covington Country Club Golf Course	1954	Joseph Bartholomew
LA	Hammond	Hammond Country Club Golf Course	1921	Joseph Bartholomew
LA	Harahan	Bartholomew, Joseph M.	c1940	Joseph Bartholomew
LA	Metairie	Metairie Golf Course	1922	Joseph Bartholomew
LA	New Iberia	Our Lady of Perpetual Help Catholic Church	x	Ferdinand Rousseve
LA	New Orleans	Ashton Theatre	x	Ferdinand Rousseve
LA	New Orleans	Beecher Memorial Congregational Church	x	Ferdinand Rousseve
LA	New Orleans	Central Congregational United Church of Christ	x	Ferdinand Rousseve
LA	New Orleans	Cherrie-Segue Medical Clinic	x	Ferdinand Rousseve
LA	New Orleans	City Park No. 1 Golf Course	1923	Joseph Bartholomew
LA	New Orleans	City Park No. 3 Golf Course	1923	Joseph Bartholomew
LA	New Orleans	Congregational Church & Parish Hall	x	Ferdinand Rousseve
LA	New Orleans	Convents Holy Ghost Catholic Church Rectory	x	Ferdinand Rousseve
LA	New Orleans	Dryades Street YMCA	x	Ferdinand Rousseve
LA	New Orleans	Fifth African Baptist Church	x	Ferdinand Rousseve
LA	New Orleans	Greater Tulane Baptist Church	x	Ferdinand Rousseve
LA	New Orleans	McDonald Dental Office	x	Ferdinand Rousseve
LA	New Orleans	People's United Methodist Church Community Ctr.		Ferdinand Rousseve
LA	New Orleans	Pontchartrain Park Municipal Golf Course	1924	Joseph Bartholomew
LA	New Orleans	Rhodes Funeral Home	x	Ferdinand Rousseve
LA	New Orleans	Rose Hill Baptist Church	x	Ferdinand Rousseve
LA	New Orleans	St. Claver's Catholic Elementary School	1921	Ferdinand Rousseve
LA	New Orleans	St. Raymond's Catholic Church	x	Ferdinand Rousseve
LA	New Orleans	Twin House	x	Ferdinand Rousseve
LA	Slidell	Pine Wood Country Club Golf Course	c1963	Joseph Bartholomew
MA	Athol	Athol Elderly Housing	1972	Henry Boles
MA	Boston	Blue Hill Avenue Fire Station	1974	Henry Boles
MA	Boston	St. Stephen's Episcopal Church Parish Hall	1961	Henry Boles
MA	Brewster	Brewster Baptist Church	1976	Henry Boles
MA	Cambridge	Harvard University Widener Library	1913	Julian Abele
MA	Camridge	Harvard University Institute of Geographical Exploration	1930	Julian Abele
MA	Cambridge	Rousseve, Ferdinand L.	x	Ferdinand Rousseve
MA	Dorchester	Brunswick Gardens	c1977	Henry Boles
MA	Methuen	Knights of Columbus Home of Council	1961	Henry Boles
MA	Methuen	Methuen Elderly Housing	1974	Henry Boles
MA	Methuen	Methuen Fire Station	1967	Henry Boles
MA	Methuen	Methuen High School	x	Henry Boles
MA	New Bedford	New Bedford Home for the Aged	1908	Elizabeth Brooks
MA	New Bedford	Sgt. William Carney House	c1930	Elizabeth Brooks
MA	Plymouth	Massachusetts Bureau of Building Construction Office & Garage	1977	Henry Boles
MA	Roxbury	Marksdale Gardens	1965	Henry Boles
MA	Roxbury	Washington Park Shopping Ctr.	x	Henry Boles
MA	South Dennis	Dennis Elderly Housing	1974	Henry Boles
MA	South Yarmouth	Captain Farris House	x	Henry Boles
MA	South Yarmouth	Boles, Henry C.	c1960	Henry Boles
MA	South Yarmouth	St. David's Episcopal Church	1970	Henry Boles
MA	Tewskbury	North Street Fire Station	1976	Henry Boles
MA	Wakefield	U. S. Post Office	1975	Henry Boles
MA	Westfield	Westfield State College Student Union-Ely Library	1973	Henry Boles
MD	Andrews Field	Keister, J. B.	1950	Clyde Drayton
MD	Ardmore	Jones, D.	1944	Clyde Drayton
MD	Baltimore	Baber-Daniels Apts.	1967	Percy Ifill
MD	Baltimore	Brown Memorial Church	1988	John Sulton
MD	Baltimore	Cherry Hill Methodist Church	1962	De Witt Dykes
MD	Baltimore	Cherry Hill Public Housing	x	Hilyard Robinson
MD	Baltimore	Colored YMCA	c1915	John Lankford
MD	Baltimore	First Apostolic Faith Church	1982	Robert Madison
MD	Baltimore	Good Hope Office Bldg.	1907	John Lankford

APPENDIX

State	City/County	Name	Year	A/AE/LA
MD	Baltimore	Holabird Homes	x	David Williston
MD	Baltimore	Morgan State College Harper Womens Dormitory	1951	Albert Cassell
MD	Baltimore	Morgan State College O'Connel Mens Dormitory	1964	Albert Cassell
MD	Baltimore	Morgan State College Soldiers Armory	1957	Albert Cassell
MD	Baltimore	Morgan State College Student Christian Ctr.	1941	Albert Cassell
MD	Baltimore	Morgan State College Talmadge Field House	1969	Albert Cassell
MD	Baltimore	Morgan State College Tubman Womens Dormitory	1941	Albert Cassell
MD	Baltimore	Morgan State University Classroom Bldg.	x	Louis Fry
MD	Baltimore	Morning Star Baptist Church	1970	John Sulton
MD	Baltimore	Murphy, Carl T.	x	Albert Cassell
MD	Baltimore	Odd Fellows Temple	11925	Albert Cassell
MD	Baltimore	Oswego Mall Public Housing	1968	John Sulton
MD	Baltimore	Provident Hospital	1927	Hilyard Robinson
MD	Baltimore	Provident Hospital	1968	Hilyard Robinson
MD	Baltimore	Provident Hospital & Free Dispensary	1928	Albert Cassell
MD	Baltimore	Southern Baptist Church	1972	Hilyard Robinson
MD	Baltimore	St. Paul's Baptist Church	1967	Albert Cassell
MD	Beltsville	RCA Educational Laboratory Animal Facility	1978	John Sulton
MD	Beltsville	U. S. Dept. of Agricultural Animal Research Facility	1980	John Sulton
MD	Bladensburg	Seton High School	1950	David Williston
MD	Bowie	Goodloe, Don S.	1915	John Moore
MD	Brentwood	Collins, Lawrence	1948	Clyde Drayton
MD	Buena Vista	Hatton, Isaiah T.	1914	Isaiah Hatton
MD	Calvert County	Cheaspeake Heights-on-the-Bay	1932	Albert Cassell
MD	Capitol Heights	Capitol Heights Metro Station	1979	Leroy Brown
MD	Capitol Heights	Faith Temple No. 2 Baptist Church	1988	John Sulton
MD	Catonsville	Crownsville Hospital Housing & Recreation Center	x	Albert Cassell
MD	Chestertown	Fairlee Methodist Church Parsonage	1964	De Witt Dykes
MD	Church Hill	Mt. Vernon Methodist Church	1961	De Witt Dykes
MD	Cloverly	Pizza Hut	1985	John Sulton
MD	Colton	Conway Hotel	1945	Clyde Drayton
MD	Colton	Hotel Golden	x	John Lankford
MD	Colton	Point House	x	Lewis Giles, Jr.
MD	Crownsville	Crownsville Hospital Housing & Recreation Center	1917	Albert Cassell
MD	Cumberland	McKendree Methodist Church	1962	De Witt Dykes
MD	Dundalk	Holabird Public Housing	1941	Hilyard Robinson
MD	Dundalk	Lawe Funeral Parlor	1948	Howard Mackey
MD	Dundalk	Soller's Point War Housing	1942	Albert Cassell
MD	Fairmount Heights	Fairmount Heights Mutual Improvement Corp	1908	William Pittman
MD	Fairmount Heights	Fairmount Heights Public School	1912	William Pittman
MD	Fairmount Heights	Fairmount Heights Village Hall	x	William Pittman
MD	Fairmount Heights	Marshall, Clement	1911	William Pittman
MD	Fairmount Heights	Pittman, William S. "Little Red Top"	1907	William Pittman
MD	Glenarden	Crawford, Susie	1947	John Holloway
MD	Glenarden	Glenarden City Hall	x	Albert Cassell
MD	Glenarden	Hawkins Manor I & II	1969	Stewart Hoban
MD	Glenarden	Smith, Raymond	1947	John Holloway
MD	Glenmont	Pizza Hut	1985	John Sulton
MD	Glenn Burnie	Maryland School for Colored Girls	1936	Albert Cassell
MD	Greenbelt	Miskan Tora Community Ctr.	1951	Howard Mackey
MD	Highland Beach	Dyson, Dr. Walter	1931	Howard Mackey
MD	Hyattsville	Sacred Heart Home	c1960	Robert Fields
MD	Kenglar	Lee Chapel African Methodist Episcopal Church	c1915	John Lankford
MD	Lanham	Glenarden Apts.	1970	Stewart Hoban
MD	Lanham	Lagana, Josephine	x	John Holloway
MD	Lanham	Scioscia, Pete	1948	John Holloway
MD	Lincoln	Calloway, Thomas J.	1910	Isaiah Hatton
MD	Lincoln	Hatton, Isaiah T.	1914	Isaiah Hatton
MD	Lincoln	Hatton, Isaiah T.	1911	Isaiah Hatton
MD	Lincoln	Seaton, Dr. Daniel P.	x	Isaiah Hatton
MD	Owings Mill	Brooks, Walter Jr."Eccleston"	1915	Julian Abele
MD	Oyster Bay	Jones, J.C.	1954	Howard Mackey

APPENDIX

State	City/County	Name	Year	A/AE/LA
MD	Seat Pleasant	Federal Housing Administration Housing	1947	John Holloway
MD	Silver Spring	Kramer, _____	1950	Howard Mackey
MD	Soller's Pt.	Soller's Pt. Homes	1941	Hilyard Robinson
MD	Sparrow's Pt.	Sparrow's Pt. Defense Housing	1941	Hilyard Robinson
MD	Takoma Park	Shop-Rite Liquor Store	x	Romulus Archer
MD	Thurmont	Camp David Trader Ctr.	1964	Francis Rassieur Roberson
MD	Turner Station	Lyon Village Defense Housing	1941	Hilyard Robinson
MI	Detroit	Aijalon Baptist Church	1950	Francis Griffin
MI	Detroit	Ambassador Bridge	1929	Cornelius Henderson
MI	Detroit	Considine Auditorium	1973	Francis Griffin
MI	Detroit	Considine Sculpture Garden	1973	Francis Griffin
MI	Detroit	Detroit-Windsor Tunnel	x	Cornelius Henderson
MI	Detroit	Ebenezer African Methodist Episcopal Church	x	John Lankford
MI	Detroit	Forest Park & Playground	x	Elon Mickels
MI	Detroit	Medical Ctr. Courts	1964	Robert Madison
MI	Detroit	Plymouth Congregational Church	1970	Robert Madison
MI	Detroit	Plymouth Estates	1970	Robert Madison
MI	Detroit	Shiloh Baptist Church	1920	Carlos Stokes
MI	Detroit	St. John's Presbyterian Church	1972	Robert Madison
MI	Detroit	St. Martins-Griggs Park & Playground	x	Elon Mickels
MI	Detroit	St. Stephen African Methodist Church	1940	Donald White
MI	Detroit	Trinity Hospital	x	Helen Parker
MI	Dexter	Dexter Skew Arch Bridge	x	Fred Pelham
MI	Dexter	Michigan Central R.R. Arch Bridge	1890	Fred Pelham
MI	Grosse Pointe	Dodge, Anna D. "Rose Terrace"	1931	Julian Abele
MI	Iron River	U. S. Post Office	x	William Cooke
MI	Muskegan	First Church of Christ, Scientist	1931	Charles Duke
MI	Pocomoke City	Mt. Zion Methodist Church	1961	De Witt Dykes
MI	Warren	Detroit Memorial Park Cemetery	1926	Cornelius Henderson
MI	Yspilanti	Armstrong Drive Apts.	x	David Williston
MI	Yspilanti	Yspilanti Public Housing	1943	Hilyard Robinson
MN	Austin	Austin Catholic Church Stained-Glass	1895	William Hazel
MN	Elk River	Elk River Creamery	1921	Clarence Wigington
MN	Grand Portage	Grand Portage National Monument Trader Ctr.	x	Francis Rassieur Roberson
MN	Hibbing	U. S. Post Office	x	William Cooke
MN	International Falls	U. S. Post Office	1935	William Cooke
MN	Minneapolis	Ft. Snelling	c1950	Clarence Wigington
MN	Northfield	Northfield Creamery	1920	Clarence Wigington
MN	Pipestone	Pipestone National Monument Visitor Ctr.	1937	Francis Rassieur Roberson
MN	St. Paul	3rd Street Esplande & Tourist Bldg.	1930	Clarence Wigington
MN	St. Paul	40 & 8 Memorial Park	x	Clarence Wigington
MN	St. Paul	Baker Playground Shelter	1938	Clarence Wigington
MN	St. Paul	Belvidere Shelter House	1936	Clarence Wigington
MN	St. Paul	Butwin, J.G.	1948	Clarence Wigington
MN	St. Paul	Chelsea Heights Elementary School	1939	Clarence Wigington
MN	St. Paul	Cleveland Junior High School	1936	Clarence Wigington
MN	St. Paul	Como Park Elementary School Entrance	1915	Clarence Wigington
MN	St. Paul	Dayton's Bluff Playground Shelter	1936	Clarence Wigington
MN	St. Paul	Edgcumbe Elementary School	1939	Clarence Wigington
MN	St. Paul	Edgecumbe Playground Shelter	1934	Clarence Wigington
MN	St. Paul	Gopher Lodge No. 105	1925	Clarence Wigington
MN	St. Paul	Griffin, James	1958	Clarence Wigington
MN	St. Paul	Hamline Playground Shelter	1938	Clarence Wigington
MN	St. Paul	Harriet Island Pavillion	1940	Clarence Wigington
MN	St. Paul	Harrison Elementary School	1923	Clarence Wigington
MN	St. Paul	Hazel Park Playground Shelter	1935	Clarence Wigington
MN	St. Paul	Highland Park Monument, Fountain & Flag Staff	1926	Clarence Wigington
MN	St. Paul	Highland Park Pavillion	1932	Clarence Wigington
MN	St. Paul	Highland Park Water Tower	1928	Clarence Wigington
MN	St. Paul	Holman Airfield Administration Bldg.	1938	Clarence Wigington
MN	St. Paul	Homecroft Elementary School	1918	Clarence Wigington
MN	St. Paul	Keller Golf Course Clubhouse	1929	Clarence Wigington

APPENDIX

State	City/County	Name	Year	A/AE/LA
MN	St. Paul	Klein, Simon	1949	Clarence Wigington
MN	St. Paul	MacAlester Junior High School	1926	Clarence Wigington
MN	St. Paul	Mann Elementary School	1939	Clarence Wigington
MN	St. Paul	Marshall Junior High School	1925	Clarence Wigington
MN	St. Paul	McVay, Catherine	1917	Clarence Wigington
MN	St. Paul	Monroe Junior High School	1924	Clarence Wigington
MN	St. Paul	Monroe Junior High School Auditorium	1938	Clarence Wigington
MN	St. Paul	Moss, Harvey	1959	Clarence Wigington
MN	St. Paul	Park Elementary School	1938	Clarence Wigington
MN	St. Paul	Pyramid Realty & Investment Co.	1923	Clarence Wigington
MN	St. Paul	Ramsey County School for Boys	1928	Clarence Wigington
MN	St. Paul	Rice & Lawson Playground Shelter	1935	Clarence Wigington
MN	St. Paul	Scheffer Playground Shelter	1934	Clarence Wigington
MN	St. Paul	Smith Memorial	1932	Clarence Wigington
MN	St. Paul	South St. Anthony Playground Shelter	1935	Clarence Wigington
MN	St. Paul	St. Anthony's Park Branch Library	1920	Clarence Wigington
MN	St. Paul	St. Claire Playground Shelter	1935	Clarence Wigington
MN	St. Paul	St. George Greek Orthodox Church	1947	Clarence Wigington
MN	St. Paul	St. James African Methodist Episcopal Church	1948	Clarence Wigington
MN	St. Paul	St. Paul Fire Station No. 17	1929	Clarence Wigington
MN	St. Paul	St. Paul Fire Station No. 5	1929	Clarence Wigington
MN	St. Paul	St. Paul Fire Station No.10	1940	Clarence Wigington
MN	St. Paul	St. Paul Public Safety Bldg.	1929	Clarence Wigington
MN	St. Paul	St. Paul Winter Carnival Ice Palace	1942	Clarence Wigington
MN	St. Paul	St. Paul Winter Carnival Ice Palace	1940	Clarence Wigington
MN	St. Paul	St. Paul Winter Carnival Ice Palace	1937	Clarence Wigington
MN	St. Paul	St. Paul Winter Carnival Ice Palace	1941	Clarence Wigington
MN	St. Paul	St. Peters African Methodist Episcopal Church	1888	Francis Jefferson Roberson
MN	St. Paul	Sterling Clubhouse	1925	Clarence Wigington
MN	St. Paul	Sylvan Shelter House	1936	Clarence Wigington
MN	St. Paul	Van Buren Elementary School	1924	Clarence Wigington
MN	St. Paul	Veterans Hospital	x	Clarence Wigington
MN	St. Paul	Washington High School	1924	Clarence Wigington
MN	St. Paul	West Minnehaha Playground Bldg.	1937	Clarence Wigington
MN	St. Paul	Wilder Playground Community Bldg.	1940	Clarence Wigington
MN	St. Paul	Wilkins Auditorium Facade	1931	Clarence Wigington
MN	St. Paul	Wilson Junior High School	1925	Clarence Wigington
MO	Diamond	Carver National Monument Visitor Ctr.	1964	Francis Rassieur Roberson
MO	Jefferson City	Jones, Lucius	x	Charles Dickinson
MO	Jefferson City	Lincoln University Fine Arts Center	x	Charles Dickinson
MO	Jefferson City	Lincoln University Greenhouse	x	Charles Dickinson
MO	Jefferson City	Lincoln University Jason Gym	x	Charles Dickinson
MO	Jefferson City	Lincoln University Journalism Bldg.	x	Louis Fry
MO	Jefferson City	Lincoln University Mens Dormitory	x	Louis Fry
MO	Jefferson City	Lincoln University Page Library	1954	Louis Fry
MO	Jefferson City	Lincoln University Student Ctr.	x	Charles Dickinson
MO	Jefferson City	Lincoln University Womens Dormitory	x	Louis Fry
MO	Jefferson City	YMCA Bldg.	x	Charles Dickinson
MO	Joplin	St. John's Hospital	1963	Golden Zenon
MO	Kansas City	Chicago, Rock Island & Pacific Bridge		Archie Alexander
MO	Liberty	Mt. Zion Baptist Church	x	John Lankford
MO	Potosi	First Presbyterian Church	1909	John Lankford
MO	St. Louis	Antioch Baptist Church	1907	Francis Jefferson Roberson
MO	St. Louis	Bush, August	x	Francis Jefferson Roberson
MO	St. Louis	Jefferson Expansion Memorial Visitor Center	x	Francis Rassieur Roberson
MO	St. Louis	Leonard Avenue Baptist Church	x	John Lankford
MO	St. Louis	Roberson, Francis J.	x	Francis Jefferson Roberson
MO	St. Louis	St. Louis Botanical Garden Greenhouse	x	Francis Jefferson Roberson
MO	St. Louis	St. Louis Courthouse	x	Francis Rassieur Roberson
MO	St. Louis	St. Louis Train Station Canopies	x	Francis Jefferson Roberson
MS	Alcorn	Alcorn State University Campus Plan	1950	David Williston
MS	Basin	Mt. Pleasant Methodist Church	1960	De Witt Dykes

APPENDIX

State	City/County	Name	Year	A/AE/LA
MS	Bay Spring	Bethlehem Methodist Church	1957	De Witt Dykes
MS	Carthage	Wesley Methodist Church	1957	De Witt Dykes
MS	Columbus	Columbus Bridge	1842	Horace King
MS	DeKalb	St. Mark's Methodist Church	1956	De Witt Dykes
MS	Handsboro	Riley Chapel Methodist Church	1959	De Witt Dykes
MS	Holly Springs	Mississippi Industrial College Dining Hall	c1910	Robert Robinson Taylor
MS	Holly Springs	Mississippi Industrial College Dormitory	c1910	Robert Robinson Taylor
MS	Meridian	Haven Institute Dormitory	x	Wallace Rayfield
MS	Mound Bayou	Taborian Hospital	1940	Moses McKissack
MS	Columbus	Jemison, Robert Jr.	1845	Horace King
MS	Yazoo City	St. Stephen's Methodist Church	1959	De Witt Dykes
MT	Lake MacDonald	Glacier National Park Trader Ctr.	1932	Francis Rassieur Roberson
NC	Ahoski	Hunter, Edward	1949	Howard Mackey
NC	Ahoski	Weaver, Dr. Joseph D.	1949	Howard Mackey
NC	Ahoskie	New Ahoskie Baptist Church	x	Harvey Johnson
NC	Apex	Larkin's Chapel African Methodist Episcopal Church	x	John Lankford
NC	Asheville	Hill Street School Auditorium & Gym	1904	John Michael
NC	Asheville	Howell, Mamie	c1921	John Michael
NC	Asheville	Michael Family Compound	x	John Michael
NC	Asheville	Michael, John H.	1920	John Michael
NC	Asheville	St. John's African Methodist Episcopal Church	x	John Lankford
NC	Bragtown	Duke's Chapel	1926	Julian Abele
NC	Cedar Knoll	Cedar Knoll Baptist Church	1930	Howard Mackey
NC	Charlotte	African Methodist Episcopal Zion Publishing House	c1912	William Smith
NC	Charlotte	Afro-American Mutual Insurance Co.	x	William Smith
NC	Charlotte	Grace African Methodist Episcopal Zion Church	c1902	William Smith
NC	Charlotte	Mecklenbug Investment Co. Bldg.	c1922	William Smith
NC	Charlotte	Parker Heights	1970	Willie Jenkins
NC	Clinton	United Grove Disciples Church	1945	Howard Mackey
NC	Concord	Coleman Cotton Mill	1898	John Lankford
NC	Concord	First Christian Church	1970	Willie Jenkins
NC	Conover	McQueen Chapel Methodist Church	1958	De Witt Dykes
NC	Durham	Berry Construction Co.	1948	Henry Livas
NC	Durham	Duke University Botany Bldg.	1929	Julian Abele
NC	Durham	Duke University Chapel	1929	Julian Abele
NC	Durham	Duke University Dormitories Nos. 1–5	1925	Julian Abele
NC	Durham	Duke University Engineers' Dormitory	1925	Julian Abele
NC	Durham	Duke University Faculty Houses No. 1–11	1930	Julian Abele
NC	Durham	Duke University Gym	1940	Julian Abele
NC	Durham	Duke University Hospital	1938	Julian Abele
NC	Durham	Duke University Library	1926	Julian Abele
NC	Durham	Duke University Physics Bldg.	1947	Julian Abele
NC	Durham	Duke University Private Patient's Bldg.	1938	Julian Abele
NC	Durham	Duke University Indoor Stadium	1939	Julian Abele
NC	Durham	Merrick, John	c1910	John Merrick
NC	Durham	Merrick, John	1881	John Merrick
NC	Durham	National Religious Training School Administration Bldg.	1910	Clarence Wigington
NC	Durham	National Religious Training School Avery Auditorium	1910	William Pittman
NC	Durham	National Religious Training School Dining Hall	1910	William Pittman
NC	Durham	National Religious Training School Mens Dormitory	1910	Clarence Wigington
NC	Durham	National Religious Training School Theology Hall	1910	William Pittman
NC	Durham	National Religious Training School Womens Domitory	1910	Clarence Wigington
NC	Durham	National Religious Training School President's Residence	1910	William Pittman
NC	Durham	North Carolina Mutual Insurance Co.	1961	William Streat
NC	Durham	Seaborough Nursery	1972	William Streat
NC	Durham	United Durham, Inc. Bldg.	x	William Streat
NC	Durham	White Rock Baptist Church	1910	William Pittman
NC	Durham	White Rock Baptist Church	1977	Willie Jenkins
NC	Elizabeth City	Shaw University Roanoke Institute	x	Harvey Johnson
NC	Enfield	Bricks Congregational Rural Life School	1890	William Moses
NC	Fayetteville	First Baptist Church	1958	William Streat
NC	Fayetteville	John Wesley Methodist Church	1958	William Streat

APPENDIX

State	City/County	Name	Year	A/AE/LA
NC	Greensboro	Alexander, Judge _____	1957	William Street
NC	Greensboro	American Federal Savings & Loan Association	1968	Willie Jenkins
NC	Greensboro	Bethel African Methodist Episcopal Church	1961	Willie Jenkins
NC	Greensboro	Carolina Nursing Home	1968	Willie Jenkins
NC	Greensboro	Coore, Dr. _____	1987	William Streat
NC	Greensboro	Country Manor	1968	Willie Jenkins
NC	Greensboro	Cumberland Office Bldg.	1964	Willie Jenkins
NC	Greensboro	Episcopal Church of Redeemer	1950	William Streat
NC	Greensboro	Gillespie Junior High School	1960	Willie Jenkins
NC	Greensboro	Greensboro National Bank	1976	Willie Jenkins
NC	Greensboro	Heart of Town Motel	1967	Willie Jenkins
NC	Greensboro	Holley, Edward	1960	Willie Jenkins
NC	Greensboro	Laughlin Memorial Methodist Church	1967	De Witt Dykes
NC	Greensboro	Lee, Atty. S. Kenneth	1960	Willie Jenkins
NC	Greensboro	Lee, Atty. S. Kenneth	1960	Jasminius Grandy
NC	Greensboro	Mt. Tabor Methodist Church Education Bldg.	1964	De Witt Dykes
NC	Greensboro	North Carolina A&T University Aggie Stadium	1980	Willie Jenkins
NC	Greensboro	North Carolina A&T University Classroom Bldg.	1966	Willie Jenkins
NC	Greensboro	North Carolina A&T University Communication Bldg.	1973	Willie Jenkins
NC	Greensboro	North Carolina A&T University Law School	1978	Willie Jenkins
NC	Greensboro	North Carolina A&T University Wiliams Cafeteria	1974	Willie Jenkins
NC	Greensboro	North Carolina A&T University Campus Plan	1975	Jasminius Grandy
NC	Greensboro	Reed, Dr. _____	1959	William Streat
NC	Greensboro	Smith Funeral Home	1967	Willie Jenkins
NC	Greensboro	St. James Presbyterian Church	1959	Willie Jenkins
NC	Greensboro	St. Matthews Methodist Church	1970	Willie Jenkins
NC	Greensboro	Streat, William A.	1962	William Streat
NC	Almance County	Three College Observatory	1987	Willie Jenkins
NC	Greensboro	Watkins, Dr. _____	1967	William Streat
NC	Greensboro	Wells, _____	1960	Willie Jenkins
NC	Guilford	Bass' Chapel Methodist Church Education Bldg.	1963	De Witt Dykes
NC	Henderson	U. S. Post Office	1970	Willie Jenkins
NC	Johns	Jerusalem Methodist Church	1966	De Witt Dykes
NC	Lake Lure	Mt. Nebo Baptist Church	1964	De Witt Dykes
NC	Lewiston	Mt. Olive Baptist Church	1957	Harvey Johnson
NC	Madison	St. Stephen's Methodist Church	1960	De Witt Dykes
NC	Midway	Brooks Temple Methodist Church	1959	De Witt Dykes
NC	North Wilkesboro	U. S. Post Office	1965	Willie Jenkins
NC	Raleigh	Masonic Lodge	1907	Gaston Edwards
NC	Raleigh	Capehart, _____	x	Calvin Lightner
NC	Raleigh	Davie Street Presbyterian Church	c1920	Calvin Lightner
NC	Raleigh	First Baptist Church	c1915	John Lankford
NC	Raleigh	Lightner Arcade & Hotel	1921	Calvin Lightner
NC	Raleigh	Lightner Bldg.	1919	Calvin Lightner
NC	Raleigh	Lightner, Calvin E.	c1907	Calvin Lightner
NC	Durham	Mechanic & Farmers Bank	1922	Calvin Lightner
NC	Raleigh	Shaw University Apts.	1973	Willie Jenkins
NC	Raleigh	Shaw University Leonard Medical School	1912	Gaston Edwards
NC	Raleigh	Shaw University Tyler Hall	1910	Gaston Edwards
NC	Raleigh	St. Augustine College Benson Library	1898	Henry Delany
NC	Raleigh	St. Augustine College Chapel	1895	Henry Delany
NC	Raleigh	St. Augustine College Taylor Hall	1902	Henry Delany
NC	Raleigh	Taylor Bldg.	x	Calvin Lightner
NC	Rock Hill	Afro-American Mutual Insurance Co.	c1909	William Smith
NC	Rockingham	Philadelphia Methodist Church	1958	De Witt Dykes
NC	Salisbury	Livingston College Aggrey Student Union	1962	Hilyard Robinson
NC	Salisbury	Livingston College Carnegie Library	1905	Robert Robinson Taylor
NC	Salisbury	Livingston College Goler Hall	c1917	William Smith
NC	Salisbury	Livingston College Harris Dormitory	1955	Hilyard Robinson
NC	Salisbury	Livingston College Hood Hall	c1906	William Smith
NC	Salisbury	Livingston College Moore Faculty House	1948	Hilyard Robinson
NC	Salisbury	Livingston College Varrick Auditorium	1963	Hilyard Robinson

APPENDIX

State	City/County	Name	Year	A/AE/LA
NC	Salisbury	Zion Hills Apts.	1970	Willie Jenkins
NC	Sedalia	Palmer Memorial Institute Boys Dormitory	1967	Willie Jenkins
NC	Tarboro	Quigless Medical Clinic	1947	John Holloway
NC	Thomasville	Thomasville Church Homes	1968	Willie Jenkins
NC	Trinity	Baptist Church	x	William Streat
NC	Weldon	Horne, Dr. W.L.	1937	William Moses
NC	Weldon	Shoffner, _____	1967	Willie Jenkins
NC	Wilmington	Avant, Dr. Frank W.	1929	John Moore
NC	Winston-Salem	Bruce, Dr. _____	1963	William Streat
NC	Winston-Salem	Coleman, Dr. _____	1961	William Streat
NC	Winston-Salem	Coley, Dr. _____	1971	William Streat
NC	Winston-Salem	Gadison, _____	1960	Willie Jenkins
NC	Winston-Salem	Goler Metropolitan Apts.	1972	Willie Jenkins
NC	Winston-Salem	Mt. Zion Baptist Church	1969	Willie Jenkins
NC	Winston-Salem	New Bethel Church Homes	1969	Willie Jenkins
NC	Winston-Salem	Oliver, _____	1960	Willie Jenkins
NC	Winston-Salem	Quick, Dr. _____	1961	William Streat
NE	Omaha	Boy's Town High School	x	Golden Zenon
NE	Omaha	Broomfield & Crutchfield Apts.	1913	Clarence Wigington
NE	Omaha	11th Street Flats	1914	Clarence Wigington
NE	Omaha	Bailey, Isaac	1908	Clarence Wigington
NE	Omaha	Britt, Leonard E.	1912	Clarence Wigington
NE	Omaha	College of St. Mary's Science Bldg.	x	Golden Zenon
NE	Omaha	Johnson, Hollis M.	1914	Clarence Wigington
NE	Omaha	North Branch Public Library	1972	Golden Zenon
NE	Omaha	Obee, G. Wade	1913	Clarence Wigington
NE	Omaha	Orr Duplex	1914	Clarence Wigington
NE	Omaha	Peterson, Thomas	1912	Clarence Wigington
NE	Omaha	Salvage Bldg.	1966	Francis Rassieur Roberson
NE	Omaha	St. Johns African Methodist Episcopal Church	1908	Clarence Wigington
NE	Omaha	Zion Baptist Church	1909	Clarence Wigington
NE	Columbus	Loup River Power Plant	1933	Archie Alexander
NE	Omaha	Creighton University Mens Dormitory	x	Golden Zenon
NE	Omaha	Creighton University Science Bldg.	1965	Golden Zenon
NE	Omaha	Creighton University Swanson Library	1966	Golden Zenon
NE	Omaha	Creighton University Womens Dormitory	x	Golden Zenon
NE	Omaha	Dominican Sisters High School	1983	Golden Zenon
NE	Omaha	Edmonson Hospital	x	Golden Zenon
NE	Omaha	Eppley Airfield Terminal	x	Golden Zenon
NE	Beatrice	Homested National Park Visitor Ctr.	x	Francis Rassieur Roberson
NE	Bellevue	Strategic Air Command Composite Hospital	1962	Golden Zenon
NE	Grand Rapids	Grand Rapids Sewage Plant	1930	Archie Alexander
NE	Lincoln	University of Nebraska College of Law	1969	Golden Zenon
NE	Lincoln	University of Nebraska Performing Arts Bldg.	1973	Golden Zenon
NE	North Platte	Union Pacific Bridge	1935	Archie Alexander
NE	Papillion	U. S. Post Office	x	Golden Zenon
NE	Sarpy County	Bryan Senior High School	1969	Golden Zenon
NJ	Englewood	Otis, Clyde	x	J. Alonzo Plater
NJ	Lawnside	Lawnside Gardens & Shopping Center	1946	Howard Mackey
NJ	Longport	Widener Memorial Home	1911	Julian Abele
NJ	Middletown	Knight, Edward C. Jr. "Stonybrook"	1927	Julian Abele
NJ	Montclair	First Church of Christ, Scientist	x	Charles Duke
NJ	Newark	Cotton Bldg.	c1920	Vertner Tandy
NJ	Newark	Ritchwood, _____	1972	Willie Jenkins
NJ	Park Ridge	Foster, George W. Jr.	1902	George Foster
NJ	Phillipsburg	U. S. Post Office	x	Samuel Plato
NJ	Plainfield	House	1922	Robert Robinson
NJ	Plainfield	Church	1930	Robert Robinson
NJ	Plainfield	Church	1921	Robert Robinson
NJ	Plainfield	Duplex	1928	Robert Robinson
NJ	Plainfield	House	1925	Robert Robinson
NJ	Plainfield	House	1903	Robert Robinson

APPENDIX

State	City/County	Name	Year	A/AE/LA
NJ	Plainfield	House	1903	Robert Robinson
NJ	Plainfield	House	1919	Robert Robinson
NJ	Plainfield	House	1926	Robert Robinson
NJ	Plainfield	House	1930	Robert Robinson
NJ	Plainfield	House	1926	Robert Robinson
NJ	Plainfield	House	1923	Robert Robinson
NJ	Plainfield	House	1923	Robert Robinson
NJ	Plainfield	House	1927	Robert Robinson
NJ	Plainfield	House	1926	Robert Robinson
NJ	Plainfield	Humphrey Hall	1928	Robert Robinson
NJ	West Long Branch	Parson, Hubert T. "Shadow Lawn"	1927	Julian Abele
NJ	Woodcliff Lake	Woodcliff Lake School	1910	George Foster
NM	Santa Fe	Hauser, Dr. Eric	1952	James Garrott
NV	Reno	El Reno Housing	1939	Paul Williams
NV	Reno	First Church of Christ, Scientist	1939	Paul Williams
NV	Storey County	Map of the Comstock Lode	1875	Grafton Brown
NV	Virginia City	Virginia City	1861	Grafton Brown
NV	Virginia City	Virginia City Territory	1864	Grafton Brown
NV	Weeks	View of Fort Churchill	c1869	Grafton Brown
NY	Astoria	Broadway-Astoria Branch Library	1958	Clinton Harris
NY	Bayside	Bayside Branch Library	1965	Clinton Harris
NY	Bedford Hills	Hillcrest Center for Children	1963	Clinton Harris
NY	Brighton	Aprilano, Frank	1955	Thomas Boyde
NY	Brighton	Axelrod, Milton P.	1952	Thomas Boyde
NY	Brighton	Eisenstat, William P.	1952	Thomas Boyde
NY	Brighton	Ferris, Newell A.	1948	Thomas Boyde
NY	Brighton	Friedman, Jules	1953	Thomas Boyde
NY	Brighton	Grossman, Milton	1954	Thomas Boyde
NY	Brighton	Heicklen, Morris	1950	Thomas Boyde
NY	Brighton	Hicks, George T.	1951	Thomas Boyde
NY	Brighton	Hoffman, Harry L.	1950	Thomas Boyde
NY	Brighton	Huntington, Harry B.	1947	Thomas Boyde
NY	Brighton	Kasdins, Jacob	1953	Thomas Boyde
NY	Brighton	Levy, Bennett	1948	Thomas Boyde
NY	Brighton	Lopatin, Harold H.	1954	Thomas Boyde
NY	Brighton	Mangurian, Harry T.	1955	Thomas Boyde
NY	Brighton	Morris, Atty. Ira H.	1955	Thomas Boyde
NY	Brighton	Papa, Frank C.	1951	Thomas Boyde
NY	Brighton	Prager, Sol L.	1952	Thomas Boyde
NY	Brighton	Queen's Colony Subdivision	1954	Thomas Boyde
NY	Brighton	Raffelson, Jacob	1948	Thomas Boyde
NY	Brighton	Rause, Arthur A.	1951	Thomas Boyde
NY	Brighton	Ritts, Donald B.	1950	Thomas Boyde
NY	Brighton	Romack, Paul	1951	Thomas Boyde
NY	Brighton	Santa, Sam R.	1955	Thomas Boyde
NY	Brighton	Segal, Morris	1953	Thomas Boyde
NY	Brighton	Sherman, Barney R.	1948	Thomas Boyde
NY	Brighton	Sleepy Hollow Motel	1954	Thomas Boyde
NY	Brighton	Thurston, Lewis M.	1949	Thomas Boyde
NY	Brighton	Weis, Linus R.	1950	Thomas Boyde
NY	Brighton	Litwin, Emil	1952	Thomas Boyde
NY	Bronx	Allerton Branch Library	1960	Clinton Harris
NY	Bronx	Bronx Municipal Hospital Ctr.	1952	Clinton Harris
NY	Bronx	East Bronx Municipal Hospital Nurses Residence	1964	Clinton Harris
NY	Bronx	Firehouse-Engine Company 96 & Ladder Company 54	1965	Clinton Harris
NY	Bronx	Fordham Regional & Children's Library	x	Clinton Harris
NY	Bronx	Grand Concourse Branch Library	1959	Clinton Harris
NY	Bronx	Jerome Avenue Garage	x	Clinton Harris
NY	Bronx	Morrisania District Health Ctr.	1955	Clinton Harris
NY	Bronx	Mosholu Branch Library	1954	Clinton Harris
NY	Bronx	University Heights Branch Library	1957	Clinton Harris
NY	Bronx	West Farms Branch Library	1953	Clinton Harris

APPENDIX

State	City/County	Name	Year	A/AE/LA
NY	Bronx	Westchester Square Branch Library	1955	Clinton Harris
NY	Bronx	Youth House for Girls Temporary Annex	1960	Clinton Harris
NY	Brooklyn	Bay Ridge Branch Library	1960	Clinton Harris
NY	Brooklyn	Bedford District Health Ctr.	1955	Clinton Harris
NY	Brooklyn	Bensonhurst Parking Field	1958	Clinton Harris
NY	Brooklyn	Borough Park Branch Library	x	Clinton Harris
NY	Brooklyn	Brooklyn Community College	1959	Clinton Harris
NY	Brooklyn	Brooklyn Domestic Relations Court	1956	Clinton Harris
NY	Brooklyn	Brooklyn Heights Public Library	1961	Clinton Harris
NY	Brooklyn	Brooklyn House of Detention for Men	1956	Clinton Harris
NY	Brooklyn	Brooklyn Supreme Court	x	Clinton Harris
NY	Brooklyn	Brooklyn Welfare Center	1955	Clinton Harris
NY	Brooklyn	Bushwick District Health Ctr.	1959	Clinton Harris
NY	Brooklyn	City Hospitals of Brooklyn Laundry	1961	Clinton Harris
NY	Brooklyn	Coney Island Branch Library	1956	Clinton Harris
NY	Brooklyn	Coney Island General Hospital	1956	Clinton Harris
NY	Brooklyn	Crown Heights Health Ctr.	1956	Clinton Harris
NY	Brooklyn	Cumberland Hospital	1961	Clinton Harris
NY	Brooklyn	Firehouse-Engine Company 202 & Ladder Compnay 101	1960	Clinton Harris
NY	Brooklyn	Firehouse-Engine Company 209 & Ladder Company 102	1965	Clinton Harris
NY	Brooklyn	Firehouse-Engine Company 214	1958	Clinton Harris
NY	Brooklyn	Firehouse-Engine Company 246 & Ladder Company 169	1960	Clinton Harris
NY	Brooklyn	Firehouse-Engine Company 330 & Ladder Company 172	1964	Clinton Harris
NY	Brooklyn	Gravesend District Health Ctr.	1953	Clinton Harris
NY	Brooklyn	Kings Highway Branch Library	1954	Clinton Harris
NY	Brooklyn	Mapleton Branch Library	x	Clinton Harris
NY	Brooklyn	Midwood Branch Library	1955	Clinton Harris
NY	Brooklyn	NYC Community College Academic & Science Bldgs.	1966	Clinton Harris
NY	Brooklyn	NYC Department of Public Works Repair Shop	1955	Clinton Harris
NY	Brooklyn	NYC Department of Sanitaition Incinerator	1961	Clinton Harris
NY	Brooklyn	Williamsburg Regional Branch Library	x	Clinton Harris
NY	Brookville	Brokaw, Howard C.	1916	Julian Abele
NY	Brookville	Clews, James B. "LaLanterne"	1929	Julian Abele
NY	Brookville	Dows, David "Charlton Hall"	1916	Julian Abele
NY	Buffalo	Lipson Furniture Co.	1952	Thomas Boyde
NY	Buffalo	McGuire Medical Office	x	John Brent
NY	Buffalo	Michigan Avenue YMCA	1926	John Brent
NY	Canandaigua	Aronson, Victor	1953	Thomas Boyde
NY	Canandaigua	Ginghamtown Restaurant & Motel	1953	Thomas Boyde
NY	Cheektowaga	Miles, Walter	c1935	John Brent
NY	Dansville	Masonic Temple	1953	Thomas Boyde
NY	Eden	Payne, Clara	x	John Brent
NY	Elmhurst	Elmhurst General Hospital	1956	Clinton Harris
NY	Far Rockaway	Far Rockaway Branch Library	1967	Clinton Harris
NY	Flushing	Auburndale-Clearview Branch Library	1967	Clinton Harris
NY	Flushing	Flushing Parking Garage-Upper Deck	1965	Clinton Harris
NY	Flushing	Flushing Regional Branch Library	1955	Clinton Harris
NY	Flushing	Hall of Science	1964	Clinton Harris
NY	Forest Hills	Forest Hills Branch Library	1958	Clinton Harris
NY	Frankfort	U. S. Post Office	x	Samuel Plato
NY	Fresh Meadows	Firehouse-Engine Company 299 & Ladder Company 152	1960	Clinton Harris
NY	Gates	Aero Industries	1953	Thomas Boyde
NY	Great Neck	Morosco, Oliver	1929	Vertner Tandy
NY	Great Neck	Phipps, Henry C.	1916	Julian Abele
NY	Greece	Davis, Harry I.	1951	Thomas Boyde
NY	Greece	Dorschel Motors	1948	Thomas Boyde
NY	Greece	Friederich, Adam G.	1955	Thomas Boyde
NY	Greece	Leonardo, Henry F.	1949	Thomas Boyde
NY	Greece	Rogacs, Joseph	1950	Thomas Boyde
NY	Henderson Harbor	Storrer, Herman L.	1954	Thomas Boyde
NY	Irondequoit	Arieno, Charles J.	1951	Thomas Boyde
NY	Irondequoit	Brodsky, Maurice	1950	Thomas Boyde

APPENDIX

State	City/County	Name	Year	A/AE/LA
NY	Irondequoit	Cellura, Alfred	1952	Thomas Boyde
NY	Irondequoit	Connors, Joseph S.	1949	Thomas Boyde
NY	Irondequoit	Dattilo, Atty. Philip B. Sr.	1948	Thomas Boyde
NY	Irondequoit	DeRyke Dairy	1947	Thomas Boyde
NY	Irondequoit	Fasino, Joseph	1955	Thomas Boyde
NY	Irondequoit	Gargano, Frank A.	1949	Thomas Boyde
NY	Irondequoit	Giordano, Joseph J.	1947	Thomas Boyde
NY	Irondequoit	Kapp, Sam	1955	Thomas Boyde
NY	Irondequoit	Lanzatella, Philip J.	1951	Thomas Boyde
NY	Irondequoit	Leonardo, Richard A.	1950	Thomas Boyde
NY	Irondequoit	LoCurcio, Ralph D.	1948	Thomas Boyde
NY	Irondequoit	Mammano, Joseph T.	1954	Thomas Boyde
NY	Irondequoit	Mercurio, Frank	1948	Thomas Boyde
NY	Irondequoit	Palermo, Biagio	1946	Thomas Boyde
NY	Irondequoit	Papa, Samuel R.	1948	Thomas Boyde
NY	Irondequoit	Parks, Joseph F.	1948	Thomas Boyde
NY	Irondequoit	Passero, Anthony P.	1953	Thomas Boyde
NY	Irondequoit	Pluto, Andrew	1953	Thomas Boyde
NY	Irondequoit	Romeo, Philip	1950	Thomas Boyde
NY	Irondequoit	Russi, Arthur M.	1947	Thomas Boyde
NY	Irondequoit	Scardino, Samuel P.	1951	Thomas Boyde
NY	Irondequoit	Schifano, Benedict F.	1954	Thomas Boyde
NY	Irondequoit	Sutphen, George T.	1953	Thomas Boyde
NY	Irondequoit	Ward, Clarence A.	1952	Thomas Boyde
NY	Irvington-on-the-Hudson	Walker, Madame C.J. "Villa le Waro"	1917	Vertner Tandy
NY	Jackson Heights	Jackson Heights Branch Library	1954	Clinton Harris
NY	Jamaica	Allen African Episcopal Church	1963	Robert Madison
NY	Jamaica	Firehouse-Engine Company 275 & Spare Trucks	1960	Clinton Harris
NY	Jamaica	Firehouse-Engine Company 298 & Ladder Company 127	1964	Clinton Harris
NY	Jamaica	Jamaica Parking Field No. 2	1960	Clinton Harris
NY	Jamaica	Queens Central Library	1965	Clinton Harris
NY	Jamaica	Queens General Hospital Nurses Residence	1956	Clinton Harris
NY	Jamaica	Queens General Hospital Stores Bldg.	1958	Clinton Harris
NY	Jamaica	Rochdale Village Branch Library	1966	Clinton Harris
NY	Jamaica	Singleton, Dr. John A.	1945	William Moses
NY	Manhasset	Grace, Joseph P.	1920	Julian Abele
NY	Maspeth	Department of Sanitation Central Repair Shop	1965	Clinton Harris
NY	Mt. Vernon	Southside Committee for Community Improvement	1963	Percy Ifill
NY	Mumford	Balonek, Frank	1952	Thomas Boyde
NY	Nanuet	Highview Avenue Elementary School	1908	Vertner Tandy
NY	Nanuet	Lewissohn Garage & Shop	1911	Vertner Tandy
NY	Queens	Firehouse-Neponsit Section	1961	Clinton Harris
NY	New York	Apartment Bldg.	1972	John Wilson
NY	New York	Public School	1971	John Wilson
NY	New York	Senior Citizen Housing	x	John Wilson
NY	New York	20th Precinct Station	1964	Percy Ifill
NY	New York	Abraham Lincoln Homes	1945	Vertner Tandy
NY	New York	American Airlines Baggage Area	1969	Percy Ifill
NY	New York	Amsterdam Avenue Housing	1971	Percy Ifill
NY	New York	Bellevue Hospital Nurses School & Residence	1956	Clinton Harris
NY	New York	Bloomingdale Branch Library	1960	Clinton Harris
NY	New York	Boys & Girls High School	1975	John Wilson
NY	New York	Brooklyn Technical High School	1933	Richard White
NY	New York	Caanan Baptist Church	1968	Percy Ifill
NY	New York	Carhart, Amory S.	1913	Julian Abele
NY	New York	Carver Savings & Loan	1962	Percy Ifill
NY	New York	Central Manhattan Repair Hqtrs.	1955	Clinton Harris
NY	New York	Children's Aid Society Bldg.	c1922	Vertner Tandy
NY	New York	Cotton, Dr. Norman F.	x	Vertner Tandy
NY	New York	Duke, James B.	1909	Julian Abele
NY	New York	East Harlem General Hospital	1959	Clinton Harris
NY	New York	East River Park Amphitheatre	x	John Wilson

APPENDIX

State	City/County	Name	Year	A/AE/LA
NY	New York	Medgar Evers State College	1971	Percy Ifill
NY	New York	Firehouse-Engine Company 11 & Ladder Company 11	1959	Clinton Harris
NY	New York	Firehouse-Engine Company 22 & Ladder Company 13	1961	Clinton Harris
NY	New York	Firehouse-Engine Company 3 & Ladder Company 12	1966	Clinton Harris
NY	New York	Firehouse-Engine Company 40 & Ladder Company 35	1961	Clinton Harris
NY	New York	Firehouse-Engine Company 58 & Ladder Company 26	1960	Clinton Harris
NY	New York	Firehouse-Engine Company 59 & Ladder Company 30	1961	Clinton Harris
NY	New York	Firehouse-Engine Company 76 & Ladder Company 22	1960	Clinton Harris
NY	New York	Firehouse-Engine Company 8 & Ladder Company 2	x	Clinton Harris
NY	New York	Franklin Plaza Subway Station	1974	Conrad Johnson
NY	New York	Freedom National Bank	1963	Percy Ifill
NY	New York	Globe National Bank	x	Vertner Tandy
NY	New York	Gouverneur Hospital	x	Clinton Harris
NY	New York	Greater Refuge Temple	1970	Percy Ifill
NY	New York	Hamilton Fish Park Branch Library	x	Clinton Harris
NY	New York	Harkness House for Ballet Arts	c1965	Booker T. Washington III
NY	New York	Harlem Hospital	1968	Clinton Harris
NY	New York	Harlem Retail Market	1955	Clinton Harris
NY	New York	Harlem River Houses	1936	John Wilson
NY	New York	Harlem River Representative Shop & Engineers' Office	1956	Clinton Harris
NY	New York	Harlem Welfare Ctr.	1952	Clinton Harris
NY	New York	Imperial Elks Lodge	1922	Vertner Tandy
NY	New York	Inwood Branch Library	1952	Clinton Harris
NY	New York	Ivey Terace Apts.	1948	Vertner Tandy
NY	New York	Kerbs Memorial Boathouse	1954	John Wilson
NY	New York	Library for the Blind	1952	Clinton Harris
NY	New York	Lincoln Hospital	x	Vertner Tandy
NY	New York	Lincoln Hospital	1956	Clinton Harris
NY	New York	Medical Examiner's Bldg.	1960	Clinton Harris
NY	New York	Metropolitan Hospital Nurses Residence & School	1961	Clinton Harris
NY	New York	Metropolitan Opera House Grand Stair	1966	Washington, Booker T. III
NY	New York	Midwood High School	c1940	Richard White
NY	New York	Milbank-Frawley Urban Renewal Site No. 2	1973	Percy Ifill
NY	New York	Morningside Health Ctr.	1959	Clinton Harris
NY	New York	Mother African Methodist Episcopal Zion Church	1923	George Foster
NY	New York	Mt. Moriah Baptist Church	1924	Vertner Tandy
NY	New York	Mt. Morris Park Senior Citizen's Housing	1960	John Wilson
NY	New York	Mt. Morris Park Swimming Pool & Bathouse	1966	Percy Ifill
NY	New York	Municipal Parking Garage	1960	Clinton Harris
NY	New York	National Monument to Black Soldiers & Sailors	1916	Edward Williams
NY	New York	New York City Public School No. 13	1969	Percy Ifill
NY	New York	New York Evening Post	1925	Julian Abele
NY	New York	New York State Office Bldg.	1974	Percy Ifill
NY	New York	NYC Municipal Court	1960	Clinton Harris
NY	New York	NYC Board of Education Early Childhood Ctr.	1975	John Wilson
NY	New York	NYC Department of Sanitiation Incinerator	1961	Clinton Harris
NY	New York	NYC Deptartment of Water, Gas & Electricity	x	Clinton Harris
NY	New York	NYC Fire Department College Training Bldg.	1964	Clinton Harris
NY	New York	NYC Institution for Female Prisoners	x	Clinton Harris
NY	New York	NYC Police Academy-13th & 15th Precincts	1964	Clinton Harris
NY	New York	NYC Police Hqtrs.	1964	Clinton Harris
NY	New York	NYC Police Station 24th Precinct	1960	Clinton Harris
NY	New York	NYC Public Health Laboratory	1966	Clinton Harris
NY	New York	NYC Terminal Market	1964	Clinton Harris
NY	New York	Pan American Bldg.	c1963	Booker T. Washington III
NY	New York	Phipps Center Police Athletic League	1967	Percy Ifill
NY	New York	Prospect Park Boathouse	x	John Wilson
NY	New York	Pulitzer Bldg.	1907	Julian Abele
NY	New York	Remand Shelter for Adolescent Boys	1964	Clinton Harris
NY	New York	Ridder Junior High School	1931	Richard White
NY	New York	Riverside Health Ctr.	1960	Clinton Harris
NY	New York	Salem Methodist Church Community Center	1965	Percy Ifill

APPENDIX

State	City/County	Name	Year	A/AE/LA
NY	New York	Sherman Creek Project	1973	Percy Ifill
NY	New York	Small's Paradise Cabaret	1925	Vertner Tandy
NY	New York	St. David's Protestant Episcopal Church	c1922	Vertner Tandy
NY	New York	St. Martin's Towers	1966	Percy Ifill
NY	New York	St. Philips Church Community Youth Ctr.	1966	Conrad Johnson
NY	New York	St. Philips Protestant Episcopal Church & Parish Hall	1910	George Foster
NY	New York	Swissair Ticket Counters	1963	Percy Ifill
NY	New York	Triborough Bridge & Tunnel	c1940	Joseph Parker
NY	New York	Throgs Neck Public Library	1972	John Wilson
NY	New York	Tri-Boro Plaza Complex	1966	Percy Ifill
NY	New York	Trinity Baptist Church	1970	Percy Ifill
NY	New York	Tuberculosis & Chronic Disease Hospital	1954	Clinton Harris
NY	New York	U. S. Post Office, Stuyvesant Station	1974	Percy Ifill
NY	New York	United Moravian Church	1973	Percy Ifill
NY	New York	Varick Community Ctr.	1970	Percy Ifill
NY	New York	Village East Towers	1964	Percy Ifill
NY	New York	Walker, Madame C.J. "Villa Le Waro"	1917	Vertner Tandy
NY	New York	Western Union Message Ctr.	1973	Percy Ifill
NY	New York	Wildenstein Gallery	1931	Julian Abele
NY	New York	World's Fair Virginia Pavillion Competition	1938	William Moses
NY	New York	Wynn Center Police Athletic League	1963	Percy Ifill
NY	Niagara Falls	St. John's African Methodist Episcopal Church	1969	Robert Madison
NY	Penfield	Gianforti, Bert C.	1954	Thomas Boyde
NY	Penfield	Ward, John C.	1941	Thomas Boyde
NY	Pittsford	Gibbin, Dr. Clifford L.	1946	Thomas Boyde
NY	Pittsford	Goldstein, David G.	1954	Thomas Boyde
NY	Pittsford	Dorschel, John	1952	Thomas Boyde
NY	Pocantico Hills	Rockefeller Barn	c1890	William Robinson
NY	Purchase	Johnson, Conrad	1950	Conrad Johnson
NY	Queens	Pan American Tower	x	Washington, Booker T. III
NY	Queens Village	Queens Village Regional Branch Library	1953	Clinton Harris
NY	Rochester	Betsy & Betty Beauty Salon	1948	Thomas Boyde
NY	Rochester	Blue Label Foods Plant	1936	Thomas Boyde
NY	Rochester	Carver House	1943	Thomas Boyde
NY	Rochester	Daltin Restauant	1950	Thomas Boyde
NY	Rochester	Dinner Bell Restaurant	1947	Thomas Boyde
NY	Rochester	Duffy's Hotel	1954	Thomas Boyde
NY	Rochester	Eastman Hotel Rainbow Lounge	1947	Thomas Boyde
NY	Rochester	Ernie's Place Restaurant	1954	Thomas Boyde
NY	Rochester	Famous Brand Shoes	1953	Thomas Boyde
NY	Rochester	Fountainbleau Restaurant & Bar	1952	Thomas Boyde
NY	Rochester	Frati, Mario J.	1953	Thomas Boyde
NY	Rochester	Frijhy, Frank S.	1950	Thomas Boyde
NY	Rochester	Genesee Steel Co.	1949	Thomas Boyde
NY	Rochester	Genesse Valley Trust Bldg.	1929	Thomas Boyde
NY	Rochester	Green, Harry Jr.	1948	Thomas Boyde
NY	Rochester	Guzetta, Matthew	1946	Thomas Boyde
NY	Rochester	H & E Sandwich Shop	1950	Thomas Boyde
NY	Rochester	Hedges Grill	1951	Thomas Boyde
NY	Rochester	Interlichia, Philip C.	1953	Thomas Boyde
NY	Rochester	Kroll's Great Expectations Shop	1949	Thomas Boyde
NY	Rochester	Matteson, Harlan J.	1947	Thomas Boyde
NY	Rochester	Miracle Diner	1954	Thomas Boyde
NY	Rochester	Monroe County Home & Infirmary	1933	Thomas Boyde
NY	Rochester	Nazareth College of Rochester Admn. Bldg.	1941	Thomas Boyde
NY	Rochester	Nazareth College of Rochester Classroom Bldg.	1941	Thomas Boyde
NY	Rochester	Nazareth College of Rochester Dormitory	1941	Thomas Boyde
NY	Rochester	Passero, Joseph D.	1952	Thomas Boyde
NY	Rochester	Pierleoni, Ennius	1951	Thomas Boyde
NY	Rochester	Piscitello, Frances	1954	Thomas Boyde
NY	Rochester	Prato, Samuel	1946	Thomas Boyde
NY	Rochester	Reagan, Edward B.	1951	Thomas Boyde

APPENDIX

State	City/County	Name	Year	A/AE/LA
NY	Rochester	Rochester Bakery	1948	Thomas Boyde
NY	Rochester	Romeo, Frank J.	1949	Thomas Boyde
NY	Rochester	Rowe, Vincent	1951	Thomas Boyde
NY	Rochester	Rutner Iron Co.	1951	Thomas Boyde
NY	Rochester	Shannon, Harry D.	1948	Thomas Boyde
NY	Rochester	Times Square Hotel & Club	1950	Thomas Boyde
NY	Rochester	Walters, Adelaide	1953	Thomas Boyde
NY	Rochester	Wilinsky, Dr. Isadore J.	1947	Thomas Boyde
NY	Sag Harbor	Meredith, Amaza L. "Azurest North"	1947	Amaza Meredith
NY	Sag Harbor	Richards, Dr. F.F. "Hillside"	1946	Amaza Meredith
NY	Sag Harbor	Spaulding, Dorothy "Edendot"	1951	Amaza Meredith
NY	Sag Harbor	Terry, Maude "Hihil"	x	Amaza Meredith
NY	Springfield Gardens	Laurelton Branch Library	1954	Clinton Harris
NY	Staten Island	Firehouse-Engine Company 165 & Ladder Company 85	1960	Clinton Harris
NY	Staten Island	Great Kill Branch Library	1954	Clinton Harris
NY	Staten Island	Richmond Central Fire Alarm Station	1960	Clinton Harris
NY	Staten Island	St. George Regional Branch Library	1952	Clinton Harris
NY	Syracuse	Noah's Ark Auto Accessories	1955	Thomas Boyde
NY	Tonawanda	Lipson, Avrome Y.	1950	Thomas Boyde
NY	Troy	Hudson Hotel Dining Room	1922	Hilyard Robinson
NY	Webster	Empire Parkway Restaurant	1950	Thomas Boyde
NY	Westbury	Phipps, John S. "Westbury House"	1911	Julian Abele
NY	x	Baird Sanitarium	1951	Thomas Boyde
OH	Ashland	U. S. Post Office	1917	William Cooke
OH	Athens	U. S. Post Office	1911	William Cooke
OH	Bluffton	U. S. Post Office	1940	William Cooke
OH	Bowling Green	U. S. Post Office	1914	William Cooke
OH	Cincinnatti	Antioch Baptist Church	x	Wallace Rayfield
OH	Cleveland	Alta Settlement House	1901	Robert Robinson Taylor
OH	Cleveland	Capt. Roth Elementary School	1965	Robert Madison
OH	Cleveland	Cleveland State Univ. Science Ctr.	1982	Robert Madison
OH	Cleveland	Hopkins Airport Concessations	2001	Robert Madison
OH	Cleveland	Hopkins Airport Continental Concourse	1999	Robet Madison
OH	Cleveland	Cleveland Trust Bank	1961	Robert Madison
OH	Cleveland	Deleon, Charles A.	1960	Robert Madison
OH	Cleveland	Boyd Funeral Home	1966	Robet Madison
OH	Cleveland	Fatima Family Ctr.	1996	Robert Madison
OH	Cleveland	Fire Fighters Memorial	1999	Robert Madison
OH	Cleveland	Eliza Bryant Homes	2002	Robert Madison
OH	Cleveland	Emmanuel Baptist Church	1958	Robert Madison
OH	Cleveland	N.A.S.A. Engineering Bldg.	1989	Robert Madison
OH	Cleveland	First Greater New Zion Baptist Church	1999	Robert Madison
OH	Cleveland	Hebrew Garden	2000	Robert Madison
OH	Cleveland	Katherine Tyler Ctr.	1967	Robert Madison
OH	Cleveland Heights	Madison, Robert F.	1960	Robert Madison
OH	Cleveland	Martin De Porres Ctr.	1984	Robert Madison
OH	Cleveland	King Jr. High School	1973	Robert Madison
OH	Cleveland	King Jr. Shopping Ctr.	1972	Robert Madison
OH	Cleveland	Medical Dental Arts Blvd.	1967	Robert Madison
OH	Cleveland	Medic's Medical Bldg.	1960	Robert Madison
OH	Cleveland	Mt. Herman Baptist Church	1958	Robert Madison
OH	Cleveland	Mt. Pleasant Family Ctr.	1999	Robert Madison
OH	Cleveland	Mt. Pleasant Medical Ctr.	1957	Robert Madison
OH	Cleveland	N.A.S.A. Research Ctr.	1978	Robert Madison
OH	Cleveland	Second Calvary Baptist Church	1978	Robert Madison
OH	Cleveland	Southeast Seventh Day Adventist Church	1985	Robert Madison
OH	Columbus	State of Ohio Computer Ctr.	1987	Robert Madison
OH	Cleveland	Union Commerce Bank	1972	Robert Madison
OH	Cleveland	Lady of Fatima Bell Tower	2000	Robert Madison
OH	Coldwater	U. S. Post Office	1940	William Cooke
OH	Columbus	No. 47 Miami Apts.	1966	Leon Ransom
OH	Columbus	Adelphia Savings & Loan Bldg.	1928	Carl Barnett

APPENDIX

State	City/County	Name	Year	A/AE/LA
OH	Columbus	Bell, Atty. Napoleon	c1967	Leon Ransom
OH	Columbus	Bethel Apts.	1968	Leon Ransom
OH	Columbus	Bolivar Arms Apts.	x	Leon Ransom
OH	Columbus	Christopher Inn Round Hotel	1963	Leon Ransom
OH	Columbus	Church of Christ Apostolic Faith	1965	Leon Ransom
OH	Columbus	City of Columbus Single-family Housing	x	Leon Ransom
OH	Columbus	Columbus Fire Station No. 8	1968	Leon Ransom
OH	Columbus	Franklin Park Medical Ctr.	c1962	Leon Ransom
OH	Columbus	Grant Hospital	1961	Leon Ransom
OH	Columbus	IGA Food Liner	c1968	Leon Ransom
OH	Columbus	Long-Garfield Filling Station	1926	Carl Barnett
OH	Columbus	Martin L. King Jr. Branch Library	1969	Leon Ransom
OH	Columbus	Mock Road Senior Citizens Housing	1969	Leon Ransom
OH	Columbus	Ohio State University Hospitals	c1961	Leon Ransom
OH	Columbus	Ohio State University Testing Laboratory	1928	Carl Barnett
OH	Columbus	Ransom, Leon A.	1957	Leon Ransom
OH	Columbus	St. Anthony Hospital	c1960	Leon Ransom
OH	Columbus	St. Paul African Methodist Episcopal Church Annex	x	Leon Ransom
OH	Columbus	St. Vincent's Orphanage	c1950	Leon Ransom
OH	Columbus	Weddington, Dr. Harold	c1969	Leon Ransom
OH	Crestline	U. S. Post Office	1941	William Cooke
OH	Dayton	Dayton Fire Station No. 13	x	Clarence Cross
OH	Dayton	Dayton Rapid Transit Office & Garage	1971	Clarence Cross
OH	Dayton	Drew Health Center	x	Clarence Cross
OH	Dayton	Greater Mt. Nebo Baptist Church	1962	Clarence Cross
OH	Dayton	Model Cities Neighborhood Facility	1971	Clarence Cross
OH	Dayton	Southwest Shopping Ctr.	x	Clarence Cross
OH	Dayton	Tabernacle Baptist Church	1958	Clarence Cross
OH	Dayton	Tabernacle Baptist Church Copeland Bldg.	1985	Clarence Cross
OH	Defiance	U. S. Post Office	1942	William Cooke
OH	East Cleveland	Chambers Elementary School	1978	Robert Madison
OH	East Cleveland	East Cleveland Municipal Bldg.	2001	Robert Madison
OH	East Cleveland	East Cleveland Municipal Courtrooms	1999	Robert Madison
OH	East Cleveland	Police Station	2002	Robert Madison
OH	Ironton	U. S. Post Office	x	William Cooke
OH	Highland Hills	Cuyahoga Community College East Campus	1986	Robert Madison
OH	Highland Hills	Cuyahoga Community College Technology Ctr.	1994	Robert Madison
OH	Highland Hills	Cuyahoga Community College Theatre Complex	1994	Robert Madison
OH	Marietta	U. S. Post Office	x	William Cooke
OH	Newburg Heights	Harvard Yard Facility	1987	Robert Madison
OH	Naperville	Naperville Transit Station	1979	Robert Madison
OH	Toledo	Banks, Louis N.	1915	Louis Banks
OH	Troy	House	1931	Clarence Wheat
OH	Walnut Hills	Brown Chapel African Methodist Episcopal Church	1929	Edward Birch
OH	Wilberforce	Central State University Hallie Q. Brown Library	1959	Leon Ransom
OH	Wilberforce	Wilberforce University Arnett Hall	c1910	John Lankford
OH	Wilberforce	Wilberforce University Heating Tunnel	c1910	John Lankford
OH	Wilberforce	Wilberforce University Womens Dormitory	c1910	John Lankford
OH	Wooster	Wayne County Justice Ctr.	1976	Robert Madison
OH	Xenia	U. S. Post Office	x	Samuel Plato
OH	Xenia	Wilberforce University School of Religion	1960	Robert Madison
OH	Youngstown	Covington Street School	1890	Plympton Berry
OH	Youngstown	Dollar Bank	1901	Plympton Berry
OH	Youngstown	First Baptist Church	1863	Plympton Berry
OH	Youngstown	First Presbyterian Church	1866	Plympton Berry
OH	Youngstown	Front Street School	1871	Plympton Berry
OH	Youngstown	Grand Opera House	1872	Plympton Berry
OH	Youngstown	Hitchcock, William	1863	Plympton Berry
OH	Youngstown	Homer Hamiltion & Co.	1861	Plympton Berry
OH	Youngstown	Howell's Business Block	1865	Plympton Berry
OH	Youngstown	Mahoning County Courthouse	1875	Plympton Berry
OH	Youngstown	McMillian Free Library	c1899	Plympton Berry

APPENDIX

State	City/County	Name	Year	A/AE/LA
OH	Youngstown	Ohio Govenor's Mansion	1868	Plympton Berry
OH	Youngstown	Rayen School	1861	Plympton Berry
OH	Youngstown	St. Columbia Cathedral	1863	Plympton Berry
OH	Youngstown	St. Joseph's Cathedral	1881	Plympton Berry
OH	Youngstown	Tod House Hotel	1869	Plympton Berry
OH	Youngstown	West Side Schoolhouse	1877	Plympton Berry
OH	Youngstown	Youngstown City Jail	1866	Plympton Berry
OK	Ardmore	First Baptist Church	1953	Leon Jackson
OK	Boley	Antioch Baptist Church	1929	William Jones
OK	Boley	Utility Plant	x	Samuel Morris
OK	Chickasha	Duncan Ranch	1952	Leon Jackson
OK	Claremore	Prince Hall Masons Bathhouse	1951	Leon Jackson
OK	Gutherie	Veterans of Foreign War Hall	1952	Leon Jackson
OK	Midwest City	Ridgecrest Country Estates	1950	Clarence Wheat
OK	Muskogee	Chandler, Jesse	1950	Leon Jackson
OK	Oklahoma City	Briscoe, Dr. Byron	1953	Leon Jackson
OK	Oklahoma City	Finely Clinic/Office	1952	Leon Jackson
OK	Oklahoma City	Jackson, Leon Q.	1951	Leon Jackson
OK	Oklahoma City	Masonic Hall	1954	Leon Jackson
OK	Oklahoma City	Perry, Rev. E.W	1950	Leon Jackson
OK	Oklahoma City	St. John Baptist Church Education Bldg.	1952	Leon Jackson
OK	Oklahoma City	Tabernacle Baptist Church	1950	Leon Jackson
OK	Oklahoma City	Wood, Carl W.	1950	Leon Jackson
OK	Wewoka	First Baptist Baptist Church	1951	Leon Jackson
OR	Clatsop County	Astoria, Clatsop County	1870	Grafton Brown
OR	Portland	Bird's Eye View of the City of Portland	1870	Grafton Brown
OR	Portland	City of Portland	c1861	Grafton Brown
PA	Belvedere	Porter, Luther	x	Calvin Hamilton
PA	Bryn Mawr	Cramp, Theodore W. "Portlege"	1910	Julian Abele
PA	Chester	Chester Recreation Ctr.	1953	Hilyard Robinson
PA	Chestnut Hill	Stotesbury, Edward T. "Whitemarsh Hall"	1916	Julian Abele
PA	Coatesville	U. S. Post Office	x	Samuel Plato
PA	Coatsville	Butler, Dr. Charles	x	Calvin Hamilton
PA	Colver	Colver Presbyterian Church	1913	Julian Abele
PA	Easton	Lafayette College Chi Phi Fraternity House	1909	Julian Abele
PA	Elkins Park	Dixon, Fitz E. "Ronaele Manor"	1923	Julian Abele
PA	Elkins Park	St. Paul's Episcopal Church	1912	Julian Abele
PA	Ford City	Second Baptist Church	1958	Clarence Cross
PA	Germantown	Henderson, Douglass	x	J. Alonzo Plater
PA	Glen Mills	Redding, Dr. Lewis	x	Calvin Hamilton
PA	Glenside	Keswick Theatre	1928	Julian Abele
PA	Harrisburg	Pennsylvania General State Authority Housing	c1973	Walter Roberts
PA	Havertown	Bell Masonic Lodge	x	J. Alonzo Plater
PA	Homewood	Westinghouse Electric Vehicle Plant	c1971	Walter Roberts
PA	Jenkintown	Grace Presbyterian Church	1909	Julian Abele
PA	Jenkintown	Jenkintown Bank & Trust Co.	1924	Julian Abele
PA	Lancaster	U. S. Post Office	1931	William Cooke
PA	Lewisburg	Bucknell University Mathewson Gateway	1923	Julian Abele
PA	Linconia Park	Livingston, W.R.	1949	J. Alonzo Plater
PA	McKeesport	Pennsylvania State University Classroom Bldg.	c1973	Walter Roberts
PA	McKeesport	St. Paul African Methodist Episcopal Church	1962	Robert Madison
PA	New Castle	Lawrence County Courthouse	1852	Plympton Berry
PA	New Castle	New Discipline Church	1868	Plympton Berry
PA	New Philadelphia	U. S. Post Office	x	Samuel Plato
PA	Oakland	Lovell, Robert	c1955	Walter Roberts
PA	Penn Hills	East Hills Shopping Ctr.	c1960	Walter Roberts
PA	Pennlyn	Smith, William G.	1951	J. Alonzo Plater
PA	Philadelphia	African Methodist Episcopal Book Concern	1926	Louis Bellinger
PA	Philadelphia	Anderson, Marian	c1940	Orpheus Fischer
PA	Philadelphia	Apex Beauty School	1948	J. Alonzo Plater
PA	Philadelphia	Beneficial Savings Bank	1923	Julian Abele
PA	Philadelphia	Bright Hope Baptist Church	1951	J. Alonzo Plater

APPENDIX

State	City/County	Name	Year	A/AE/LA
PA	Philadelphia	Chateau Crillion	1928	Julian Abele
PA	Philadelphia	Clanerda Presbyterian Church	1912	Julian Abele
PA	Philadelphia	Continental Hotel	1922	Julian Abele
PA	Philadelphia	Eisenlohr, Otto	1911	Julian Abele
PA	Philadelphia	Emmanuel Methodist Church	1965	De Witt Dykes
PA	Philadelphia	Episcopal Hospital	1933	Julian Abele
PA	Philadelphia	Fifth Baptist Church	1924	Julian Abele
PA	Philadelphia	Free Library of Philadelphia	1917	Julian Abele
PA	Philadelphia	Grady, James	1948	J. Alonzo Plater
PA	Philadelphia	Hahneman Medical College Out-Patient's Bldg.	1947	Julian Abele
PA	Philadelphia	Jefferson Medical College Curtis Clinic	1929	Julian Abele
PA	Philadelphia	New Apostolic Church of North America	x	J. Alonzo Plater
PA	Philadelphia	North Broad Street Station	1928	Julian Abele
PA	Philadelphia	Northern Home for Children	1927	Julian Abele
PA	Philadelphia	Philadelphia Stock Exchange	1912	Julian Abele
PA	Philadelphia	Philadelphia YMCA	1912	Julian Abele
PA	Philadelphia	Ritz-Carlton Hotel	1911	Julian Abele
PA	Philadelphia	Star of Hope Baptist Church	1962	Alonzo Plater
PA	Philadelphia	Sullivan, Dr. J.W.	1933	Howard Mackey
PA	Philadelphia	Supreme Liberty Life Insurance Co.	1949	J. Alonzo Plater
PA	Philadelphia	U. S. Post Office	x	J. Alonzo Plater
PA	Philadelphia	United Sports Club	1940	J. Alonzo Plater
PA	Philadelphia	University of Pennsylvania Irvine Auditorium	1928	Julian Abele
PA	Collindale	Widener, Peter A.B. Mausoleum	1915	Julian Abele
PA	Philadelphia	Zoological Society	1912	Julian Abele
PA	Pittsburgh	House	1922	Louis Bellinger
PA	Pittsburgh	Allegheny County Housing Authority	c1973	Walter Roberts
PA	Pittsburgh	All-Pro Chicken	c1973	Walter Roberts
PA	Pittsburgh	Beedy, Carol	x	Clyde Drayton
PA	Pittsburgh	Bellinger, Ethel	1928	Louis Bellinger
PA	Pittsburgh	Bethel African Methodist Episcopal Church	1959	Robert Madison
PA	Pittsburgh	Burchett Apts.	1923	Louis Bellinger
PA	Pittsburgh	Business and Jobs Development Corp.	c1973	Walter Roberts
PA	Pittsburgh	Carnegie Institute Gate	c1937	Walter Roberts
PA	Pittsburgh	Carnegie Library of Pittsburgh	c1973	Walter Roberts
PA	Pittsburgh	Ciaramella, John	1929	Louis Bellinger
PA	Pittsburgh	Colonial Church	c1931	John Lankford
PA	Pittsburgh	Crunkleton, J.H.	1945	Louis Bellinger
PA	Pittsburgh	Cutts, Dr. W.G.	1927	Louis Bellinger
PA	Pittsburgh	East End Middle School	1976	Walter Roberts
PA	Pittsburgh	Greenlee Store	1933	Louis Bellinger
PA	Pittsburgh	Hill House Ctr.	c1974	Walter Roberts
PA	Pittsburgh	Hiram Masonic Lodge	c1973	Walter Roberts
PA	Pittsburgh	Iron City Lodge Post No. 17	1945	Louis Bellinger
PA	Pittsburgh	Johnson, Luther H.	1945	Louis Bellinger
PA	Pittsburgh	Keystone Park Multi-family Housing	c1973	Walter Roberts
PA	Pittsburgh	Knights of Phythias Temple	1927	Louis Bellinger
PA	Pittsburgh	Knott Apts.	1932	Louis Bellinger
PA	Pittsburgh	Lincoln Avenue Church of God	c1973	Walter Roberts
PA	Pittsburgh	Mutal Real Estate Co.	1928	Louis Bellinger
PA	Pittsburgh	Pittsburgh Board of Public Education Office	c1973	Walter Roberts
PA	Pittsburgh	Pittsburgh Housing Authority	c1973	Walter Roberts
PA	Pittsburgh	Pittsburgh Police Station	1923	Louis Bellinger
PA	Pittsburgh	Pittsburgh Presbytery	c1973	Walter Roberts
PA	Pittsburgh	PPG Industries	c1973	Walter Roberts
PA	Pittsburgh	Prince Hall Temple Association Lodge & Apts.	1928	Louis Bellinger
PA	Pittsburgh	Reed-Roberts Street Housing	c1971	Walter Roberts
PA	Pittsburgh	Rodman Street Baptist Church	1929	Louis Bellinger
PA	Pittsburgh	Selma Burke Art Ctr.	c1968	Walter Roberts
PA	Pittsburgh	Sixth Mt. Zion Baptist Church	1930	Louis Bellinger
PA	Pittsburgh	Smith, Robert T.	1928	Louis Bellinger
PA	Pittsburgh	St. John's Evangelical Baptist Church	1943	Louis Bellinger

APPENDIX

State	City/County	Name	Year	A/AE/LA
PA	Pittsburgh	Three Rivers Youth, Inc.	c1973	Walter Roberts
PA	Pittsburgh	Urban Redevelopment Authority of Pittsburgh	c1973	Walter Roberts
PA	Pittsburgh	West Funeral Home	c1973	Walter Roberts
PA	Pittsburgh	Youth Opportunities Unlimited	c1973	Walter Roberts
PA	Radnor	Berwind, Herminie "Knollnut"	1908	Julian Abele
PA	Rosemont	McFadden, George H.	1923	Julian Abele
PA	Rydal	Ogontz School for Girls	1916	Julian Abele
PA	Somerset County	Zimmerman, Daniel	1915	Julian Abele
PA	Trevose Twp.	St. Matthew's Methodist Church	1959	De Witt Dykes
PA	Uniontown	Lewis Clinic	x	William Moses
PA	Villanova	Brooke, George A. "Almonbury"	c1925	Julian Abele
PA	Villanova	Darlington, H.S.	1911	Julian Abele
PA	Villanova	Montgomery, Robert R. "Androsson"	1911	Julian Abele
PA	Wilkinsburg	St. Mark African Methodist Episcopal Church	1927	Louis Bellinger
PA	Windber	Windber Hospital	1930	Julian Abele
PA	Wyncote	Martin, John C.	1922	Julian Abele
PR	Humacao	Presbyterian Hospital	c1920	Vertner Tandy
RI	Newport	Drexel, John R. "Fairholm"	1910	Julian Abele
RI	Newport	Rice, Eleanor E. "Miramar"	1930	Julian Abele
SC	Abbeville	Williams & Ferguson College	1910	William Pittman
SC	Abbeville	Williams & Ferguson Industrial Academy	1909	John Lankford
SC	Aiken	Danziger, William H.	1931	John Holloway
SC	Aiken	Langley, Howard E.	1932	John Holloway
SC	Bamburg	Mt. Carmel Methodist Church Education Bldg.	1962	De Witt Dykes
SC	Bennettsville	St. Michael's Methodist Church	1918	Miller Whittaker
SC	Bowman	Antioch Baptist Church	x	John Blanche
SC	Brancheville	Wesley Methodist Church	1963	De Witt Dykes
SC	Bucksport	Salem African Methodist Episcopal Church	1944	Wade Ford
SC	Bucksport	St. John African Methodist Episcopal Church	1927	Wade Ford
SC	Camden	Trinity Methodist Church Education Bldg.	1962	De Witt Dykes
SC	Charleston	E.G. Haselton Undertaking Establishment	1914	Thomas Pinckney
SC	Charleston	Guenveur, E. L.	1923	William Streat
SC	Charleston	People's Federation Bank	c1921	John Lankford
SC	Clover	Green Pond Methodist Church	1962	De Witt Dykes
SC	Columbia	Allen University Chapel	x	John Lankford
SC	Columbia	Allen University Chapelle Administration Bldg.	1922	John Lankford
SC	Columbia	Allen University Girls Dormitory	1950	John Blanche
SC	Columbia	Allen University Ministers' Hall	x	John Blanche
SC	Columbia	Benedict College	x	John Blanche
SC	Columbia	Big Bethel African Methodist Episcopal Church	1921	John Lankford
SC	Columbia	Francis Burns Methodist Church	1963	De Witt Dykes
SC	Darlington	Bonnoit, M.	c1890	Lawrence Reese
SC	Darlington	Early, W.F.	c1890	Lawrence Reese
SC	Darlington	Hart, M.S.	c1895	Lawrence Reese
SC	Darlington	Hennig, Henry	c1895	Lawrence Reese
SC	Darlington	Hyman, Abraham	c1900	Lawrence Reese
SC	Darlington	Kirven, J.K.	c1893	Lawrence Reese
SC	Darlington	Lucas, C.L.	c1895	Lawrence Reese
SC	Darlington	Lunn, E.E.	c1895	Lawrence Reese
SC	Darlington	Lunney, Dr. John	c1895	Lawrence Reese
SC	Darlington	Mertz, G.O.	c1895	Lawrence Reese
SC	Darlington	Muldrow, J.O.	c1895	Lawrence Reese
SC	Darlington	Sanders, Edward	c1900	Lawrence Reese
SC	Darlington	Spears, J. Monroe	c1890	Lawrence Reese
SC	Darlington	West, E.J.	c1890	Lawrence Reese
SC	Darlington	Western Railway Station	1911	Lawrence Reese
SC	Darlington	Wilson, J.F.	c1895	Lawrence Reese
SC	Denmark	Voorhees Industrial School Administration/Classroom Bldg.	1914	William Pittman
SC	Denmark	Voorhees Industrial School Washington Hospital	1905	William Cooke
SC	Easley	John Wesley Methodist Church	1967	De Witt Dykes
SC	Erhardt	Friendship Methodist Church	1962	De Witt Dykes
SC	Florence	Mt. Zion African Methodist Episcopal Church	x	John Blanche

APPENDIX

State	City/County	Name	Year	A/AE/LA
SC	Florence	Salem Methodist Church Education Bldg.	1962	De Witt Dykes
SC	Greenville	Wesley Methodist Church	x	William Cooke
SC	Greenwood	Trinity Methodist Church	1966	De Witt Dykes
SC	Hartsville	Centenary Methodist Church	1962	De Witt Dykes
SC	Holly Hill	Lovely Hill Baptist Church	x	John Blanche
SC	Jefferson	Hopewell Methodist Church	1958	De Witt Dykes
SC	Lake View	Ford, Wade A.	1937	Wade Ford
SC	Laurens	Bethel African Methodist Episcopal Church	c1910	Columbus White
SC	Laurens	St. Paul First Baptist Church	1912	Columbus White
SC	Laurens	White, Columbus B.	1908	Columbus White
SC	Laurens	Whitner, Mary	c1896	Columbus White
SC	Mechansville	Mechansville Methodist Church	1961	De Witt Dykes
SD	Mitchell	James River Bridge	x	Archie Alexander
SC	Mullins	Mt. Olive Baptist Church	1922	Wade Ford
SC	Orangeburg	Blanche, John H. "Home on the Hill"	1945	John Blanche
SC	Orangeburg	Claflin University Chapel	1890	Robert Bates
SC	Orangeburg	Claflin University Lee Library	1898	William Cooke
SC	Orangeburg	Claflin University Main Bldg.	1899	Robert Bates
SC	Orangeburg	Claflin University Main Bldg.	1900	Robert Bates
SC	Orangeburg	Claflin University Manual Training Bldg.	x	Robert Bates
SC	Orangeburg	Claflin University President's Residence	x	William Cooke
SC	Orangeburg	Claflin University Science Bldg.	x	John Blanche
SC	Orangeburg	Claflin University Slater Training Bldg.	1900	William Cooke
SC	Orangeburg	Claflin University Soules Home for Girls	1905	William Cooke
SC	Orangeburg	Claflin University Souvenir Cottage	1898	William Cooke
SC	Orangeburg	Claflin University Stokes Girls Dormitory	1904	William Cooke
SC	Orangeburg	Claflin University Tingley Hall	1908	William Cooke
SC	Orangeburg	Daniels, Harry	x	Miller Whittaker
SC	Orangeburg	Fordham, Atty. John	1903	William Cooke
SC	Orangeburg	Horne Ford Dealership	1949	Miller Whittaker
SC	Orangeburg	Limehouse, Frank	c1930	Miller Whittaker
SC	Orangeburg	Lowman Hospital	1920	Miller Whittaker
SC	Orangeburg	Orangeburg Lutheran Church	1949	Miller Whittaker
SC	Orangeburg	Slumberland Motel	x	John Blanche
SC	Orangeburg	South Carolina State College Bradham Hall	1916	Miller Whittaker
SC	Orangeburg	South Carolina State College Creamery Bldg.	c1929	Miller Whittaker
SC	Orangeburg	South Carolina State College Dukes Gym	c1929	Miller Whittaker
SC	Orangeburg	South Carolina State College Felton Training School	1920	Miller Whittaker
SC	Orangeburg	South Carolina State College Floyd Dining Hall	1932	Miller Whittaker
SC	Orangeburg	South Carolina State College Hodge Hall	1928	Miller Whittaker
SC	Orangeburg	South Carolina State College Home Economics Bldg.	1925	Miller Whittaker
SC	Orangeburg	South Carolina State College Lowman Mens Dormitory	1917	Miller Whittaker
SC	Orangeburg	South Carolina State College Manning Hall	1016	Miller Whittaker
SC	Orangeburg	South Carolina State College Mechanical Industries Bldg.	1938	Miller Whittaker
SC	Orangeburg	South Carolina State College Poultry Plant	c1929	Miller Whittaker
SC	Orangeburg	South Carolina State College White Hall	1920	Miller Whittaker
SC	Orangeburg	South Carolina State College Wilkinson Library	1937	Miller Whittaker
SC	Orangeburg	South Carolina State College Wilkinson YWCA Hut	1924	Miller Whittaker
SC	Orangeburg	South Carolina State University Dukes Gym	1931	John Blanche
SC	Orangeburg	Staley, Frank M.	x	Miller Whittaker
SC	Orangeburg	Trinity United Methodist Episcopal Church	1928	Miller Whittaker
SC	Orangeburg	Wilkinson, Robert S.	c1930	Miller Whittaker
SC	Orangeburg	William Chapel African Methodist Episcopal Church & Parsonage	c1950s	John Blanche
SC	Orangeburg	Holiday Inn Motel	x	John Blanche
SC	Pendleton	Bethel Methodist Church	1961	De Witt Dykes
SC	Pinnopolis	John Wesley Methodist Church	1967	De Witt Dykes
SC	Reevesville	Greenville Methodist Church	1963	De Witt Dykes
SC	Ridgeville	Canaan Methodist Church	1967	De Witt Dykes
SC	Spartanburg	Trinity African Methodist Episcopal Church	1922	Wallace Rayfield
SC	St. George	St. Marks Baptist Church	x	John Blanche
SC	Sumter	Asbury Methodist Church	1961	De Witt Dykes

APPENDIX

State	City/County	Name	Year	A/AE/LA
SC	Sumter	Morris College Home Economics Bldg.	x	John Blanche
SC	Umbia	Bethel African Methodist Episcopal Church	1921	John Lankford
SD	Custer	Custer National Memorial Park	x	Francis Rassieur Roberson
SD	Custer	Custer National Memorial Park Visitor Center	x	Francis Rassieur Roberson
SD	Hot Springs	Wind Caves National Park Visitor Center	x	Francis Rassieur Roberson
SD	Keystone	Mt Rushmore National Memorial Park Visitor Center	1925	Francis Rassieur Roberson
SD	Pennington County	Badlands National Park Museum	1939	Francis Rassieur Roberson
TN	Jackson	CME Publishing Board Office	1931	Calvin McKissack
TN	Jackson	CME Publishing House	c1920	Calvin McKissack
TN	Jackson	Lane College Campus Plan	1945	David Williston
TN	Jackson	Lane College Cleaves Womens Dormitory	1920	Calvin McKissack
TN	Jackson	Lane College Hamlett Mens Dormitory	1914	Calvin McKissack
TN	Jackson	Lane College Health Bldg.	1942	Moses McKissack
TN	Knoxville	Appalachian Exposition Negro Bldg.	1910	John Michael
TN	Knoxville	Bentley Street Christian Church	1966	De Witt Dykes
TN	Knoxville	Johnson Recreation Ctr.	1977	De Witt Dykes
TN	Knoxville	Clinton Chapel African Methodist Episcopal Zion Church	1977	De Witt Dykes
TN	Knoxville	Dykes, DeWitt S. Sr.	1953	De Witt Dykes
TN	Knoxville	Emmanuel Presbyterian Church	1964	De Witt Dykes
TN	Knoxville	Golden Age Retirement Village	1982	De Witt Dykes
TN	Knoxville	Henderson Community Home & Apts.	1911	John Michael
TN	Knoxville	Knoxville College Bldg.	x	John Michael
TN	Knoxville	Knoxville College Boarding House	x	William Jones
TN	Knoxville	Knoxville College Faculty Cottage	x	John Michael
TN	Knoxville	Knoxville College Greehhouse	x	John Michael
TN	Knoxville	Knoxville College McMillan Chapel	1914	William Jones
TN	Knoxville	Lenon-Seney United Methodist Church	1976	De Witt Dykes
TN	Knoxville	Logan Temple African Methodist Episcopal Zion Church	1963	De Witt Dykes
TN	Knoxville	Lonsdale Day Care Ctr.	1988	De Witt Dykes
TN	Knoxville	Martin Chapel Methodist Church	1960	De Witt Dykes
TN	Knoxville	Michael, John H.	1909	John Michael
TN	Knoxville	Mt. Calvary Baptist Church	1974	De Witt Dykes
TN	Knoxville	Mt. Olive Baptist Church	1969	De Witt Dykes
TN	Knoxville	Mt. Zion Baptist Church Parsonage	1911	John Michael
TN	Knoxville	Seney Chapel Methodist Church	1965	De Witt Dykes
TN	Knoxville	Sertoma Sunshine Ctr.	1976	De Witt Dykes
TN	Knoxville	Shiloh Presbyterian Church	1967	De Witt Dykes
TN	Knoxville	Unity Mortuary	1978	De Witt Dykes
TN	Knoxville	World's Fair Merchanding & Snack Shops	1982	De Witt Dykes
TN	Memphis	Collins Chapel Hospital	x	Moses McKissack
TN	Memphis	Fraternal Savings & Trust Bank	1924	Walter Bailey
TN	Memphis	Mammoth Life Insurance Co.	x	Moses McKissack
TN	Memphis	St. Stephens Baptist Church	1929	Calvin McKissack
TN	Memphis	Universal Life Insurance Co.	1930	Calvin McKissack
TN	Milan	Phillips Chapel Colored Methodist Episcopal Church	x	Moses McKissack
TN	Nashville	AME Sunday School Union Publishing House	1930	Calvin McKissack
TN	Nashville	Avery Apts.	1930	Calvin McKissack
TN	Nashville	Avoca Apts.	c1920	Calvin McKissack
TN	Nashville	Bastian, Nate A.	1921	Calvin McKissack
TN	Nashville	Boyd Park Community Ctr.	x	Moses McKissack
TN	Nashville	Bransfort Realty Co.	1920	Calvin McKissack
TN	Nashville	Cameron Junior High School	1940	Calvin McKissack
TN	Nashville	Capers Congregational Methodist Episcopal Church	1925	Calvin McKissack
TN	Nashville	College Hill Housing	1951	Moses McKissack
TN	Nashville	Comer, Montgomery	1920	Calvin McKissack
TN	Nashville	Eaton Day Care Home	x	Moses McKissack
TN	Nashville	Ewing, Edward B.	1919	Calvin McKissack
TN	Nashville	Fairfield Baptist Church	1927	Calvin McKissack
TN	Nashville	First American Bank	x	Moses McKissack
TN	Nashville	Fisk University Landscape Plan	c1900	David Williston
TN	Nashville	Fisk University Burris Music Hall	1945	Moses McKissack
TN	Nashville	Fisk University Carnegie Library	1908	Calvin McKissack

APPENDIX

State	City/County	Name	Year	A/AE/LA
TN	Nashville	Fisk University English Department Bldg.	1952	Moses McKissack
TN	Nashville	Fisk University Henderson-Johnson Gym	1950	Moses McKissack
TN	Nashville	Fisk University Parker-Johnson Hall	1954	Moses McKissack
TN	Nashville	Ford Green Public School	1939	Calvin McKissack
TN	Nashville	Glenn, Dr. L.C.	c1920	Calvin McKissack
TN	Nashville	Griswold, Norman W.	1919	Calvin McKissack
TN	Nashville	House, John	1919	Calvin McKissack
TN	Nashville	Hubbard, Dr. George	1920	Calvin McKissack
TN	Nashville	Jackson, Granberry, Sr.	1905	Calvin McKissack
TN	Nashville	Kayne Avenue Baptist Church	x	Moses McKissack
TN	Nashville	Kings Lane Elementary School	x	Moses McKissack
TN	Nashville	Knights of Pythias Bldg.	1924	Walter Bailey
TN	Nashville	Masonic Temple	1928	Calvin McKissack
TN	Nashville	Meharry Medical College Hubbard Hosptial	x	Moses McKissack
TN	Nashville	Meharry Medical College Mental Health Ctr.	x	Moses McKissack
TN	Nashville	Meharry Medical College Sciences Ctr.	x	Moses McKissack
TN	Nashville	Meigs Public School	1933	Calvin McKissack
TN	Nashville	Morris Memorial Bldg.	1924	Calvin McKissack
TN	Nashville	North Nashville Community Ctr.	x	Moses McKissack
TN	Nashville	Payne Chapel African Methodist Episcopal Church	1921	Calvin McKissack
TN	Nashville	Pearcy, G.C.	1919	Calvin McKissack
TN	Nashville	Pearl High School	1935	Calvin McKissack
TN	Nashville	Riverside Sanitarium & Hospital	1948	Moses McKissack
TN	Nashville	Roberts, Albert	1937	Calvin McKissack
TN	Nashville	Roger Williams University Dormitory	c1920	Calvin McKissack
TN	Nashville	Sexton, Daniel P.	1921	Calvin McKissack
TN	Nashville	Smith Towers	1980	Leon Jackson
TN	Nashville	Tennessee Agricultural & Industrial Home Economics Bldg.	x	Moses McKissack
TN	Nashville	Tennessee Agricultural & Industrial School of Business	x	Moses McKissack
TN	Nashville	Tennessee Agricultural & Industrial Engineering Bldg.	1950	Moses McKissack
TN	Nashville	Tennessee Agricultural & Industrial Physical Education Bldg.	1951	Moses McKissack
TN	Nashville	Tennessee Agricultural & Industrial President's Residence	x	Moses McKissack
TN	Nashville	Tennessee Agricultural & Industrial Administration Bldg.	1926	Calvin McKissack
TN	Nashville	Tennessee Agricultural & Industrial Library	1927	Calvin McKissack
TN	Nashville	Tennessee Centennial & International Exposition Competition	1897	William Hazel
TN	Nashville	Tennessee State University Campus Plan	1948	David Williston
TN	Nashville	Washington Junior High School	1927	Calvin McKissack
TN	Powell	Haven Chapel Methodist Church	1966	De Witt Dykes
TN	Pulaski	Pulaski Public School	1937	Calvin McKissack
TN	Shelbyville	Turner Normal & Industrial Institute Administration Bldg.	1912	Calvin McKissack
TN	Nashville	Jackson Courts Housing	x	Moses McKissack
TX	Austin	Tillotson Institute	x	Vertner Tandy
TX	Dallas	Knights of Pythias Temple	1915	William Pittman
TX	Dallas	St. James African Methodist Episcopal Temple	1918	William Pittman
TX	Dallas	Universal Life Insurance Co.	c1940	Moses McKissack
TX	Fort Worth	Allen Chapel African Methodist Episcopal Church	1914	William Pittman
TX	Hawkins	Jarvis Christian College Dining Hall	x	Hilyard Robinson
TX	Houston	Colored Carnegie Branch Library	1913	William Pittman
TX	Houston	Odd Fellows Office Bldg.	1924	Robert Robinson Taylor
TX	Houston	United Order of Odd Fellows Lodge	1924	William Pittman
TX	Houston	Wesley Chapel African Methodist Episcopal Church	1926	William Pittman
TX	Marshall	House	1920	Robert Robinson Taylor
TX	Prairie View	Prairie View Agricultural & Mechanical Gym	1929	Louis Fry
TX	Prairie View	Prairie View Agricultural & Mechanical Womens Dormitory	1928	Louis Fry
TX	Prairie View	Prairie View Agricultural & Mechanical Veterans Hospital	1925	Louis Fry
TX	Prairie View	Preston, Ann C. "Anndot"	1956	Amaza Meredith
TX	San Antonio	United Brothers of Friendship Lodge	1915	William Pittman
TX	Tyler	Texas College Carter Womens Dormitory	1937	Calvin McKissack
TX	Tyler	Texas College Glass Library	1954	Moses McKissack
TX	Tyler	Texas College McKinney Administration Bldg.	1954	Moses McKissack
TX	Tyler	Texas College President's Residence	1954	Moses McKissack
TX	Tyler	Texas College Taylor Gym	1940	Moses McKissack

APPENDIX

State	City/County	Name	Year	A/AE/LA
TX	Tyler	Texas College Wiley Mens Dormitory	1913	Calvin McKissack
TX	Waco	Quinn College Grant Hall Dormitory	1921	William Pittman
TX	Waxahachie	Joshua Chapel African Methodist Episcopal Church	1917	William Pittman
UT	Bryce Canyon	Bryce Canyon National Park Museum	1929	Francis Rassieur Roberson
VA	Alexandria	Alexandria Housing Authority FHA Housing	x	Stewart Hoban
VA	Alexandria	Carpenter Medical Office	x	Stewart Hoban
VA	Arlington	Arlington View Terrace	x	Stewart Hoban
VA	Arlington	Callan Motors Office & Garage	x	Stewart Hoban
VA	Arlington	Carver War Housing	1942	Albert Cassell
VA	Arlington	Cherry, Jeff	1950	Clarence Wheat
VA	Arlington	Liggio Housing	x	John Holloway
VA	Arlington	Lyon Village Apts.	x	David Williston
VA	Arlington	Nauck Heights	x	Stewart Hoban
VA	Arlington	Shelton, J.E.	x	Howard Mackey
VA	Beaverdam	St. James Baptist Church	x	Ethel Furman
VA	Charlottesville	Ebenezer Baptist Church	c1910	John Lankford
VA	Chesterfield County	Edwards, Thomas N.	c1950	Ethel Furman
VA	Chesterfield County	Mt. Pleasant Baptist Church	x	Ethel Furman
VA	Covington	Johnson Office Bldg. & Apts.	1957	William Moses
VA	Danville	Loyal Street Baptist Church	1924	Romulus Archer
VA	Parksley	Metompkin Baptist Church	1958	Harvey Johnson
VA	Ettrick	Johnson, Dr. James H.	1954	Amaza Meredith
VA	Ettrick	Meredith, Amaza L. "Azurest South"	1938	Amaza Meredith
VA	Ettrick	Reed, _____	n.d.	Amaza Meredith
VA	Ettrick	Virginia State University Alumni House	1949	Amaza Meredith
VA	Fairfax	Oakland Manor Apts.	x	Stewart Hoban
VA	Falls Church	Industrial School	1909	John Lankford
VA	Falls Church	Second Baptist Church	x	George Ferguson
VA	Ft. Lee	Jonesburg Land Improvement Co. Cottages	1906	John Lankford
VA	Franktown	Allen Chapel Methodist Church	1921	John Lankford
VA	Glen Allen	Snead, Junius	1968	Ethel Furman
VA	Goochland County	Cauthorne, Leland S.	1955	Ethel Furman
VA	Goochland County	Dickerson, Isaac	c1950	Ethel Furman
VA	Goochland County	Snead, Mack	1968	Ethel Furman
VA	Goochland County	Snead, Samuel	c1968	Ethel Furman
VA	Goochland County	Snead, Thomas M.	1965	Ethel Furman
VA	Goochland County	St. James Baptist Church	1972	Ethel Furman
VA	Hampton	Blue, Alllie	x	William Moses
VA	Hampton	Butler Oak Park War Housing	1944	William Moses
VA	Hampton	Carter, W.H. Jr.	x	William Moses
VA	Hampton	Colonial Tavern	1938	William Moses
VA	Hampton	Cooper, Lajoie	1955	William Moses
VA	Hampton	Davis, Don	1955	Hilyard Robinson
VA	Hampton	Frazier, Dr. Maurice	1956	William Moses
VA	Hampton	Hampton Institute Dixie Cottage	1936	William Moses
VA	Hampton	Hampton Institute Harkness Dormitory	1954	William Moses
VA	Hampton	Hampton Institute Holley Tree Inn & Monestery	1964	William Moses
VA	Hampton	Hampton Institute Laundry & Dry Cleaning Plant	1951	William Moses
VA	Hampton	Hampton Institute Long Range Plan	1963	William Moses
VA	Hampton	Hampton Institute President's Residence	x	William Moses
VA	Hampton	Hampton Institute Tuskegee Memorial Sun Dial	1957	William Moses
VA	Hampton	Hampton University Armstrong Hall	1964	Hilyard Robinson
VA	Hampton	Hampton University Davidson Dormitory	1954	Hilyard Robinson
VA	Hampton	Hampton University Harkness Dormitory	1954	Hilyard Robinson
VA	Hampton	Harris, Lemuel	x	William Moses
VA	Hampton	Hayes, Ernest H.	1939	William Moses
VA	Hampton	Jones, Edward N.	1939	William Moses
VA	Hampton	McAlister, Dr. H.A.	1941	William Moses
VA	Hampton	Peoples Building & Loan Association Bank	1937	William Moses
VA	Hampton	Scott, Dr. A.J.	1941	William Moses
VA	Hampton	Scott, Dr. Anderson T.	1950	William Moses
VA	Hampton	Virginia School for Colored Deaf & Blind	1945	William Moses

APPENDIX

State	City/County	Name	Year	A/AE/LA
VA	Hampton	White, George L.	1948	William Moses
VA	Hampton	Williams, L. Anthony	x	William Moses
VA	Hampton	Williams, Paul	x	William Moses
VA	Hampton	Wilson, Earl	1944	William Moses
VA	Hampton Roads	Jamestown Ter-centennial Negro Bldg.	1907	William Pittman
VA	Hanover County	Springfield Baptist Church	1976	Ethel Furman
VA	Henrico County	Mt. Olive Baptist Church	1974	Ethel Furman
VA	Kent County	Mt. Nebo Baptist Church	x	Ethel Furman
VA	Lawrenceville	St. Paul's College President's Residence	1953	William Streat
VA	Lawrenceville	St. Paul's College Saul Bldg.	1943	William Streat
VA	Lawrenceville	St. Paul's College Student Ctr.	1952	William Streat
VA	Lynchburg	Virginia Baptist Convention School	1924	Romulus Archer
VA	Lynchburg	Virginia Seminary & College Dormitory	x	Howard Mackey
VA	Lynchburg	Virginia Seminary Administration Bldg.	c1920	Romulus Archer
VA	Lynnhaven	First Baptist Church	x	Harvey Johnson
VA	Nauck	Lomax African Methodist Episcopal Church	x	John Lankford
VA	Newport News	Aberdeen Gardens	1935	Hilyard Robinson
VA	Newport News	Crown Savings Bank	1918	Isaiah Hatton
VA	Newport News	Foreman, Madeline	1943	William Moses
VA	Newport News	Jones, Robert	1949	William Moses
VA	Newport News	Miller, Alfred Z.	x	William Moses
VA	Newport News	Patterson Laundry Bldg.	1951	William Moses
VA	Newport News	Uganda Ballroom	1943	William Moses
VA	Newport News	Whittaker Memorial Hospital	1942	William Moses
VA	Noel	Mt. Carmel Church	1955	Ethel Furman
VA	Norfolk	Alston's Esso Service Station	c1920	Harvey Johnson
VA	Norfolk	Attucks Theatre	1919	Harvey Johnson
VA	Norfolk	Brooks, J. C.	1921	Harvey Johnson
VA	Norfolk	Burke, Dr. _____	1946	William Moses
VA	Norfolk	Central Baptist Church	x	Harvey Johnson
VA	Norfolk	Cook, _____	c1925	Harvey Johnson
VA	Norfolk	Diggs, _____	1921	Harvey Johnson
VA	Norfolk	First Baptist Church	x	Harvey Johnson
VA	Norfolk	First Baptist Church Home for the Aged	1948	William Moses
VA	Norfolk	First Church of Christ Holiness	c1922	Harvey Johnson
VA	Norfolk	Garrett Christian Methodist Episcopal Church	1920	Romulus Archer
VA	Norfolk	Grant Street Holiness Church	1920	Romulus Archer
VA	Norfolk	Hale Funeral Home	c1933	Harvey Johnson
VA	Norfolk	Handy, Dr. James	1921	Harvey Johnson
VA	Norfolk	Kelly, Emma V.	c1925	Harvey Johnson
VA	Norfolk	McAdoo, John	c1920	Harvey Johnson
VA	Norfolk	Mother Church of God in Christ	1959	Harvey Johnson
VA	Norfolk	Mt. Gilead Baptist Church	1952	Harvey Johnson
VA	Norfolk	Mt. Olive Baptist Church	1919	Harvey Johnson
VA	Norfolk	Mt. Pleasant Baptist Church	x	Harvey Johnson
VA	Norfolk	Community Lutheran Hosptial	x	Golden Zenon
VA	Norfolk	Queen Street Baptist Church	1910	John Lankford
VA	Norfolk	Queen Street Baptist Church	1957	Harvey Johnson
VA	Norfolk	Rich, William	1919	Harvey Johnson
VA	Norfolk	Riddick, _____	c1922	Harvey Johnson
VA	Norfolk	Second Calvary Baptist Church	1919	Harvey Johnson
VA	Norfolk	St. John African Methodist Episcopal Church	1952	Harvey Johnson
VA	Norfolk	St. John's African Methodist Episcopal Church & Parsonage	c1907	John Lankford
VA	Norfolk	St. Luke Congregational Methodist Episcopal Church	x	Harvey Johnson
VA	Norfolk	St. Mark Reformed Zion United Apolostolic Church	1919	Harvey Johnson
VA	Norfolk	St. Paul's Colored Methodist Episcopal Church	1920	Harvey Johnson
VA	Norfolk	Trigg, _____	1921	Harvey Johnson
VA	Norfolk	Turpin, _____	1922	Harvey Johnson
VA	Norfolk	Zion Bethel Church	1958	Harvey Johnson
VA	Norfolk	Carter, Charles S.	c1925	Harvey Johnson
VA	Petersburg	First Baptist Church	x	Harvey Johnson
VA	Petersburg	Gillfield Church Education Bldg.	1964	Amaza Meredith

APPENDIX

State	City/County	Name	Year	A/AE/LA
VA	Petersburg	Harrison Street Baptist Church	x	Harvey Johnson
VA	Petersburg	Robbins, Dr. C.A.	1949	William Moses
VA	Petersburg	Tabernacle Baptist Church	1966	Harvey Johnson
VA	Petersburg	Zion Baptist Church	1959	Harvey Johnson
VA	Portsmouth	Corprew, Maggie	x	Harvey Johnson
VA	Portsmouth	Cumberland Street Houses	x	Harvey Johnson
VA	Portsmouth	Ebenezer Baptist Church	1936	Harvey Johnson
VA	Portsmouth	Ebenezer Plaza Apts.	1968	Harvey Johnson
VA	Portsmouth	Emanuel African Methodist Episcopal Church	c1907	John Lankford
VA	Portsmouth	Federated Colored Womens Club	x	William Moses
VA	Portsmouth	First Baptist Church	1919	Charles Russell
VA	Portsmouth	First Baptist Church	1940	Harvey Johnson
VA	Portsmouth	France, Dr. J. J.	c1918	Harvey Johnson
VA	Portsmouth	Grove Baptist Church	c1928	Harvey Johnson
VA	Portsmouth	Holland, Catherine	1956	Harvey Johnson
VA	Portsmouth	Jackson Cleaners	1952	Harvey Johnson
VA	Portsmouth	Jackson Memorial Baptist Church	1948	Harvey Johnson
VA	Portsmouth	Jackson, Dr. J. A.	1939	Harvey Johnson
VA	Portsmouth	Mt. Hermon Baptist Temple	1924	Harvey Johnson
VA	Portsmouth	New Bethel Baptist Church	1952	Harvey Johnson
VA	Portsmouth	St. John Baptist Church	1919	Harvey Johnson
VA	Portsmouth	Union Commercial Bank	1919	Harvey Johnson
VA	Portsmouth	Union Holiness Church	1954	Harvey Johnson
VA	Portsmouth	Waters, W. E.	x	Harvey Johnson
VA	Portsmouth	Watts, Dr. Irvin	1953	William Moses
VA	Powhatan	Pleasant, Nathan	c1950	Ethel Furman
VA	Princess Anne Courthouse	Mt. Zion African Methodist Episcopal Church	c1910	John Lankford
VA	Quinton	Union Baptist Church	x	Ethel Furman
VA	Richmond	Apostolic Faith Church	x	Ethel Furman
VA	Richmond	Attucks Theatre	1919	Charles Duke
VA	Richmond	Belgian Friendship Complex	1939	Charles Russell
VA	Richmond	Cedar Street Memorial Bpatist Church	x	Ethel Furman
VA	Richmond	Dammalls, Issaac	1890	Daniel Farrar
VA	Richmond	Davis, D. Webster	c1905	John Lankford
VA	Richmond	Dismond, Dr. Samuel H.	1890	Daniel Farrar
VA	Richmond	Ebenezer Baptist Church	x	Charles Russell
VA	Richmond	Fourth Baptist Church	1961	Ethel Furman
VA	Richmond	Henderson, William	1890	Daniel Farrar
VA	Richmond	Hewen, Atty. J. Thomas	x	Charles Russell
VA	Richmond	Hill, Robert T.	1891	Daniel Farrar
VA	Richmond	Hughes, Dr. W.H.	1915	Charles Russell
VA	Richmond	Johnson Hall	1910	Charles Russell
VA	Richmond	Jones, Dr. Robert E.	1891	Daniel Farrar
VA	Richmond	McCurdy, Hugh A.	1891	Daniel Farrar
VA	Richmond	Quarles, Alexander P.	1890	Daniel Farrar
VA	Richmond	Richmond Beneficial Insurance Co.	1911	Charles Russell
VA	Richmond	Riverside Baptist Church	1914	Charles Russell
VA	Richmond	Robertson Apts.	c1907	John Lankford
VA	Richmond	Robertson, Atty. J. C.	c1907	John Lankford
VA	Richmond	Shepherd, John M.	1890	Daniel Farrar
VA	Richmond	Sixth Mt. Zion Baptist Church	1925	Charles Russell
VA	Richmond	Snead, James	1968	Ethel Furman
VA	Richmond	Southern Aid Society Bldg.	1907	John Lankford
VA	Richmond	St. James Holiness Church	1956	Ethel Furman
VA	Richmond	St. James Holiness Church	1939	Ethel Furman
VA	Richmond	St. Luke's Hall	1919	Charles Russell
VA	Richmond	St. Luke's Penny Savings Bank	1910	Charles Russell
VA	Richmond	Strother, Charles	1890	Daniel Farrar
VA	Richmond	Taylor Apts.	1907	John Lankford
VA	Richmond	Taylor, Rev. W. L.	1907	John Lankford
VA	Richmond	Thompson, Atty. J. W.	x	Harvey Johnson
VA	Richmond	Trainum, Alexander	1890	Daniel Farrar

APPENDIX

State	City/County	Name	Year	A/AE/LA
VA	Richmond	True Reformers Meeting Hall	1895	Daniel Farrar
VA	Richmond	Turner, Beverly F.	1890	Daniel Farrar
VA	Richmond	United Order of True Reformers	1890	Daniel Farrar
VA	Richmond	Virginia Union University Classroom Bldg.	x	Charles Russell
VA	Richmond	Virginia Union University Hartshorn Dormitory	1928	Hilyard Robinson
VA	Richmond	Virginia Union University Huntley Hall	x	Charles Russell
VA	Richmond	Walker, Maggie L.	c1920	Charles Russell
VA	Richmond	Wilder, Robert J.	c1923	Ethel Furman
VA	Richmond	Wood, J. P.	x	Harvey Johnson
VA	Richmond	Wyatt, William	1890	Daniel Farrar
VA	Roanoke	U. S. Post Office	1960	Willie Jenkins
VA	Sanston	Rising Mt. Zion Baptist Church	1976	Ethel Furman
VA	Smithfield	Wren, Fred D.	1946	William Moses
VA	South Portsmouth	First Baptist Church	1919	Harvey Johnson
VA	Staunton	Community Methodist Church	1962	De Witt Dykes
VA	Stauton	Allen Chapel African Methodist Episcopal Church	1922	John Lankford
VA	Suffolk	First Baptist Church	x	Harvey Johnson
VA	Suffolk	Phoenix Bank of Nansemond	1936	Harvey Johnson
VA	Suffolk	Tynes Street Church	1936	Harvey Johnson
VA	Warrick	Reynolds, T.A.	1953	William Moses
VA	Kent County	Union Hope Baptist Church	x	Ethel Furman
VA	Yorktown	Rooks, Rev. Shelby	1948	William Moses
WA	St. Helen's	Plan of the Town of St. Helen's	c1875	Grafton Brown
WA	Walla Walla	Walla Wall, Washington Territory	1866	Grafton Brown
WI	Appleton	U. S. Post Office	x	William Cooke
WI	Columbus	U. S. Post Office	1938	William Cooke
WI	Millville	U. S. Post Office	1939	William Cooke
WI	Milwaukee	Fourth Church of Christ, Scientist	1931	Charles Duke
WI	Sheboygan	U. S. Post Office	1933	William Cooke
WVA	Beckley	Brown-Payne Business Complex	x	John Norman
WVA	Charleston	Community Center	x	John Norman
WVA	Charleston	Municipal Auditorium	x	John Norman
WVA	Charleston	Cabell Junior High School	x	John Norman
WVA	Charleston	Catalina Business Complex	x	John Norman
WVA	Charleston	Connelly Business Complex	x	John Norman
WVA	Charleston	Faulkner Hardware Store	x	John Norman
WVA	Charleston	Ferguson Business Complex	1919	John Norman
WVA	Charleston	Fisher, _____	x	John Norman
WVA	Charleston	Frankel's Men's Apparel Store	x	John Norman
WVA	Charleston	Gamble, Dr. _____	x	John Norman
WVA	Charleston	Gamble, Katherine	x	John Norman
WVA	Charleston	Garnet High Schol	x	John Norman
WVA	Charleston	Greenbriar Theatre	x	John Norman
WVA	Charleston	Jones, Joseph R. Sr.	x	John Norman
WVA	Charleston	Knights of Pythias Bldg.	1905	Albert Brown
WVA	Charleston	Pfizer Chemical Store	x	John Norman
WVA	Charleston	Saunders, W.W.	x	John Norman
WVA	Charleston	Shanklin, _____	x	John Norman
WVA	Charleston	Staats Hospital Complex	x	John Norman
WVA	Charleston	Washington Manor Complex	x	John Norman
WVA	Charleston	Wells, Dr. Ira J.K.	x	John Norman
WVA	Charleston	West Virginia State College Auditorium	1941	John Norman
WVA	Charleston	West Virginia State College Faculty Houses	1933	John Norman
WVA	Fairmont	American Legion Post No. 37	1945	Louis Bellinger
WVA	Fairmont	Mt. Zion Baptist Church	x	Carl Barnett
WVA	Fairmont	Watson, James E. "High Gate"	1909	Julian Abele
WVA	Huntington	Commercial Bldg.	x	Robert Washington
WVA	Huntington	Barnett Elementary School for Negroes	x	Robert Washington
WVA	Huntington	Barnett, Caroline C.	x	Robert Washington
WVA	Huntington	Brown Brothers & Co.	1921	Robert Washington
WVA	Huntington	First Baptist Church	x	Carl Barnett
WVA	Huntington	Frances, D.S.	1942	Carl Barnett

APPENDIX

State	City/County	Name	Year	A/AE/LA
WVA	Huntington	McClain, C.S.	1921	Robert Washington
WVA	Huntington	McClain's Funeral Home	1921	Robert Washington
WVA	Huntington	White Pharmacy	x	Robert Washington
WVA	London	London High School	x	John Norman
WVA	Malden	Booker T. Washington Memorial	1926	Albert Cassell
WVA	Montgomery	Simmons High School	x	John Norman
WVA	Morgantown	U. S. Post Office	1931	Samuel Plato
WVA	St. Albans	St. Paul Baptist Church	1920	Albert Brown
WY	Devils Tower	Devils Tower National Monument Visitor Ctr.	1950	Francis Rassieur Roberson
WY	Laramie	Ft. Laramie Cavalry Barracks	1953	Francis Rassieur Roberson
WY	Laramie	Ft. Laramie Commissary Store	1952	Francis Rassieur Roberson
WY	Laramie	Ft. Laramie Guardhouse	1955	Francis Rassieur Roberson
WY	Laramie	Ft. Laramie Officers Quarters	1954	Francis Rassieur Roberson
WY	Laramie	Ft. Laramie Old Bedlam	1957	Francis Rassieur Roberson
WY	Laramie	Ft. Laramie Sutler's Store	1951	Francis Rassieur Roberson
WY	Laramie	Ft. Laramie Visitor Ctr.	x	Francis Rassieur Roberson
WY	Moose	Grand Teton National Park Trader Ctr.	1950	Francis Rassieur Roberson
WY	Norris Junction	Yellowstone National Park Ranger Museum	x	Francis Rassieur Roberson
WY	Sheridan	Potato Chip Factory	1908	Clarence Wigington

Country	City	Name	Year	A/AE/LA
Brazil	Sao Paulo	Aranha, Paulo	1986	Georgia Brown
Brazil	Sao Paulo	Beer, Robert	1979	Georgia Brown
Brazil	Sao Paulo	Behmer, _____	1968	Georgia Brown
Brazil	Sao Paulo	Bohlen und Halbach Ranchero	1967	Georgia Brown
Brazil	Sao Paulo	Bottene, Brown	1975	Georgia Brown
Brazil	Sao Paulo	Carrera, Bermudez	1976	Georgia Brown
Brazil	Sao Paulo	CIT Co.	1978	Georgia Brown
Brazil	Sao Paulo	dos Reis, Jair Sorbelini	1977	Georgia Brown
Brazil	Sao Paulo	Elene, Nilson	1980	Georgia Brown
Brazil	Sao Paulo	Ericsson of Brazil	1972	Georgia Brown
Brazil	Sao Paulo	Fagundes, Jose Otavio	1979	Georgia Brown
Brazil	Osasco	Ford Motor Company of Brazil	1957	Georgia Brown
Brazil	Sao Paulo	Fourth City Centennial	1955	Georgia Brown
Brazil	Sao Paulo	Frederick Reydon, Frederick	1979	Georgia Brown
Brazil	Sao Paulo	Guglielmi, Julio	1974	Georgia Brown
Brazil	Sao Paulo	Hoverter, _____	1980	Georgia Brown
Brazil	Sao Paulo	Hughes, Peter A. E.	1974	Georgia Brown
Brazil	Sao Paulo	Kodak of Brazil, Industrial & Commercial Division	1970	Georgia Brown
Brazil	Sao Paulo	Marchesini, Hugo B.	1987	Georgia Brown
Brazil	Sao Paulo	Marchesini, Hugo B.	1976	Georgia Brown
Brazil	Sao Paulo	Matarazzo, _____	1967	Georgia Brown
Brazil	Sao Paulo	Michineves, Eduardo	1978	Georgia Brown
Brazil	Sao Paulo	National City Bank of New York	1954	Georgia Brown
Brazil	Guarulhos	Pfizer Corporation of Brazil	1960	Georgia Brown
Brazil	Sao Paulo	Pravaz—Recordati Laboratories	c1963	Georgia Brown
Brazil	Sao Paulo	Ruthofer, Eva M.	1977	Georgia Brown
Brazil	Sao Paulo	Sampaio, Marcio	1986	Georgia Brown
Brazil	Sao Paulo	Terron, _____	1975	Georgia Brown
Brazil	Sao Paulo	Von Erlea, _____	1968	Georgia Brown
British Columbia	Vancouver	Second Narrows Bridge	1925	Cornelius Henderson
Canada	Cooper Cliff	Ontario Refining Co.	1913	Cornelius Henderson
Canada	Edmonton	Edmonton High Level Bridge	1913	Cornelius Henderson
Canada	Falconbridge	Falconbridge Nickel Co.	1920	Cornelius Henderson
Canada	Frood	International Nickel Co. Mill Bldgs.	1917	Cornelius Henderson
Nova Scotia	Sydney	Dominion Iron & Steel Co.	1910	Cornelius Henderson
Canada	Ontario	Thousand Islands Bridge	1937	Cornelius Henderson
Canada	Ottawa	Canadian Supreme Court	x	Cornelius Henderson
Canada	Ottawa	Royal Canadian Mounted Police Hqtrs.	x	Cornelius Henderson

APPENDIX

Country	City	Name	Year	A/AE/LA
Canada	Hazleton	Skeena River Viaduct	x	Cornelius Henderson
Canada	Peterborough	General Electric Company Factory	1929	Cornelius Henderson
Canada	Quebec	Quebec Bridge	1917	Cornelius Henderson
Canada	Rouyn	Noranda Mines Factory	1927	Cornelius Henderson
Canada	Trenton	Royal Air Force Hangars	x	Cornelius Henderson
Canada	Welland	Welland Vertical Lift Bridge	1930	Cornelius Henderson
Canada	Windsor	Dominion Forge & Stamping Co.	1910	Cornelius Henderson
China	Pusan	Baptist Mission Hospital	1954	Arthur Ferguson
Columbia	Bogota	Hotel Granada	1946	Paul Williams
Columbia	Bogota	Ribon Apts.	1948	Paul Williams
Columbia	Bogota	Villegas, Don Luis Toro	1948	Paul Williams
Columbia	Medelin	Nutibara Hotel	1955	Paul Williams
Ecuador	Guayaquil	Tubercular Hospital	1948	Paul Williams
France	Paris	United Nations Bldg.	c1953	Paul Williams
Guinea	Bissau	Guinea Government Complex	1962	Percy Ifill
Korea	Seoul	Chamber of Commerce	1954	Arthur Ferguson
Korea	Seoul	Korean Housing Corp.	1954	Arthur Ferguson
Korea	Seoul	National Library	1954	Arthur Ferguson
Korea	Seoul	Seoul Central Bldg.	1954	Arthur Ferguson
Korea	Seoul	Son Dai Moon Police Station	1954	Arthur Ferguson
Korea	Seoul	Suwon Agricultural College	1954	Arthur Ferguson
Korea	Seoul	Suwon Agricultural Laboratory	1954	Arthur Ferguson
Liberia	Harbel	Booker T. Washington Institute Trade School	1950	Donald White
Liberia	Harbel	Roberts Airfield	1941	Hilyard Robinson
Liberia	Harbel	Roberts Airfield	1941	David Williston
Liberia	Monrovia	Agricultural Experiment Station	1953	Henry Boles
Liberia	Monrovia	Centennial Victory Exposition Ctr.	1946	David Williston
Liberia	Monrovia	Mines & Geology Bldg.	1955	Henry Boles
Liberia	Monrovia	Monrovia Elementary School	1954	Henry Boles
Nigeria	Lagos	Ojike Memorial Medical Ctr.	1962	Percy Ifill
Puerto Rico	Ponce	Ponce Medical Center	1950	Conrad Johnson
Puerto Rico	Humacao	Presbyterian Hospital	c1920	Vertner Tandy
Senegal	Dakar	Deputy Chief of Mission Residence	1965	Robert Madison
Senegal	Dakar	Staff Apts.	1965	Robert Madison
Senegal	Dakar	U.S. Embassy Office	1965	Robert Madison
Sierra Leone	Njala	Njala University Master Plan	1976	Edward Pryce
South Africa	Capetown	Cosmic Metropolitan African Methodist Episcopal Church	c1920	John Lankford
Sudan	Kharutoum	Khartoum Technical Institute Administration Bldg.	1958	Granville Hurley
Sudan	Kharutoum	Khartoum Technical Institute Trades Bldg.	1959	Granville Hurley

Index

Abele, Julian Francis, **1–4,** 104, 149, 203
Aberdeen Gardens, 128, 352, 353
Abita Springs Golf Course, 27
Abraham Lincoln houses, 391, 392
Adams, Charles, 265
Adams Elementary School, 334
Addison Road Metro Station, 385, 386
Adelphia Savings & Loan building, 23, 24
Aero Industries, 54
African Baptist Church, 363
African Methodist Episcopal Book Concern, 30, 32
African Methodist Episcopal Publishing House, 273
African Methodist Episcopal Zion Publishing House, 371, 372
Afro-American Mutual Insurance Co., 371, 372
Agricultural Experiment Station, 46
Aijalon Baptist Church, 178
Aiken, Ernest, 265
Aiken apartments, 41, 265
Alabama Agricultural & Mechanical College
    Palmer Hall, 255
    saw mill, 255
    Seay Hall, 255
    steam plant, 255
Alabama Agricultural Fair Negro Building, 395
Alabama Christian College, 334
Alabama Courts apartments, 171
Alabama State College
    Arena-Auditorium, 161
    classroom buildings, 161, 428
    dining hall, 161, 428
    library, 161, 428
    men's dormitory, 161, 428
    Science building, 161
    swimming pool building, 161
    women's dormitory, 161, 428
Alabama State Courthouse, 247
Alabama State Fair Negro Building, Montgomery, **5–6,** 17
Alabama State Teachers College
    community center, 437
    dormitory, 437
    extension service building, 437
    gym, 437
    Science building, 273, 437
Alcorn State University, 455

Alexander, Archibald Alphonse, **7–9**
Alexander, John A., 265
Alexander, Judge, 383
Alexander Chapel Methodist Church, 132
Alexandria Housing Authority FHA housing, 209
Al Jolson Memorial, 450
Allegheny County Community College, 350
Allegheny County Housing Authority, 350
Allegheny County Rehabilitation Corp., 350
Allen, Joseph R., 461
Allen African Methodist Episcopal Church, 269
Allen Chapel African Methodist Episcopal Church
    Ft. Worth, TX, 321
    Stauton, VA, 255
Allen Chapel Methodist Church, 255
Allen Realty Co. house, 14
Allen University
    Chapel, 255
    Chapelle administration building, 255
    girls dormitory, 40, 41
    Laymen Hall and Reid's Hall, 40
    Ministers Hall, 41
Allerton Branch Library, 190
All-Pro Chicken, 348, 350
Almonbury, 3
Alston's Esso Service Station, 239
Alta Settlement House, 394, 395
Alter Mack Copper Co., 201
Altgeld Gardens Public Housing, 398, 399
Ambassador Bridge, 200, 201
Ambler, George M., 419
American Airlines, 223, 236
American Beach, 64
American Federal Savings & Loan Association, 232
American Legion Post No. 7, 32
American Negro Exposition, 296, 297
AME Sunday School Union Publishing House, 273
Amsterdam Avenue housing, 223
Anchor apartments, 14
Anderson, Eddie, 450
Anderson, Marian, 149, 150
Angelus Funeral Home, 449, 450
Anthony, Isham H., 50, 51
Antioch Baptist Church
    Augusta, GA, 210, 211
    Bowman, SC, 40, 41

519

INDEX

Antioch Baptist Church (*continued*)
    Cincinnati, OH, 36, 339
    St. Louis, MO, 343, 344
    Washington DC, by Hatton, 194
    Washington DC, by Melby, 279
Apartments
    by Archer, 13, 14
    by Bankhead, 18, 20
    by Bellinger, 30, 31, 32
    by Bow, 48
    by Bowman, 50, 51
    by Boyde Jr., 53, 54–56
    by Brown, G.L.H., 74
    by Brown, L.J.H., 80
    by Buffins, 84, 85
    by Cassell, A.I., 92–93, 94
    by Duke, 128, 129
    by Ferguson, 146
    by Fry, 160, 161
    by Garrott, 165, 167
    by Giles Sr., 171, 172
    by Hamilton, 181, 182
    by Hilliard, 204–205
    by Hoban, Sr., 207, 209
    by Holloway, Jr., 211
    by Ifill, 223, 224
    by Johnson, Jr., 235, 236
    by Lankford, 255
    by Mackey, Sr., 265, 266
    by C. McKissack, 273
    by M. McKissack, 276
    by Melby, 278, 279
    by Ransom, Jr., 336, 337
    by H.R. Robinson, 352, 353, 354
    by Sealey, 369
    by Tandy, 391, 392
    by Taylor, 397–399
    by R.A. Vaughn, 414–417
    by Williams, 450, 451, 452
    by Wilson, Jr., 456, 457, 458
Apex Beauty School, 323
Apostolic Faith Church, 164
Appalachian Exposition Negro Building, **10–11,** 286, 287
Aprilano, Frank, 54
Aquilar Cigar Factory, 255
Aranha, Paulo, 74
Archer, Romulus Cornelius, Jr., **12–14,** 322
Ardrosson, 4
Argentine Embassy, 4
Arieno, Charles J., 54
Arkansas Valley Lodge No. 21, 421, 422
Arlington View Terrace, 207, 209

Armstrong, Samuel Chapman, 183–184
Aronson, Victor, 54
Arrowhead Springs Hotel, 449, 450
Arthur Capper public dwellings, 353
Asbury Garden apartments, 182
Asbury Methodist Church
    Lynchburg, SC, 132
    Washington DC, 14
Asbury United Methodist Church, 80, 110, 111
Ashton Theatre, 363
Athol, elderly housing, 45, 46
Atkins, Jack P., 448, 450
Atkins, Louise, 354
Atlanta Life Insurance Co., 291
Atlanta University, President's residence, 455
Attucks Theater
    Norfolk, VA, 238, 239, 364–365, 366
    Richmond, VA, 364, 366
Auburndale-Clearview Branch Library, 190
Augusta, A. T., 59
Austin Catholic Church, 198
Avant, Frank W., 293, 294
Avery apartments, 273
Avoca apartments, 273
Axelrod, Milton P., 54

Baber-Daniels apartments, 223
Badagry Hotel, 236
Badlands National Park, Museum, 346
Bailey, Isaac, 445
Bailey, Walter Thomas, 5–6, **15–17,** 128, 204, 215
Bainbridge, Griffin, 437
Baird Sanitarium, 54
Baker, Raymond T. "Marly," 3
Baker playground shelter, 445
Balonek, Frank, 54
Band, Louis M., 265
Bankhead, Lester Oliver, **18–20,** 167
Bank of America, Vermont/Slauson Branch, 369
Banks, Louis Harvey, **21–22**
Bannister, C. C., 145
Baptist Academy, 255
Baptist churches
    by Abele, 4
    by Archer, 13, 14
    by Bailey, 17
    by Bankhead, 19, 20
    by Barnett, 23, 24
    by Bellinger, 32
    by Berry, 35
    by Blanche, 40, 41
    by Boles, 46
    by Bow, 48

by Brent, 58, 59, 60
by Brown, A. G., 70, 71
by Brown, L.J.H., 80
by Brown, R. L., 83
by Cassell, A. I., 93, 94
by Cross, 116, 117
by Drayton, 126
by Dykes, Sr., 131, 132, 133
by Ferguson, 145, 146
by Fields, 147, 148
by Ford, 154, 155
by Furman, 163, 164
by Giles Jr., 169
by Giles Sr., 172
by Griffin, 178
by Hamilton, 181, 182
by Hatton, 194
by Hoban, Sr., 207, 209
by Holloway, Jr., 210, 211
by Hutchins, 218, 219
by Ifill, 223, 224
by Jackson, 227
by Jenkins, 232, 233
by Johnson, 238, 239, 240
by Lankford, 256, 257
by Livas, 262
by Mackey, Sr., 265, 266
by Madison, 269, 270
by C. McKissack, 273
by M. McKissack, 276
by Miller, 290, 291
by Pittman, 321
by Plater, 323, 324
by Plato, 325, 326, 327
by Price, 331
by Rayfield, 338, 339, 340
by Roberson, 343, 344
by Rosemond, 359, 360
by Rousseve, 363, 363
by Russell, 365, 366
by Spears, 380
by Streat, Jr., 383
by Sulton, 385, 386
by Tandy, 392
by R.I. Vaughn, 419, 420
by Walker, 421, 422
by C.B. White, 433, 434
by Williams, 451
Baptist Mission Hospital, 143
Baptist Seminary, 255
Barber Daniels Garden apartments, 236
Barker Electrical Appliance Store, 419
Barnett, Carl Eugene, **23–24,** 425

Barnett, Caroline C., 425, 426
Barnett Elementary School for Negroes, 425, 426
Barnum, H. B., 20
Barry Farm public housing, 386
Bartholomew, Joseph Manual, Sr., **25–27**
Bass Chapel Methodist Church, Education building, 132
Bastian, Nate A., 273
Bates, Robert Charles, **28–29,** 99, 108
Bay Ridge Branch Library, 190
Bayside Branch Library, 190
Bay View Hotel, 54
Beason, J. T., 59
Becker Brothers Photographic Studio, 129
Becket (Beckett), John W., 463, 464
Becket, L. M., 59
Beckley, M. D., 59
Bedford District Health Center, 190
Beecher Memorial Congregational Church, 363
Beer, Robert, 74
Behmer, 74
Belgian Friendship complex, 366
Bell, Napoleon, 337
Bellevue Hospital, 190
Bellevue Hospital, nurses school & residence, 190
Bellinger, Louis Arnett Stewart, **30–32**
Bell Masonic Lodge, 323
Bell Tower, Lady of Fatima, 269
Belvedere Department of Social Services, 369
Belvidere shelter house, 445
Benedict College, 40, 41
Beneficial Savings Bank, 3
Bennett, Helen Z., 171
Bennett College, Dett Cottage, 383
Benning, H. S., 211
Bentley, Eugene M. III, 301
Bentley Street Christian Church, 132
Berenson, Bertram, 185–186
Bergan-Mercy Hospital, 467
Bernheimer, L., 171
Berry, Plympton Ross, **33–35**
Berry Construction Co., 262
Berwind, Herminie "Knollhunt," 3
Beth-Eden Church, 211
Bethel African Methodist Episcopal Church
    Deland, FL, 255
    Detroit, MI, 437
    Greensboro, NC, 232
    Laurens, SC, 433, 434
    Little Rock, AR, 269
    Malvern, AK, 255
    Pittsburgh, PA, 269
    Stamford, CT, 269
Bethel apartments, 336, 337

INDEX

Bethel Methodist Church, 132
Bethlehem Baptist Church
    Bay Spring, MS, 132
    Washington DC, 126
Bethlehem 8th Street Baptist Church, 181, 182
Betsy & Betty Beauty Salon, 54
Beulah Baptist Church, 169
Beverly Hills Hotel Polo Lounge, 449, 450
Bevins, L. M., 125, 126
Bibleway Temple, 269
Biff's Coffee Shop, 416
Big Bethel African Methodist Episcopal Church
    Atlanta, GA, 254, 255
    Columbia, SA, 254, 256
Bill's Friendly Inn, 209
Birch, Edward Eginton, **36–37**
Birch, Ernest Octavius, 36, **38**
Birdville African Methodist Episcopal Zion Church, 256
Birmingham Art Club, 339
Birney Elementary School, 93
Black Arts Festival housing, 236
Blackie's House of Beef, 125
Blanche, John Henry, Jr., **39–41**
Blodgett, Joseph Haygood, **42–43**
Blodgett, Louis M., 450
Bloomingdale Branch Library, 190
Blount, R. A., 339
Blue, Allie Congregational, 297
Blue Hill Avenue Fire Station, 46
Blue Label Foods Plant, 54
Bodger County Park Director's building, 167
Bogota Country Club, 450
Bohlen und Halbach ranchero, 74
Boles, Henry Clifford, **44–46**
Bolivar Arms apartments, 337
Bonnoit, M., 342
Booker, Nelson, 59
Booker T. Washington Institute Trade School, 437
Borough Park Branch Library, 190
Bottene, Brown, 74
Bow, Cyril Garner, **47–48**
Bower, Mattie, 256
Bowman, Charles Sumner, **49–51**
Bowman, Theodore A., 211
Boyce, Jacob, 211
Boyde, Thomas Wilson, Jr., **52–56**
Boyd Funeral Home, E.F., 269
Boyd Park Community Center, 276
Boy's Town High School, 467
Boy's Town Visitor Center, 467
Bradfield, E. R., 250
Bradfield building, 247

Brandeis Crossroads Shopping Center, 467
Brandon, Julia B., 461
Brandywine Village I, 181, 182
Bransfort Realty Co., 273
Branson, Stephen, 59
Brent, Calvin Thomas, **57–60,** 61
Brent, John Edmonson, 59, **61–63**, 215, 463
Brewer, George, 380
Brewster Baptist Church, 46
Bricks Rural Life School, 295, 297
Bridges
    by H. King, 245–248
    by J.T. King, 249–250
    by Pelham, 315, 316
Bridges, James L., 297
Bright Hope Baptist Church, 323
Briscoe, Byron, 227
Britt, Leonard, 445
Broadway-Astoria Branch Library, 190
Broadway Temple African Methodist Episcopal Zion Church, 326, 327
Brock, David C., 380
Brodsky, Maurice, 54
Brokaw, Howard C., 3
Bronx Municipal Hospital Center, 190
Brooke, George A. "Almonbury," 3
Brookins, Sanford Augustus, **64–65**
Brookland Union Baptist Church, 419
Brooklyn Community College, 190
Brooklyn Domestic Relations Court, 190
Brooklyn Heights Public Library, 190
Brooklyn Hospital, 423, 424
Brooklyn House of Detention for Men, 190
Brooklyn Supreme Court, 190
Brooklyn Technical High School, 439
Brooklyn Welfare Center, 190
Brooks, E., 169
Brooks, Elizabeth Carter, **66–68**
Brooks, J. C., 238, 239
Brooks, J. R., 14
Brooks, Walter, Jr., 3
Brooks Temple Methodist Church, 132
Broomfield-Crutchfield apartments, 443, 445
Brown, Albert Grant, **69–71**
Brown, Arthur M., 338–339
Brown, Calvin, 274
Brown, Georgia Louise Harris, **72–74**, 308
Brown, Grace A., 171
Brown, Grafton Tyler, **75–77**
Brown, John, 276
Brown, Laurelia, 59
Brown, Leroy John Henry, **78–80,** 206, 215
Brown, Mary Ramsay Channel, 163

Brown, Richard Lewis, **81–83**
Brown, R. W., 321
Brown, Sterling, 171
Brown, W. T., 126
Brown Brothers Confectionery 425, 426
Brown Chapel African Methodist Episcopal Church, 36, 37
Brown Memorial African Methodist Episcopal Church, 386
Brown-Payne business complex, 303, 304
Bruce, Dr., 383
Brummel Manor, 386
Brunswick Gardens, 45, 46
Bryan, Julius, 125, 126
Bryan Senior High School, 467
Bryce Canyon National Park, Museum, 346
Bucknell University, 3
Buffins, Robert Lester, **84–85**
Bull, Gustavus N., 13
Bunche, Ralph J., 352, 354, 455
Burchett apartments, 32
Burke, Dr., 297
Burns Methodist Church, 132
Burton store and apartments, 211
Bushwick District Health Center, 190
Business and Jobs Development Corp., 350
Butcher apartments, 211
Butler, Alberta Jeannette Cassell, **86–87**
Butler, Charles, 182
Butler Brothers Garage, 256
Butler Oak Park War Housing, 296, 297
Butwin, J. G., 445
Byrd, David R., 301

Caanan Baptist Church, 223
Cabell Junior High School, 304
Calistoga Motel, 167
Callan Motors Office & Garage, 209
Calloway, Thomas J., 193, 194
Calvary Baptist Church
    Washington DC, 194
    Wichita, KS, 421, 422
Calvary Hospital, 424
Camellaci, Raymond, 54
Cameron Junior High School, 273
Campbell Ave. Church, 93
Campbell Chapel African Methodist Episcopal Church, 256
Campbell Chapel Church, 318
Campbell Friendship House, 111
Campbell Heights elderly housing, 386
Camp David Trader Center, 346
Camp Jackson barracks, 434

Canaan Methodist Church, 132
Capehart, 260
Capers Congressional (Christian) (Memorial Christian) Methodist Episcopal Church, 271, 273, 275
Capitol Heights Metro Station, 79, 80
Capitol View Baptist Church, 14
Capitol View public housing, 386
Capitol View Realty Co., 278, 279
Captain Arthur Roth Elementary School, 269
Captain Farris house, 46
Cardozo, Dr., 265
Carhart, Amory S., 3
Carlisle, Alma Fairfax Murray, **89–90**
Carnegie Institute, Gate, 350
Carnegie Library of Pittsburgh, 350
Carney, William H., 67, 68
Carpenter Medical Office, 209
Carolina Missionary Baptist Church, 386
Carolina Nursing Home, 232
Carrera, Bermudez, 74
Carson County Public Library, 167
Carter, Charles S., 239
Carter, W. H., Jr., 297
Carter Lake School, 346
Carver House, 54
Carver National Monument, Visitor Center, 346
Carver public housing, 93
Carver Savings and Loan Bank, 223
Cass, Louis, 450
Cassell, Albert Irvin, 47, 53, 86, **91–94,** 104, 125, 159, 168, 177, 189
Cassell, Charles Irvin, 86, **95–96,** 168
Catalina business complex, 304
Catholic Diocese, 92, 93
Catholic University of America, 455
Caton apartments, 171
Cauthorne, Leland S., 164
Cedar Knoll Baptist Church, 265
Cedar Street Memorial Baptist Church, 164
Cellura, Alfred, 54
Centenary Methodist Church, 132
Centennial Missionary Baptist Church, 331
Centennial Victory Exposition Center, 455
Central Baptist Church, 239
Central Congregational Church of Christ, 363
Central Heights Normal & Industrial School, 256
Central Manhattan Repair Headquarters, 190
Central Methodist Episcopal Church, 256
Central State University, Brown Library, 336, 337
Central Union Baptist Church, 324
Central Valley Methodist Church, 132
Century of Progress Exposition, **97–98,** 128
Chamberlain Vocational High School, 80

INDEX

Chamber of Commerce, Seoul, Korea, 143
Chambers Elementary School, 269
Chandler, George M., 14
Chandler, Jesse, 430, 431
Chandler Normal School, Webster Hall, 392
Chaney, Lon, 448, 450
Chang, San Yee, 84, 85
Chapel of Faith Baptist Church, 19, 20
Chapman, Michael A., 301
Charles Drew Health Center, 116, 117
Charlton Hall, 3
Chase Knolls apartments, 415, 416
Chasen's Restaurant, 450
Chateau Crillon, 3
Cheevers, Samuel R., 299, 301
Chelsea Heights Elementary School, 445
Cherrie-Segue Medical Clinic, 363
Cherry, Jeff, 430, 431
Cherry Cove Night Club, 416
Cherry Hill Methodist Church, 132
Cherry Hill public housing, 354
Chesapeake Heights on the Bay, 93, 95–96
Chester Recreation Center, 354
Chicago, Rock Island & Pacific Bridge, 9
Chicago Avenue Bridge, 129
Chicago Tribune, house competition, 297
Chicago War Memorial, 264, 265
Children's Aid Society building, 392
Christian Reformation Church, 176
Christopher Inn, 336, 337
Christ Presbyterian Church, 211
Chrysler Corp., 200
Churches
    by Abele, 3, 4
    by Archer, 13, 14
    by Bailey, 15, 16, 17
    by Bankhead, 19, 20
    by Barnett, 23, 24
    by Bellinger, 32
    by Berry, 35
    by Birch, Edward, 36, 37
    by Blanche, 40, 41
    by Boles, 45, 46
    by Bow, 48
    by Brent, 57–60
    by Brown, A. G., 70, 71
    by Brown, L.J.H., 80
    by Brown, R. L., 82, 83
    by Cassell, A. I., 93, 94
    by Cooke, 110, 111
    by Cross, 116, 117
    by Drayton, 126
    by Duke, 127–129
    by Dykes, Sr., 131, 132, 133
    by Ferguson, 145, 146
    by Fields, 147, 148
    by Ford, 154, 155
    by Foster, Jr., 156–158
    by Furman, 163, 164
    by Garrott, 167
    by Giles Jr., 169
    by Giles Sr., 171, 172
    by Greene, 176
    by Griffin, 178
    by Hamilton, 180, 181, 182
    by Hatton, 194
    by Hazel, 196, 198
    by Hoban, Sr., 207, 209
    by Holloway, Jr., 210, 211
    by Hutchins, 218, 219
    by Ifill, 223, 224
    by Jackson, 227
    by Jenkins, 232, 233
    by Johnson, 238, 239, 240
    by Lankford, 254, 255, 256, 257
    by Livas, 262
    by Mackey, Sr., 265, 266
    by Madison, 268, 269, 270
    by C. McKissack, 271–272, 273
    by M. McKissack, 276
    by Miller, 290, 291
    by Persley, 318
    by Pittman, 321
    by Plater, 323, 324
    by Plato, 325, 326, 327
    by Price, 331
    by Rayfield, 338, 339, 340
    by Roberson, 343, 344
    by Rosemond, 359, 360
    by Rousseve, 363, 363
    by Russell, 365, 366
    by Smith, 370, 371, 372
    by Spears, 379–380
    by Streat, Jr., 383
    by Sulton, 385, 386, 387
    by Tandy, 390–391, 392
    by R.I. Vaughn, 419, 420
    by Walker, 421, 422
    by C.B. White, 433, 434
    by, D.F. White, 436, 437
    by Whittaker, 442
    by Wigington, 446
    by Williams, 450, 451
. Church for David Smith, 171

Church of Christ Apostolic Faith, 337
Church of God
    Washington DC, by Archer, Jr., 14
    Washington DC, by Giles Sr., 171
    Washington DC, by Woodson, 461
Church of the Redeemer, Presbyterian, 268, 269
CIT Co., 74
City Hospital of Brooklyn Laundry, 190
City Mills Co., 247
City Park golf courses, 25, 27
City Terrace Park Pavilion and Pool, 167
Claflin Library, 28
Claflin University
    administration building, 111
    Chapel, 28, 29
    Dunton boy's dormitory, 109, 111
    Lee Library, 108, 111
    main building, 28, 29
    Manual Training building, 29, **99–100**
    President's residence "Dunwalton," 111
    Science building, 40, 41
    Slater Manual Training building, John F., 28, 109, 111
    Soules Home for Girls, 109, 111
    Souvenir Cottage, 108, 111
    Stokes girl's dormitory, 109, 111
    Tingley Memorial Hall, 109, 111
Clandny apartments, 171
Clanerda Presbyterian Church, 3
Clapp's Textile Factory, 247
Claramella, John, 32
Clark, Michael, 59
Clark College
    landscaping, 455
    McPheeters-Dennis Hall, 291
Clarke, Thomas H., 59
Clemons, Lester Jr., 301
Cleveland Junior High School, 445
Cleveland State University, Science & Research Center, 269
Cleveland Trust Co. Bank, 269
Clewman, Nelson, 419
Clews, James B. "La Lanterne," 3
Clinton Chapel African Methodist Episcopal Zion Church, 132
Coar, John M., 339
Coastline apartments, 129
Cockatoo Hotel Restaurant & Garage, 369
Cohen, Samuel L., 171
Colbert, Robert R., 59
Cole, Laura P., 419
Coleman, Dr., 383
Coleman, Frank, 265
Coleman, J., 256
Coleman, Katherine W., 301
Coleman, William Emmett, Jr., **101–103**
Coley, Dr., 383
College Hill housing, 276
College of St. Mary, Science building, 467
College Street Viaduct, 9
Collins, Lawrence, 54, 126
Collins, William, 450
Collins, William K., 169
Collins Chapel Hospital, 276
Colonel Wolfe School, 17
Colonial Church, 256
Colonial Tavern, 295, 297
Colored Carnegie Branch Library, 321
Colored Masonic Temple, 317, 318
Colored Methodist Episcopal Publishing House and Board Office, 273
Colored State Normal School Library, 321
Colored YMCA building, 256
Columbian-Presbyterian Medical Center, 423, 424
Columbus, housing in city of, 337
Columbus Bridge, 247, 250
Colver Presbyterian Church, 3
Comer, Montgomery, 273
Comme Investment Trust and Financial Co., 222, 223
Community Methodist Church, 132
Como Park Elementary School entrance, 445
Coney Island Branch Library, 190
Coney Island General Hospital, 190
Confederate defensive obstructions, 247
Confederate Naval Iron Works Rolling Mill, 247
Congregation Beth Am Synagogue, 415, 416
Congregation Mogen David, 416
Congress Heights Recreation Center, 386
Congress Park homes, 386
Connelly business complex, 303, 304
Connors, Joseph S., 54
Considine Auditorium, 178
Considine Sculpture Court, 178
Conter African Methodist Episcopal Zion Church, 171
Continental Concourse "C," 269
Continental Hotel, 3
Convents Holy Ghost Catholic Church, Rectory, 363
Conway Hotel, 126
Cook, 239
Cook, Julian Abele, **104–105**
Cook, Ralph Victor, 47, 91, 101, **106–107**
Cooke, William Wilson, 12, 100, **108–111**, 241, 292, 418

INDEX

Cookman Institute
    Dining Hall and Girls' Home, 109, 111
    main building, 109, 111
Cooper, Lajoie, 297
Coppin Chapel, 308, 309
Cord, Everett L., 448, 450
Corinthian Baptist Church, 93
Cornell, harry W., 323
Cornerstone Chapel African Methodist Episcopal
    Church, 256
Corprew, Maggie, 239
Correll, Charles, 448, 450
Cosmic Metropolitan African Methodist Episcopal
    Church, 256
Cosmopolitan Temple Baptist Church, 256
Cotton, Norman F., 392
Cotton building, 392
Cotton States and International Exposition, Negro
    Building, 11, **112–114,** 249
Country manor, 233
County Line Methodist Church, 132
Covington Country Club Golf Course, 27
Covington Street School, 35
Cramp, Theodore W. "Portlege," 3
Crawford, Susie, 211
Credit Union, 308, 309
Creighton University
    men's dormitory, 467
    Science building, 467
    Swanson Library, 467
    women's dormitory, 467
Criminal Courts building and prison, 190
Crockett, Edward, 93
Cross, Clarence, **115–117**
Crown Heights Health Center, 190
Crown Savings Bank, 194
Crownsville Hospital Housing & Recreation Center, 93
Crunkleton, J. H., 32
Cuerin, Leon G., 450
Cumberland Hospital, 190
Cumberland office building, 233
Cumberland Street houses, 239
Curtis, J. S., 14
Curtis Wright Defense Plant housing, 327
Custer National Park
    Museum, 346
    Visitor Center, 346
Cutts, W. G., 32
Cuyahoga Community College
    East campus, 269
    Technology Learning Center, 269
    theatre complex & classroom, 269

Dallis & Edmundson, 250
Daltin Restaurant, 54
Dammals, Isaac, 140
Dandridge, W. B., 194
Daniels, Harry, 442
Danziger, William H., 211
D'April Brothers housing, 14
Darlington, H. S., 3
Dattilo, Philip B., Sr., 54
David, George, 14
Davie Street Presbyterian Church, 258, 260
Davis, Don, 354
Davis, D. Webster, 256
Davis, Earl F., 383
Davis, Elizabeth, 59
Davis, Harry I., 54
Davis, James A., 301
Davis, Stephen, 161, 428
Davis apartments, 171
Dayton Fire Station No. 13, 116, 117
Dayton Rapid Transit Office & Garage, 117
Dayton's Bluff playground shelter, 445
Deal Funeral Parlor, 265
Deanwood Professional Arts building, 169
Dearborn Street subway station, 409
Decatur, William Jefferson, **119–120,** 213
Decotah Elementary School, 450
Deepdale Golf Clubhouse, 4
Del Aire County Park Director's building, 167
Delany, Henry Beard, **121–122**
Delaware Avenue Baptist Church, 147, 148
Delaware State University
    boundary wall, 181, 182
    Conrad Hall, 180
    Luna I. Mishoe Science building, 180
    Washington Herbarium, 181, 182
    women's dormitory, 180, 182
Delaware Technical and Community College, Terry
    building, 181, 182
DeLeon, Charles A., 269
Dennis, elderly housing, 45, 46
DeRyke Dairy, 54
De Saible cabin, Jean Pointe Baptiste, **97–98,** 128
Des Moines River Highway Bridge, 9
Des Moines Sewage Disposal Plant, 9
Detroit Memorial Park Cemetery, 200, 201
Detroit-Windsor Tunnel, 200, 201
Develon, Thomas, Jr., 3
Devils Tower National Monument, Visitor Center, 346
Dexter Skew Arch Bridge, 316
Dickerson, Isaac, 164
Dickinson, Charles Edgar, **123–124,** 159

INDEX

Diggs, 239
Dillard apartments, 14
Dinner Bell Restaurant, 54
Dinosaur National Monument Trader Center, 346
Dismond, Samuel H., 140
Dixon, Fitz E. "Ronaele Manor," 3
Dixon, J. A., 172
Dobbins, A. G., 339
Dodd, Randolph, 172
Dodge, Anna, 3
Dollar Bank, 35
Dolphin, Woodrow B., 301
Dominican High School, 467
Dominican Sister High School, 467
Dominion Forge & Shipping Co., 200, 201
Dominion Iron & Steel Co., 200, 201
Dorschel, John, 54
Dorschel Motors, 54
dos Reis, Jair Sorbelini, 74
Douglas, Dr., 262
Douglass "Cedar Hill" home, 196–197, 198
Downing, Lewis K., 300
Dows, David "Charlton Hall," 3
Drake Hotel, 416
Drayton, Clyde Martin, 47, **125–126**
Drexel, John R. "Fairholme," 3
Duchess apartments, 85
Dudley High School, gymnasium, 231, 233
Duffy's Hotel, 54
Duhart, Harry L., 380
Duke, Charles Sumner, 84, 97, **127–129**, 204, 300
Duke, James B., 3
Duke Chapel, 3
Duke University
　Botany building, 3
　Chapel, 3
　dormitories 1–5, 3
　Engineers' dormitory, 3
　faculty houses 1–11, 3
　gymnasium, 4
　hospital, 4
　indoor stadium, 4
　Perkins Library, 4
　Physics building, 4
　private patient's building, 4
Dunbar Hotel
　Birmingham, AL, 339
　Los Angeles, CA, 416
Dunbar Theatre, 193, 194
Duncan Ranch, 227
Dunn, James A., 301
Durkee Gardesn, 64, 65

Dutton, Benson L., 185
Duvall, Malcolm, 172
Dykes, DeWitt Sanford, Sr., **130–133**
Dyson, Walter, 265

Earls, Julian M., 301
Early, W. F., 342
East Bronx Municipal Hospital, nurses residence, 190
East Capitol Church of Christ, 169
East Cleveland
　municipal building, 269
　municipal courtrooms, 269
　police station, 269
East End Middle School, 348, 350
East Harlem General Hospital, 190
East Hills shopping center, 350
Eastland Gardens apartments, 211
Eastman Hotel Rainbow Lounge & Coffee Shop, 54
East River Park Amphiltheatre, 458
Eaton Day Care Home, 276
Ebenezer African Methodist Episcopal Church
　Detroit, MI, 256
　Indianapolis, IN, 256
Ebenezer Baptist Church
　Charlottesville, VA, 256
　Chicago, IL, 339
　Portsmouth, VA, 238, 239
　Richmond, VA, 366
　Wilmington, DE, 181, 182
Ebenezer Baptist Church, Christian education building
　(Atlanta, GA), 290, 291
Ebenezer Methodist Episcopal Church parsonage, 59
Ebenezer Plaza apartments, 239
Eccleston, 2
Edgcumbe Elementary School, 445
Edgcumbe playground shelter, 445
Edgewater Hyatt House Hotel, 369
Edmondson, Gladys, 172
Edmonson Memorial Hospital, 467
Edmonton High Level Bridge, 201
Ed Murphy's Supper Club, 125
Edward, Joseph T., 450
Edwards, Gaston Alonzo, **135–137**
Edwards, Thomas N., 164
Edward Waters College, Centennial Hall, 81–82, 83
Effigy Mounds National Monument, Visitor Center, 346
18th Avenue Community Center, 227
860 North Lakeshore Drive apartments, 204, 205
Eisenlohr, Charles, 3
Eisenlohr, Otto, 4
Eisenstat, William P., 54
Eisinger, Jane, 172

INDEX

Elene, Nilson, 74
Eliza Bryand cluster homes, 269
Elk River Creamery, 445
Elks Lodge Hall, 207, 209
Elks Lodge No. 85, 419
Elks Rest Home, 395
Ellington School of the Arts, 207, 209
Elliott, Curtis Graham, 36, **138**, 215
Ellis, Lacy B., 172
Elmendorf Farm, 4
Elmhurst General Hospital, 190
El Mirador Hotel, 450
El Reno housing, 450
Emanuel African Methodist Episcopal Church, 256
Emmanuel Baptist Church
    Cleveland, OH, 269
    Jacksonville, FL, 218, 219
Emmanuel Methodist Church, 132
Emmanuel Presbyterian Church, 132
Empire Parkway Restaurant, 54
Engineering Services building, 269
Ephesus 7th Day Adventist Church, 14
Episcopal Church of the Redeemer, 383
Episcopal Hospital, 4
Eppley Airfield Terminal, 467
Ericsson of Brazil, 74
Ernie's Place Restaurant, 54
Eufala Covered Bridge, 246
Evans, James C., 301
Ewing, Edward B., 273
Executive Motel, 14
Ezion Methodist Episcopal Church, 181
Ezion-Mt. Carmel United Methodist Church, 180, 181, 182

Fabcrete Demountable housing, 354
Fagundes, Jose O., 74
Fairfield Baptist Church, 273
Fairholme, 3
Fairlee Methodist Church parsonage, 132
Fairmount Heights
    Mutual Improvement Corp., 321
    public school, 310, 321
    village hall, 319, 321
Fairview apartments, 172
Faith Temple No. 2 Baptist Church, 386
Falcon Bridge Nickel Co., 201
Famous Brand Shoes, 54
Farrar, Daniel J., Sr., **139–141**
Far Rockaway Branch Library, 190
Fasino, Joseph, 54
Father Flanagan Alternative High School, 466, 467
Fatima Family Center, 269

Faulkner Hardware Store, 303, 304
Federal City College, feasibility study, 207, 209
Federal Housing Administration housing, 211
Federal Life building, 144, 145, 461
Federated Colored Women's Club, 297
Fellowship Christian Church, 262
Ferguson, 256
Ferguson, Arthur Wilfred, **142–143**, 214
Ferguson, George Alonzo, **144–146**, 168, 418
Ferguson business complex, 302, 304
Ferris, Newell A., 54
Fides Settlement House, 126
Fields, Robert Lionel, **147–148**
Fifth Baptist Church, 4
Files, Herbert, 126
Fine, Maurice T., 369
Finley, Gravely E., 227
Fire Engine Company No. 2 (Washington DC), 80
Fire Fighters Memorial, 269
Firehouse-Neponsit section of Queens, 191
Firehouse stations
    Columbus, OH, 336, 337
    New York, 191
    St. Paul, MN, 443, 446
    Tewksbury and Boston, 45, 46
First African Methodist Episcopal Church
    Athens, GA, 318
    Gary, IN, 110, 111
    Los Angeles, CA, 450
    Pasadena, CA, 450
First American Bank, 276
First Apostolic Faith Institutional Church, 269
First Baptist Church
    Ardmore, OK, 227
    Detroit, MI, 437
    Fayetteville, NC, 383
    Huntington, WV, 23, 24
    Marion, IN, 326, 327
    Norfolk, VA, 239, 262
    Petersburg, VA, 239
    Portsmouth, VA, 366
    Raleigh, NC, 256
    South Portsmouth, VA, 239
    Washington DC, by Archer, Jr., 14
    Washington DC, by Vaughn, 419
    Wewoka, OK, 227
    Youngstown, Ohio, 35
First Baptist Church Home for the Aged, 296, 297
First Baptist Church of Georgetown, 265
First Baptist Church of Oakland, 360
First Born Church of the Living God, 218, 219
First Christian Church, 233
First Church of Christ, 211

First Church of Christ, Scientist
    Montclair, NJ, 129
    Muskegan, MI, 129
    Reno, NV, 450
    West Palm Beach, FL, 4
First Church of Christ Holiness
    Norfolk, VA, 172
    Washington DC, 172
First Church of Deliverance, 16, 17
First Colored Baptist Church, 256
First Congregational Church, 339
First Greater New Zion Baptist Church, 269
First Presbyterian Church
    LaGrange, GA, 250
    Potosi, MO, 256
    Youngstown, OH, 35
First Rising Baptist Church, 386
First Rising Mt. Zion Baptist Church
    adult center, 386
    education building, 386
First Union Bank, 4
Fisher, Orpheus Hodge, **149–151**
Fisher, Robert E., 265
Fisher brothers, homes, 304
Fisk University
    Burris Music Hall, 276
    Carnegie Library, 273, 274, 276
    English Department building, 276
    Henderson-Johnson Gym, 276
    landscaping, 455
    Parker-Johnson Hall, 276
Flanner House Social Center, 354, 455
Flat Rock Methodist Church, 132
Flat Shoals Creek Bridge, 250
Flint, Katherine, 450
Florence-Firestone Health Clinic, 167
Florence-Firestone Sheriff's Station, 167
Florida Agricultural & Mechanical University, School of Architecture, **152–153**
Florida Masonic Grand Lodge, 256
Fluer Drive Bridge, 9
Flushing Regional Branch Library, 191
Fon-Ri Bowling Alley, 416
Fontaine warehouse, 247
Ford, Wase Alston, **154–155**
Ford Green Public School, 273
Fordham Regional & Children's Library, 191
Fordman, John Hammond, 109, 111
Ford Motor Co.
    of Brazil, 74
    of Canada, 200, 201
Foreman, Madeline, 296, 297
Forest Hills Branch Library, 191

Forest Park & playground, 289
Fort Gaines Bridge, 247
Fort Laramie Park
    cavalry barracks, 346
    commissary store, 346
    guardhouse, 346
    officers quarters, 345, 346
    Old Bedlam bachelor quarters, 346
    Sutlers store, 346
    Visitors Center, 346
Fort Larned National Historic Site, Trader Center, 346
Fort Lincoln Elementary School, 160, 161
Fort Snelling, 445
Fort Valley State College, student center, 273
Foster, Clyde, 301
Foster, George Washington, Jr., **156–158**, 390
Founders Church of Religious Science, 450
Fountainbleau Restaurant & Bar, 55
Fourth Baptist Church, 163, 164
Fourth Church of Christ, Scientist (Milwaukee, WI), 129
Fourth City Centennial, 74
Fourth (Metropolitan) Baptist Church, 58, 59
Fowler, Dr., 354
Fox West Coast Theatre, 450
Frakes fire station, Kentucky, 132
France, J. J., 239
Frances, D. S., 24
Francis, John R., 59
Francis Scott Key Bridge, 9
Frankel's Men's Apparel Store, 303, 304
Franklin, Homer, 14
Franklin Bridge, 247
Franklin House Restaurant, 55
Franklin Park Medical Center, 337
Franklin Plaza subway station, 236
Fraternal Savings & Trust Bank, 17
Frati, Mario J., 55
Frazier, Maurice, 297
Frederick Douglass Homes, 53
Frederick Douglass Memorial Estate apartments, 8, 9
Frederick Douglass public housing, 354, 427, 429
Freedom National banks, 223
Free Library of Philadelphia, 2, 4
Freeman, Daniel, 256
Freeman, Frank, 172
Freeman, William L., 59
Frelinghuysen University, administration building, 254, 256
French, Alfred, 59
French Cleaners, 339
Friederich, Adam G., 55
Friedman, Jules, 55

INDEX

Friendship Baptist Church
    Ehrhardt, SC, 93
    Washington DC, 145, 386
Friendship Methodist Church, 132
Frijhy, Frank S., 55
Froe, R. A., 211
Froe, U. M., 14
Froe apartments, 211
Front Street School, 35
Fry, Louis Edwin, Sr., 123, 125, **159–161**, 168, 207, 215
Fulton, Robert J., 450
Furman, Ethel Madison Bailey, **162–164**

Gadison, 233
Galbrieth Chapel African Methodist Episcopal Church, 256
Galilee Baptist Church, 14
Gamble, Howard and Katherine, 303, 304
Garfield Elementary Public School, 319, 321
Gargano, Frank A., 55
Garnet High School, 304
Garrett Congregational Methodist Episcopal Church, 14
Garrott, James Homer, 19, **165–167**, 204
Garrott office building, 167
Gas station, 279
Geiman apartments, 172
General Electric Co., 200, 201
Genesse Steel Co., 55
Genesse Valley Trust building, 55
Georgetown University, Theatre, 148
Georgetown Visitation Preparatory School for Girls, 148
George Washington Carver public housing, 354
Georgia State Industrial College for Colored Youth, Meldrim Hall, 108, 111
Gianforti, Bert C., 55
Gibbey-Simon, 450
Gibbin, Clifford L., 55
Gibson, T. J., 126
Gilder Elementary School, 467
Giles, Gladys W., 172
Giles, Lewis Wentworth, Jr., **168–169**
Giles, Lewis Wentworth, Sr., **170–172**
Gillespie Junior High School, 233
Gillfield Baptist Church
    education building, 281, 282
    Family Life Center, 262
Ginghamtown Restaurant & Motel, 55
Giordano, Joseph J., 55
Girls Detention House, 227
Glace Bay Power Plant, 149
Glacier National Park, Trader Center, 346
Glass Bridge, 248

Glenarden apartments, 207, 209
Glenarden City Hall, 93
Glenn, L. C., 273
Glenside Baptist Church, 324
Globe National Bank, 392
Golden Age Retirement Village, 132
Golden Grove Church, 265
Golden Rule shopping center, 269
Golden State Elks Lodge, 450
Golden State Mutual Insurance Co.
    Los Angeles, CA, by Garrott, 165, 167
    Los Angeles, CA, by Williams, 449, 450
Goldstein, David G., 55
Goler Metropolitan apartments, 233
Golf courses, by Bartholomew, Sr., 25–27
Good Hope, office building, 256
Goodloe, Don S., 292, 294
Good Wife Restaurant, 416
Gopher Lodge No. 105, 445
Gore, Dr., 383
Gospel Hall Home, 4
Gott, Howard S., 172
Gouverneur Hospital, 191
Grace, Joseph P. "Tullaroan," 4
Grace African Methodist Episcopal Zion Church, 372
Grace Methodist churches, 132
Grace Presbyterian Church, 4
Grady, James, 323
Grady, Washington, 59
Grand Avenue Bridge, 129
Grand Concourse Branch Library, 191
Grand Opera House, 35
Grand Portage National Monument, Trader Center, 346
Grand Rapids sewage plant, 9
Grand Teton National Park, Trader Center, 346
Grandy, Jasminius Wilsonni Rudolphus III, **173–174**
Grant, Bradford, 186
Grant, Duane, 185
Grant Hospital, 337
Grant Memorial African Methodist Episcopal Church, 256
Grant Street Holiness Church, 14
Grave of the Unknown Sailor, 450
Gravesend District Health Center, 191
Gray, James C., 161, 429
Gray Funeral Home, 181, 182
Greater Life Missionary Church, 19
Greater Nebo Baptist Church, 116, 117
Greater Refuge Temple, 224
Greater St. John Church, 211
Greater Tulane Baptist Church, 362, 363
Great Kill Branch Library, 191
Great Neck School admin. building, 4

INDEX

Green, Harry, Jr., 55
Green, William O., 380
Greenbaugh, Kevin, 301
Greenbriar Theater, 304
Greene, Beverly Loraine, **175–176,** 236, 308
Greenlee store, 32
Green Pond Methodist Church, 132
Greensboro National Bank, 233
Greenville Methodist Church, 132
Greenwood Missionary Baptist Church, 290, 291
Gregg, William H., 126
Gregory, F. A., 419
Griffin, Francis Eugene, **177–178**
Griffin, James, 445
Griffith, Corrine, 448, 450
Griswold, Norman W., 273
Gross, William E., 172
Grossman, Milton, 55
Grove Baptist Church, 239
Guenveur, E. L., 383
Guglielmi, Julio, 74
Guilford Baptist Church, 48
Guinea government building complex, 224
Guzetta, Matthew, 55

Hadneman Medical College, Out-Patient's building, 4
Hale Funeral Home, 239
Hale Junior High School, 467
Hall, Alvin C., 172
Hall of Science, 191
Hamilton, Calvin Pazavia, **179–182**
Hamilton, Sara A., 265
Hamilton, Thomas, 450
Hamilton Fish Park Branch Library, 191
Hamilton Methodist Church, 167
Hamilton Printing Co., 144, 146
Hamline Methodist Episcopal Church, 14
Hamline playground shelter, 445
Hammond Country Club Golf Course, 27
Hampton University, 36, 78
    Armstrong Hall, 354
    Davidson dormitory, 354
    Department of Architecture, **183–186**
    Dixie Cottage, 295, 297
    Harkness Hall men's dormitory, 296, 297, 354
    Holley Tree Inn & Monastery, 297
    laundry building, 262, 297
    model house, 262
    President's residence, 297
    Tuskegee Memorial Sun Dial, 297
Hancock, Richard Mason, **187–188**
H & E Sandwich Shop, 55
Handy, James, 239

Hardy recreation center, 386
Harkness House for Ballet Arts, 423, 424
Harlem Community Center, 224
Harlem Hospital, 191
Harlem Retail Market, 191
Harlem River Houses, 456–457, 458
Harlem River Representative Shop & Engineers' Office, 191
Harlem Welfare Center, 191
Harriet Island Pavilion, 443, 444, 445
Harris, Clinton Stevens, **189–192,** 251
Harris, Garry A., 301
Harris, Lemuel, 297
Harris, Mortimer, 354
Harris, Rose P., 323
Harris Methodist Church, 132
Harrison Elementary School, 445
Harrison Street Baptist Church, 239
Harris Temple Methodist Church, 132
Hart, M. S., 342
Harvard University
    Institute of Geographical Exploration, 4
    Widener Library, 4
Harvard Yard Service Facility, 269
Hatton, Isaiah Truman, 170, **193–194**
Hauser, Eric, 167
Haven Chapel Methodist Church, 132
Haven Institute, dormitory, 339
Haven Methodist Episcopal Church, 254, 256
Haven United Methodist Church, 182
Hawkins Manor I and II, 207, 209
Hayes, Ernest H., 297
Hayes-Taylor YMCA, 231, 233
Haynes, Gilbert A., 301
Hays, Will H., 448, 450
Hazel, William Augustus, 91, 156, **195–198,** 213, 263, 343
Hazel Park playground shelter, 445
Heart of Town Motel, 233
Hebrew Cultural Garden, 269
Hedges Grill, 55
Hedges-Rayfield Motor Co., 129
Heicklen, Morris, 55
Henderson, Cornelius Langston, Sr., **199–201,** 300
Henderson, Douglass, 324
Henderson, William, 140
Henderson Community Home & Apartments, 286, 287
Henley, Stewart, 269
Hennig, Henry, 342
Herrick, Glen C., 8
Hersh, Ben, 419
Hewen, J. Thomas, 366
Hicks, George T., 55

531

INDEX

Higbee, Geroge F., 7
High Gate, 4
Highland Park Monument, fountain & flag staff, 445
Highland Park pavilion, 445
Highland Park water tower, 443, 445
Highview Avenue Elementary School, 392
Hi-Hat Club & Bar, 415, 416
Hill, Joseph E., **202–203**
Hill, Robert T., 140
Hillcrest Center for Children, 191
Hill House Center, 349, 350
Hilliard, Leroy, **204–205**
Hillside Memorial Mausoleum, 449, 450
Hill Street School
  auditorium, 287
  gym, 287
Hiram Masonic Lodge, 350
Hirsch apartments, 172
Hitchcock, William, 35
Hite, Ronald T., 172
Hoban, Stewart Daniel, Sr., **206–209**
Hoffman, Harry L., 55
Hoffman, Jarrett F., 59
Holabird public housing, 354, 455
Holden, Robert, 450
Holiday Inn Motel, 40, 41
Holiday Lanes Bowling Alley, 416
Holland, Catherine, 239
Holley, Edward, 233
Holloway, John Bunyon, Jr., **210–212**
Holly, William C., 301
Holman airfield administration building, 443–444, 445
Holman Reynolds, Libby "Treetops," 101–103
Holy Trinity Apostolic Church, 14
Holy Trinity Church
  Washington DC, by Giles, 172
  Washington DC, by Vaughn, 419
Homecroft Elementary School, 445
Homer Hamilton & Co., 35
Homestead National Park, Visitor Center, 346
Hopewell Methodist churches, 132
Hopkins Airport, Cafe Connection concession, 270
Horne, W. L., 297
Horne Ford dealership, 442
Hostetter Elementary School, 450
Hotel Andrews, 249, 250
Hotel Golden, 256
Hotel Granada, 450
House, Christopher C., 265
House, John, 273
House of Prayer, housing, 386
Hoverter, 74
Howard, Damely E., 301

Howard, J. H., 59
Howard, Opie, 450
Howard Chapel Methodist Church, 132
Howard High School, 181, 182
Howard Inn, 385,, 386
Howard University
  Aldridge Theatre, 354
  Armory, 93
  Baldwin Hall, 94
  Bethune Hall dormitory, 354, 431
  Biology building, 354
  Blackburn student center, 431
  Building and Grounds Department, 36, 177
  Burr gym, 94, 431
  Cancer Research building, 431
  Carnegie Library, 104, 105
  Carver dormitory, 221
  Chemistry building, 79, 80, 94, 148, 159, 189, 431
  Clark Hall, 105
  classroom buildings, 431
  College of Medicine, 94
  Cook dormitory, 354
  Cook Hall, 427, 450
  Cramton Auditorium, 354
  Crandall women's dormitory, 94
  Dental building, 431
  Department of Architecture, **213–215**
  Dining Hall & Home Economics building, 91, 94, 197, 198
  Douglass Hall, 159, 189, 214
  Douglas men's dormitory, 94
  Drew dormitory, 354
  East of the River Health Clinic, 386
  Engineering & Architecture building, 354
  faculty offices, 431
  Fine Arts building, 354
  Founders Library, 53, 92, 94, 159, 189, 214, 431
  Frazier women's dormitory, 94
  Greene Stadium and Football Field, 94
  hospital, 432
  hospital parking structure, 386
  Human Ecology building, 432
  Locke Hall, 432
  Medical/Dental Library, 432
  Mudd Medical Research building, 385, 386
  Museum, 148
  power plant, 94, 159
  President's Home, 94
  School of Business, 386, 432
  School of Communication, 432
  School of Dentistry, 354
  School of Human Ecology, 354
  School of Pharmacy, 354

Seley Mudd building, 432
Slowe dormitory, 354
Slowe Hall, 148
snack bar, 265
Student Bookstore, 148
Truth women's dormitory, 94
Wheatley Hall, 94
women's gym, 94
Howell, Mamie, 287
Howell's Business Block, 35
Hubbard, George, 273, 275
Hudson Hotel dining room, 354
Hudson Ledell Medical Office Building, 451
Huff, George, 4
Hughes, Peter A., 74
Hughes, W. H., 366
Hughes Memorial United Methodist Church, 386
Humphrey Hall, 355, 356
Hunter, Edward, 265
Huntington, Harry B., 55
Hurley, Granville Warner, Sr., 104, 215, **216–217**
Hutchins, James Edward, **218–219**
Hyman, Abraham, 342

Ida B. Wells Homes, 17
Ifill, Percy Costa, 175, **221–224**
IGA Food Liner, 337
Imani Church, 270
Imperial-Compton Hotel, 451
Imperial Elks Lodge, 391, 392
Independence Avenue Bridge, 9
Independence Square, 416
Independent Benevolent Order Lodge No. 1, 339
Independent Order of Odd Fellows Temple
    Savannah, GA, 256
    Waycross, GA, 256
    Washington DC, 256
Industrial Bank of Washington, 270
Industrial Savings Bank, 194, 265
Industrial School, 256
Inn at Georgian Place, 4
Institute for Colored Youth, School of Industrial Art, 202–203
Interlichia, Philip C., 55
International Nickel Co., mill buildings and furnace, 201
Inwood Branch Library, 191
Iowa apartments, 419
Iowa condominiums, 386
Iron City Lodge Post No. 17, 32
Irwinton Bridge, 248
Isaacs, Hart, 451
Israel Baptist Church
    Washington DC, by Ferguson, 146
    Washington DC, by Vaughn, 420
Ivey Terrace apartments, 391, 392

Jackson, F., 14
Jackson, Granberry, 274, 276
Jackson, J. A., 239
Jackson, Leon Quincy, **225–227**
Jackson, T. S., 339
Jackson Boulevard Bridge, 129
Jackson Cleaners, 239
Jackson Courts Housing, 276
Jackson Heights Branch Library, 191
Jackson Memorial Baptist Church, educational building, 239
James Creek public housing, 93, 94
James Lee Memorial Church, 326, 327
James River Bridge, 9
Jamestown Ter-centennial Exposition Negro Building, **228–230,** 254, 319, 321
Jarvis Christian College, dining hall, 354
Jason, Robert S., 172
Jefferson Expansion Memorial, Visitor Center, 346
Jefferson High School, 467
Jefferson Medical College Curtis Clinic, 4
Jemison, Robert, Jr., 248
Jenkins, Willie Edward, **231–233**
Jenkintown Bank & Trust Co., 4
Jennings, James J., 301
Jerusalem Baptist Church, 194
Jerusalem Methodist Church, 132
Jessup, Cedric, 324
Johnson, Catherine W., 172
Johnson, Conrad Adolphus, Jr., 175, 223, **234–236**
Johnson, Conrad A., Sr., 235, 236
Johnson, Fielding, 211
Johnson, Frank, 395
Johnson, Harvey Nathaniel, Sr., **237–240,** 365
Johnson, Hollis M., 445
Johnson, James H., 282
Johnson, Joseph, 354
Johnson, Luther, 395
Johnson, Luther H., 32
Johnson, Morris, 14
Johnson, Paul E., 300
Johnson, Walter A., 212
Johnson G. Smith University, men's dormitory, 383
Johnson Medical Center, 467
Johnson office building and apartments, 297
Johnson Recreation Center, 132
Johnson's Hall, 364, 366
John Wesley African Methodist Episcopal Zion Church, 256

INDEX

John Wesley Methodist Church
    Easley and Pinnopolis, SC, 132
    Fayetteville, NC, 383
Jones, Clarence A., 165, 167
Jones, Cleo, 59
Jones, D., 126
Jones, Edward N., 297
Jones, George Maceo, 84, **241–242**
Jones, J. C., 265
Jones, Joseph R., 303, 304
Jones, Lucius, 124
Jones, Robert, 296, 297
Jones, Robert E., 140
Jones, William Thomas, **243–244**
Jones, W. W., 146, 420
Jonesburg Land Improvement Co., 254, 256
Jones Memorial Methodist Church, education building, 14
Jones Memorial Methodist Episcopal Church, 461
Jon-Jose Beauty Salon, 55
Jordan, Isaiah, 461
Joshua Chapel African Methodist Episcopal Church, 321

Kapnick apartments, 14
Kapp, Sam, 55
Kasdins, Jacob, 55
Kathryn Tyler Neighborhood Center, 270
Kaufman Store & apartments, 172
Kayne Avenue Baptist Church, 276
Keister, J. B., 126
Keith, John, 59
Keller Golf Course Clubhouse, 445
Kellom Knoll apartments, 467
Kelly, Charles H., 265
Kelly, Clayton, 13
Kelly, Emma V., 239
Kelly Miller Smith Towers, 227
Kentucky Normal & Industrial Institute
    Hume Hall, 321
    Trade School, 38, 321
Kerbs Memorial Boathouse, 456, 458
Keswick Theatre, 4
Keystone Park multi-family housing, 350
Khartoum Technical Institute
    administration building, 217
    classroom building, 217
Kimball Elementary School, 94, 386
King, Cornelius, 212
King, Horace, **245–248**
King, Jimmy, 301
King, John M., 279
King, John Thomas, 112, **249–250**

King, Lawrence P., 301
King, Martin, Jr., 291
King, Stuart, 451
Kings Highway Branch Library, 191
Kings Lane Elementary School, 276
King's "X" Restaurant & Bar, 416
Kirven, J. K., 342
Klein, Simon, 445
Knight, Edward C. Jr. "Stonybrook," 4
Knights of Columbus Home of Council, 46
Knights of Pythias Bath House & Sanitarium, 17
Knights of Pythias Hall, 69, 70, 71
Knights of Pythias Temple
    Birmingham, AL, 339
    Chicago, IL, 15–16, 128
    Dallas, TX, 319–320, 321
    Pittsburgh, PA, 30–31, 32
Knollhunt, 3
Knott apartment, 31, 32
Knox, Ellis O., 420
Knox Hill
    elderly housing, 386
    recreation center, 386
Knoxville College
    faculty cottages, 287
    faculty house, 244
    greenhouse, 287
    McMillan Chapel, 243, 244
Kodak Brasileire Comerico, 63, 74
Korean Housing Corp., 143
Kramer, 265
Kramer, J. W., 14
Kramer, Leon A., 14
Kramer, V. W., 14
Kroll's Great Expectations Shop, 55
K Street elevated highway, 8

Laborers Building and Loan Office, 321
Lafayette College, *Chi Phi* House, 4
Lagana, Josephine, 212
LaGrange Cotton Oil Factory, 249, 250
Laguna Park Senior Citizen building, 167
Lahr, Bert, 414, 416
Lake Shore Davis apartments, 74
Lake Street Bridge, 129
Lakewood Transit Center, 334
Landis, John, 451
Landis, Sylvia, 48
Landscapes, by Williston, 454, 455
Lane College
    Cleaves women's dormitory, 273, 274
    Hamlett men's dormitory, 273, 274
    Health building, 276

INDEX

landscaping, 455
Langley, Howard E., 212
Langon, Willenton, 265
Langston Terrace, 79, 80, 189, 352, 353, 354, 427, 449, 451, 454, 455
Lankford, Arthur Edward, 189, **251–252**
Lankford, John Anderson, 12, 177, 189, 214, 228, 241, 251, **253–257**, 300, 319
Lanzatella, Philip J., 55
Larkin's Chapel African Methodist Episcopal Church, 256
Laughlin Memorial Methodist Church, 132
Laurelton Branch Library, 191
Lavengood, David, 326, 327
Lawe Funeral Parlor, 266
Lawndale Administrative Center Health Clinic, 167
Lawndale Administrative Center Library, 167
Lawnside Gardens & Shopping Center, 266
Lawrence, Phillip, 212
Lawrence County Courthouse, 35
Lawson, Belford, 354
Lawton-Pratt Funeral Home, 42, 43
Lee, J. Kenneth, 231, 233
Lee, Robert, 48
Lee, S. Kenneth, 174
Lee Chapel African Methodist Episcopal Church, 256
Lee County, courthouse and jail, 248
Lenon-Seney United Methodist Church Sanctuary, 132
Lentral Valley Methodist Church, 132
Lenvox Transit Station, 334
Leonard, Abraham, 278, 279
Leonard Avenue Baptist Church, 256
Leonardo, Henry F., 55
Leonardo, Richard A., 55
Le Rendezvous Restaurant, 363
Levy, Bennett, 55
Lewis, Douglas L., 266
Lewis, John W., 194
Lewis, Kathye E., 301
Lewis, R. A., 172
Lewis, S. W., 354
Lewis building, 172
Lewis clinic, 298
Lewissohn Garage and Shop, 392
Liberian Centennial, 221
Liberty Colored Baptist Church, 59
Library for the Blind, 191
Liggio housing, 212
Lightbrown store, 279
Lightner, Calvin Esau, **258–260**
Lightner Arcade & Hotel, 259, 260
Lightner building, 258–259, 260
Limehouse, Frank, 442

Lincoln Avenue Church of God, 350
Lincoln Hospital
    Bronx, NY, 191
    New York, NY, 392
Lincoln Memorial Theatre & Office Building, 321
Lincoln Place apartments, 414, 415, 416
Lincoln Ridge Colored Institute
    Belknap dormitory, 392
    Berea Hall, 392
    Industrial building, 392
    North dormitory, 392
Lincoln University
    Fine Arts Center, 124
    greenhouse, 124
    Jason Gym, 124
    Journalism building, 159, 161
    men's dormitory, 161
    Page Library, 159, 160, 161, 428, 429, 437
    Scruggs Student Center, 124
    women's dormitory, 161
Lipson, Avrome Y., 55
Lipson Furniture Co., 55
Lithographs by G.T. Brown, 75–77
Littles, Italy, 380
Litwin, Emil, 55
Livas, Henry Lewis, 78, 185, **261–262**, 301
Livingston, W. R., 324
Livingston College
    Aggrey Student Union, 354
    Ballard Hell, 371, 372
    Carnegie Library, 395
    Goler Hall, 371, 372
    Harris dormitory, 354
    Hood Hall, 371, 372
    Moore faculty house, 354
    Varrick Auditorium, 354
Lockett, Jesse, 182
LoCurcio, Ralph D., 55
Logan, Rayford, 354
Logan Temple African Methodist Episcopal Zion Church, 132
Lomax African Methodist Episcopal Church, 256
London, Julie P., 450
London High School, 304
Long Cane Creek Bridge, 250
Long-Garfield Filling Station, 23, 24
Longshoremen's Hall, 181, 182
Lonsdale Day Care Center, 132
Lopatin, Harold H., 55
Los Angeles County Courthouse, 449, 451
Los Angeles County Psychiatric Hospital, 451
Los Angeles County/USC Medical Center
    admitting and minor trauma, 369

INDEX

Los Angeles County/USC Medical Center (*continued*)
    diagnostic and evaluation, 369
    employees cafeteria and kitchen, 369
    north parking garage, 369
    premature nurseries, 369
Los Angeles International Airport, Theme building, 448, 449
Louisiana Colored Teachers Association building, 363
Loup River Power Plant, 8
Love, Heilbron B., 301
Lovell, Robert, 350
Lovely Hill Baptist Church, 40, 41
Low-income housing (Rochester), 55
Loyal Street Baptist Church, 14
Loyd, James, 248
Loyd building, 249, 250
Lucas, C. L., 342
Lucas, William E., 59
Lunduer apartments, 172
Lunn, E. E., 342
Lunney, John, 342
Lunt Lake apartments, 74, 205
Lutes, Bertie M., 172
Lutheran Community Hospital, 467
Lycee Francais, 3
Lyons Hospital, 37
Lyon Village, landscaping, 455
Lyon Village Defense Housing, 354

MacAlester Junior High School, 445
Macedonia Baptist Church
    Los Angeles, CA, 451
    Washington DC, 14
Mackey, Howard Hamilton, Sr., 44, 78, 104, 147, 160, 177, 213, 215, **263–266**, 322
Madison, James G., 59
Madison, Robert Prince, **267–270**
Mahoning County Courthouse, 34, 35
Malcolm X Elementary School, 79, 80
Malibu Inn, 416
Mammano, Joseph T., 55
Mammoth Life Insurance Co., 276
Mangurian, Harry T., 55
Mann Elementary School, 445
Mapleton Branch Library, 191
Maps by G.T. Brown, 77
Marchesini, Hugo B., 74
Margolis, Ben, 167
Marie Reed Elementary School, 160, 161
Marilynn apartments, 420
Marina Del Ray Junior High School, 451
Marksdale Gardens, 45, 46
Marly, 3

Marrs Junior High School, 467
Marshall, Clement, 321
Marshall, Faith, 279
Marshall Junior High School, 445
Martin, George W., 146
Martin, John C., 4
Martin Chapel Methodist Church, 132
Martin de Porres Center, 270
Martin Luther King Jr. High School, 270
Martin Luther King Jr. Public Library, 336, 337
Martin Luther King Jr. Shopping Plaza, 270
Maryland School for Colored Girls, 94
Masonic Hall, 227
Masonic Lodge, 254, 256
Masonic Temple
    Dansville, NY, 55
    Nashville, TN, 273
    Raleigh, NC, 135, 137
    Washington DC, 92, 94
Massachusetts Bureau of Building Construction Office and Garage, 46
Matarazzo House, 73, 74
Mathewson Gateway, 3
Mathews/Phillips, Inc., 350
Matteson, Harlan J., 55
Matteson, Ralph E., 451
Mattingly, Robert, 144, 146
Mayfair Garden (Mansion), 91, 93, 94, 177
McAdoo, John, 239
McAlister, H. A., 298
McClain, C. S., 426
McClain's Funeral Home, 426
McClare's Main building, C. H., 28
McCulloch apartments, 420
McCurdy, Hugh A., 140
McDonald Dental Office, 363
McDuffie, Clyde, 48
McFadden, George H., 4
McGuire, Myron, 62, 63
McIntosh, Ernest W., 212
McKendree Methodist Church, 132
McKissack, Calvin Lunsford, 215, **271–273**, 301
McKissack, Moses III, 168, 215, **274–276**
McMartin, Pauline Scott, 451
McMillan Chapel, 243, 244
McMillan Free Library, 35
McQueens Chapel Methodist Church, 132
McVay, Catherine, 445
Mechanic & Farmers Bank, 260
Mechanics Bank building, 139
Mechanicsville Methodist Church, 132
Mecklenburg Investment Co., building, 371, 372
Medgar Evers College, 224

INDEX

Medical Center Courts, 270
Medical Dental Arts building, 270
Medical Examiner's building, 191
Medic's Medical building, 270
Meharry Medical College
    Hubbard Hospital, 276
    Mental Health Center, 276
    Sciences Center, 276
Meigs Public School, 273
Melby, John Alexander, **277–279**
Melody Cocktail Bar, 415, 416
Mentrotone Baptist Church, 14
Menuhin, Moshe, 451
Mercurio, Frank, 55
Meredith, Amaza Lee, 163, **280–282**
    "Azurest North" subdivision, 281, 282
    "Azurest South" house, 280, 281, 282
Meridian Hill Baptist Church, 419, 420
Merrick, John, 101, **283–284**
Mertz, G. O., 342
Metairie Golf Course, 25, 27
Methuen, elderly housing, 45, 46
Methuen Fire Station, 46
Methuen Junior High School, 45, 46
Metompkin Baptist Church, 239
Metro North, Department of Social Services, 368, 369
Metropolitan African Methodist Episcopal Zion Church, 340
Metropolitan Baptist Church, Monument Hall, 146
Metropolitan Baptist Church, service building, 420
Metropolitan Hospital, nurses residence & school, 192
Metropolitan Opera House, 423, 424
Metrotone Baptist Church, 172
Metzler, I. S., 416
Miami apartments (No. 47), 336, 337
Michael, John Henry, 10, **285–287**
Michigan Boulevard Garden apartments, 397–398, 399
Michigan Central Railroad, arch bridges, 316
Michineves, Eduardo, 74
Mickels, Elon Howard, **288–289**
Midway and Wake dormitories, 327
Midwood Branch Library, 192
Midwood High School, 439
Milbank-Frawley Urban Renewal Site, 224
Miles, Mitchell, 62
Miles, William, 451
Miles Memorial Colored Methodist Episcopal Church, 59
Miller, Alfred Z., 298
Miller, Charles M., 212
Miller, Edward Charles, **290–291**
Miller Factory, 248
Milton Medical Clinic, 437

Mines & Geology building, 46
Minter, Sylvester, 126
Minton, Theophilus J., 60
Miracle Baptist Church, 19, 20
Miracle Diner, 55
Miramar, 4
Miskan Tora Community Center, 266
Mission Church, 321
Mississippi Industrial College
    dining hall, 395
    dormitory, 395
Missouri Mews, 386
Mitchell, Frank P., 4
Mobile & Girard Railroad Bridge, 248
Mock Road, senior citizens housing, 337
Model Cities Neighborhood Facility, 116, 117
Momence Country Club, 17
Monmouth College, Wilson Hall, 4
Monroe County Home and Infirmary, 52–53, 55
Monroe Junior High School and auditorium, 446
Monrovia Elementary School, 44, 46
Montana Terrace public housing, 161, 427, 429
Montgomery, Robert "Ardrosson," 4
Moore, Grace, 448
Moore, John Aycocks, 197, 261, **292–294**
Moore drug store, 321
Moorer, A. A., 420
Moore's Bridge, 246, 248
Morehouse College
    Archer building, 291
    Bennett dormitory, 291
    Chemistry building, 291
    Danforth Chapel, 291
Morgan State College
    Harper women's dormitory, 94
    O'Connel men's dormitory, 94
    Soldiers Armory, 94
    Student Christian Center, 94
    Talmadge Field House, 94
    Tubman women's dormitory, 94
Morgan State University, classroom building, 161
Morningside Health Center, 192
Morning Star Baptist Church, 386
Morosco, Oliver, 392
Morris, Ira H., 55
Morrisania District Health Center, 192
Morris Brown College, Central Heights Industrial building, 256
Morris College, Gymnasium and Home Economics buildings, 40, 41
Morris Furniture Store, 266
Morris Memorial Building, 272, 273
Mosaic State Temple building, 17

INDEX

Moses, William Henry, Jr., 104, 184–185, **295–298**
Mosholu Branch Library, 192
Moss, Chester M., 166, 167
Moss, Harvey, 446
Mother African Methodist Episcopal Zion Church, 157–158
Mother Church of God in Christ, 239
Mounsey, Ethel N., 461
Mt. Airy Baptist Church, 146, 207, 209, 420
Mt. Bethel Baptist Church
    Washington DC, by Mackey, 146, 266
    Washington DC, by Vaughn, 419, 420
Mt. Calvary Baptist Church, 132
Mt. Calvary Baptist Church and Community Center, 223
Mt. Carmel apartments, 160, 161
Mt. Carmel Baptist Church, 148
Mt. Carmel Church, 164
Mt. Carmel Methodist Church, Education building, 132
Mt. Gilead Baptist Church, 240
Mt. Gleason Junior High School, 369
Mt. Herman Baptist Church (Cleveland, OH), 270
Mt. Hermon Baptist Temple (Portsmouth, VA), 240
Mt. Jezreel Baptist Church and parsonage, 60
Mt. Joy United Methodist Church, 182
Mt. Meigs School for the Deaf, 437
Mt. Moab Baptist Church, 256
Mt. Moriah Baptist Church
    New York NY, 392
    Washington DC, by Ferguson, 146
    Washington DC, by Vaughn, 420
Mt. Moriah Lodge No. 28 Free & Accepted Masons, 17
Mt. Morris Park
    senior citizen's housing, 456, 458
    swimming pool and bath house, 223, 224
Mt. Nebo Baptist Church
    Kent County, VA, 164
    Lake Lure, NC, 132
Mt. Nebo Methodist Church, 132
Mt. Olive African Methodist Episcopal Church, 82, 83
Mt. Olive Baptist Church
    Henrico County, VA, 164
    Knoxville, TN, 132
    Lewiston, NC, 238, 240
    Mullins, SC, 154, 155
    Norfolk, VA, 238, 240
    Washington DC, 420
Mt. Pilgrim African Baptist Church, 340
Mt. Pisgah Church, 212
Mt. Pleasant Baptist Church
    Chesterfield County, VA, 164
    Norfolk, VA, 240
    Washington DC, 266
Mt. Pleasant Family Center, 270
Mt. Pleasant Medical Center, 270
Mt. Pleasant Methodist churches, 132
Mt. Pleasant Sayreton Methodist Church, 132
Mt. Rushmore National Monument, Visitor Center, 346
Mt. Sinai Baptist Church, 385, 386
Mt. Tabor Methodist Church, Education building, 132
Mt. Vernon Salem Methodist Church, 133
Mt. Zion African Methodist Episcopal Church
    Florence, SC, 40, 41
    Princess Anne, VA, 256
Mt. Zion Baptist Church
    Fairmont, WV, 23, 24
    Liberty, MO, 256
    Washington DC, by Madison, 270
    Washington DC, by Vaughn, 420
    Winston-Salem, NC, 233
Mt. Zion Baptist Church, parsonage
    Knoxville, TN, 287
    Washington DC, 60
Mt. Zion Church, 212
Mt. Zion Methodist Church, 133
Muhammed, Elijah, 205
Muldrow, J. O., 342
Murphy, Carl T., 94
Murray, Daniel, 60, 256
Murray Palace Casino, 193, 194
Murray Shoe Store, 55
Murray's Ice Cream Factory, 256
Muscogee County courthouse, 248
Music Corporation of America building, 448, 451
Muttontown Golf Club, 3
Mutual Real Estate Co., 32

Naperville Transit Station, 270
National Benefit building, 144, 145, 146, 420
National City Bank of New York, 74
National Library, Seoul, Korea, 143
National Negro Fair, 254, 256
National Pythian Temple, 15–16
National Religious Training School
    administration building, 443, 446
    Avery Auditorium, 321
    dining hall, 321
    dormitory, 321
    men's dormitory, 443, 446
    President's residence, 321
    Theology Hall, 321
    women's dormitory, 443, 446

National Technical Association
　formation of, **299–301**
　members of, 13, 31, 48, 79, 125, 128, 138, 178, 201, 255, 262, 272, 308, 312, 322, 407, 430, 438
　presidents of, 300–301
National Training School for Women and Girls
　Chapel, 146
　dormitory, 146
　Jubilee Arch, 292, 294
　laundry, 292, 294
　model house, 292, 294
Nauck Heights, 209
Naylor, William T., 60
Nazareth Baptist Church, 80
Nazareth College of Rochester
　administration building, 55
　auditorium, 55
　classroom building, 55
　dormitory, 56
Neiman-Marcus department store, 222, 224
New Ahoskie Baptist Church, 240
New Apostolic Church of North America, 324
New Bedford Home for the Aged, 67, 68
New Bethel African Methodist Episcopal Church, 218, 219
New Bethel Baptist Church, 240
New Bethel Church homes, 233
New Discipline Church, 35
New Hope Baptist Church
　Danbury, CT, 151
　Los Angeles, CA, 451
New Hope Church, parsonage, 172
New Hope Free Church Parsonage, 14
New Hope Methodist Church, 133
New Jerusalem Missionary Baptist Church, 19, 20
Newman, Nelson, 420
Newman Club, 126
Newmark, Robert, 451
New Mt. Calvary Missionary Baptist Church, 380
New Mt. Olive Baptist Church, 172
Newton, Frontis J., 266
New World Laboratory, 209
New York City
　Board of Education, Early Childhood Center, 456, 458
　Department of Public Works Repair Shop, 192
　Department of Sanitation Central Repair Shop, 192
　Department of Sanitation Incinerator, 192
　Fire Department College Training building, 192
　Institution for Female Prisoners, 192
　Municipal Court, 192
　Police Academy, 192
　Police Headquarters, 192
　Police Station, 24th Precinct, 192
　Public Health Laboratory, 192
　Public School No. 13, 224
　Terminal Market, 192
New York City Community College, Academic & Science buildings, 192
New York Evening Post, 4
New York State Harlem office building, 222, 223, 224, 236
New York University, 176
　Institute of Fine Arts, 3
Nickerson Gardens public housing, 449, 451
Nikki's Dress Shop, 416
92nd Street Bridge, 129
Nite-club, 279
Nix, Theopholis, 182
Njala University, 334
Noah's Ark Auto Accessories (Rochester and Syracuse), 56
Noranda Mines Factory, 201
Norman, John Clavon, Sr., **302–304**
North Branch Public Library, 467
North Broad Street Station, 4
North Carolina Agricultural & Technical State University, 173, 174
　Aggie Stadium, 231, 233
　classroom building, 233
　Communication building, 233
　Law School building, 233
　McNair School of Engineering, 231, 233
　School of Mechanical Arts, **305**
　Williams Cafeteria, 233
North Carolina Central University, Law School building, 231
North Carolina Mutual Insurance Co., 383
Northeast Baptist Church, 420
Northern Home for Children, 4
Northfield Creamery, 446
North Hollywood Manor apartments, 415, 416
North Nashville Community Center, 276
North Street Fire Station, 46
Nutibara Hotel, 451

Oakhaven Old People's Home, 129
Oakland Manor apartments, 207, 209
Obee, G. Wade, 446
Odd Fellows office building, 395
Odd Fellows Temple, 94
Ogontz School for Girls, 4
Ohio Governor's Mansion, 35

INDEX

Ohio State University
    hospitals, 337
        Testing Laboratory, 24
Ojike Memorial Medical Center, 224
Okert, D. M., 14
Old Post Office, 207–208, 209
Oliver, 233
Oliver, Annie, 97
Olivet Baptist Church, 17
Omega Psi Phi fraternity headquarters, 94, 384, 386
O'Neal, Kenneth Roderick, 72, 175, **307–309**
Ontario Refining Co., 201
Opportunities Industrialization Center, 350
Orangeburg Lutheran Church, 40, 41, 441, 442
Orange Lanes Bowling Alley, 416
Orr duplex, 446
Oswego Mall public housing, 384, 386
Otis, CLyde, 324
Ottawa Supreme Court building, 200, 201
Our Lady Queen of Peace Church, 148
Oyster House Restaurant, 415, 416

Paducah Junior College, Anderson Hall, 302
Palermo, Biagio, 56
Paley, William, 448, 451
Palmer Memorial Institute, boys dormitory, 233
Palm Springs Tennis Club, 449, 451
Pan American building, 423, 424
Papa, Frank C., 56
Papa, Samuel R., 56
Paradise Bowling Alley & Amusement Center, 437
Park Elementary School, 446
Parker, Arthur H., 340
Parker, Evelyn L., 282
Parker, Helen Eugenia, **311–312**
Parker, Joseph Lincoln, **313–314**
Parker Heights, 233
Parker House Sausage Co., 85
Parks, James B., 420
Parks, Joseph F., 56
Parkside Dwellings, 79, 80, 266, 455
Park Wilshire Hotel, Mardi Gras Room, 415, 416
Parnell, William J., 256
Parson, Hubert T., 4
Parsons, James A., 300
Passero, Anthony P., 56
Passero, Joseph D., 56
Patternmaking, 187
Patterson laundry building, 298
Paul Quinn College, Grant Hall dormitory, 321
Payne, Clara, 62, 63
Payne Chapel African Methodist Episcopal Church, 273
Peace Baptist Church, 461

Peachy, Katherine, 451
Pearcy, G. C., 273
Pearl High School, 273
Pelham, Frederick Blackburn, 199, **315–316**
Pemberton, Stafford, 94
Pendleton, William H., 126
Penn, Garfield A., 146
Pennsylvania General State Authority, 350
Pennsylvania State University, classroom building, 348, 350
Penny Savings Bank
    Birmingham, AL, 340
    Waycross, GA, 392
Peoples Building & Loan Association Bank, 295, 298
People's Church & Metropolitan Community Center, 129
People's Federation Bank, 256
People's Settlement, 182
People's United Methodist Church, Community Center, 363
Pere Marquette Hotel, 4
Perino's Restaurant, 449, 451
Perry, E. W., 227
Perry, L. D., 212
Persley, Louis Hudson, **317–318**
Peterson, Thomas, 446
Petitfils, Anna S., 451
Pfizer Chemical Store, 303, 304
Pfizer Corp. of Brazil, 73, 74
Phalanx housing, 46
Pharrow, Ed, 340
Phelps High School Greenhouse, 161, 429
Philadelphia Free Library, 2, 4
Philadelphia Methodist Church, 133
Philadelphia Stock Exchange, 4
Philadelphia YMCA, 4
Philander Smith College, 455
Phillips Chapel Colored Methodist Episcopal Church, 276
Phipps, Henry C., 4
Phipps, John S. "Westbury House," 4
Phipps Center Police Athletic League, 224
Phoenix Bank of Nansemond, 238, 240
Phylis apartments, 172
Pierce, V. Mott, 451
Pierleoni, Ennius, 56
Pierre, William, 60
Pilgrim African Methodist Episcopal Church, 94, 172
Pilgrim Baptist Church
    Washington DC, by L.J.H. Brown, 80
    Washington DC, by G.A. Ferguson, 146
    Washington DC, by Vaughn, 420
Pincus apartments, 172

INDEX

Pine Wood Country Club Golf Course, 27
Pipestone National Monument, Visitor Center, 346
Piscitello, Frances, 56
Pittman, William Sidney, 38, 61, 109, 193, 202–203, 228, **319–321**, 338, 423
    "Little White Tops," 321
Pitts, ZaSu, 448, 451
Pittsburgh Board of Public Education, 350
Pittsburgh Housing Authority, 350
Pittsburgh Police Station, 30, 32
Pittsburgh Presbytery, 350
Plater, James Alonzo, 215, **322–324**
Plato, Samuel M., 12, 144, 278, **325–327**
Platonian apartments, 326, 327
Pleasant, Nathan, 164
Pleasant Hill Methodist Church, 133
Plummer, Robert, 94
Plummer, Roy U., 172
Pluto, Andrew, 56
Plymouth Congregational Church, 270
Plymouth Housing Estate, 270
Plymouth Theatre, 212
Ponce Medical Center, 235, 236
Pontchartrain Park Municipal Golf Course, 25, 26, 27
Porter, Luther, 182
Portlege, 3
Potato chip factory, 443, 446
Powell apartments, 420
Power, Tyrone, 414, 416, 448, 451
PPG Industries, 350
Prager, Sol L., 56
Prairie Court apartments, 74
Prairie View Agricultural & Mechanical College, 44
    duplex, 437
    Evans Hall, 159, 161
    gym, 161
    Hospital, 159, 161
    Registrar's Office, 437
    School of Architecture, **328–329**
    unmarried men's dormitory, 437
Prato, Samuel, 56
Pravaz-Recordati Laboratories, 74
Preminger, Otto "Rock House," 451
Presbyterian Church (Washington DC), 386
Presbyterian Hospital, 392
Preston, Ann C. "Anndot," 281, 282
Price, Henry James, **330–331**
Prince Hall Grand Lodge, 256
Prince Hall Masonic Temple, 394, 395
Prince Hall Masons bath house, 227
Prince Hall Temple Association Lodge and apartments, 32
Prince High School, gym, 291

Princess Kaiulani Hotel, 309
Professional Associate Medical building, 262
Progressive Architecture Rich Competition, 298
Prohaska apartments, 172
Promontory apartments, 74
Promotory Point apartments, 204, 205
Prospect Park Boathouse, 458
Provident Hospital and Free Dispensary, 92, 94, 354
Prudential Bank, 420
Pryce, Edward Lyons, **332–334**
PSU Southerland Hall, 4
Pueblo Del Rio public housing, 449, 451
Pueblo Gardens subdivision, 451
Pulaski Public School, 273
Pulitzer building, 4
Purce, C. L., 325, 327
Purity Baptist Church, 169
Pyramid Realty & Investment Co., 446

Quarles, Alexander P., 140, 212
Quebec Bridge, 200, 201
Queens Central Library, 192
Queen's Colony subdivision, 56
Queens General Hospital
    nurses residence, 192
    stores building, 192
Queen Street Baptist Church, 240, 256
Queens Village Regional Branch Library, 192
Quick, Dr., 383
Quigless Medical Clinic, 212

Rabbinical College, 4
Raffelson, Jacob, 56
Rahn, Joseph, 172
Ramsey County School for Boys, 446
Randall, John, 172
Randall Memorial United Methodist Church, 386
Randall Universal United Methodist Church, 148, 266
Ransom, Leon Andrew, Jr., **335–337**
Rause, Arthur A., 56
Raussieur, Francis, 169
Rayen School, 34, 35
Rayfield, Wallace Augustus, 36, **338–340**
RCA Educational Laboratory Animal Facility, 386
Reagan, Edward B., 56
Red Cap building, 256
Redding, Lewis, 182
Reed, Dr., 383
Reed, J. D., 212
Reed house, 281, 282
Reed-Roberts Street housing, 349, 350
Reese, Lawrence, **341–342**
Refoe, Herman L., 380

541

INDEX

Remand Shelter for Adolescent Boys, 192
Render, 248
Reno store, 279
Repass, Maurice A., 8
Research Analysis Center, 270
Residence Deputy Chief of Mission, 270
Reydon, Frederick, 74
Reynolds, T. A., 298
Reynolds Residence Hall, Hobson, 262
Rhines, John T., 172
Rhines Funeral Home, 386
Rhodes Funeral Home, 363
Ribon apartments, 451
Rice, Eleanor "Miramar," 4
Rice & Lawson playground shelter, 446
Rich, William, 240
Richards, F. F. "Hillside," 282
Richardson, Patricia, 301
Riches department store, 222, 224
Richmond Beneficial Insurance Co., 364, 366
Richmond Central Fire Alarm Station, 192
Ridder Junior High School, 439
Riddick, 240
Ridell, A. F., 279
Ridgecrest Country Estates, 227
Ridgely, Marion, 212
Ridgeway, Edwin, 451
Riley Chapel Methodist Church, 133
Ring, Ellis, 56
Rising Mt. Zion Baptist Church, 164
Ritchwood, 233
Ritts, Donald B., 56
Ritz-Carlton Hotel, 4
River Power Plant, 9
Rivers, W. N., 420
Riverside Baptist Church, 365, 366
Riverside Health Center, 192
Riverside Sanitarium & Hospital, 276
Robbins, C. A., 298
Roberson, Francis Jefferson, 196, **343–344**
Roberson, Francis Rassieur, 343, **345–346**
Roberts, Albert, 273
Roberts, James E., 266
Roberts, Walter Lenox, Jr., **347–350**
Roberts Airfield, 354, 455
Robertson, J. C., 256
Robertson apartments, 256
Robinson, Alvin F., 266
Robinson, Bill, 448, 451
Robinson, Hilyard Robert, 44, 79, 128, 142, 159, 168, 189, 213–214, 221, 235, 272, 296, 322, **351–354**
Robinson, H. J., 14
Robinson, Jackie, 190

Robinson, Rev., 257
Robinson, Robert L., **355–356**
Robinson, William J., **357–358**
Rochdale Village Branch Library, 192
Rochester Bakery, 56
Rock Creek Baptist Church, 172
Rockdale Park, 224
Rockefeller Barn, 358
Rockefeller University, 423, 424
Rodman Street Baptist Church, 32
Rogacs, Joseph, 56
Rogers, J. L., 60
Rogers, Madeline P., 266
Roger Williams University, dormitory, 273, 274
Romack, Paul, 56
Romeo, Frank J., 56
Romeo, Philip, 56
Ronaele Manor, 3
Rooks, Shelby, 298
Rose Hill Baptist Church, 363
Rosemond, John Henry, **359–360**
Rosenthal, J., 369
Rose Terrace, 3
Ross Funeral Home, 4
Rounds, T. S., 321
Rouse, Charles C., 420
Rousseve, Ferdinand Lucien, **361–363**
Rowe, Vincent, 56
Royal Air Force, hangers at Trenton, 200, 201
Royal Canadian Mounted Police headquarters, 200, 201
Rubbert, M. Frank, 172
Rucker building, 119, 120
Russell, Charles Thaddeus, 184, 237, 296, **364–366**
Russell County Bridge and courthouse, 248
Russell Funeral Home, 383
Russi, Arthur M., 56
Ruthofer, Eva M., 74
Rutner Iron Co., 56

Sacred Heart Home, 148
St. Anthony Hospital, 336, 337
St. Anthony's Park Branch Library, 446
St. Augustine College
   Benson Library, 122
   Chapel, 121–122
   Taylor Hall, 122
St. Augustine Episcopal Church, 262
St. Augustine Roman Catholic Church parish, 337
St. Claire playground shelter, 446
St. Claver's Catholic elementary school, 363
St. Columbia Cathedral, 35
St. David's Episcopal Church, 45, 46
St. David's Protestant Episcopal Church, 392

542

INDEX

St. Edmund's School, 308
St. Elizabeth Ann Catholic Church, 467
St. George Greek Orthodox Church, 446
St. George Regional Branch Library, 192
St. James African Methodist Episcopal Church
    St. Paul, MN, 446
    Sanford, FL, 379–380
St. James African Methodist Episcopal Temple, 321
St. James Baptist churches, 164
St. James East Thomas Methodist Church, 133
St. James Holiness churches, 163, 164
St. James Methodist Church, 133
St. James Presbyterian Church, 231, 233
St. John African Methodist Episcopal Church (Marion, SC), 155
St. John African Methodist Episcopal Church, auditorium (Norfolk, VA), 240
St. John Baptist Church
    Portsmouth, VA, 240
    Washington DC, 172
St. John Baptist Church, education building (Oklahoma City, OK), 226, 227
St. John Missionary Baptist Church, 380
St. John's African Methodist Episcopal Church
    Asheville, NC, 257
    Indianapolis, IN, 257
    Niagara Falls, NY, 270
    Norfolk, VA, 257
    Omaha, NB, 443, 446
St. John's Baptist Church, 276
St. John's Evangelical Baptist Church, 32
St. John's Hospital
    Gary, IN, 110, 111
    Joplin, MO, 467
St. John's Presbyterian Church, 270
St. John Tabernacle Baptist Church, 257
St. Joseph's Cathedral, 35
St. Jude's Catholic Hospital, 363
St. Jude's Children's Hospital, 451
St. Louis Botanical Garden Greenhouse, 344
St. Louis courthouse, 346
St. Louis Union Station Canopies, 344
St. Luke Episcopal Church Parish, 94
St. Luke Hall, 366
St. Luke Penny Savings Bank, 364, 366
St. Luke's Baptist Church, 60
St. Luke's Church, 354
St. Luke's Episcopal Church, 57, 60
St. Mark African Methodist Episcopal Church, 32
St. Mark Reformed Zion United Apostolic Church, 240
St. Mark's Baptist Church, 40, 41
St. Mark's Methodist Church, 133
St. Martins-Griggs Park, 289

St. Martin's Tower, 223, 224, 235, 236
St. Matthew's Methodist Church, 133
St. Matthews United Methodist Church, 231, 233
St. Michael's Methodist Church, 442
St. Nicholas Orthodox Church, 451
St. Nicholas Park Urban Renewal area, 236
St. Paul African Methodist Episcopal Church
    Columbus, OH, 337
    Jacksonville, FL, 218, 219
    McKeesport, PA, 270
St. Paul Baptist Church, 70, 71
St. Paul Congregational Methodist Church, 14
St. Paul First Baptist Church, 434
St. Paul Methodist churches, 133
St. Paul Public Safety building, 446
St. Paul's African Methodist Episcopal Church, 196, 198
St. Paul's Baptist Church, 94
St. Paul's College
    President's residence, 383
    Saul building, 383
    student center, 383
St. Paul's Colored Methodist Episcopal Church, 240
St. Paul's Episcopal Church, 4
St. Paul's Parish Church, 338, 340
St. Paul Winter Carnival Ice Palace, 443, 446
St. Peter's African Methodist Episcopal Church
    Minneapolis, MN, 343, 344
    St. Paul, MN, 196, 198
St. Philip's Church, Community Center, 224, 236
St. Philips Episcopal Church, 458
St. Philip's Protestant Episcopal Church and Parish House, 156–157, 158, 390–391, 392
St. Phillip's African Methodist Episcopal Church, 257
St. Raymond's Catholic Church, 363
St. Stephen African Methodist Episcopal Church, 436, 437
St. Stephen's African Methodist Episcopal Church, 257
St. Stephen's Baptist Church, 273
St. Stephen's Episcopal Church Parish Hall, 45, 46
St. Stephen's Methodist churches, 133
St. Vincent's orphanage, 337
Saks Fifth Avenue (Beverly Hills, CA), 448, 451
Salem African Methodist Episcopal Church, 155
Salem Manor Housing, 467
Salem Methodist Church
    Community Center, 224
    Education building, 133
Salvage building, 346
Samaritan Order building, 318
Sampaio, Marcio, 74
Sanchon Beerup, 451
Sanders, Edward, 342

543

INDEX

Sanitarium, 437
San Marcos Hotel Golf Club House, 416
Santa, Sam R., 56
Santa Ynez Inn, 416
Sara Lawrence College, Theater, 176
Sargent Memorial Presbyterian Church, multipurpose building, 387
Sash and Blind Factory, 250
Saterwhite store, 14
Saunders, W. W., 303, 304
Saunders apartments, 146
Savoy, Archie, 324
Scardino, Samuel P., 56
Scheffer playground shelter, 446
Schifano, Benedict F., 56
School No. 2 (Weaver, IN), 325–326, 327
Schwab Drug Store, 416
Scioscia, Pete, 212
Scott, A. J., 298
Scott, Anderson T., 298
Scott, Armond, 354
Scott, M. M., 212
Sealey, Roy Anthony, **367–369**
Searborough Nursery, 382, 383
Seaton, Daniel P., 193, 194
Seaton Elementary School, 94, 387
Second Baptist Church
    Ford City, PA, 116, 117
    Marion, IN, 325, 327
    Los Angeles, CA, 448, 451
    Santa Ana, CA, 416
Second Calvary Baptist Church
    Cleveland, OH, 270
    Norfolk, VA, 240
Second Narrows Bridge, 201
Second Street Bank, 139, 141
Segal, Morris, 56
Selma Burke Art Center, 348, 350
Selma University, Dinkins Memorial Chapel, 318, 394, 395
Seney Chapel Methodist Church, 133
Sensenbrenner, August, 451
Seoul Central building, 143
Sertoma Sunshine Center, 133
Sessoms Drug store and office, 257
Seton High School, 455
Settle, R. T., 212
Seventh Day Adventist Education building, 383
Seventh District Police Station (Washington DC), 80, 385, 386
Sexton, Daniel P., 273
Seymour, R. W., 340
Shanklin, 303, 304

Shannon, Harry D., 56
Sharpe Health Center, 387
Shaw Junior High School, 387
Shaw United Methodist Church, 14
Shaw University
    apartments, 233
        Leonard Medical School, 135–136, 137
        Roanoke Institute, 240
        Tyler Hall, 137
Shelton, J. E., 266
Shephard, O'Donne, 146
Shepherd, John M., 141
Sheppard, John J., 451
Sheridan Beach Hotel, 129
Sherman, Barney R., 56
Sherman Creek project, 224
Sherman Shopping Center, 416–417
Shiloh Baptist Church, 257
Shiloh Presbyterian Church, 133
Shiloh Seventh Day Adventist Church, 129
Shoffner, 233
Shop-Rite Liquor store, 14
Short, Clarence, 48
Shuwarger, 451
Simmons High School, 304
Simmons University, Stewart Hall, 326, 327
Simms, Edgar R., 212
Simon apartments, 172
Simpson Memorial Methodist Church, 133
Simpson Memorial United Methodist Church, 359, 360
Sinatra, Frank A., 449, 451
Singleton, John A., 296, 298
Sixteenth Street Baptist Church, 338, 339, 340
Sixth Avenue Baptist Church, 338, 340
Sixth Mt. Zion Baptist Church
    Pittsburgh, PA, 32
    Richmond, VA, 366
Skeena River Viaduct, 201
Sleepy Hollow Motel, 56
Slumberland Motel, 40, 41
Small's Paradise Cabaret, 392
Smallwood Memorial Institute, administration building, 130, 141
Smith, Alwyn M., 250
Smith, Colin H., 451
Smith, Darr, 417
Smith, J. W., 112
Smith, Raymond, 212
Smith, Robert T., 32
Smith, William G., 324
Smith, William W., **370–372**
Smith Chapel Methodist Church, 133
Smith Funeral Home, 233

Smith-Gaston "Hill Top," 340
Smith Memorial Arch, 446
Snead, James, 164
Snead, Junius, 164
Snead, Mack, 164
Snead, Samuel, 164
Snead, Thomas M., 164
Society and Business building, 257
Soldier's Home, 327
Soller's homes, 354
Son Dai Moon Police Station, 143
South Carolina Interstate and West Indian Exposition Negro Building, **373–375**
South Carolina State University
    Bradham Hall, 442
    Creamery building, 442
    Dukes gymnasium, 39, 40, 41, 441, 442
    Felton Training School, 442
    Floyd dining hall, 442
    Hodge Hall, 440, 441, 442
    Home Economics home, 442
    Lowman Hospital, 442
    Lowman men's dormitory, 442
    Manning Hall, 442
    Mechanical and Engineering building, 40, 441, 442
    poultry plant, 442
    White Hall, 442
    Wilkinson Hall, 441, 442
    Wilkinson YWCA hut, 440–441, 442
Southeast Seventh Day Adventists Church, 270
South Elyton Baptist Church, 340
Southern Aid Insurance of Virginia building, 193, 194
Southern Aid Society building, 257
Southern Appeal building, 257
Southern Baptist Church
    Baltimore, MD, 354
    Washington DC, 14, 266
Southern Female College, administration building, 248
Southern University, School of Architecture, **376–378**
South St. Anthony playground shelter, 446
Southside Committee for Community Improvement, 224
Southwest Land & Lake Tunnel, 129
Southwest Shopping Center, 116, 117
Sparrows Point Defense housing, 326, 327, 354
Spaulding, Dorothy "Edendot," 282
Spears, J. Monroe, 342
Spears, Prince W., **379–380**
Spencer, A. L., 266
Spencer, John H., 186
Springfield Baptist Church, 164
Staats Hospital complex, 303, 304
Staley, Frank M., 442

Stanwyck, Barbara S., 451
Star of Hope Baptist Church, 324
State of Ohio Computer Center, 270
State Street subway station, 408, 409
Stein, Ben, 369
Sterling clubhouse, 446
Stevenson, Louis, 301
Stewart, Carrington H., 301
Stewart, Edward, 60
Stewart, William A., 58, 60
Stewart Memorial Settlement House, John, 110, 111
Stewarts Chapel & Undertaking, 257
Stillman, Robert, 212
Stoddard Baptist Home, 420
Stoddard Baptist Home for the Aged, 266
Stoller's Point housing, 93, 94
Stonybrook, 4
Storrer, Herman L., 56
Stotesbury, Edward T. "Whitemarsh Hall," 2, 4
Stowe, Thomas H., 321
Strategic Air Command Composite Hospital, 467
Strawbridge, T. S., 340
Streat, William Alfred, Jr., **381–383**
Strickland, Edwin D., 380
Striner, Benjamin, 172
Strong Undertaking Co., 340
Strother, Charles, 141
Suffolk Community Hospital, 262
Sugar Hill single-family housing, 42, 43
Sullivan, J. W., 266
Sulton, John Dennis, 352, **384–387**
Sumter Masonic Lodge, 257
Sunset Plaza apartments, 449, 451
Supreme Liberty Life Insurance Building, 322, 324
Supreme Liberty Life Insurance Co., 266
Sutphen, George T., 56
Suwon Agricultural College, 143
Suwon Agricultural Laboratory, 143
Swissair, 224, 236
Sylvan shelter house, 446
Syphax, Douglass P., 60

Tabernacle Baptist Church
    Oklahoma City, OK, 227
    Petersburg, VA, 240
    Washington DC, 14, 169
Tabernacle Baptist Church, Parks Copeland building (Dayton, OH), 116, 117
Taborian Hospital, 276
Takoma Elementary School, 160, 161, 427
Talbert, E., 182
Talbert, Ella M., 172
Tallassee Bridge, 248

INDEX

Tandy, Vertner Woodson, 47, 52, 61, 156, 189, 295, 338, 351, **389–392**, 456
Tater, William, 172
Taylor, Edward W., 301
Taylor, Francis Jefferson, 169
Taylor, Robert Robinson, 2, 28, 109, 165, 168, 210, 215, **393–396**
Taylor, Robert Rochon, 169, **397–399**
Taylor, Van, 451
Taylor, W. L., 257
Taylor apartments, 257
Taylor building, 260
Temple of Gailean Fisherman, 321
Tennessee Agricultural & Industrial University
    administration building, 273
    Brown Library, 272, 273
    Engineering building, 276
    Health Center, 227
    landscaping, 455
    Library, 276
    Music building, 227
    Physical Education building, 276
    President's residence, 276
    Residence Economic building, 276
    School of Business, 276
Tennessee Centennial and International Exposition Negro Building, 156, 196, **400–401**
Tepper, Joseph L., 172
Terron, 74
Terry, Maude, 282
Texas Centennial Exposition, Hall of Negro Life, **402–404**
Texas College
    Carter women's dormitory, 273, 276
    Glass Library, 276
    McKinney administration building, 276
    President's residence, 276
    Taylor Gym, 276
    Wiley men's dormitory, 273
Tex's Sporting Goods Store, 451
Third Baptist Church, 60, 209
Third Church of God, 461
Third National Bank, 227
3rd Street Esplanda & Tourist building, 445
Thirty-Second Avenue Baptist Church, 340
Thirty-Second Street Elementary School, 369
Thomas, Edward, 94
Thomas, Frederick W., 13
Thomas, George, 172
Thomas, Leonard E., 301
Thomas, Valerie L., 301
Thomas Public School, 340
Thomasville Church homes, 233

Thompson, C. T., 257
Thompson, Martha Ann Cassell, 86, **405–406**
Thompson, J. W., 240
Thornton, William Ferguson, 210, 212, 301, **407–409**
Thousand Islands Bridge, 200, 201
Three College Observatory, 231, 233
Three Rivers Youth, Inc., 348, 350
Throgs Neck Public Library, 458
Thurston, Lewis M., 56
Thurston, Thomas C., 266
Tidal Basin Bridge and Seawall, 8
Tift Nelson Bridge and keeper's house, 248
Tiller's Chapel Methodist Church, 133
Tillotson Institute, 392
Times Square Hotel & Club, 56
Tod House Hotel, 35
Tod mansion, 33
Tooks, H. Y., 257
Trader, Dr., 383
Trainum, Alexander, 141
Triborough Bridge and Tunnel Authority, 313, 314
Tri-Borough Plaza complex, 224
Trigg, 240
Trinity African Methodist Episcopal Church, 340
Trinity Baptist Church
    Birmingham, AL, 338, 340
    Los Angeles, CA, 20, 451
    New York, 224
    Washington DC, 257
Trinity Hospital, 312
Trinity Methodist Baptist Church, 380
Trinity Methodist churches and education building, 133
Trinity Methodist Episcopal Church, 110, 111
Trinity North Washington Church, 321
Trinity United Methodist Episcopal Church, 442
Triumph the Church, 218, 219
Troup County courthouse, 250
True Reformers Meeting Hall, 139, 140, 141, 228, 254, 257
Trumbauer, Horace, 2
Tubercular Hospital, 451
Tuberculosis & Chronic Disease Hospital, 192
Tucker, M. O., 451
Tudor apartments, 129
Tufeld, Richard, 167
Tuggle Institute, 340
Tullaroan, 4
Turner, Beverley F., 141
Turner Memorial African Methodist Episcopal Church, 420
Turner Normal & Industrial Institute, administration building, 273, 274
Turpin, 240

Tuscaloosa Bridge, 248
Tuskegge Army Airfield (Chehaw, AL), 352, 353
Tuskegge Institute (University)
   administration building, 395
   Andrews Hospital, 161, 291, 334, 395, 429
   Armstrong Science building, 395
   Butler Chapel, 393–394, 395
   Carnegie Library, 318, 395
   Carver building, 334
   Carver dormitory, 334
   Cassedy Hall, 395
   Chambliss Hotel, 437
   Chapel, 161, 334, 427, 428, 429
   cottage no. 34, 437
   Davidson Hall, 395
   Dorothy Hall, 396
   Douglass dormitory, 396
   Dresge Center, 334
   Drew dormitory, 334
   Emery dormitories, 396
   Engineering Nuclear building, 270
   fire-safe model house, 437
   food processing plant, 161
   Harvey Hall, 291
   Hollis Burke Frissell Library, 396
   Huntington Memorial building, 321, 396
   Infantile Paralysis Hospital, 161
   James Center, 334
   James Hall, 318, 396
   Kay barn, 437
   landscapeing, 334, 454, 455
   laundry building, 396, 437
   Logan Hall, 396
   Logan Hall Gym, 318
   Mechanical Industries Department, **410–412**
   men's dormitory, 161, 429
   Middle School, 334
   Millbank building, 396
   Moton Airfield cadet classroom, 290, 291
   Moton Airfield entrance gate, 290, 291
   Moton Airfield hangars 1 and 2, 290, 291
   Moton Airfield landscaping, 455
   Moton Airfield warehouse, 291
   Moton Hall, 161, 334
   Nurses Home, 429
   Roberts housing, 334
   Rockefeller Hall, 321, 396
   Russell barn, 437
   Sage dormitory, 396
   Sage Hall, 318
   School of Engineering, 334
   School of Nursing, 161, 334
   School of Veterinary Medicine, 334
   Science Hall, 318, 396
   student housing, 407, 409
   Tantum dormitory, 334
   Tantum Hall, 396
   Thrasher dormitory, 334
   Thrasher Hall, 393, 396
   Tompkins dining hall, 396, 437
   Trade buildings, 94, 198
   Tree Inventory, 334
   Tubman dormitory, 334
   Veterans Hospital, 334
   Vocational building, 161
   white dormitory, 396
   women's dormitory, 161, 429
   Woodruff Food Plant, 334
20th Precinct Station, 223
Tynes Street Church, 240

Uganda Ballroom, 296, 298
Union Baptist Church
   Kent County, VA, 164
   Washington DC, 420
Union Bethel African Methodist Episcopal Church, 257
Union Commerce Bank
   Cleveland, OH, 270
   Portsmouth, VA, 240
Union Holiness Church, 240
Union Hope Baptist Church, 164
Union Pacific Railroad Bridge, 8, 9
Unionville Methodist Church, 133
Union Wesley American Methodist Episcopal Zion
   Church, 60
Union Wesley Methodist Church, 133
United Brothers of Friendship Lodge, 321
United Durham, Inc., 383
United Grove Disciples Church, 266
United House of Prayer, 161, 427, 429
United Moravian Church, 224
United National Bank, 387
United Nations, Paris headquarters, 176, 452
United Order of Odd Fellows Lodge, 321
United Pacific Insurance Co., 452
United Revelation Church of God in Christ, 19, 20
United Sports Club, 324
U.S. Army, airfield at Chewhaw, Alabama, 8
U.S. Customs Court, 455
U.S. Department of Agriculture, animal research
   facility, 387
U.S. Embassy, in West Africa, 270
U.S. Naval Reserve Air Base, 451
U.S. Navy
   Foundation Exploration Destroyer Base, 451
   Roosevelt Fleet Base, 451

INDEX

U.S. Post Offices
    by Boles, 46
    by Cooke, 109, 110, 111
    by Ifill, 224
    by Jenkins, 233
    by Plater, 322, 324
    by Plato, 326, 327
    by Williams, 451
    by Zenon, Jr., 467
Unity Funeral Chapel, 176
Unity Methodist Church, 250
Unity Mortuary, 133
Universal Life Insurance Co., 272, 273, 276
University Heights Branch Library, 192
University of Arkansas, Theater, 176
University of California-Los Angeles
    Botany building, 449, 452
    Chi Omega sorority house, 452
    Franz Hall, 452
    Kappa Sigma fraternity house, 448, 452
University of Iowa, Power and Steam Plants, 7–8, 9
University of Nebraska
    College of Law, 467
    Performing Arts building, 467
University of Pennsylvania
    Irvine Auditorium, 4
    President's Residence, 4
University of the District of Columbia
    administration building, 96
    Auditorium, 96
    Library, 96
    Life Sciences building, 96
    Music & Dance building, 96
    Physical Activities Center, 96
    Physical Science building, 96
    Power Plant, 96
    Technology building, 96
Urban Redevelopment Authority of Pittsburgh, 350
Urban Village, 207, 208, 209
Urico, Raphael, 266

Van Buren Elementary School, 446
Varick Community Center, 224
Vaughn, Ralph Augustine, 215, **413–417**
Vaughn, Roscoe Ingersoll, 12, 144, **418–420**
Veterans Administration Hospital, 455
Veterans Administration Housing, 417
Veterans Hospital, 446
Veterans of Foreign War Hall, 227
Viaducts, by Alexander, 9
Victoria County Park Director's building, 167
Village East Towers, 223, 224
Village of Robbins town hall, 212

Villegas, Don Luis Toro, 452
Vine City Transit Station, 334
Vine Street Café, 167
Virginia Avenue School, 326, 327
Virginia Baptist Convention School, 14
Virginia Pavilion Competition, 298
Virginia School for Colored Deaf & Blind, 298
Virginia Seminary & College, dormitory, 266
Virginia State University, Alumni House, 282
Virginia Theological Seminary, administration building, 14
Virginia Union University
    Hartshorn women's dormitory, 92, 94, 354
    Huntley Hall, 366
Von Erlea, 74
Voorhees Industrial School
    administration and classroom building, 321
    Booker T. Washington Hospital, 109, 111

Waddington, Harold, 337
Wales, S. S., 60
Walker, Josiah Joshua, **421–422**
Walker, Maggie L., 366
Walker, Mrs. C.J. "Villa le Waro," 390, 391, 392
Walker, T.H.B., 257
Walker-Jones Elementary School, 207, 209
Walker Memorial Baptist Church, 257, 420
Walters, Adelaide, 56
Walters African Methodist Episcopal Zion Church, 129
Walton's Cafe, 340
Ward, Clarence A., 56
Ward, John C., 56
Warren Temple Christian Methodist Episcopal, 250
Warren Temple Christian Methodist Episcopal Sabbath School, 248
Warrior Manufacturing, 248
Washington, Booker Taliaferro III, 6, 42, 49, 112, 229, **423–424**
    "The Oaks," 394, 396, 455
Washington, George F., 301
Washington, Robert Edward Lee, **425–426**
Washington Boulevard apartments, 129
Washington Chapel African Methodist Episcopal Church, 270
Washington High School
    St. Paul, MN, 446
    Tuskegee, AL, 334
Washington Junior High School, 273
Washington Manor complex, 303, 304
Washington Memorial, Booker T., 93
Washington Park shopping center, 46
Washington Street Bridge, 129
Washington Vocational School, 94

Waters, W. E., 240
Watkins, Dr., 383
Watkins Hotel, 417
Watson, James E. "High Gate," 4
Watts, Irvin, 298
Wayne County Better Homes, 437
Wayne County Justice Center, 270
Weaver, Joseph D., 266
Web Park Golf Course, 27
Webster Avenue Bridge, 129
Weis, Linus R., 56
Welch, John Austin, 160, 290, **427–429**
Welland Canal, vertical lift bridges, 200, 201
Wells, 233
Wells, Ira J.K., 303, 304
Wells, Samuel, 60
Wells Homes, Ida B., 128, 129
Wesley African Methodist Episcopal Zion Church and parsonage, 60
Wesley Chapel African Methodist Episcopal Church, 321
Wesley Methodist Church (Carthage, MS), 133
Wesley Methodist Church (Greenville, SC), 111
Wesley Methodist Church (Brancheville, SC), 133
West, E. J., 342
Westbury House, 4
Westchester Municipal building, 166, 167
Westchester Square Branch Library, 192
Western Railway Station, 342
Western Union Message Center, 224
Western University, Stanley Industrial Hall, 49–51
West Farms Branch Library, 192
Westfield State College, Student Union-Ely Library, 45, 46
West Funeral Home, 348, 350
Westinghouse Electric vehicle plant, 348–349, 350
West Los Angeles Synagogue, 417
West Minnehaha playground building, 446
Westover subdivision, 326, 327
West Point Bridge, 248, 250
West Point Female College, 248
West Point Public Library, 467
West Side Schoolhouse, 35
Westtown square and village, 181, 182
West Virginia State College
    Auditorium, 304
    Fleming Hall, 303
    houses, 302–303, 304
    Library, 304
Westwood Medical building, 452
Wetumpka Bridge, 248
Wheat, Clarence Buchanan, Sr., 47, 215, **430–432**
White, Columbus Bob, **433–434**

White, Donald Frank, 177, 301, 311, **435–437**
White, Drank, 383
White, George H., 461
White, George L., 298
White, Richard Cassius, 202, 300, **438–439**
Whitehurst Freeway, 8
Whitelaw Hotel, 193, 194
Whitemarsh Hall, 2, 4
White Oak Bridge, 248
White Pharmacy, 426
White Rock Baptist Church, 232, 233, 321
Whitlock print shop, 212
Whitner, Mary, 434
Whittaker, Miller Fulton, 39, **440–442**
Whittaker Memorial Hospital, 296, 298
Whitted, Harold L., 266
Widener, Peter A.B., 3, 4
Widener Memorial Home, 4
Wiggins, Elsie C., 172
Wigington, Clarence Wesley, 196, **443–446**
Wilberforce University
    Arnett Hall, 254, 257
    heating tunnel, 257
    School of Religion, 270
    women's dormitory, 257
Wilcox Hotel, 417
Wildenstein Gallery, 4
Wilder, Robert J., 162–163, 164
Wilder playground community building, 446
Wiley College building, 396
Wilinsky, Isadore J., 56
Wilkins Auditorium facade, 446
Wilkinson, Robert S., 442
William Anderson Community Center, 181, 182
Williams, Arthur C., 266
Williams, J. W., 212
Williams, L. Anthony, 298
Williams, Paul, 298
Williams, Paul Revere, 18, 19, 142, 166, 214, 352, 368, **447–452**
Williams & Ferguson Industrial Academy (College), 257, 321
Williamsburg Regional Branch Library, 192
Williams Chapel African Methodist Episcopal Church and parsonage, 40–41, 257, 442
Williams office building, 257
Williamson, Alphonso, 172
Williamson, Willard O., 301
Willis, M. J., 420
Williston, David Augustus, 215, 272, 332, 352, **453–455**
Williston, Thomas, 266, 354
Willow Grove Baptist Church, 262
Will Rogers Park community house, 452

INDEX

Wilma Gardens apartments, 172
Wilmington, city of, 181, 182
Wilson, Earl, 296, 298
Wilson, J. F., 342
Wilson, John Louis, Jr., **456–458**
Wilson, J. Woodrow, 326, 327
Wilson High School, 452
Wilson Junior High School, 446
Wilson Manor apartments, 172
Wilson Pine Garden apartments, 262
Winberg, Charles, 452
Winchester-Hood Garden apartments, 204, 205
Windber Hospital, 4
Wind Caves National Park, Visitor Center, 346
Windslow Stable, 257
Wineburg, C., 417
Wineland, Lloyd G., 172
Winestock, Reba, 212
Winston, Leon, 212
Wise, Lee L., 12
W.J. Sloane Department Store, 452
Wolk, Paul, 56
Women
    Brooks, Elizabeth Carter, **66–68**
    Brown, Georgia Louise Harris, **72–74**
    Brown, Mary Ramsay Channel, 163
    Butler, Alberta Jeannette Cassell, **86–87**
    Carlisle, Alma Fairfax Murray, **89–90**
    Furman, Ethel Madison Bailey, **162–164**
    Greene, Beverly Loraine, **175–176**
    Parker, Helen Eugenia, **311–312**
    Thompson, Martha Ann Cassell, 86, **405–406**
Women's Clinic, 383
Wood, Carl W., 227
Wood, J. P., 240
Woodcliff Lake School, 158
Woodmen of Union Bath House, 17
Woods, James A., 212
Woods, Lawrence, 126
Woodson, Howard Dilworth, 144, 292, 418, **459–461**
Workers housing, 327
World's Fair Corp., 347–348, 350
World's Fair Merchandising and Snack Shops, 133

Wormley, Garrett, 58, 60
Worther, Edmund C., 266
Wren, Fred D., 298
Wrights Chapel Methodist Church, 133
Wyatt, William, 141
Wynn Center Police Athletic League, 224

Yellowstone National Park, Ranger Museum, 346
Yenching Palace Restaurant, 14
YMCA
    Baltimore, MD, 256
    Buffalo, NY, 62, 63
    Greensboro, NC, 231, 233
    Hollywood, CA, 448, 450
    Los Angeles, CA, 448, 450
    Nashville, TN, 227
    New Orleans, LA, 363
    Washington DC (12th Street), 319–320, 321
    Washington DC (Wheately), 94
Yonge, William Penn C., 248
Young, Edward Walter Owen, **463–464**
Young, Frank M., 419, 420
Young, John L., 420
Young, Lucius, 266
Youngstown Board of Education building, 35
Youngstown City Jail, 35
Your Flower Shop, 56
Youth House for Girls, temporary annex, 192
Youth Opportunities Unlimited, 350
Ypsilanti public housing, 354, 455

Zenon, Golden Joseph, Jr., **465–467**
Zimmerman, Daniel, 4
Zion Baptist Church
    Petersburg, VA, 240
    Omaha, NE, 443, 446
    Washington DC, by Brent, 60
    Washington DC, by Madison, 270
    Washington DC, by Pittman, 321
Zion Bethel Church, 240
Zion Hills apartments, 233
Zion Hope Baptist Church, 218, 219
Zoological Society, 4

9780415929592